HIGHLAND
HERITAGE

Glencoe taken near Ballachulish

HIGHLAND HERITAGE

Barbara Fairweather

Published by Glencoe and North Lorn Folk Museum

Dust jacket: *A painting of Glencoe by Horatio McCulloch reproduced by kind permission of Glasgow Art Gallery and Museum*

First published 1984
© Glencoe and North Lorn Folk Museum
ISBN 0 905 806 11 5

Printed by Nevisprint Limited, Fort William, Scotland.

Contents

Acknowledgements

First we are indebted to the Glencoe Foundation Trust Inc of U.S.A. for their generous grant without which it would not have been possible to print this book.

We have three publishers which we wish to thank for permission to print from books still in copyright.

Random House Inc, Alfred A. Knopf Inc for permission to print an extract from The Letters of Chopin collected by Henryk Opiesnki translated by E Voynich 1932.

Permission to reprint an extract from 'Dugald Christie of Manturia' by his wife published by James Clarke & Company Ltd.

Permission to reprint an extract from Journal of a Tour in Scotland by Robert Southey. As the travels were not published till 1929 the work is in copyright but we have been given permission to reprint an extract by Messrs John Murray.

Permission to use photographs of Eilean Munda from Mr Paton, Fort William.

Permission to use photograph of dog at work on Mountain Rescue for Mr Hamish MacInnes.

For the drawing of seals and Eagle we wish to thank Mr Paige, and to the West Highland Museum, Fort William we wish to thank for the use of their library.

We would also like to thank the many visitors who have handed in old photographs to add to our collection - many are given anonymously.

Chapter 1 **Glencoe: a short history**

By sea, the men of the Bronze age came here, where important archaeological finds have been made. At North Ballachulish a wooden figure about five feet was found preserved in a peat bog, while nearby were the remains of a wattle shrine. This find is known as the Ballachulish figure and is now preserved in the National Museum of Antiquities in Edinburgh. It is not certain who the figure represents, it may be any pre Christian goddess. The two nearby bronze age graves are in poor shape as they have been used as quarries in the past. On a nearby tidal island by Altshealach, carved cup markings can be seen on the rocks. These are common throughout Europe but their use is uncertain. At Onich is a fine Standing stone known as "Clach a' Charra".

Vikings harried the coast. At the narrows where the Ferry used to run, now spanned by a bridge, the straight is called "Caoles-Mhic Pharuig", or the Channel of Patrick's son. A raiding Viking ship foundered there. The young prince was drowned though his father tried to save him. The father managed to save himself by clinging to a rock near the south shore. This is visible at low tide, it is called Clach Pharuig. Before the channel was dredged and deepened the rock would not have been so near the shore. There are two Viking graves in Ballachulish. They were opened at the beginning of the century but no record was made of what was found in them.

It was to Glen Etive that Deidre and Naisi came when they fled from Ulster. Much legend and poetry has grown and entwined itself with her name including the beautiful Gaelic song translated as "Farewell to Albyn". Fine Burial cairns are found at Benderloch and not far off a vitrified fort. At one time there was a lake dwelling or Crannog near the Cairns but the land is now drained.

The Pictish monk St. Kenneth first brought Christianity to Glencoe, but he travelled on to Fife. Later St. Findan Munda came. He built his church on an island in Loch Leven known as St. Munda's Isle or Eilean Munda.

Glencoe is so associated with the MacDonalds, it may surprise some to learn they were not always here. The land belonged to the MacEanruig (or MacHenry or Henderson). The founder of the Glencoe branch of Clan Donald was Iain Og Fhraoich (heather) sometimes called Iain Abrach (Lochaber where he was fostered). Iain was a natural son of Angus Og of Islay King of the Isles (the Lordship came later). Iain's mother was the daughter of Dugall MacEanruig Chief of the Glencoe MacEanuruigs or Hendersons.

Angus Og of Islay helped Bruce in his fight for Scotland's freedom from the English. Some Scots fought against Bruce and after he had stabbed the Red Comyn in a church the Comyns joined those fighting against Bruce. The MacDougalls were connected to the Comyns and they joined against Bruce too. There is no record of the part taken by the MacEanruigs, but their lands were part of the territory held by the MacDougalls. After Bannockburn, Bruce gave the lands of "Durrour and Glencoe and the Isles of Mull and Tirree" to Angus Og who had supported him throughout his campaign, and whose men had held the right wing at Bannockburn. Angus Og in turn gave them to his son Iain Abrach. The Hendersons accepted him and became the hereditary pipers to the Chiefs of the MacDonalds of Glencoe. Iain Abrach died in Knapdale in 1358. He was buried on Iona near his father. He was followed by eight Johns. This makes history difficult and it is only now and then records show how life in the Glen went on. The MacDonalds of Glencoe had no known charter nor were they crown vassals but were included in charters of John of Islay. After the fall of the Lordship in 1493 they became vassals of the Stewarts of Appin and the Campbells of Argyll.

During the Civil War Montrose raised an army for the King. He had the famous Alasdair Cholla Chiotaich as his lieutenant. Most of the army was Highland and it included the Glencoe MacDonalds. A Glencoe man Angus MacAlain Dubh acted as his guide through Argyll. He promised Montrose that his army would live well "If tight houses, and cattle, and clear water would suffice". Another Glencoe man has a claim to fame in that campaign. He was a poet known later as Raonull na Sgèithe that is Ranald of the targe or shield. In the ranks of the defeated army there was a soldier who spoke disparagingly of the way the Highlanders fought. He offered to fight anyone with sword against a Highlander armed with sword and targe, and to gain his freedom if successful. Raonull offered to fight him with dirk and targe. He assured the dragoon that his clansmen would desert if the bargain was not kept. Alan of Dalness, who was an excellent swordsman said "The sword alone is better than the dirk and targe; and there is no knowing what will become of you". Ranald replied "I don't know what will happen to me, but the very devil is going to happen to him". Ranald won.

With the help of his guide Montrose reached right into the heart of Argyll, Campbell country and even to Inverary which the Campbells had hitherto thought impregnable. Montrose wintered in Argyll but in spring marched off.

In 1688 the Whig faction in England invited William of Orange over, as king, to replace the Stuart King James VII of Scotland and II of England. The movement against James was partly political and partly religious. When William landed in England James sent his army to meet him under the command of the Churchill who later became Duke of Marlborough. He changed sides and lost England for James.

Dundee raised an army for James in Scotland, again it was largely Highland. The Glencoe MacDonalds joined him. They are described in a poem which translated is "Next came Glencoe, terrible in unwanted arms, covered as his breast with new hide, and towering far above his whole line by head and shoulders. A hundred men all of gigantic mould all mighty in strength accompany him as he goes to war. He himself turning his shield in his hand flourising terribly his sword, fierce in aspect, rolling his wild eyes, the horns of his twisted beard curled backwards seems to breath forth whenever he moves".

Dundee was victorious at Killiecrankie, but he was killed and this unfortunately left the Highlanders without a good leader and the army melted away. The Glencoe MacDonalds (often referred to as the MacIains) made a big creach (cattle lifting etc.) on their way home to Glencoe, on the Campbells of Glenorchy taking cattle and much else. With the death of Dundee Scotland was lost for James and sometime later Ireland too.

William held the land by the sword, he did not wish to continue fighting in Britain as he wished to concentrate on his continental war. So, he tried to pacify the Highlands. First he tried bribery, John Campbell of Breadalbane was given £12,000 for this work. A meeting was held at his castle at Achallader on the 30th June. It was not a peaceful meeting for Breadalbane told MacIain that any money that was due to him would be used to pay for the cattle lifted by him and his clan on their way home from Killiecrankie. MacIain replied that he was being given remission for the killing of a few red coated soldiers at Killiecrankie but it appeared that the lifting of a few cattle was without pardon. He added that no money would take their loyalty from their rightful king. At the meeting the Chiefs agreed not to rise before October of that year (1691). There were certain private resolutions made but of which there is no documentary proof. These include (1) The previous agreement about not rising should lapse if a Rising took place, (2) James had to give his consent before the Chiefs would submit to William, (3) Messengers to James to be allowed free and safe passage to James, (4) If William's forces were withdrawn the Clans would rise, (5) If there was a Rising Breadalbane undertook to rise with 1000 men. Later when Breadalbane was asked to account for how the money was spent, he said "My Lord the Highlands are quiet, the money is spent and that is the best way of accounting among friends".

On the 27th of August 1691 a proclamation was made in Edinburgh pardoning and indemnifying all those who had taken up arms, if they took an oath of allegiance to William before January 1st 1692. By the beginning of December there had been few submissions, but from then on they began to come in till almost all had submitted except the MacDonald Chief of Glencoe and Glengarry, another MacDonald Chief. MacIain wished to hear from James before taking the oath, and he did not hear till 29th December. He set off for Fort William then known as Inverlochy. He came before Col. Hill the Governor who told him that the oath must be taken by a civil magistrate, and the nearest was at Inveraray. Col. Hill gave MacIain a letter to the Sheriff explaining the circumstances and asking him to take in "the great lost sheep". He also gave MacIain a letter of safe conduct. The Chief was an old man (for those days) nearing seventy, the weather was bad with thick snow which delayed progress. In spite of the safe conduct letter from Hill, MacIain was captured by some soldiers of Argyll's regiment and had to spend New Year's Eve in Barcaldine Castle as a prisoner. The time expired at midnight but the next morning MacIain was set free and he continued on to Inveraray. He reached there on the 2nd of January. The Sheriff Campbell of Arkinglass was away from home and did not return till the 5th of January. At first he refused to receive the oath but MacIain pleaded with him to do so. The Sheriff had MacIain return the next day and having noted Hill's letter duly received the oath, and MacIain returned to the Glen.

Ardkinglass sent off the oath along with Hill's letter and his own description of how earnest MacIain had been in taking the oath. He asked that the three documents should be presented to the Privy Council. The letters went first to Colin Campbell Sheriff Clerk of Argyll, he took them to the Clerks of the Council who would do nothing about them, then Campbell took it to some of the Privy Counsellors one of whom was the father of Stair, who objected. Then the documents went to Lord Aberuchill, a Campbell. It was decided to give the papers to the Clerk when it was in session. Later when the Royal Commission was set up to inquire into the Massacre they were blamed for this.

Stair, John Dalrymple the Secretary of State for Scotland, a man who had the King's ear, had started his schemes for the Massacre before the deadline of 31/12/91. He wrote on the 3rd of December to Col. James Hamilton "The MacDonalds will fall into the net. That is the only popish clan in the kingdom, it will be popular to take a severe course with them". There were in fact other popish clans beside the MacDonalds. In a letter to Sir Thomas Livingstone Commander in Chief of forces in Scotland dated 7th January Stair wrote "the troops at Inverness and Inverlochy will be ordered to take the house of Invergarry, and destroy entirely the country of Lochaber, Lochiel's lands, Keppoch's Glengarry's Appin and Glencoe ... I assure you your power shall be full enough, and I hope the soldiers will not trouble the Government with prisoners ..." On the 9th of the month Stair again writes to Livingstone "I could have wished the MacDonalds had not divided and I am sorry that Keppoch and Glencoe are safe ..." Later he wrote that he had heard from Argyll that Glencoe had no taken the oath "at which I rejoice ..."

There is on record a letter of instructions from William of Orange to Livingstone signed by the King at the beginning and again at the end. The last paragraph reads "If M'Ean of Glenco and that tribe can be separated from the rest, it will be a proper vindication of Public justice to extirpat that sect of thieves".

The first sign of all the coming disaster to the Glen was on February first 1692. A company of 120 of Argyll's regiment came into the Glen under Robert Campbell of Glenlyon. Glenlyon said the Inverlochy garrison was overcrowded and he also had taxes to collect. This was accepted especially as Glenlyon's niece had married McIain's son. The rank and file of the soldiers were offered and accepted the hospitality of the Glen and lived with the MacDonalds. Ceilidhs were held, games of shinty were played and all was friendly. Glenlyon dined with MacIain in friendship. This continued till the 12th.

On the 12th Glenlyon received his final instructions from Robert Duncanson a Major in the Argyll Regiment. The document is now in the National Library of Scotland in Edinburgh. It is as follows: "You are hereby ordered to fall upon the rebels the MacDonalds of Glenco, and to put all to the sword under seventy. You are to have a special care that the old fox and his sonnes do not escape your hands. You are to secure all the avenues that no men can escape your hands. You are to put in execution at five of the clock precisely. And by that time, or very shortly after it, I will strive to be at you with a stronger party. If I do not come to you at five, you are not to tarry for me but to fall on. This is by the King's special commands, for the good and safety of the countrie, that the miscreants be cutt off root and branch. See that this be put in Execution without fear or favour. Else you may expect to be dealt with as one not true to King or Government, nor a man fitt to carry a commission in the King's service. Expecting you will not fail in the fulfilling hereof, as you love yourself, I subscribe this at Ballychylis the 12th of February 1692."

The resulting activity and the doubling of the guards troubled Alistair Og the son of the Chief who went first to his brother, then the two of them went to see their father. MacIain did not believe any harm threatened them, and sent them home.

About 5 am soldiers were seen approaching Alistair's home and seeing their fixed bayonets he and his wife fled. He met his brother and between them got some of their people to safety.

MacIain and his wife were awakened by the soldiers knocking on the door led by Lieutenant Lindsay who said they had urgent business. The soldiers were let in and MacIain called for drinks but before they could be enjoyed MacIain was shot dead. His wife who went to help him was seized and her rings wrenched off her finger by the teeth of the men and her clothes taken from her. She escaped but died next day. The servant in the house was killed and also an old man of 80 who sometimes called with letters and chanced to be in the house.

At Inverigan the nine men living there were bound and then shot. At Achnacon the soldiers under sergeant Barbour shot at 8 men and killed six. One of the men still alive though wounded asked if he might die outside rather than indoors. This request was granted and when outside he threw his plaid over the guns and leaped into the darkness and escaped. At Larach (Note at this date the land of the MacDonalds continued to the Glencoe side of the Laroch river in Ballachulish. The other side of the river was Stewart country). Ranald of the Shields was shot and his son killed. Ranald was badly wounded but not dead and crept into a house but when it was set alight he was not able to escape. Later two further MacDonalds were shot at Inverigan one of whom was a boy of seven. In all 38 were shot; but as the houses were fired and the cattle driven off, leaving neither shelter nor food it is not certain how many died as a result of the Massacre.

Major Duncanson arrived at Inverigan after the shooting and it was he who found the extra man and the boy. However Hamilton arrived late. He had come in awful weather from Kinlochleven over the Devil's staircase. He only found one man of eighty whom he killed.

To some of the soldiers it was a shocking thing to attack the unsuspecting and hospitable MacDonalds. There would have been no disgrace in killing them in a fair fight, but once they had accepted hospitality it was another matter. Nowadays some who have little thought of history belittle the Massacre as having killed so few. But whatever the present day standard of what constitutes a massacre may be, the Massacre of Glencoe shocked the people of the day. Some of the MacDonalds received warnings from the soldiers who were to exterminate them. This showed their Highland code came before the risk of military action if found out.

It is said that Glenlyon's piper himself tried to convey a warning. They say, those who know the pipes well, that the pipes can talk in Gaelic and that it is possible to convey a message by music without the use of words. There have been a number of instances in Highland history when this has happened. Then too there was the tale of the fairy piper of legend who is said to have led the soldiers a wild trail after him through the bogs and over rocks and so gave time for clansmen to escape. Two officers of Hamilton's, Francis Farquhar and Gilbert Kennedy (both lieutenants) refused to continue the killing and were put under arrest. One soldier is said to have run away.

Several of the common soldiers gave warnings to their hosts. One soldier seeing a nurse with a child, sat by the fire and called to the dog stroked it, and said "Ah many a good thing may happen good dog, during the long winter night, yes, many a good thing may happen, but it may not be so tomorrow". One soldier at Brecklet as he saw the father of the household come in and take off his plaid, said "Yours is a good plaid," "It is not bad" the man replied. The soldier continued "Were this plaid mine I would put it on and go out and look for cattle" as the man (a Robertson) said nothing a second soldier said "No one knows to whom the plaid may belong tomorrow" Robertson said "I would like to see the man who would take my good plaid from me." Looking steadily at him the soldier said "Were that plaid mine I would put it on at once and take every male child with me and go

The Henderson Stone (Clach Eanruig). It was to this stone that a soldier spoke before the Massacre and so warned one family of impending disaster, for they took to the hills and escaped the Massacre.

3

This Monument was erected in 1884 by Mrs
Burns MacDonald. It states:
  "This cross is reverently erected in
  memory of McIan Chief of the
  MacDonalds of Glencoe
  Who fell with his people in the Massacre
  of Glencoe 13 Feb 1692
  By his direct descendant Ellen Burns
  MacDonald August 1883
  Their memory liveth for evermore."

and drive the cattle away to a safe place" Robertson took the warning, the house was fired as instructed but later the soldiers came back and put out the flames.

In another instance while a game of shinty was being played on the eve of the Massacre a soldier was heard to say "A Clach glàs tha anns a gleann S' mórdo chor air a bhi ann, na be mise thusa cho a bhithin idir ann". Translated is "Yon grey stone which is in the Glen much is your right to be here, but if I were you I would not be there at all". This stone is still to be seen and is known as the Henderson Stone. At Inverigan a woman fled with her child. When the child began to cry a soldier was sent to kill the child. The soldier not wishing to do this cut the little finger of the child to get blood on his sword to satisfy his superiors. Years later this soldier took refuge in an inn at Appin in the depth of winter. He spoke of the Massacre as being the worst time he had known as a soldier. Further questioned as to the part he had played the soldier told the tale of cutting the child's pinkie. The host held up his hand and there the pinkie or little finger was missing. The soldier remained at the inn for the rest of his life as an honoured guest. A very similar story is told of a soldier on being sent to kill a crying child found the mother singing to her child and it was the same song that his wife had sung to his child. In this case, he wrapped his plaid round her, and gave her what food he had and left her. Coming on the body of a young woman being eaten by a wolf, he killed it and got blood on his sword.

Again the fairies were said to have helped in their own way. Fairy women were seen washing the shrouds in the river Coe of those about to be killed. Many of these stories are confirmed and some have come down orally. Certainly many made their escape, and were welcomed and helped by the people of the territory they took refuge in. Some escaped through the passes to Appin, or to Glen Etive. The alarm coming in the middle of the night when it was dark and in wild weather hindered escape but also hindered the soldiers.

Great feeling was aroused throughout the country when the news of the Massacre slowly filtered through. Ministers of the Crown tried to stifle the feeling but the clamour was so great that a commission was appointed to inquire into the "Slaughter of the people of Glencoe."

Among other points raised is the fact that shortly after the Massacre there came a clansman from Campbell of Barcalden, steward to the Earl of Breadalbane to the two sons of the dead chief. He wished them to declare that the Earl of Breadalbane was clear of any guilt of the Massacre and if they would so agree to declare this they would be sure of Breadalbane's help in getting remission and restitution.

The findings of the Commission were first, that it was a great wrong to discount the oath which MacIain had taken, and that it "seemed to have had a malicious design against Glencoe". That Stair knew he had taken the oath. There was no instruction for the slaughter nor far less as to the manner of it. And fourthly that Stair's letters were the only warrant for what the commission called "Slaughter under Trust".

The findings were presented to Parliament. It was voted that the execution of the Glencoe men was murder. They requested to the King that he send home from Flanders the soldiers Major Duncanson; also Glenlyon, Drummond; Lt. Lindsay, Ensign Lundie and Sergeant Barbour should be sent home for the "Murder of the Glencoe men under Trust".

William certainly signed the document both at the top and bottom of the letter. It was claimed he did not read it, which hardly excuses him when it affected so many lives and above all, the fact that he did not prosecute. Stair retired temporarily. A gift of certain rents and feus of Glenluce from the King followed shortly and in 1703 he got an earldom. Livingstone was raised to the peerage in 1698. None of the soldiers were sent home.

In late August the Clan were allowed back to their land. Houses were repaired for winter. Food and help came to them from Keppoch, Locheil and the Stewarts of Appin from far distant Heiskir the laird sent a birlinn of meal.

The Clan were out in the '15 and again in the '45. During the last campaign the Jacobite army came to Newliston where nearby was a house owned by the then Lord Stair. The Prince feared that there might be some reprisal in revenge for the Massacre so he ordered a guard to be put round the house. The MacDonald Chief demanded that his men should guard the house to show that the purity of the cause was smirched by no "vileiny of hate". So the Clan of Glencoe men guarded the house and saw no damage was done to it.

The present Monument to the MacDonalds who perished in the Massacre was erected in 1884. There is an open air service at the Monument on the anniversary of the Massacre 13th of February.

The Story of James of the Glen is in Lismore, Duror & Strath of Appin.

Chapter 2   Lismore, Duror & Strath of Appin

Castle Stalker lies out from the shore at Strath of Appin. It was a stronghold of the Stewarts. The rock on which it stands is known as "Craigan Scart", the Cormorant Rock.

The Island of Lismore in Loch Linnhe lies off Port Appin. It is ten miles long and about one and a half miles broad. It is a fertile island and its Gaelic name means "great garden". Port Appin is about two miles from the small townships of Strath of Appin.

Duror lies six miles to the North East. They were all part of one parish, that of Kilmaluag named after Saint Maluag. This parish did extend from Lismore, Appin, Glencoe and Kingairloch in the seventeenth century but now consists of Lismore and Appin. The area known as Appin includes Duror, Glencreran and Strath of Appin.

There are the remains of prehistory in all three areas. A Standing Stone at Duror 13 ft. in height is an impressive sight. It can be seen from the main road. It is in a field which belongs to Achara House. There is the remains of a stone circle on Balnagowan, an island in Loch Linnhe not far from Cuil Bay, Duror. In the sixteenth century the island was described as "full of woods" but now it is without trees. At Inverfolla in Strath of Appin is a Standing Stone, but it has fallen down and now lies on its side. It is said to mean death within the year if anyone raises it. On Lismore the Standing Stone has been broken about three feet from the base. It is near the old remains of the Cathedral, now the Parish Church.

Lismore has a fine broch. These circular buildings were built for defence. They are more plentiful in the North and East. This is far South for the West coast. None are to be found in their completed state. We do not know if they were roofed or not. A broch is made of two walls with an inner space between them, with access for people to climb between the walls. It has an easily guarded entrance. The centre of the broch is not built on. The whole is constructed without mortar or lime. The one on Lismore is known as Tirfuir (cold land). Both on Lismore itself, and on the surrounding small islands there are archeological remains.

The early Christian history begins with St. Maluag who arrived at Lismore somewhere between 561 and 564. He was born in Ulster in 525 and died at Ardclaich in 592. While he is rightly associated with the island, he travelled over a considerable part of Scotland as a missionary. A rock on the Island is known as St. Maluag's Chair. By natural processes it appears carved in the form of a chair. It is said that sitting in this chair will give help to those suffering from rheumatism. St. Maluag's pastoral staff is under the care of the hereditary guardian and stays on the island. The family of Livingstones known as "The Bachull" have had the care of this staff for many centuries. The "Bachull Mor" the pastoral staff had many powers, it ensured safety at sea, truth on land, was guard against plague and murrain (infectious disease among cattle) was able to preserve women in labour. It was said that as long as those responsible for looking after it were true to their trust, it would return home if stolen. What is believed to be St. Maluag's Bell is now in the National Museum of Antiquities of Scotland in Edinburgh.

Another Saint associated with the island is St. Kieran of Clonmacmois who worked so well in the Argyll area he became known as the "Apostle of Kintyre". There are the remains of his chapel at Port Kilchieran.

On the island of Bernera at the South West of Lismore is the remains of a small chapel. It is said that St. Columba held services on the Island under the shadow of a large yew tree. These trees were grown for their use in making bows. St. Columba foretold the destruction of the tree. "The pride and greed of man would hew down the noble tree but retribution would overtake the vandals who did so, and their crime would be expiated only by water, blood and three fires."

As late as the nineteenth century Campbell of Lochnell ordered the tree to be cut down for the staircase of his Lochnell Castle. When the tree fell, one workman was crushed and killed and the tree and the surrounding ground were marked with blood. The boat taking the logs to the mainland was swamped by a sudden storm and lives were lost, and on three occasions Lochnell Castle was burnt down with the staircase escaping each time. The tree has started to sprout again.

The Cathedral Chapter was constituted in 1249 but the building was finished about the middle of the fourteenth century during the time of Bishop Martin. The Cathedral was burnt down at the reformation but the remains of the Choir or chancel of the Cathedral is now the Parish Church. It was re-roofed in 1749 and the wall height reduced by 9 feet. It is now small but delightful. Near the Cathedral is a Sanctuary Cross. A criminal was safe if he reached it and stayed within the area of four Crosses for a year and a day, he had then paid for his crime and was free. He was allowed outwith the area to go to church on Sunday but on no other occasion.

The Gaelic word "lios" as well as meaning garden also means Cathedral, fort, or enclosed space. So it is possible one of the last three is the derivation of its name for all three are on the island.

Besides the rest of the coast of Scotland, Lismore was harried by Vikings. One heroine of the island was Eilidh Mhor. When the Vikings were seen approaching the Island everyone hid except Eilidh Mhor. She hid her one cow in a hollow and watched. Three Vikings found the cow and started to drive her away, when Eilidh Mhor came on them, and in great anger swung her flail. She took them by surprise, and killed all three. She threw their bodies over the cliff on to the shore below where the other Vikings were gathered. Then Eilidh Mhor rolled big boulders from the cliff down on to the shore and killed the Chief Viking. The others fled.

In spite of such a victory, the Vikings did land and settle on Lismore. One of them built Castle Coeffin. There, lived Princess Boathail and her brother. Her father was king of Lochlan. Her brother was said never to rest his oars nor let his arms rust, but his sister made friends with the people and was much loved. When she learnt that her lover had died in Lochlan she would not be consoled. She declined and died. She was buried on Lismore, but could not rest in her grave. She haunted her brother and her father begging to be buried in the same grave as her beloved in Lochlan. This distress caused arrangements to be made to wash her bones and take them for reburial in Lochlan. However she still did not rest, for some of her bones had been left in the well when they were being washed, on Lismore before the journey. This was found to be true, for two of her toe bones had been left in the well. Again an expedition was sent to Lochlan to bury the two bones. After this, the Princess rested in peace.

One of the most photographed sights in the area is Eilein Stalcair known in English as the Island of the Hunter or some authorities say Falconer. The island is rock and is known in Gaelic as "Craigan Scart" the Cormorant Rock. It is the Appin slogan. According to the Ancient Monument Authorities, there may have been a building of sorts in the time of the MacDougall's before 1388. But this was restored by Dugald 1st of Appin (died 1498) and his son Duncan.

Both James IV and James V visited the Castle and traditionally hunted from it. But more important the two Kings had the loyal support of their kinsman who alone in the West Highlands both kings could depend upon. The Castle was rebuilt in its present form by James V. Duncan Stewart was appointed hereditary keeper of the Castle

There is a tale told, that over some wine Sir Donald Campbell persuaded Duncan Stewart to sell the Castle for a small wherry. It is certain that the Castle changed hands and remained in Campbell hands for many years. However, it is more likely that Sir Donald Campbell of Ardnamurchan afterwards of Airds was put in under pressure on a weak Stewart Chief by the Marquis of Argyll about 1620–25. In the reign of James VII the Castle was restored after a Stewart lawsuit which alleged this pressure. It was lost again in 1689, and garrisoned by the Hanoverians in 1745. 1705 was the last year it was lived in, and in 1840 the roof fell in. It was bought by Mr. Charles Stewart of Achara. Recently it was sold again and has been restored as a dwelling place. Modernisation has taken place inside, the outside has been unaltered.

Castle Shuna on the Island of Shuna is in ruins. It is uncertain when it was built, but it may be 15th century or 16th century. The Island lies off the shore from Appin. A description written about the 1630's described the Island, "It is verie fertill of Corne and abundance of butter and cheese and milk, and fish to be slaine in the sea next to this Illand".

In the Episcopal Church yard at Portnacrois is a monument to the Battle of Stalc. On it is written "1468 Above this spot was fought the bloody Battle of Stalc, in which hundreds fell, when the Stewarts and the MacLarens their allies in defence of Dugald, Chief of Appin, son of Sir John Stewart, Lord of Lorn and Innerneath defeated the combined forces of the MacDougalls and the MacFarlanes".

The events leading up to this are long and involved. In the fourteenth century both the "Lordship" the great MacDonald Kingdom, and the MacDougalls, Lords of Lorn, were considerably more powerful in their own areas than was the central government. Both considered themselves as independent princes. The MacDougalls fought against Bruce and were antagonistic towards the Stewart kings who followed. Bruce had killed the "Red Comyn" which antagonised that Clan, and as the MacDougalls had connections with the Comyns they were also antagonised. One of the MacDougall titles was "Lord of Lorn". In 1388 the title was lost to them through a political marriage and it came to Sir John Stewart. In 1439, the third to succeed to the title was another of the same name, Sir John Stewart. At this time the Campbells had risen from an unimportant Clan to a powerful one, both in their own territory and at court. Sir John had three daughters, all married to Campbells. To these he gave land as dowries. He had a brother Walter who regarded himself as heir, and one illegitimate son Dugald MacLaren. Sir John being a widower, decided to marry Dugald's mother to make his son legitimate. The Earl of Argyll (Campbell) wished to acquire the title "Lord of Lorn" and make a pact with Walter to aid him if need be. Sir John, knowing the difficulties ahead, gave much land including Dunollie Castle, back to the MacDougall Chiefs who understandably resented the loss of their title. Sir John also made him guardian of his heirs.

The marriage was arranged, and it was to take place at Dunstaffnage Castle, seat of the Lords of Lorn. While the marriage was about to take place Sir John was stabbed by Alan M'Coule an illegitimate son of the MacDougall Chief. Sir John lived long enough for the marriage to take place. The MacDougalls revolted. This was organised by the Earl of Argyll who also arranged support for them from the MacFarlanes from Loch Lomond. Dugald, still a young lad, retreated up Glen Orchy with the MacLarens and the men from Lorn who remained loyal to his father. It should be remembered at this point, that the Stewarts were not a Clan as for instance the MacDonalds or MacDougalls, but were superiors over a number of smaller Clans such as the MacColls and the Livingstones and the Caermichaels.

The monument to the Battle of Stalc fought in 1468. The writing on the monument reads as follows: "1568 Above this spot was fought the bloody battle of Stalc in which hundreds fell, when the Stewarts and the Maclarens their allies in defence of Dugald, Chief of Appin, son of Sir John Stewart, Lord of Lorn and Innerneath defeated the combined forces of the MacDougalls and the MacFarlanes". The monument is in the grounds of the Scottish Episcopal Church of Portnacrois Strath of Appin.

There was a battle at Leac-a-dotha. Dugald was heavily defeated and there was a heavy loss of life on both sides, and this included the MacFarlane Chief. Dugald retired to Appin and then occurred the "Inveich Mor" or "Great Flitting", when many from the lower part of Lorn who were neither MacDougall nor Campbell supporters, joined Dugald. There was a battle in 1468 when the MacDougalls and MacFarlanes landed at Airds Bay, and nearby in the Churchyard area was fought the Battle of Stalc, when Dugald was victorious.

There was then a complex situation. The king was a minor and the Earl of Argyll was Justiciary of Scotland, and while Dugald was the rightful heir he had had neither experience, nor was he powerful. Walter got the title but relinquished this in return for land and the Campbell Earl became Lord of Lorn. Dugald remained in Appin. When King James IV became of age he confirmed Dugald in Appin and other lands and made him King's Chamberlain of the Isles.

Donald of the Hammers Domhnull nan Ord is one of Appin's heroes. He was the son of Alexander 1st of Invernahyle known as "Tiochail" or peaceful. One morning he visited an island called Eilean-nan-Gall which at low water can be reached on foot from Stalcair. He laid his Lochaber axe to one side. At that time there was a feud between his family and that of Campbell of Dunstaffnage. While he was on the island Cailean Uaine brother of Dunstaffnage landed on the island along with some of his men. He came on the axe and lifting it said "This is a good axe if it had a good handle to it." Alexander said "Has it not that?" He laid his hand on the axe and a struggle followed. Alexander was surrounded by Colin's men and was killed. Possibly news of the murder reached Invernahyle before the Campbells, for the nurse escaped with the infant son of the dead Alexander. She hid him in a cave up in Glen Hyle. She tied a lump of fat round his neck, which, being a small baby he sucked, and this kept him alive for three days till she was able to escape with the baby to her own country of Moidart. There she and her husband brought up the baby as one of their sons. His foster father Raibeart's work was held in great regard so that it became a saying "Is that a Moidart-made sword you are wearing?" Donald grew up and showed great physical strength and mental powers. He was able to lift two of the heavy hammers one in each hand and wield them without apparent effort. He is said to have been able to dive in to the deepest pool of the River Shiel and come up with a salmon in his hands. His foster father made a special sword for Donald and told him of his birthright. Donald was offered help from his foster brothers and from his uncle who recognised his claim. The Chief too returned Invernahyle to him which during his supposed death had reverted to the Chief. Donald attacked Dunstaffnage and after several fights Colin was killed. As his clansman saw Colin die he said, "That is clean blood you have given the Lyon salmon today". Donald replied, "Not so clean as you gave without cause one fine morning to the crabs of Eilean 'n Stalcair".

In 1692 the Massacre of Glencoe occurred. Some of the MacDonalds managed to escape and some reached Appin where they were given a kindly welcome. In the original Order for the Massacre signed by King William, it said "to destroy entirely the country of Lochaber, Lochiel's lands, Keppoch's Glengarry's Apine and Glenco."

There is a story of a woman with an infant at the time of the Massacre. The baby cried and a soldier was sent to kill the child. He told the mother to keep the child quiet, and he cut off the child's pinkie and got blood on his sword and reported he had killed the child. Years later, on a wild stormy night an old soldier came to the door of an inn at Appin. As everyone talked, someone asked the soldier what was the worst time he had had as a soldier. He said it was at the Massacre of Glencoe. The landlord stiffened but asked the soldier what part he had played. The soldier told of the cutting off of the little finger of the baby. The landlord help up his hand which had no pinkie and the soldier remained at the inn as an honoured guest for the rest of his life.

Besides the warring humans, Lismore, Appin and Duror, had a population of fairies. Mermaids have been reported resting in the windows of Stalker Castle combing their yellow hair with silver combs. Lismore had two horrifying characters who were slain by the Fienn. They hunted over the parish (including Glencoe) besides many places in Scotland. There are many places named after them. The Fienn are the legendary heroes of the Celts. Tales of their exploits were handed down orally (and on paper) through the centuries. They possessed all the great Celtic virtues, were good soldiers and brave fighters, hospitable, generous, as time went on they became larger than life and giants. The poet of the Fienn, Ossian, left a record of their lives and activities.

One of the famous sons of Lismore was the Dean of Lismore who in the sixteenth century collected Gaelic Manuscripts. From this collection (which has been published in part) it is possible to see some of the old tales of Ossian written down. It is a pity Dr. Johnson did not visit Lismore where he would have seen the Manuscripts and talked to people who understood them. The Rev. Donald McNicol who was a nephew of Stewart of Invernahyle was minister of Lismore from 1766 to 1802. He was in fact in charge of the huge parish which included Kingairloch from Shian Ferry to Kingshouse some 559 square miles. He was a Gaelic scholar and collected old Gaelic poems some of which have been preserved.

Duror had a glaistig whose face was like a lichen covered stone. She received a libation of milk daily. Oddly enough when this libation was stopped I have been told that the family who had previously enjoyed good health, had more than their share of illness. One girl who was going to the burn for water at night said she was not afraid of the glaistig. As she walked she felt a slap on her cheek which twisted her head to one side. But the next day she got a slap on the other side and this put the matter right. The glaistig is variously described as being half woman and half fairy or sometimes half goat. She usually wears green. There was a glaistig on Lismore. She enjoyed startling travellers. Like the rest of her kind she was attached to places rather than to people. She was able to utter powerful and effective curses so it did not do to offend her. Lismore had Bodaich who were spectres who were not accepted in any spiritual home, and because they were bored spent their time frightening people. In Appin there is the story of Bladderunm. A small kitten used to come in every evening to sit at the huntsman's fire. One day when the hunter was out he shot a wild cat. Before it died it said, "Say to the kitten at the fireside, 'I have killed Bladderunm.'" The hunter went home and repeated this to the kitten who said, "You have killed my sister." At that, the kitten swelled up and grew to a huge size and killed the hunter.

The Chief of Stewart of Appin had their loyal followers, but unlike most clans these followers were not all Stewart or branches of the Stewarts. The Livingstones are descended from the Macbeths or Beatons, the great medical family who held the hereditary post of doctor to the Lords of the Isles. When this was broken up, the family maintained their medical skill on behalf of different chiefs. Dr. Livingstone's grandfather had connections with the North Lorn area before he went to Ulva in Mull and later the family moved to the South.

The MacColls arrived in the Lorn area round Loch Crearan about 1350. The MacColls had a great attachment to the Appin Stewarts and the Achnacon Stewarts have a MacColl at either side of their coffin. The Caermichaels were also to be found fighting under the Stewart Banner.

The Stewarts were out on the side of Montrose and again rose for Dundee. They were engaged in both the '15 and the '45. In this last they were led by Stewart of Ardsheal acting for the Chief. After Culloden, Ardsheal returned to his home country and for a while took shelter in a cave on the hillside of Beinne Bheir and escaped to France in September 1746.

His clansmen had to pay rent to the government as they had been forfeited by Ardsheal. But voluntarily and at some risk, they sent a second rent to France to Ardsheal. One of the collectors of rent was Colin Campbell. He not only took the rent, but under Government orders he evicted those of a strong Jacobite sympathy and replaced them with tenants who had Whig sympathies or were at least neutral. He had a quarrel with James of the Glen, but this was made up. One day when Colin Campbell of Glenure (known as the Red Fox), was coming from Fort William to do some more evicting, as he made his way towards Kentallen, a shot rang out and he was killed. James of the Glen was arrested. He was in Duror at what was then an Inn known as Inshaig. The house, no longer an Inn, still stands. James of the Glen was taken to Inverary and tried by a jury of eleven Campbells and the Duke of Argyll. He was condemned, though it was known witnesses were prevented from coming forward, and to the end James protested his innocence which is largely accepted today. He was hanged at Ballachulish just near the Ballachulish Hotel. He was not given burial but his bones hung for over a year and when they dropped they were wired up. Finally the body was collected and buried at Kiel Churchyard in Duror. There is a monument to him at the place where he was hanged.

Above: Grave of James of the Glen at Keil Church in Duror of Appin. This church is in ruins it lies on the Oban side of Duror. The best approach is from the shore. There are some interesting graves in the churchyard though not of the importance as that of James of the Glen.

Above right: The Monument to the memory of James of the Glen. It was at this spot he was hanged and the stone on the top of the monument was one he used to sit on according to local legend. This monument is at the south Ballachulish side of the new bridge.

In Duror there is a house where, local oral tradition says, he was born. This lies up in the Forestry area. It is certain that the house he lived in, though now a sad ruin, is visible. It lies in the grounds of a house at present called Invernahyle, previously Acharn (further back in its history Invernahyle). But the old home of James of the Glen has no connection with this house.

The Stewarts of Appin saved their Banner which was at Culloden. It was one of the few to reach home in safety, the rest being burnt by the public hangman in Edinburgh. It was rescued by Donald Livingstone who tore it from the flag pole and wrapped it round his body and brought it back to Appin. At the present time it is in the Museum at the Castle in Edinburgh. A replica is shown in the Scottish Episcopal in Appin.

At Appin in the old Kinlochlaich church, is a stone from Culloden, a memorial to those who died at Culloden from the Appin area. The moving spirit behind this monument was Lt. Col. Alexander Stewart of Achnacone. It was done by public subscription but he was the organiser. As well as this, he was responsible for the monument to the Battle of Stalc and that of James of the Glen.

A point of interest is, that Scott in his tale "Waverley" used a true fact as a basis of the tale. Col. Whiteford of Ballochmyle was the prisoner of Stewart of Invernahyle and the behaviour of the two men was followed in "Waverley".

Chapter 3 **Eilean Munda: the burial island in Loch Leven**

St. Munda or St. Munde is an island at the head of Glencoe in Loch Leven midway between South Ballachulish on the one side, and Callart on the other. Loch Leven is salt water and changes its name to Loch Linnhe at the narrows at Ballachulish Ferry. It changes its name several times before it reaches the open sea at Oban. The Island is called after St. Fintan Mundus who built his church on the Island.

The first Christian missionary to come to Glencoe was St. Kenneth the Pictish monk who later went to work in Fife. He chose a smaller island nearer Ballachulish Ferry called Eilean Choinneich. It was a custom for these early missionaries to choose islands for their homes and for the building of their churches. They were away from the forays of war, and the world, yet accessible. Also the wolf survived in Scotland till the 18th century, and by having the graves on an island they were safe from these beasts. As a side issue there is a local tale of the last wolf in the area being killed by a man who wrapped his plaid round his hand and pulled out the wolf's tongue, the plaid protecting his hand while he did so.

For a while St. Kenneth according to the legend lived in a sunless part of Glencoe. One day an angel appeared before him and offered to remove the mountain and cast it into the sea, but St. Kenneth refused to allow this. However, if you look at Aonach Eagach you can still see the fissure in the rock where the angel had started.

St. Fintan Mundus was the son of Tailchen or Tulcan and he was related to Columba, and like him of royal blood, a scion of the family of Niall of the nine hostages. His mother was Feidelmia or Fedelyn and was of the race of Maine, perhaps this is where his surname came from. His sister was St. Coinchenn the Devout, Abbess of Cill-Sleibh, now Killeavy. She died in 654.

Tulcan brought his young son to Iona where he meant to become one of St. Columba's monks. It is said, though with uncertain authenticity, that Baithene one of Columba's most gentle monks said to Columba "This Laic loves his boy more than the Lord, therefore they should be separated". Columba then ordered Tulcan to throw his son off a cliff into the sea. Tulcan with a heavy heart started to obey, but at that moment St. Kenneth appeared. He had been sailing to Ireland and come to visit Iona on the way. He was much angered and stopped this act. He is said to have said "Henceforth we cannot be friends, for that thou hast given so cruel and impious a command, and has afflicted this miserable stranger". It is also said that Columba later blessed the boy and said "Thou shalt be reckoned among the greater saints of Ireland".

Columba himself passed through the area known as Loch n-Apor (Lochaber) and sailed up An Linne Dhubh (Loch Linnhe). There are four tales of his miracles told of him in the area. First there is the story of Nesan the Crooked, who lived in the district that borders upon the lake of river-mouths. He was very poor but at once received Columba with joy as his guest. Columba asked him how many cows he had and was told "Five". The Saint had them brought to him so he could bless them. They were blessed thus "From this day, your small number of five little cows will increase up to one hundred and five cows". Nesan had a wife and children so the blessing went on "Your seed will be blessed in your sons and grandsons".

Nearby was a rich man Vigenus who was mean and who had slighted Columba and on him Columba prophesied thus "The riches of that greedy man who has spurned Christ in pilgrim guest, will from this day be gradually diminished, and will be reduced to nothing. And he himself will be a beggar and his son will run from house to house with a half-empty bag. And he will die, struck with an axe by one of his enemies, in the trench of a threshing-floor".

Another host who received Columba had his cows blessed and in both cases when the number fixed by the Saint had reached the 105 cows it would not increase for any beasts over that number were carried off and not seen again except any that might be used for charity.

Another poor man of Loch n-Aper came to Columba for alms. Saint Columba told him "Take from the forest near by a stick of wood and bring it to me quickly". The man obeyed. The Saint shaped it into a spike, sharpened it and blessed and gave it to the man, saying "Keep this spike carefully. It will, I believe, have power to hurt neither man nor cattle but only wild animals, and also fish. And so long as you have this stake there will never be wanting in your house an abundant supply of venison to eat".

The man returned and set the spike in a part where there were wild animals and the next morning he went to his spike and found a fine stag had fallen on it. Every day he would find some beast or other had fallen on the spike. His house was full of meat and he sold the surplus to his neighbours. But his wife had misgivings for she was a foolish woman and said "Take up the spike from the ground. For if people, or if cattle should perish upon it, you yourself and I, with our children, will either be put to death, or led into slavery". Though the man tried to reassure her with the words of the Saint that the spike would never harm man or cattle, she persisted and so lifted the spike and took it into the house. His dog fell upon it and was killed and his wife said that one of the children would fall upon it and be killed. So her husband took it to very dense part of the forest and fixed it to a thornbrake where he thought no beast could be hurt by it. But next day he found a goat had been killed. He then took it and put it in the waters of the "Black Goddess" (Lochy) but when he went back he found a large salmon on the spike. He then placed the spike on a high part of his roof but a raven flying past was killed by it. Then the man on the advice of his wife chopped the spike into small pieces and threw them into a fire. From then on he returned to the life of begging and regretted his rash action in destroying the blessed spike.

Fintan Mundus sometimes Fentan Munnu went back to Ireland where he became a shepherd boy for a while. He was in training for eighteen years in the famous Monastery at Clonard under Finnian. Fintan Mundus dearly desired to become a monk on Iona and consulted with a wise old priest named Colum Crag. When Colum Crag heard of his desire he advised thus "Who can forbid your desire inspired, as I think, by God, and devout; and say that you ought not to sail over to the holy Columba?". However at this time two monks from Iona arrived at the Monastery with the news of Columba's death (597 A.D.). But on hearing that Baithene, Columba's foster son, had become Abbot Fintan Mundus sailed for Iona.

He was at first received as a guest who was unknown but the next day he met Baithene. When Baithene learnt his name he said "I ought indeed to give thanks to God at your coming; but this you must know for certain, you shall not be our monk". Fintan is reported to have said "Perhaps I am unworthy of becoming a monk?" "Nay" answered Baithene "Thou art not unworthy and I would fain have thee, but I dare not disobey the command of Columba by whom the Holy Spirit prophesied of thee. For he told me that after his decease one Fintan, son of Tailchen, would come and seek for enrolment. But in God's prescience it is not predestined for him to become a monk of any abbot, but he has long since been chosen by God as an abbot of monks, and as leader of souls to the Kingdom of Heaven". "Be it unto me according to the prophecy and the marvellous foreknowledge of Columba".

St. Fintan worked in Ireland for some time and then came over to Scotland where he built churches in various parts of the country. He was a leper and was described as "The torch with the ascending flame, Fintan, pure tested gold the powerful abstenious flame, Son of Tulcan, a warrior, religious and crucified".

Towards the end of his life St. Kenneth now 84 felt death was near and wished to receive the Holy Sacrament. He said "God will send me another holy man named Fintan, and from him I may receive the Body of the Lord". Fintan Mundus then arrived and after administering to him, St. Kenneth died on the 11th October 600 A.D.

St. Fintan supported the Celtic Church against the Romans in the great argument. It might be well here to make a slight digression and deal briefly with the Celtic Church, the Roman Church and the Picts. Both the Celtic Church and the Roman Christian Church had the same theology and sprung from the same source, both acknowledged the seniority of the See of Peter. But owing to the wars of the last three centuries the Celtic Church had been cut off from the Roman Church and there had been little communication between them. Various differences had arisen. In the Celtic Church, Mass was said only on Sundays and Holy days, more than one Priest might take part in the consecration. The tonsure of the monks differed, the work of the Bishops varied, and Easter was celebrated on a different day. This last is what really brought matters to a head. They had different ways of calculating the date, the Celtic Church calculated by an astronomical formula which Rome had dropped as being inaccurate. With the two Churches being out of communication the differences had widened with the result that in the court of Northumbria, King Oswiu (an Angle) was celebrating Easter while his wife (a Saxon) was still holding Lent. At the famous Synod of Whitby in 664 representatives of the two Churches met. It was here that the story goes the King who presided at the synod, gave his vote in favour of St. Peter's lest when he came to the Gates of Heaven there should be none to open them.

The Picts were an older race in Scotland than the Scots, who came from Ireland. The Picts were a pastoral people to whom their greatest treasures were their dogs, their flocks, and their pasture. They were hunters on foot and on horse. They were fine horsemen. They have left us some excellent carved stones which tell us much of what we know of them. We have not got much in the way of written records or language and we do not know the key to many of the symbols carved on their stones: but one that is easily recognised is the wool comb. These were no barbaric tribe wearing little but paint. In many of the carvings the men are depicted in long woollen capes. Some say they stripped for battle and may have used painted symbols and so acquired their name from the Romans. Pictish and Celtic carving are both of great artistic merit but are quite different in spirit and craftsmanship.

It was the Picts who built these massive Brochs for defence. These are large circular towers with only one entrance which could be protected by a door and easily guarded. Some had springs for water. Most of the Brochs are to be found in the North and East of the Country and on the Islands. Lorn is not in the Pictish country, but our first missionary was the Pictish St. Kenneth and we do have a Broch on the Island of Lismore.

The church that St. Fintan founded on Eilean Munda was used till 1495 when it was burned down. It happened thus: one of the congregation consulted the Dalness wiseman over the bewitching of one of his cows. He was told to take a quern and place it above the church door on the next Sunday, which was St. Barnabus Day. He was to say as each man came out "Trioblaid air do shuil a dhuine", translated is "Trouble on thine eye my man". The man followed his instructions and when one man came out, the quern fell upon him. The owner of the cow attacked him, and a general fight started. One man made a torch with some hay and set the thatched roof on fire. It was repaired in the 16th century and used up to 1653. By the way a quern consists of two circular stones used for grinding corn.

There is a Latin life of St. Fintan which gives some details of his life though with some discrepancies from the details of him in Adomnan's Life of Columba. According to this Life, St. Fintan's mother was warned by an angel to go to a secret place for her son's birth and was told that her son would be a holy man. It is reported that Columba on a journey went out of his way to visit a holy boy (Fintan) who was living at Cluain in Ireland. He went to live in Clonenagh and began to build a famous monastery there. Fintan had the land ploughed and worked with his hands. He respected all animals. They did not keep a cow and when anyone offered anything with either milk or butter they would not accept it, and the vessel was immediately broken with a divine rod as the Saint so wished it. They were a very strict order and no one dared to offer them meat. Some of the holy men in the area came to Fintan and asked him to relax some of the severity. The night before their arrival an angel came to Fintan and told him to go along the road where he would meet a man and he was to do what the man told him. The man told him that he, Fintan, was not to relax anything which he had begun for God, but he was to beware that his severity did not let others be tempted "because one jug is more fragile than another".

A fire broke out in the monastery diningroom. The monks lost their heads, but St. Fintan blessed the fire which became extinguished on the spot.

One day his monks were working outside in the fields. When St. Fintan appeared among them, they playfully held him by the hand as was the custom of labourers with their masters and asked for refreshments. "The Lord can give on my behalf dearest sons what you ask". The cook had only country vegetables but chariots and wagons arrived with food for the monastery at that hour.

Most interesting of all is St. Columba's description of Fintan Mundus. "He is a certain holy man, a famous member of your race (this was being said to an Irishman) with a red face, bright eyes, and a head with few hairs" ... "He is a good shepherd of the flock ..."

The chronicler ends "No one could ever tell in this fleshy life on earth the love, humility, gentleness to others, vigour on himself, self-restraint, heavy fasting, nightly vigils kneelings and love surrounding all Christians of the blessed old man Fintan. He died on the 17th of February, 635 A.D.

The following extracts from the Minutes of the Synod of Argyll from 1639–59 give something of the history of the church on the island.

In 1649 there is a report that the church on the Ile of Munn in Glencoan has been vacant for five years. Several other churches in the area have also been vacant, and the assembly "appoynts Mr. Ar Me Calman their collector for uplifting the foirsaid vacencies, and to be comptable to the next syned".

In 1642 there is under discussion the question of separating the different charges "Considereing the discommodiousenes of the united kirks of Lesmore and Apine, pairt wherof being ane yle and pairt a continent, and everyone of them being both a considerable congregation and a sufficient maintenance, it is thought expedient that the yle of Lesmore be dismembered from the continent, which is Appine, and be served by a minister: And the said Appine and Durer, which is the continent, be erected in a paroach by itselfe and a minister provyded to serve the cure at the new builded kirk at Appine And Elen-Min (which includes Glencon and Mamore) to be annexed to Appine, and the preaching to be the 3rd Sunday at Elin Mun".

In 1651 there is as follows. "The saides commissionares have dismembret and disjoyned Appyne and Durror fra Kilmaluag in Lismore, as also Glencoan fra the kirk of Illanmoune, to be erected a new paroach to be bigged at Kilcallumkill in Durror, And ordanines the Ile Lismoir with the lands of Kengerloch to remaine a distinct paroach ..." In 27th of the same year the Synod minutes report "... and sicklyk dismembers the lands of Mammoir fra the kirk of Illan mowne and annexes the samen to the said kirk of Kilmalzie And mofefies for a constant locall stipend to ilk ane of the saids twa kirks ane thousand marks money and twa chalder meall with twenty punds for the communione elements, And appoyntes sufficient manses and gleebs for the minister of the said kirks of Kilmalzie and Kilmaneveg. And ordaines the saids stipends to be payed out of the first and readiest of the teynds of the said paroaches".

Among other details to be learnt is that Lorn got into trouble for not keeping its "presbyterie booke".

In the year 1770 in July Bishop Forbes sailed up Loch Leven and visited Ballachulish and Glencoe. Bishop Forbes was a noted Episcople and a staunch Jacobite. He had been going to join the Prince in 1745 but was arrested before he could do so. After the Rising he collected stories of those who had been "out" and went to great pains to get even small details exact. This work was published at the end of the last century by the Scottish Historical Society under the name of "The Lyon in Mourning". It is the major source book for those writing on that period.

The Bishop writes "We likewise come in view of the Island of St. Munde, who was abbot and Confessor in Argile, ... His anniversary in April 15. Upon the Island is the Ruine of a little Chapel, all four walls are still entire dedicated to St. Munde. Though the Isle has little Depth of Earth, being rocks, the MacDonalds and Camerons still bury there." The Nests of Jack Daws are sometimes found in the Sculls of the Dead ... Up from this Island is the House Of MacDonald of Glenco ..." On another visit he writes "Out of the Leith ship we got two more hands and rowed by favour of a delightful morning up the North side of the Island of St. Munde. I had full view of it, which is much larger than I imagined it to be, being devided by Interactions at High Water, but one continued Island at Ebb."

This stone has early Celtic carving and is likely to date back to the 15th century. Unfortunately sea air and weathering is hard on the stone but this one is in good condition. There are three stones of this date showing above ground possibly others under the turf.

There are three landing places on the Islands called the Ports of the Dead. The Island was used by the MacDonalds of Glencoe, the Stewarts of Ballachulish and the Camerons of Callart for burial and each had a recognised port. If for some reason it was not suitable to use their own port the boat would return to the mainland and try again. Near to Eilean Munda is Eilean a' Chomhraidh or the Isle of Discussion, a meeting place to discuss disputes on questions of land ownership and other matters. When a dispute had been settled they would sail up to Eilean na Bainne, the Isle of Covenant or ratification, where agreements were drawn up and sealed. On Eilean a' Chomraidh the men left their caps before going on to the burial island. After the funeral before rowing back they would land here and have whisky and oatcakes and cheese.

The ownership of the Island has long been disputed. It was the custom for the MacDonalds of Glencoe and the Camerons of Callart to take a crop of hay off it on alternate years. It is at present unknown who owns the Island. The Museum would like to raise money to preserve the Church but till the actual owner is located this is not practical. It might be as well at this point to read a letter written by Bishop Forbes. In his letter to Mr. Stewart Ballachulish dated Leith Nov. 15 1770 "As the walls of his chapel with you are still standing, and appear to be entire, I would heartily wish that those will still bury on the Island would put a roof upon the chapel. Surely they could so it at a small charge, as there is plenty of wood in the country, and that your slate quarry is at hand. In this case I could have worship in it when God may be pleased to favour me with a return to the delightful Bottom of Ballachulish. I would gladly contribute my mite for patching the walls of the chapel and putting on the roof". In 1872 Bishop Ewing in the Scottish Guardian writes "In the island which fronts the quarries and on which fig trees grow, lie buried the bodies of most of the inhabitants of Glencoe, of Ballachulish, and Lochaber".

There are many interesting graves on the Island. One of the most fitting is perhaps that of MacIain the Chief of the MacDonalds of Glencoe at the time of the Massacre. When he was taken for reburial on the Island, the legend of his great size and bull hide jacket was confirmed. At the beginning of the century Mrs. Chinnery Haldane's father took the remains of a MacDonald House from near the farm at Invercoe and put it by the grave. As the date on the stone was 1708 it can't have been that Chief's own house as he was murdered in the Massacre of 1692. But it may have been the home of the succeeding chief or his brother.

Another grave of great interest and originality is that of William MacKenzie shown taking a dragoon off his horse at Preston Pans. The whole incident being carved with considerable vigour.

There is one grave with the warning verse

My glass has run
Yours is running
Be warned in time,
Your hour is coming

There are three very old graves with Celtic carvings possibly going back to the 15th century. There is the grave of Allan Dall MacDougall, a Glencoe born poet. Allan Dall was apprenticed to a tailor. He had a very sharp tongue and he angered his fellow apprentices and one day one of them in anger put a needle in his eye. Allan Dall used his skill at music and verse and had his works published and became Bard to MacDonald of Glengarry. On his death he was brought for burial in Glencoe in 1829. The Gaelic word Dall means blind.

There is also buried there the slate quarry worker who was accidentally killed in the quarry and to whom flew a bird and put a leaf of ivy on his brow.

On looking at the graves one is struck by the very fine writing and carving upon them. It is a fact that people of this area were noted for their skill at this work. The slate graves have worn well, some of the stone ones have suffered from time and salt spray.

There are several superstitions about the Island. One is the one common to a number of island burial grounds, that the last person buried had to keep watch over the island and could not get free to Paradise till the next person was buried on the island. There used to be an old custom of dropping coins into the graves to repay the hospitality of the earth. There is the story of the Tailor who for a bet agreed to stay all night on the Island and make osan or garters or in some versions knitting stockings who to win his bet had to wait in the church till the job was finished. A voice from the grave said to him "do you see these two hands tailor", the tailor continued hard at his work but replied that he did. "Can you see this" and at this a head appeared; the tailor working as hard as he could said yes he could see it. Then the voice said "Can you see and feel this Tailor". The tailor said yes but he would knit till he finished and just as he put in his last stitch the body rose from the grave but the tailor leaped for the door and safety. The Thing grabbed at him, missed and caught the door and left his prints on it. They are still there as evidence so the tale goes. Another tale is that of young Cameron who fell in love with a MacDonald girl. He swore to be true to her while his head was on his shoulders. He broke this vow and fell in love with another girl. Not long after he took a fever and died. He was buried on the Island. But the peace of the Island was from then on disturbed with shrieks and groans. One day a brave man went out to the Island to see what was the cause of this unrest. He found the young Cameron buried but with his head above ground and the young Cameron asked the man to behead him with his sword. This was done and peace returned to the Island.

The last two times that the church was used for a service were firstly on 2nd July 1653 probably by Mr. Reid when Donald Campbell of Blarmafoldach one of several persons

Top: This is a spirited drawing of one "William MacKenzie taking a dragoon off his horse at Preston Pans" This grave is in the interior of the church.

Right: The remains of the old church on Eilean Munda. This church was built in the sixteenth century to replace one which was burned down by accident.

Below: This gravestone shows the excellent lettering for which the local men were noted.

Bottom right: This is the grave of MacIain the murdered Chief. He was buried on the island when the clansmen returned to Glencoe. This grave lies at the opposite end of the island from the church.

The interior of the church on Eilean Munda.

excommunicated for joining "the crewell and bloodie rebels of James Grahame and Alexander MacDonald" was relaxed from his sentence. This last from Carmichael's book 'Lismore in Alba'. The last service of all was held in February 1954 when a commemoration service was held inside the church. It is still sometimes used for burial.

The Church of Scotland for Glencoe, is called St. Munda. It is in what is now called Ballachulish. In the old days the boundary between the MacDonald lands at Glencoe and the Stewart lands was the river Laroch which runs through the township of Ballachulish, though still situated in present day Ballachulish it still calls itself Glencoe Church. The Roman Catholic Church in Ballachulish is called St. Muns which also commemorates St. Fintan Mundus.

The flora and fauna of the island are like the mainland. Seals lie on the rocks, there is a heronry. Gulls and other sea birds frequent it. In the old days whales of different kinds sailed past it. Swans are still nesting there and some of the small song birds of the mainland. The flowers are about a fortnight ahead of the mainland and butterflies are more plentiful. I find it a delight, a peaceful and fascinating island, but I do know those who find it gloomy and fearful.

Chapter 4 **Ballachulish slate quarry**

The story of Ballachulish slate quarries goes back to 1693, when the West Quarry was opened. In 1694 the East Quarry was opened. There is a tradition that it was some slate quarry workers passing through the village who first observed the type of rock at Ballachulish. It was their report which caused investigations to be made. This has been claimed both for the slate workers from Easdale when they were returning from work at Aberfoyle and came by Rannoch Moor and Ballachulish and from slate workers from Northumberland. It has also been claimed by workers from Dunkeld who are said to have passed on their way to look for work.

Before going further, it may be as well to say that the minerals found in slate include quartz, white mica, and chlorite, while other minerals which may or may not be present are pyrites, haematite, magnetite, graphite, biotile, rutile, tourmaline, and ziron. A characteristic of slate is that it splits with a perfect cleavage.

By 1791 there were 74 families of 322 people engaged in the industry. From the Statistical Account of that year we learn that a great quantity of slates were sent to Leith, the Clyde, to England, Ireland and even to America. Ships of any "burden" could be loaded easily as the fine smooth sand came so near the shore and there was no swell. The method of loading was that a few planks were thrown between the ship and the shore, the men formed what they called a "rank" and passed the slates by hand to each other in a chain till all the slates were safely in the hold. This is the local tradition though early travellers mention that a wheel barrow was used.

In 1770 Bishop Forbes in his Journal writes "We rowed up the Loch with two hands only, till we came to some ships anchored at Ballachulish Slate Quarry, the South side of the Loch, by which he (the then Stewart of Ballachulish) gets 2 or 300, if not £400 sterl. a year". In Lord Teignmouth's Sketches, he writes of the bustle and industry of a crowded population. John Leydon writing in 1800 said that the quarries were near the bottom of the hill, and that the working was done with little danger. He added that the workmen were chiefly from Cumberland. Dorothy Wordsworth in her journal writes of the many ships and their tall masts in the harbour.

By 1845 there were 300 employed in the quarry. The average wage was about 12/- a week but a well-matched crew might earn £1 or more each. The pay for a day-labourer varied from 1/6 to 1/- or 10d. a day. Three-quarters of the men employed had houses on the Ballachulish Estate. The houses had three rooms "all plastered" with chimneys and grates in the principal rooms and an open garret above. Most of the houses had a "cowhouse" attached, and pasture on the nearby hill. Almost every family had a cow. The annual rent for the best type of house was £2. 5s. and pasture for a cow £1. 6s. and the ground for growing potatoes and vegetables 15/-—£4. 6s. in all. They also paid 5/- a year for a stretch of the seashore to gather kelp for their potatoes. The shore stretch used was from the march at Ballachulish to the Ferry. The men were paid quarterly at first and later every six weeks. There was a store where they could chalk up an account for goods such as flour, salt, herring, etc. This meant that when the wages were due, there might in fact be little money available, as the account at the quarry store was paid before the rest of the wage was paid over. This was stopped at the passing of the Truck Act. Local shops were helpful. I have heard the story of how one man went to a shop to say he could buy no more, nor pay for what he had had already. The shop owner lifted a bag of meal and one of flour and put them in a cart and delivered them. It was reckoned that this would last six weeks.

The Statistical Account of 1845 (known as the New Statistical Account) described the quarry. The height from the top of the quarry to the lowest level was 216 ft. and about 536 ft. in length. The first level was at 28 ft. above the half-tide mark. In 1955 the levels were 280 ft. from the top of the quarry to the road level, 130 ft. to the lowest bit below the road level. All levels were entered from the North and at the end which abutted upon the sea. A tram road extended along the face of the rock to a bank formed in the sea by the rubbish of the quarries. Along this road, the whole of the quarried rock was carried in waggons. The second level was 66 ft. above the first and it communicated with another bank also formed in the sea, by an arch thrown over the high road. This arch was built in 1822 and it was known as Glaic-an-Tobair. At present one arch remains, but before the present road was built there were two arches. These arches were built of slate. The third level was 74 ft. above the second. The slate from this level was taken down the slope by means of a fly-wheel to the same bank as the second level. At that date all the quarry levels were above sea level and as they were open to the sea there would be no trouble of flooding as the water would be drawn back to the sea if it rose.

By this time (1845) the men were local and descended from local people. By 1875 there were 587 men employed in the quarry. This included blacksmiths, carpenters, and other craftsmen. In the year 1875 there were 26 million slates made and shipped. In the largest quarry there were 11 and a half miles of railroad laid for waggons. There were six levels, two below and four above the road. The depth of the quarry was then 497 ft. It employed 12 horses and had four stationary engines and one locomotive. Later another locomotive was added.

Originally the quarry was worked by the proprietor, a Stewart of Ballachulish. This continued for some generations. Sometime after 1780 the quarries were let first to a Mr. Stevenson and later to a Mr. Rawse. Then the last Stewart proprietor took over for a while. He worked the quarry using a system known as the "Level System". This helped to develop and expand the quarry, but it was costly and he had to borrow money to try and keep going till he recovered his losses. Either his system did not work, or he wasn't allowed enough time to repay his debt, for the Bond Holders appointed as their agent Mr. MacGregor, a solicitor from Fort William and a clerk in the estate office, Mr. MacInnes, as works manager.

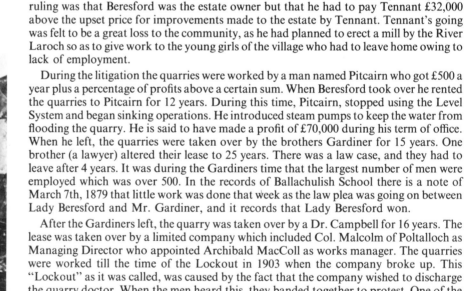

Some of the trucks which were used to move slate

At the end of the first year the Bond Holders decided to sell the estate, and advertised it for sale. It was bought in 1862 by an Englishman, who sent his agent, a Mr. Tennant, to buy the estate, who bought it for himself and took possession. He spent a lot of money on improvements. He built a large number of workmen's houses and a large hall for social activities. He employed an architect to make plans for a large house near the present Ballachulish House. The ground was even measured out for this house. Then he was sued by Beresford for "unlawful possession". The case was heard in Edinburgh. The judge's ruling was that Beresford was the estate owner but that he had to pay Tennant £32,000 above the upset price for improvements made to the estate by Tennant. Tennant's going was felt to be a great loss to the community, as he had planned to erect a mill by the River Laroch so as to give work to the young girls of the village who had to leave home owing to lack of employment.

During the litigation the quarries were worked by a man named Pitcairn who got £500 a year plus a percentage of profits above a certain sum. When Beresford took over he rented the quarries to Pitcairn for 12 years. During this time, Pitcairn, stopped using the Level System and began sinking operations. He introduced steam pumps to keep the water from flooding the quarry. He is said to have made a profit of £70,000 during his term of office. When he left, the quarries were taken over by the brothers Gardiner for 15 years. One brother (a lawyer) altered their lease to 25 years. There was a law case, and they had to leave after 4 years. It was during the Gardiners time that the largest number of men were employed which was over 500. In the records of Ballachulish School there is a note of March 7th, 1879 that little work was done that week as the law plea was going on between Lady Beresford and Mr. Gardiner, and it records that Lady Beresford won.

Above: The device for moving trucks of slate.

After the Gardiners left, the quarry was taken over by a Dr. Campbell for 16 years. The lease was taken over by a limited company which included Col. Malcolm of Poltalloch as Managing Director who appointed Archibald MacColl as works manager. The quarries were worked till the time of the Lockout in 1903 when the company broke up. This "Lockout" as it was called, was caused by the fact that the company wished to discharge the quarry doctor. When the men heard this, they banded together to protest. One of the old bill posters reads: "Highland News, Ballachulish Lock Out. Another great meeting of the men shoulder to shoulder for Dr. Grant. Full report today." The men gained their point, and Dr. Grant remained the quarry doctor, till the company dissolved shortly after.

At the beginning of the Great War the quarry closed down for lack of men and want of trade. After the war it was seen that no individual or company was interested in restarting the quarry. A meeting of the men was called, and it was decided to ask Sir William Haldane of Auchterarder and Mr. Brodrick Chinnery Haldane of Glen Eagles, for help. They had always shown a keen interest in the community. Chiefly through their efforts, and that of their friends a company was formed under the Industrial and Provident Societies Act. Sir William Haldane was made chairman and Mr. Brodrick Chinnery Haldane and two workmen as directors. A scheme was started by which all employees became shareholders to the value of £20, by deducting a percentage off their earnings each week. In October 1922, work began without any assets other than enthusiasm and co-operation. By 1926 engines had been installed making compressed air so that the men could drill mechanically, as before this all drilling was done by hand. This continued for 18 years so that it can be said that it was successful. While there were good and bad patches, unemployment was not as bad as in many other places. It should be realised that this enterprise succeeded in spite of starting with little equipment, so that boring had to be done by hand, but after three years, modern machinery was put in to make the quarry one of the best equipped.

By the 1930's the men got 10d. an hour, and 4/- per 1,000 slates. On good rock and with good weather they might take home £3 but bad weather and poor rock would reduce this amount.

In the last Statistical Account of Argyll, 1951, only about 20 men were employed. The competition from lighter and cheaper materials was being felt. But there was an output of over a million slates annually. The quarry closed down in 1955 though for a few years some of the older men carried on. At the present date the quarry is entirely idle, but there has been hope raised that the waste slate may, after processing, be used in the building of tall buildings of the multiple storey type. After the processing the slate becomes very light, and may be used as insulating material.

The men of the quarry were of a kindly nature. In the time of Stewart of Ballachulish (one of the earliest of that name to work the quarries) the men were not clear about certain workings of the quarry. He got some Englishmen in to help. They all left but one man who married a MacDonald. When she died and he was too old to look after himself, his fellow quarrymen looked after him, he stayed one week at one house then moved on to the next home and so on till the end of his life.

There is a true legend of the quarry. A young slate worker was accidentally killed by a premature explosion while shot firing, and as he lay dead a dove was seen to come and place a leaf of ivy on the man's forehead. This incident is recorded on his grave on Eilan Munda, the burial island in Loch Leven.

There is also on record an instance of the second-sight. A man called Ewan MacColl had this uncanny and unwanted gift. Once when trimming slates with a boy beside him splitting them, Ewan became agitated and lifted the boy's legs off the path saying as he did so, "The spirits of the living are too strong". A friend came near and saw how pale Ewan was and asked if he were ill. Ewan replied that he was well but there was an awful fate in store for a mutual friend. The friend asked if it could not be averted, but Ewan said that it could not. Soon after, a large boulder rolled down the hill and crushed the friend seen by Ewan in his vision. The men going to the rescue carried an oak lever. Their path crossed the spot where Ewan had lifted the boy's legs.

In the Statistical Account of 1845 we get a good account of how the quarry was worked. The slate was manufactured by contract, the rock being let annually to parties of 4 and sometimes 6 men. Each party was called a crew, and was paid at a stipulated rate for the number of slates which they made within the period of agreement. The workmen bought their own tools and paid for the powder that was used in blasting the rock, while the master maintained the tram roads, and furnished wagons. Crews sometimes hired men and boys to assist them but all were under the master's control. Boys from 10 to 15 years were paid 6d. to 1/- a day, lads from 15 to 20 years were paid 1/- to 1/6 a day.

The price of slate at the Easdale quarry in 1862 was on average £2 per thousand, likely those from Ballachulish averaged much the same. The colour of the slate is deep blue, spangled with pyrites called by the workmen "diamonds". The different types of slate were the Duchesses 24″ × 12″, Countesses 20″ × 10″, Marchionesses 22″ × 12″, Princesses 24″ × 14″, Imperials 30″ × 24″, Queens or Rags 36″ × 34″, Sizeable 14″ × 8″ and undersized 10″ × 6″. The Ballachulish quarry chiefly produced sizeable and undersized. They produced one much larger than any mentioned and it stands on a low hillside by the road beyond Ballachulish. It was put there as a monument to Queen Victoria's Jubilee. By 1845 the number of slates produced annually was from 5 to 7 million. Ballachulish slates got 5/- more per thousand than any other Scottish, Welsh or English slate because of their superior quality. They were less liable to break so this extra could afford to be given for them. There are tales of these slates being sold second hand fifty and more years after they had been first used.

When it was decided to bore a hole in the rock (for blasting) a sedan chair, as it was called, was lowered by a rope, a man climbed to the chair, and front there he started to bore two small holes each about 4 ins. deep and about 3 ft. apart. This chair upon which he sat was much like an ordinary chair, but its front legs were cut off, and a stay was tied from the edge of the seat to the back legs. Into each of the bored holes was placed a stage pin, and on these stage pins were laid three planks of wood each 4 ft. long by 12 ins. wide and 1 in. thick. After this, two other men climbed up onto the stage and they pulled up by quarry line two double hand-hammer each of seven pounds and the required number of drills, or "jumpers" as they were called. One man sat in a stool holding the jumper which the other two men hit in rotation. Between each blow the jumper was moved round in the hole. When it had been bored to about 8 ins. water was used to clean out the filings. This in turn thickened with the filings and became almost like porridge in consistancy. This made it difficult for the man rotating the drill and he would straighten his forefinger which was a signal to the hammer men to stop drilling so that he could clean the filings out with a cleaner. When the hole was bored to the required depth, the hole was dried out and all the filings removed. After this, it was filled a quarter to a third of its total length with black powder and safety fuse inserted. The hole was then filled up with dried clay. The staging was then removed, and when everyone had gone under shelter, one man lit the fuse then

Top: A slateworker on his sedan chair. He has his drill inserted making a hole for blasting.

right: Machinery being used in the quarry.

ran to shelter. When the fuse reached the powder, it exploded and dislodged the rock. Two men then climbed the rock face to clean up all the loose rock. The men of Ballachulish were said to be the best at blasting rock in Scotland. In the old days, the powder for blasting was carried in the horn of a Highland Cow. The thick part near the head had a wooden block fitted in it, while the tip was used for pouring (it could be poured slowly from the twisted tip) and it was closed with a wooden stopper when not in use. Later pitchers of a nonsparking metal were used. The powder was brought to the quarry in small wooden barrels. The fuse in early days was made of straw taken from the fields. The straw would be about 3 ft. long, and if a straw longer than this was required the tip of another straw would be cut off and inserted in the first straw so that the required length could be obtained. The top end of the outside straw was split with a knife and match paper inserted. This fuse led down to the powder. The powder used in the straw fuse was made as fine as dust, usually a pile of powder was spilled on top of a slate and then rolled with a bottle. The match paper used was often old copies of the Oban Times, it being made of coarse paper was especially suited for this work. The paper was soaked in saltpeter and dried in the workers' homes.

When the straw fuses were being used the practice was, after putting the powder in the hole, to use a copper pricker. This was a rod of turned copper up to 6 ft. long. One end was inserted into the powder after which the clay was rammed onto the top of the powder and hammered hard. The pricker was then twisted by hand and the pricker withdrawn leaving a hole suitable for inserting the straw.

When all levels of the quarry were working the method of blasting was as follows, a warning whistle would sound to tell everyone to get into shelter except those firing a shot. Five minutes after a double whistle was blown, which was the signal to light the fuses. Thereafter those on the bottom level lit theirs, then each level in turn till the top. This insured that no man was in the open when the first shot was fired. The blasting was done at 10 a.m. and again at 3 p.m.

In the early days they used to carry the slate blocks after blasting in creels to the slate cutting banks. After the railway was introduced these blocks were put into wagons and drawn by horses to the dressing sheds. Each crew had its own mark chalked on the wagons to ensure that it would reach the proper shed. Everything was done by hand then. In the early days the rock was split by making a wedge of soft wood and putting it into the fissure of rock and pouring water in for the wood to swell. They also used dry lime shell and poured cold water on it and left it overnight to swell and split the rock. Later came air compressors for boring and once the decision where to bore had been taken the work which used to take hours was done in a short time.

The blocks of rock which contained the slate were separated from the rubbish within the quarries before being taken to the banks, where they were split to the proper thickness and shaped to the right size. When the rock was easy, one man splitting kept their cutter busy splitting and shaping. The average was that for every ton of slate used there was roughly seven tons of waste. This waste found a use, as it made two banks which gave the harbour shelter from wind. This must have been important, for one should realise that if Ballachulish had not been by the sea its products could hardly have developed beyond local needs, there being no roads for transporting the slate.

Between the different levels rails were laid. A drum was used one end of it had an iron rope. This connected to a handbrake at the foot of the Quarry. When a bogie had been filled, and had to get to the foot, it was tied to the top rope and at the same time an empty bogie was tied to the lower rope, as the full bogie went down so the empty one came to the top.

The slate workers tools were specialised. He had a drill for boring holes to hold the powder for blasting. It might be anything from 15 ins. to 6 ft. This is the "jumper" mentioned earlier. There was the wedge. It was held on line with the cleavage of a large piece of rock. This wedge then being struck by a heavy hammer split the rock. This would occasion considerable jarring when being worked, so the men used to make handles for their wedges. In the old days, they would get hazel branches and twist them round the handles. If the hazel was not green, they would steam the branches till they were mallable. These hazel handles were used till they broke. The men would take a pile to work for replacements. Later lengths of hose pipe were used in the same way. When a slate was being dressed into thin pieces, one man used a mallet and a slate chisel, to split the block, while another man got hold of the split pieces, then held it on a slate stand and shaped the pieces the right size. To divide an extra large split, the dresser made a series of small holes in the slate with a pointed hammer, so that it broke in a straight line. He then used a slate worker's knife to shape the slate to size. The slate worker was a skilful craftsman and those of Ballachulish made their village known many miles from their home. It was considered necessary to serve a seven year apprenticeship before being qualified as a slate worker, dresser and splitter.

Besides the various kinds of slate used for roofing, there were slates made for gravestones, pavements, and soles for drains. Though these were shipped so far afield. Around Ballachulish, you can still see excellent small sheds made entirely of slate, a most practical use of local raw material. The slate gravestones are of outstanding craftsmanship with beautiful printing and in some cases fine drawings, showing considerable artistic ability. I have heard of someone who has found a cross made of slate which is surely an unexpected use of the material.

Slate was sold in 100's. But for every 20 an extra slate was added and for every 100 slates an extra 20 was added so that if a 100 slates were bought the actual number delivered was 126.

There was a long tool used for handling the heavy blocks of slate before trimming. It is called a "coraig". It has been suggested that when the North country men were at the quarry they called it a coal-rake, only their accent made it sound like caurake, which was then turned into Gaelic sounding words. Likewise wedges became haddies, not because of any likeness to a fish, but because the English said "haud it" which in turn became the name for the tool.

Even the children were drawn into the work of the quarry and used to carry tea down to the men working during their lunch break. They used slate in school but were delighted when they were allowed to use paper instead. It was usual for the men working in the quarry to wear "moleskin" trousers. Moleskin is a heavy, strong, cotton fabric of the Fustian class, an uncut velveteen with a smooth surface, often dyed black giving it a likeness to moles skin. Corduroy is a variant of a similar material. The Oxford Dictionary gives as an example of usage "our agricultural labourers who wear corduroys or moleskins" (The Times 1858). Moleskin was so hard wearing that it came to be used as a synonym for "sound", "good", and "true". The men working at the quarry used white

Men working preparing slate.

Shaping slates using slaters knife and slateworkers table.

moleskin. It was the pride of their women folk to send them out each day clean and well turned out. This involved hard work for the women who in early days had to use the burns and the river. Old photos confirm the fine appearance of the men. The men used to wear a short blue jacket rather like a blouse with a belt, this belt crossed at the waist to avoid having any flapping parts when using the hammer. The women made these jackets which were called "carsackies".

It may be of interest to know that it is believed that slate was used for roofing in Scotland as far back as four centuries ago, and that Stalker Castle was roofed with slate from Easdale quarry in 1631.

This short account of one of the oldest industries of the North Lorn area and indeed of the Highlands itself, has largely been collected from the men who worked in the quarry, and who knew of the traditions of the quarry from the earliest times. The older generation had a rich store of knowledge and tales of older times and this is largely being lost with the change in the way of life of the present times. It would be a pity if so much local history should be lost.

Chapter 5 **Living in old Glencoe**

Background information

In the period covered by this book, people built their own homes. First the foundations were cleared and suitable stones collected; then, neighbours would be asked to help—perhaps by a young couple wishing to get married. When the stonework was finished a long tapering tree was laid end to end, at the highest points of the gable. "Tossing of the Caber" at Highland Games has its origin in this work. In both cases, the caber must fall on the exact place planned. After the caber was laid wood, 3 inches thick and tapered at both ends, was placed from the caber to the walls. A layer of turf was placed on top followed by the thatching; which might be of heather, rushes, or bracken. The thatch was pegged down with hazel and finally rope weighted down with stones held it all in position.

Old Glencoe showing water pumps in the street also some thatched cottages.

Much earlier there were the "black houses" which had no chimney and from which smoke escaped from holes in the roof. A later type of building was the "Cruck" where the bearing beams of the walls did not rest on the roof, but continued down the inside walls of the cottage.

The fuel was peat, which was dug from the Loch (Stratoran) near where the hospital now is. Lord Strathcona made this artificial loch. He bought the MacDonald lands from Mrs Burnes MacDonald. His Canadian wife was homesick, so Lord Strathcona made "Little Canada" by planting pine trees and maples round the newly formed loch.

For light, cruisie lamps were used; they were not unlike the Roman lamp, with a lower drip holder. Fish oil was used and a wick at one end. The cruisie had a long metal hook which was used on unmortared walls like byres. Candles were made in moulds. The wick (originally rushes but later, candlewick) was put in the mould and hot fat (often mutton) was poured in.

Cooking might be done with a swee. This is a mobile metal arm which swings over the fire. The girdle, when baking bannocks (big scones) or oatcakes, hung from the swee. After baking, the oatcakes were then toasted before the fire. Pots, with broth or porridge hung, from the swee. A pot, when used as an oven, was put on the fire, with hot peats round it; the lid was then inverted and also filled with hot peats. Sometimes a slabhraidh was used— this is a chain slung from a chimney beam, which hangs down the chimney with a metal pot hook on the end. The pot hangs from the pot hook over the fire.

In winter food was short. Every family used to salt salmon (called lax, here, as in Norway) for winter. They would buy a fat cow at the start of winter and pickle it. At one time everyone had a boat and some had two; a large one and a smaller one, nets also! Fish were dried on the Ballachulish slates for winter. Salt herrings and potatoes made many a meal. Fish were plentiful and fishermen came from as far as Buckie for the herring which came up the Loch. Much cheese, both simple crowdie and longer keeping cheese, was made, and butter and milk was available. Shop bread would not be available, so oatcakes would be used. Within living memory there were three shibeens where illicit whisky was made in Glencoe. The old mill has not been in use for many years. Heather ale was made but the local recipe lost. Only the flower bells were used. Pennant in 1771 wrote that it was made using "2/3 of the tops of young heather and one of malt".

Wool was spun and dyed and at one time woven in the Glen, but the weaving stopped before it can be recalled by living memory. People walked over the hills to Creran carrying bags of wool to be woven.

The blankets were washed by the River Coe, the water was heated in cauldrons, and wooden wash tubs were used to hold the blankets which were "trampled" clean. The Slate Quarry workers wore white moleskin trousers; sometimes the women would wash these on the rocks at the river, or use the big slate slab-bridges (over the burns which used to flow through the village). The men always went out clean to work and many women made their own soap.

Winters were harder than now. Snow used to come right up to window sills, and stay for many months. Summers were warmer and drier. A wedding party once walked over the ice from Coalasnacon to Kinlochleven, and it was possible to skate along the road from Ballachulish to Glencoe. Winters are not now, normally, as severe as this. A shinty match would be played, on New Year's day, between Glencoe and Ballachulish. Everyone turned out for it. The Glencoe Shinty team once beat the Vale of Leven, for the Celtic Trophy, in 1880. The team went to Mull and thence travelled to Glasgow by boat. They returned by train to Tyndrum and walked back to Glencoe all through the night. At six o'clock they arrived at a shepherd's house, they knocked and asked for a glass of milk. The woman of the house woke suddenly and said "Oh! I have not lifted the cream yet". The Shinty boys called up "We could lift the cup, so we can lift the cream for you". The cup returned to the Glen in 1911.

There were two cobblers in the Village. Shoes were made and sold untanned to allow the workmanship to be seen.

Behind the ferry and Ballachulish hotel, there used to be a Smithy; at Glencoe the smith stayed at, what is now, the end house in the Village—which had earlier been a school. The blacksmith made a hole in the wall through which he threw his shoes to cool in the small burn which ran by the side of the place.

Boats were usually made at Lismore but some were built in the Glen. The heavy boat, used to take coffins to the Burial Island, was made in the Glen by a wandering carpenter.

The Slate Quarry gave employment to the Village and the men were paid every six weeks. Local shops were helpful, even when money was unlikely to come in. One man said he could buy no more nor pay for arrears. The shop owner lifted a bag of meal and one of flour into his cart and delivered them. It was reckoned this would last 12 weeks. The school children used to take tea to the men at the Quarry during the school lunch. Many of the local graves were of slate finely carved for the men were noted for their skill.

Many villagers had no English language, so they met in the evenings at a Mr Robertson's house, where he read the newspapers to them. After, there was a discussion which in time became known as the Glencoe Parliament.

As many people had the same surname (and possibly even the same Christian name), nicknames were used a great deal; they were often chosen in childhood and stuck for life.

Usually Glencoe and Ballachulish are taken together for numbers of population. An authoritative guess is that there were about 200 MacDonalds at the time of the Massacre. In 1745, 120 men joined the Prince and by 1771 there were said to be about 400. In 1871 Glencoe and Ballachulish (including the Quarry) numbered 1529 and in 1875, with the Quarry working fully to capacity, it was 2500. By 1881 it had fallen due to emigration to 1444 and in 1891, to 1480; of whom 1221 were Gaelic speakers.

Dolamite was worked at Duror and Gleanna' chaolais. From Lagnaha, between Duror and Kentallen, china clay was sent South and returned as china. Kentallen had both a lime and a granite quarry. A quarry at upper Clachaig provided the marble for St John's, Ballachulish; it was sent to Aberdeen to be polished.

Before the old Bridge of Coe was built, the river was crossed by big flat stones located about 400 yards below Greenpool. The old Glencoe boundary then extended to the Laroch River, now part of Ballachulish.

In the old days, there was often great sadness at the death of tiny babies, hardship, and scarcity; but still life in the Glen was in many ways better than that lived in the town. There was hunting and fishing in plenty and the resources of shell fish, fish, seaweed and wild plants for both food and medicine. There was peat for the fire and homes could be built when needed. There were cattle for wealth and for milk, butter and cheese—all health giving foods. Grain was cultivated and also distilled. There was poetry and song—which is still part of the Glen's life; shinty and other sports, piping and dancing. There was the telling of tales, and these historians are vivid and dramatic in their telling (as I know). In the Highlands each member of the Clan had access to his Chief, who was related perhaps distantly to all. The oldest son was sent to be fostered out in a humbler home where he was brought up with great devotion. In this way the Chief could understand the problems of his people. Whatever may be said against the Clan system, there is no doubt that the Clansmen were devoted to their Chiefs, and it seems that such devotion, still true under extreme trial, must have been founded on good reason.

Religion (Churches in Glencoe)

The story of the coming of Christianity to this countryside and of the early Church has been told in another Museum publication—"The Burial Island Eilean Munda".

When the Scottish Episcopal Church was persecuted, Glencoe and Ballachulish were largely of that faith. They were served by licenced lay readers, itinerant priests, or catachists. They had no church (nor would have been allowed one) and meetings were held at Rudha-na-glaslic, near the shore, in front of the Slate Quarries, at Laggan-na-bhainne, between Ballachulish Ferry and the present church and oral tradition says, at Carnglas— where Loch Leven Hotel (N. Ballachulish) now stands. The clergy wore grey to avoid

It was the custom in Scotland for a girl once she was married to wear a mutch. Before marriage she would go bareheaded.

detection. Sentries were posted against military surprise and sentences against clergy were heavy and often included transportation.

The Rev Donald MacColl was ordained in 1784 (a native of Appin) and he was the first Episcopal clergyman to pray for a Hanovarian king. One congregational member rose to her feet and publicly protested.

The Church of Scotland "St. Munda" built in Glencoe (now part of Ballachulish, though, within the old boundary) was built in 1836. The Roman Catholic "St. Muns" was built in 1830, St. John's Episcopal Church, Ballachulish, was built in 1842 and the United Free Church in 1874. St. Mary's Episcopal Church was built in Glencoe in 1880.

St. John's has a silver Chalice and patten, first used in 1723—and still in use. Stewart of Ardsheil had communion from it before going off to the '45.

A small Communion cup was discovered when alterations were being made to an old cottage; the cup was hidden from view during the period the Church was being persecuted.

There is now a happy relationship among the different churches, a mutual help at sales of work and a joining together in carol singing and also at special services—making for mutual and happy understanding.

A brief history of secedings from the Church of Scotland and their uniting. 1733 there was the first seceding. In 1761 the Relief Church broke from the main body. In 1820 The New Light Seceders were formed. In 1843 came the Great Disruption when 474 ministers left the Church of Scotland and formed the Free Church. In 1847 the New Light Seceders joined with the Relief Church to form the United Presbiterian Church. In 1852 the Old Light Seceders joined the Free Church but a minority remained outside till 1956. In 1900 the United Free and the United Presbiterian joined but again a minority remained outside this join, and became the "Wee Frees". In 1929 the Church of Scotland joined the United Free.

A local school.

Education

The Statistical Account of 1791 records a school, at the Slate Quarry Glencoe, which was endowed by the Society for Christian Knowledge. There were 60 to 80 Scholars; the schoolmasters salary was £18 and the probable amount of fees £8. The expense of education, per quarter, ranged from 1/- to 2/6 for common branches of instruction. For book-keeping and mathematics, 3/- and Latin 5/- per quarter. There were few between six and fifteen who were not at school, and few under 40 who could not read and write.

In 1849 the Scottish Episcopal Church built a church school by subscription on land given by Mr. Stuart of Ballachulish. The master was paid £15 annually by the Church Society along with fees. The pupils were taught the "common elements of reading, writing and arithmetic", and a little Latin and geography was taught.

As already mentioned, the last house in Glencoe was once a school. Later a Church school was built in Glencoe which has been replaced by a modern building. Secondary education is had at Kinlochleven and Oban or Fort William although even now, Kinlochleven does not do the final year.

The cost of living in the Glen

The Statistical Account of 1791 reports that a salmon was 2d or 3d per pound, a taylor had 6d to 8d and his victuals per day and a day's wages might range from 8d to 1/- a day. A barrel of herrings cost 3/- each and held 500 to 800 fish.

An account book gives figures for the army but does not make it clear if this is the whole of their pay or what they paid for billets. It is headed "The Pay Bill of Captain Ronald MacDonald Compy. G.B.F. from 3rd till 9th May 1799".

3 Sergeants @ 9/5	£1	8	3
1 Corporal @ 6/-		6	
2 Drummers @ 5/8 1/4		11	4½
38 Privates @ 4/6			
	£11	2	11½

An account book of a local shop, now no more, dated 1857 gives the following:

4lbs sugar @ 7½ 2/6
4lbs butter 4/8
6 Candles 6d
1 pair of shoes 1/6
buttons ½ each

The same shop in 1863:

3 yds of velvet @ 5d 1/3
Soft soap 1d
2lbs sugar 1/1

From Messrs Barr's stores stocktaking list (undated but about 1890):

14 lbs of mottos (sweets) 2/9
1 lb of whole peppers 6d
24 cups and saucers 3/-
6 kettles at 1/3
1 bonnet box 1/6
2 umbrellas 3/6

Barr's 1898:

Frillings £1
Mufflers £2

Barr's 1890:

8 lead pencils @ 9d
6 Greek books @ 1/6
11 tins of knife powder @ 4/1½

The price of sugar in 1857 shows how dear it was in comparison to other items. Sugar came in a block or cone and had to be broken. Knife powder may surprise younger people, knives were not stainless and had to be constantly cleaned. 1lb of whole peppers seems a lot for a small shop but possibly no ground pepper was available. What did impress is that this small shop sold Greek books and French ones also.

Communications—road, rail and boat

Early communication was by sea and, till the coming of the motor, boats called at the many piers which are now derelict. A visit to Oban might be made by boat, whereas a horse and carriage would not get there and back in a day. By 1791 the Statistical Account reported that a "road from Shian Ferry to Kingshouse at Lubmanart Glencoe was mostly finished". A road to Glencrerran was opened in 1790. In 1788, and for many years, the nearest post office was at Inveraray—where a runner went once a week to bring the mail. Smeaton of Touch, who bought an estate at Appin, got a post office there. By 1845 it was possible to get a newspaper, published in Glasgow in the morning, in Appin by night.

At one time Ballachulish was a posting station and from there a coach ran to Kingshouse where they changed horses and, using the old road to Tyndrum, went to Glen Etive.

The road to Kinlochleven was built by German prisoners of War in 1914–18.

The Ballachulish railway was constructed between 1898 and 1903. It was a beautiful run and is missed by many since it closed in 1966.

Hotels and inns

Wade started road building in the Highlands. The road through Glencoe (the old road) is popularly called Wades road but he was dead before it was built. Roads were built for the quick passage of Government troops in the event of a Jacobite Rising. Kingshouse, our oldest Inn, was built for housing the troops employed in building the road, hence the name King's House. Early records show that its hospitality and comfort left much to be desired. Many travellers declared it to be the worst Inn in Scotland. Dorothy Wordsworth in 1803 described it as a wretched place "as dirty as a house after a sale on a rainy day". Another traveller described it as having "more the appearance of a hog sty as an Inn".

Southey found conditions much better, with lamb, hens eggs, and, surprisingly, turkey eggs and cream for tea. One does not easily visualise turkey wandering on Rannoch Moor. Southey writes of the great contraband trade in salt carried on the road. Salt was taxed—a sore burden on the Scottish fishermen and a man who had formerly worked on the roads made a bargain with Kingshouse to deliver salt, by which both made a good profit. Southey writes "The landlord of Kings house took that Inn ten years ago and only had a captital of £70 to begin with. This year he has taken a large farm and laid out £1500 in stocking it".

Dickens enjoyed a meal at Kingshouse which included kippered salmon, broiled; a broiled fowl, hot mutton ham and poached eggs; pancakes, oatcakes; wheaten bread; butter; bottled porter, hot water, lump sugar and whisky. He enjoyed his meal but did not like the mountains.

The Hotel (no longer an Inn) has been enlarged and so modernised that, although it is one of the oldest Inns in Scotland, it might be in London, except for the view from the windows.

I have always liked this picture which was made into a postcard. I wondered who the children were and what were their lives. One day I was asked to tea at a house in Ballachulish to collect some items for the Museum. I happened to mention this and found that my hostess was one of the children and the other child was her sister. They were frightened of being late for school but the photographer persuaded them to wait long enough for their photo to be taken.

About 500 yards away was a drovers Inn known as "Queens House", of which only a few stones remain. Clachaig Inn is an old coaching Inn, on the old Glencoe road, and nearer the Village now is the Youth Hostel. The "Glencoe Hotel" was built in 1933 when the new road was opened. At the ferry is Ballachulish Hotel, where an old Inn used to be and in Ballachulish is Laroch House Hotel; besides many small boarding houses and bed and breakfast places where an assured welcome can be expected.

The British Aluminium factory at Kinlochleven
At the beginning of the century British Aluminium obtained Parliamentary authority to develop water power. In 1904 the Loch Leven Water and Electric Power Company (which later merged with the B.A. Co.) was set up to build a reduction factory. The building of the dam, power-house and factory altered the life of the area. Before this advent there were few houses and the loch was too shallow for large boats to reach the head. While the building was being done, there were between 2 and 3 thousand workmen who lived in huts in the hills; all the foremen had to be bilingual—in both English and Gaelic. The first metal was produced in 1907, in a temporary smelter, which closed when the main smelter began working in 1909.

The Kinlochleven hydro-electric scheme is based in the Blackwater dam, a storage reservoir with a capacity of about 3930 million cubic feet. It is a gravity dam, 3112 feet long, and 86 feet high, made across the Blackwater river. From this, a $3\frac{1}{2}$ mile, long-roofed conduit, runs a small forebay where six, 39 inch diameter, pipes, one and a quarter miles long, takes the water to the power station at the factory. If they worked at the factory, men who lived at Glencoe had either to walk on the hillside or go by boat as the road was not made till 1914; when this was constructed by prisoners of war.

Glencoe Hospital (Medical services)
Glencoe House was built by Lord Strathcona and was built on modern lines, with electric light and central heating (about the end of the last century). He employed 24 gardeners. His grand-daughter gave the house to the County for use as a hospital. In April 1948, Glencoe Maternity Hospital had patients and by July of that year it was taken over by the National Health. In 1955, maternity work was transferred to Oban hospital and Glencoe hospital was used for the benefit of local people. At first 15 beds only were available, but it expanded to deal with 28 patients.

In 1970 it became a geriatric hospital, in which many of our older local people now come to spend their last days in comfort and kindliness and in the companionship of others of their own generation and spirit.

Wild life in the Glen
To the Geologist, Glencoe and the countryside around has much of interest. The hills are said to have rock, going back 400 million years. Fossils have been found, at the foot of Buachaille Etive Mor, of the lower Old Red Sandstone period.

Many years ago there were wild boar, bison and wolves—by tradition, the last as late as the Massacre. Pennant, in 1771 wrote "The principle native animals on the mountains of Glencoe are Red Deer, Alpine Hares Foxes . . . It is remarkable that the common hare was never seen either here, in Glen Crean, in Glen Ety, till the military roads were made. There are neither rats nor vipers".

The mole is common here . . . under the name of "The little gentleman in black velvet" he may have been toasted. William of Orange, who signed the order for the Massacre, died from an injury caused by his horse stumbling over a molehill.

There is a rich bird life. We even have a bird legend. A man injured in the Quarry many years ago lay dying when a dove is said to have flown down and placed an ivy leaf on his brow. The incident is depicted on his tomb on Eilean Munda.

Derivations

Alt, ault-Allt a burn Altnafeigh feigh-deer
Allt-a-mhulin allt—a burn, Mhulin—a mill
Achnacoan—Ach—field, coan—dogs
Achnambeith—field of the birches
Ballachulish—Balla—town, Chaolais—narrows
Buachaille Etive Beag—the little herdsmen of Etive
Buachaille Etive Mor—big herdsman
Caolasnacoan—narrow of the dogs
Carnoch cairns—piles of stones
Claichaig—clach—a stone, little stones
Gleann-leac-na-muidhe—the glen of the flat stone of the churns
Balnagowan (Island of Duror) town of the smith
Dalnatrat—the field (Dal) of the shore
Kinlochleven—from ceann, a head—meaning the head of the Loch
Oban—small bay, from Ob nooe—Norse for bay
Larach—Site of ruin

Search and rescue dog.

Mountains and mountaineering in Glencoe

There are many excellent publications for those interested in the mountains therefore this is but a brief guide. The most famous mountain is Buachaille Etive Mor, 3345 feet. Buachaille Etive Beag is 3129 feet and is the easier of the Glencoe hills to climb; but, the North and East slopes should be avoided. Aonach Eagach is the ridged centre portion, but the name is used for the range from the Pap of Glencoe, or, Sgor na ciche at 2430 feet; Sgor nan Fiannaidh, 3168 feet; Stob Coire Leith, 3080 feet to the Chancellor and Am Bodach, 3085 feet. The summit is Meall Dearg 3118 feet.

There is a walk over the old road, from Altnafeadh to Kinlochleven, by the Devil's Staircase. Another walk is by Beinn Fhada over a track through Lairig Eilde, which leads from Glencoe to Glen Etive.

Many climb these hills and unfortunately accidents do happen. There is a volunteer rescue team of about 20; one of the team is Mr. MacInnes of Allt-an-righ, a well known Scottish and Himalayan climber, who has also written a book on "Search and Rescue Dogs". Alsatians and collies are the most worked dogs and were used in Switzerland, during the War, to find escaping prisoners of war. In 1963 Mr. MacInnes went to Switzerland for a course in dog training. He is Secretary of the Society for Search and Rescue dogs.

Winter courses are held here, when dogs come from all over Britain. Training is long (three years) and hard, but through this voluntary work, lives have been saved which would have been lost. The dogs work by a sense of smell, and it is estimated that one dog is worth 20 men—but where the victim is covered in snow, the dog is worth even more men.

Glencoe Mountains are also becoming well known for winter sports; there are, however, records of ski-ing here going back almost as early as the motor car. In the summer of 1955 came the first ski-tow on the top thousand feet of mountain followed in 1959 by the first commercial ski-ing in Scotland.

In the season, many enjoy winter sports here.

Chapter 6 **Pictures of the past**

Introduction

This collection of old photographs comes from the archives of Glencoe Museum. Most of the pictures were taken around the turn of the century and show something of the life of the people in many aspects—work and play, war and peace, costume and social life.

Please note: the caption of the picture on the back cover which reads "Scene of the Massacre" is not, strictly speaking accurate. The Massacre took place throughout the territory of the Macdonalds of Glencoe.

If you have any old photographs we would be interested to see them, and to take copies, returning the originals.

Above: Changing Pastures, Glencoe.
Left: Upper Carnoch, Glencoe.
Below: Tighpbuirst.

Right: The Village, Ballachulish
Below left: By the fireside.
Below right: Teatime.
Botttom: Ballachulish School.

Left: Ballachulish 'Sunday Best'.
Below left: Picnic in the garden.
Below right: Time for a quiet smoke!
Bottom: A lively game of shinty.

Left: Family Group.
Middle: The Doctor ready for his visits.
Bottom: Doctor and patients.

Mrs MacInnes and Mrs MacPherson washing and wringing blankets in Glencoe.

Waulking Song.

Ballachulish Rural Choir.

The Stores, Ballachulish and the Postman goes his rounds.

Above: The East Harbour, Ballachulish loading slates.

Left: Keeping the home fire burning!

Right: The Launch 'Cona' transporting workmen to Kinlochleven.

Haymaking at Invercoe.

32

The Battle Fleet on Exercise in Ballachulish Bay.

Rifle Drill, near Ballachulish.

Territorial Army at the Drill Hall, Ballachulish.

Peace Celebrations 1918

Unveiling the 1914-18 War Memorial, Kinlochleven.

Chapter 7 The folklore of Glencoe and North Lorn

In this short account of the local folklore, I am including the obvious fairy and witch tales, ghost stories and accounts of healing by faith, and I have also included tales of second sight. This last is not to be confused with mythical personages from Fairyland but a genuine occurrence. There were many strange instances of this in the Glen. But I think the thread that binds them is that they might all be mentioned at a Ceilidh. By that, I don't mean the present type of Ceilidh, delightful as they are, in which money is paid at the door, but of the older type in which people of the Glen would meet for an evening's entertainment, in which they each contributed their share, by song, music or tale.

The following stories have been told to me by some of the older inhabitants of the village, and, as far as possible, I have told the stories in their words.

At one time, there were thousands of fairies round Glencoe and Ballachulish. They used to come into the houses and sit by the fire. They were good-looking people "looking like princesses" I was told. Another said that they were like little maidens dressed in green. They did not like mortals to wear their favourite colour. When Dundee was killed at Killiecrankie some felt it was because he had worn green on that day, and the little people had been annoyed. They were very musical people, fine singers and wonderful dancers. Besides that they made the most beautiful music. They had their homes in "Sithean" or Fairy knolls.

The local dragon lived on these hills.

The fairies of the Glen were not like the "story book" fairies in the south with their magic wands. They were a race of people who had their own customs and personalities. Sometimes they mixed happily with the mortals of the Glen, but at other times there were awkward encounters. There was one woman in the village who used to put up big branches of holly on the lintel inside her doorway every Christmas and New Year, to keep out fairies and witches, who are said to be particularly mischievous at that time of the year. The woman insisted on big branches saying that twigs were no use at all. I have also heard that one reason why rowans were so effective in keeping out fairies is that the fairies like to play with the berries of both rowan and holly. Certainly there is a widespread tradition that rowans keep witches away and this in turn degenerated to them being called "lucky". They should be planted at the front of a house and an elder at the back.

One Hogmanay an old man from the village went for whisky at Strontian (a place that got its name from "sron"—nose or promontory, "ans sith"—fairy). He and a companion were coming along home with the whisky when they met some fairies and were asked into their "sithean". The door was open and they could hear the most wonderful and enticing music. So the men entered, meaning to stay for a little while. The old man's companion struck his knife into the doorway so that the door was unable to shut (cold iron is not friendly to fairies and breaks their magic). When he had had enough he left by the open door, but his friend, the old man, stayed on longer. Finally he thought that he too, had better be off home, so he left. When he got back home he was in time for the next year's Hogmanay. People asked what he had been doing all the time, but he felt the time to have been only a few hours. Another version is that only one man entered the sithean, the other going home. He returned the next year and saw his friend still in the sithean and dancing to the reels. He went in, leaving his knife in the door, and pulled his friend out by force. The latter objected that he had just entered and begun to dance.

Like many such tales, it appears in different parts of the country with variations. But the following tale I have not seen in any other part of the country though it may exist.

There was a shepherd living in a lonely place. He was sitting by the fire, drowsing, his wife was in bed with their small child, and his dog, a collie called Deargain, was nearby. A knock on the door, and a woman in green asked for shelter. He let her in (in some versions she appears without being let in). His wife suddenly gave a shout, for there was the fairy woman trying to get the baby. The shepherd took a big burning stick from the fire which he was going to hit the woman with, the dog Deargain growled and went for the fairy woman. She asked him not to hit her and to call off his dog, which he did. However, she again went to lift the child, so he put some snuff on his dirk and held it to the fairy, who fled. In some versions the snuff made her sneeze, in others not. In yet another version, it says that after he had called off the dog, the fairy asked for snuff, but the shepherd would only give it to her from off his dirk, while she in turn asked for it on a piece of wood. Possibly this was to avoid any contact with cold metal, possibly she did not like a dirk held too near her.

It is said that the reason that fairies tried to carry off mortal children is that they hoped to rear one who would be their leader and fear not cold iron. They hoped this leader will drive out the mortals who have stolen the land from them. Fairy mothers are very fond of their children and cannot be persuaded to part with them, so it is usually an elderly and often grumpy elf who is used as a changeling.

A young man saw some people dressed in green coming out of a "sithean". Each one called upon a person by name to fetch his horse, a fine beast came at once and each mounted and flew off. The young man also called for a horse, using the same name. The horse appeared, he mounted and went off with the fairy troop. He was with them for nearly a year and during this time they wandered the country visiting fairs, weddings and feasts, mixing unseen with mortals. They ate the food, danced to the music, and sang, all unseen and unheard. At one wedding feast the bridegroom sneezed. The young man said "God bless you". This annoyed the fairies who told him not to do it again. Again the bridegroom sneezed and the young man called out "God bless you." When they left the feast the fairies knocked the young man off his horse and he fell down a precipice. He was not hurt and got up and went back to live with mortals.

Dr. I. F. Grant, the founder of "Am Fasgadh" the Highland Folk Museum at Kingussie, has given me permission to quote from her book "Highland Folk Ways" the following account of fairies at Appin. She has been writing on music in the Highlands and goes on "the Highlander also played on a humbler instrument—the Jew's Harp—generally called 'the trump'. The earliest allusion to it that I have met with is in the record of a trial at a Justice Court held at Inveraray in 1677. A certain Donald McIlmichall, vagabond, was accused of stealing a cow and consorting with evil spirits. Donald told the court that one Sunday evening he had noticed a lighted opening in a hill in Appin, and on entering, he had seen a crowd of men and women dancing in a place having many lighted candles. He said he did not know who they were but judged them 'not to be worldie men'. He admitted that he had returned to meet them in various 'shians' (fairy mounds) 'on ilk Sabbath nights and that he played the trumps to them when they danced'. To reward him they told him of stolen cattle so that he might claim the 'Tascal Money' (the reward paid to an informer). Poor Donald was found guilty on both charges and hanged. I have heard that a trump, being of metal, had been considered a safe thing to play on entering a fairy mound."

The first of Glencoe's long line of bards was Ossian. Ossian's father was Finn mac Cumhal who was renowned for his courage and hospitality. Before he married Ossian's mother he had a fairy sweetheart. She was annoyed at being jilted, and being a fairy, had the power to avenge herself. She used a power known as the fith-fath. This was the transformation of someone into some other creature, while still keeping their own personality. Men were usually changed into horses, bulls, or stags and women into cats, hares, or hinds. Ossian's mother was changed into a hind. When Ossian was born she possessed so much of the hind in her nature, that she licked her son's forehead, but her woman's nature was so strong that she stopped at the one lick. Many years later she met Ossian when he was hunting and she was able to stop him shooting her with his arrows and she told him who she was. Then she took him to her underground home where she was able to cast off her fith-fath and become a most beautiful woman. While he stayed with her, she taught him much, including minstrelsy.

Another version tells how Finn was hunting with his hounds, Bran and Sceolaun. They chased a faun which lay down and let the hounds lick her. The faun followed them to the Dun of Allen. That night Finn woke to find a most beautiful woman standing before him. Her name Saba (or Sabha, Sava). She told him that she had been put under enchantment by the Dark Druid of the fairy people, but if she were ever to reach the Dun of Allen she would turn into a woman again. Finn made her his wife. When word reached him that Norse ships had sailed into Dublin bay and honour demanded his going to aid the men of Erin. When he returned he was told that a figure like his own had appeared at the castle wall and that Saba had rushed outside to greet it, only to be turned into a hind again. In the rush of men and dogs that followed she was lost. Finn searched for seven years without trace till one day he came on a beautiful boy on Ben Gulban. The boy told how he had been reared by a gentle hind till a dark man had come entreating her to go with him, though she clearly feared to go; the boy's limbs were spell-bound and he could not help her and none ever saw her again.

Another mortal who had a fairy sweetheart was one of the first MacIntyres to come to live in Glencoe. This MacIntyre lived at Inverawe wih his elder brother, the fairy lived in Ben Cruachan. The young MacIntyre used to ask the fairy's advice when he got into difficulty. The brothers go on well together till the elder one married. Then he told his younger brother to be off to Glencoe with all that he owned. The young brother asked what was his and was told that the white cow and all those that would follow her were his. He then went to consult his fairy sweetheart. She told him to go back and spend the night in his brother's house. She told him that it would snow during the night and that in the morning he was to set off for Glencoe. He was to call the white cow after him and to carry a sheaf of corn. He did as she told him and he found that the larger half of the herd came after him to Glencoe. He reached there safely and settled there. He built a house and married. His wife took seriously ill and he wondered what he should do. He remembered his fairy sweetheart, but he was afraid she would be too jealous to help. Then he decided to ask her help but to say it was his grey mare that was ill. He went to see the fairy who told him to take five turfs and put them under the left knee of the mare and in a short while she would be well again. He did this, and his wife soon recovered.

There was once a postman, Donald, who used to go between Ballachulish and Fort William. The road was full of fairies and bogles. One Hallowe'en, Donald was coming back to Corrie Chaorachain when he saw a dozen fairies dancing. One of the fairies wished to take Donald with them but another would not let her as he was the postman who went to the farm where her home was. Donald saw many more fairies but they all disappeared. He got safely home and never saw them again but sometimes he heard them at the same spot.

In Appin a certain clergyman after his evening service had a habit of going to a mound at the back of his house and giving the same sermon to what he regarded as the fairies. He was fully of the opinion that he heard the fairies singing with him.

The song "Crodh Chailein" or "Colin's Cattle" was said to have been composed by a young girl of Glencoe who had been sent to the milking at the sheiling. She is said to have overheard it being sung by the fairies. It is said to have been a favourite of Robert Burns.

At the time of the Massacre, the soldiers were led astray by the sound of piping and tradition says that they tramped over bog and rock trying to catch the piper, whom the officer thought was trying to rally the MacDonalds. It was a fairy piper, and is still spoken of and used to be heard playing. He does not appear to be identified with the original piping. It is merely recounted that there is said to be a fairy piper up at Leac an Tuim. This is where the older tale of the piper leading the soldiers astray is located. At one time there was a fairy fiddler along the old road. It is possible that he has been confused with the fairy piper. Boys of the village used to play pranks on the nervous by playing after dark nearby.

The Maid of Duror was a fairy woman though I have heard her called a Glaistig (sometimes spelled Glaistrig) which is a much less attractive personage. A Glaistig is a mortal woman who has been put under enchantment. She wears green but her face, instead of being beautiful, is pale and grey. Her name in fact comes from "glas" meaning grey. She is often to be found working with cattle or haunting castles. In some versions the Maid of Duror was said to have lived as a mortal 200 or 300 years ago and to be a true glaistig. There was a man who used to go to Duror to cut rushes for his house near her home on the south side of Beinne Bhair. She used to help him, and when other people heard of this, they went there too, and she helped them also. Some came from as far away as Glencoe and Ballachulish. Many were helped in this way. She also helped people in Achindaroch Farm, Duror. She was given a bowl of milk and, in return, saw the cows gave a good supply of milk. If she got her milk, all would be well the next day, but if it was forgotten the cows would be dry and the calves out of their pen. When the custom of leaving her the milk was stopped all kind of trouble came to the farm, ill-health to a family that had not known of such a thing before and general bad luck. She was often with the cattle. If she liked one tenant better than another she took special care of his cattle. At flitting time she would try to place obstacles in the way of lifting the cattle. She was last seen about 1880.

By the river Coe lives the Bean-nighe. When she is seen washing something in the river, it is the shroud of the viewer, and foretells their own death, or that of a member of the Clan. She is said to have been seen before the Massacre.

Then there is the Coineag who also foretells death. It is possible to speak to the bean-nighe but not to speak or approach the Caoineag. The latter sheds tear for those who are killed in battle. She is rarely seen, but her wailing might be heard in lonely places. She was heard for several nights before the Massacre. The following song is said to have been sung by her before the Massacre.

Tha Caoieachag Bheag abhroin, A dortadh deoir a sula,
Fath mo leoin! Nach d'eisd an cula!
The little weeping one of sorrow, is shedding tears from her eyes,
Alas, my grief! would that ye had given heed to her cries.

It is said that one woman at least heard the singing and escaped.

There must have been a glaistrig at one time at Ballachulish, or so it would seem. The point of the shore nearest to the Burial Island is known as Rudh na Glaistrig. Rudh means the point. Unfortunately there are no tales left to tell of her.

An Uruisg used to haunt a waterfall near Tyndrum. An Uruisg is a solitary being and harmless to mortals. They are said to be a cross between a fairy and a mortal. They are big and grey and often sit on rocks watching travellers. The Uruisg stayed in the corries in the summer but in winter came down to the lower ground. They would enter houses at night for warmth, sometimes they would work for a farmer at threshing and such jobs. It liked presents of food and clothing. The Uruisg at Tyndrum was banished to Rome by St. Fillan. Its home is still known as Na-h-Uruisg.

Round Rannoch Moor lived an unfriendly glaistig who would attack mortals. There were fairies there too. Once a farmer heard, but could not see them. They were saying "Some of it for me, some of it for me". When the farmer realised that it was the fairies who were saying this, he did so too. That night the cows gave such a yield of milk that before the dairymaid had milked half the cows, all the milk pails were full. Milk was not plentiful on the other farms that night.

There is the story of how Ben Doran came to be free from bracken. There was a farmer named Echain, gaelic for Hector. He lived in the area but was very lazy and one day he kept saying "if only the fairies would cut the peats". The fairies heard him and came to help him. They cut his peats, dried them and stacked them. The fairies had a great wish to do more work for him, so he sent them to pull all the bracken off Ben Doran. They did this job and came back for yet another job, calling "Obair, obair, Echain", (or "Work, work, Hector"). The farmer to be rid of them sent them to make string out of the sand. In the old days string was not available for harvest work and a substitute was made by raking hay in strands and twisting it. The fairies tried to rake the sands but found that they could not do the job so they went away.

Besides fairies, there were fairy beasts. I have heard of one tale of a water horse or Each Uisge in Glencoe, also there was one at Appin. The Appin beast used to wait at Lagan-nan-gillean and, as it was a very fine horse, any boy who saw it wished to ride it, whereupon it went, in this case, to a cavern where the burn disappeared (usually they go to lochs and rivers). One day, as happened in many instances, it took five boys, but one of them was lame and he managed to slip off the beast's back and come home and tell the tale.

Again an Each Uisge has the power to become a finely dressed and handsome man. In this instance he engaged the attention of a very bonnie girl from Appin. One day he fell asleep with his head on her knee and she noticed that he had sand and water in his hair. She undid her apron and slipped away home as fast as she could. The Each Uisge woke up and went after her, but just as he was about to overtake her he was attacked by a Tarbh Uisge or Water Bull. The water bull was repaying a debt to the farmer whose daughter the girl was. This story is widespread but the incident about the water bull coming to the rescue is unusual and gives a different slant to the story.

There is the tale of Snian Rouh Uisge. As Domhuill Mor Drobhain was returning from a "drove" to Falkirk or Pitlochry, his way home lay across Rannoch Moor. Night fell, but as he knew the way well he walked on till at midnight he rested beside a small lochan to eat his bannock and cheese, stooping to drink from the lochan he saw shining in the moonlight a bright object in the water. He fished it out with his cromag and saw that it was a bridle with silver bit and mountings. He carried it home and examined it by daylight. The silver was hot to the touch and the reins etc. were made of the finest supple beautifully worked leather. He had never seen anything so beautiful and was overawed. So he sent for the local "Wise Woman". She told him it was a water-horse's bridle—srian each uisge. The silver was mined in the deep caverns at the centre of the earth, the leather was made from the skins of a large species of water serpent, that lived in the same water as the Each Uisge. She told Doimhuill Mor to hang the Srian on a rowan cromag by his door. So long as the cut ends of the cromag pointed upwards prosperity would be his, but if the ends should point downwards evil from the Bridle would overtake him. Domhuill Mor Drobain lived long and prospered.

It is interesting to know why such a beast as a water horse should wear a bridle at all. It is because that one day "Thomas the Rhymer" with a large troop of Scots from fairyland will come mounted on water horses and will give battle and drive out foreigners and the crown will go to the rightful heir and Scotland become a free and happy country.

Loch Achtriochtan, the home of Tarbh Uisge.

Glencoe had a very famous water bull or tarbh uisge. It lived in Loch Achtriochtan. This beast, unlike the water horse, was quite harmless. It was rarely seen but has been described as being of small size, black and slippery and shaped like a bull. It would come out of the loch at night to graze. It ate far more than any mortal beast and if it should get amongst crops or corn did much harm. Another trouble was that it cross-bred with mortal cows and the resulting calves were very poor and weak. There are several descriptions of these calves. As the bull had no ears, the calves may have pendulous ears and wide-webbed spreading jet black hoofs. Another says that the calves have short ears as if the upper part had been cut off, others say they had slit ears. It is interesting to know that the cross between a water horse and a mortal mare can be recognised for their clean limbs, large flashing eyes, red distended nostrils and their fiery spirit.

Neither of these fairy beasts nor fairies or witches could cross running water. The problem for the water horse and water bull arose where a river ran through their loch. They had a special pact with the devil by which they could pass under the flowing river so that they could move about their home freely.

Fairy dogs were not so good as mortal dogs. The fairies tried to improve their breed with the help of mortal dogs. Fairy dogs were green with gold eyes. They were not harmful to humans, but if they got near enough to you for you to hear them bark three times, it was a death summons. But this fate could be averted if you threw a stone at the dog at the first bark. Fairies had cattle quite distinct from the tarbh uisge. They were usually white. One suspects that they owned some of the white native cattle of the same breed as the Chillingham.

Many years ago there lived on Beinn Bheithir a dragon. She used to catch the unwary traveller. But when she had seven young the whole countryside was alarmed, fearing that their land would be emptied of life. But a young man, Charles the skipper, sailed up Loch Linnhe and anchored at Ballachulish. He offered to free the country from the dragon. First he made a causeway between the boat and the shore. It was made of barrels with a loose set of planks on top. He put a roast pig on the boat and set fire to the boat which he left burning. The dragon smelt the roast pig and came down from her lair for it, leaving her young in the cave. She crossed the causeway, disarranging the planks as she went and got into the burning boat to get the roast pork. By that time, though, the boat was well on fire and her escape was cut off and, as the causeway had now no planks on the barrels, she was either burnt to death or drowned. Some say that the barrels were spiked and that these spikes were covered with the planks and when they went into the sea, it was the spikes which killed the dragon when she attempted to return. The local poeple killed off the young as they were not yet large enough to be dangerous.

There was a strange beast not so far off, in Mull. A young boy, Alistair by name, was walking along a footpath when he stopped to pick up a small nut. With a knife he bored a hole in it. Out from the hole crept a very small creature, it lay in his open palm and he noticed that it breathed out deeply and as it did so, it grew. It grew and grew, soon it was too big to hold in his hand, so he put it on the ground. Still it breathed out deeply and at each breath grew larger yet. Then it turned to Alistair and said "Now Alistair, I am going to eat you". Alistair protested in vain. He said to a cow which was nearby, "This creature is going to eat me". The cow said "Well, it's bigger than you and if it says it's going to eat you I expect it will". Then Alistair turned to a frog and told him the tale. The frog asked the creature where he came from for "I have never seen anything like you before". The creature said that he had come out of the nut. The frog replied that that was a likely story, which he did not believe. The creature then breathed deeply and at each breath grew smaller, then it crept back into the nut which Alistair swiftly sealed up again. I heard this from a Henderson though not from the Glen. He had heard it orally.

If a cock was heard crowing during the night, someone went to the hen-house to see which direction the cock was looking, and to feel whether his feet were warm or cold. If warm it was a good omen, if cold an evil omen, and the news came from the direction in which the cock was looking.

When a homestead was infested with rats someone composed a rhyme—always in praise of rats. They were never miscalled, or blamed for causing damage or destruction. This rhyme was spoken or sung at each corner of the steading and the rats were invited to go to another homestead, always across running water. It is said that the rats immediately disappeared from the first place and arrived in hoards at the place named in the rhyme.

There was once a fairy stone in the village. It was round and very smooth. It is said to have been thrown after an inhabitant of the village when walking not far from the quarry. In many parts of the Highlands people were troubled with fairy arrows or elf shot. These were shot at man, or more usually beast, and could kill. The arrows when found, have been prehistoric arrow heads.

There are by tradition two sithean of importance in the area. One lies at the end of the part of the village known by its old name of "Carnoch" and the other is the small hill near the Rectory at Ballachulish. This last appears to have been "inhabited" within living memory, and from it could be heard beautiful music, and when something annoyed the fairies, like the cutting down of some of the trees on the hill, their annoyance was quite audible to those outside the sithean.

Highland witches had considerable powers attributed to them. They had the widespread power of making images of people to whom they wished ill, sticking these with thorn or pin and letting them disintegrate in streams, as they did dissolve, so the person whose image it was slowly wasted away. They could raise storms or winds. Many a sailor in the days of sail has bought a special rope for such a purpose. The rope would have had three knots in it. If the sailor untied the first knot, a good breeze would come and fill his sails, if he untied the second knot, a very strong wind followed. He would be warned not to undo the third knot, and those who did so found themselves in a wild gale.

Witches had the power to transform themselves into animal form, cats and hares were usual. Transformed into such animals, hares in particular, they could cover a wide area of country quickly and unsuspected. There have been many tales of hares and cats being shot and injured in some way, and of finding some unsuspected, or suspected, person suffering from a like injury. One such story of the village is told of how a Ballachulish woman fared.

A man from the village was out shooting early one morning, he shot and wounded, but did not kill, a hare. He walked to Laroch and he found, sitting by the wheel of the old ruined sawmill, a woman that he knew by her face marked with pellets. She said to him "You are up early today", and he replied "You were up early yourself".

Witches had the power to take the goodness out of the milk and butter, so it was wise not to give her any of your own butter, milk or even fire, as this aided her in her schemes. There were charms and incantations to prevent this. Rowan branches hung up outside acted as a safeguard and here honeysuckle was hung in the byres. They possessed the power of the evil eye by which they would cause mischief or harm without actual contact. For boats they used riddles and eggshells. It was the custom in the Highlands for empty eggshells to be broken to prevent them being used by witches. An old Highland friend of my youth used to do this, but I am fairly certain that she did not know why she did so. While harmful in many ways, the people made use of witches as they were called and were helped. Cures against evil spells, charms, love potions, and help in misfortune and illness, and sometimes a forbidden look into the future.

To avert the evil eye from the home an oatcake should be toasted until it smoked, and burned and this was supposed to clear the house of evil spirits. Carvy (carraway) oatcake was sewn into women's bodices to ward off evil spirits. If a cow under the spell of the evil eye stopped giving milk a bannock of oatcake with a hole in the centre was fired and the cow was milked through the hole till she gave milk again.

Kenneth MacLeod writes of witches and their work as patriots, for they caused mists to hinder armies invading Gaeldom, and caused storms to beset enemies in ships. Among themselves they were said to be convivial and that after the business of the coven was finished they would dance and sing and there would be drinking too, for in old trials they speak of taking their tassies with them.

The broomstick is well-known to us as a means of transport, but real horses might be used, and a horse thus used would be known as it would be exhausted next day, and would have hagknots in its mane, which had been used as stirrups by its witch rider. Straw might be used as in Burns' poem on the witches of Fife.

"Some horses were of the broom cane formit
And some of the green bay tree,
But mine was made from ane humloke straw
And a stout stallion was he."

There was one famous witch of Glencoe who was known far from her home. This was Corrag, daughter of Iain Bhan (Ian the Fair). Another Glencoe witch of lesser fame was Cas a' Mhogain Riabhaich (grizzled shoe or greyish shoe). They would join with Gormshuil of Moy (Blue Eyes), Doideag of Mull, Laorag of Tiree, Maol-odhar of Kintyre (Maol meaning Mull and Odhar meaning drab or dun). This powerful team of witches were able to sink ships. Some accounts have it that they sank the ship of the Armada that found its way to Tobermory. Others say that it was a MacLean who did this, and that a punitive ship under Captain Forrest, was sunk by the witches at the request of the people of Mull to save them from the Captain's vengeance. There is another tale in which a Spanish ship with a beautiful princess aboard attracted the attention of all the men of the Island and the women made arrangements with Doideag to sink the ship, others again say that a princess died in Mull and was buried in unconsecrated ground, and that her spirit returned to Spain to tell her people, who sent a punitive expedition under Captain Forrest against Mull. In Glencoe the story is different in that the ship sunk by the witches was an emigrant ship, but again under the command of Captain Forrest. In all accounts the witches turned themselves into ravens and by their magic sunk the ship.

While Corrag was considered to have been of outstanding badness, she was nevertheless to have been given a Christian burial on the Holy Island of Eilean Munda, the local burial island. It had always been a fact that, though the sea was stormy and rough, it always became calm for a funeral. On this occasion the sea remained stormy, gales raged, and it was impossible to take the boats out to the island. So Corrag was buried near the present road, through Tigh Phuirt. Before the new road of the early thirties came, and ran through the burial place, there used to be a mound on which the grass never grew long. This was Corrag's grave. There was considerable local opposition to the obliteration of the grave, but in spite of this no mark was left, nor were the remains taken care of.

Another local witch whose name has come down to us is that of Dubhac nic an rachain. She was a Ballachulish witch and lived near Craig Rannoch, at the cutting through which the railway used to run, there is a high rock and a black pool beyond. Around there dwelt this witch. The rock has been named after her, but no tales have come down about her and she seems to have been less powerful.

The great Gormshuil of Moy is said to have caused the split in the rock known as Clach Pharuig (this rock gets its name from a Viking who saved himself by clinging on to it). It happened that Gormshuil had met with Sir Ewan Cameron, who was an old enemy of hers. Sir Ewan kept just one step ahead of her. She followed saying "Step on beloved Ewan", and he replied "Step for step". When they reached Ballachulish Ferry, Sir Ewan was still ahead by one step, he leapt on to the ferry boat, pushing it off from the shore. She, fearing to lose her chance of vengeance, called out "The wish of my heart to thee". Sir Ewan replied "The wish of your heart be on yon grey stone". The stone instantly split in two.

One amusing remark made by a local child on seeing the Forestry fire-fighters' brooms was to ask if it was a witches' parking place.

Cailleach Bheinn a' Bhric was not a witch at all but rather a spirit, sometimes described as the Autumn Hag. She is described as having grizzled locks, wearing a tawny, tattered plaid, and grey hose. Though she was reputed to be fierce, she was also noted for her kindness to wanderers. She would appear to them as a woman of huge size, wearing a 'kerchief, either stripped or mottled. Sometimes she wore mocassins and at others, buckskin, but she always had her tawny plaid.

Another such spirit was Cailleach Bheur who was a winter hag of great age. The winter storms are caused by the Cailleach tramping her blankets and the howl of the wind is the song she sings when she is milking her goats. She keeps the earth bare by beating it with her pestle till she is defeated by the return of the sun. Another such spirit, some say her twin sister, is A'Mhuileartach, who is responsible for the storms at sea. All three of these spirits are known over a wide range of the Highlands and have left their names on landmarks and hills and rocks

There are not a great many ghosts in this area. Kingshouse was at one time haunted. One man remembers that when he was a boy, he was sitting in the kitchen at Kingshouse, beside the fire. The kitchen door was fastened by a latch which was lifted up with the thumb. He saw the kitchen door open, having watched the latch rise up, but nobody appeared. This happened three nights in succession, and the proprietors said it occurred often and they hardly noticed it any more. A woman had been murdered there some years before, and she was the only spirit that was likely to walk, so far as they knew.

The old Ballachulish House was burnt down after the '45, but the present house is said to be haunted by an Appin Stewart who gallops to the door, dismounts and vanished on the threshold. There is also a grey lady.

At the beginning of this century the owners of Ballachulish House decided to let their home. It was advertised. One viewer came to see over the house. She said that she knew it well as she had visited it often in her dreams. The owner of the house said "Yes, you are the woman we often see wandering through the house."

At Ardshiel, another old house burnt after the '45 and rebuilt, there are two ghosts. One a grey lady who appears to the most unlikely persons, but not to the usually psychic, apparently preferring the sceptical. The other ghost is Headless Peter who appears at a gate half way up the drive. Who he is and why he haunts is not known. The only possible clue is that there were some very old pre-Christian graves in a field nearby which were disturbed and are now no more.

There is a story of two men walking one evening towards Ballachulish. One of them said, "Do you see those people?" The other man didn't at first, but did later. They were soon among a crowd of villagers who had been dead for some time. On the same road a minister walking alone came to a man standing in the middle of the road. He would neither walk nor speak. The minister walked all round him and when he went back the next day he saw his own footprints in the snow, but there was no sign of the man's footprints.

The Rectory at Ballachulish is said to be haunted. Mysterious lights have appeared and a man on horseback or sometimes the horse alone, have appeared.

A coachman who lived at the steading at Invercoe Farm and worked for Lord Strachcona, opened a stable trap-door and saw a soldier in full dress uniform of some centuries earlier. Others too, have felt a presence there.

At the time when one of the MacDonald Chiefs (about 1890) died, there were people of a different name living at Invercoe House, the home of the chiefs of Glencoe, there was an unaccountable happening. One night one of the maids was talking at the back door, with a boy friend, when they saw a carriage driving up on the other side of the water. They wondered where it was going at that time of night. Then they saw by the direction of the light that it had gone on the road that came to the house. So they decided that the boy should open the gate, and that the maid would go through the house to open the door when the carriage arrived. They did this. In a few minutes they met again at the back door. The boy said that nothing had passed him but a cold wind. The maid had seen the light, but upon opening the door there was nothing to be seen. But in fact the body of the MacDonald Chief was brought on a carriage from the posting stables at Ballachulish that very night. There is a sequel to this story, but, as it deals in the second sight, I have left it in the meantime.

It is interesting that ghosts in the Lowlands and beyond are clad in white but those in the Highlands are clad in normal clothes. Highlanders were buried in their ordinary clothes, lowlanders were buried in white winding sheets.

There are many tales of Second Sight in the village and the neighbouring countryside. This is the ability to see into the future in an uncanny way, it is usual to see things ahead in a vision by those who possess this gift, one which they have no control over, and which they would mostly prefer to be without. I would like to add to those who have not met with it before, its authenticity is beyond doubt, though how or why it works, is beyond our ken.

Dean MacInnes was known to have the sight, and many tales are told of his visions. One day he was walking with a friend near where the station is at Kentallen. At the time the line had been plotted on paper but nothing further had been done. Suddenly, the Dean grabbed his friend to one side and said, "Man, that was a close one!" The friend asked what was close? The Dean said "Did you not see the train?" "No, I did not" said the friend. Again after the rails had been laid, these two were on the line, this time at Ballachulish Ferry Station, when suddenly the Dean raised his hat. "Why do you do that" asked his friend. "Do you not see the child's coffin taken from the train?" As yet no train had run on the line, but the first train into the station had a child's coffin on it.

To return to the ghost story of Invercoe House, this is the sequel. It was told of the Dean. One evening looking down the Loch, he saw a procession of boats put out from the pier, making for the Burial Island. He was astonished to see that there were thirteen boats when there were only twelve boats between Glencoe and Ballachulish. But on the day of the funeral, thirteen boats turned up, the thirteenth being from Kinlochleven. The boats he had seen previously being visions of the funeral that followed, which was that of the MacDonald Chief.

When Major Fernside's wife died and was buried at St. John's, Ballachulish, a ferryman who was at the funeral and who had gone to call on a relative, had the sight. On his way home, he came on a funeral cortege, which had a riderless horse with it. A week later the Major died, and at his funeral his favourite horse followed the cortege, riderless.

At upper Carnoch at one time, lived a wee woman with six fingers. She went missing. A local man dreamed that she appeared before him and told him she was not content where she was, and he was to go to the new barn by the narrows and get her remains, which were behind a stone by the boat. The man went to the place and found her remains.

There is a story of a young woman who looked out of her door and saw a funeral pass and knew all the people in the procession. She told it all in detail, to an older woman, her companion at the time. The older woman told her she would never see the like again because she had discussed it so fully, and she never did see another such vision.

When Gorton Farm was only fields and had no buildings, the field was walled. Someone saw a vision of a pig walking on the wall and was told that the next tenant would be a Campbell. This happened as foretold. The boar is the Campbell's crest.

Apart from the Dean's experiences with the railway, it is interesting to learn that the B.A. Factory was also subject to second sight. There were some who heard the hammering at the place where the factory was afterwards built, long before the factory was ever thought of. Others too saw the men on ladders.

It is difficult to decide where the story of the Callart Light should be placed. It was a well-known happening in the Glen. It was a mysterious light seen across the water from Glencoe before the road was built, and seen within the last fifty years. A light appeared at night and travelled down the loch to the ferry and back again. This could hardly be explained by ships. The teller of the tale went on to say "I know for certain a ship came up the Loch which was too big to go beyond the Ferry, or the pilot was not there. The ship's watch definitely saw the light, and indeed saw it travelling about". Scientific people tried to find an explanation but so far as we know, found none. Callart Light was brighter on stormy nights, and at times came across the water almost to the houses at the cross-roads. It was a blueish light. It was seen by many people and I have heard many accounts of it from those who saw it.

There was a man who worked on the Farm at Invercoe who had his fortune told. He was told that he would drown before the year was out. He was much upset by this, and avoided crossing the water to Callart (there used to be a ferry from this side to Callart). One day he was asked specially to take someone across, he tried to refuse but was pressed and finally yielded. He got across safely, landed his passenger, but was drowned on his return trip. It was nearly on the last day of the year.

It is said that the famous Brahan Seer foretold the Massacre.

There is a healing brooch in the area. It is of great interest and its history is as follows: Euphemia MacKenzie had the brooch as a betrothal gift about 1760. Since then it was used by a natural healer. It was used along with certain sayings from the Bible, also certain water had to be used. Where this water came from, and if from a Holy Well or any other source, is not now remembered. The late owner from whom I got my information remembered hearing someone say that they would have to "go to the water". She was a child at the time, but she remembered it being used by her father's sister on a brother. She knew of specific cures both in and outside of the family. People came a distance for the healing. As far as she could remember, the brooch was used in a specific way, e.g. folded up in a silk ribbon, and she added that there was quite a lot of secrecy attached to the procedure. She was a child when it was last used and never learnt the full story of how it was used. I was allowed to handle and photograph it. The brooch was of old gold with a swivel pin holder. It was on a gold chain and held on a gold coloured ribbon.

Up the hillside beyond Creagan Inn there are two healing wells. One of them, the Eye Well, is shaped as an eye. The other is the Knee Well into which one put one's knee. There is also nearby a large rock which was used for curing rheumatism. The cure consisted in sitting on the ground and rubbing one's back against the rock.

A little way there is a wishing well into which one dropped coins for the fairies. One last rather unusual item is a large rock on which is carved a ship which is near the two healing wells.

At Tyndrum there was a wee Chapel beside the river with two pools. Its waters were used for healing and people were taken from Glencoe, Ballachulish and further afield. It was used especially for mental illness. There were two pools, one for men and one for women. The upper was Poll nam Bean for the women and Poll nam Fear for the men. Patients were led three times round the pool, sunwise, first in the name of the Father, Son and Holy Ghost. Then they were dipped in the pool in the name of the Trinity. After that they were taken to the Church of St. Fillan and stretched on their backs between two sticks and bound in a simple way. If the patients had got themselves untied by morning they were expected to recover, if not there was no hope for them. Some say the ordeal was only used on men and that women were simply dipped into the pool. One day someone brought a mad bull and dipped it in, and from then on, the pool never healed.

I have heard that there is, somewhere in Argyll, a stone that was used at the time of the Massacre to stop a haemorrhage. It was smooth and flat and would be entirely practical but that part of its effectiveness was thought to be because it had red flecks on it, representing blood. I have not seen this stone but simply heard of its existence.

There was a seventh son of a seventh son who healed the King's Evil. He lived some distance away. He cured his patients by dipping in water, and saying the Lord's Prayer over them. Another seventh son I heard about used to cure epileptics by rowing them sunwise round a certain loch. The teller in this case was a hospital nurse who said it went against her training but that he did have many cures to his credit. I have also heard a doctor tell how, as a young man, he found all his patients going to a local wise woman to have their warts charmed off. Again it worked, though how or why it could do so he could never think.

The eye well used to cure eye troubles.

The knee well used for ailments of the knee.

Chapter 8   The Highland calendar and social life

Many dates in the calendar still have a special significance in Scotland especially for the Highlander. In the past, these special days were observed to a greater degree than at the present time. New Year's Day is a great day all over Scotland. This includes the evening of December 31st, which is known as Hogmanay. Not only is the New Year brought in, but "First Footing" is widespread. For this many families don't go to bed but spend the time from midnight onwards calling and visiting friends. There they meet other friends doing likewise.

Housewives will have had a busy time baking special food such as black bun, short bread and other Scottish fare for some days before the New Year. The health of the New Year and of friends will be drunk and the baking eaten. Housewives would receive gifts. In fact it is a widespread custom to give something on entering a home around that date and small gifts are sometimes exchanged among friends. These gifts are known as a ne'erday gift.

It is still considered lucky if a dark haired man is the first to cross the threshold after midnight has struck. A fair haired woman is considered the least lucky. In parts of the Highlands for long, and possibly still in some households, householders held the Old New Year. That is, 12th January, the date on which New Year would have fallen if the calendar had not changed in the eighteenth century. New Year's Day is a general holiday in Scotland with shops, offices and works closed.

The 25th of January is celebrated both in Scotland and abroad by those of Scottish descent. It is the birthday of Robert Burns. In the olden days Burns was not widely read in the Highlands where many had only Gaelic, but at the present time many Highland villages have their Burns Club which celebrates the 25th. Haggis is on the menu and it is piped in with some ceremony. Usually it is served with "bashed neeps" i.e. mashed turnips. Perhaps the meal begins with a cock-a-leekie or Scotch broth and the Scotish flavour of the food is maintained through the meal. Whisky will be drunk. It is usual for all the guests to be male, though some clubs allow women too. Someone proposes the "immortal memory" and there are recitals from Burns.

February 1st is the day of St. Bride, invoking the old Celtic Festival of spring. Bride was much loved. She was the saint of poetry, smithwork, and of healing. She loved animals, birds, and motherless children. Before the Christian St. Bride, there was an older Celtic goddess of the same name, and some of the legends of the first have been interwoven with the second. St. Bride lived between 452 and 525 A.D.

Old Candlemas, February 2nd, was the date of the first calfing, for in the past little winter feeding was available for the beasts, so the cows went dry. St. Brides day was something of a milk festival; milk, butter, and cheese being very important to the Highland people.

February 13th is the anniversary of the Massacre of Glencoe in 1692. For many years there has been a service conducted round the Monument to those who were massacred. This outdoor service is held in wind and rain, snow or sun. It is very impressive, with a piper playing the lament, and unaccompanied singing amidst the hills.

On Maundy Sunday, that is the Sunday before Easter, in some places in the Highlands an offering of meal and gruel was made to the sea. This practice belongs to the distant past. Easter itself is celebrated, but with few customs not common on the rest of the country. Children get coloured hard-boiled eggs which they roll down hillocks; the sun is said to dance for joy on rising to celebrate the Risen Christ.

The first of April, known in many parts of the world as April Fool's day, in Scotland is often called "hunting the gowk". The word "gowk" means fool or cuckoo. In the Highalnds it is considered a good day to start a new enterprise.

In the Highlands many will remember April 16th, the anniversary of Culloden Moor. There are many Highlanders here and abroad whose forebears fought and died on that field. The reprisals that followed caused more deaths, loss of homes, and families. Often those who had not taken part suffered too. As late as 1749 Dr. Cameron, Lochiel's brother was captured and condemned to death.

The first of May was a landmark. It was Beltane, the date of the fire festival. The origin goes back into the distant past, certainly into pre-Christian days. It still survived when Pennant toured Scotland in 1770 and in places lasted much later. Vestiges still remain, such as the parties who go up Arthur's Seat in Edinburgh on the first of May.

The domestic fire which had burned day and night throughout the year was put out on Beltane's Eve. Two large bonfires with a passage between them were built on a hill. On the morning of Beltane the people drove the cattle and other beasts before them to the bonfire which had been lit as the sun rose. The cattle were driven through the passage between the fires three times to receive protection from murrain. The people followed the same practice and blackened each other's faces with the ashes. Torches were made of dried sedge or heather and were carried by those who were returning home. When they reached their own land, they walked round it sunwise carrying their lit torch, then round their home, which they re-entered, and relit their fire which would remain lit till next Beltane's Eve.

In the meantime, the elder folk who had remained at the bonfire had a special task. It is described by Pennant. "They cut a square trench in the ground, leaving the turf in the middle; on that they make a fire of wood, on which they dress a large caudle of eggs, butter, oatmeal and milk; and bring besides the ingredients of the caudle plenty of beer and whisky; for each of the company must contribute something. The rites begin with spilling some of the caudle on the ground, by way of libation; on that everyone takes a cake of oatmeal, upon which are raised nine square knobs, each dedicated to some particular being, the supposed preserver of their flocks and herds, or some particular animal, the real destroyer of them; each person then turns his face to the fire, breaks off a knob, and flings it over his shoulders, says, This I give to thee, preserve thou my horses; This to thee, preserve thou my sheep; and so on. After that, they use the same ceremony to the anxious animals; This I give to thee, O Fox! Spare thou my lambs, this to thee, O Hooded Crow! This to thee, O Eagle".

The bonfire at the Beltane Festival was always started with need fire, that is a fire started by friction. Steel and flint were never used for the Beltane Fire. Need fire was made by rubbing two large planks of wood (preferably oak sacred to the Druids) till by friction a spark was made and this was kindled into a flame. The work was done in shifts by nine men in shifts of nine, so 81 men took part in all—naturally this only where there was this number of men available.

A May day custom that has lingered longer is that of washing your face in the May dew. It was regarded as a beauty aid.

Sometime in May the people took to the life of the shieling, when the young ones left the main township and went to live a simple life in the hills. There they made butter and cheese for winter. At this time of year it was practical to take the beasts to the hill grazing for a few weeks. The grass was at its best in the heights then, and it allowed the inby fields to be rested. Those going to the shieling set off in gay mood with dairy equipment, some wool and spinning equipment and the simplest of cooking pots and other necessities.

June 9th is St. Columba's Day. He was held in high regard by the Gael. In many parts of Scotland special fairs or festival were held. Thursday was dedicated to the Saint. It was a good day to start a new enterprise, since it was one of the days of the week when the fairies were less likely to be active. In their case, they did not like Friday any better, because Friday was the day of Redemption and they had no part in it. Thursday was the day to send sheep to prosperity, cow to calf, or web to loom. It was also the day to put the coracle out to sea, put the flag in the staff, to die or to hunt the heights, to send herds to pasture or put horse to harness. It was also a good day for prayer. Friday was not a good day to kill a beast, or count your stock. It was unlucky to set off by boat, and a bad day to cut hay or to make a purchase. Hair should be cut on a Thursday, and nails on a Monday. Tuesday was a good day for reaping. In the Lowlands there is a saying "Saturday flit a short sit," but in the Highlands Saturday was a good day for moving if you were going from South to North. If however you were going from North to South the best day was Monday. May was (and still is) considered to be an unlucky month for marriage. The best day for that ceremony was Thursday. The phase of the moon was taken into consideration, for it was thought that beef or other food grew less if salted or boiled when the moon was waning but grew larger when the moon was waxed fat. When planting seeds the state of the moon was taken into consideration. I understand that this last is being investigated by some scientists.

On the eve of St. Columba's Day many mothers made a cake of barley or rye. The cake was toasted in rowan, oak or yew fire where possible. Into the cake the mother put a small silver coin. In the morning the cake was cut into as many pieces as there were children. This was put in a basket, the children were blindfolded and each chose a piece of cake. The one who got the coin got the lamb crop for the year. Sometimes this child got so many of the lambs and the rest were divided among the other children.

While the Day of St. Columba was 9th June this was always celebrated on the 2nd Thursday of the month. While Thursday was lucky and dedicated to the Saint, this was not so if Beltane fell on a Thursday.

June 10th, White Rose Day, is the birthday of James VIII and III, known to the Whigs as the Old Pretender. He was never officially crowned, but some evidence exists that he may have been at Scone Palace. The proclamation was issued for January 23rd and in letters from the Bishop of Rochester the Bishop writes "... the anniversary of your Majesty's Coronation" meaning the date 3rd February which would be correct allowing for the change in the calendar. In Scotland, and in England too, there are still some who like to wear a white rose on James' birthday as others do the oak leaf and oak apple on the 29th May to commemorate the escape of Charles II. The white rose was a Jacobite emblem.

On Midsummer's Day we Scots like to remember the great victory won by Robert the Bruce at Bannockburn. This was followed by the Declaration of Arbroath. Bannockburn was fought in 1314 and the Declaration of Arbroath was signed in 1320.

In mid July comes the Glasgow Fair. At one time all works closed during the Fair Fortnight and there was a general exodus from the city. Many Highlanders returned home for a brief spell. Nowadays works stagger their holidays and no longer are there the huge crowds waiting at railway and bus stations or departing by car.

August 1st was the Celtic Festival of Lammas, originally a day of the sacrifices of the fruits of the soil—a pagan harvest festival. In many parts of the country races were run and

The head of the Highland pony is covered to prevent it getting frightened with the sight of the stag.

bonfires lit. On that day too, many of the cattle returned from the shieling. Children received a small cheese from the day's milking for luck. Though there was great joy in setting out for the shieling, there was also great pleasure in the return.

On August 12th grouse shooting begins. At one time, when many thousand acres were devoted to grouse moors, this was of some financial profit to the Highlands. Landlords gained the rent and many were employed on the moors as beaters. The deer forests too were let for high rents and again helpers were wanted not only on the moor but in the "lodges" as well. In Scotland the words "deer forest" are misleading as it largely means hill country barren of trees but frequented by deer, this though the deer is by nature a forest creature. Unfortunately much of the work was seasonable and ended when the shooting season ended.

At some date in October the Mod is held each year. This is the biggest gathering of the Gaels nowadays. Individual competitions are held for both singing and speaking Gaelic for both adults and children. Choirs compete and fiddlers too, along with poetry competitions. The winner of this last section is crowned Bard for the year. Gold medals are awarded to the top singers. An Comunn Gaidhealach, a society which has done much to save Gaelic culture, organises the Mod. Beautiful songs encourage singers to learn Gaelic to understand what they sing and so to sing with more feeling. It should be remembered that at the beginning of the 20th century if a child uttered one word of Gaelic in school he or she was thrashed. Many children in those days went to school knowing no other tongue. This harsh treatment continued throughout schooling, and was not confined to the classroom but even in the playground Gaelic was forbidden.

Halloween falls on the 31st October. This is the time of year when the fairies move home. Whilst they are flitting it is the time to rescue any mortal they may have stolen and forced to live amongst them. Both witches and fairies are powerful at this time, and it is indeed a chancy time for as well as fairies and witches the spirits of the dead are abroad too. At Halloween between sunset and sunrise it is possible to gain admittance to a fairy shian. A shian is the home of the fairies.

On Halloween bonfires were lit. It is still a festive time in Scotland especially for children who dress up and go from door to door collecting apples, nuts, cake or pennies. Each child is expected to sing, tell a story, or dance. Ducking for apples is a special delight. Apples are put in a tub of water where they float. The children may duck in turn and try to catch an apple in their teeth, or they may kneel on a chair, hold a fork in their mouths and drop the fork over the back of the chair into the tub of moving apples. If the fork lands on an apple they get it. Sometimes a scone covered in treacle is hung by a string from a height. The children have to try to get a bite out of it. Another ploy is a dish of mashed potatoes or champit tatties with small favours in it. At one time there used to be tiny china dolls, silver 3d. pieces, little thimbles, buttons and horse shoes. If you got something in your helping, it told your fortune. Halloween cakes also have favours and are decorated usually with witches, black cats and the like. The children who dress up are known as guisers. often they carry a turnip lantern which is made by taking the inside out of a swede turnip. (The inside pulp is usually eaten raw.) A face is made out of the shell of the turnip and a candle put inside the turnip.

Another way of foretelling the future was the visit to the kailyard. The young girls go out after dark and with their eyes shut pull the first kail (or cabbage) they touch. As it is in appearance so will be their future husband—tall, short, thin or fat, straight or crooked, and by the amount of earth carried with the plant so the tocher or dowry will be either large or small. If the heart is sweet so will be the disposition of the future husband. If sour, then so will he be. If there are knots under the earth then there will be no children. There are many local variations of this and other fortune telling rites.

Martinmas falls on November 11th. It is an old Scottish term day. Many flitted on this date, and it was the day that many farm labourers were fee'd. A simple feast was given to those departing and those arriving.

The 30th November is St. Andrew's Day. Tradition has it, that the bones of St. Andrew in 1210 (when Constantinople fell) were taken to Amalfi but that certain bones were taken aside. A holy abbot by the name of Regulus who was in charge of the bones was visited by an angel who commanded Regulus to sail to the West. There he was shipwrecked and built a church to the Glory of God and St. Andrew. The ship had been wrecked off what is now known as St. Andrews and there was the great cathedral built. St. Andrew is the Patron Saint of Scotland.

Christmas day was not celebrated a great deal in Scotland after the reformation. Now it is treated as a very special day but at the beginning of the century shops were not shut for the day, nor was there any public notice taken of the day. Now it is a holiday.

Song lightened much of the work in the Highlands. Hearts were cheered by song, and hard toil made easier by the rhythm keeping all together. Cows were said to give more milk when their favourite songs were sung, and dealers buying cows from the Islands gave less money saying the cows would not give as high a yield where the songs and the Gaelic were different on the mainland. Butter was churned to song, the grinding of corn at the quern was made easier by song, and in the home the spinning wheel and the cradle both had their own songs. The waulking of cloth was worked with song, the rhythm keeping all those taking part in harmony. The men sang as they rowed, and as they fished. They sang as they sowed and as they reaped. You may remember Wordsworth's poem on the Highland lass reaping?

In the Highlands it was, and to a much lesser degree still is the custom through the long winter for people to meet in each other's homes and each in turn would help in the general entertainment. Perhaps the first would sing a song in Gaelic, and the next tell a tale, an old traditional one, a later one, or a romantic legend. One might play the fiddle, another the pipes or perhaps the chanter. One might recite the geneology of the Chief of the Clan or tell tales of the Feinn. This entertainment was called a Ceilidh (pronounced Kailly). Naturally food would be provided. The man of the house, in Gaelic *Fear an Tighe* would be master of ceremonies. At the present time, this has largely died out, though not entirely. There is a new style of ceilidh held for the purpose of raising money. It is usually held in the Village Hall where one pays to enter. The type of entertainment is based on the older type of ceilidh, though fewer tales are told and these short. To some extent the atmosphere is flavoured by the old tradition. The singers encourage the audience to join in the choruses. If your *Fear an Tighe* is good, the audience can feel themselves part of the ceilidh.

So many natural poets came from Glencoe that if a native born in Glencoe showed no aptitude for poetry their parentage might be doubted. Much of the poetry is lost as it was not printed and only retained in memory and with time this has failed. Some was printed. Allan Dal, the blind MacDougall poet, was born in Glencoe. He was apprenticed to a tailor and by his quick wit annoyed his fellow apprentices. One stuck a needle in his eye and Allan then got the Gaelic word *dal* attached to his name, meaning blind.

Iain Lom from Lochaber wrote on the wars of Montrose. A contemporary of Ronald was Iain Raomuill Oig who wrote pastorals, a MacDonald known as the Muck Bard for going to live on the Island of Muck, wrote a poem on the Massacre. Songhus MacAlasdair Ruiadh wrote a long poem on Killiecrankie, and a grandson of Ronald of the Shields wrote humorous poems, satires, and a poem on Sherriffmuir. It should be realised that by no means all Gaelic poems were laments; the Gael wrote in many moods. The famous Duncan Ban MacIntyre stayed not far from Glencoe and took part in a poetic contest with MacAlisdair when he, Duncan, was a young man.

Mention must be made of Ossian, who is said to have lived in a cave on Anoch Dubh which is a most unlikely place for anyone to choose to live, but that he was familiar with the area of Glencoe and wrote of the district is true.

Bagpipes were not confined to Scotland but Scottish pipes differ somewhat. In Ireland a bellows on the arm blows the bag. The Ceol Mor or classical music was brought to its peak by the MacCrimmons about 250 years ago and some is older still. While the real enthusiast prefers the classical music the pipes may also play reels, strathspeys and other lighter music. A good piper is said to speak to those who have an ear. Tales tell of pipers giving information or warnings with their pipes. The lighter music is known as ceol beag, while the classical music is piebaireachd. As a symphony is written to a pattern so is the piebaireachd. The theme is played first. This is the ground or urlar. Variations follow; the bithis or doubling consists of fingering movements; the quickening movements are the taorluath and the crunluath, and then follows the closing movement of the crunluatha'mach.

The chanter is hollow, with seven finger holes and an extra for the thumb. Tartan or velvet covers the bag. The tone is reinforced by three drones. The blow stick has a flap valve to prevent the back rush or air into the piper's mouth. The chanter is connected to the bag, which must be air tight. Beginners practise on a smaller practice chanter alone.

Scotland's greatest composer of fiddle music was Niel Gow. There have been many others. Macpherson's Rant was composed by himself before his execution for reiving. A reprieve was on its way, but it is said that the magistrates advanced the hour on the town clock and as the bringer of the reprieve came in sight so Macpherson hanged. Unfortunately in many parts of the Highlands the ministers condemned the fiddlers and referred to them as "the wee sinful fiddlers". Many fiddles were broken and the playing stopped. But in recent times they have regained their popularity. The BBC meeting of Scottish fiddlers at Blair Castle was a great occasion and gave widespread pleasure.

The Clarsach is a small harp which originally came from Ireland but is of a great age in Scotland. It may be strung with metal or gut. If strung with gut the harp was held against

Ballachulish shinty team is playing away from home in this match.

the right shoulder with cushion of fingers, the right hand taking the treble. If strung with wire it was held on the left hand side and plucked with nails which had been left to grow long, and in this case the treble was taken by the left hand. If the musician was using a harp strung with wire and he did not give pleasure he could be disgraced by having his nails cut in punishment. The Chiefs would have their own harper, as they had their own piper and bard, and like these the post was usually hereditary.

For long the study of geneology and family trees has been a Scottish and particularly a Highland interest. The Bards used to recite the descent of their Chief and of the Clan through the ages from mythical personages to historic persons.

Scottish country dances have a special flavour and many touch on Scottish history. In the Highlands the puirt-a-beul or mouth music was used when the music of the fiddle or pipes was not available for dancing. The words are not important and may be without sense, but the song gives the rhythm and timing to the dancers. The sword dance in which the dancers dance over crossed swords was originally an auger for the dancer's fate in battle. If his feet touched the sword it was a bad omen. In many dances the dancer's hands are raised above the head in a curve to represent the antlers of a stag. The Sean Triubhas tells of the delight of the Highlander when the law which prescribed the wearing of the tartan was revoked. This banning of the tartan was one of the many laws against the Highlander after the '45. Its harshness was felt by those with little money who risked death or deportment if found wearing their usual clothes. This act did not take into account those who had not been "out" or even out on the other side. In the dance, the dancers go through the motions of throwing off the loathed garments. In recent times the dance "The reel of the 51st division" was designed by prisoners of War in German camps.

Fairs were social occasions as well as a commercial undertaking. Cattle, ponies, and sheep were the mainstay of many Fairs but produce and booths were set up also. Carts, people on horse and on foot crowded the road to get there. It was a day out and a meeting of friends, a holiday when these were not plentiful. At some markets farmers got men to work for them and the men in turn found work.

Shinty is called Camanach in Gaelic. It somewhat resembles hockey but it is a more vigorous game. Shinty players say they may take up hockey in their old age. Recorded in old Irish records shinty has ancient pedigree. In Ireland at the present time they play a similar game called hurley. James II of Scotland declared the game illegal as the time spent on shinty would be better spent at the butts for the safety of the realm. James IV was, however, a keen player.

There are 12 players on each side. Their club is a caman or camain in the plural. The curved part is the "bas" and the shaft the "cas". Shinty sticks varied in design from one part of the country to another. Not only may the player raise his stick above his shoulder, but in some parts "Capachs" were allowed when a player might catch a ball in mid-air, throw it up again, and drive it with the caman. In the old days balls were made of wood in many parts, but according to local tradition the Glen made theirs of the fungus Fomes fementarious which grows on birch trees. It hardens and resembles cork. This was covered in wool and put in a leather bag. Later string was added to the wool, and cork used for the centre. For many years in the past, each New Year's Day Glencoe played Ballachulish, but this match no longer takes place.

Scotland has many golf courses, and Glencoe had a course at one time. Fort William, Spean Bridge and Oban all have courses. A favourite Scottish game is curling. Ice conditions used to be tested by putting a wet handkie on a hedge and checking on its stiffness. A cat washing and passing her forepaw over her ear was the sign of a thaw. Brooms were made of twigs of broom bound together. The tee marker or dolly used to be a bawbee (old 1 penny), snuff, or a button. Tassles of coloured wool were used on the handles for identification. Curling is called the "roaring game" because of the roar of travelling stone. The earliest Scottish stone dates back to 1511. No other country has a stone as old as this.

Skating was popular and in past winters during the first half of the century, much skating was even carried out in the evenings with lights. In one hard winter when the water of Loch Leven froze by the shore a wedding party skated from Ballachulish to Caolasnacone about halfway to Kinlochleven, a distance of five or six miles.

August is the favourite month for Highland Games. Tossing the caber, seen at the games, is said to originate in the need to toss the long "roof tree" on to the gable ends when building a cottage. Tossing the caber needs skill as well as strength, and so too both were needed in building the house. At a wedding a toast might be drunk to this same "roof tree", and in some parts so scarce was timber that when the family moved the roof tree went with them to their new home.

At Braemar, the caber for the society and its members is 17 feet 3 inches long and weighs 91 lbs. The caber for open competition is 17 feet, but weighs 114 lbs. There is also a famous Braemar caber which is 120 lbs and is 19 feet 3 inches long. In less well known Games if the competitors are unable to toss the caber, a foot may be sawn off, and all competitors try again till it is thrown. In the actual tossing, some men, two or maybe three, hold the caber upright with the thick end at the top. The competitor rests the caber against his shoulder; works down to the base and gets his hands under the smaller end. He gradually raises the caber which rests against his shoulder. When the caber has been raised he comes forward a few steps and then tosses it. The aim is not so much the distance but that it should fall straight in front of the competitor. With the impetus of the toss it lands first on the heavy end and then somersaults over so that the light end is furthest from the competitor.

In putting the stone, a stone or a metal ball may be used. It is said to have originated from the "clach neart" or stone of strength so often used as a test of strength. The river provides the rounded stones. In putting the stone, the athletes do not throw the stone, for the hand may not be further back than the elbow and he may not make a run of over $7\frac{1}{2}$ feet. The stones may vary from 16 lbs to 23 lbs. The record shot-putt was at Fort William by Donald Kennedy and was 55 feet 6 inches.

In throwing the hammer the weights used may be anything from 16 to 22 lbs. Weight throwing competitions are also competed. A 56 lb weight is thrown for distance and weight; the 28 lb weight is thrown for distance only. Besides these athletic competitions some Games will have tug-of-war, hill races, wrestling and pole vaulting. There are also piping competitions and sometimes competitions of children's Highland dancing.

Fishing provides fine salmon trout and sea trout, while shooting and before that bow and arrow provided sport and food. In modern times the Highlands provides mountaineering and skiing.

The betrothal ceremony was known as the "reiteach". The parents of the bride were visited by the prospective groom accompanied by a friend. After some general talk, the friend began to praise the groom and advocate the match. The girl, if she approved the match stayed, but if she went away it was a sign that she was not willing. Her father would then say "if she is willing I am willing, and if this were not so, this would not be so". The reiteach would follow, a betrothal feast of importance and happiness.

Recently a friend told me of a custom which is forgotten and possibly was never widespread. The bridegroom at the time of the betrothal gave the girl a shoe and after the wedding the bride was given the second shoe. At first the shoes were for wearing, but later shoes of brass and copper for mantelpiece ornaments were given.

A Highland wedding is still an occasion, but a shade of its former self. The ceremony was more often held at the Manse or the Rectory than the Church. The bride's party and the best man met at her home and rode or walked to the manse. The groom's friends and the best maids met at his home and they too set off for the manse. Both parties were piped, and young men fired shots into the air. Both parties returned to the groom's home after the ceremony. When within a mile of the house, the two fathers, the best man and the best maids raced for the house and the first to enter and announce the news was given a bottle of whisky and a glass. He went to meet the wedding party, usually meeting them before they entered the township of the new couple and he distributed whisky among the guests.

Previous to the wedding, friends were asked to the bride's home. The housewives of those invited families repaid this visit by bringing presents of ham, beef, butter, cheese, whisky or whatever was likely to be needed. Usually there was more than enough presented to start the young couple off on their housekeeping.

Sometimes a penny wedding was held. Then the bridegroom provided the feast, which anyone might attend. Each guest gave money which helped the new home. Usually a fiddler played. Impoverished musicians were glad to play at such weddings. They were paid by the guests. A variation of this practice was when employers might arrange a penny wedding for one of their servants. The employers asked their own guests, who paid something towards the future of the young couple.

Handfast marriages were not uncommon, where a couple met at an appointed place, joined hands and lived together for a year. At the end of that time they met again and were married for life or parted company. In Scotland a young girl went bareheaded before marriage, but on her marriage she wore a mutch; this is a slight cap of linen or cotton. Often these were finely embroidered and sewn with tiny stitches. Many have survived the years and come down to us.

An unchristened child had to be protected from many hazards. The fear of the fairies stealing the child and leaving a changeling was real. Fairies wished for a mortal child as a leader who feared not cold iron, and who would help them to recover their lost lands. Some say the fairies were the Bronze age folk who lost their lands to the Iron age people. Certainly cold iron was always regarded as a barrier for magic. The mother might have some cold iron in bed for protection. The Christening was held as soon as possible, as it was a great protection to the baby. It was considered lucky to take the child upstairs rather than downstairs for the first time out of the mother's room. Where there was no upstairs, a ladder or a chair was used.

Burt writing in the early 18th century says "The Moment a Child is born, in these Northern Parts, it is immersed in cold water, be the Season of the Year never so rigorous. When I seemed at first a little shocked at the mention of this strange extreme, the Good Woman told me the Midwives would not forego that Practice if my Wife, though a Stranger, had a Child born in this Country."

Pennant writing in 1770 told how "In many parts of the Highlands at the birth of a child, the nurse puts the end of a green stick of ash into the fire, and while it is burning receives into a spoon the sap or juice which comes out at the other end and administers this to the new born babe."

Going to the Christening the woman carrying the baby had a parcel of bread and cheese which she presented to the first person she met. It was considered important that this should be accepted. It was also thought lucky if they walked a little way with the Christening party.

It is still "lucky" to cross a new baby's hand with silver on first seeing the baby. A Christening feast was held, friends sending food to help. A friend has this account of the seriousness of "luck". She writes "I called to see a Ballachulish lady several years ago with her baby son. She told me he would be 'lucky' as the nurse, who was herself 6 feet tall, had stood on a chair and raised him above her head so he would rise in the world and had worn her stockings outside in for luck." When the baby was taken out of doors for the first time he must not be taken in the direction of the cemetery, as this might mean an early death. He was to be carried in the direction of a place of business where money was handled. In this case he was carried in the direction of the railway. In later years he became a station master.

The true Highlander will never speak of the death of a person by the common words "bass" and "Basaich". An animal dies—a friend departs. Sometimes under the announcement of a death the words "Tir nan Og" are written. This is the paradise of the Gael—the land of the ever young. It lies to the West of Scotland.

In the distant past in the Highlands a dance was held at the time of a death. Not as a mark of disrespect or impiety, but to express joy that the departed was removed from the troubles of the world. By the late 18th century it was disappearing. Neighbours attended these dances, which began when the nearest relative led to solemn music. The dance was repeated till after the funeral.

In Appin the bier was broken when the grave was filled in to prevent witches or fairies carrying away the bodies of the dead.

In the past, the virtues of the deceased had to be sung in special music. Often this was done by a professional mourning woman. It was thought to make the passage to the next world easier. There was the song sung in the home, and outside another called the "coronach" was sung. Salt and earth unmixed were put on a wooden platter and buried with the corpse, salt being the symbol of the spirit, and earth of the body. In many cases there was a long walk to the grave, over hills and rough ground. Along the route a cairn of stones was built at each resting place. Every member of the cortège added his stone. The size of the cairn denoted the number of mourners and told of the esteem in which the deceased was held. The burial of a Chief was important and was managed with a great deal of display and circumstance. Before the funeral would be the wake and before that and afterwards a lavish amount of hospitality offered and much food and drink lasting up to seven days. People would come for many miles for the death of a kinsman, even though travelling was not easy. At one time a "riachaid" was used. This was a stick which was notched to count the number of rounds of whisky at a funeral. I heard of a local man, a minister, who went out to a charge to Tiree. He was distressed at the amount of whisky consumed at a funeral and tried to moderate this. One old man came up to him and said, "Take it easy, there was whisky drunk at funerals before you came to the Island, and there will be whisky drunk at funerals after you go, so take it easy."

In the Highlands, Communion was held in great solemnity. While it is still solemn, it is less noticed when many churches hold Communion three or four times a year. Long ago one church covered a widely scattered congregation who had to travel miles by road, sea or loch to attend. The crowds drew attention to themselves as they made for sevice, by sheer weight of numbers. Lord Teigmouth wrote of fifteen hundred persons assembling for Communion on Skye. he writes of the preparations on the Thursday before and the Monday after, when there were sermons and services. The prospective communicant was tested before Communion and if their way of life and state of grace passed, they were issued with a Communion token. Those who failed to pass received no token and received no Communion.

These various assemblies, both happy and sad, commercial or of the spirit, let people from different clans meet, and friends and relatives keep in touch. For the social Ceilidh people would walk miles over the hills for the pleasure of the meeting. Though winter was hard and the people toiled, song lightened life and labour. The skill the women showed in dyeing their wool, in knitting, and the setting of patterns for the weaver allowed for artistic expression. The men with music in their bones played pipes or fiddles, sang at work and made poetry.

Many of the customs of the old Highlands have now gone, but still, at the Highland games held all over the area, the old sports, music and dances are practised; shinty matches are held and eagerly followed, and today's Highlander is still famous for his warm hospitality.

The Ballachulish Highland Games

Chapter 9 **Highland livestock and its uses**

From the days of pre-history the celt has been a noted stockman. The terrain moulded the breeds produced in the mountains of the Scottish Highlands and those of Wales. Hardiness was required and the ability to thrive on poor feeding and this has produced the Highland Cattle and Welsh Black Cattle. In Ireland the lush green grass has produced many fine horses. Brittany and Cornwall both produced their own breeds.

Horses

Many horses were kept in the Highlands, and their descendants are still with us. There were, and are, three separate types coming from different parts of the country. The Mainland breed of Highland Garron or work horse is the largest. In modern times 14 or 15 hands though earlier writers say 12 to 13 hands which is 54 inches. The older men held that greater height only meant longer legs, which made loading the beast with a stag more difficult. If need be, a garron can carry two stags. Sometimes when crossing a river the stalker would get on the garron's back along with the stag. The ponies used for this work are trained to walk and not to trot. There are photographs of Edward VII riding this type of pony. The stags themselves weigh up to 18 stones. The other breeds are those from the Western Islands, which are smaller than the Mainland breed, and the very small Shetland ponies. Other Scots breeds are the Galloway and the Clydesdale. At the present time Highland ponies are used for pony trekking and for hauling timber for the Forestry Commission.

Highland ponies with foals.

The value of these ponies was great in a land without roads, and transport had to be by sea or by pony. The horses were also used to work the farms or crofts, and pack ponies traversed the country carrying goods for sale to parts of the country where there were no shops. These beasts wore special packsaddles with wooden hooks to carry the packs. They went in a long single string, head to tail, and needed few humans to manage them.

The Highland pony is distinguished by a black eel stripe that runs along the ridge of the neck and the back. They are noted for their sure footedness, and hardiness, walking in safety through dangerous boggy ground or climbing rocks. They will refuse to go where the danger is too great, and are extremely intelligent.

A friend told this story. Her father and uncle went 21 miles to the blacksmith's to have Dandy shod. On their return, it grew dark, specially going through a thick wood. My friend's father and uncle dismounted, the reins of the younger horse were tied for safety and he was sent off. My friend's father put a white hankie at his back and held on to Dandy's tail. The uncle was able to see the white hankie and Dandy acted as guide. If my friend's father stumbled and he lost his grip on the tail, Dandy stood still, till contact was made again. When they got out of the wood, the other horse was waiting for them, and by moonlight they got home safely.

One traveller describes the Highland pony as "Large, low before, long in the back, short on the legs, upright in pastern, rather slow in his pace and not unpleasant to ride except in a canter. His habits make him hardy for he is rarely housed in summer or winter". The Rev. Hall writes in 1807, "When these animals come to any boggy ground, they first put their noses to it, and then pat on it in a peculiar way, with one of their fore feet, and from the sound and feel of the ground they know whether it will bear them. They do the same with ice and so determine in a minute whether it will bear them, then proceed".

Burt in the early 18th century writes, "The horses swim very well at first setting out; but if the Water be wide, in Time they generally turn themselves on their Sides and patiently suffer themselves to be dragged along". Again he writes, "Having passed the Hill, I entered the River, my Horse being almost at once up to his Midsides; The Guide led him by the Bridle, as he was sometimes climbing over loose Stones which lay in all Positions, and many of them two or three Feet in diametre; at other Times with his Nose in the water and mounting up behind. Thus he proceeded with the utmost Caution never removing one Foot till he found the other firm, and all the while seeming impatient of the Pressure of the Torrents, as if he was sensible that, once losing his Footing, he should be driven away and dashed against the rocks below".

Sir John Sinclair in his Statistical Account (1812) writes, "In general the tenants pay no manner of attention to their stallions, or breeding mares, but leave them almost entirely to chance. In summer, and early autumn, one half of the horses and mares range freely and unconfined amidst the mountains whence they are not brought to the different farms and hamlets for work until the harvest is ended, and the crops carried home, and the peats or fuel secured. They are then hunted after like so many wild beasts, and each tenant or proprietor endeavours to procure his own, which he has not seen for many weeks before. They are driven into enclosed fields or penfolds, frequently into bogs or morasses, before they can be laid hold of, and sometimes injured severely in the process. Their manes are then cut and the hair laid up for rope work and other purposes, and the young horses are gradually broken in for labours and cruel hardship of winter".

Walker in his Economical History (early nineteenth century) writes, "The Highland horse is sometimes only 9 and seldom 12 hands high. He is too often short necked, chubby headed and thick, flat at the withers forming altogether a bad forehand though fitted for strength. Others of them are hollow-backed. The hindhand is generally plump and of a better shape. He is well set on his limbs, which are clean; the hooves narrow and are like iron. He has rounded lips, small narrow nostrils, and contracted eyes, which have a peculiarly sly and sagacious look. Many of them however are free from some of these defects in this description and are of an excellent form. They have great strength in proportion to their size, and a great deal of agility and spirit without being vicious".

"Scarce any horse can go through so much labour and fatigue upon so little sustenance; and, when well kept, they are almost indefatigable. To become highly useful and profitable, the Highland horse requires only to have his breed carefully preserved, and his size enlarged".

"An excellent horse of this kind, taken in a manner wild from the hills, was travelled for three months in a very laborious journey through the Highlands. He was firm, active and strenuous yet good tempered and docile though almost in a state of nature. He had never felt a spur, and being astonished at such a new attack, he stopped, and returned the kick with hind foot, which the rider would have received to his cost, had he not suddenly shifted his leg forward. Having never tasted oats, when they were thrown into the manger at the first inn he came to in the Low country he was alarmed and rushed out of the stable. Yet, though unacquainted with the civilised life of a horse, he possesses all the good qualities of the animal ... The Captain of Clanranald, who was killed in the year 1715 at the Battle of Sheriff Muir, had been a colonel in the Spanish service. On his return home, not long before that action, he brought with him some Spanish horses which he settled in his principle island of South Uist. These, in a considerable degree altered and improved the horses in that and the adjacent island. Even in the year 1764 not only the form, but the cool fearless temper of the Spanish could be discerned in the horses of that island, especially those in the possession of Clanranald himself, and his cousin MacDonald of Boysdale ..."

Clanranald is the title of the Chief of a branch of Clan Donald whose territory covered Moidart and the Hebridean Islands of North and South Uist.

Thornton describes horses being taken across a river where the beasts were not wearing bridles but "branks" that is two pieces of wood through which a halter runs, generally made of twisted birch which, when the rider wished the beast to stop, he pulled and this pinched the pony's nose.

In Loch Awe dwelt an Eelhorse which had twelve legs and at Ardnamurchan there was a horse which could carry its owner over land or sea. In Skye, to dream of a horse was very lucky, varying colours denoting different fortunes. To meet a piebald horse was lucky, and a rider on a white horse was supposed to be able to name a cure for any illness. There are proverbs connected with horses. "*Gheibh an t-easgaidh a luchd.*" The willing horse gets the load. "*Ma 's math an t-each, 's math a dhreach.*" If a horse is good his colour is good. "*Is fhiach each breab a leigeadh leis.*" A good horse may be forgiven a kick. "*Millidh an t-srathair an t-each.*" The pack saddle will spoil the horse.

In some parts of the Highlands the horses were taught English as well as Gaelic so that if they were sold to the Lowlands they could understand the commands of their new masters. Lismore was noted for its grey and dappled horses and the skill of the islanders with horses was recognised. About 1790 the price of Highland ponies was between £4 and £6.

Marjoram was used as a fomentation for stitches and pains in horses. An infusion of broom tips was given to cure grass sickness.

Cattle
The cattle of the Highlands were the Kyloe cattle of the type known today as Highland Cattle. In those days black beasts were preferred. Like the horses, there were three

BRITISH KYLOE.

Kyloe cattle. In the past the black beasts were much preferred as they were considered to be hardier.

different types, those from Argyll being considered the best. The others came from the Islands and other parts of the Mainland.

Sir John Sinclair describes a beast of 1812, "A bull of the Kyloe breed should be of middle size, capable of being fattened to fifty stone avoirdupois. His colour should be black (that reckoned the hardiest and most durable species) or dark brown without any white or yellow spots. His head should be rather small, his muzzle fine, his eyes lively and prominent, his horn equable, not very thick, of a clear green colour and waxy tinge ... his neck should rise with a gentle curve from his shoulders and should be small and fine where it joins the head. His shoulders moderately broad at the top joining full to his chine and chest ... His general appearance should combine agility, vivacity and strength and his hair should be glossy, thick and vigorous, indicating a sound constitution and perfect health. For a bull of this description Mr MacNeill of Colonsay lately refused 200 guineas; and for one of an inferior sort he actually received £170 Sterling. Mr MacDonald of Staffa bought one nine years old at 100 guineas."

"The general properties of this breed are great hardiness of constitution which, as they are driven to distant markets, is an essential one, being easily maintained and speedily fattened on pasture where large animals could scarcely subsist—and produce beef of fine grain and well marbled or intermixed with fat. Their milk is rich, but small in quantity".

Dr. Johnson writes of Skye, observing, "The price regularly expected is from two to three pounds a head. There was once one sold for five pounds. They go from the Island very lean, and are not offered to the buyer till they have been long fattened in English pastures". A contemporary writer again on Skye, says, "If the cows calve before the first of March it will be sometimes a month or six weeks before they have sufficient milk to feed the calves. The best cows on the Island afford only a Scots Quart of milk a day, of which the calf gets a choppin in the morning and the same quantity in the evening, but many of them yield not daily above a pint (sic) milk". Note that a Scots pint is equal to two English quarts.

"One of the best and one of the worst Milk cows yield together during the summer season about two stones of butter and 4 stones of cheese, sometimes in all 7 stones but seldom 8. The butter they afford is always one third of the cheese".

From the gentleman farmer of 1815.

A dairy may be turned to great account. A good cow, during the six summer-months, will give at a medium twelve Scotch pints of milk daily; the butter of which, with the skimmed milk, may amount to eighteen pence per day, and thirteen pounds ten shillings in the six months—the grazing of such a cow for that time, will not cost above forty shillings of profit.

These Highland cattle yield only four, or five and rarely six Scots pints of milk (i.e. nearly so many half English gallons) daily; while cows in the Lowlands give double that quantity. The first is, however, by far the richest milk.

53

Dr. Lightfoot wrote that the cattle often weighed heavily and one in Braemar weighed 18 stones. He also recorded the fact that both cattle and deer would go down to the sea shore to eat wrack even if they were out of sight of the sea.

Walker (Highland Economy) writes, "The Highland cattle lie abroad all the year round and have little or nothing to eat during the winter and spring but what they can pick up in the fields. The richest milk is always produced upon the poorest pasture; and where ever it is in small quantity it is usually superior in quality. The best cows in parts of the Highlands, afford only a Scots Quart ... The milk, however, is like cream, compared to that of large cows fed on clover, which gives from fourteen to eighteen Scots pints of milk a day ... In consequence of this superior quality of the milk the butter made in the Highlands is generally excellent. Where there is a large herd of cows, the milk is churned from sweet cream, and it is from this only that butter of the most exquisite flavour and sweetness can be obtained. The richness of the milk is also very remarkable in the quality of Highland cheese, wherever it is made of the entire milk it is richer than any other cream cheese in the kingdom, that is formed without any addition of cream".

Cattle formed the greatest part of the wealth of the Highlands. Rents and wages were often paid in kind and little real money circulated. Pennant states that the Glencoe men servants were paid in kind. He says from the area £700 worth of cattle were sold annually. The cattle went to the fairs on the hoof under the charge of a drover. He sold them on behalf of the owner, or sometimes bought them for himself often not paying for them till they were resold. As the beasts journeyed south they would finally leave the soft grassy drove roads and come to the hard roads. They were then shod. The main fairs were at Crieff and later at Falkirk. Besides these main ones there were many local ones. One for black cattle was held at Shian (near Port Appin) where the ferry used to be before the road came on the mainland. The fair was held on Friday before the last Wednesday in October. There was a fair at Appin on Friday before Martinmas and one at Duror on the Saturday before the last Wednesday in May and in October and one held on Lismore on the last Tuesday of October.

'The manner of disposing of their dry cows, or young bullocks, is somewhat curious. When the drovers, from the South and interior of Scotland, make their appearance in the Highlands, which always happens during the latter end of April, or beginning of May, they give intimation at the churches, that upon a particular day, and in as central place of the district, they are ready to purchase cattle from any who offer them for sale. This is a most important and anxious time, to both buyers and sellers. The price of the commodity, like all others is regulated by demand. The farmers have only two ways of judging of the demand; first by the number of drovers that appear in the country; and, secondly, by epistolary correspondence with persons in the South, who have their confidence. The drovers are of two descriptions: either those who buy by commission, for persons of capital, who being diffident of their own skill, or averse from fatigue, choose to remain at home; or those who purchase cattle on their own account ... Their anxiety on both sides is sometimes so great, that the cattle are given away upon a conditional contract; that if the price rises within a limited time, the seller will receive so much more; but if the lean cattle fall in value, the drover will get a reduction. Ready money is generally given for the cattle; and this is the reason for the banks to circulate their paper money,' Robertson General View of the Agriculture of Inverness 1808.

In the book "The Farm and the Village" the author writes about East Anglia. He was told that near Needham market there was a field called Oxlands. This field was used to rest the cattle coming down from Scotland. They stayed for a while in Norfolk to fatten after their long journey. Naturally some of the cattle did not make this long journey but were used in Glasgow, Edinburgh and other parts of Scotland.

When times were hard during the long winter the cattle were bled and the blood was used to make black puddings. In the distant past, when spring came the cows having had little winter feeding were often so weak as to need help to get out of the byre into the fields. The cattle were bedded in bracken for the winter.

When an animal was killed every part was used. Beef was salted and the perishable parts used in different ways, the leather and horn were also of value. The suet apart from its use in the kitchen, was used in the making of candles. Butter and cheese were stored for winter. There was the old Gaelic proverb, "*Cha dean corrag-mhilis im, 's cha dean glaimsear caise.*" Sweet tooth will make no butter nor will Gobble-it-up make cheese.

Here follow some old recipes.

Meate Pye

Of chopped meate of ye ox or stag to fill ye trencher, put to it sweet herbes of basil and thyme, salt, nutmeg, and much pepper if it be ripe. Put all into a basin and sprinkle with Madeira wine. Leave to steepe 1 hour. Put ½ a pint of water, ½ a lb of fat (lard if hogges be kept) but good fat of other kind will do, add some salt in the pan and bring to the boil. Then mix in flour and it should take up nearly 2 lbs of best flour. Kneed it well, much kneed it well for nigh on ½ an hour. Put most to line ye dish, put in ye meate and wine, and if liked, a chopped anchovy. Cover it in and bake at once.

Another recipe from the same source.

Mince Meate

1 lb of lean chopped fine beef, 1½ lbs of chopped fine beef suet from ye kidney, 1 lb of moist brown honey sugar, 2 oz candied lemon peel, grated rind and juice of two lemons, 1 small nutmeg, grated, also a little sweet spice, half a pottle of chopped apples without peel or pips, ½ a pint of best whisky. From other lands 2 lbs Valencia raisins cut in flour, 1 lb

Corinth currants. Mix all but the whisky adding it to the last. Put in a large jar, and keep out the air with a stretched bladder. It will be ready for use in 3 weeks. If one does not care to use his best whisky French brandy makes it nearly as good. Note a pottle is roughly 2½ lbs, 2 lbs of apples peeled and cored and chopped make up the right amount. As will have been seen, in the old days mince meat was meat and not fruit.

When a cow has newly calved the milk is called beastings and in the old days, it was given to the sick or weakly children. The milk was kept warm at the side of the fire when it turned into a thick custard like cream. A little sugar and cinnamon was added if liked. Nowadays this is usually thrown away if not fed to calves.

Neat's foot oil

This was specially prized by old people. It was used for sore throats and other ills externally and internally. It was made by boiling cow's feet for a long time until the oil could be taken off the top with a saucer.

Crowdie

Crowdie, the simple cheese, was made, and also the harder better keeping cheese. Crowdie is simply sour milk slowly heated, but never boiled, the solids separate from the liquid. It is then drained of all liquid and the solid part is put in a muslin cloth and hung to drip. This may be done on a tree outside or inside on a hook. The cheese can be flavoured with herbs and salt, and I have known butter added and even sugar. This type of cheese does not keep. The hard cheese kept well and lasted through the winter.

Hard cheese

To make hard cheese, the milk was heated to blood heat, and the rennet added and this was allowed to set. Then the curd was broken and the mixture was strained through a cheese cloth and hung up till it dripped. This may be done for a few days until enough curd to fill the vat is obtained. The curd is crumbled and salted to taste and put into a dry cheese cloth and placed in a vat under pressure for a few days. The cheese is taken out and put into a fresh dry cheese cloth and returned to the vat under pressure every few days. In about a fortnight the cheese should be ready. It is then rubbed all over with butter or lard, to seal all cracks, and placed on a shelf to mature. It may be eaten at this stage as a mild cheese, or kept for later use. Sometimes the ashes of burnt seaweed were used to preserve cheese instead of salt.

Rennet

To make rennet, take a suckling-calf's stomach, wash it and tie one end, fill with sweet milk, add a handful of salt, tie the other end and place in a covered jar and leave till fermented. When ready, empty the rennet into a clean jar and use as required. Add a little fresh milk to keep the jar filled for further use. Keep in a warm place. Some wild plants were also used to make rennet.

Boswell writes about frothed milk which was a favourite drink among the Highlanders, "... and they brought us out two wooden dishes of milk, one of them froathed like a syllabub. I saw a woman preparing it with such a stick as is used for chocolate, and in the same manner". Pocock describes the making of froathed milk. "A great pot of whey was over the fire, of which they were making frau. (Fro' or Froth Frau whisked cream.) They have a machine like that which they put on the churn with stiff hairs round it, this they work round and up and down to raise a froth, which they eat out of a pot with spoons, and it had the taste of new milk." Syllabub is a pudding much favoured in the 18th century. It was made in different ways. Here is one kind.

Syllabub

Grate the rind from a lemon then extract its juice, strain and mix with the rind, gradually thicken with 1 pint of thick cream, then stir in ½ a pint of white wine. Sweeten with caster sugar if liked. Whip it up well, then put through a sieve. Pour a little more wine, white or red, into the bottom of the serving glasses. Pour the cream into glasses and chill. Though there are many variations the basis is always milk in some form or other.

The stick used to make froathed milk was usually about 1½ feet. It had a cross at one end which had strands of horse or cow hair wound round it. Sometimes oatmeal was added to the drink.

The first of February was St. Bride's Day which evokes the old Celtic Festival of spring. Old Candlemas was on February second and it was the date of the first calving, for owing to lack of winter feeding beasts went dry in winter. St. Bride's was a kind of milk festival. Milking songs were used and the cows appeared to enjoy the Gaelic songs they heard, so much so, that dealers from the mainland would not give the full price for Island cows as the Gaelic songs to which they were used and the Gaelic itself would differ from that of the mainland. This would mean less milk.

The horns were used to make buttons, spoons, drinking horns, snuff mulls, etc. Horn is not easy to work and was worked by the tinkers. They were secretive about their methods. Horn has to be heated to become malleable. British horn is softer than the horn imported today. Skill is needed in cutting the horn to avoid waste. Horn is hollow except at the tip. When being worked it was heated by a gentle flame, if the heat was too strong the horn got damaged, if the heat was too little the horn returned to its original shape after it had been moulded. The horn might be used whole to give an animal medicine, sometimes they were used thus as powder horns for gunpowder. Horn is made of two materials, the outward case of horn and an inner cone shaped material. These might be separated by a blow against wood. The horn was cut in three. The lowest part was made into combs after being flattened several times. The middle was flattened with heat and oiled to make it transparent and split into layers for making lanthorns, the sides of which were horn not glass. The tip was used for making knife handles. The material inside was boiled down for fat and used for making yellow soap while the liquid was used as glue. The chippings ended up as manure.

The skins of the beasts were cured for clothing or rugs or tanned to make leather. They might also be sewn up and filled with air and used as buoys.

In the Highlands shoes were made of rough leather, uppers sewn on to the soles. Hen feathers were used to push the strong thread through the thickest parts of the sole at the heel. Leather thongs were used with one lace to each shoe. When shoes were made to order, and not at home, it was the custom to deliver them untanned so that the workmanship could be inspected. It was a reproach to sell them otherwise, and it became a term of reproach to describe anyone as a "blackener of shoes". The early brogues were made with holes to let out the water. They were for protection over rough ground rather than for keeping feet dry; somewhat on the principle of the sandals being worn today. Tormental was used for tanning leather and sometimes oak chips.

Dr. Johnson made some observations on brogues, "In Skye I first observed the use of Brogues, a kind of artless shoe stitched with thongs so loosely that though they defended the foot from stones, they do not exclude water. Brogues were formerly made of raw hides, with the skin inwards, and such are perhaps used in rude and remote parts, but they are said not to last above two days. Where life is somewhat improved, they are now made of leather tanned with oak bark, as in other places, or with the bark of birch or roots of tormental ... My inquiries about Brogues gave me an early specimen of Highland information. One day I was told that to make a pair of Brogues was a domestic art, which every man practised for himself, and that a pair of Brogues was the work of an hour. I supposed that the husband made the brogues as the wife made the apron. Next day it was told me that a brogue-maker was a trade and that a pair of brogues cost half a cown ..."

John Buchanan in 1790 writing of his travels in the Western Hebrides says "Their brogues (shoes) are made of cow or horse leather, and often seal skins, that are commonly well tanned by the roots of tormentil which they dig out of the hillocks and uncultivated lands about the seaside. This properly pounded and prepared, without lime or bark, is sufficient to make the hides pliant and fit for wearing. It answers their purpose much better than leather tanned with lime or bark because they seldom grow hard or shrink when dried, even though wet through all day; which is the case with such as are burnt with lime. They never use tan-pits, but bind the hides fast with ropes, and hold them for several days in some remote solitary stream, until the hair begins to come off, of its own accord; and after that, the tormentil roots are applied as above described ..."

Leather was important for the making of targes or shields used by the Highlanders in time of war. These are large round thick pieces of wood covered with leather and studded with large brass nails or studs worked to a pattern. Sometimes there was a spike in the centre as an extra weapon. This could be removed for safety when carrying the targe.

The targe is round, usually 19 to 21 inches in diameter, made of two layers of light wood, possibly fir. The grain of one layer crossing the other at an angle, the pieces were then dovetailed together. A covering of leather is stretched over the wood tightly and hide, often calf skin, over the back.

Skins were used for making sieves used for riddling grain. One traveller writes, "They make sieves of sheep skins and sift meal on plates made of grass onto large goat skins placed on the floor". Osgood MacKenzie wrote that he had never seen a wire riddle but only stretched sheep skins with holes made with a red hot needle.

MacIain, the murdered Chief of the Glencoe MacDonalds wore a leather bull's hide jacket, and this type of garment is still worn by the family.

The Patron Saint of cattle was Saint Columba though he would not have any on Iona. "*Far am bi bo bidh bean, is far am bi bean bidh buaireadh.*" Where a cow is, a woman will be, and where a woman is, will be mischief, trouble or temptation.

A spoon made from a horn, lost from a living cow, was thought to heal many ills when used to eat food. Many references to the fine complexion of dairy maids were made. This was the result of their catching cow pox and thus escaping small pox. Innoculation was first brought to this country by Lady Wortly Montagu from Turkey. The origin of the black patches worn by women started with the desire to hide small pox scars. These patches became fashionable in their own right and even mildly political, Tory ladies favouring the right cheek and Whig ladies the left.

Proverbs about cows are plentiful. "*An t-eolan a rinn Calum-cille dh'aona bho no caillich.*" The charm of St. Columba to the old woman's cow, plenty of milk if well tended. "*Cha 'n fhaodar a bho a reic 's a bainne ol.*" You can't sell the cow and drink her milk.

"*Cho glan ri imideal.*" Clean as a covering skin, needs some explanation. In the old days cows were not brought to the byre to be milked and in fact were never in the byre from Candlemas till Hallowe'en. They were brought or more usually came of their own accord, to an area known as the cuidhe or the cuidh. This would be a sheltered hollow. It might be some way from the township but where the grazing was good. Home made sieves were used to strain the milk into a dish known as "stop" or "stoup". It was tub shaped, except that the staves sloped inward, the result being that the mouth was smaller than the bottom. The hoops were usually of hazel. Two hoops were made at the top edge. When the milk was in the stop a prepared piece of sheep skin was put on top. This skin had been prepared with alum and was as white as linen and as clean. It fastened over the top of the stop and was tied with string made from horses hair and tied in the hollow between the two hoops.

Thus no milk was spilt on the journey home. When two stops were being carried to the same house a bag was made stitched with bullrushes. The bag was flat at the bottom and the sides could stand on their own. The stopan went into the bag and the mouth was drawn together with straw rope drawn through the eyes. The emptied stop was scalded and the corners scrubbed with marran grass. The leather part or "imideal" was scrubbed in cold water and scraped on a flat stone and finally put in cold water with salt to keep pliable. Sometimes this imideal was made flat and was strapped on the back of the carrier, sometimes when the people were going to the shieling, to keep the calves following the top was not secured so tightly as usual and the drops of spilt milk encouraged the calves to follow.

In some parts of the Highlands where the milk vessels were of wood, to clean and sterilise them stones would be heated in the fire till red hot, the vessels would be filled with cold water and the hot stones dropped in, gradually the water temperature was raised to boiling. Another simple adaptation in the Highlands was the use of scallop shells to skim off the cream, holes being made in the shell to allow the cream to collect.

Illness among stock had to be treated with traditional cures. The lask or scour was difficult to cure but an infusion of tormentil boiled till it had acquired a styptic quality and a similar infusion of oak bark, neither of them stronger than summer water (clear water) carefully strained through a cloth. A Scots pint of it was poured into the animal which was not allowed to swallow any other liquids. When milk was scarce calves were given an infusion of hay; this was made with boiling water and cooled. It was found to be nourishing. For inflammation of heifers' udders there were several cures, the simplest being made by boiling the roots of docks till the juices were extracted, in a quantity of butter, straining the infusion through a linen cloth and mixing it with flowers of sulphur or brimstone. In autumn cows ate the coarse dying grass and got constipated. In Glencoe they were given an infusion of slippery elm bark. This is an American tree but it was here previously, or more likely planted by Lord Strathcona, but the tree was used within living memory. Turnips were considered the proper food for cows after calving. Bulls were inclined to get cataract, for which the old treatment was to grind a piece of crystal to a fine powder and sprinkle a little into the animal's eyes. The action of the eyelid cut out the film of the cataract. It was said to be effective. However I must add that our local vet said it was not to be recommended. In fact these remedies are folklore, not veterinary medicine.

One remedy from an old book deals with the swelling of the belly caused by swallowing small spiders. The cure was a musket charge of gun powder given in cold water. Should this fail a Scottish quart of watered milk given warm and poured down the animal's throat, would purge it and remove the disorder.

During an illness an animal may lose the cud, and will be unable to ruminate and thus fall into a decline. A drench made of hot ale, oatmeal gruel, $\frac{1}{4}$ oz of ground ginger and $\frac{1}{2}$ lb of treacle (black) will restore the rumination. A simple method was to chew a little grass and place this behind the animal's back teeth where the cud is held, thus a fresh cud enables the animal to "bring up the cud" and ruminate.

Many cures were made with the help of tar, and according to local tradition foot and mouth disease was cured with it. An injury in the Quarry, as well as to any animal, was dressed with archangel tar mixed with fat. The bandage was smeared with it and this was put on. By the way, archangel tar is from pine trees and is a vegetable product not like the tar used on the roads. Though this too was considered curative and as a child I was told to breathe deeply and inhale the smell of the hot tar when we passed a tar boiler at work on the roads. It was said to be healthy and to cure colds.

In the spring the young people would likely suffer from boils and skin complaints. The cure was to use the fresh voidings of a young heifer and put it on the boil while hot. The boil was cured without any ill effect. This by the way was more sensible than some of the fashionable cures used by early doctors. Mercury was used in medicine internally at an alarming rate. Then they did have to cure some strange ailments such as flying gout or the Rising of the Lights, the only cure for which seemed to be the drinking of a paste made of flour and water.

During the summer pond weed was gathered and made into bundles. On New Year's Day an infusion was made of it and this was fed to the cows. It helped them to give a better yield of milk and also protected them against the wiles of witches who were said to be able to steal the milk from the cows by charming it away and this was done without coming near the cows.

In the first Statistical account (1791) there is a surprising account of farmers changing from oxen for ploughing and then going back to the oxen. "The practice of ploughing with oxen was for several years almost totally given up, till of late, that some of the farmers have begun to revive the ancient practice. In strong stoney land, which is frequently to be met with in this parish, oxen are preferable to horses. The oxen move at a slow, but persevering pace, and take the draught along with them; whereas the metal of the horse is soon raised by resistance and the whip; he becomes restive and unmanageable. The oxen have also the advantage of the horses in point of economy, being maintained at much less expense. The chief objection against oxen ploughs is the slowness of their movement; but, when the superior execution of their work is considered, where the ground is cross and stoney, and that they can continue in the yoke two hours longer than the horse without any injury, the objection has little or no weight".

Sometimes the ploughs were drawn by a mixture of horse and oxen. The old Scots plough usually required two men and four horses while the new plough used one man and two horses. Sometimes four oxen and two horses were used with the old plough sometimes even as many as eight oxen were used. "The man who holds the plough walks by its sides and directs it with a stilt or handle fixed on the top of it. The driver . . . goes before the oxen and pulls them on a rope tied round their horns. Some people with spades follow who level the furrow and break the clods".

Scotland has produced other breeds of cattle besides the Highland type. The Ayrshire is a most popular breed mostly for milk. The Aberdeen Angus is a noted beef breed. Besides these there are the Galloway, and the belted Galloway and the Shetland and Orkney. At one time there was a Fife breed which has died out. A new breed is the Luing cattle. A herd of them are to be seen in Ballachulish.

The large wild ox auroch or Boa primoganeus was hunted to extinction many years ago. However many escaped cattle lived in the woods and are the Urus. These are park beasts and their descendants are confined largely to three herds at Chillingham, Charley and Cadzou. They are white, but the inside of the ear is black or red and from time to time black or red calves are born. These are culled. These cattle are descended from Bos longifrona. The word longifrona means "long forehead" that is the part of the head between the horns and the nose. These beasts came with the Celts and archaeologists have found their remains in Celtic settlements.

Dr. Lightfoot describes these cattle thus, "Of a milk white colour; having black ears and muzzles and orbits; horn fine and bending out; slender legs; very fierce and dangerous when wounded, attacking their assailant with great fury. Never approach the cattle-yards but when compelled by hunger in very severe weather always lie out; their hides on that account tougher and more valued by curriers than those of tame cattle. The carcass of an ox of their kind weighs 38 stones English, of a cow 28 stones". Dr. Lightfoot visited Scotland along with Pennant, who was one of the early travellers to visit Scotland.

> Four-and-twenty tailors
> Went to catch a snail
> The best man amongst them
> Durst not touch her tail;
> She put out her horns
> Like a little Kyloe cow.

Soay Sheep

Sheep

The earliest type of sheep in Scotland was the Soay. They are of Mediterranean origin and appear to be related to the Mouflon, the wild sheep of that area, Cyprus, Sardinia and Corsica. Though the Soays are not common, there are still some of them in Scotland.

As a breed they are more individualistic and more intelligent than other breeds. Dr. Grant (founder of "An Fasgadh" Museum in Newton More) tells a story of her own small flock which perhaps illustrates this as well as anything. Her sheep were grazing in a field, and by some mischance a flock of passing sheep got into the field and became mixed with the Soays. The shepherd came apologetically to Dr. Grant to tell her, and said he would work his dogs to get the two flocks separated. Dr. Grant told him not to put a dog near them or the Soays would end up in another county. But, she added, she would call her sheep to one side. The shepherd thought this impossible till Dr. Grant went to the field and called "Sheepy, sheepy, sheepy" whereupon all her sheep left the mixed flock and came to her side.

To look at, the Soay have the general appearance of goats. They come in a range of colours—white, reddish brown, which is called "moorit" faun, brownish black and grey. They have soft wool which can be spun to make fine threads for fleecy knitting.

The Soay of today has bones very similar to the bones of sheep found in Neolithic graves. As a breed they have the largest lambs in proportion to their size. It is possible that they were the first breed to become domesticated.

Other old Scottish breeds still living though in small numbers, are the Shetland, whose wool is plucked not shorn; the Orkney, a great eater of seaweed; the Moorit, with reddish fleece and the St. Kilda. There is a breed with a mutant genetic factor of producing four or even six horns. Often they have only two, but in popular opinion at any rate the four horned sheep is typical of St. Kilda. There is the Keerie or rocky sheep of Caithness. These all have Scandinavian blood.

Scotland had several small "soft Wool" sheep varying according to the locality. But in general all were small, lightly built, tails of medium length so that they had to be cut. They were horned, but the horns were short and slender in the ewes and not unlike the blackfaced in the rams. They were of various colours, frequently the face remained brown (hence the Dun faced sheep so often met with). They were very resistant to disease. They were also island sheep which are mainly of Scandinavian origin, and short tailed.

In the Statistical Account the old breeds are described. Their bodies were long and squat made, their heads erect, having either small horns or no horns at all, their legs short, their faces white, or sprinkled with black or brown spots, their fleece soft, and mostly of the longest kind of carding wool; their tails were not so short as those of the Muirland sheep but descended almost to the knee joint and seldom below it. Walker describes the sheep, "The smallest of its kind, of thin, lank shape, with short straight horns, face and legs white, tail extremely short and wool of various colours, i.e. black, white, sometimes bluish grey, brown, deep russet, etc. Frequently the same animal was blotched with three of these colours or tints. The wool however was generally of the finest, except in the mountain sheep which had often four and sometimes six, horns. The souming of sheep was eight or ten to one cow and two cows to one horse." The word "souming" is used to denote the number and type of animal a crofter can run on common grazing. It varies from place to place. Garnett (another traveller) says, "the sheep of this Island (Mull) were till lately, of the small Highland breed, with very good wool, and sweet delicate flesh". While Osgood MacKenzie describes the old sheep as having pink noses and fine wool.

On the other hand, in 1812 the old sheep of Aberdeen are described as having yellow faces and legs and generally fine wool. Elgin at the same date also had yellow faced sheep which are described as the old native Highland breed. "That have been too long neglected. They have fine wool; their mutton (7 or 8 lbs per quarter) is of excellent quality, and they are very hardy, consequently well-adapted to an Alpine pasture."

In 1782 Anderson writes, "Among animal productions these islands possess two articles singularly precious which have scarcely yet been considered as of any value by the inhabitants, one of which is wool of a kind extremely valuable, being not only fine in quality, but possessing a peculiarly silky softness and elasticity that is not to be equalled by any other wool known in Europe. Of the finest of this wool some ladies here (in Skye) have made shawls nearly, if not equal, in fineness and softness to those of India ... Yet, on account of the laws that under severest penalty prohibit the carriage of wool by sea, the natives have been obliged to rely on cattle as their principle stock."

Before the large scale sheep farms in the Highlands began, only a few sheep were kept by each family. The small flocks provided the family with wool, milk and cheese and mutton.

Stephens, in his Book of the Farm writes, "More as a curiosity than a matter of interest ... The original breed of Scotland, very few of them now remain. A small lot was exhibited at the show in Inverness in 1839 where I saw them. They were small keen active looking creatures. The face was tawny, the eyes lively and not unpleasant in aspect. The horns yellowish-brown and curved in the form of the black faced. The muzzle small. The wool was not unlike that of the black faced but rather more hairy. The legs of the colour of the face whether white or tawny. The head, face and horns of the breed have a strong resemblance to those of the Black faced breed and may have been the foundation upon which it was reared; but with what cross the face became black does not appear, although a late writer remarks that a black-faced sort from England was said to have originated that of Scotland.

Tydebber in 1912 writes in The Sheep and its Cousin, "Scotland was in former days the home of various breeds of small sheep belonging to what is known as the soft-woolled type; but even half a century ago these had been so altered by crossing with larger and more profitable breeds from the South that only a few purebred flocks remained and these chiefly in the central Highlands and the Hebrides."

He quoted from Low's Domesticated Animals of the British Islands, "These sheep presented different breeds, according to the nature of the localities in which they were reared; but they may be described in general as being of small size and lank, agile form; as having slender horns; and as having soft wool, fitted for the making of flannels, but not well adapted for felting ..." The issue is confused by different authorities giving different descriptions. One authority describes them as wild, and another that they were tame enough to be milked, and there appear to be two definite types, one described as having a short tail and the other as having a long tail. The description by Stephens is that the wool was coarse, while others have it that the wool was fine. Some authors say the breed was noted for being hardy, others that they were brought into shelter at night, partly for fear of foxes and because they were not hardy like the other beasts. What is claimed by Low is that some beasts came originally with the Celtic settlers and that others came by means of Scandinavian pirates.

In 1812 Sir John Sinclair writes, "It was the common practice to milk the ewes for six, seven, or even ten weeks; but in some farms milking is totally discontinued and in others the period much shortened. The song, "The Flowers of the Forest are a' wede awae" starts with the line, "I've heard them lilting at the ewe milking, Lassies a' lilting before break of day.""

Dr. Johnson says that in Skye the sheep gave a pint at a milking. Sheep's milk is thicker than that of cows. It is never eaten before it is boiled; as it is thick it is liberal of curd. When making ewe cheese, all the watery whey must be extracted. This is done by spreading a cheese cloth over the curds in the tub, pressing gently at first then force against the curds. The curds are put in a coarse linen bag. A cheese barrow made of three or four spokes about two inches broad and the three apart. The bag of curds is put over the tub in the cheese barrow; a plank is laid on it; a woman stands, or sits, one at each end of the plank, and by a seesaw movement, the whey is squeezed out.

As the cheese has a strong taste the loss of whey improves it. Then the curds are broken by hand into very small pieces and salted. They may be resqueezed and the lost salt replaced, then put into a cheesal under a press, for twenty four hours.

An old farm account book gives these figures; 380 ewes gave 75 stone of English cheese in six weeks at 4/4 per stone giving £16 5s. 0d.—12 stone of butter at 5/6 per stone £3 19s. 11d. The wages for the women (there were four of them) £2 8s. 0d.; the wages of the eweherd were 18/-. The whey made from the milk was more than equal to the maintenance of the five servants.

The cheese was considered indigestible when new but when older was much enjoyed. In some parts ewe milk churned was considered an excellent remedy for consumption.

St. Fond, when travelling in Scotland, noticed the practice of tarring sheep. "So that in November the shepherd sets off with two barrels of tar and butter. This was boiled together and the stuff when cool is rubbed on to the sheep. It was said that this kept the sheep healthier and produced more wool, but the wool sold for less and it had to be cleaned by soaking in warm water in which butter had been added. This was done in the Highlands, but not on the higher parts." (It is not certain whether the writer means further north or the higher hills.) He writes to say that English sheep (Blackfaced) sold for half a guinea or sometimes 12/-, whilst a Scottish one would fetch 6/- to 8/-. The wool was sold by weight, 24 lbs being called a stone; this usually was valued at from 6/- to 7/-.

In the second half of the eighteenth century, so the story goes, and it may be true, an innkeeper bought some blackfaced sheep from the south and took them to his native Perthshire. He was a careless shepherd and did not bother to bring his sheep in at night over the winter. He was completely surprised on the return of spring to find his sheep alive and flourishing. Whether this tale is true or not, and variations of it exist, blackface sheep did come north of the Border about that time and later the Cheviots followed. The blackfaced sheep are the most usual to see in the Highlands at this present time. They are hardy and so nimble on their feet, in spite of heavy wool, and they can jump fences and walls (particularly into gardens) that visitors from abroad have asked what kind of goat they are. They have, as their name denotes, black faces and black legs. The Cheviots have white faces and white legs.

A black sheep was said to be lucky in the flock, but several unlucky. It was also believed to be the form witches assumed. A sheep should not be killed on a Friday but "*Dih-aoine la' 'lle Chaluim chaoin, Latha chaorach an seabh.*" Thursday, gentle St. Columba's day, the day to put sheep to pasture. Again, "*Caora luideagach 'theid san dris; fagaidh i 'h-plainn Is an dos.*" The ragged sheep that goes into the briars will leave wool here wool there. "*Caora dhubh a thilgeas ceud lomara geal's a bhliadhna Groideal.*" The black sheep that casts a hundred white fleeces in a year—the griddle on which cakes are baked. There is the following proverb which has a story behind it. "*Tha a' mharachd-shidh air.*" He suffers from fairy passing. It is used for those who suffer from a form of paralysis. There used to be a belief that in cases of "Sturdie" where the beast has a trembling sickness, the cause was a witch in the form of a dormouse who had crossed over some part of the sheep. The cure was to find the identical dormouse and then pass it over the sheep in the opposite way from the previous time. The impossibility of finding the right dormouse in the first instance and knowing the original path over the sheep prevented a cure. A somewhat similar illness was prevalent in England. Here Gilbert White writes of a shrew-mouse which afflicts the beast that it runs over. He writes that the old people always had on hand a "shrew-ash". This was got by boring a hole with an auger into an ash tree trunk or bole, a live shrew-mouse was then put into the hole and the hole was plugged up with the live shrew-mouse. It was then possible to take a twig from the tree which could be applied to the sick animal, in this case it might be sheep, cow or horse. The shrew ash never lost its virtue no matter how many times it was used.

Queen Victoria describes how the sheep were "Juiced". "A large trough was filled with liquid tobacco and soap and the sheep were dipped into this. They were turned on their backs, then an assistant held them by the legs and gave them a good dipping. After dipping they were put into another pen to dry. There was a cauldron boiling nearby which held the tobacco and soap and this, with water from a nearby burn, kept the trough filled as needed."

As with the cattle, when a sheep was killed every part was used. Mutton was salted down. The tripe and intestines were cleaned and scraped. The liver and lights were made into haggis. Skirly in the pan was made. This is made by heating a pan very hot, adding finely chopped suet and when melted add one or two finely chopped onions. Brown these, add oatmeal to absorb the fat and make a thick mixture. Serve this with potatoes.

To make haggis use one pluck (heart, liver and lights of sheep) 2 cups of toasted oatmeal, 1 onion chopped, ½ lb chopped suet, salt, black pepper, Jamaica pepper to taste. Carefully wash and scrape the tripe, leave in cold salted water. Boil the pluck for about an hour, leave the windpipe attached and hang over the side of the pot. This allows any impurities to drain off. Remove the pluck (retain stock) discard the windpipe. Mince the pluck, add the other ingredients, soften with stock, turn into the tripe leaving room for it to swell, sew up the opening. Put it in to the pot with boiling water, prick occasionally to allow air to escape. Boil for three hours. Serve with mashed turnips and jacket potatoes.

The sheets of suet covering the intestines if not needed for these would be hung up and

Sheep shearing time. Farms join together for this work.

dried and kept for future use such as dumpling. These were made locally thus: 5 cups of flour, 2 teaspoons bicarbonate of soda, 1 teaspoon Cream of tartar, pinch of salt, 1 teaspoon mixed spice, $\frac{1}{2}$ teaspoon of cinnamon, 2 cups stoned raisins, 2 cups of chopped suet, 2 cups of sugar, 1 desertspoon of treacle, water to mix to a soft dough. Put in a well floured cloth, tie, allowing room to rise, place in a pan of water, boil for 5 hours.

Some of the fat would be rendered down for dripping, candles, soap, etc. Kidneys were stewed or used for soup, the tail was salted and boiled and eaten cold and was a great delicacy. The head was singed till bare of wool and hair, opened to remove nostrils and eyes which were discarded. It was made into sheep's head broth or potted head. The brains were made into brain cakes. The pancreas or sweetbreads were used. The spleen, gall bladder and heart valves were discarded. The bladder was blown up for a child's balloon. Sometimes bladders were used to cover food being preserved. Sometimes lard was used for this work. It is from this use of lard that we get the word "larder".

Mutton was cut up and pickled in brine. The gigots might be spiced and dried as hams and hung from rafters to smoke; the trotters were singed and boiled. Tallow was used to make candles.

There used to be held a great "Wool Fair" in Inverness in July each year. Here many hundreds of sheep were sold annually. This Fair was most unusual in that not a single beast was on view, and the buyer depended on the description and honesty of the seller along with the knowledge of the type of livestock he was known to have. The farmers took a great pride in the fact that there was never any legal query or proceedings from misrepresentation of stock sold at the "Fair".

Pigs

Pigs were not generally popular in the Highlands. Dr. Lightfoot writes that they were small, fierce, with long prick ears, high backs, long bristles and slender noses. Pork soup was considered a remedy for consumption and pigs blood was among the many cures for warts. Pig skin was held in great regard and from it the best shoes were said to be made. Lismore was one of the places where pigs were to be found.

There was a breed of pig known as the Orkney pig. It was also found in Shetland and to some extent in the Hebrides. It was known to exist as late as the first half of the 19th cent. As a breed they were almost wild moving in herds and finding their own food. They were wild not to say savage but were hardy and thrifty. The meat was good and there was a trade in selling them to ships. The long hairs of the beast were used to make rope used when collecting bird's eggs.

Black puddings were made. To make black puddings, use the skin of a cleaned gut if available. If not, they could still be made. Suet was put in a pan, and the strained blood added, with oatmeal, salt and pepper. This was stirred continuously till solid. If there was a skin, the mixture when cold was used to fill the skin and then both ends were tied. When it was to be used, it was placed in boiling water and pricked continuously and boiled till heated through, or it might be sliced and fried. White or mealy puddings, are made with oatmeal, shredded suet and salt. The skins are filled and the ends tied and it is cooked as before. A variation is white sweet pudding made from flour, shredded suet, raisins or currants, sugar to taste. Cook as before. From pigs, home made sausages were made and hams sugared, cured and smoked.

Goats

There were goats in the Glen and they had a considerable value. People observed that goats on free range rarely took TB and that children drinking this milk would remain in good health. From that observation, followed the belief that goat's milk was a cure. People went to the Highlands to drink goat's milk, and sometimes to take goat's whey. Goats on free range were almost wild and as they kidded in March, by May when food was in short supply, a kid was welcome for the pot, and as goats usually have two kids, this did not diminish the flock. Still another reason was that goats would eat the grazing off the dangerous places so the sheep were not tempted to try for these titbits and so get themselves into danger. The hides of goats were valuable. The suet made the best candles, the skin dyed well, and barbers used the hair for wigs and paid 1 guinea per skin.

Walker writes, "Though the goat is accounted an unprofitable article of stock compared with the sheep, he is not without his advantage in a mountainous country. No quadruped better endures the extremities of heat and cold. On the most stormy hills, he needs no housing, no shelter, no smearing, nor any artificial provender. His tallow is equal to that of the sheep; his skin gives a better price and is still more valuable, when dressed with the hair, for the purposes of knapsacks and holsters. Even the hair, though neglected in the Highlands, was it shorn in due time and properly sorted, would sell to different artists, for more than the fleece of a sheep on the same pasture. The value of his carcase in the Highlands, is but little, if at all inferior to that of sheep, nor is he subject to disease and mortality. He cannot, however bring so good a price when exported out of the country and must, therefore, in general give way to sheep. . . . Flocks of goats, on account of the milk as medicine, will always be kept in many places. On some rocky and abrupt mountain or where the fox still prevails, it may be still advisable to retain him. In these cases the breed and the culture of the animal are very deserving of notice."

"*Is gearr gu 'm bithear am minnean na's miosa na'n t-seana bhoc.*" The kid will soon be worse than the old buck. "*Is ann mar a mheagairt a ghobhair a dh'aithlis a 'mhinnean.*" Tis as the goat bleats the kid responds.

Scotland owes a debt to the wild goat. Once when Robert the Bruce was escaping from his enemies, (in this case the MacDougal after his defeat at Dalrigh) he reached Inversnaid where he took shelter in a cave. It was a very cold night with heavy snow. A herd of goats came into the cave, and accepted Bruce without trouble. When Bruce was secure on his throne, he remembered these goats with gratitude both for their tolerance and for the warmth that they brought to the cave, so he said that goats were to be "Mail free" (rent free) for ever, that is the goats of Craigroyston.

When Bishop Forbes made a Tour of his diocese, he visited Ballachulish and Glencoe and rowed up to Kinlochleven. On his journey he wrote, "Just before leaving the Boat we saw one of the largest Flocks of Goats moving up a Hill that could be well seen". At Bridge of Orchy he had a "Draught of Goat-Milk" and here he saw another herd of goats though smaller than the previous one.

Pennant had the idea of introducing goats to the Hebrides. He writes, "Goats might turn to good advantage if introduced into the few wooded parts of the Island. These animals might be procured from Lochness for being naturalised to the climate would succeed better than any imported from the southern parts of Europe or from Barbary. As an inducement, I must inform the natives of the Hebrides that in the Alpine part of Wales, a well-haired goatskin sells for seven and sixpence or half a guinea." Anyone who has seen a goat at work on trees knows the result! Some landlords began banning goats to their tenants because of the depreciation among trees.

Dogs

Argyll and notably Glencoe, was noted for its dogs. In a poem in Gaelic written at the time of the Massacre (1692) "*Mort Gleanne Comhan*" there is a line, "*Clann Iain nan gadhar.*" Clan Iain noted for their hounds. There is another poem of a later date, again in Gaelic, written by Ronald MacDonald Vic John Ronald, who wrote the following on his dog.

An cu bh'aig Raonull-mac Raonuill-'ic-Iain
Bheireadh sithionn a beinn,
Ceann leathann eadar 'dha shuil, ach biorach
'S bus dubh air gu 'shroin;
Uchd gearrain, seang leasrach 's bha 'fhionnadh
Mar fhrioghan tuirc nimheil nan cos;
Donn mar airneag bha shuil; speir luthannach lubta,
Is faobhar a chnamh mar gheinn;
An cu sud bh'aig Rainull-mac-Raonuill-'ic-Iain
Is tric thug e sithionn a beinn.

Ronald-son-of-Ronald-son of John's good dog
He could bring venison from the mountain;
He was broad between the eyes, otherwise
Sharp and black muzzled to the tip of his nose;
With horse-like chest he was small-flanked, and his pile
Was like the bristles of the den-frequenting boar
Brown as a sloe was his eye,
Supple-jointed (was he) with houghs bent as a bow
All his bones felt sharp and hard as the edge of a wedge
Such was Ronald-mac-Ranald mhic John's good dog,
That often brought venison from the mountain.

A print of a deerhound around 1560 shows them to be much the same as they are today. In early days hunting with deerhounds was an entertainment of the Chiefs, where a vast amount of game was driven unwounded towards the hunters. Later, the breed was used for deer stalking. They were popularised by Sir Walter Scott, who had Maida as his special companion. In the first of the Waverley novels, Waverley, a Highland hunt with deerhounds is described.

Dr. Lightfoot describes them, "Highland grey-hound now rare; large, strong, deep chested and covered with very long and rough hair; was in great vogue in the old times and used in great numbers by Chieftains in their magnificent huntings".

Dr. Johnson describes them, "They have a race of brindle greyhound, larger and stronger than those with which we course hares, and these are the only dogs used by them for the chase". St. John writes of coursing with these dogs and says that the breed had nearly died out, but that it was again gaining popularity and that a good specimen would cost about £50 (in 1892). "This for a first class dog, while tolerable ones fetch about 20 to 30 guineas." He describes one dog, "Bran, an immense but beautifully made dog of light colour, with black eyes and muzzle; his ears of dark brown, soft and silky as a lady's hand, the rest of his coat being wiry and harsh, though not rough and shaggy like his comrade, Oscar, who was longhaired and of a dark brindle colour, with sharp, long muzzle".

James VI referred to the terriers from this part of the world as, "Earth dogges out of Argyllshire". He was speaking of the breed we now call the West Highland White Terrier. He wished for some of these dogs to give as a present to the King of France. He gave special instructions that they should be sent in two ships in case one was lost. There is a story that a ship of the Armada carried two small white dogs of the West Highland type to catch rats on board. In The West Highland Terrier, by Mary Dennis, she writes that the West Highland terriers were found in Skye and the West coast generally, including Ballachulish and it is not a recent breed produced by the Portalloch estate, as is sometimes claimed.

Sheepdogs are bred with an instinct for their work among sheep. That is, if off a working strain. The many sheep dogs which frequent Glencoe today, would not have arrived here till the sheep came in large numbers at the end of the eighteenth century. These wonderful dogs are well known. Some years ago there was a cairn erected in Glenetive in a memory of a faithful collie. A shepherd, tending his sheep, was caught in a blinding snow storm. He lost his way and fell to his death over a precipice. His collie returned home and made the shepherd's wife realise that something was wrong. The dog acted in such a way that she knew he wished her to follow him. She did go, and he led her straight to where his master's body lay.

In the Highlands there is a tradition of a dog now extinct. It was smaller than a collie, but very intelligent and had keen scenting powers. It was short haired and dark, but under the tail was about an inch of long white hairs and the tip was also white. It was known as the "conachair". There used to be in the south another breed no longer with us, the Clydesdale Terrier. This had long silky hair. It was a small breed, Scotland's only "toy". It was a great favourite with the Paisley weavers. Pennant says the bloodhound is a Scottish breed. The following certainly are Scottish breeds, The Cairn Terrier, The Scottish Terrier, The Dandie Dinmont Terrier (a border breed). This was mentioned in Scott. The Border Terrier, The Gordon Setter, a gun dog, the show Collie (the breed that produced the film dog "Lassie"), The Border Collie, the bearded Collie and the elegant Shetland Collie or Sheltie.

Gaelic proverbs about dogs include the following. "*Ge be nach beathaich na coin cha bhi iad aige latha na seilge.*" He that does not feed his hounds wont have them on the hunting day. "*Bidh nadur a choin mhoir 's a chuilein.*" The big dog's nature will be in the pup. "*Tigh gun chu tigh gun ghean gun ghaire.*" A house without a dog is a house without cheerfulness and laughter.

There is a rather nice story just slightly connected with this area. There was a foxhound named Rover. He hunted in Yorkshire. He developed mange and at this time (1752), there was no cure. It was decided to destroy Rover. In these days dogs were hanged, not shot. Rover was hanged and the body was thrown into a deep sulphur mine. This mine was habitually used as a dumping place in which to deposit every sort of rubbish. A dead donkey had been thrown in about the same time as Rover. Some weeks later the hounds were hunting in the vicinity and giving tongue. An answering call came from the sulphur mine. The Hunt stopped to investigate. It was Rover. He was pulled up and was found to be well, and completely cured of mange. Rover rejoined the pack and continued to hunt for two more years. A picture of Rover was painted and this was copied and brought back to this area by someone with connections in both places—Yorkshire and North Lorn.

Poultry

Sir John writes in 1812 on poultry. He is writing on Murray. "The indigenous breed are hardy, easily fattened and fully naturalised to the climate and the substance of the country. In upland districts where this breed is yet uncrossed and pure, it resembles in some respects the common pheasant and is superior in respects of delicacy at the table. To the pheasant it is doubtless nearly allied, or from them. There is reason to believe that this breed may have originally sprung under the title of Hebrysal pheasants . . . This valuable kind may be managed in such a manner as to breed twice in the year; and the hen properly kept, besides rearing both broods, will lay nearly 200 eggs.

"The second most valuable variety is distinguished by the name of the "Hamburg Breed". It has nearly all the good qualities of the indigenous race, except the glossy plumage which individuals of that species possess and it cannot provide so effectively for its own subsistance, but it attains to a much larger size. It generally has five toes on each foot, is adorned by a ruff of feathers round the neck and ears, and is commonly of a mixed, though not very bright, white colour. The Game bird is the third variety frequently to be seen in every quarter. They weigh about 4lbs, but produce few eggs and being delicate when young, they are not a profitable breed for the farmer. A fourth variety known by the name of the bantam breed, is distinguished by being covered with feathers to the toes, which greatly incommodes them when walking in snow, while any advantage of this distinguishing mark is not obvious. They weigh scarcely more than 2 lbs but they produce a great number of small eggs.

"The fifth species is also a small breed called the 'French Fowl' having feathers partly erect and for the greater part curled towards the head. Similar to the bantam breed, they only weigh about 2 lbs, and they produce a great number of eggs, but as they are very imperfectly protected by their plumage from the cold and from the rain, they are rather delicate for this severe climate.

"The sixth variety is peculiarly marked, by having neither rump nor tail. They weigh more than either the bantams or the French Fowl, yet less than the native, laying never a greater number of eggs than any of the other kinds, the shape of the egg being globular, more than what may be called oval. A bolus of butter and oatmeal about the size of a pigeon's egg, given daily, will in four or five days cure the disorders to which they are generally subject. In summer with a little boiled potato, cabbage or turnip, they will thrive on grass with the assistance of worms, seeds, and insects which their own industry procures. In winter they may require a little corn (oats or barley). To make a hen lay daily in that season she must have a mess of warm oatmeal porridge or something warm and equally nutritive besides the common feeding."

At that date (1812) the cost of a turkey was 4/- or 5/- and the price of a hen 1/6. Chickens were nearly half as much, and eggs 4d. a dozen.

By 1854 the Polish was considered the best layer, with between 130 to 200 eggs per bird per year, and up to 223. From bantams, from March to October, 130 to 150 eggs might be expected, and if well bred, 185 eggs from January till 31st March by six bantams. Spanish will lay 4 days out of 5 a week from the end of January till the end of September and Dorkings 140 to 175 eggs and good flesh-producing birds. Seven Cochin China's laid 40 eggs one Christmas week. Cobbet, writing in England, reports that, "The French give their hens barley boiled and given warm, curds, buckwheat, parsley and other herbs chopped fine, leeks chopped the same way, also apples and pears chopped very fine, oats and nettles, or dried nettles harvested in the summer and boiled in winter. Some give them ordinary food, and, once a day, toasted bread sops in wine. White cabbages chopped up, are very good in winter for all sorts of poultry. This is a great deal of pains; but the produce is also great and very valuable in winter".

Cockburn of Ormistoun, in his letters to his gardener, speaks of his poultry, "Be sure you neither set eggs for my Wife nor give any to the people upon my Estate but of the very finest large top'd and pure white leg'd hens. We have enough of our own now to propagate a good Breed from the very best without setting of the Hamburgh kind, so give none of the Hamburg to any upon my ground, for though they have large tops, they are smaller fowls and have not pure white legs, so if mixed with our own they'l spoil our Breed as to size and whiteness of Legs and Bills, . . . Who ever inclined to have a really good Breed should keep none but the finest cock, for one little cock will spoil a whole Breed tho' they have the best hens. Feb. 19th 1743. As the earliest Chickens grow generally the largest, having more of the summer before them, the sooner they set the Eggs the better. If they keep above six hens to one Cock their Breed will degenerate and dwindle away to small fowls. Five hens are enough for a year old Cock. Greed, hurt and disappointed many upon several occasions. Whoever sets too many Eggs will have the smallest and poorest Chickens . . . You tell me you have set one for my Wife, and you say she has three fine Muf't and Top'd hens. Get as soon as you can a setting of 9 eggs all of muf't and Top'd hens only, and set them under the first hen that will sit. If you'l keep the Eggs covered carefully in Bran and turn the Eggs carefully every day, they'l keep for sometime till a Hen sits . . ."

These figures may have been impressive when written, but in modern times the Guiness book of Records mentions one hen which in one year laid 363 eggs. On the other hand the older hens were not laid out early and went on for several years, about three years in their prime. They were hardy and did not have the balanced diet of today. The old way of rearing chickens before the days of hatcheries meant that a good broody hen might be of greater value as a mother than the extra eggs of one that did not go broody.

MacCulloch writes about the poultry in some parts where the fowls came into the house to partake of the fire in wet weather and as a result laid as well in the winter as in the summer . . . "When they do not lay, indeed it is in the time of harvest to the great distress of gentlemen travellers; as it is usual to tether them by the legs to a tree or plough or a cart, and thus starve them to prevent them from defecating on the corn. Southern tourists will also be amused to see them cased in gloves or boots or stockings to prevent them from destroying the new laid thatch. When not the objects of sale they are a medium of rent in the shape of kain fowl, as are the eggs. Recently however, higgling vessels have begun to make periodic voyages through the maritime Highlands, collecting them principally for the markets of Glasgoe and Greenock and raising the price to double the former one, greatly to the benefit of the people" (1824).

The Beauties of Scotland, describes a strange hen, "A variety of the dunghill fowl has sometimes been found in the mosses and domesticated by taking the eggs from the wild bird's nest, and taking care to have them hatched and reared by the common hen. This variety is called the Heath fowl and is but rarely found here or in the northern counties of Scotland. It is not so large as the common dunghill-fowl; but the eggs for the most part are equally large as duck eggs and are very fine. The hen continues to produce eggs for a long time, and seldom to hatch. When the eggs are hatched by another hen, care must be taken to break the shell after it has chipped, for it is frequently so hard that the young chick cannot break it so as to disengage itself. The colour of the chick very much resembles that of the common partridge; but when the fowls come to maturity the colour is commonly red or brown, mixed with spots of white and grey. Both cocks and hens are round crested, and often the crests are so large that they hang over the eyes, and must frequently be clipped. They are smooth legged and the length of the leg is in proportion to the body. The heels of the cock are short, and not very well adapted for fighting. Both cocks and hens, however, fight keenly with the bill, which is thick, short and hooked. Although they are fully domesticated they are fond of swamps and woods, and are extremely greedy of worms and of reptiles, in quest of which they wanter to a considerable distance. They will frequently leave their companions of the dunghill and follow any plough that may be in the neighbourhood. They are more easily supported than the common fowl, and their eggs bring nearly double the price of ordinary eggs.

In the Highlands the fat round the gizzard of a hen was melted by the fire, strained and used for skin irritations and rubbed on the chest. It was bottled for use. It was also sometimes used to preserve boots and shoes. To preserve eggs it was the custom to get them fresh and smear them over with butter, mutton suet, or lard, immediately on being taken from the nest. However, local tradition was to store them in salt.

The Scots dumpy. This is a very rare breed now.

"*An gog mor 's an t-ubh beag.*" Loud cackle little egg. "*Beiridh cearc dhubh ubh geal.*" A black hen will lay a white egg. "*An uair a ghlaodhas an t-sean choileach foghlumaidh an t-og.*" As the old cock crows the young one learns. "*Far am bi cearcan bidh gracan.*" Where hens are, will be cackling.

Here is an old recipe. "Take a capon and scalde hym, and draw hym clene, and chop hym in two across the waist; take a needle and thread and sew the forepart of the capon to the after part of ye pig. Put hym on a spit and roast hym. And when he is done, glaze thou hym with yolk of eggs and powdered ginger root and saffron. Then with the juice of parsley without. And serve it forth. The capon may be ornamented with the tail of the pig in the bill of the capon."

Folklore has supplied several tales about hens. Eggs should be set under hens during ebb tide for pullets and during flow for cocks. A cock crowing on his roost shortly before midnight meant coming news. He should be caught. If his legs are warm, it is to be good news, but if cold, bad news or even death. The direction his head had pointed would give the direction from where the news was to come. When the hens are preening themselves extra carefully it means coming bad weather. A black cock buried under the bed of an epileptic was said to effect a cure.

There are two noted Scottish breeds of poultry. The Scots grey which is still with us though in small numbers. It is a breed which can be a full sized bird or bantam. It has been bred in Scotland for over 200 years. It is, "Cuckoo feathered in a blue and white." The other breed which appears to be nearly extinct and seems to have died out about the end of the last War, was known as the Scots Dumpy. They were low built with short legs; rather like a Dorking for colouring.

Cock fighting took place in the Highlands as elsewhere. It was usual for the local schoolmaster to arrange a fight on Shrove Tuesday, Fastern's Eve. It was of economic importance to the master as he received the carcases of defeated birds and nonfighters, also money from each boy who entered a cock for the fight.

Bees

Bees were kept and their honey was valued, specially when sugar was not available. In the older straw skeps which were used in the past, it was necessary to kill the bees or overcome them before taking the honey. Puff balls were used in some parts. The spores had the effect of chloroform or so it is said. In the nineteenth century the modern hive was produced, which meant working the bees without harming them.

Athol Brose was made and still is. Stoddart, writing in 1801, "Atholl Brose: a composition of whisky, honey and eggs, which is considered an indispensable dainty to the feast, and no unimportant addition to the materis medical." Burt, at an earlier date, wrote (he had been writing on whisky), "When they choose to qualify it for Punch they sometimes mix it with Water and Honey or Milk and Honey; at Othertimes the mixture is only Aqua Vitae, and Butter; this they burn till the Butter and Sugar are dissolved." The usual recipe is of honey, whisky and oatmeal, and cream.

From Monymusk Papers:

> Cause gairdners in winter nights make bee scaps & elks & baskets, and at least 40 or 50 moll traps, that they may all be set in spring to destroy that hurtful creature. Cause ym keep the furrs of those they catch, & also urge him to be reading and explaining to his apprentices books of gairdening & husbandry.

Bees have the reputation of helping sufferers from rheumatism and modern science is inclined to the view that some forms of rheumatism are indeed helped by the stings. The older type of British Black bee was hardy and would fly out on damp days. This species was largely wiped out by Isle of Wight disease at the beginning of the century. Though some were left, bees were imported from the Continent, and the old strain lost as a pure strain; though some of this strain has crossed, no true Black bee remains. Some of the cross bred bees are indeed cross and noted for bad temper.

There is now a society which is trying to preserve breeds of livestock which are getting scarce or even near extinction. It is called the Rare Breeds Survival Trust and under their guidance several native British breeds are being saved. Once lost, they can't be reproduced.

Chapter 10 **Highland wildlife**

The countryside round Glencoe has a varied flora and fauna which in the past was greater. Some wild life was used as food, some as medicine, and others had folktales and magic attached to them.

Red deer

A Red Deer stag.

Red Deer (*Cervus elaphus*) roam the hills in herds. In winter they come down from the heights and at that time, in a drive from Glencoe to Crainlarich in the early morning or at dusk, many beasts may be seen. They pay little heed to moving cars, provided the doors are not opened or the car does not stop suddenly. The summer sees them in the heights.

The young, known as calves, are born about the end of May or early June. Their hair is dappled with white spots which disappear when they grow their first winter coat in about two or three months. During their first week they are unable to stand. The hind hides her calf in bracken or heather, leaves it, and returns to suckle it. Later the calf will follow her and remain with her for about two years. At three years the hinds breed. The horns of the young males first appear during their second year and then only the frontal knobs known as knobblers. The next year a pair of single spiked horns and the following year another point is added, and this continues until the full number is reached. Some stags never develop horns and are known as hummels. A twelve pointer is a "Royal" and a fourteen pointer is an "Imperial". The stags lose their antlers in March and April, and often eat the cast off horn. New antlers start to grow immediately. They are covered in a sensitive velvet. In April, pestered by flies, the beasts return to the tops.

The weight and size of a full grown stag varies according to the feeding. Park deer which are winter fed may weigh thirty stones, while a good Highland stag may weigh eighteen stones or as little as twelve stones (that is when gralloch or gutted). The height at shoulder is four feet.

The deer remain in herds of one sex except during the autumn mating season, or "rut", when the stags can be heard roaring challenges to one another. The stags round up as many hinds as they can. They challenge and are challenged and fights occur, but serious injury is uncommon. Sometimes both beasts may get their horns interlocked and so perish, but this is rare.

The deer usually feed in the evening or early morning. They eat grass, young heather shoots, moss, seaweed, leaves and shoots of trees. While the red deer is by nature a forest animal, in the Highlands it lives in what are known as "deer forests" but which in fact are moorland and mountain. In Scotland the deer are stalked and shot with a rifle and not hunted with packs of hounds, as in the south. Stalking a red deer requires skill and patience. The deer have good eyesight, keen hearing and above all an excellent sense of smell. From a mile off, they can smell a human if the wind is blowing in the right direction. So the stalker has often to make a long detour to get up wind of the beasts, keeping out of sight meanwhile, and making no noise. The shooting season for stags is from the 1st July to the 30th October, and for hinds, from the 31st October till the 15th February.

The art of cooking venison is in seeing that the meat does not dry up. Mrs. Glasse, in her book in 1796, gives the following: "To roast venison—Take a haunch of venison and split it; take four sheets of paper well buttered; put two on the haunch; then make a paste with some flour, a little butter and water; roll it out half as big as your haunch, and put it on the fat part, then put the other sheets of paper on, and tie them with some packing thread; lay it to a brisk fire and baste it well all the time of roasting; if a large haunch of twenty four pounds it will take three hours and a half except it is a very large fire, then three hours will do it, smaller in proportion. When it is near done, take off the paper and dust it well with flour and baste it with butter; when it is a light brown dish it up with brown gravy."

Rowan jelly makes an excellent accompaniment to venison. This jelly may be made with half apple half rowan, or rowan alone.

Venison is excellent eating and may be cooked in many ways—minced as collops, roasted, and even venison haggis was sometimes made. Nowadays it is not easily bought as there is a big trade to the Continent where a bigger price is obtained.

Apart from venison, deer grease was much valued in the Highlands. As the deer is not a fat animal, this makes what fat there is, more valuable. There is a Gaelic saying, "*Geir feidh a muigh 's a stigh, mar leighis sin thu cha 'n 'eil do leighis ann.*" The fat of the stag (applied) externally and internally; if that cures you not, your cure is not to be. This grease was sometimes stored in a container in a peat bog.

The antlers of the stag were made into a jelly and used in cases of consumption and debility and this jelly was known as *Segh Caber Feigh*. Wash the horns and saw them into 3 inch lengths, put in a pot with one large breakfast cup of water to each piece of horn, cover closely and simmer slowly for five hours. Strain, sweeten with candy-sugar and add a little rum. Allow to set. A tablespoon of the jelly to be taken frequently.

To make Hartshorn Flummery: "Boil half a pound of the shavings of hartshorn in three pints of water till it comes to a pint, then strain it through a sieve into a basin and set it by to cool; then set over the fire let it just melt, and put half a pint of thick cream scalded and grown cold again, a quarter of a pint of white wine, and two spoonsful of orange-flower water; sweeten it with sugar, and beat it for an hour and a half, or it will not mix well nor look well; dip your cups in water before you put in the flummery, or else it will not turn out well; it is best when it stands a day or two before you turn it out. When you serve it up turn it out of the cups and stick blanched almonds cut into long narrow bits on top. You may eat them with wine or cream.

The antlers were also used to make knives for cutlery, i.e. carving knives, etc. and for making buttons.

There is a heavy mortality among deer calves. Sometimes when the hind has been killed the newly born deer calf becomes a pet for children. It would be reared by hand and become quite tame with the family but would rush off if strangers appeared. The following story has been told to me of one such hand reared calf. It was reared in a gamekeepers family. It formed a special attachment to the calf of a cow. They grew up together and were inseparable. The day came when the calf of the cow (now a cow itself) had to be sold. The keeper set off to walk to the nearest township. Shortly after leaving home the pet hind "Daisy" overtook them and refused to be sent home.

When they approached the village Daisy became frightened of the strangers and the dogs, and squeezed in between the keeper and the cow and pressed her trembling body against his. As he had to return home by boat, he was obliged to put Daisy and the cow into the deer-fenced park, and leave them there. He boarded the boat with only minutes to spare and so arrived home by an entirely different route. Hardly had he reached home when Daisy arrived too. She had leapt the ten foot fence and followed the boat along the road.

In folklore, deer were called "fairy cattle". It was said that the fairies milked them on the mountain tops. One noted witch *Cailleach Beinn-a-bhric* was thought to be in the habit of so doing. She was said to have used a *buarrach* or a cow fetter. As all good dairymaids did, she sang to her "cattle". The deer of the Forest of Reay were specially protected by the witch *Cailleach mhor Chilibric* who made them bullet proof. A stag's leap, or *sinteag feidh* (thirty feet) was used as a measure. *Caberfeidh* is the war cry or slogan of the MacKenzies. Sometimes fairies assumed the guise of deer, and they could also put humans into this form. Ossian's mother was under an enchantment for a considerable part of her life, thus, and only resumed her human form when in her underground home. Ossian was the poet of the *feinn*.

Proverbs include the following, "*Bu dual do laogh au fheidh ruidh a bhi aige*". It is natural for the calf of the deer to be swift on foot. "*Cha trom lies an fhiadh a chabar*". The deer does not feel his horns heavy.

Roe deer

The roe deer (*Capreolus capreolus*) is a reddish brown in summer but changes to a varying grey tone in winter. The fawns arrive at the beginning of June. They are usually twins. They are able to follow the doe at a fortnight old. They are spotted like the red deer and like them they lose these spots at three months. The yearling fawns are driven off by their dam in May before the new fawns arrive. Unlike the red deer roe deer prefer family parties rather then herds. The height of the roe varies from 2 feet 1 inch to 2 feet 5 inches. Their weight can be anything from 35 lbs to 60 lbs. The horns are cast in November and are usually free from velvet by mid March, though young bucks are later to cast and later to shed velvet. in the first year a buck usually has a single spike or fork. The "rut" is in July or August.

In general the roe deer is a woodland animal though in the Highlands it is not always so confined in its habitat. They are shy, mostly feeding at night, though in Glencoe district they are quite often seen eating in the daytime. They eat grass, shrubs, leaves, corn, turnips, clover, hips, moss, bracken, and fungi.

Like the red deer their venison is excellent. There are a few proverbs which relate to roe deer rather than to the red deer. "*Cha tig athas na-earba gun na coin a chur rithe.*" A tip for the stalker—the roe deer does not have the keen sense of smell of the red deer.

Fallow deer and other types of park deer have occasionally escaped in Scotland and may be met with, but it is unlikely. The reindeer has been reintroduced in the Cairngorm area, and it will be interesting to see how it does.

Seals

The Atlantic or grey seal (*Halichoerus grypus*) and the Common Seal (*Phoca vivulina*) both breed in Scotland and in the Highlands, but the present range of the Atlantic seal does not extend to this district. However it is worth noting the different way of life. One young pup is born to the grey seal in early September to mid-October. The pups are born with a white woolly coat which disappears at about six weeks. The adult colouring is yellow dappled with grey. They are gregarious. The young are born in a "rookery". During the breeding season September and October the bulls collect as large a harem of cows as they can, and there is fierce fighting. They live entirely on fish.

The Common seal pup is born in June. It has already shed its prenatal white coat and looks like the adult. The sexes remain together in winter but then separate before the birth of the pup. The breeding season is in September. These seals may sleep under water, rising to breathe every fifteen minutes.

In 1777 Pennant wrote that the skins of the adult sold for 4/- (20p) to 4/6 (22p) each and were used for trousers, trunks, and shot flask and pouches. Eight gallons of oil was

Seals.

obtained from each seal. The oil sold for 6d. to 9d. (2½p to 4p) per gallon. The skin of a young seal sold for 6d. to 12d. (2½p to 5p).

A broth used to be made from seals which was considered good for the chest, and the meat was astringent. The liver was dried and pulverised and taken in milk for flux. A purse made of seal skin was considered good and "lucky". A girdle of seal skin was considered good for sciatica. It was eaten as fish in lent. A proverb says, "*Is fhada bho'n uair sin bho'n a bha cluas air ron.*" It's a long time since the seals had ears. "*Cho reamhar ris an roin.*" As fat as a seal. "*Ismath am biadh feamanaich aran seagail agus saill roin.*" Good food it is for sea weed workers, rye bread and seal's flesh.

In folktales seals were said to be the children of kings under enchantment. Seal folk appear in many tales. Usually the seal takes off her skin and goes bathing in human form. A young man steals the skin and sometimes gets a promise of help in fishing but more often he marries the woman and keeps the skin safely hidden. Sooner or later, in varying ways, the woman finds the skin, puts it on, and returns to the sea. The MacCodrums claim to be descended from such a woman.

Porpoises (*Phocaena*) and even some of the larger whales and Killer whales have been seen in Loch Leven within living memory. It may well be that they were hunted at one time, but I do not have any record of it being done in this area.

At one time the walrus was a visitor to our shores and its tusks a matter of commerce in a small way in Shetland. It must be a considerable time since one visited Scotland. It is unlikely that any ever reached this part of the country.

A unicorn was seen on Skye and in the Hebrides. It was called *Biand na agroguig*. It was described as clumsy, inelegant, awkward, with a single horn on the forehead. It is now considered to have been a narwhal which had strayed from its Arctic home.

Badgers

There are still badgers around. The badger (*Melex melex*) being a nocturnal animal is not often seen. Some say that badgers hibernate in part in winter, but this is doubtful. In Sweden they do. Badgers have keen scent and hearing. They are notably clean animals and have their latrines some way from the set. A badger funeral has been witnessed when a dead badger was carefully removed from the set and buried. The two to four cubs are born some time between January and April, usually February and March. The female is called a sow and the male a boar. The adult boar may weigh 25 lbs though some have been recorded as much as 40 lbs. The length is about 28 inches with another 8 inches of tail. They eat roots, fruit, honey, slugs, wasp grubs, beetles, moles, young birds and rabbits. They also eat rats and earth worms in considerable quantity.

Badger grease was used as an excellent cure for wounds. The hair was used for making paint brushes. Many sporrans are made from badger skin. The sporran was originally a bag used to carry meal, and later it became a purse. Badger skin was also used to make pistol cases. In some places the hams of badger are eaten though I do not know of this happening in the Highlands.

Otters

The badger is a member of the weasel family, as is the otter (*Lustra lustra*). The otter is not often seen being nocturnal for the most part. Cubs may be born at any time of the year, but spring is most usual. The holt, where around three cubs are born, may be a hole under the bank of a river, in a hollow tree, or in some parts a dry bed in rushes and reeds. Otters are adapted for swimming, the ears are short and close under water, as can the nostrils. The weight of an adult male (the dog) is about 20 to 25 lbs and for the female (bitch) 15 to 18 lbs.

Otters can be seen by river, loch or sea. They can travel a distance over dry land but the water is their home. They are intelligent animals and very playful. They spend hours sliding on steep grassy banks or in snow. They eat fish, mollusca, eels, failing this rabbits, frogs, ducks and moorhen. Even fishermen should approve of this killing of eels and the sick and cannibal fish.

At one time in the Highlands it was thought that there was some magic about an otter. It was said that the otter was vulnerable at one white spot under the chin or under the forearm. It was believed that there was a jewel in the beast's head. As a result the skins became valuable and had magic properties: a charm against drowning, efficacious in childbirth, and as an antidote against smallpox and fever. Otter skins are used for sporrans. A proverb about otters is the following: "*Mar dhobhran am bun uisge, tha bean mic gu 'mathair-cheile.*" Like otter at a river mouth is the son's wife to his mother—watchful.

Weasel

The weasal (*Mustel nivalis*) does not change colour in winter. It is also smaller than the stoat. Weasels help to keep down the number of mice, voles and rats. It will also eat toads and frogs. There are usually 4 to 6 young born in May or June. The male is 7 inches long plus two inches of tail. It weighs about 3 ozs. In the old days one might hesitate to kill a weasel as it might be a witch. It was considered unlucky to meet one first thing in the morning. However a purse made of weasel skin was considered a money getter and a money saver. There was said to be a larger form of weasel which could kill a cow with its breath.

Stoat

The stoat (*Mustela erminea*) is larger than the weasel, the males being about $10\frac{1}{2}$ inches with a $4\frac{1}{2}$ inch tail. The change to ermine in winter varies according to the climate and many do not make the full change. The stoats on Ben Nevis remain white all year round. Stoats eat voles, mice, rats, birds eggs, and sometimes carrion.

The pole cat (*Mustela putorius*) and the pine martin (*Martin martes*) are no longer in this area.

Fox

The Highland fox (*Canis vulpes*) lives in the hills and has its holt among rocks. Three to eight cubs are born in spring. The food of the fox is varied, fish, flesh, fowl, frog, crabs, worms, some lambs. In the Highlands many live on hares (the blue ones) ptarmigan and grouse and a considerable amount of carrion.

Duncan Ban Macintyre blessed the fox as a sheep destroyer. "*Mo bheannachd aig na balgairean a chionn 'bhi sealg nan caorach.*" My blessings on the cunning ones (foxes) for hunting the sheep. This sentiment was because of his strong feelings on the Clearances. There are a number of Gaelic proverbs about foxes. "*Am fear a bheir car as an t-sionnach feumaidh e eiridh moch (or mocheiridh) a dheanamn.*" He who would cheat the fox must rise early. "*Be sin an t-sionnach a searmonachd do na geoidh.*" That was the fox preaching to the geese. "*Is eallach earball fhein do'n t-sionnach tha sgith.*" Even his own tail is a burden to the weary fox. "*Tha biadh 'us ceol an seo mu 'n dubhairt a' madadh-ruadh 's e ruith air falbh lies a phiob.*" There's meat and music here—as the fox said when he ran away with the bagpipes.

Wild cats

There still are Scottish Wild cats here. The wild cat (*Felis solvestris*) is one of the fiercest animals. Beside the true wild cat there are a number of domestic cats which have gone wild. They fend for themselves and have little dependence on humans. There is a difference between the two types. The Wild cat is bigger 11 to $11\frac{1}{2}$ inches in the tail and 22 to 25 inches long in the body. The wild cat has a short blunt ringed tail, compared to the longer, tapering tail of the domestic cat. Wild cat litters of two to five kittens are usually born in May. They are entirely carnivorous, eating hares, grouse, black cock, etc.

In folklore it was said that if a cat was cast over a patient with fever this would act as a cure. Proverbs include, "*A mhic a chait d'am bu dual am bainne ol.*" Son of a cat born to drink milk. "*Cha dean cat miotagach sealg.*" Cats with mittens wont catch mice. "*Tigh gun chat tigh ghean gun ghaire.*" A house without a cat, a house without cheerfulness or laughter. "*Nuair a dh'-fha'gas na cait am baile, bidh na luchain a' dansa (rinca).*" When the cat leaves the place the mice dance.

Hares

Pennant wrote of the mountain hare (*Lepus timidus*) saying that till the road came there was no other hare in the district. There are few brown hares, (*Lepus europaeus*) in this district till one gets to Duror. A hare's sleeping place is her "forme" which is a "Print" of her form, and from this comes the use of the word "forme" by printers.

The blue hare is 20 inches long, with ears of $3\frac{1}{4}$ inches, weighing 5 to 7 lbs. These hares do not make a forme but hide among stones or find shelter. It changes to white in autumn. Blue hares eat grasses, rushes, young heather and moss.

The brown hare is larger, 22 to 24 inches, and ears $4\frac{1}{2}$ inches; weighs 7 to 13 lbs. The leverets (two to five) are able to run when born and are covered in hair. The tradition of the Mad March Hare is fully justified and during the main breeding season when the bucks appear to lose fear of man.

At one time fried hare was considered a great delicacy in this part of the country. Hare soup was also much enjoyed and was made thus: Skin the hare and carefully preserve the blood. Boil the bones with mixed vegetables and a tablespoonful of peppercorns for stock. Strain. Add the blood and the fine flour of oatmeal for thickening. Bring to the boil stirring continuously. Season to taste.

Rabbits

As late as 1806 there were no rabbits (*Oryctolagus cunniculus*) in Argyll except those on an island in Loch Awe which the Duke of Argyll kept as a warren. They are now plentiful, having recovered numbers after the outbreak of Myxomatosis.

Rabbit skins were tanned. They were washed well and the skins let soak from three to eight hours, depending upon the thickness, in lukewarm water in which had been dissolved $\frac{1}{4}$ cup each of salt alum and saltpetre to the gallon. The skins were pulled and worked while being washed. Then they were wrung out well and stretched flesh side up on a board and powdered alum, half part arsenic were rubbed in. Plenty of the mixture was used and it was rubbed well in, care was taken to see there were no wrinkles at the edges. The skins were then placed flesh sides together with the edges folded in and rolled tightly. They were kept in a warm place. Every two or three days the mixture was rubbed in and the skins worked well each time. The fur was not injured by the juice brought out of the skins by the mixture.

The skins would be tanned in about two weeks, depending upon the amount of working they have had. When the mixture had gone through the skin, the fur was cured. The skins were then rinsed well in lukewarm water to remove all the mixture and then washed in strong lukewarm soap suds using a wash board. If the fur was badly tangled and matted, it was combed while under water, with a coarse comb. It was then wrung out and the fur shaken and hung·up tail end down in the sun to dry. The more the skin was worked and pulled while drying, the softer it would be. The same applied all through the process. It was important never to use hot water, barely lukewarm was enough.

Small mammals

The red squirrel (*Sciurus vulgaris*) is now rare with us. And so far we do not have the grey squirrel (*Sciurus carolineunsis*). Usually two or three young squirrels are born naked and blind, in April. They may take a time of sleeping in winter, but do not hibernate. The nest or drey is built in February and March. Additional nests are built so the young can be moved if danger threatens. The Red squirrel is diurnal. It is very quick, climbing trees the far side from the viewer. It eats acorns, nuts, beech masts, haws, pine seeds, bark fungi, sometimes eggs and young birds. A Gaelic proverb says, "*Ge h-ainneamh an fheorag, gheibhear seol air a faotainn.*" Though scarce be the squirrel there is a way to find her.

The brown rat (*Rattus norvegious*) and the black rat (*Rattus rattus*) are both pests to mankind. The latter has been largely replaced by the former though the black is the usual ship's rat. Their cleverness has been woven into folklore. Rats coming to a house foretell a flitting, their leaving, a death in the household or a fall of the deserted building. They detest the smell of goats which drives them away. If one was plagued by rats and the usual methods appeared not to be having any effect, a rat incantation was used, whereby the rats were encouraged to leave and go elsewhere. The incantations were in rhyme and most generally in praise of the rat, rather than miscalling it. They were asked to cross running water. The rhyme was said at each corner of the steading.

The house mouse (*Mus musculus*) a lesser pest than the rat, had some proverbs connected with it. "*Tha fios aig an luch nach 'eil an cat a's tigh.*" The mouse knows the cat is not in the house. "*Is bean-tighe (neo bana-mhaighistir) an luchag 'n a tigh fein.*" The little mouse is mistress in her own home. "*Is fheairrd an luch samhchair, mar a thuirt luch a mhonaidh ri luch a bhaile.*" The mouse is the better of quiet, as the moor mouse said to the town mouse.

There are other rodents, but with no special distinction to the Highlands nor have they folklore connected with them.

The hedgehog (*Erinaceus europaeus*) seems to be diminishing in these last years. Possibly wet summers, and poorer insect life, possibly heavier traffic on our roads, or the use of insecticides. This loss is general throughout the country and quite noticeable in this district.

Hedgehogs usually have two litters a year, one in May–July and the other August–September. The young are born blind, and have soft spines which harden in three weeks. Hedgehogs hibernate. In summer they are largely nocturnal, but may be seen in the evenings. They eat insects, slugs, worms, frogs, young birds, young rats, mice, sometimes birds' eggs. They may eat vegetables such as turnips.

In the old days the hedgehog was an article of diet. A simple way to cook it was to wrap the animal in sea weed from the loch, to mask the spines, and then encase it in peat mud and roast it on hot ashes of the peat fire. When unrolled, the spines and skin came off with the baked mud crust, leaving "a succulent small beastie for ane man or two weans". It is said that the hounds enjoyed the entrails and the outer crust, spines and all.

Another recipe said to be from Glencoe: Take pigs' maws and scald them well, take chopped pork and kneed it well with powdered ginger root, salt, pepper, and a little honey. Put it in the maw, but fill it not too full, then sew it with a fair thread and put them on a spit, as men do pigs. Take of almonds and blanch them and cut them into long sharp spikes and fry them in pig's grease and sprinkle with sugar.

"Take a little spike and make holes in the cooked Yechouns, and into each hole, put a spine of ye cooked almonds. Lay them near the fire and when they be roasted glaze them with some wheat flour and milk of almonds and some blood, and let them not brown too much, and serve them forth. These eat as a lykness to pork whych is the next best wylds fleshe." This recipe is said to have been enjoyed by the Chiefs when visiting France in the 16th and 17th centuries.

It used to be a toast to drink a health to "The little gentleman in black velvet". This is the mole (*Talpa europaea*). The reason for this toast was that William of Orange (the king who signed the order for the Massacre of Glencoe) died as a result of a fall from his horse which tripped over a mole hill.

There is usually one litter a year, of from two to seven moles. When they are born the young are hairless and pinkskinned and their eyes do not open for the first three weeks. They leave the dam when they are about five weeks old, usually late June or July. The mole digs deeper in winter. They eat worms and insects. In captivity one mole can eat sixty worms in a day. It may also eat frogs, larvae and small mammals. They are rarely above ground but do come up for water, or when a shower of rain brings the worms to the surface or in spring when the males chase each other.

In folk medicine, the ashes of the mole or its ashes decocted in wine, were said to be good for scrofula. The blood of the mole made the hair grow. There is a Gaelic proverb, "*Far am faighear (oir neo far am bi) famh bi fuithir.*" Where a mole is found good land will be.

Shrews were said to have bewitching powers and their bite was venomous. It was cured by taking the head, boiling it in water and then drinking the water.

Mink are sometimes seen, having escaped from the well known Mink farm at Appin.

There is a proverb about bats: "*Thainig iultag a steach, bidh frasan a mach air ball.*" A bat has come in—showers will be out directly. (It's going to rain.)

Wilson in 1842 reported a surprising animal when he stayed at Oban. "In the evening we went ashore to see some llamas, beautiful creatures of the camel kind (of course the natives of Argyllshire call them Campbells) from South America, originally imported, and afterwards bred in this quarter, through the care bestowed by Mr. Stevenson. Though at this time under cover they are said to be hardy and were obviously gentle and familiar. An elderly female (the grand llama) mother, we believe of almost all the rest, had a young one with her only a fortnight old, a high-legged, staring infant with a combination of grace and awkwardness so usual in the young of the larger quadrupeds. Those animals produce only a single offspring at a time and go with the llama for eleven months."

Before leaving the animal world, mention might be made of the use of food used for animals, converted to human use.

Syrup of linseed was made thus: Infuse 2 oz of linseed and half an oz of senna leaves in boiling water and let it stand by the fire for a few hours covered with a quart of boiling water. Strain it, and add to the juice 2 oz molazzie juice which is the purest black sugar, the same of candy sugar or heather honey and a teacupful of good vinegar. Let this mixture be kept by the fire closely covered, for use. A wine glass in the morning before breakfast and the same between meals during the day was used for constipation. Linseed jelly was taken for sore throats, which it soothed. In 1793 Heron wrote: "Linseed oil was then esteemed highly medicinal; and a glass of whisky mixed with a glass of this oil was a favourite dram".

Bran tea was taken. Put a cupful of nice fresh bran into a clean saucepan, pour a quart of boiling water over it, stirring it all the time; let it boil a few minutes; strain through a fine sieve. Dissolve 1 oz of pure gum, add it to the water and sweeten with honey; put into an earthenware tea pot, keep by the fire and drink it moderately warm. Bran jelly was considered a valuable nerve food. It was made with two breakfast cups of water, one breakfast cup of bran, and this was placed in a covered jar in a slow oven for four or five hours. It was then strained and sugar and lemon juice added to taste. It should stand overnight to jell.

In times of great scarcity which sometimes occurred in the Highlands in winter, neep broth was made. Peel and chop a good turnip, cook in salted water, strain on to it oatmeal to make brose, add a nob of butter and season to taste. Mash the turnip with a nob of butter and season. This was eaten as a main meal.

Birds

As there are so many varieties of birds it is not practical to deal with all of them. Mention will only be made of a bird which is essentially Highland, was used in the economy of the country or had some traditional folklore associated with it. In some cases a number of species are dealt with under the one heading, such as "gulls" so no Latin name is included.

The blackbird is well known to most people. In the Highlands there is a legend that its yellow bill came because the blackbird dug its bill into a mass of gold in an enchanted cave. The blackbird appears in a number of Gaelic poems. James VIII or III was nicknamed "The Blackbird" owing to his dark colouring.

The Capercailzie became extinct in the Highlands, but has been re-naturalised from Sweden. The bird eats fir shoots among other things, and its flesh tastes of resin. This is overcome to some extent by soaking overnight in milk.

The cormorant, a sea bird, was used to make soup. I have been told it resembles hare soup. It was the custom to bury the bird in the earth for a few days to extract the strong fishy taste before it was cooked and eaten. The fat of the young birds is so strong that it used to be burned with a wick drawn through the body which was used as a candle. The bird has a reputation as a glutton.

The corncrake is now rare. Its call when made frequently, foretold the coming of rain. Another belief was that when it began to call, all danger of frost injuring the crops was past. The call is a rasping one like someone stroping an old fashioned razor. If a man killed a corncrake, he would die and if he knocked out its feathers, he would become ill—or so the story goes.

There are various members of the crow family in the Highlands. The ashes of crows were said to be good for gout, but how they were used is no longer remembered. There are some proverbs about crows. "*An taobh a theid an fheannag bheir i feaman leatha.*" Wherever the crow goes she will take her tail with her, "*Bheireadh e a suilean nam feannag e.*" he would take it from (beneath) the crow's eyes. "*Is caraid (no dithis) dhuinn sin, mar a thuirt an fheannag ri 'casan.*" That's a pair (or two) of us as the crow said to her feet.

The cuckoo haunts Gaelic poetry and folklore. It is connected with the fairies. A cuckoo calling from the chimney meant death to one of the household, within a year. On the other hand heard calling from the right hand side it was considered lucky. Proverbs include, "*Chubhag gun bhiadh' am bhroinn.*" I heard the cuckoo while fasting. (A foretelling of misfortune for the year.) "*Luath no mall g'an tig an Maigh thig a chubhag.*" Late or early as May comes, so comes the cuckoo. "*Nuair a ghoireas (no a ghairmeas) a chubhag air an sgitheach lom, diol (no reic) do bho, a's ceannaich arbhar.*" When the cuckoo calls on the bare thorn, sell your cow and buy corn. "*A chuir a ruith na cubhaig no air gnothach na cuthaig.*" On the cuckoo or the gowk's errand. Sending anyone to chase the cuckoo. April fool. In the Lowlands the cuckoo is known as the gowk.

The fat of the diver was said to be a cure for sciatica. It was considered lucky to see a wild duck on the first day of the year. "*Cha chudthrom air loch an lach.*" The wild duck burdens not the loch.

The Golden eagle is a bird of the hills. Eagle plumes were and are worn on the bonnet of a Chief. Three from the wing for the Chief at the side of his bonnet, and for his family, or a woman Chief, two feathers, and some others are entitled to wear one. In some instances it has been known for Highlanders to visit the eagle's eyrie (nest) and remove food from it for themselves, hares, grouse, etc. When Prince Charlie was approaching Scotland an eagle was seen from the ship. Tullibardine considered it a good omen and said, "The King of birds is come to welcome your Royal Highness on your arrival in Scotland".

Finches coming into a house were said to bring luck.

August 12th is the traditional day for the start of the grouse shooting. Many Highland estates found that their income was much augmented by the rent got by the letting of their moors for this sport. The red grouse is an indigenous bird to Scotland, though some have been taken over the Border and beyond, to provide shooting. The hen has been called, "*A chearc ghearrghoback riabhach*". The short beaked hen. Alasdair MacAlasdair called the cock, "*An coileach craobhach nan gearr sgith.*" The woody cock of the short wing. The rendering of its cry in English is, "Go back, go back". In Gaelic it is, "*Co chaidh mo chlaidh*". Who went, my sword. Like a sentry making a challenge.

Young gulls are said to be excellent eating. They used to be preserved by being "salted" with the ashes of burnt sea weed in cow hides. The fat of sea fowls was made into puddings in the stomach of the fowl. It was said to be a sure cure for wounds and bruises. Some Highlanders will not touch the gull, considering it unclean food.

It was lucky to see a hawk first thing in the morning. The screaming hawk is said to mean a change of weather.

The lark, it was said, could curse anyone who stole her eggs in as many ways as there were spots on her eggs. "*Cha 'n 'eil deathach an tigh na-uiseige.*" There is not smoke in the lark's house.

The Magpie was the messenger of the Campbells, but except for any of that name it was an unlucky bird. However this could be modified under certain circumstances. If it jumps out on the road in front of a traveller it is a good omen, and if seen on the right hand side it is still good, but seen on the left hand side, it is a bad omen. It is unlucky to see the bird before beakfast as the first living thing seen that day, but if seen hopping near the home it meant good news. To shoot one was unlucky. Eating the leg of a magpie was said to be a cure for anyone who was bewitched.

The Osprey is now carefully guarded and with help from mankind may one day be back on the list of breeding British birds. The skin of the bird with the feathers left on was applied warm to cure colic.

"*Tha chomhachag ri bron, tha na tuiltean oirnn.*" When the owl mourns the rain comes. "*Tha mi na's eolaiche air coille na 'bhi fo eagal na caillich-oidhche.*" I am more accustomed to a wood than to be afraid of an owl.

The petrel or fulmar was an important source of food in St. Kilda. A piper of the island composed a tune on the notes of this bird. When the fulmar was heard on St. Kilda the people used to say, "*Paisg mo chaibe, faigh mo ribe, chuala mi gug-gug 's a chuan.*" Lay by my spade, get me my rope (snare) I heard the goo-ggok on the sea. The rope meant a hair rope used for rock climbing or for lowering down the cliff face. In the later days it was made of hide thongs, three ply, covered with sheep skin to prevent chaffing. This was a most valuable possession and was even used as a dowry.

To this day, the men of Lewis, by a special Act of Parliament may go and collect eggs of sea birds or the young who are not able to fly.

Ptarmigan live on the hill tops and change to white plumage in the winter. The Puffin was valued on St. Kilda. It provided food and oil and feathers. These were valuable as once cleaned, the army found that no bed bugs etc. were harboured in these feathers, so this crop helped to pay the rent (paid in kind for many years). "*Far am bi an-t-iasg 's ann a bhios na h-eoin.*" Where the fish are, there the sea birds will be.

It was unlucky to see a raven, if it was seen by more than one person at a time. "*Tha gliocas an ceann an fhithich or fice ceann na fithich.*" There is wisdom in the raven's head. Pennant writes that raven quills sold for 12/- (60p) per 100. They were used for tuning the lower notes of harpsicords.

When the robin sings cheerfully in the summer evening, it is a sign of good weather coming, even if it is poor at the time, but if it cheeps or is silent, this means coming rain. It was thought that the bark of a rose briar in which a robin had a nest would make a decoction that would cure some ills. Oil from the Great crested grebe was used for rheumatism. Heron oil was used for guns.

It was thought lucky if a snipe rose in front of the cattle when they were being driven to the shieling. The solan goose or gannet is a seabird which was eaten in St. Kilda and in the Hebrides. It is a very salty and strong tasting bird and an acquired taste for those not used to it. The oil from the bird was used for many cures and was said to cure cancer. The stonechat was said to have its eggs looked after by a frog or toad when it left its nest. It was not considered a lucky bird to meet. A wagtail coming near the house meant bad weather. If seen between the person and their home it meant eviction.

There is a tale of an artful wren. A wren was building his nest and looking for suitable material. He found some which he could not get at. Along came a fox who heard the wren's tale. "What will you give me if I help you?" "Oh," said the wren, "when I have threshed out my grain in the autumn I may pay you something." "How much will you give me," said the fox. The wren thought and said, "*Peic 'us ceannan.*" (A peck and two pecks.) The fox agreed to the terms, shifted the material and went off. Autumn came, so the wren was busy threshing grain with his twelve sons, when along came the fox. However the fox could not distinguish between the father and the sons and finally said, "What a different stroke the father has from the sons". The proud wren stepped forward, "Tis well you said this". The fox then reminded the wren of his promise made in the spring. "Certainly," said the wren and jumped on to a dyke. Looking towards the house he called, "it was Peic 'us Ceannan was it not, Peic 'us Ceannan," whereupon two dogs from the house on hearing their name called, came running, and the fox made a quick departure. "*Is farsuing a sgaoileas an dreathann a chasan 'n a thigh fhein.*" The wren spreads his feet wide in his own house.

The yellow hammer was supposed to cure jaundice. The patient had only to look at the bird. Otherwise the bird was considered to be unlucky.

Fish

In March, on Maundy Sunday, that is the Sunday before Easter, in olden times it was the custom in many parts of the Highlands to make an offering in the sea of meal and gruel. Fish was a most important food for those who lived near the sea. Salt smuggling was a most profitable occupation, much safer than whisky smuggling as it could be got rid of so easily. The salt tax was a sore burden to the fishing industry. When Southey visited this part of the country he wrote of the great contraband trade and of the Inn Keeper at Kingshouse, who made considerable wealth in that smuggling trade.

At one time, so good was the herring fishing in Loch Leven, that the boats came from as far away as Buckie to fish here. Pennant writing in 1770 said that the women got 1½d. per hour and that they could make 15d. (7p) per day. The fish were laid in the barrel on their backs with a layer of salt between layers of fish. The entrails were boiled and about 8,000 fish gave 10 gallons of oil which sold at 1/- (5p) per gallon. The barrels cost 3/- (15p) and held 500 to 800 fish. Garnett writing in the same century records, "The herring industry commonly begins in July and sometimes continues till the first of January. The country express the quantities of herring abounding here in very strong language. At these seasons they say the lake contains one part water and two parts fish (he is writing of Loch Fyne) . . . It is believed that there have been caught and cured in one season upwards of 20,000 barrels valued at 25/- (£1.25) each.

Part of each boat is covered with a kind of sailcloth to form a covering for the four men who compose the crew . . . These men may be said to live in their boat the whole fishing season, for they seldom quit it during the time . . . The night is the time for fishing; the day is employed in gutting the fish that they have taken, in sleep, or in singing Celtic tales to the sound of the bagpipes. Each boat clears upon average between 40/- and 50/- (£2 and £2.50), and in some seasons, 100/- (£5.00), besides a quantity of fish which they preserve for their own families. In the evenings a number of boats form a line across the Loch and uniting their nets produce a chain often more than a hundred fathoms long. The herring swim at very uncertain depths so that it is necessary to sink the nets to the depths the shoal is known to take, hence it is evident that the success of the fishers must in great measure, depend on their judgement or good fortune in taking the proper depth . . . The nets are kept up by buoys consisting of blown bladders or leather bags filled with air . . . They often boil or soak their nets in strong decoction of oak bark which prevents putrifaction in water. When they have caught as many as they can during the night, they gut them, and throw them into a tub with a sprinkling of salt, and after standing in this manner for few weeks they are repacked into other barrels and sent to different parts of the world ... a barrel holds about 500 of the best kinds of herring but 700 of medium—if the number be greater they are reckoned poor. The gut affords a considerable quantity of oil."

Herron in 1793, writes of fishing in Stornoway. "We found ... the fish being carefully laid flat layer above layer, and each kind, whether cod, ling, grey-lords (sethe) being made up in separate stacks, each consisting of about a couple of tons. Previously to curing they are bled, cut open nicely clensed and the backbone for nearly two thirds of its length from the head cut away. They are then immersed for a certain time in large pickling tubs, and finally spread out to dry upon the stony beach, which seemed excellently adapted to the purpose. A gently blowing breeze is of more consequence at first than sunshine, one fine bright day being of most importance towards the conclusion of the course of cure. The stakes are covered at night, and during wet weather by canvas ... haddocks ... selling at 1/- (5p) a dozen in spring and at other seasons for a half penny each."

Saithe and herring were hung to dry and fish were also dried on the slated roofs of Ballachulish and Glencoe for use in winter. Mackeral were smoked with pine cones.

The oil left in the brine residue was used in the old days to dress leather. "*Cha 'n ioghnadh boladh an sgadain a bhi de 'n t-soitheach 's am bi e.*" Tis no wonder that the herring vessel smells of herring. The lower jaw of the haddock was said to cure toothache. Crappit heads was a Scottish dish in which the heads of haddock were cooked with a stuffing of oatmeal suet, onions and pepper. Reistes haddocks are those which have been smoked. Another cure for toothache was from the backbone of the dogfish. The Chief of the MacDonalds of Clanranald kept a man whose only duty was to catch dogfish. The eel is generally considered unwelcome on the table in Scottish homes. However it was used in the Highlands. Soup made from it was considered to be a cure for many internal ills, and the skin was used for cramps. The oil was also used medically. The skin too was used as a sling. "*An easgunn ag ith' a h-earball fein.*" The eel eating her own tail. (Speaking evil of one's own relations. "*An t-iasg a chriomas gach boiteag, theid a ghlacadh uaireigin.*" The fish that bites every worm (bate) will be caught some time.

As there is a considerable likeness between the haddock and the whiting, children are taught this rhyme.

Ball dubh air an adaig
Gob fad air a chuideig.

A black spot on the haddock, a long black snout on the whiting.

A Gaelic proverb says, "*A's t-Earrach 'n uair a bhios a chaors caol bidh an maorach reamhar.*" In spring when the sheep are lean, shellfish are fat. (A dispensation of Providence.) Certainly the shell fish were a most valuable food for the people who lived near the shore. Winkle soup was popular. It was made thus: Cover the winkles with cold water and salt and boil them for twenty minutes, then take the winkles out of their shells and to the stock add chopped onions, the shelled winkles and a handful of oatmeal to thicken, and simmer for ten minutes. The yellow or large white periwinkle gives a purple dye, but these were not eaten. The black and white forms were said to make good soup for nursing mothers. The broth and the shells pounded small and boiled then strained was said to be good for the gravel. "*Buirn teith do 'n fhaochaig.*" Hot water to the buckie— never boil them. "*Cunnstaidh iad na faochagan.*" They will count the buckies. Said about extra penurious people.

Limpets should be boiled with peeled potatoes and eaten together. Fried cockles are delicious. They should be collected and left in a bucket of sea-water until the sand has been expelled. They are then boiled for half an hour in sea water. The water is poured off and after the shells have cooled, the meat is removed and put in a shallow pan, containing a pint of fresh milk and allowed to simmer for $\frac{3}{4}$ hour. It must not boil. Add pepper and 1 oz of butter; serve with toasted bread. Whelks are good cooked like oysters, stewed or fried. The dried fish was soaked and boiled and milk was added. Soup from razor shell was delicious. Shell fish were said to cure stomach ulcers. Mussels should be well boiled. Other shell fish become tough with over cooking.

Lobsters got a poor reputation, not in the kitchen but as an epitaph. Crab was used for bait, but its real name must not be used when baiting.

There is a saying attributed to a mermaid whose seal skin had been stolen by a young man who married her. Before she returned to the sea she gave as a parting gift this advice, "*Na h-ol an saile 'm feasd gun sioladh, 'S ioma biasd tha 's a chuain.*" Never drink sea water without filtering. There's many a beast in the ocean. This refers to the minute life of the ocean plankton. There was an old belief among the Celts that birds had originally been fish.

Sea sand was used for crops, being a good source of lime. Seaweed was and is used as an excellent plant food. Seaweed was enjoyed by cattle and when boiled with meal is said to be very good for them. When cloth was being waulked, if it was of a blue colour it was harder to do, but this was overcome by coating the cloth (which had much oil in it) with boiled seaweed. Some seaweeds were used as poultices. By the shore grows lovage which was eaten raw as a salad or boiled as greens. Dulse broth was made and thickened with oatmeal. It was also eaten raw. Carageen was made into a pudding after it had been dried and beached; it was then simmered in milk, adding flavouring if desired. When it thickened, it was strained and left to set.

From the shore, sand was collected and was used with soap (home made) to scrub and scour wooden furniture till it whitened and the furniture was then washed with water. In very early times when houses had earth floors, sand was sometimes put on top of the earth floor.

The ash of seaweed could be used to scour flaxen thread better and make it whiter than anything else. Seaweed was used for making kelp, which for a while was a great Highland industry. The seaweed *fucus linearis* was used in Jura and Skye as cattle food. It also made a black salt powder, helpful in cases of scorbutic laxity of the gums. When the plant was used to preserve cheese without salt, the ashes of the weed were so salt that 5 oz of the ash would contain half its weight in salt. Another seaweed *Laminaria lamour* was eaten by men and cattle. It was considered to strengthen the stomach and restore the appetite. Purple melic grass was used in Skye for making nets, and excellent nets they made with it. In some parts marram grass was used for making horse collars.

Some domestic lamp oil was got by collecting the livers of any fish, which were put in a pot and left till they had melted down to a semi liquid state. The decayed livers were then put on a slow fire to dissolve. When this was done the good oil was stored and the remains put on the manure heap. The good oil was a dark colour and looked like port wine.

St. Fond wrote that salmon up to 150 lbs were caught at Oban. These were dried in peat smoke. In February 1785 a fishery on the Lochie was taking 200 barrels of salmon, each barrel containing about 25 to 27 fish. These barrels were sold at £7 at their highest, but could be done to £5 10s. 0d. The word somersault is a corruption of salmon-sault, or leap.

At one time salmon fishing on rivers was done at night. A flare on a stick, or a flare of burning peat was carried in a metal pot. This attracted the fish which were then speared with a leister, or salmon spear, something like a trident.

Salmon were kippered. To do this in the local way take $\frac{1}{4}$ lb brown sugar, 1 lb salt, 2 oz saltpetre, $\frac{1}{4}$ teaspoon black pepper, a little allspice—mix. Lay the fish on a board and cover with the above mixture. Lay aside for three days. Dry in the sun ready for use.

In some Scottish rivers fresh water mussels may contain a pearl. These pearls can be very fine. In "The Beauties of Scotland" an account is given of how they were fished. "They are fished with a kind of spear consisting of a long shaft, and terminated by two iron spoons, forming a kind of forceps. The handles of the spoons are long and elastic, which keeps the mouth closed, but they open upon being pressed against anything. With this machine in his hand by way of a staff, the fisher, being up to his chin in water, gropes with his feet for the mussels, which are fixed by one end in the mud and sand. he presses down the forceps which opens and grabs the shell, and enables him to pull it to the surface. He has a net bag hanging by his side to carry the mussels till he comes ashore where they will be opened."

In many parts of the Highlands you will see Riga bowls from Russia. These were obtained by barter by our fishermen in the Baltic when they met the Russian fishermen.

Sea shells were used to make excellent lime for buildings and particularly for plastering. They were sold at 4d. (2p) and 6d. (2½p) per barrel.

Lightfoot in the late eighteenth century writes of basking sharks. They were hunted and harpooned for their oil, a good fish giving 8 barrels of oil. The rest of the fish were discarded. The commissioners of the forfeited estates tried to encourage this type of fishing, but it was not a success and only private ventures continued. The shark when first harpooned, may carry a 70-ton boat through a gale, and it may take 12 to 24 hours to land or secure the fish. When first struck in the gills, it may pay little heed till two men with all their strength force the harpoon deeper.

Insects

There are a few folk tales of, and uses for insects and reptiles. One of the Beatons (a hereditary line of doctors) a Mull man—his soul was said to go on aerial journeys in the form of a butterfly. This insect was thought to contain the soul or ghost of someone who had died. Caterpillars were used to cure toothache. The caterpillar (one of the hairy kind) was wrapped in a rag and placed under or near to the painful tooth. The ashes of a burned frog were used to stop haemorrhage and the spawn was used for erysipelas. A frog was often kept in the dairy for luck and to catch the insects. "*Cha 'n ann far am bi uisge bhios mag, ach am bi mag bi uisge.*" Tis not where water is a frog will be, but where a frog is, water will be.

A snake will not bite a MacIver. There is said to be a pact between the MacIvers and snakes not to molest each other. When a snake was killed, the head was preserved and put in to water. The wound of the next person to be bitten was washed in the water. If an ointment made of snake grease were used to anoint the eyes, it enabled one to see the fairies. Snake skins were used by the fairies to make clothes. It is unlucky to dream of a snake.

Pennant tested an old belief that toads cured cancer, but found it to be untrue. The snail is unlucky if seen on a hard surface. Soup made from snails was said to be very nourishing. Also, it was thought that if someone suffering from corns on the toe put a snail on a thorn where two laird's lands meet, a cure would be effected. A cure for jaundice was thought to be the drinking of water which had had a snail in it. Pounded snails were used as a poultice for bruises, and were laid on the forehead when no leeches were available.

Chapter 11 **Old Highland farming**

Through the centuries the peoples of the Highlands and Lowlands of Scotland were divided by hills into two separate races. They spoke a different language, for though at one time Gaelic was the language of Scotland it had receded to the hills for many years. The culture of the two parts of the country was different, as was their social structure. The very soil they tilled and the climate were different. The difficulties of communication were increased by lack of roads save only tracks through the passes used by the cattle drovers. In the south the memory of cattle stealing had left a suspicion of the Highlander, and though this was dying out by the eighteenth century, the Clansmen of the north were mistrusted and feared. In the north the Highlander looked down on the Lowlander as comfort-loving, without pride of race, or the appreciation of music and poetry.

For many years the main traffic between the two parts of the kingdom had been limited to the travelling cattle drovers passing south with their beasts to the Fairs or Trysts as they were called. Later some went to the south for the work of the Lowland harvest, which they finished, then travelled north to their own harvest which was later. In the south trade in cattle, furs, charcoal, etc., sometimes lured the Lowlanders to the north.

The first roads in the Highlands were made by General Wade. After the '15 Jacobite Rising he was called in by the Government to advise on ways to prevent any further rising. He advised the making of military roads through the Highlands. Lowland troops being at a great disadvantage when it came to fast travel in the hills. As it turned out, in the '45 it was the Jacobite army which made use of the military roads in their quick march south. Many of the Highlanders were not enthusiastic about the new roads, for they did not suit the feet of their cattle, so the old drove roads continued to be used for many years.

There were few travellers to the Highlands till after Pennant in 1769, when he was followed by Dr. Johnson, Boswell and others. It was the publishing of the Waverley novels and Queen Victoria's love of the Highlands that started the many tours to the Highlands. From the north, travel was mostly to Edinburgh or to the Continent. The great smuggling industry must have necessitated some travel, but in general it may be seen that there was little communication between north and south for ideas to be exchanged.

Agriculturally the Highlands and Islands lagged behind the rest of the country. They had no iron, and in the Islands especially, they had no wood, and money was scarce. The climate is harder, the soil poorer and the wind harsher. Markets for surplus produce were non-existent. The Islanders had often to make a voyage of 30 to 70 miles for wood before they could make a plough or even a small tool from wood. They faced a considerable danger in carrying timber in an open boat.

The ownership and tenure of the land differed greatly between the north and the south. In the Highlands before the '45 the land was divided into the territories of the different Clans. The land was owned by the Chief. Unlike the southern landowner he was accessible to all, and his men claimed kinship with him. The Highlanders were largely a pastoral people, and their wealth was in the cattle they possessed. After the '45 much land owned by Jacobites was confiscated and run by the Commissioners of the Forfeited Estates. Towards the end of the eighteenth century much of this land was returned to the Chiefs, but the old link between the Chief and his people was largely broken.

The Chief of the Clan would let out a good portion of his land to Tacksmen. These men, who were often closely related to the Chief, were usually men of intelligence, well educated, and with some financial means behind them. The tacksmen in turn let out a considerable amount of the land to the clansmen. They in turn might sublet still smaller pieces of land. The Tacksmen were responsible to the Chief for the rents.

Walker (The Economical History of the Hebrides) states "when a number of tenants jointly occupy a farm they pay rent according to their separate valuations; some have penny, some half-penny and others only a farthing land. Each has his number of cattle soumed or proportioned to his rent, which go in a common herd. But all join in labouring the arable part of the farm land and, according to their valuation, receive a proportion of its produce. As in this situation their separate interests must frequently interfere, the harmony in which they live and the good will they bear to one another is truely surprising."

The souming and the rents and the area of land vary in different parts of the country. Walker goes on: "The pennyland may support four or five cows and their followers, that is a calf, a beast of a year old, and another of two years and possibly one of three years, so that with the cow there are five beasts. But as there are losses and sales it is not usual for the number to be the full compliment. But with the different tenants grazing, the land may carry twenty to twenty-five head of cattle of the old Highland breed. Nearly always they were black which was considered to be the hardiest type. Besides the cattle there would be some horses and sheep. The half-penny land is about half the value of the penny land and may carry eight or nine shares of perhaps four cows, three horses and ten sheep." The sheep at this time (*c.* 1800) were not in general kept in large flocks, as later, but just a few were kept by each family to provide wool for themselves. "Sometimes sheep were omitted and there might be six cows and six horses." The value and the variety of the work of the horse was great. It was the horse that worked the land, or at least much of it, and for any journey beyond walking the Highland beasts (more ponies than horses) were invaluable. They were surefooted and able to scramble over rocks and to avoid bogs. They were very hardy. Land known as farthing land might have four cows and their followers, perhaps four horses with some arable land for sheep. The rent for this being about 30/- to 50/- (the second half of the eighteenth century) "Possibly about five or six bolls* of grain would be grown in the area".

There were two other ways land might be rented. Steelbow meant that the tacksman sublet a farm, stocked it with his beasts which were valued at the entry of the tenant, and at the end of the lease the stock was again valued and any loss of value was made good by the tenant. The last method of tenure was known as half foot. In this case the tacksman bought the seed and the tenant did the tilling, sowing and harrowing and the crop was divided between them.

Money might be borrowed from the land when a Wadset was taken. This was a form of mortgage, a deed from the debtor assigning the rent of the land till the debt had been paid.

The old system of Run-rig (sometimes called run-dale) continued in the Highlands till a much later date than it did in the south. Under this system the arable land was divided into strips, and each man drew a lot. In his lot there would be so much land that was good, and so much of it would be poorer land. In this it was fair, all getting so much good land and so much of the poorer. But next year, or sometimes after three years, the lots were drawn again, and everybody got a different strip. The great fault of this system was that it discouraged good husbandry. There could be a reluctance to keep weeds under control on ground that would go to someone else at the next drawing of lots. A hard working man might hand over land in good heart and get comparatively weedy and uncared for land for the next year's crop. But in general, the system worked reasonably well over a long number of years. No doubt in a small community no one would wish to be known as the one who returned dirty land, and many would take a pride in handing over the land in good heart.

In Perthshire the land cultivated under the run-rig system was about 20 to 40 feet long. The cultivated lines were often not straight but bent to avoid natural obstacles. A wavy line of corn might be followed by piles of stone which marked the end of one man's area, and the beginning of the next plot.

In the old days, and in some parts still sometimes seen, the cropping, usually potatoes, was done in the "lazybed" method. This is called "Feannagan" in Gaelic. The name "lazybed" is misleading as much hard work is involved. A strip of land is dug, and the top soil is lifted off it, on to the next strip of land. This would have been dug previously and would have a layer of manure or more likely seaweed on top, or more simply the top turf turned face down, so with the fresh earth making a sandwich with the top layer of soil and the lower layer of earth making the "bread" while the layer of seaweed made up the filling. The land is worked in strips. Thus the strip from which the top of the sandwich was taken is now considerably lower than the top of the sandwich and this acts as drain and in wet areas such as the West Highland and Islands it is most useful especially on boggy land. The raised part benefits by getting the greater depth of soil, and because it is drained it is warmer. In some places the natural depth of the soil is very shallow, and may be only inches in depth. The continued use of the lazybed method with its additional depth of manure or seaweed will help to build up a greater depth of soil through the years. Lime was used, very often shell particles from the shore. On Lismore however lime was worked and lime was exported. That Island is very fertile and the Gaelic name means the great garden.

The thatched roofs of the cottages were removed each year and used as manure, and replaced with fresh thatch. The smoky peat reek which solidified and festooned the inside of the house gave good feeding for crops. This was especially true of a "black house". This was the old type of cottage where the fire was in the middle of the floor and without any chimney, the smoke finding its way out of the room through a hole in the roof.

It should be mentioned that much of the rent paid in the Highlands in the old days was paid in kind; woven material, cheese, hens, eggs, etc., also with a day's work. The main source of money to come into the Highlands was from the sale of cattle at the great Trysts in the south to which the cattle went on the hoof. This way of paying rent worked to the benefit of all, there being no markets or shops to hand for the purchase or sale of goods.

One of the main reasons (according to those who lived at the time) why agriculture was so far behind in the Highlands was the short leases. The "Improvers" all claimed that a good length of lease would make for a great improvement to the land and give great satisfaction to crofter or farmer. Another source of difficulty was this giving of a day's service in lieu of rent. The Improvers suggested that a higher rent for the landlord and no service would be appreciated by both.

Like many mountainous countries, the hill grazing was used in the summer when it was practical to do so and when there would be rich grazing in the heights. In the Highlands the men went up first to do any repairs to the simple dwellings they had there, and heather was cut for beds. Most of the people of the township went to live a very simple life in these huts in the hills. They might go in May or June, and stay six weeks or more. They would only take the bare necessities, cooking pots, blankets, dairy utensils, and wool for spinning.

While they were up in the hills they made butter and cheese for the winter. The rich hill grass produced a good flow of milk. In this way they not only made use of the hill grazing

* 1 boll = 140 lbs.

The cas chrom.

at the only possible time, but thus rested the inby fields. It was a time much looked forward to and enjoyed. It gave freedom to young children, and the older ones enjoyed music, dancing and ceilidhs in the long light evenings. I have met one person who remembers going to the Shieling as this life in the hills was called, but in general this annual trek has been discontinued for many years.

In many parts of the Highlands and Islands the land was prepared for the cultivation of crops with a foot plough called a cas chrom. This is a curved piece of wood fitted with a flat shoe of iron at the front. Dr. Johnson describes it thus: "The soil is turned up by manual labour, with an instrument called a crooked spade, of a form and weight which to me appeared very incommodious, and would perhaps be soon improved in a country where workmen could be easily found and easily paid. It has a narrow blade of iron fixed to a long and heavy piece of wood, which must be a foot and a half above the iron, a knee of flexture with the angle downwards. When the farmer encounters a stone which is the great impediment of his operation, he drives the blade under it, and bringing the knee or angle to the ground, has in the long handle a very forcible lever." The handle is about 5½ feet long, and is of naturally bent wood. It was usual for a man about to make a cas chrom to go out into the woods and select a piece of growing wood of the right shape. The idea of so choosing wood suited to the task in hand was general in the Highlands. Wood for prows of boats, for cas chroms, for shinty sticks and other items were selected in this way.

The cas chrom was worked backwards by one man. The work was heavy, but a man skilled in its use could do a good job of work. The iron foot which is shaped like a plough was put into the ground, a foot was put in what Dr. Johnson called "A knee with the angle downwards". The man would give a jerk and this would turn over the soil. The tool is now more or less obsolete as a working implement, but may be seen in many Highland Museums. In the Glencoe and North Lorn Folk Museum we had an interesting resurrection of the cas chrom. One of our committee members had bad back trouble and could no longer use a spade in his garden. He copied the design of the cas chrom in the museum and got one made and when he used it he found he did not hurt his back as he did with the spade. In the past in some parts of England a not dissimilar tool was used.

When the work of the plough and the cas chrom are compared the reason for the long use of the latter is better understood. Walker writes "Upon poor land a boll of oats raised with the plough will bring in only three bolls, but if raised with the spade it will produce 5 bolls. But in such land the third crop after the plough is sometimes better than the third crop after the spade." Another writer says "It appears in general that a field laboured with the cas chrom affords usually one third more crop than if laboured with the plough. Poor land will afford usually one half more ... The cas chrom is a beneficial instrument in cultivating the rocky tracks of the Highlands which are inaccessible to the plough."

Again in Durnish "The instrument in use among them is called caschrom literally the crooked leg, a kind of clumsy spade or rather a very rude and primitive plough, probably the primitive one which was subsequently so much improved on in various ways in parts of the world. The cas chrom is pointed with a piece of iron nearly half an inch thickness about

Scottish eighteenth century ox plough.

ten inches in length and four in breadth, which may be called the sock. Into this is fixed the sole, a strong piece of wood from two to three feet in length, and to the sole is fastened, by means of nails, the handle or stilt, which is about five feet in length—considerably thicker than a man's wrist, and forms a very obtuse angle with the sole of the lower part. At the junction of the sole and handle there is a wooden pin, called sgonnan, fixed in at right angles to the sole, for the foot to rest upon when the impliment is digging . . . When oats or barley are put in the ground, ploughed by the cas chrom, it is harrowed, sometimes by means of a large rake, made for the purpose, sometimes by a light harrow made of the ordinary shape, but having wooden teeth and drawn hither by men and women. I have seen this kind of harrow drawn by a horse; but it was fastened by a very primitive way and to me a very new mode. The whole harness consisted of two straw ropes one of which was attached to the head and the other to the tail of the animal. The one supplied the trace of reins and the other the traces of collar and hems (Hains). The harrow was tied to the tail by this straw rope, and the horse pulled away apparently not much incommoded by the weight fastened to it."

Walker writes, "With a cas chrom a Highlander will open up more ground in a day and render it fit for the sowing of grain than could be done by two or three men with any other spades that are commonly used. He will dig as much ground in a day as will sow more than a peck* of oats. If he digs from about Christmas to near the end of April he will prepare the land for 5 bolls, after this he will dig as much land in a day as will sow two pecks of bear; and in the course of the season, will cultivate as much land with his spade as is sufficient to supply a family of seven or eight persons, the year round, with meal and potatoes.

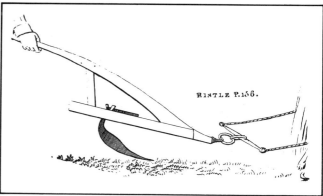

Above: Oliver plochilled plow.
Above right: Ristle plough.

Ploughs in the Highlands and Islands were primitive. The one known as the Hebridean or Highland plough had a beam and only one stilt or handle to guide it. Fastened to the beam and handle in a somewhat casual manner was a slight mould board. A ring held together the coulter and the sock and shares. Usually four horses were used for this plough. They walked abreast, in front of them walked the driver with the reins fastened to a crosspiece. On the left-hand side the ploughman went to hold the one handle and guide the plough. Behind came a man who turned the turfs cut by the plough. The reason why this last man was needed was the lack of a true moulding board. A good type of plough of that date could do the work of one man and two horses.

There was the ristle or sickle plough. It is about the same size as the previous plough, similar in shape, again with one handle and a beam. The coulter is shaped like a reaping hook, but a bit stronger. It is without sock or share. One horse can draw it worked by two men, one to see to the horse and the other to direct the restle, for it is the coulter which cuts the ground. The restle is first used on land to clear it of roots and other hazards and to cut turf etc., so that the plough which follows will not be damaged.

Highland harrows too were feeble, more like hay rakes. Some were worked by hand and others by horses. They were light in weight and had wooden teeth and were not used much in newly ploughed land. Owing to there being neither roads nor carts in the Highlands in

* 1 peck = 2 gals or 14 lbs.

many parts it meant that everything had to be moved on horse or human back or on sledges. This included seaweed for manuring the ground, the crop of hay or corn when harvested, peat and any other item. In many cases it was the women who carried the seaweed and peat in baskets on their backs.

Buchanan writes of the old Scotch plough: "It is quite simple and has a sock and coulter, with two handles almost like the English plough, drawn by four little horses; but so weak that another kind of plough, called the rissle, with a crooked iron resembling a hook, passing through a stick of four feet long, and drawn by one horse cuts the furrow before that drawn by four horses so making it easier for the plough. Cromman-gadd is a simpler plough than the old Scotch, and drawn by two or more little horses. It has only one handle, and the ploughman goes with his left side foremost ..."

In the Highlands and Islands harrows had wooden teeth, and carts were without iron on their wheels. Sledges, and similar means were used to transport their crops; baskets were used for carrying peat manure and so forth, but while they appeared slow and out of date, they served the purpose for the job, cost little or no money and could be made by the crofter or farmer at his leisure. As there were no roads in many parts and only poor ones in others, the carts of the south would have been of much less value in the north. Those who wished to improve their estates in the late eighteenth century (1775 or thereabouts) had to import ploughs, etc. from the south as there were no trained carpenters or smiths available. But as more people became interested in improvements some young men were persuaded to train in the south and return to the country with their skills.

By the 1800s the improved Scottish ploughs became more plentiful and with them harrows, thrashing machines, and carts. There was also a brakeharrow drawn by one horse used to clean couch-grass and to pulverise the soil. In the eastern area in Inverness, there was a machine used to bruise the tops of furze, which was used to feed the horses in time of scarcity. Those who had not the machines used to beat the furze with a flail.

In Barra and the Long Isle bear was sown in the same way as potatoes in lazy beds. It was sown on the prepared bed in May and it was harrowed by a hand harrow. The islanders sowed thin and got very good crops.

Lismore has a soil that, unlike the rest of the area, is full of lime. The fields had many spear thistles and hempagrimony and wayside thistle. The people of the island made a special tool for removing thistle. It was fashioned as a long pair of pincers about 3 feet 8 inches long, the pincers themselves being about ten inches long and the handle two feet ten inches. It was called in Gaelic Clou-mait or timber tongs. When the thistles were ready to be removed a man went over the field and drew the thistles out by the root. It was a much better way than trying to remove the thistles by the gloved hand as was done in other areas. At Gortlec they used a small knife crooked at the point and having a wooden handle.

What became known as the Old Scots plough was a strong machine about 13 feet long, and 4 feet from the sock to the back of the head. It was used to cultivate rough stony ground. The point was sharpened and the sock, which is long and tapering, slips past obstacles. The weight of the plough makes it less easy to overturn.

In 1837 the Statistical Account reports that: "The work formerly done by five men and five horses at the plough is now performed by one man and two horses. It is not more than 20 years since the old plough with one stilt named cromnan-gad was entirely discontinued and now it was only a few years ago that the small plough called the ristle which was used for cutting the ground to enable the other plough to turn the sod with more ease was disused ... formerly the tenants had all their potatoes in lazy beds in narrow rigs three or four feet broad in lea strong ground."

In parts of the country horse and oxen were used together for ploughing. On light soils 4 or 6 oxen might be used alone, but in general farmers preferred to use horses when the weather was good to get work finished before it changed. There was also an economy as by the use of horse no driver was needed. Gradually the use of oxen became obsolete.

Sir John Sinclair describes the grain grown: "Black oats, this variety is little known in the best cultivated districts of Scotland, but sown in cold exposed situations. It receives its name from the dark colour of its husk ... yet its meal is as white and good as any other kind ... It ought only to be sown on the poorer soils requiring pulverisation and on low rented grassland..." "The time of sowing barley follows that of oats and the most proper seed time is the later part of March or the beginning of April, though good crops are often produced from a much later seed-time, even to the middle of May. Bear or Big may be sown much later than barley as it grows and ripens with great rapidity ... Under the old system of Scottish husbandry seldom sown till after the middle or about the end of May." He goes on to describe the barley. "This kind has been shown in Scotland from time immemorial, and is of the hot-seed or quick growing of Horedeum distinction. It admits of great latitude in the season of growing, having in some cases been sown so late as the 12th of June and produced a satisfactory crop. It is seldom, however, sown after the middle of May; Bear or Big is a distinct species of the barley genus known to botanists by the name of quadrangular barley, as its ear or spike has four rows of grains, while all the varieties hitherto mentioned have only two rows. Its ordinary Scots name is rough-bear or simply bear."

To add to the difficulties of the farmer the price for barley altered with the law which fixed the price of the malt duty which was the same in England and Scotland. In Scotland it was harder to get the barley and it was rarely as good as that from the south, so the distillers, if they had to pay the malt tax, bought the dearer English barley rather than the Scottish. When at Inverness the cost of barley was 25 shillings a boll, home-grown barley fetched only 16 to 18 shillings a boll.

The seed was sown broadcast. There is an art in this as the sower steps carefully over the ground sowing seed by hand so that there are no bare patches, nor those thrown too thick. When the crop grows the skill of the sower is shown, and nothing can hide the work of the unskilled.

To clean the grain for seed a sloping screen made of iron wires with small intervals which was part of the winnowing machine or they were separated by the use of sieves with small mesh through which the weed seeds fell but which held the grain. The weed seeds were fed to the poultry.

There is a lack of information about crop failure from disease or pests and any remedies

The crofts round Glencoe in the past.

which may have been used. However by the 17th century (in the south at least) infected seed was not sown, though still eaten as food. By the early 18th century there is a reference to dressing seed-corn with arsenic or a mixture of salt and lime. The custom of leaving ground fallow helped to reduce disease by not providing a host plant, and improving the land fertility by the rest.

In general in Scotland and in the Highlands in particular crops were not fenced to protect them from cattle. It was the work of boys to guard the crops from the cattle.

It was usual to use the saw-edged sickle or reaping hook at harvest, though a smooth sickle was introduced in the late eighteenth century. It was the custom to have six or seven reapers grouped with their binder. These binders collected the corn and made it into sheaves which they tied at the ear end.

Hay was usually harvested at the beginning of July and bog hay in August. The wages for any harvest were 1/6 to 2/- with their keep. When hired by piece work the cost would be 2/6 to 3/- an acre. Some farmers reported the difficulty in getting labour for the work as the young men of their area preferred to go to work at the illicit stills.

A good mower could cut an acre a day at the cost of 5/- with food, and two experienced women could bind this work which cost 7/- the cost of the horse rake would be 6d per acre (*c.* 1810).

The hay barns were made open to allow the air to circulate, by building the gable ends with the walls no higher than the walls at the side, the gap being only filled with stakes, wound with broom or brushwood. When damp hay is brought in, frames are put up from floor to ceiling and the hay is spread on these to dry.

Rye was not grown a great deal on the mainland, but was grown on the sandy soil of the Isles and manured with the seaweed.

Sir John Sinclair writes of three unusual crops which might be cultivated. Madder he thought a suitable crop owing to the high premium offered by the Highland Society for growing madder in the Highlands which it was discovered dyed cotton a turkey-red. The root gave a colour as good as cochineal and the top of the plant a yellow. One acre produced 3 or 4 tons and an ounce of seed would produce enough plants to fill an acre. During the American War efforts were made to grow tobacco. It grew well in the Borders and was reasonably successful in Perthshire. The Duke of Atholl (1810 or thereby) cultivated a considerable area but the public liking things foreign largely rejected the Scotch grown plants.

The first potatoes planted in the Highlands was in 1743 in South Uist. Clanranald was on a visit to his cousin MacDonnel of Antrim and saw potatoes. When he was returning home he brought back seed potatoes. When he arrived home, his tenants were gathered together and told how to plant and cultivate the crop, but they all refused. They were imprisoned for a while, but after a short time let out when they agreed to plant the roots. When the crop was lifted the whole crop was laid at the Chief's home. The tenants said that the Laird might indeed insist that the foolish roots were planted, but he could not force them to eat them. It was not long before the inhabitants began to value the roots. "The price of potatoes in years of abundance seldom exceeds 7 or 8 shillings a boll.

"Unmarried servants are engaged for six months only, they are maintained in the farmer's house and their wages are from ten to twelve pounds for a whole year. Women are hired at from 3 to 4 pounds for the same time. Married men-servants who are commonly hired by the year charge the same as unmarried together with six bolls of livery-meal, and ground for half a boll or sometimes more of potatoes. Their house and garden is rent free."

In many districts in the Highlands regular farm servants were quite unknown and the work was done by the family. On other farms too many were employed. Reports from differing sources vary as, no doubt, did the work on the land. In one way Scotland was in advance of the rest of the world, by the forming of Agricultural Societies, the first being created as early as 1723.

Reapers who came from a distance were supplied with their food whether they were working or not which included Sunday. But they were only paid on the days they worked. Accommodation had to be provided for them.

Shepherds were generally allowed a boll and a half of meal besides keeping two cows and sixty or seventy sheep. The hire of a common labourer by the day was one shilling besides his maintenance or sixpence more without food from his employer.

Woman planting potatoes.

Flax is a plant that needs moisture, so it was not difficult to grow in the Highlands, though it also needed some shelter from the north and full sun. It was harvested by hand, this being done before the seeds ripened. If the harvest is left till later the oils in the plant leave the stem for the seeds and this makes the stems brittle and difficult to work. The flax is soaked in water for something like ten to twelve days. When taken from the water it is spread on the land to dry and this process is called being "grassed". The previous soaking being called "retting".

If as sometimes the plants were left to form seed, they were then "rippled"; that is the heads are pulled through an instrument rather like a comb. The flax can then be got ready for spinning, or left till needed. It should have reachd the stage of being dry and brittle so that the fibres can be easily separated.

Rushes were cleared by draining and then mowed as closely as possible twice in a season. The cut rushes were used to bed cattle. Ferns were cut by hand, and used as thatch in some parts, or they might be burned for their ash which was sold for bleaching. Broom was used sometimes for thatching the peat stack and the corn. It was also used to feed cattle in winter. It was cut green and bruised with flails. Up until about 1756 hay was not grown in the Highlands and cattle and horses were kept on the moors like sheep, getting only straw to eat and any remains of the summer pasture.

On the east coast what were called "Broom Parks" were grown. This was a field of pasture where the brooms were allowed to increase and overrun the field till the plants were up to 6 or 7 feet in height. All the cattle of the farm wintered there, and found both food and shelter. After seven or eight years this field was ploughed and with the heavy dunging it had received was fertile and gave a very good yield.

An iron furnace was started in Bonawe, Argyll about 1740, and later, more furnaces began in this district. Such was the demand for charcoal and for oak bark that the value of woods was realised by landowners for the first time, so they cared for, cropped, fenced and improved their woodland.

From an estate in Ardnamurchan a manufacturer in Glasgow bought wood to the value of £7,000. Naturally some wood was more valuable than others. Oak was most generally used, but the makers of gunpowder preferred above all the charcoal of apple-leaved willow as it fired quicker and thus brought in the highest price. Willows were used in the Highlands and were available in many parts. The wood is light, soft and tough and lasts well both wet or dry. It could be made into platters, bowls, or clogs and outside it was used for whetting steel and water wheels. It was used for hoops, creels for carrying manure and seaweed, peats, etc. In the Hebrides the willow was used for the making of bridles, and even to hold the anchors of ships. The people of Colonsay and Tiree used to tan hides with the bark of willow. It was also of value to tanners, and their cattle ate the leaves of the tree in Autumn.

Scotland maintained connections with France and the continent. Scottish nobility were frequently abroad and on their return set out to improve their estates and to make gardens. On Iona and other places where there had been monasteries or convents the remains of gardens could be seen. Small landed gentry and farms and farm servants had their kale yards. Certain flowers were used in simples and for dyes so some of these were probably grown, though many were collected wild. We know that cherries were grown in Ballachulish, for Bishop Forbes speaks about them. Certain wild fruits were much liked in the Highlands, but gathered wild, not cultivated.

In the past the general food of farmworkers was oats, barley or bigg. Higher up the social scale both wheat and rye was used. The latter was used to make sour cakes at Christmas for the poor. Where peas were cultivated there was a certain amount of peasemeal. The cabbage and colewort were practically the only vegetable in general use. They were thickened with meal and made into porridge, or more simply the juice was poured onto the meal for brose and cabbage eaten with bread. The general winter farm breakfast had what was known as tartan purrie which was porridge made with the liquid of boiled coleworts. The coleworts themselves had been eaten for supper the previous evening. Before the planting of turnips, milk was very scarce in winter. It was the water in which the vegetables were boiled that provided the liquid. When summer came, milk was in good supply and was used to save meal.

In 1810 a writer speaks of the food available, potatoes, turnips, cows milk ... butcher meat in use in all towns and indeed most villages and with this and potatoes and vegetables there was a great saving in meal! But in spite of this writer's remarks, meat was not so general in the diet, but milk, oats and cheese were staple, with fish and shell-fish being eaten a great deal around the coast. The coming of potatoes to the Highlands must have been a welcome addition to the monotonous fare, for while oat cakes and cheese make a splendid meal, some variety must have added spice.

What are known as "grits or grouts" are the kernel of the oat and used to be used for broth. These grits not used thus are then ground again into a coarse rough meal, varying in different districts as to how fine. The meal is then sifted and so remove the thin inner skin of the husk. These skins called seeds (which still retains some of the fine powder of the kernel) is steeped in water and is called sowens, A kind of jelly is made by boiling and it is eaten with milk. Some of the dust separates from the oats which is used for feeding stock. The main product of oat is the oatmeal which is usually used to make porridge or pottage ... When travelling with droves of cattle to the different fairs, the Scotch Highlander usually ate oatmeal in cold water which food they ate for a good while and on it walked many miles.

One of the dishes taken by the Highlander was "Stapag" which was cream with some

oatmeal stirred in and "Onaich" which is frothed whey which was formed by using a stick with a cross at the end, with a cord made of cow hairs.

In many parts of Scotland barley bread was eaten, to this was added peas and bear up to a third or fourth part. The meal was sieved through a coarse sieve to take off the fibrous husk, was then kneaded with water and salt without yeast and formed into round cakes about an inch thick. They were fired on a girdle, and turned then when cooked fired toasted in front of a fire. In some parts barley flour was used and finely sieved and baked with yeast and again the cakes were made from barley flour mixed with boiling water or milk and made thin, cooked on the girdle and served warm with butter.

A Scottish acre of oats averaged $6\frac{1}{2}$ bolls after the seed corn had been deducted and 4lbs of potatoes were equal to 1lb of oats.

The Drovers when they took their beasts to the trysts often sustained themselves on oatmeal, moistened with cold water and did this for days on end. On this they walked more or less the length of Scotland.

There were a number of important agricultural improvements made in Scotland which though not originating in the Highlands eventually affected all parts of the country.

One of the earliest plant breeders was a Scot, Patrick Sherriff who in the late 18th century when living in East Lothian collected seeds from plants of the best quality. He once carefully picked out with a pin 99 grains of wheat from a plant growing in a field at Drim. This was the source of Hopetown Wheat which gave 36 bushels per acre.

Dr Johnson said "A tree might be on show in Scotland as a horse in Venice." Sir Archibald Grant (1696–1778) planted some 5 million trees of ash, oak, elm, and pine. When he started he found not an acre enclosed, no timber, lands full of stones, and the soil poor from lack of manure and cultivation. But like many other pioneers in agriculture both in Scotland and England the many improvements produced a good fertility.

In 1178 the first practical threshing machine was built by Andrew Meekle. His father had been accused of "making the devil's wind" when using a winnower from Holland. At nights when the horses were stabled the barn was still busy threshing when 6 strong men worked the drum.

Hugh Wilson of Keelor began with six cows and one bull to try to improve his stock of Aberdeen Angus. One cow known as "Granny" lived for 35 years, had 25 calves but was finally killed by lightning. She is No. 1 in the Aberdeen Angus herd book.

Smith when he took over a farm at Deanston found the land wet, covered in stones and thick with rushes. To improve it he did not follow the practice of his day which was to leave open furrows to drain off the water, instead he dug parallel ditches 20 feet apart and 30 inches deep which were filled with broken stones and earth. This was then ploughed. But as the fields remained wet, he decided that the subsoil was not letting the water get away, so he invented a subsoil plough to break up the pan. It was very heavy (100 lbs) and needed 4 to 8 horses. Smith made his 200 acres of poor soil and sour land into a place where farmers from all Britain came to see the improved land.

There were many such improvers throughout the land.

Chapter 12 **Highland plant lore**

A n luibh nach fhaighear cha'n i a chobhras
The herb that cannot be found can never heal a wound.

Through the ages many people have made use of wild plants as food, as medicine, as dye plants, and in magic. In the Highlands they were used as Clan badges. Some of these uses are listed in this book, but please do not use any plant unless you are sure of its identity. Many wild flowers look similar and mistakes can have serious results.

In 1950 the body of a man was dug from a peat bed in Tollund in Denmark. He had been buried there some 2000 years ago but it was still possible for scientists to tell what he had eaten for his last meal. It had been of plants, Fat hen (Chenopodium album) Black bindweed (Polyganum convolvulus) Pale persicaria (P. lapathifolium) Corn spurrey (Spergula arvensis). Similarly the contents of the stomach of a frozen mammoth had the remains of Alpine foxglove (Alopecurus alpinus). A woman's body dating back to the bronze age contained seeds of bramble (Rubus fruticosus), rose (rosa) and Orache (Atriplex).

In historic times not only were wild flowers and plants collected for medical and other uses, but John Reid in the Scots Gard'ner of 1683 gives a list of wild plants to be brought into cultivation as "Physick—Herbes".

This list includes:

> wormwood comfrey, Solomon's-seal, callamint (calamint), elecampane, masterwort, wall-pellitory, garden beatony (beatony), camomile, swallowwort, suthernwood (southernwood), lovag (lovage), spignall (spignel), agrimony, briony (bryony) bear's breach, madder, dog mercury, dward-elder, hart's-tongue, maiden hair, asrum (ararabacca), dropwort, brithwort, and thornapple among others. The names in brackets are the modern spelling of the old names for plants now in use.

When looking for plants, you will have to remember that seasons vary, so that flowers may bloom three weeks ahead or behind their usual flowering time, and that sheltered spots and cold shady places can make some weeks of difference. For instance I have seen primroses in flower in December in sheltered corners, and seen some still in bloom in July in a colder shady spot. In 1970 the primroses were late and flowered in masses in May instead of April, though some had been out in March. In 1971 a mild January brought forward coltsfoot which flowered in February instead of late March or mid-April which is usual with us. I have seen it flowering in mid and late May. Apart from this, sometimes one may find a stray plant in flower quite out of its normal flowering time, as for instance a yellow pimpernel in flower in the last week of October.

Plant life changes through the ages. Draining the land alters the habitat and so does the addition of lime which causes plants which are intolerant of lime to become scarce or to die out. Recent weed controls have diminished plant and insect life. This last affects the pollination of some plants.

Present day travel has brought changes too. It has been said that the great spread of the rosebay willow herb (Chamaenerion augustifolium) was caused by the Canadian soldiers of the 1914–18 War unwittingly bringing it with them. But the plant was here long before. Possibly the lack of manpower on the land allowed the willow herb to get a real grip. It only reached Glencoe during the next War 1939–45. Perhaps the new road of 1933 helped it to travel. It was reported to be at Crianlarich in 1777 by Dr Lightfoot. He visited Scotland along with Pennant who wrote his well known "Tour of Scotland", while Dr Lightfoot published his work "Flora Scotica".

At picnic places one may sometimes see a plant not usual to the district. A striking example of a plant spread away from its usual habitat is near the station at Loch Eilt on the Fort William to Mallaig line, where there grows some yellow toadflax (Linaria vulgaris) along with the moorland plants in their natural habitat. It may have come as seed on passengers' clothing, or seed may have been caught up by the train, for it is often found growing by railway lines. In my own garden grows the great water parsnip (Sium latifolium). It appeared in the herbacious border. Normally it is a plant of wet places, and I don't know how it came to be in my garden. Once a plant of woad (Isatis tinctoris) appeared brought by chance, I believe, from a nursery in the south along with some purchased plants. Possibly I have these strays in my garden because I rarely use my hoe, and so I get some delightful surprises as treasures, but also alas a good many tiresome weeds.

There is a classic example of the change of habitat in plants. The Romans wrote of how some of the people of this country used to paint themselves with woad. This plant now only grows wild in two tiny areas in the South of England.

The true Scotch Thistle (Onopordum acanthium) is another case in point. It is not common in Scotland. The reason why it became the national emblem of Scotland is that during one of the many Norse invasions a Danish force marching on the Scots to take them by surprise walked barefoot. One man was badly pricked by a thistle and let out a cry, this alerted the Scots who drove off the invaders.

The thistle, along with the oak, is the Clan badge of the Stuarts. In an inventory made after the death of James III of Scotland there was listed a hanging embroidery with "thrissils". When James IV of Scotland married Margaret Tudor of England, the Scots poet Dunbar wrote a poem, "The Thistle and the Rose", in honour of the occasion (1503). James V had a gold badge of a stemless thistle among his possessions. In 1540 the Order of the Thistle was founded. It languished, but was revived later. Mary Queen of Scots is said to have planted milk thistles (Silybum marianum) at Dumbarton. This plant was reported growing there by Dr Lightfoot which would confirm the legend. James VI of Scotland and I of England had thistles on his coins. James VII of Scotland and II of England revived the "Most Noble and Most Ancient Order of the Thistle", in 1685 with the motto "Nemo Me Impune Lacessit". James made it to consist of eight knights—lapsed again during the Revolution, but was revived by Queen Ann in 1703, when it was restored to the original twelve knights. By a statute of 1827 the Order consisted of the Sovereign and sixteen knights.

Dr Lightfoot reported that the Scottish Thistle grew near Edinburgh where they were eaten like artichokes, and used medically for the treatment of cancer. John Bartam the American naturalist wrote of how, two hundred years ago, the thistle reached America. "A Scotch minister brought with him a bed stuffed with thistle down on which contained some seed. The inhabitants having plenty of feathers, soon turned out the down and filled the bed with feathers. The seeds coming up filled that part of the country with thistles".

A plant associated with the Stuarts, is the sea-bindweed (Calystegia soldanella). In 1745 Prince Charles Edward landed on the Island of Eriskay, and from his pocket he scattered seeds of this white striped pink convolvulus which he had gathered while waiting to embark from France. These seeds grew and seeded themselves in turn and are still to be found growing at this spot and nowhere else in the Outer Hebrides.

Conversely, a Scots widow emigrated to New Zealand and took with her one plant of the sweet briar. It grew well in its new home, and it spread, till finally one whole valley was choked with it.

Not only does man alter the environment of plants, but plants themselves change. When the dahlia first came to this country, it was a stove plant. Now it has adapted in part to this country and its climate, and up and down the country it may be seen in gardens flowering come warm summer or cold.

In recent years there has been a sad diminishing of native plants, among other sufferers has been the primrose (Primula vulgaris). While it is still plentiful in Glencoe and district, in some parts so many have been lifted for gardens that they are becoming scarce. It is hard for town people to realise this can happen when they see a wood turned lemon gold with primroses. However repeated inroads can eventually clear a wood.

Floral art too, affects plant life. Some come from the town and invade woods and hedgerows, hack at what they want, often regardless of damage to trees by pulling and tearing and not cutting, nor considering subsequent growth of the shape of the tree. Many are careful, but there is a tendency for town people to collect "wild hedge branches", all considered "free". People cut into a hedge for autumn leaves, regardless of whether by doing so the hedge is worn thin and dies back, or is rendered useless for the keeping of stock safe. Many hours and much skill is needed to make a hedge stockproof, so that an exasperated farmer may well turn to fencing, with a loss to all—the pleasure of seeing hedges for those who pass by, the useful windbreak for plants whether cultivated or wild, the loss of nesting sites for birds, and for some insects the loss of their larder. And as sad as any, is the loss of a traditional country skill.

Plants have been used of old, and in our day new uses are being found. A tropical form of periwinkle has been found useful in the fight against cancer, and Cleopatra's aloe is now being used for radiation burns.

In the Highlands plants were used in many ingenious ways. Bell heather (Erica cinerea) and Ling (Calluna vulgaris) were used for thatching roofs. They were made into rope and the big roots (hardened by charring) were made into nails. This last is typical of the Highlands alone, but in many cases plants were used throughout the country and over the Border and beyond these shores in much the same way. Books of healing came from the south and from overseas, and from the north there are surviving manuscrips in Gaelic dating from the 14th to 16th century. In the Highlands, it was the custom for many occupations to be held by heredity, Pipers, Bards, and Doctors too, came down through the years in the same family. Not always father to son, sometimes uncle to nephew. The most famous of all these doctors were the Beatons or MacBeths. They were the doctors to the Lordship of the Isles, the great MacDonald kingdom. When the Lordship fell in 1493 the Beatons became physicians to several Highland families—the Macleans of Duart, the Macleods of Skye, and to the MacDonalds of Sleat among others.

One of the Beatons translated into Gaelic the Lilium Medinae by Bernard Gordon, a famous professor of physics at the University of Montpelier. The work was written in 1305. This cost as much as sixty milch cows to translate, and was considered so valuable that when the doctor crossed the sea by boat from one arm of the land to another, he sent the book by land by a trusted messenger on horseback.

Martin Martin who travelled in the Western Islands of Scotland at the end of the seventeenth century (1695) met Neil Beaton in Skye. Neil was one of the old line of doctors. Martin writes of him thus. "He considered his patients' constitution before any medicine is administered to them; and he has formed such a system for curing disease as

Bindweed (Calystegia soldamella). Known as the Prince's flower. When Prince Charles Edward landed on the Island of Eriskay he scattered some seed of this plant which he gathered in France before embarking. It grew and still does on the shore of the beach. It is the only spot in the Outer Isles where it grows.

served for a rule to him upon all occasions of this nature … He had the boldness to cut a piece out of a woman's skull broader than half-a-crown, and by this restored her to perfect health".

From Carmina Gadalica we learn "A gland in the throat of human beings and animals is called in Gaelic 'Brisgein', in English, the thyroid gland. It is sometimes imperfect in a child from birth, in which case the child is dwarfed in mind and body. To remedy this the people applied the 'brisgein' thyroid gland of a sheep in the form of an extract … Not the least curious thing about the old Gaelic remedies is that many of them have been adopted in medical practice. Dr Donald Munro Morrison … remarked that the Highlanders had cures for all the common ailments of man and beast, but where or how they had acquired them he could not understand; he had analysed the plants, earths and other remedies they used, and in no instance were these mis-applied. On the contrary their ingredients were those now used by practitioners in more concentrated form".

Cameron (author of the Gaelic names of plants) says that in the early days the Highlander believed that where a distress was prevalent, nearby would be found the plant which would cure it. With this in mind they experimented with many plants and so found their virtues. Sometimes in these early days, as many plants as possible were gathered and used as a bath.

There was a widespread belief among herbalists of old in what is known as the "Doctrine of Signatures". By this belief, they looked at a plant and from its appearance decided what it resembled and that would be what it would cure. Many yellow plants were used to cure jaundice. Eyebright (Euphrasia officinalis) reminded them of the human eye, so it was used for eye trouble. Lungwort (Pulmonaria officinalis) has a spotted leaf and pink flower turning to blue. This reminded the herbalists of lungs and so was used for lung troubles. There were many others, but as it happens both eyebright and lungwort are still used for these troubles by modern herbalists.

Early in the recognition of microbes the Highland people described them as "fridich bheaga, bhideach, brònach, làn nimhe, neamha agus nàimhdeis". Microbes small, minute, full of spite, venom and hostility.

The gathering of plants for use as medicine, requires considerable knowledge. They must be gathered at the right time, before, during, or after flowering. It is necessary to know the right part to use, for plants vary in their parts, as for instance the potato whose green tomato-like fruit is poisonous, or the leaf of the rhubarb which is also poisonous. Plants may vary in their chemical make-up according to whether they grow in sun or shade, in one type of soil or another. This variation is one of the reasons why modern medicine prefers to get drugs by other means so that they are uniform. The drying and storage of plants is most important, as badly dried plants lose much of their goodness. Both for medicine and for domestic use, plants should be pulled on a dry day in the early morning or early evening. Some plants are volatile; that is they give off fragrance with the heat of the sun, and if pulled at midday will have lost some of their essential oils. The plants should be dried in a warm airy place, out of direct sunshine, for sunlight can cause them to lose their colour. If an ointment is to be made, then some form of fat would be used as a base. In the old days many ointments were made from clarified mutton fat, lard and the like. The herbs might be simmered at the side of the oven in the fat, or might be on the top of the range. If the mixture was not thought to be strong enough, the first herbs might be squeezed out and a fresh bunch added to the fat. Sometimes the herbs might be pounded in a mortar with a pestle and the resulting juice added to the fat. In some instances rhymes and jingles were used in making these and other healing stuffs. This originated from the very sound reason that people did not have clocks and by reciting a rhyme one got the idea of the correct time to boil a pot, etc. with a fair accuracy. Through time some of these rhymes became part of the cure. This does not mean charms and incantations were not used in the Highlands as elsewhere, but that is a different thing altogether. When they talked of "simples" in the old days, they meant that only one herb was being used for medicine etc. but where several were being used they were known as compounds.

The gathering of plants for use as dyes requires knowledge too. Not only do different plants give different colours, but one part of the same plant can give one colour; and a distinct variation or alternate shade can be got from another part. It is necessary to know when to pick. Another consideration is that by the use of a different mordant the same part can give an alternative colour. The mordant is the substance used to retain the colour in the wool so that it remains fast after dyeing. Each fabric will react to dyes in its own way. Wool was by far the commonest fabric to be dyed in the Highlands. Flax was usually left natural or bleached.

Sheep have two types of coat: what we call wool which is a lock, and short hair like a dog. The hair varied according to the climate as the hair gives protection in wet weather. In the wool trade this hair is known as kemp. The wool from different parts of the individual sheep varies in quality. Each part reacts to dye and even to water in a different way. Garments made from dissimilar parts of the same animal will tend to shrink and lose shape as the fibres do not react to water and dye in the same way. The breed of sheep, feeding, and climate, all have a part in the formation of the fleece.

Wool must be carefully handled and stored once it is off the sheep's back. It must be washed before use. Soft water must be used, preferably rain water. In Glencoe and district the water is soft and caused no problem but where it was hard bran was added to the water to soften it. Before washing, the fleece had to be opened up and soiled parts or bits of vegetation removed. Usually the water was heated to hand heat; soap was added to make a

Yellow toadflax (Linaria vulgaris) a plant out of its usual habitat likely carried by the train or by the clothing of passengers.

lather and then the fleece put in to the water. The fleece had to be moved with care to avoid felting. It would be rinsed in several waters, each a little cooler than the one before, and then dried.

In some parts of the country the wool was first spun and then dyed in the hank, in others it was dyed first then spun. Apart from cleanliness, it was necessary to wash the wool before dyeing as the lanolin in the wool prevented the dye from taking. Dyeing requires skill and judgement. One person may get a good clear colour while another from the same plant might have a poor muddy shade. Usually the wool was put in the cauldron, a very large one, with a layer of wool and a layer of the dye plant alternately and the cauldron filled up with water and the desired mordant added. This might be in layers too. The whole would be boiled and, with a stick, the dyer would ease out some of the wool to test it, and if not satisfied with the colour would continue till the result was satisfactory. In some cases the plant was boiled in the water first, then removed, and the wool already mordanted was dyed in the resulting water.

Before the use of alum, Fir Club Moss (Lycopodium selago) was used as a mordant. This plant is the Clan badge of the MacRaes and the Monroes. There is some doubt in certain cases as to which badge was used by each Clan. In these cases I have used what I believed to be the best authority. Staghorn Moss (Lycopium clavatum) was also used as a mordant, Copperas, mostly for black was used, as was salt and urine. This last was kept in a special container.

Before the wool is spun it is carded. This is done with carders. They get their name from the French word "cardere" which means teasel, the wild plant (Dipsacus fullonum) for in the old days this plant was used to tease the wool, remove stray bits of vegetation and to arrange the fibres so that they all ran the same way. Carders have been made for many years. They look like butter pat makers, or Scotch hands, only they have metal spikes fitted to the leather on the inside. The wool is combed by these metal spikes or teeth which makes the wool softer and ready for spinning. This may be done by a spinning wheel, or by a distaff and spindle. The latter is much slower, but a woman could spin on her way to market or when carrying peat on her back. The spinning wheel did not become common in the Highlands till about 1750.

The distaff was about 27 inches long, made of wood and often carved. The spindle was about 10 inches long. When using the spindle and distaff the wool to be spun was loosely attached to the distaff and held under the left arm, the wool itself being in a soft ball with the end of the distaff inserted into it. The spindle was a small tapering piece of wood with a weight of stone or earthenware at the bottom, and on top there was often a split to take the thread. The art of spinning is to get the threads to lie lengthwise and then to twist them— this makes the thread. The spindle was made to rotate and recede from the spinner by a twist; the thread was drawn out between the forefinger and the thumb of the right hand while the spindle twisted. More wool was put on and so it continued. The spinning wheel was used in this area till the 1914–18 War though some may have continued after this date.

After the wool was spun and dyed it would be used for knitting or weaving into cloth or blankets. Unless the man of the house was a weaver, it would not be done in the home but taken to a weaver. The pattern was chosen by the spinner who marked it on a piece of wood. Martin describes it. "The plaid worn by men is made of fine wool, the thread as fine as can be made of that kind. It consists of diverse colours so as to be agreeable to the nicest fancy. For this reason the women are at great pains, first to give an exact pattern of the plaid upon a piece of wood, having the number of every thread of the stripe on it . . ." The principles employed in weaving are much those of the homely darn. The warp is set up, that is the thread which goes from one end of the loom to the other, and the shuttle weaves the weft in and out of the warp.

When the cloth was returned from the weaver it had to be fulled. This was done by the women. It was called waulking. The purpose was to shrink the cloth and by so doing make it closer woven and warmer, and stop further shrinkage when made up. The woven cloth was first wetted with soapy water or ammonia in the form of urine. Often the women would be seated round a stout door which had been taken off its hinges for the job, or failing that, some planks nailed together. The web would be laid on this and by pounding the wet fabric by hand it would be felted and shrunk. The leader would start at a slow pace which would increase, the rhythm would be kept by song. The cloth was passed sunwise round the group, but going to opposite sides of the group backwards and forwards in a zigzag fashion.

When this was finished the cloth was rolled in its web form and the younger ones would remove shoes and stockings and sit on stools or on the ground and kick at the cloth, again in rhythm. All the time the cloth was kept soapy and wet. When the waulking was finished two or three strong men would roll up the cloth on a narrow board as tightly as they could. It would be left thus for a few days, and then unrolled and dried in the sun.

Flax (Linum usitatissimum) was grown in many parts of the Highlands. It is recorded being grown and spun in Appin and thus likely in Glencoe, in both cases for home consumption and not for commercial purposes. Flax is a tall plant with blue flowers. Though it is not difficult to grow, it is not easy to prepare for spinning. The flax is pulled after the flower has faded and before the seed has formed. It is never scythed but pulled from the ground.

To prepare flax for spinning it is necessary to free the fibres from the vegetable part of the plant. This is done in various ways, usually by rotting (or retting as it is called) the plant in water. After various processes the flax is hackled and the remaining bits of vegetation removed from the fibres. The hackle is on the same lines as a carder, but much heavier with teeth about six inches long. But the design varied in different parts of the country.

If we take the plants roughly in the months that they flower, it may help to give a quick reference.

January

In January there would be few flowers open and not enough to be worth using. But pine cones might be available. The Scots pine (Pinus sylvestris) is the Clan badge of the Macgregors, the Grants, the MacAlpines, the MacQuarries and the MacAulays. These badges were worn on the side of the bonnet.

The bark of the pine is astringent and was used for agues, and in some cases the buds were used for scurvy. As a dye the cones gave a soft dull light brown, but if the cones had been picked in early autumn it was possible to get a reddish yellow from them.

In some parts of the Highlands, Rannoch Moor is one of them, the roots of old pine trees were found in the bog. These roots were cut into slivers and used for light. They were held in a metal clamp usually set in a wooden base or sometimes a metal one. They were said to give an excellent light. At one time in Scotland when a wandering beggar or gaberlunzie man came begging he got his supper and his bed but he had the job of holding the light. Later, when the tall iron light stand came in, it became known as the "puirman". There was an old Scottish saying about an unsociable person "He'll neither dance nor hold the candle".

Cruisies were also used for light. They looked like the old Roman lamp but had an under part to catch oil. They burned fish oil and had a rush or cotton wick. They did not give a good light and smelt as they burned.

Rope was made from pine roots. The fibres were cut and plaited together. This made strong rope. Rope was also made from heather. In this case the work was done by two people, one feeding in the heather and the other walking backwards twisting the heather with a stick clockwise. Straw rope was made in the same way.

As well as pine slivers, soft rushes (Juncus effusus) were used to make candles. In this case the longest rushes were cut in summer when they were at their best—likely midsummer. They were soaked in water for forty-eight hours, then dried in the sun. The rushes were then peeled, all but a thin strip of the outer green skin which was left to hold the pith in one piece. The rushes were then coated with fat several times (usually mutton fat) and stored for winter use. They too were held in the middle by metal clamps of the rush light holder, and thus came the saying about "burning your candle at both ends". For the extravagant might indeed allow both ends to burn giving double light. Later when candle moulds became available the rushes were prepared as before and put into the moulds and the hot fat was poured in. Then the rushes were replaced by candlewick, and this in turn was used for embroidery. Small plaited rush rattles were made having small stones inside a rush compartment—a most satisfactory rattle.

Rushes were used for chair seats, bedding and for strewing floors of houses and churches. Fines imposed by the Church for delinquency included money for the poor and rushes for the church, often for the roof as well as the floor.

The bulrush (Scirpus lacustris) is the Clan badge of the MacKays. The aspen (Populus tremula) is the Clan badge of the Fergussons.

From the oak (Quercus robur) a rich dull brown or a black dye could be got. The bark was used for tanning. Every part of the tree is styptic. The bark was used for a gargle for sore throats. The 29th of May was Royal Oak day which commemorated Charles II's escape after the Battle of Worcester when he hid in the Boscobel oak. Oak apples used to be worn on the 29th.

The bird cherry (Prunus padus) the bark would dye wool a soft light brown. In the old days in the Highlands no woman would measure her dye stuffs but work by instinct rather like someone who bakes without measuring, having got their eye trained to assess amounts. In modern charts weights and times are often given as a guide.

The silver birch (Betula verrucosa) the bark dyes wool a soft light brown of dull tone. Later in the year the birch leaves give a greenish yellow dye. The outer rind of the birch tree was called "meilleag" in Gaelic and was used in place of candles. The birch is the Clan badge of the Buchanans.

February

Much would depend upon the season as to what flowered this month. We will assume that it is an early season as this helps not to crowd too many flowers into the later months.

Coltsfoot might be in flower. It is somewhat similar to a dandelion, but has the distinction that the flower comes up first, and when this dies down the leaves appear. The leaves are large for the size of the flower and give it one of its popular names, another is Son before father. Coltsfoot (Tussilago farfara) was considered so valuable that in Paris it was used as a sign of the apothecary's shop.

The fresh leaves or the juice or syrup are all good for a dry cough but the dried leaves are best for rheume. Herbal tobacco contains coltsfoot which is still used in herbal medicine. Coltsfoot candy used to be made for coughs. When coltsfoot goes to seed it does in a somewhat similar way as dandelion. However the seed is thicker and used to be collected and used to stuff pillows.

Ivy (Hedera helix) flowers in winter but is easily recognised at all times of the year. The leaves boiled and mashed till the water was dark, was used in cleaning black silks. It was

Scots pine (Pinus sylvestris). This used to cover a large area of the country but is now confined to small areas.

also used to take the shine out of serge. The leaves soaked in vinegar and applied to corns, was most effective I am told. The twigs boiled in butter made a cure for sunburn. Ivy is the Clan badge of the Gordons.

Some gorse (Ulex europaeus) would be in flower. There is the old country saying that "Kissing is out of flavour when there is no gorse in bloom". Stray flowers are to be seen all the year round. When the fodder for cattle was in short supply in winter, gorse used to be pounded and fed to them. The ash of gorse mixed with clay was used as a soap substitute and for scouring. The plant gave a yellow dye. Bakers used to burn the plant in their ovens to heat them for making bread.

Hazel catkins might be blooming. This tree (Corylus avellana) is the Clan badge of the Colquhouns. It is generally considered unlucky except to the Colquhouns, but two hazelnuts growing together were considered lucky.

The lesser celandine (Ranunculus ficaria) was used by beggars. The irritating juice of the plant caused sores with which it was hoped to get greater alms from the compassionate.

The dandelion (Taraxacum officinale) is St. Bride's plant. Her day is the 1st of February. The white juice of the plant was thought to be good for lambs, who were fed dandelions. The leaves can be used as a salad and an old local cure for ulcers was dandelion leaves between bread and butter. The white juice can be used to cure warts, but it has the disadvantage of blackening the skin temporarily. The plant dyes a soft dull brown if the root alone is used, but the whole plant gives magenta. The root was dried and ground and used as a substitute for coffee. Children like to play with the seed head and play "clocks" with it. This dispersal it to be discouraged as it is an invader but a handsome one. It has another means of survival for it gives off ethylene gas which inhibits the growth of nearby plants.

The laurel (Prunus laurocerasus) the leaves of this plant were used to remove stains. It is the Clan badge of the Maclarens.

The ash (Fraxinus excelsior) is the Clan badge of the Menzies. The bark of the ash can give a blue dye. The seeds of the ash are known as "Keys" and were pickled at one time. Pennant noted a strange use for the ash. He writes "In many parts of the Highlands at the birth of a child, the nurse puts the end of a green stick of ash into the fire, and while it is burning receives into a spoon the sap or juice which comes out at the other end and administers this to the new-born babe".

March

Perhaps the primrose is the best loved of spring flowers. The primrose (Primula vulgaris) had many uses, the leaves were used as a salve for wounds, the flowers could be made into a pudding or pottage and wine made from the petals. Chickweed (Stellaria media) was made into poultices for carbuncles and abscesses. The water in which chickweed was boiled, was drunk as a slimming aid. The plant chopped and simmered in lard made a good healing ointment. Bracken (Pteridium aquilinuma) is the Clan badge of the Chisholms and the Robertsons. The roots would dye yellow and the leaves and young shoots a brownish green. Bracken was used for bedding for cattle and dried and used for filling mattresses. This was renewed each year. Dr Lightfoot writes of it "In the North the inhabitants mow it green and burning it to ashes, make these ashes into balls with a little water. These are dried in the sun and they are then used to wash linen instead of soap". Fern ash was a commercial proposition in the Highlands and in 1764 barrels of fern ash sold at 7/- per barrel and were exported to Liverpool. The ash was sold to manufacturers of glass and soap. In some parts of the country it was used for thatching.

Hart's-tongue fern (Phyllitis scolopendrium) made into an ointment was an old Highland cure for burns. Polypody (Polypodium vulgare) leaves dyed wool a soft clear yellow using alum as a mordant. The plant was also used for the cure of catarrh. Spleenwort (Asplenium trichomanes) was used for disorders of the spleen. Male fern (Dryopteris filix mas) was used for worms. Ferns in general were supposed to have magic properties. As they had no obvious flowers and the spores at the back of the leaf were ignored magic seemed the best way to account for its increase. Moonwort (Botrychium lunaria) could by magic take the shoes off horses which crossed their territory.

The daisy (Bellis perennis) made a healing ointment for cuts and bruises. It, like the dandelion is capable of restricting the growth of neighbouring plants by giving off a toxic substance. It has been noticed by flower arrangers that if shasta daisies (a relative of the common daisy) is put in water with other plants that it can cause them to wither. The common daisy is a great favourite with children though I have seen fewer daisy chains in the last ten years than I used to see. I hope this activity has not declined.

From groundsel (Senecio vulgaris) a lotion was made for chapped hands, boiling water was poured over the plant and the resulting liquid used. Boiling water poured over groundsel then thickened with oatmeal was excellent for a festering wound. Horses tail (Equisetum arvense) was used for cleaning pans and gave a grey dye. A similar plant common Mare's tail (Hippuris vulgaris) has the ability to extract minute traces of gold which resides in some soils, not however practical to recover in economic terms.

Spurge laurel (Daphne laureola) was used for rheumatism. Sanicle (Sanicula europaea) was used externally and internally as an astringent and vulnerary.

April

The violet (Viola riviniana) was used in cases of fever. The plant was boiled in whey and the decoction was considered very good. In the Highlands violets were used as a cosmetic. This is shown in the following lines.

Bog Asphodel (Narthecium ossifragum) flowers in July and August. It is common and typical of the wet bogland.

Above: Flag Iris (Iris pseudacorus) a plant with an interesting history of different uses.

Above right: Sea Aster (Aster tripolium) this plant of the sea shore is shown growing in a tidal pool. Its narrow fleshy leaves which can withstand the effect of salt water.

Sail-chuach as bainne ghabhar
Suadh re t-aghaidh
'S cha 'n 'eil mac righ 'air an domhain
Nach bi air do dheigh.

Anoint thy face with goats milk in which violets have been infused and there is not a young prince on earth who would not be charmed with thy beauty.

The leaves of the violet are antiseptic and were used for skin diseases. The marsh violet (Viola palustris) was used as rennet on milk.

The cuckoo flower or Lady's smock (Cardamine pratensis) which flowers at the end of April, but is more plentiful in May, is a fever plant, and had at one time a reputation for helping in cases of epileptic fits. It was used as a spring salad and was helpful in cases of scurvy.

The sycamore (Acer pseudoplatanus) is the Clan bade of the Oliphants. Butterbur (Petatites hybridus) was used for cases of fever and dropsy. Dog's mercury (Mercurialis perennis) was used for wounds, and gave a good dull yellow ochre when used as a dye, however with long boiling it produced a blueish tone. Bilberry (Vaccinium myrtillus) used with alum gave a violet dye, without the alum it gave a blueish dye. Dr Lightfoot writes "The berries have an astringent quality . . . given in diarrhoea. The Highlanders frequently eat them in milk, which is a cooling and agreeable food, and sometimes they make them into tarts and jellies, which last they mix with whisky to give it relish to give to a stranger".

93

Blackthorn (Prunus spinosa) is not common here but is plentiful in the island of Lismore. The flowers were used as a laxative, and later in the year the berries were used in fevers and dropsy. Sloe jelly was used for a relaxed throat and the berries were used as ink. Wool can be dyed red or blueish black according to which part of the plant is used. The flowers made into an infusion were used externally for scabies. A decoction of the root and bark was used for asthma. Wood sorrel (Oxalis acetosella) is a plant that has leaves which children enjoy eating. It used to be used to allay fever. It was boiled in water and the resulting liquid quenched the thirst and reduced the fever. A green sauce was made by pulping the leaves and adding sugar and vinegar. The plant was also used to take rust marks out of linen. Wood Avens (Geum urbanum) sometimes called Herb Bennet, was boiled as pottage. Mountain avens (Dryas octopetala) is a plant of the moors. I have known those who made jam of the fruit but have not seen this in any book. Fat hen (Chenopium album) gives a reddish to reddish gold dye. It was used as a pottage in the Highlands where the leaves were boiled, pounded and had butter added. Its near relation Good King Henry (Chenopodium-henricus) is an old fashioned perannial vegetable and can be used in the same way.

May

In some parts of the country tea was made from ground ivy (Glechoma hederacea) this tea was drunk two or three times a day for consumption and coughs. The tea was sweetened with honey. Snuff was made from the dried leaves of ground ivy and this was used in cases of asthma and to clear headaches. From periwinkles (Vinca major and minor) an ointment was made with lard or other fat to heal bruises. The leaves too were healing for skin irritations. Bog bean (Menyanthes trifoliata) was used in the village within living memory. The plant was put in a stone jar and simmered on the old range. The resulting water was drunk as a spring tonic. Sometimes the stems were boiled for two hours, pulped, left to cool, the liquid strained and bottled for winter. A teaspoon three times a day for a persistent cough was most effective.

The common nettle would be getting plentiful by now, though not perhaps in flower. The plant (Urtica dioica) had many uses. It was an excellent spring tonic used as a pot herb. This is the only time to use it internally for once it is over six inches it develops acid crystals which are harmful. The young spring nettles bring to mind the old rhyme:

If they wad drink nettles in March and eat muggins in May
Sae many braw maidens, wadna gang to clay.

Muggins is the Scots word for the plant Mugwort (Artemisia vulgaris) a plant which dyes yellow. It was considered that travellers who carried mugwort with them would not tire. It has a bitter taste but it is said to strengthen the stomach and create an appetite.

The nettle gave a yellow dye if salt was the mordant used. If alum was used it would dye green. Rennet can be made from nettles. The fibre of the nettle can be spun instead of flax. The Scots poet Campbell said of the nettle "In Scotland I have eaten nettles, I have slept on nettle sheets, and I have dined off a nettle tablecloth. The young and tender nettle is an excellent pot herb. The stalks of the old nettles are as good as flax for making cloth. I have heard my mother say that she thought nettle cloth more durable than any other species of linen". In Scotland nettles were forced as an early vegetable and in Sir Walter Scott's Rob Roy, Andrew Fairservice, the gardener, raised early nettles under glass. Nettle pudding was made with leeks or onions, broccoli or cabbage and rice boiled in a muslin bag served with butter and gravy, cut up and dried it was eaten with relish by beasts. The nettle is the food plant for a number of caterpillars and if you have the space a small clump of nettles can mean butterflies in your garden. At one time a spray was made with nettles and used for mildew. Old tea leaves boiled with a few nettle tops were used to clean nankeen or Holland linen.

The docken (Rumex obtusifolius) was sometimes used in place of bog bean. A decoction taken internally was said to be good for scurvy. Used with alum it gave a yellow dye. Water dock (Rumex hydrolapathum) was used as a dentifrice.

The rowan would be in flower. This tree (Sorbus aucuparia) is sometimes called the mountain ash in the south. The tree was considered most valuable for keeping witches and fairies away from the home, and one was often planted in the front of the house. The berries make an excellent jelly to eat with mutton or venison. It is the Clan badge of the MacLauchlans. A good gargle can be made from the berries by boiling them till pulp, then they should be squeezed through a muslin and strained for use. According to Dr Lightfoot the Highlanders often eat the berries when ripe. This is not now considered wise.

The scurvy plant or more usually scurvy grass (Cochlearoa officinalis) as its name denotes was used against scurvy. This was a prevalent disease when so little fresh food was available in winter and so much dried and salted food eaten instead. Scurvy was not only gathered wild, but it was also cultivated, and as late as the 19th century was taken at breakfast.

White clover (Trifolium repens) is the Clan badge of the Sinclairs. This is one of the weatherwise plants, in dry weather the leaves are relaxed but in wet weather they are held erect. Red clover (Trifolium pratense) was used for eczema.

The May or hawthorn (Crataegus monogyma) may or may not flower in May. It got its name before the calendar was changed in the 18th century. Both the flowers and the leaves were made into decoctions for sore throats. The berries were eaten. Both flowers and berries can make good wine. Children used to eat the young shoots.

Brooklime (Veronica beccabunga) is a small plant of the damp ditches. It was used as an anti-scorbic eaten as a salad. Evergreen alkenet (Pentaglottis sempervirens) is the Clan badge of the Ogilvies. Ox eyed daisy (Chrysanthemum leucanthemum) is known as gowans in Scotland. It was used for asthma. The juice of the plant boiled with honey was used for coughs, and externally for wounds. Herb Robert (Geranium robertianum) was used for cancer, and at times in veterinary medicine for horses. Bishop weed (Aegopodium podagraria) also known as ground elder was at one time cultivated and used in cases of gout. A poultice of the plant was used too in cases of sciatica. It was also used as a pot herb.

Some of our wild orchids were at one time used to make salop, particularly two blade (Listera ovata). In the 18th century salop (or dried ground orchid) sold at 1/- per ounce.

Cherry (Prunus avium) is called gean in Scotland. A tissane of the stalks of the cherries made an astringent. The gum from the bark dissolved in wine was used for colds, the root will dye purple red, the bark a cream to tan colour. Couch grass (Agropyron repens) was used for wounds. Ivy leafed toadflax (Cymbalaria muralis) was an antiscorbic plant. Shepherds purse (Capsella bursa-pastoris) was used for diarrhoea and also for external and internal haemorrhages in man and beast. The alder (Alnus glutinosa) was used as a gargle, the bark and twigs would dye a warm brown. The plant was also used to cure green wounds and ulcers. Tormentil (Potentilla erecta) was used to tan leather. An infusion of the root was used to cure dysentery. Dr Lightfoot writes "A spirituous extract of the plant stands recommended in the sea-scurvy and to strengthen the gums and fasten the teeth". Islesmen used tormentil roots to tan their nets. Common sorrel (Rumex acetosa) gives a red dye. It is another antiscorbic plant. It was also used to heal wounds and sores.

During the spring when milk was scarce it was the custom to give the calves an infusion of hay and this appeared to be nourishing. The roots of docks (Rumex obtusifolius) boiled till the juice was extracted in a quantity of butter, strained through a cloth and mixed with flowers of brimstone was used in cases of inflamed udders of heifers. Broad pond weed (Potamogeton natans) was gathered in the summer and dried and made into bundles. These were fed to the cattle in the form of an infusion. It was said to improve the milk yield and to protect the cows and their milk from the wiles of witches.

Ramsons, a form of garlic (Allium ursinum) was much appreciated. There is the Gaelic couplet "Is leigheas air gach tinn, Creamh 'us im a Mhaigh". Garlic and May butter are the remedies for every ill". The leaves were boiled as a vegetable. The root was added to other plants and used in cases of scabies and ringworm. Garlic has a hollow stem and it was under the Doctrine of Signatures thus used for windpipe disorders. It is an antiseptic herb and was used as late as the 1914–18 War to deal with suppurating wounds. Crab apple (Pyrus malus) is the Clan badge of the Lamonts. Deer grass (Scirpus cespitosus) is the Clan badge of the MacKenzies.

June

The meadow sweet or Queen of the meadow (Filipendula ulmaria) was used in soups or stews, an infusion of the dried leaves and flowering tops was used for colds. A distilled water made from the flowers was used for the complexion. It was one of the old strewing herbs. Used with alum the plant minus the root gives a greenish yellow dye, while the root alone will give red. It makes an excellent wine.

Thyme (Thymus drucei) is the Clan badge of the Drummonds. Thyme is still used in the kitchen, and in modern medicine under the name of thymal. In older days it was used to help in cases of whooping cough when the fresh herb was mixed with syrup. It was also used in cases of colic to relieve the pain. Bog cotton (Eriophorum augustifolium) is the Clan badge of the Hendersons and the Sutherlands. It was sometimes used for stuffing pillows, and if very fine quality was needed the green part was removed. In parts of the Highlands a girl was not considered fit for marriage till she had made a shirt for her lover and stockings for herself from bog cotton. Wicks for candles have been made out of it.

The leaves of Flag Iris (Iris pseudacorus) made a green dye, and the root a black dye or a dark grey. The root was used medically to make snuff for colds. The iris is the origin of the Fleurs de lis. King Louis of the Franks was threatened by a Goth army at the bend of the Rhine at Cologne but noticed flag iris growing out into the river, and realising the water must be shallow there, he forded the river with his army and escaped the larger Goth force.

The elder (Sambucus nigra) was a guard against witches and fairies. Often an elder tree was planted at the back of the house while the rowan guarded the front. Elder blossom was used to make elderflower water which was used for the complexion and clear away freckles. The leaves were disliked by flies and they were used to rub meat as a protective measure. Both the blossom and the berries make good wine. In the 18th century Mrs Glasse gives a recipe for "Elder shoots in imitation of bamboo". But probably that was not in general use. The Glencoe recipe is "Boyle in burn water elder flower heads with some rough birch bark, this is strained and taken as a spring tonic". An ointment was made for dressing wounds and burns. The flower heads were infused in warm lard. Dr Lightfoot writes that the inner green bark was put in wine, half an ounce to one ounce of the expressed juice and used as a mild purgative. The infusion of the flowers made a mild laxative. Elder jelly or rob (that is the juice of the fruit reduced by boiling with syrup and used as jam and pickles and chutney were made from elder. An old street cry used to be "Here's elder buds to purge your blood". Sea Aster (Aster tripolium) was used as a wound herb.

Long before the coming of the potato in the Highlands the plant silverweed (potentilla anserina) which has a tuberous root, was eaten and even cultivated. The tubers were boiled, roasted, or dried and ground for porridge. It was a most valuable food, for it was

Silverweed (Potentilla anserina) a food crop and a medical one.

both palatable and nutritious, not like some famine foods used in time of stress. It used to be said that a man could live in his own length in a square of ground cultivated with silverweed. When cultivated it grew to a considerable size. Apart from this use, the plant made an excellent gargle when infused and sweetened with honey.

St John's wort (Hypericum) is the Clan badge of the MacKinnons. It was said to stop evil and more prosaically used as a tonic and to heal gangrenous wounds. There is a story that St Columba found a small boy watching cattle night and day, weeping with fear when night came on. The Saint plucked some St John's wort, put it under the boy's arm and bade him sleep and fear not. Dr Lightfoot writes "The superstitious in Scotland carry it about with them as a charm against dire effects of witchcraft and enchantment. They also cure, or fancy they cure their ropy milk which they suppose to be under some malignant influence, by putting this herb into it and milking afresh upon it". The flowers were used in hair lotions and gargles. The plant without the root dyes yellow, the flower buds in vinegar dyes crimson.

Woundwort (Stachys arvensis) was used to heal wounds. It gave a yellow dye. Stamped in vinegar and used as a poultice it took away wens and inflammations. Woundwort was still cultivated and sold in markets as late as 1812—possibly later nasturtiums were on sale as a vegetable. Bugle (Ajuga reptans) might well have flowered in May, and later a very similar plant known as selfheal (Prunella vulgaris) appears. Both plants are astringent and were used for kidney and liver diseases.

Enchanters nightshade (Circaea lutetiana) gave protection from evil though in the south it was considered to be associated with evil. Ragwort (Senecio jacobaea) will dye orange. In some parts of the Highlands it was plaited into rope. By tradition it is said to have come to Scotland first in the fodder that was used by the horses under the command of Butcher Cumberland. It is known as "Stinking Willie" in Scotland after Cumberland.

> Let Warlocks grim, an' ragwort wither'd nags,
> Tell how wi' you on rag-weed nags,
> They skim the muirs, and dizzy crags,
>   Wi' wicked speed;
> And in kirk-yards renew their leagues
>   Owre howkit dead.—*Burns*

The plant acquired an unenviable reputation as Burns shows.

Meadow Cranesbill (Geranium pratense) was used as an astringent herb and in cases of colitis. It was used too, for stopping the bleeding after a tooth had been pulled out. The species known as bloody cranesbill (Geranium sanguineum) was held in special repute in the Highlands because of its astringent and vulnery properties. Woodsage (Teucrium scorodonia) was used for making poultices for external cancers and as a blood purifier. It was sometimes used as a gargle. Meliot (Melilotus officinalis) was used boiled in lard or fat for ulcers. Water avens (Geum rivale) was used to cleanse the breath, the root being chewed. The seeds of stonecrop (Sedum anglicum) were used with a linen rag to stop the itch. The wild dog rose (Rosa canina) provided hips which were used as late as the War of 1939–45 to provide vitamin C for the children. I might add that the white rose became the emblem of the House of Stuart. Various theories have been put forward as to why this was chosen and it has been considered likely that they chose the white rose as being in the legitimate line as was the York line, against the usurping Lancaster line with its red rose. The 10th of June is white rose day when the Jacobites wore a white rose. It was the birthday of James VIII of Scotland and III of England. Many of the fine Jacobite glasses had a rose or rose and buds engraved on it.

Angelica (Angelica sylvestris). The wild form of this plant grows here by the shore. Whether it was used locally or not I have not made certain, possibly not, but old cook books have recipes for angelica tarts as well as the more usual candied form. It also makes an excellent jam along with rhubarb $\frac{3}{4}$ rhubarb and $\frac{1}{4}$ angelica or thereby. Bog myrtle (Myrica gale) is the Clan badge of the Campbells and the MacIntyres. The cones of the plant give off a scum-like wax, when boiled. This was used to make candles. The root gives a yellow dye and the dried leaves give linen a delightful fragrance. The dried leaves (or fresh) may be added to stews and other such dishes. It repelled fleas. Bog myrtle beer is sometimes made. Sweet cicely (Myrrhis ororata) was used for constipation, for coughs and debility. The dose was a handful of leaves or some of the root sliced and taken daily. Hemlock (Conium maculatum) a poisonous plant but one which was used under strict medical supervision and helped in cases of cancer. The guilder rose (Viburnum opulus) was used for cramp. Rosebay willow herb (Chamaenerion augustifolium) was used for asthma. The down of the seeds was at one time manufactured and the young underground shoots were eaten. The dried seeds of sticky Willie or goosegrass (Gallium aparine) were used as a substitute for coffee, and a tissane made from the plant was used for sleeplessness and for comfort in colds. As a slimming recipe it was taken in soup. The plant gives a red dye.

Mention must be made of the Machar. This is the low-lying sandy shore by the sea. It is fertile and provides an early bit. Some parts having a living carpet of wild flowers.

Houseleek (Sempervivum tectorum) was used for shingles and for burns and mixed with cream for earache. For fevers it was given warm in milk. Box (Buxus sempervirens) is the Clan badge of the Macphersons and the Macintoshes. It was used for fevers. Scullcap (Scutellaria galericulata) was used in nervous disorders.

Milkwort (Polygala vulgaris) was said to improve the supply of milk to beasts and it might also be given to nursing mothers. It was eaten raw, a few plants a day. It was also considered a safe purge. It was used in fevers as a decoction. The seeds were used to cure worms, and the powdered root was used for pleurisy. The leaves give a green dye. Butterwort (Pinguicula vulgaris) was used in dairies for the coagulation of milk. It was also distilled for a summer drink. Lady's bedstraw (Galium verum) perhaps more likely to flower in July, had its roots scraped to make a red dye, and it was also used to colour the butter yellow. Woodruff (Galium odoratum) was used as an anti moth herb giving off a pleasant smell. It was used to help sufferers from chest complaints and consumption, and it was said to increase the milk yield.

Kidney vetch (Anthyllis vulneraria) was used to make an ointment for cuts and bruises. Soapwort (Saponaria officinalis) was used for washing and makes quite a lather. It is still used for washing fine tapestries. Ragged robin (Lychnis floscuculi) was used for cleaning. The wild hyacinth (Endymion non-scripta) sometimes called the bluebell in the south dyes a soft blue, not usually used as a dye plant but was so used in this area with good result. The bulb provides starch for the laundry. The plant is styptic. Horse chestnut conkers (Aesculus hippocastanum) were used to make soapy water. The bark was used for tanning, and it gave a warm brown dye. Soap was not an easily come by commodity so this natural material was most welcome. Even within living memory people living in out of the way places had to depend on their own efforts to make soap.

Figwort (Scrophularia nodosa) was used for food in time of famine, but it had an unpleasant taste and little nourishment. It was, however, useful in healing; figwort poultices for ulcers, skelfs, abscess, wounds and so forth. It was said to help sufferers from measles and was used for scab in pigs. It was also used in scrofula. Comfrey (Symphytum officinale) was sometimes called knitbone. It was used for curing wounds, for healing broken bones and again in lung troubles, quinsey and coughs. At one time the young leaves were eaten as a salad. It is said to be excellent on the compost heap. It is however very invasive so care must be taken.

Spignel (Meum athamanticum) the leaves are said to taste of celery and can be used in salads. Highlanders used to chew the roots, used as a spice and carminitive. Oyster plant (Mertensia maritima) is a plant of the stony shore. It has become rare. It has bluey green leaves the shape of a mussel (or perhaps oyster) these are held stiffly, the flower is blue. The leaves can be eaten and taste similar to oysters, but nowadays even if you come on one don't feed on it—it's much too scarce.

July

Honeysuckle (Lonicera periclymenum) was used for asthma and an ointment was made from the plant for freckles and sunburn. A tissane made from it was used to cure headaches. It can also make wine. The berries however, are poisonous. Feverfew (Chrysanthemum parthenium) was used to cure fevers and it was said to be good for flatulence. A fly repellent could be made by using two teaspoons of the plant to half a pint of cold water. Purging flax or fairy flax (Linum catharticum) was considered a safe purge, a handful of plants were infused in whey or water or the plants could be pulverised and a drachm taken. Toadflax (Linaria vulgaris) was used for jaundice and boiled in milk or whey it was used to kill fleas. Foxglove (Digitalis purpurea) is well known for its use in heart trouble. It was William Withering, a Shropshire doctor, enquiring into local treatment of dropsy who from that research began to use foxglove tea. He wrote a book on this, published in 1785. In it he writes "It has power over the motion of the heart to a degree yet unobserved in any other medicine ..." Though digitalis is still used it is now obtained from other sources than the foxglove. An ointment made from the leaves was used in scrofulous cases. The plant is the Clan badge of the Farquharsons.

Roseroot (Sedum rosea) is a plant of the hills. It is the Clan badge of the Gunns. The plant was used to heal malignant ulcers. It is a remedy for scurvy. A fragrant kind of rosewater can be distilled from the roots. Hemp agrimony (Eupatorium cannabinum) was used as a wound herb. Sometimes an ointment made with lard or fat and at other times the fresh bruised leaves were used. The wild strawberry (Fragaria vesca) was said to keep tartar off the teeth and to keep gout at bay. The leaves were used for diarrhoea. The leaves slightly heated were used for inflamed places.

Honeysuckle (Lomicera periclymenum) the plant that scents the evening air in summer.

97

Sundew (Drosera rotundifolia) one of our few native insect eating plants, grows in damp places on the hills. It was used for asthma and whooping cough. The juice of the plant was used for warts and corns. It gave a yellow dye but if the root alone was used the colour this gave was purple. Salad burnet (Poterium sanguisorba) has pleasant cucumber flavoured leaves. Barberry (Berberis vulgaris) was used for jaundice and the inner bark steeped in wine was a purgative. The berries were cooked and used for tarts and preserves. Privet (Ligustrum vulgare) berries with alum gives a green dye, and with salt added, a blueish green; with alum and cream of tartar the leaves and branches give a yellow dye. Golden rod (Solidago virgaurea) was used to heal broken bones and if picked before flowering will give a yellow dye. Broom (Sarothamnus scoparius) is the Clan badge of the Forbes. Broom tops were at one time a special delicacy and were so used at the coronation of James VII of Scotland and James II of England. The seeds were used as a substitute for coffee, the plant was used for thatching in some parts and of course brooms were made of it. A proverb of 1562 "The greene new bourne sweepeth cleene". Juniper (Juniperus communis) was used to cure dropsy. Broom and juniper were used together to cure dropsy. The dwarf cornel (Chamaepericlymenum suecicum) was known as the gluttony plant as it was used to restore the appetite after illness. Ribwort plantain (Plantago lanceolata) had its roots brewed for fevers and the leaves were used for healing. Waterlily (Nymphaea alba) roots were used to dye wool black or dark blue. The white form was considered best, but the yellow (Nuphar lutea) could be used in the same way. The roots of both plants were used to heal boils.

Watercress (Rorippa nasturtium-aquaticum) was used for fevers. But the plant had one disadvantage for, with its help witches could steal milk by "charming" it (that is stealing from the cow by magic and without direct contact with the cow). The plant was cut and the witch chanted something like this, "'S leumsa leth do chuidsa". "Half thine is mine". This charming of milk could be prevented by the aid of groundsel, if the plant was put in the milk or cream. Watercress is an excellent antiscorbic plant. Burdock (Arctium minus) was used in the form of a decoction for jaundice and fevers. The bruised leaves were applied outwardly to ringworn. The roots and stalks were eaten and found nourishing, this before the flowering period. The rind was pulled off and the rest was taken raw with oil and vinegar or boiled. Corn marigold (Chrysanthemum segetum) gives a clear bright yellow dye. Vervain (Verbena officinalis) was used for nervous diseases. Cow wheat (Melampyrum pratense) gives a rich golden hue to milk and this milk makes the best butter. Stitchwort (Stellaria holostea) was used for the stitch. Cudweed (Filago germanica) was used for sciatica. Common cromwell (Lithospermum officinale) was used for the stone. Rest harrow (Ononis repens) has a sweet sticky root which used to be chewed. Petty spurge (Euphorbia peplus) juice was used to cure warts. Bog asphodel (Nartheciun assifragum) is typical of the acid, boggy soil in the Highlands.

August

Devil's bit scabious (Succisa pratensis) was a plant of great repute. It was believed that the devil had bitten off a part of the root because he was so jealous of the benefit that mankind got from the plant. The same root was boiled in wine against the plague. The juice was used to cure green wounds, and the root was used for toothache. With alum the plant gave a greeny-yellow dye. Scabious was used as its name denoted for scabies.

The tuberous bitter vetch (Lathyrus motanus) known in Gaelic as "Cairmeille" was dried and the roots were chewed to ward off hunger when going on a long journey. It was made into a liqueur when bruised and steeped in water. Dr Lightfoot writes "The Highlanders have a great esteem for the tubercles of the root of this plant; they dry and chew them in general to give a better relish to their liquor; they also affirm them to be good against most disorders of the thorax and that by the use of them they are enabled to stand hunger and thirst for a long time ... They have a sweet taste something like the root of liquorice and when boiled we are told are well flavoured and nutritive in times of scarcity have served as a substitute for bread".

Willow was used to make baskets and creels. When we remember that roads were few and far between and that even the best were poor by modern standards, and that most people living in the Highlands would have to carry stuff by hand or by horse, it is easy to see how important the willow was in the economy of the croft and the home. Fish would be carried in willow creels, the seaweed to be used as manure carried from the shore to the land, and the peat from the peat bed to the home. All had to be carried by horse or by hand. Even the knitting of the women was carried in a willow basket. Medically the willow was used for the ague and as a sedative. It had a most unpleasant taste and upset many stomachs. Research into the plant isolated the healing parts and it was reproduced and manufactured under the name of "asperine". There was a saying "It is time to be steeping the withies" meaning "it is time to go". At one time the harness of the horse was made of withies (willow) and when the withies were laid aside for a while they became stiff and brittle and it would be necessary to soak them in water to make them malleable again. Willow ropes and bridles were made.

Knapweed (Centaurea nigra) was used as a dye and gave a good green. Yarrow (Achillea millefolium) was used as a styptic. A salve was made from the flowers. Yarrow tea was drunk for colds and rheumatism. If going a journey it was the custom to kneel down and say while the right hand was on the plant "In the name of the Father and Son and Spirit journey prosper". The plant was used for consumption, and sometimes eaten as a salad. Heather (Calluna vulgaris) gave a green dye. Heather is the Clan badge of the MacDonalds and the bell heather of heath (Erica cinerea) is the Clan badge of the MacDougalls. Heather honey is held to be one of the best of honeys. Many beekeepers move their hives near the heather to get this delicacy. Heather ale was an old drink of the Picts. By tradition the receipt was lost, however, heatherwine and ale may still be made with modern recipes. Wild plants adapt to their habitat. The sedum grows where water is scarce or drains away quickly and has leaves which store water. The plants of the mountain tops grow in small compact clumps giving protection from the strong winds, while those of the sea aster (Aster tripolium) and the sea pink or thrift (Armeria maritima) have fleshy narrow leaves that can withstand sea water. The photo shows sea aster covered by the tide yet surviving.

September

Brambles (Rubus fruticosus) makes good jam, jelly and wine. The roots taken from the ground in February and March and boiled with honey was an old remedy for dropsy. The fresh young shoots give a warm grey dye and the full plant gives an orange dye. The bramble is the Clan badge of the MacLeans. The seed of bramble is so viable that it has been known to germinate after it has been made into jam.

Spagnum moss was used to dress wounds as recently as the last War. It was collected locally from the hills for this work. There is a tradition that the Highlanders used it after Flodden.

Lichens were a most valuable source of dyes. Crotal is the best known of them. It is one of the easiest plants to use for dyeing. Crotal (Parmena saxatalis) colours wool a good warm reddish brown to dark brown. Lichens were scraped off the rocks. Nowadays this is considered best gathered in August after rain and may be used fresh or dried in the sun. In the old days, it was scraped off and cleaned and steeped in urine for three months, then taken out and made into cakes and hung to dry in bags. When the cakes were to be used, they were reduced to powder and the colour fixed with alum, though in this case care had to be taken not to use too much as it hardened and coarsened the wool. At one time crotal used to be gathered and dried and sold to the Glasgow dyers. This lichen had another use. Highlanders used to sprinkle it on their stockings before going on a long journey as it was believed to help prevent inflamed feet. There is a Gaelic saying about crotal "Siridh air mointeach or air clachan"—"Cattle on the hill gold on the stones". Wool dyed with crotal was never used for seaman's jerseys. There was an old superstition about "rock to rock" meaning that as crotal had grown on rock, so rock would claim it back. Hooker in his "Flora Scotica" of 1821 writes "Leanora tartareus or cudbear is employed to produce a purple dye ... in the Highland districts many an industrious peasant gets a living by scraping this lichen with an iron hoop and sending to the Glasgow market. When I was in Fort Augustus in 1807 a person could earn 14/- a week at this work selling the material at 3/4d. the stone of 22lbs.

Sea weeds though hardly regarded as wild flowers were used as both food and medicine. Hooker in Flora Scotica writes "Ulva lactuaca or green laver oyster-green served occasionally stewed with lemon juice is esteemed good as indeed almost all esculent vegetables are for scrophulous habits". Carrageen makes an excellent pudding with milk. The great kelp industry did not touch our shores in Glencoe, but briefly, the process was this; seaweed was collected and dried on the shore then put in trenches between layers of peat where it was burned for its ash. This ash was used for bleaching linen and for making glass and soap. The cause of the boom was due to the Napoleonic War the imported barilla from Spain became difficult to get. But in 1820 barilla* was again imported and the kelp industry declined. At one time kelp cost about £15 a ton. Seaweed was used a great deal for manure for which it is excellent. Shell sand was used as lime on the land. Again this is excellent. The beasts both domestic and wild came down to the shore to eat the seaweed. The Clan badge of the MacNeils is seware.

Sneezewort (Achillea ptarmica) this plant was dried and used as snuff. Holly (Ilex aquifolium) was used for the lungs; the leaves were used in fractures and the berries for dropsy. The inner bark was boiled and left to ferment and made bird lime. Grass of Parnassus (Parnassia palustris) was used for liver complaints. Mistletoe (Viscum album) was used for epilepsy. Puff ball (Lycoperdon giganteum) was used for wounds. The common field gentian (Gentianella campestris) was used in cases of "croodling" in horses. In this ailment the front and hind feet are drawn together. In autumn the needles of the larch (Pinus larix) were used to dye brown. It is said that one of the first larches to come to Scotland was brought by one of the Dukes of Athole. The gardener tended it carefully in a pot in a greenhouse but slowly it went back and finally he threw it outside in disgust whereupon it grew and thrived. Juniper (Juniperus communis) is the Clan badge of the Murrays. It was used to give a brown dye. The cloudberry (Rubus chamaemorus) was the Clan badge of the Macfarlanes. The blueberry (Rubus caesius) is the Clan badge of the Macnabs. The cowberry or whortleberry (Vaccinium vitis-idaea) is the Clan badge of the Macleods. The yew (Taxus baccata) is the Clan badge of the Frasers. At one time it was ruled that in Scotland churchyards must grow yews as a source of arrows. The wallflower (Cheiranthus cheiri) is the Clan badge of the Urquharts. Goatsbeard (Tragopogon pratensis) was used for stomach troubles and gave a green dye. Orphine (Sedum telephium) was used for burns and sores. Wild pansy (Viola arvensis) cured diahorrea in children.

The campanula rotundifolia known as harebell in the south and recognised as the bluebell of Scotland in the north would flower but was not used so far as I know for medicine or other use. Also in flower at this time would be Mountain everlasting

* Barilla is the name for glasswort or marsh samphene (Salicornia herbacea).

Wild carrot (Dancus carota) was used medically.

(Antennaria dioica) known as the Scotch edelweiss, it is an attractive low growing everlasting. A nice story about plantains, not in the Highlands but in the south. At the time of the War between Stephen and Maud, Stephen was besieging Newbury Castle held by John Gilbert who asked for a truce. At that date it was forbidden to take in reinforcements during a truce. The truce was granted and Gilbert handed over his four-year-old son as hostage. He took in reinforcements and it was suggested that the boy be catapulted into the Castle. Stephen vetoed this but was going to hang the child then changed his mind. The child, in later years Earl of Pembroke, used to tell how he and Stephen made "war" with the plantain stalks strewn on the floor.

Bladder campion (Silene vulgaris) was eaten and was said to taste like green peas. From Fumitary (Fumaria officinalis) a yellow dye was obtained. The roots of elecampane (Inula helenium) were candied.

On Michaelmas Day (29th September) some of the Hebridean Islands held a festival in which the wild carrot (Daucus carota) featured.

A poultice of carrot eased the pain of cancerous ulcers, and the leaves with honey cleaned sores and ulcers. Lovage (Scotch) (Ligusticum scoticum) was used in the Hebrides as a pot herb and also an infusion in whey was given to calves as a purgative.

The homely blackcurrant (Ribes nigrum) was used for sore throats usually given as a rub or jelly or a drink and an infusion of the leaves was considered cleansing. The gooseberry (Ribes uva-crispa) got its name because it was eaten with goose in the old days.

Besides these few plants listed there are many more. A great many more than these few listed were used for even more aids for I have not mentioned all the various uses to which some plants were put. Many more were possibly used but in what way has not come down to us. The reason why the Latin name is given is that there are many wild plants which have different names in different areas which can lead to confusion.

Apart from the use of wild flowers in medicine, as dye plants etc., quite a number of garden plants had their uses. Marigold (Calendula officinalis) gave a yellow dye. The petals were used in soup something which Charles Lamb disliked so much. Marigold cheese was made and also a skin ointment. Charles I wrote "The Marigold observes the sun more than my Subjects me have done".

The raspberry (Rubus idaeus) provided a gargle made from its leaves and this same mixture (1 ounce dried leaves to 1 pint of boiling water) was used to wash wounds and ulcers. An infusion of the leaves was said to make a confinement easier. Tansy (Taracetum vulgare) sometimes growing wild but often a garden escape plant was used to repel flies so meat was often rubbed with it and bunches kept in the larder. Tansy was used for fever in horses. Easter pudding was made with tansy, a very little of the plant which has a strong taste. Tansy tea was given to children with tantrums "I'll gie ye tansy tea for temper, an' a better bairn ye'll be". Onion and sugar juice was used to remove coffee stains. Potato water made from raw potatoes grated and strained was used to sponge flowered silks and white satin was cleaned with soft stale bread and blue rubbed over the article then shaken and dusted with a clean soft cloth.

In 1793 a MacDonald published his discovery that mice could be kept from the store cupboard by putting sprigs of mint there. Onion, by using the outer skin gave a golden brown dye, the outer leaves of cabbage dyed yellow. Soot, especially from the base of the pot, gave crimson.

Earlier it was seen that some plants could harm their neighbours, there are also some which help. The French marigold (Tagetes patula) and to a lesser degree Mexican Marigold (Tagetes minuta) can inhibit eel worm in potato, and the Mexican form is said to repel weeds such as ground elder and twitch grass or couch (Agropyrum repens).

Saffron (Crocus sativis) sometimes called Meadow saffron is not a native British plant but was imported from the near east. It came to the Highlands and saffron shirts were worn but in most cases this was a yellow shirt dyed with some other plant as saffron was and is expensive. It takes 40,000 blooms to make a pound of saffron. Only the stigma is used. In the past is was used for cures of jaundice, measles and oppression. It is a poisonous plant and had to be used with care. It is not now so used. Saffron is still used in cooking particularly in Cornwall. There is a modern use for the plant. It contains colchicine which has the ability to double the number of chromosomes in a plant which makes saffron a valuable helper in hybridization.

Again some animals were used in medicine apart from their uses as food. The skin of an eel was used as a sling for sprains. Stag horn jelly was used for debility and there are many more.

On the whole, these country remedies in their day were sounder than many of the so called sophisticated remedies of the town where quite fearful ingredients were used. Some quite useless ones also figured such as the one which called for black sheep's wool to be put in the ear to cure toothache.

Perhaps to end we should recall the prayer of the old Highlanders, for preservation from the disorder that whisky would not cure.

Chapter 13 **Travels around Glencoe in olden days: 1760–1900**

Right Rev. Robert Forbes, M.A.: *Journals of the episcopal visitation—1762 & 1770*

Friday July 6.—Sail'd up Loch Leven to a Store House belonging to Ballachelish, where preached from Acts 8, 14 etc., Mr Allan Cameron resuming in Gaelic. Baptized between 60 and 70, and confirmed 170, Old Ballachelish for one (Alexander Stewart of Ballachelish, who was present at the battle of Sheriffmuir in 1715 and Culloden, died in 1774 at a great age). Mr Cameron and I were obliged to officiate standing in the Door of the Store House, with our Face towards the multitude on the grass, as the House could not hold a 4th of them. In sailing up, I saw the Rowers very careful, and Ballachelish Junior, directing them, to avoid a Rock, or rather a very large Stone, on the right Hand, quite overflowed at high Water, but bare all round at Ebb, which is called Peter's (in Gaelic Clach farick i.e. Peter's Stone) Rock, because a Son of the King of Denmark of that name is said to have perished here by the Boat's striking on the Stone. The Ferry (in Gaelic Keulisfarick, i.e. Peter's Ferry) at Ballachelish is likewise called by his name.

Before Dinner visited the spot where Glenure fell, and the Bush from behind which he received the Shot, and very near indeed to his Person, but so concealed that the Murderer could not be seen by the human Eye. His Horse threw him, and fractured his skull. The Country People have gathered together a Heap of Stones upon the Spot where the Body was found dead. The Road is so narrow that two cannot ride side by side, so that his Servants were a good way behind him when the Discharge happened, and he was dead by the time they got up to him. . . . July 8 the 4th Sunday after Trinity—Twixt 8 and 9 in the morning baptised Katherine MacDonald an adult, in Ballachelish's House. When making ready to go to the foresaid Store House for Worship, I spied an old venerable grey headed man looking wistfully at me, and Solicitous to carry Books, or any other thing. In setting out for the Boat, Stewart of Invernahyle met us, and, after common compliments, told me that this was John Og Ean MackDonell, the Principal of the eight Glenmoriston men in 1746, who had come 36 long miles to see me. Upon this, making up to him to take him by the Hand he fell flat on his Face to the Ground, on the Eastern manner, from which I soon raised him up, the Tear starting in my Eye as well as in his, and asked by an Interpretor, as he could speak nothing but Gaelic, how he had found me out? He answered that, "hearing I was in the Country, he well knew that Ballachelish would be my Head-Quarters, and therefore he had come hither". Old Ballachelish, turning about just as we were ready to go on Board the Boat, and pointing to the valuable Hero, said "There is the man that did more for HIM sir, than us all"! I gave him some small thing to bear his Charges in footing the Journey, but not so much as I inclined, not having it to spare from the unexpected Jaunt to Argileshire. I asked Invernahyle seriously if it was true, that John had been a Thief. "Yes" said he, "as damned a Thief as ever was in the Highlands; but, since he had the Honour to have a hand in preserving his Master in his greatest Distress and Danger, no man dare say he has ever been guilty of a dirty or ungentlemanly Action."

The Reason why John had taken such a Journey to see me is that for some years past I had been so lucky as to make up a small Pension of five £-a-year for him, which pays his farm. . . . It was Evening before we could sail down to Ballachelish, where at Dinner we ate ripe cherries, so large one was apt to take them for Heart-Cherries. . . .

Thursday July 5—The little Mount on which Jas Stewart was put to Death is hard by Ballachelish, and in sight of the Wood, though not of the very spot, where Glenure fell. This day we visited the Mount, and saw the Hole in which had been fixed the very high Gibbet, covered over with Bars of Irons; but the body was soon blown down with the excessive hard Gales, that are ordinary from the West, up Loch Leven. The Justice-Clerk, Lord Milton ordered the Body to be fixed up again, with severe Threatenings. However, the violent winds soon blew down the Body, Bone by Bone. Ballachelish Junior carefully gathered the Bones, and had them placed in the same Coffin with the Body of the Mournful Widow, Ballachelish's Daughter, then of about 10 years of age, washing the Scull with her own hands. . . .

We likewise came in view of the Island of St Munde who was Abbot and Confessor in Argile, and flourished about the year 962. His anniversary is April 15. Upon this Island is the Ruine of a little Chapel, all the four Walls of which are still entire, dedicated to the same St Munde. Though the Island has little Depth of Earth, being rocky, the MacDonalds and Camerons still bury there. The Nests of the Jack Daws are sometimes found in the sculls of the Dead. Up from this Island is the House of MacDonald of Glenco, the Massacre of which Family and Clan is a piece of Shocking History well known. Glenco, a delightful fertile Bottom, and the House has Plenty of Wood about it, at the Back of which is a Top, or Hill, rocky, called Scurnakeich, i.e. a Woman's Pap, which it resembles very much.

Bishop Forbes was a noted Jacobite. He wished to join the Prince in 1745 but was arrested before he was able to do so. He was not set free till after the Rising was over. He then wrote or spoke to everyone he could who had been "out", or who had any knowledge of the events of the Rising. He cross-checked all information even to small details. His recordings were published in the 19th century by the Scottish Historical Society in three volumes known as *The Lyon in Mourning*. From these three books comes much of our knowledge of the Rising.

Bishop Forbes was of the Scottish Episcopal Church not Church of England. The Scottish church was a disestablished church worshipping under difficulties. It had not recognised the Hanoverian succession. When the first American churchman was elected Bishop, the Church of England Bishops would not consecrate him as he would not swear allegiance to, nor pray for King George III, so the American came to Scotland and was duly consecrated. At the present time not only are the two churches in communication but they are also in communication with Episcopal Churches throughout the world.

I. Lettice: *Letters on a tour through various parts of Scotland—1792*

We landed in that part of the Highlands called Lochaber, celebrated in Scottish song. We did not, however sing *Lochaber no more* for much were we rejoiced at setting foot upon solid ground.

It was on this coast, July 7, 1745 that Charles Edward, son of the Chevalier St George, landed, for the conquest of the British empire, with seven officers, and arms for two thousand men. Hands were found, however, for three fourths of them, in this quarter. The Highland chiefs, hastening to join his standard, brought him fifteen hundred men. You recollect how much the audacious spirit of this attempt surprised all Europe; how it excited the apprehensions of the pusillanimous in England, the pity of the wise, and the loyalty of the kingdom in general.

Lochaber is a poor, but pleasant country, more cultivated, at present for potatoes, than oats; though the latter are not wanting. Pretty large flocks of sheep, herds of goats, and some black cattle occupied the hanging steeps on our right. The estuary of Loch Leven ran on the other hand of this agreeable valley.

John Leyden: *Tour in the Highlands & Western Islands—1800*

After passing the slate quarries we entered Glenco, and saw, by the side of the river, the ruins of the ancient mansion where MacDonald was murdered. ... We made the usual enquiries to Captain Stewart concerning the authenticity of the Poems of Ossian, and were informed that numerous persons in Appin and Lochaber were still able to repeat them; and the Captain declared that he had frequently heard them himself. You will not be surprised that my scepticism was vanishing like the morning mist, and it is now extremely probable that my next epistle may contain an explicit recantation of my former infidelity.

Leyden, a geologist and friend of Sir Walter Scott, was interested in the controversy over Ossian.

T. Garnett: *Observation on a tour through the Highlands and part of the Western Islands of Scotland—1800*

At the distance of four miles from Connel, we crossed Loch Creran, at Shean ferry, and soon entered the extensive plantation of Airds.... Riding round the head of this arm of the Loch, we came to the inn of Portnacraish, about five miles distant from Shean ferry; here we breakfasted, and Mr Watts afterwards took a sketch of the Castle and surrounding scenery.

Soon after we passed Appin House, we saw several enormous blocks of Quartz lying close to the shore: a few miles farther, Loch Leven opens to our view, with a great deal of grandeur and sublimity; it is a branch of Loch Linnhe, and is nearly surrounded by lofty mountains. After riding for some miles along the banks of this loch, we reached Ballichelish, where is a ferry towards Fort William, which place we could easily have reached this evening, had we not wished to see the celebrated Glencoe. We therefore determined to take our residence here for the night, and after dinner walked along the banks of the Loch.

... On the side of the road, near the head of the Loch, is a very fine quarry of blue slate. A considerable number of workmen are employed here, and great quantities of slate sent annually to Leith, the Clyde, England, Ireland, and even to America. Vessels of any burden can load most commodiously in fine smoothe sand, and so near to the shore, that nothing more is necessary than to throw a few planks between the vessels and the shore, and carry the slates on board in wheelbarrows.

We found the accommodation both for ourselves and our horse at the ferry-house of Ballichellish very uncomfortable, but being fatigued by the labour and heat of the proceeding day, we slept tolerably, and early the next morning (July 26) set off for Glencoe.

An old print of Glenetive the land associated with Deidre of the sorrows.

Stoddart: *Remarks on Scotland—1801*

At a point of the hills, two miles north from Connell ferry, some rocks, of a noble and tremendous height, overhung our path; they were composed of a coarse pudding-stone, resembling those near Oban; their vast detached fragments, and their nodding ruins, bound with ivy, appeared awfully grand. They bear the name of Dunvallanrie, (Gaelic dun—a fortified hill; baile—a town; ri—a king) from a fortress formerly built on their brow, and overlooking Beregonium, a royal city. This latter is called by the country people Baragoudie, or Dun MacSnich (probably the fortress of the son of Usnich, as an island in Loch Etive is called Eilean Usnich, from that prince); and its remains are easily traceable, at some little distance on the left, where a level mound of gravel extends a considerable way, overgrown with grass, and terminated by an eminence, on which the royal palace is supposed to have stood. This causeway is called Sraid mharagaid or Market Street; another near it Sraid namin, or Meal Street; a third the Queen's Road, etc. The place was evidently destroyed by fire; the line of the walls being marked by stones resembling the scoria of a foundry, partly vitrified and partly reduced to the state of pumice. Some naturalists contend that these effects are volcanic; popular credulity believes them to have been produced by fire from heaven; but the most probable cause is a hostile conflagration, as has been suggested concerning the vitrified forts hereafter to be mentioned.

The road crossing the peninsula, by a flat moor, about two miles long, passes the old castellated house of Barchaldin, whose appendages, such as the large iron gate, the hollow stone for pounding corn, etc., are marks of ancient feudal superiority. Hence, winding to the left by the edge of the wood, on a gentle eminence you descend upon Loch Creran. The view of this beautiful estuary is one of the most exquisite pieces of lake scenery in Scotland. Though a branch of the sea, it appears entirely shut in, to the westward, by an island, which stretches across its mouth; and winding away to the north-east, it is lost among wild, lofty mountains, which retire with a fine gradation of softening shades. Immediately in front, it spreads into a wide, tranquil bason, singularly divided by a reef of rocks near the ferry-house, which stretch almost the whole way across the lake. The opposite shore rises with a gentle swell, most beautifully broken into small woody hills; and these form the base to the immense ridge of towering mountains, which bounds the deep glen of Creran.

Crossing the ferry at Shean, we took the direct road over the hill, among the beautiful plantations of Airds, which, at about two miles, brought us to the Strath of Appin. This pleasant walk is interspersed with cottage farms, whose appearance may be imagined from their Gaelic names, such as Leat grianach, the sunny slopes, etc. Strath is the name usually given to the broader vales through which a river flows; and Appin is the distinction of this large and beautiful district. The stream discharges itself into that arm of the sea, called in the maps Linnhe Loch; but by the natives simply Linnhe.

Our next excursion led us back through the Strath of Appin, passing the inn at Portnacroish, the church, and the bridge, and thence taking the left-hand road up the Strath to Invernaheil. Hence, ascending an eminence by a stony precipitous road, we descended into Glen Creran, near the narrows of the lake, a most dangerous pass, where, confined by two mountain barriers, the waters rush with great rapidity. Above this, the lake, again expanding, flows with a varied outline, between towering mountains: those on the north side, which we skirted, are woody; the opposite ones mostly bare, but rearing their tremendous summits to the clouds. Among them may be remarked Drum-avuich, the buck's ridge; Ben Sculour, the mountain of yelping; and Meall Dearg the red heap. . . . Airds is about four miles from Appin House, whence, taking leave of Mr Campbell, with many thanks for his obliging attentions, we departed for Ballachulish, about eleven English miles. The distinction of English and Scottish, or of measured and computed miles, is very necessary to be observed; for the latter, which is to the former as three to two, is that by which the country people usually reckon. . . . The cottages are numerous, simple, and prettily clustered; and their inhabitants surpass most of the Highlanders in freshness and beauty. Perhaps, indeed, these remarks may be partly owing to the bright and cheerful weather, which now attended us. . . . Four miles from Appin, are the bridge and mill of Daltraut, where the road quitting the lake, runs behind a hilly promontory through the glen of Duror. On the face of a mountain here, at a considerable height is seen a tremendous chasm, which during the rebellion of 1745, served as a retreat to Mr Stewart of Ardshiel, a staunch supporter of the Pretender. In this asylum he lived many months, and notwithstanding his great size and corpulency, underwent many fatiguing hardships. . . . A mile or two more brought us to Ballachulish, where we experienced the warmest welcome from Captain and Mrs Stewart. . . . The landscape is continually varied, by cottages, by the great slate-work of Ballachulish, by a lime-kiln, and various other objects on the wayside; by the islands in the lake; and by the woods and residences, at the base of the mountains. At the point, where the river Coe joins the lake, is Invercoe, the property of MacDonald Esq. of Glen Coe, but the present residence of Major Cameron. The old house, the scene of the infamous massacre, is at a little distance, a perfect ruin. . . . Afterward varying our route, we explored the upper parts of Loch Leven. . . . The wind blowing down the Loch, our boat was a considerable time in passing the Narrows; but we were recompensed by the varying scenery, and by the descriptive remarks of our obliging guides. The rock of Clach Varig, said they, is so called from a Danish prince, who leaping on shore, to invade this country, was killed at the head of his troops. Farther on, in the bosom of a noble bay, is the Isle of Mun, so called from St Mungo: the remains of a chapel dedicated to him, are still to be seen, and the ground around it is held sacred. . . . Kinloch Leven, which is about eleven miles, in a straight line, from Ballachulish . . . and which as its name imports is the head of the lake, also exhibits some beautiful scenery of a similar kind. The water of Baa here joins the Leven, but previously to its junction, forms a shooting fall, called Eass Baa, seventy feet in height, which gushing in a narrow spout, from a dark thicket above, spreads wide as it descends into the rocky chasm below. ...

The Leven itself, for five miles higher up its course, is one continued succession of the wildest scenery that can be imagined. The whole district has no other name than Branahaoun, i.e. the banks of the river. A great part of it lay on the tracks of the old military road, between the King's House, and Fort William, which passing by the head of Glencoe, crossed a zigzag ascent, emphatically termed the Devil's Staircase, to Kinloch Leven. ... The water coming from a chain of small lakes, far in the mountains, begins to descend rapidly as soon as it enters the glen. In the course of five miles it falls considerably more than a thousand feet, sometimes rumbling over great rocks ... frequently precipitating itself in cascades. ... Eass na Smudh the general name of these cataracts or smoke cascades, well describes their appearance, ... they present themselves in long perspective succession; falls beyond falls tumbling over the rudest rocks. ...

The Burial Island is not called after St Mungo but after St Fintan Mundus and the Island is known as Eilean Munda.

An old print of the Three Sisters of Glencoe.

Coleridge: *From his letters—1803*

But hearing from the gude man of the house that it was (40) miles to Glen Coe, of which I had formed an Idea from Wilkinson's Drawing—and having found myself so happy alone—such blessing is there in perfect Liberty!—that I have walked off—and have walked 45 miles since then—and except for the last mile, I am sure, I may say I have not met with ten houses. For 18 miles there are but 2 Habitations:—and all that way I met no Sheep, no Cattle—only one goat!—all thro' Morelands with huge mountains, some craggy and bare, but the most green with deep pinky channels is worn by Torrents—Glen Coe interested me; but rather disappointed me—there was no superincumbency of Crag, the Crags not so bare or precipitous, as I had expected ...

Dorothy Wordsworth: *From her journal—1803*

We travelled under steep hills, stony or smooth, with coppice-woods and patches of cultivated land, and houses here and there; and at every hundred yards, I may almost venture to say, a streamlet, narrow as a ribbon, came tumbling down, and crossed our road, fell into the lake below. On the opposite shore, the hills—namely, the continuation of the hills of Morven—were stern and severe, rising like upright walls from the water's edge, and in colour more resembling rocks than hills, as they appeared to us. We did not see any house, or any place where it was likely a house could stand, for many miles; but as the loch was broad we could not perhaps distinguish the objects thoroughly. A little after sunset our road led us from the vale of the loch. We came to a small river, a bridge, a mill and some cottages at the foot of a hill, and close to the loch.

Did not cross the bridge, but went up the brook, having it on our left, and soon found ourselves in a retired valley, scattered over with many grey huts, and surrounded on every side by green hills. The hay grounds in the middle of the vale were unenclosed, which was enough to keep alive the Scottish wildness here blended with exceeding beauty; for there were trees growing irregularly or in clumps all through the valley, rocks or stones here and there, which, with the people at work, hay-cocks sprinkled over the fields, made the vale look full and populous. It was a sweet time of the evening: the moon was up; but there was yet so much of day that her light was not perceived. Our road was through open fields; the people suspended their work as we passed along, and leaning on their pitchforks or rakes, with their arms at their sides, or hanging down, some in one way, some in another, and no two alike, they formed most beautiful groups, the outlines of their figures being much more distinct than by day, and all that might have been harsh or unlovely softened down. The dogs were, as usual, attendant on their masters, and, watching after us, they barked aloud; yet even their barks hardly disturbed the quiet of the place.

I cannot say how long this vale was; it made the larger half of a circle ... before it opened again upon the loch. It was less thoroughly cultivated and woody after the last turning— the hills steep and lofty. We met a very tall stout man, a fine figure, in a Highland bonnet, with a little girl, driving home their cow; he accosted us, saying that we were late travellers, and that we had yet four miles to go before we should reach Ballachulish—a long way, uncertain as we were respecting our accommodations. He told us that the vale was called the Strath of Duror, and when we said it was a pretty place, he answered, Indeed it was, and that they lived very comfortably there, for they had a good master, Lord Tweeddale, whose imprisonment he lamented, speaking earnestly of his excellent qualities. (The Marquis of Tweeddale being in France in 1803, was detained by Boneparte, and died at Verdun in 1804.) At the end of the vale we came close upon a large bay of the loch, formed by a rocky hill, a continuation of the ridge of high hills on the left side of the strath, making a very grand promontory, under which was a hamlet, a cluster of huts, at the water's edge, with their little fleet of fishing-boats at anchor, and behind among the rocks, a hundred slips of corn, slips and patches, often no bigger than a garden such as a child, eight years old, would make for sport; it might have been the work of a small colony from China.

There was something touching to the heart in this appearance of scrupulous industry, and excessive labour of the soil, in country where hills and mountains, and even valleys, are left to the care of nature and the pleasure of the cattle that feed among them. It was, indeed a very interesting place, the more so being in perfect contrast with the few houses at the entrance of the strath—a sea hamlet, without trees, under a naked stony mountain, yet perfectly sheltered, standing in the middle of a large bay* which half the winds that travel over the lake can never visit. The other a little bowery spot, with its river, bridge and mill, might have been a hundred miles from the sea-side. . . .

Hastening back again to join the car, but were tempted to go a little out of our way to look at a nice white house belonging to the laird of Glen Coe which stood sweetly in a green field under the hill near some tall trees and coppice woods. At this house the horrible massacre of Glen Coe began, which we did not know when we were there; but the house must have been rebuilt since that time. . . . We turned up to the right, and were at the foot of the glen—the laird's house cannot be said to be in the glen. The afternoon was delightful,—the sun shone, the mountain-tops were clear, the lake glittered in the great vale behind us, and that stream of Glen Coe flowed down to it glittering among alder-trees. The meadows of the glen were of the freshest green.

Mrs Murray Aust

My carriage was once two hours in getting over Connel Ferry, although it was a fine day, and at proper tide; and almost as long a time at Sheean Ferry. The tediousness at both these ferries is generally owing to the want of hands to put the carriage into the boat. I mention this, to caution you to set out early from Oban, if you are bound for Bailechoalish in one day. It is only abot 26 miles from Oban to Bailechoalish, and it took me near twelve hours to go it.

The price for a carriage and pair of horses, with the attendants, is, at Connel Ferry, five shillings, and you may, if you please, give one for the boatmen to drink your health. Ditto, at Sheean Ferry, seven shillings, and one for the boatmens' drink.

Should the weather be fair when you are at Connel, I would advise you to be ferried over in a small boat, and leave the management of the carriage to the driver. Walk on the road about two miles, till you come to a huge rock hanging over your head to the right, and a blacksmith's shop on the left. You will there get a guide to what is commonly called Berigonium. Make your guide take with him a hammer and axe, and be provided with a coarse bag; for on the top of the little hill where the forts of Berigonium stood, you will, by the help of the axe and hammer, procure very curious and perfect pumice stone. By the time your carriage gets over the ferry, you will have secured a cargo of stones, that will swim in water, and be ready to join your vehicle at the foot of the hill. When at the top of the hill, look around you, and you will have as fine a view as can be seen. . . . At Sheean Ferry you will have a view of some charming woods and estate of Airds. After you have crossed Sheean Ferry, you will come to a division of the road, both leading to Port-na-Craish. The left hand road goes by Airds and Port Appin, in my opinion the most beautiful; but it is to Port-na-Craish a mile more than the right hand road, which is also very pretty.

About a mile and a half north of the ferry, on the Airds and Port-Appin Road look to the right and you will see a very pretty wooded glen.

At Port-Appin there is a very good carpenter, a smith, and a shop where many useful articles may be had.

From Port-Appin walk by the sea round the black rock; at the south end of it you will come to a very curious aperture, through which you will see the peaks of Ben Cruchan etc. . . . Five miles short of Bailechoalish, where the road runs again close to the seashore, you will see, to the west of the road a few huts, by which is a small bridge, leading to a road at the base of stupendous rocks, covered with wood to the brink of the sea. Behind that beautiful, rocky, woody, promontory-like mountain, lies an enchanting place, called Ardshiel. It cannot be seen from the great road, except a glimpse of it, at about two miles north of the little bridge leading to it. A carriage might drive to Ardshiel on its way to Bailechoalish, and it would scarcely make an hour's difference in the drive.

The inn at Bailechoalish is small; but in 1801 it was neatly kept by a new landlady. In general it is ill kept.

Halt a few days at Bailechoalish; for the scenery at, and all around that enchanting place, is amazingly fine. Go to the very head of Glencoe, even as far as King's House, 15 miles by carriage road, where you may bait your horses, and return leisurely to Bailechoalish. I cannot, in my own mind, clearly decide whether it be more grand to go up Glencoe, or to go down it.

. . . When I was at Tyndrum I wished to see Glencoe. . . . My horses were tired I therefore hired a cart with one horse, and a Highlandman to lead it, and went 9 miles into Glencoe; for which I was charged nine shillings.

Mrs Murray was the Hon Mrs Murray of Kensington. She wrote more than one guide. Born in 1744 she married the Hon William Murray, younger brother of the Earl of Dunmore. After his death she married George Aust. She travelled to see Scotland and to write a guide book.

* Kentallen.

R. Southey: *Journal of a tour in Scotland—1819*

The evening was glorious. To the west the Linnhe Loch lay before us, bounded by the mountains of Morven. Between those two huge mountains, which are of the finest outline, there is a dip somewhat resembling a pointed arch inverted; and just behind that dip the sun, which has not been visible during the day, sunk in serene beauty, without a cloud; first with a saffron, then with a rosy light, which imbued the mountains, and was reflected upon the still water up to the very shore beneath the window at which we stood, delighted in beholding it. It is only at the equinox that the sun sets just behind that opening; and it is but seldom that so clear and spotless a sky is to be seen these latitudes. The effect was such that I could almost have wished I were a believer in Ossian. ... About three miles from the summit, 14¾ from the ferry, is the Kings House, a solitary inn, upon level ground, about 1200 feet above the level of the sea.

There were two beds in the room wherein we breakfasted. For the first time upon our journey, the house could supply no bread, but in apprehension of this at other places we had brought on loaves from Fort Augustus. There were, however, turkey as well as hen's eggs, a shoulder of lamb, and cream for the tea, which we had not found either at the Ferry or Fort William. Both here and at the Ferry there was handsome English china. Goats are kept here, and they make goat hams, which I was desirous of tasting, but they had none drest, nor in a state for carrying on, for they were in salt, and had not yet been smoked. ...

A great contraband trade in salt is carried on upon these roads. ...

Tynedrum is said to stand on higher ground than any other house in Britain. The abominable candles here have almost blinded me. They are of home manufactory, made of the tallow of braxie sheep (this is Mitchell's explanation)—that is, of sheep who died of some disease, I know not exactly what. I fancied that the tallow had been salted, and that the unexcised salt had spoilt the unexcised candles; something however it is which concretes round the wick, and snuffing is of no use.

[Note that duty was payable on both candles and salt.]

Southey, friend of Coleridge and writer of prose and verse, became Poet Laureate. As his travels in Scotland were not published until 1929 it is still in copyright and we have kindly been given permission by the publishers Messrs John Murray, to print this extract.

Larkin: *Sketches of a Tour in the Highlands of Scotland*

The road passing over the bridge of Etie at the King's House, stretches along the moor to the Glenco pass, where the drove road to Kinlochleven, which may be taken by travellers on horseback, strikes off to the right, being the shortest and most direct way to Inverlochy. But the road through Glenco by the ferry of Ballachelish, although longer by about six miles, is much better, and was chosen on this occasion for that reason, and also from a desire to see the scene of the massacre. Buachailetie, the edge of that wedge-like range of mountains, which rise between Glenetive and Glenco, guards the entrance into the two passes. ... The Glenco men were in the rebellion of 1745, and were on one occasion accidentally quartered near the house of the Secretary Stair's son. When the circumstances came to be adverted to, some apprehension was entertained that the men might seize the opportunity to avenge the massacre; and orders were given to remove them to another situation. The Glenco men prepared to return home; and, when asked the reason, replied that they were insulted, since they were thought capable of making an innocent man suffer for the crime of his father ... The road to the ferry, passing through much wood of this description, stretches about half way between the foot of Glenco and the ferry, along the base of the celebrated slate mountain, on the sides of which are seen crowds of labourers busily employed in preparing the slates, and conveying them to the quay, and shipping them. On the west side of the mountain appears the village of Ballachelish with its long neat rows of slate-covered cottages, the habitations of the quarries and retailers of such commodities as are in constant demand in that situation. The crowd, the activity, noise, and bustling industry of this place, contrast agreeably with the stillness solitude and silence of the scene behind ... Argyll seems to be the chief slate county of Scotland, about five millions of slates being made annually at Easdale, and its other islands, and three millions at Ballachelish and other quarries in the mainland, forming nearly one half of the slate produce of the whole of the rest of Scotland. The revenue derived by the proprietors of Argyll-shire quarries for the slate is said to be about £14,000 per annum and of this a considerable portion is brought into the division of Upper Lorn for the fine blue Ballachelish slates, for which there is a great and constant demand. The quarry is most conveniently situated for sea carriage, the waters of Loch Leven washing the side of the mountain from which a pier stretches into the lake. To the end of this pier may be lashed vessels of considerable burden, into which the slates are thrown from hand-barrows, rolled from the quarry; so that on the same spot the article is raised from the ground, manufactured, and shipped for any quarter in the world.

In this tract, between the bases of the mountains and the lake, appear some extensive and well-cultivated level fields, on which immense quantities of potatoes are raised. A portion of this produce intended for winter consumption is housed, and the rest is usually buried in pits with earth heaped over them, which is found to secure the potatoes from frost. This valuable plant, together with herrings and milk, constitutes the food of the west

Highland population during the greater part of the year; and is fortunately cultivated with success, not only on low fields but among the interstices of many wild and bleak mountains.

Lord John Russell: *Letters written for the post and not for the press—1820*

I regret being only a week here, as it seems a doubtful point our returning. You may figure us setting off with quantities of those beautiful Tartans flying about the back of the carriage; for old Sam has a pride, I see, in dressing as well as packing, the carriage; and, I am told, all English tourists are known by the Plaid, as they call it, being displayed so as to look as much, what they suppose, like Scottish people as possible; then the tumbling in of books, writing-cases, and portfolios, with the space Fredrick's dandy gun-case takes is a work of some nicety. The distinguishing marks of a return-party from a Highland Tour are sometimes curious enough; and they say at our hotel, a gentleman arrived last year with a live eagle strapped on the back of his carriage; but I own I cannot believe that.

Apropos to these tartans, they are beautifully displayed from a corner shop, near a whole cluster of hotels; and, I suppose regularly expand their glowing colours there, as the butterflies in your flower garden every season ...

Glencoe surpassed all my expectations ... and we drove up this magnificent glen before six o'clock in the morning. The rich tinge of a morning sun, and the singular points of the hills, had, all together a charming effect.

Murray: *Handbook for Scotland—1894*

On the little island in the loch are ancient burial places—one for the inhabitants of Glencoe and the other for those of Lochaber. In the former repose the bones of McIan the chief who was shot in the Massacre of Glencoe. The road to Glencoe and Kingshouse runs by the S. shore of Loch Leven, past the village (about 3 miles above the hotel) and the Bridge of Coe (5 miles). On a wooded eminence stands Invercoe Ho. (Trs. of Mrs B MacDonald). A portion of the old house of MacDonald, the head of the clan ... now a ruin—may be seen above the trees ...

James Johnson: *The recess, or autumn relaxation in the Highlands and Lowlands—1834*

James Johnson visited in 1834 "The road to Ballachulish displays a lively and moving picture, boats and various vessels gliding to and fro, on Loch Linnhe. ... We therefore pushed forward ... found ... a colony of Highwaymen, now dignified with the title of Macadamisers warring only against the granite, making, mending, and moving along the road over the Black Moor at the rate of a mile a month."

Lord Teignmouth: *Sketches of the coast of Scotland—1836*

A parliamentary road proceeds between steep and lofty ridges to Loch Linnhe, and under the mountains of Ardgowar to Connal Ferry. On setting foot on the opposite shore, we entered a region remarkable for its striking, varied, and contrasted interest. Ash and other trees enrich the scenery between the Ferry and Ballachulish, at which spot the channel of Loch Leven forms a rapid, so narrow and powerful as to expel the salt from the upper part of the lake. The residence of Mr Stewart is near to it: a gentleman descended from a younger branch of the Stewarts of Appin. The Stewarts were the original proprietors of a large part of Argyllshire, and displaced by the Campbells, a clan of Irish extraction, who were designated "greedy", in having gradually obtained possession of nearly the whole country. The branch of Appin was regarded as the head of the Episcopalians in this part of Scotland, in which they abound: prevailing as far as Fort William ... At Ballyhulish the slate-quarries divert the attention awhile to the bustle and industry of a crowded population.... The descent to Loch Leven from the Moor, which is considerably elevated, significantly called the Devil's Stair-case, is tedious and difficult, down the almost precipitous side of a deep ravine, through which the river Leven foams and tumbles, in its rapid progress from a hill-encircled basin to the lake, rolling smoothly during the later part of its course over a rich and inhabited valley. Two men passed us as we approached the lake, one of whom bore on his shoulder a keg of spirits, whilst the other, who gently whispered to us as he hurried by, that he would speedily join us, was pointed out to me by my guide as the boatman who had been engaged to await us at the upper extremity of the lake. He had availed himself of the opportunity to convey a smuggler to the public-house in the valley. ...

St Mungo's Island, the cemetery of Glenco, is the repository of the remains of the victims of the Massacre ... a ruined chapel contains some monuments ... It bears the representation, very well sculptured, of a dragoon struck from his charger by a Highlander armed with sword and targe; above is the name of Duncan Davidson, and beneath it the following inscription; "The fate of an English dragoon, who attacked Duncan Davidson at the battle of Preston Pans where he fought under Prince Charles Stuart."

Note: While the story is true, it should read William MacKenzie not Duncan Davidson.

Above: Glencoe

Catherine Sinclair: *Scotland and the Scotch—1840*

Today we resolved "to progress" through the celebrated Glencoe and being unable to find a chariot and four at the Ferry of Ballachulish, we stepped into an elegant green Tax-cart, not furnished with the newest patent axle or spring, but nevertheless very endurable, and committed ourselves to the guidance of an old ambling grey horse, whose paces would have made no great sensation at Tattersals, but perfectly suited our purpose of viewing at leisure the succession of magnificent landscapes claiming our admiration along Loch Leven—not Queen Mary's Loch Leven, but another much more beautiful, an arm of the sea, or rather, a mere finger, as it is so narrow, that those who live on the banks often cross and recross it four times in one day to pay visits. ... Among the savage mountains of Glencoe Ossian was born, if ever he was born at all, which some people doubt.... Ossian's cave, one of the most striking objects in Glencoe, looks like a lion's den, excavated in the centre of a precipice, and is nearly inaccessible to the foot of man. One enterprising shepherd formerly scrambled high enough to reach his hand in, and pluck a tuft of grass. Tradition says too, that a man actually did succeed in getting in, but has never since been heard of; therefore some say he is dead, other that he is alive, but for my part, like the Irishman, I believe he is neither the one nor the other. ... When leaving Glencoe, our minds filled with recollection of murder, massacre, and banditti we turned a sharp corner of the road, and I was startled to perceive a party of men advancing, armed with pistols. They came straight towards us in a body, and I had only time to calculate how many notes were in my purse, when the whole troop touched their hats and passed on. This turned out to be a party of excisemen going to seize contraband whisky, a service of no small difficulty and danger.... You would be pleased to observe, that the horses we employ here as well as in some other Highland places, always endeavoured to stop when we approached the Church, being evidently accustomed to carry their employers regularly there; and on one occasion we were nearly upset before the worthy quadrupeds could be prevailed on to proceed. In many remote places the high road terminates at the church door.

Dickens: *From his letters—1841*

Today we had a journey of between 50 and 60 miles, through the bleakest and most desolate part of Scotland, where the hill-tops are still covered with snow, and the road winds over steep mountain passes, and on the brink of deep brooks and precipices. The cold all day has been intense, and the rain sometimes most violent. It had been impossible to keep warm, by any means; even whisky failed. The wind was too piercing even for that. One stage of ten miles, over a place called the Black-Mount, took us two hours and a half to do; and when we came to a lone public called the King's House, at the entrance to Glencoe—this was about three o'clock—we were well nigh frozen. We got a fire directly, and in twenty minutes they served us up some kippered salmon, broiled; a broiled fowl; hot mutton ham and poached eggs; pancakes; oatcakes; wheaten bread; butter; bottled porter; hot water, lump sugar, and whisky; of which we made a very hearty meal. All the way, the road had been among moors and mountains with huge masses of rock, which fell down God knows where, sprinkling the ground in every direction, and giving it the aspect of the burial place of a race of giants. Now and then we passed a hut or two, with neither window nor chimney, and the smoke of the peat fire rolling out at the door. But there were not six dwellings in a dozen miles; and anything so bleak and wild, and mighty in its loneliness, as the whole country, it is impossible to conceive. Glencoe itself is perfectly terrible. The pass is an awful place.... To get from Ballyhoolish (as I am obliged to spell it when Fletcher is not in the way: and he is out at the moment) to Oban, it is necessary to cross two ferries, one of which is an arm of the sea, eight or ten miles broad. Into this ferry-boat, passengers, carriages, horses, and all get bodily, and are got across by hook or by crook if the weather be reasonably fine. Yesterday morning, however, it blew such a strong gale that the landlord of the inn, where we had paid for horses all the way to Oban (thirty miles), honestly came upstairs just as we were starting, with the money in his hand, and told us it would be impossible to cross.

Charles Weld: *Two months in the Highlands, Orcadia and Skye—1860*

I left the steamer at Bannavie, passed the night in the excellent hotel, supped with one tourist, an American, who was in raptures with the Highlands, and had seen them leisurely and well, and the next morning dressed by candle-light and left by the huge van-like coach for Loch Lomond via Glencoe.

It was the last journey for the season, and a strange journey it was. For at every place between Bannavie and Loch Lomond where we stopped, we took up various establishment; brushes and buckets, horse-clothes and harness, with an enormous quantity of whisky contained in living barrels, said barrels being the ostlers'. The fact is, the coach was returning to its winter quarters to be laid up in ordinary until the ensuing season; and as no passengers were expected, everybody considered that he had full license to get drunk.

How the coach got through Glencoe is a mystery to me. I walked, and arrived at King's House long before the coach reeled up to that lonely abode. Here more ostlers full of whisky were taken up, with the result, of course, of increase in the drunken confusion of everybody; and so we galloped down that long hill across the shoulder of the Black Mount, and through Lord Breadalbane's forest to Tyndrum, scattering, to the dismay of their shepherds, thousands of sheep that were being driven to the Falkirk cattle Tryst, and which whitened the road for many miles. That the coach, with its motley and tremendous load, arrived whole at Tyndrum, is highly creditable to its builder, for so erratic were its motions that I momentarily expected to find myself sprawling on the road, and see the vehicle break up into innumerable fragments.

Weld visited Skye and Orcadia in his two months.

Captain Basil Hall: *Patchwork*

The road along which we travelled past King's House on our way to the great quarries of Balahulish, is the only line of Highway in that part of the world, being one of those originally made by the Government, though now kept up by the county. As we were winding slowly up the southern side of a weary black mountain, we came most unexpectedly in sight of a great waggon or caravan—which seemed to our eyes strangely out of place—for what, we thought, could induce any one to bring wild beasts to a still wilder country? On coming nearer to it, we discovered eight or ten men standing round a fire, kindled in a respectable-looking moveable grate; and from the windows of the caravan we detected several curly heads thrust out, evidently attracted by the unusual sound of carriage wheels. Round about lay wheelbarrows, pickaxes, and shovel—whence we soon found that this was a party of roadmakers, or rather road-menders. As the country is entirely desolate, and quite destitute of inhabitants, except at long intervals, it would be impossible to maintain workmen steadily at the proper places, without some contrivance of this nature. Like your provident snail, therefore, these poor fellows carry their house and provisions about with them, and go a-voyaging over the moors pretty much in the style that we seafaring people do over the ocean.

The crew belonging to this caravan or ship of the mountains consisted of sixteen souls—there being eight beds, or one for every two men—and close stowage, too, as it appeared, since space must have been left for packing away their working tools, provisions, and clothes. Two stout horses, ready to be employed in drawing cartloads of gravel and stones to the road under repair, grazed near the caravan, upon what they could catch among the heather. When the vehicle was required to be got under weigh, in order to engage with a new piece of road, the gravel-carts were towed behind, and the horses being yoked in front, the whole mass moved ahead together. In this manner, without entering a house, indeed scarcely seeing even a hut, much less a village, these hard pioneers of the hills continued at work during the whole of the fine season, that is, from the beginning of May to the middle or even to the end of October which is generally a very favoured month in Scotland. In this interval they go backwards and forwards along the whole line from Tyndrum to Balahulish; a distance of about thirty-three miles.

Black: *Tourist guide—1869*

From the Ballachulish Ferry on Loch Leven, noted for its slate quarry, the West Highland road penetrates the savage vale of Glencoe. On certain days the steamer lands the passengers for Glencoe at Ballachulish Ferry. When this is not done they must land at Corran Ferry, from which the distance to Ballachulish is four miles. A cart, said by its owner to have springs, may be hired from one of the boatmen at a charge of one shilling per mile to carry Tourists to Ballachulish. ...

Alexander Smith: *A summer in Skye—1865*

Oban, which, during winter, is a town of deserted hotels, begins to get busy by the end of June. Yachts skim about in the little bay; steamers, deep-sea and coasting, are continually arriving and departing; vehicles rattle about in the one broad, and the many narrow streets; and in the inns, boots, chamber-maid, and waiter are distracted with the clangour of innumerable bells. Out of doors, Oban is not a bad representation of Vanity Fair. Every variety of pleasure-seeker is to be found there, and every variety of costume. Reading parties from Oxford lounge about, smoke, stare into the small shop windows, and consult *Black's Guide*. Beauty, in light attire perambulates the principle street, and taciturn Valour in mufti accompanies her. Sportsmen in knickerbockers stand in groups at the hotel doors; Frenchmen chatter and shrug their shoulders; stolid Germans smoke curiously-curved meerschaum pipes; and individuals who have not a drop of Highland blood in their veins flutter about in the garb of the Gael, "a hundredweight of Cairngorms throwing a prismatic glory around their persons". All kinds of people, and all kinds of sounds are there. From the next street the tones of the bagpipe come on the ear; tipsy porters abuse each other in Gaelic. Round the corner the mail comes rattling from Fort William, the passengers clustering on its roof; from the pier the bell of the departing steamer urges passengers to make haste; and passengers who have lost their luggage rush about, shout, gesticulate, and not unfrequently come into fierce personal collision with one of the tipsy porters aforesaid. A more hurried, nervous frenzied place than Oban, during the summer and Autumn months, it is difficult to conceive. People seldom stay there above a night. The old familiar are the resident population. The tourist no more thinks of spending a week in Oban than he thinks of spending a week in a railway station. When he arrives his first question is after a bedroom; his second, as to the hour at which the steamer from the south is expected.

And the steamer, be it said, does not always arrive at a reasonable hour. She may be detained some time at Greenock; in dirty weather she may be "on" the Mull of Cantyre all night, buffeted by the big Atlantic there: so that he must be a bold man, or a man gifted with the second sight, who ventures anything but a vague guess as to the hour of her arrival at Oban. . . .

Smith was a lace pattern designer in Glasgow. He wrote some poetry and essays.

J. Reid: *Art rambles in the Highlands & Islands of Scotland*—1873

I met a man in the Glen who seemed to know every spot, and gave me the Gaelic names of all the corries. . . . He pointed out to me the "Thief's Corrie" a dismal place only accessible at one point—that point the apex of a rocky and almost perpendicular water-course; he said that one man could hold the pass against five hundred, and I inclined to agree with him. Now, this place had inside grazing for several hundred head of cattle, so that the dwellers of Glencoe could harry a goodly herd and keep them safely there. A number of Gaelic-shouting plaided Highlanders, with sticks and dogs might drive them up the steep hill, and then roll a large stone to prevent their escape. . . .

The mouth of the Coe valley is unlike the bare and dismal glen, for it boasts many sylvan monarchs; and a fertile strath through which the waters having left their wild dancing when they bade adieu to the rocky bed farther up, now flow peacefully. The extensive slate Quarries, and the long rows of cottages occupied by those who work there, are a strongly-marked feature in the day's walk; while many of the walls are entirely composed of slates fixed into the ground and placed upright; in the churchyard many of the tombstones were slate slabs, with painted inscriptions.

As I walked along the road that skirts the southern shore of Loch Leven I met two fair ones, a Minna and a Brenda, walking leisurely, having as companion a jackdaw. He hopped close to my foot, and waited till I presented him with a bun all to himself, and he had hard work nibbling it and taking it along with him to his home. Most of the cottagers in the neighbourhood keep one or more of these quaint pets.

Black: *Picturesque tourist guide of Scotland* (pedestrians copy)—1875

As we advance towards the northern extremity of the glen signs of desolation disappear, and the country gradually becomes cultivated and wooded. After passing Invercoe House, the road for four miles skirts the banks of Loch Leven, a narrow arm of the sea running eastwards from the head of Loch Linnhe, bounded by lofty mountains, some of which are grouped in grand combinations. From its mouth to its farther extremity this loch is one succession of beautiful landscapes. Passing the slate-quarries, we reach Ballachulish with its fine new hotel, beautifully situated near the mouth of Loch Leven, and a few minutes' walk from the steamboat pier.

A guide with a difference—a pedestrian guide.

Miller: *Royal tourist handbook to the Highlands and Islands*—1882

Ballachulish, the name of a district, is situated on both sides of Loch Leven. North Ballachulish is in Inverness-shire, and South Ballachulish in Argyllshire. Both places derive their name from Caolas, the narrow stream of the sea which runs between them. South Ballachulish extends over five miles from east to west. It is some 26 miles north-east from Oban, 12 miles south of Fort William, and 36 miles west of Tyndrum via Glencoe. It is in the parish of Appin and Lismore, and in the immediate neighbourhood of Glencoe; steamers call twice a week in winter, and daily during the tourist season; two mails leave and arrive daily—one by the north, and one by the west. There are two postal and telegraph offices, money order office, Bank of Scotland branch office; Ballachulish Hotel, depot for stage coaching and hiring; Established, Episcopalian, Free, and Roman Catholic churches; a pier, erected in 1863, three-quarters of a mile west of the hotel, where coaches wait the arrival of passengers for Glencoe. Passengers pay 3d. each, and 6d. per coach to the hotel. A van from the hotel carries luggage free.

The lovely valley on the right is Glenachaolais. The residence of Lady Beresford is seen through the trees. Two higher peaks are named Sgur-Chonuail and Corry-Van. The little one, like the sprout of an old tree, is called Sgur-a-chaolais . . . The hotel is locally known as Tigh-a-Chnaip, House of the Knap. The "Knap" is that woody eminence opposite the hotel. An innocent gentleman was hanged there 126 years ago: . . . The Slate Quarries come now into view. The enormous heaps of slate refuse above and under the sea have taken upwards of 90 years to form ... A little further on and the little village of Invercoe is reached, and still farther on is the entrance to Glencoe, where the river Coe rushes down the Glen to mingle its waters with those of Loch Leven. The stream is crossed by a bridge at the opening of the glen, where the road passed through a grove of birch, beech, pine, and other kinds of trees, through which can be seen the house of Invercoe the residence of MacDonald of Glencoe. On the bank of the river, below the bridge, the gable of the dwelling of MacIan, chief of the MacDonald of Glencoe at the time of the massacre, still stands; and the tourist should alight there, and enter at a small gate which opens to the old homestead. It is approached by a noble avenue of ash and plane trees, which must have existed at the time of the massacre. Into the old house a stone has been inserted in the wall, with the letters *M.D.* elaborately entwined, and bearing the date of 1706. ...

When nearly out of Ballachulish, in the direction of Glencoe, the grave of "Corac" the witch lies beside the road. The story goes that she was one of the company that destroyed the Spanish Armada in the Sound of Mull. The people tried to bury the corpse in the island, but stormy weather preventing them, they placed the remains beside the road.

Dunstaffnage Castle. The Stone of Destiny was kept in the Castle for sometime. Originally a MacDougall castle but now a Campbell one. It is open to the public.

Cumming: *In the Hebrides—1883*

From Dunstaffnage we overlook a desolate tract of wide flat moorland, known as Loch Nell Moss, lying between the blue waters of Loch Etive and the broad Atlantic.

Here various traces have recently been discovered of the homes and graves of our Pagan ancestors, suggesting dim and shadowy visions of their life in far remote ages. Half way across the Moss rises a large cairn, built of rounded water-worn stones, and surrounded by stunted trees. This has recently been excavated; and in the heart of the tumulus were found two megalithic chambers, containing human remains and urns. Also divers white quartz stones such as various pagan nations were wont to bury with their dead. ...

Turning from these dwellings of the dead, to the sunny shores of Loch Etive we next come on traces of a lake village, of considerable size, and in fair preservation. Here, on removing accumulations of peat-moss which would seem to have been the growth of twenty, or perhaps thirty centuries, a series of oval palings were found, still surrounded by wooden stakes, which doubtless once supported conical thatched roofs, like those dwellings of the old Gauls described by Strabo as circular, with lofty tapering roofs of straw.

These cairns can be seen by taking the Bonawe road. Once past Benderloch they are on the right hand side of the road. The ground is boggy so be prepared.

Queen Victoria: *More leaves from the journal of a life in the Highlands—1883*

After three miles we passed a few cottages called Onich, the high hills of Glencoe beginning already to show. All was so bright and green, with so much wood and the loch so calm, that one was in perpetual admiration of the scenery as one went along. Four miles more from Corran Ferry brought us to Ballachulish at a little before one o'clock. The situation of the hotel—the larger one—on the opposite side, at the foot of the hills close to the ferry, is extremely pretty. There was a smaller and less handsome inn on the north side, by which we had come. Here we got out, after all our things—cloaks, bags, luncheon baskets, etc—had been removed from the carriage, which we had to leave, and walked down to the boat. The small number of people collected there were very quiet and well behaved. Beatrice and Jane Churchill and I, with General Ponsonby and Brown, got into the boat, and two Highlanders in kilts rowed us across to the sound of pipes. On the opposite side there were more people but all kept at a very respectful distance and were very loyal. A lady, (a widow), Lady Beresford, who owns the slate quarries, and her daughter, in deep mourning, were at the landing place, and one of them presented me with a bouquet. We got at once into two carriages (hired, but very fair ones), Beatrice, Jane, and I in a sort of low barouche, Brown in the box. We had a pair of horses which went very well. the two gentlemen occupied the second carriage. The drive from Ballachulish looking both ways, is beautiful, and very Alpine. I remember Louise and also Alice, making some sketches from here when they were on tour in 1865.

We went winding under the high green hills, and entered the village of Ballachulish, where the slate quarries are, and which is inhabited by miners. It was very clean and tidy— a long, continuous, straggling, winding street, where the poor people, who all looked very clean, had decorated every house with flowers and bunches or wreaths of heather and red cloth. Emerging from the village we entered the Pass of Glencoe, which at the opening is beautifully green, with trees and cottages dotted about along the verdant valley. There is a farm belonging to a Mrs MacDonald, a descendant of one of the unfortunate massacred MacDonalds. The Cona flows along the bottom of the valley, with green "haughs", where a few cattle are to be seen, and sheep, which graze up some of the wildest parts of this glorious glen. A sharp turn in the rough, very winding, and in some parts precipitous road, brings you to the finest, wildest, and grandest part of the pass. Stern, rugged, precipitous mountains with beautiful peaks and rocks piled high one above the other, two and three thousand feet high, tower and rise up to the heavens on either side, without any signs of habitation, except where, halfway up the pass, there are some trees, and near them heaps of stones on either side of the road, remains of what once were homes, which tell the bloody, fearful tale of woe. The place itself is one which adds to the horror of the thought that such a thing could have been conceived and committed on innocent sleeping people. How and whither could they fly? Let me hope that William III knew nothing of it.

To the right, not far on, is seen what is called Ossian's Cave; but it must be more than a thousand feet above the glen, and one cannot imagine how any one could live there, as they pretend Ossian did. The violence of the torrents of snow and rain, which coming pouring down, has brought quantities of stones with them, which in many parts cover the road which is very rough. ... When we came to the top, which is about ten miles from Ballachulish, we stopped and got out, and we three sat down under a low wall, just below the road, where we had a splendid view of these peculiarly fine wild-looking peaks which I sketched. ...

A short distance from where Ossian's cave is shown there is a very small lake called Treachtan through which the Cona flows; and at the end of this was a cottage with some cattle and small pieces of cultivated land. We drove down on our return at a great pace. As we came through Ballachulish the post-boy suddenly stopped, and a very respectable, stout-looking old Highlander stepped up to the carriage with a small silver quaich, out of which he said Prince Charlie had drunk and also my dearest Albert in 1847, and begged that I would do the same. A table, covered with a cloth and with a bottle on it, was on the other side of the road. I felt I could hardly refuse, and therefore tasted some whisky out of it, which delighted the people who were standing around. His name, we have since heard, is W. A. Cameron.

Cockburn: *Circuit journey—1888*

On getting there (the Bunaw ferry), my prediction of the risk of not sending word a day before was confirmed, for after wasting an hour and a half entreating and trying to bribe, and even letting off the red Lord, we could not get a single man to move at the opposite side, where alone tourist boats are kept, and which Ivory crossed to. I thought our expedition ended when three stalwart quarriers from our own side volunteered their services, and the coachman, doffing his livery coat, volunteered his. They found a boat, our provisions were put on board, and the voyage began. I never saw so good a Highland crew. Tall, strong, sensible, cheerful, willing fellows, and excellent rowers, but the coachman clearly the best.

We got up at two, having taken rather less than three hours to do the fourteen miles. ... After an hour's contemplation and refreshment, we sailed again, homeward bound. Three hours and a half, stoppages included, brought us back to Bunaw. We there parted with our three maritime quarriers, on very good terms on both sides; and the coachman took us back to the ferry, where we, on equally good terms parted with him. ... So I have seen Loch Etive. There are few things in this country better worth seeing.

From the Bunaw Ferry Loch Etive runs about fourteen or fifteen miles up the country, is nearly straight, and from one mile to three wide. The boat men said that for about seven miles up, on the right side, there was, since they remembered, a profusion of birch, which the Bunaw furnaces had cleared away. Whether this be true or not, there is scarcely one observable stem or leaf there now.

... There is a passage, I think, in one of Scott's novels in which he makes somebody who is lamenting the encroachment of civilisation on Highland solitude say, but only as an extreme result, that he should not wonder if the mail-coach horn should one day be heard in Glencoe. Alas, alas! it has been heard all this summer. A romantic tourist pinched for time can now be hurried from Fort William to Edinburgh in one not long day. A coach left Fort William all this season at about six in the morning, and after blowing away to Ballachulish, up Glencoe to Kingshouse, and from thence to Tyndrum and down Glenfalloch to Tarbet, which it reached about two, its passengers could get into a steamer there and reach Glasgow in time for the five o'clock train, which landed them at Edinburgh about seven. Spirits of Fingal and of Rob Roy! what say ye to this.

Cockburn was a criminal judge who moved on the judicial circuit.

Fort William to Glasgow on foot (printed in the Banffshire Journal)—*c.* 1900

At last I turn my back upon Loch Linnhe, and pass through the pleasant little village of Onich at the junction of Loch Linnhe with Loch Leven. North Ballachulish, a long row of houses on the north shore of Loch Leven soon follows, and I arrive at the ferry connecting North with South Ballachulish on the opposite shore. While the boatman was having his supper there was time to survey my surroundings. ... About a mile eastward an island on the loch is used as a burial place and in it generations of MacDonalds sleep their last sleep. Here at last comes the boatman and throwing their shadows far across the waters ... the trade carried on in this district is speedily revealed by a remarkably large slab of slate at the roadside, bearing an inscription announcing it is erected in honour of Queen Victoria's reign of fifty years.

Chapter 14   Travellers' tales from the Highlands

Thomas Grey: *Correspondence—September 1765*

We cross'd at the Queen's Ferry in a four-oar'd yawl without a sail & were toss'd about rather more than I should wish to hazard again. Lay at Perth, a large Scotch Town with much wood about it, & came by dinner time to Glamis, being (from Edinburgh) 67 miles wch makes in all from Hatton 197 miles; the Castle stands on Strathmore (i.e. the Great Valley). Wch winds about from Stonehaven on the East-coast to Kincairdinshire obliquely as far as Stirling near 100 miles in length, & from 7 to 10 miles in breadth, cultivated every where to the foot of the hills on either hand with oats or bere-barley, except where the soil is mere peat-earth (black as coal) or barren sand cover'd only with broom & heath, or a short grass fit for sheep. Here and there appear just above the ground the huts of the inhabitants, wch they call Towns, built of & cover'd with turf, and among them at great distances the Gentlemen's houses with enclosures & a few trees round them.

Heron: *Scotland delineated—1799*

The cattle and sheep are small, but much valued for the delicacy of their flesh; and the fleece of the Scottish sheep often emulates the finest Spanish wool. Even the shepherd's dog peculiar to Scotland, so hardy, docile, and sagacious, is not unworthy of mention.

Though the cattle in the high ground may be diminutive, yet in many parts of the country the horses and cows are not inferior in size and beauty to those of the English breed ... The hills of this country feed many small cattle, sheep and goats.

Dunkeld ... Its romantic situation, and the advantages of drinking goat whey invite much genteel company to this place ...

Falkirk is a considerable town, containing about four thousand inhabitants. It is chiefly supported by the great markets for Highland cattle, called Trysts, which are held in its neighbourhood thrice a year. Fifty thousand head of cattle are sometimes sold at one Tryst. These are for the most part sent to England and fattened for the butcher.

There is a smelting house at Strontian, on the north side of Loch Sunart. A new kind of earth found there has its name from the place.

Loch Leven, a branch of the bay called Linnhe Loch, and Loch Etive, another arm of the sea forms a peninsula, comprehending part of the district of Appin. Near the shore the lands are cultivated; but the high grounds are remarkably wild. There is one sheep-farm about twenty-seven miles in length. A solitary cottage named King's House, in the eastern part of the district, is almost the only habitation to be found in a tract of about thirty miles in circuit. Near the head of Loch Etive, lies the vale of Glenco, ... At Larroch in Glenco is Bailichelish slate-quarry from which great quantities of excellent slate are annually exported.

In the neighbourhood the road from Tyndrum inn to Fort-William, is, by various windings, cut across a steep mountain called the Devil's Staircase. On the sea coast to the south of Loch Etive, stands the rising village of Oban, an excellent fishing station, where there is a custom-house and post office. It contains about six hundred inhabitants, has a capacious harbour, with good anchoring ground, and is likely to become, in a short time a place of considerable size.

Douglas: *Tour to the Hebrides—1800*

We reached the celebrated Rest and be Thankful ... in safety, about half way betwixt Arrochar and Cairndoe, but there, the carriage containing our fellow travellers broke down ... and the young lady was glad to take refuge in ours, whilst the gentleman continued the remainder of the stage on foot ...

It was nearly midnight before we arrived at Oban, where we found our friends waiting supper for us, and every apartment of the small inn occupied by tourists. We contrived notwithstanding, to obtain three miserable beds in one room, and after our fatigues slept soundly ...

Before sitting down to breakfast a footman handed round a glass of mountain dew to the individuals of both sexes assembled, and no one declined the offer. Indeed, I presume that the moistness of the climate requires this antidote, and no love of intemperence need be inferred from this its moderate but diurnal use at the same hour ...

There is almost no tillage, (Aros) as the farms are kept in grass for cattle which are generally sold lean. There is, indeed, a miserable attempt here and there at a hay crop, and some small fields of dwarf oats which are said not to be easily shaken in exposed situations ...

The seat of Mr Campbell of Airds, situated on the margin of the lake, with its fine wood, interspersed with much cultivation and distant views of the fine mountains of Glenco delighted us so much, and after crossing another shocking ferry we took up our abode for the night at the village of Portnacroish, where we found a small but clean country inn ...

Loch Etive is a charming lake, or rather arm of the sea, which has sometimes been compared to the archipelago, and is indented with small islands, some of which exhibit the interesting ruins of ancient castles.

From Airds there are distant views of Mull, Lismore, and other islands, which we have just left behind.

Notwithstanding torrents of rain we proceeded to Bailichelish famous for its slate quarries, to breakfast. We passed Appin, the seat of Mr Campbell, en route, finely situated on the margin of Loch Leven, and much beautiful mountain scenery ...

The vale of Glenco is situated near the head of Loch Etive, and holds a remarkable place in history in consequence of the cruel Massacre ...

We were in due time overtaken by our carriage, and after achieving the celebrated Devil's Staircase, and a no less alarming morass, we reached that most desolate of all human habitations, King's House ...

Even potatoes, the innkeeper told us would not grow there, and loaf bread was a luxury unknown to them.

Our fare was of course not sumptious, and the charge high, so we hurried on, after a very wretched meal, to Tyndrum ...

The Rev. Hill: *Journal of a tour through Scotland and second tour—1800*

Having given them a sermon at Fort-William, we proceeded down the most beautiful arm of the sea, affording a prospect very various and pleasant. We passed some vales, the most striking and romantic. Some Highlanders were building their cottages, and this they contrived to do without the use of a single nail or a particle of iron; the rafters and the ribs were pinned together with wood, and twisted withes answered for the hinges and fastenings of the door.

With much difficulty, and much loss of time, we passed a Ferry; the boat being bad, and my horse not a little fearful, we were under the necessity of swimming him over this arm of the sea. The scenery continued the most enchanting and wild, the inlet of the sea giving it a very pleasant variety. We soon met with mountains of the most rugged and terrible appearance. The road finds its way up a narrow rocky glen, where one would suppose no road could have been formed, called the Devil's Staircase. This gives entrance into a country the most dreary and barren; not a single tree, scarcely a blade of grass; all a wide-extended bog for many miles. In the centre of this dreary part of the Highlands, having met with such delays, we were obliged to take up our night's lodging at a place called the King's House. The accommodations, however, ill suited the name of the place; a little tea, a few eggs and oatcakes, were our only repast. Our poor horses had neither hay nor straw, and it was with difficulty that we could procure for each of them a feed of corn at night, and another in the morning, while our chamber accommodations were of a similar description.

We made our early escape from this miserable habitation, which has not a single cot nearer than nine miles and after a dreary journey of near twenty miles, came to Teyndrum, a village of some decent appearance for those parts ...

Rev. P. Homer: *Observations on a short tour in the summer 1803 to the Western Highlands of Scotland*

We left Oban before breakfast, and proceeded towards Fort William. In going along, we were considerably retarded by two ferries the first of which we found very inconvenient, with no key, or the least attempt at facilitating the mode of conveying a horse and a gig. We passed over it, however, with no other accident than breaking a thin leather in the bridle. Our road lay chiefly along the seashore and as far as I recollect was generally very good ...

In the evening we reached Ballachulish. Here we were obliged to put up with very poor accommodations. The people however, were very civil, and we took the will for the deed. In the morning we crossed the ferry, and made a late breakfast at Fort William ...

We had here an abundance of excellent goat's milk and whey. Malt liquor is very scarce in Scotland; and what is drank of this kind in the Highlands is, I believe, imported from England. The constant beverage of this country is a nauseous and abominable spirit that is called whisky. The natives are very fond of it ... The common food of the Highlanders is oat or barley cakes, potatoes and milk. In the Highlands they milk not only cows, but goats and ewes.

All the gentlemen in the Highlands are farmers; but they differ from our ideas of a farmer; because they are persons of good education, and elegant manners. They dispose of their cattle to English purchasers; who buy them without seeing them; and rely upon a general knowledge of the kind of stock that is bred upon particular farms, and upon the character and credit of the person with whom they deal. What is not found answerable to the representation of the seller is returnable upon his hands. The mode of selling them, is by holding fairs twice a year at Fort William, where the Scotch and the English farmers meet to make their bargains. No cattle are produced or could be conveniently, on account of the distances. They are sold upon honour at so much a head, and the purchaser sends for them. They could not be fattened in Scotland, as the winters in the north are very long, and the summers very short, the turnips not much in fashion. Whether it will ever answer in the north of Scotland to fatten sheep on turnips, or whether the soil will not admit it, I am not farmer enough to decide; but I am told that the sheep which are sold in August at thirty shillings a head, will fetch fifty in England the following spring.

As milk is very abundant on these great farms, it is served up at table in a variety of forms. A favourite dish in the Highlands is sour cream, with sugar and whisky Curd with fresh milk was set before us at New Kelso. I tasted both of these; but I liked plain milk better than either. We had also a dish called flummery which I did not venture to touch. The aspect of it was very forbidding. It resembled paste that had been made for two or three days and had stood in an upholsterer's shop. It was a preparation of oats steeped in water. The children seemed to be very fond of it.

Cruttwell: *Tours through the whole island of Great Britain—1806*

About seventy years ago there were not above seven tea-kettles, as many pair of bellows, and as many watches; now not a house is without the two first nor a servant without the last. About the same time four stone of beef might have been purchased for five shillings, and other things in proportion; an ox, worth at that time about forty shillings, supplied the flesh market of Forfar eight days of a fortnight excepting the extraordinary occasions from Christmas to Lammas. Between Hallowess and Christmas when the people laid in their winter provisions, about twenty-four beeves were killed in a week; the best not exceeding sixteen or twenty stone. A man who had bought a shillings worth of beef, or an ounce of tea, would have concealed it from his neighbour like murder. Eggs were bought for one penny a dozen, butter 3d. to 4d. per pound, and a good hen thought high at a groat.

The river Keith, a natural cascade considerably improved by art; is so constructed that the salmon, which repair the great numbers to it, cannot get over it unless the river is very much swelled. The manner of fishing here is probably peculiar to this place. The fishers, during the day, dig considerable quantities of clay, and wheel it to the river side immediately above the fall. About sunset the clay is turned into mortar, and hurled into the water; the fishers then ply their nets at different stations below, while the water continues muddy; this is repeated two or three times in the space of a few hours. It is a kind of pot-net, fastened to a long pole, that is used here. The river is very narrow, confined by rocks composed of sand and small stones ...

With respect to their dress, their brechcan, or plaid, consists of twelve or thirteen yards of a narrow stuff, wrapt round the middle and reaching to the knee. It is often fastened round the middle with a belt, and is then called brechcan feill; but in cold weather is large enough to wrap round the whole body from head to foot; and this is often their only cover, not only within doors, but on the open hills during the whole night. It is frequently fastened on the shoulders with a pin, often of silver, and before with a broache (like the fibula of the Romans), which is sometimes of silver, and both large and expensive; the old ones very frequently have mottos.

The stockings are short and tied below the knees. The cuaran is a sort of laced shoe, made of a skin with the hairy side out, but seldom worn. The truis were worn by the gentry, and were breeches and stockings made of one piece. The colour of their dress was various, as the word brechcan implies, being dyed with stripes of the most vivid hues; but they sometimes affect the duller colours, such as imitated those of the heath in which they often reposed.

The feil-beg, i.e. little plaid also called kelt, is a sort of short petticoat reaching only to the knees, and is a modern substitute for the lower part of the plaid, being found to be less cumbersome, especially in time of action, when the Highlanders used to tuck their brechcan into their girdle. Almost all have a great pouch of badger and other skins, with tassels, dangling before in which they keep their tobacco and money.

Their ancient arms were the Lochaber-axe, now used by none but the town-guard of Edinburgh; a tremendous weapon; the broad sword, and target; with the last they cover themselves, and with the first reached their enemy at a great distance.

The Black Mountain is certainly the most lofty public road in Great Britain. The King's House was built for the accommodation of the army when marching through this desolate country. It is built on a plain.

To the west of the King's House is Glenco remarkable for the infamous massacre in 1691,* and celebrated for having, as some assert, given birth to Ossian. Towards the north is Morven, the country of his hero Fingal.

---

* The date of the massacre is 1692.

In times long before, the ancient Scotch used round targets, made of oak, covered with hides of bulls, and long shields, narrow below and broad above formed by pieces of oak or willow, secured with iron.

Sir John Carr: *Caledonian sketches on a tour through Scotland in 1807*

Upon my return from Leith I could not help stopping and admiring a very handsome display of Scottish carriages, at a coach-builder's, of the name of Crichton, a person of great respectability and ingenuity, a Lieutenant-Colonel of a battalion of volunteers, and the inventor of a machine for the speedy conveyance of troops, and the easy carriage for wounded soldiers ... The carriages appeared to be extremely well built, and to unite lightness to elegance; and were more than one-third cheaper than in England. Many of them are exported to the West Indies; and before the blockade there was a great demand for them in the north of Europe.

On the downs where the volunteers were reviewed I had frequent opportunity of seeing an amusement peculiar to this country, called the Golf. The art of this highly favourite game consists in parties of one, two, three, or more on each side, endeavouring to strike a hard ball, about the size of a tennis-ball, into one hole, or several small holes, successively, distant from each other about a quarter of a mile, with the fewest strokes. There are several bats or clubs used in the course of the game; that by which the ball is struck is formed of ash, slender and elastic, about four feet long, crooked in the head, faced with horn, and having lead run into it. The Scotch are in general extremely expert in this exercise; and so highly was it formerly esteemed that the dress usually worn on the occasion, and one of the bats, form the decoration of many a male in a family picture.

On my way from Hopetoun-house to Linlithgow I saw the process of tramping, that is, of washing. The washerwomen firsts soaps the linen, and next puts it in a tub of cold water; she then kilts her coats, that is, raises her petticoats above her knees, and dances round the tub with her face outwards, until she presses out the dirt with her feet; she then rinses the linen in the river or stream and dries it on the grass. If the tub is large, and the work much, two women will dance round, hand-in-hand, laughing and singing all the time.

Misfortune has always strong claims upon the feelings of a Highlander, and I could not help being highly gratified by a little rebuke I received in this town (Inverness) from one whose loyalty and devotion to the august family now on the throne are exemplary; upon designating the royal exile by the usual name of the Pretender—"Do not call him the Pretender" said he, "He was the Prince Charles."

A lady of rank, who had a Highlander in her service, whom she employed as her hairdresser, one morning as he was adjusting her hair, asked him how many traditional poems concerning Fingal still remained amongst his countrymen; to which he replied, "When any stranger entered a Highland Cottage, the first question always was from the family to the guest, "Know you anything of Fingal or Ossian, or Oscar?" If he did, he was called upon to recite what he knew; if he did not, they recited it to him; and upon the lady asking how they could treasure up in their memories so many poems, he said "oh madam, before we had so many schools, we had long memories."

Most of the vessels belonging to Inverness convey to London the produce of the manufacturers, the fish caught in the river Ness (which is considerable), the skins of hares, foxes, goats, rabbits, otters, roes, and return with hardware, haberdashery, and other articles of use or luxury, which are retailed by the tradesmen to the town and country. A shipload of juniper-berries, were some time back, to be sent annually to Holland from this place; the juniper grows in great profusion upon the neighbouring hills. The herring-fishering upon the coast is, of late rather precarious. The Highlanders are very fond of this fish, and hail its first visit, as the Dutch do, with jubilee joy. I saw very fine wheat growing in the neighbourhood of this town, a very rare circumstance in the west part of the Highlands; and the wheaten bread is very good. The crops here are mostly more forward than on the western coast, owing to the climate and the soil being much more favourable than the western Highlands.

It has been said, but I doubt the fact, that oatmeal is sometimes supped dry, undressed, or baked, by putting a handful in the mouth, and washing it down with water. I was told that the very poor Highlanders boil the blood of their cattle, when killed, with a quantity of salt, and that, when it becomes cold and solid, they cut it up into pieces, and use it for food. At Inverness I saw some poor people in the act of carrying blood in bowls, and, upon my asking what they intended to do with it, they said "To make puddings with it." A very favourite Highland dish, of the higher class, is composed of sour cream, sugar, whisky, curds, fresh milk and flummery, a paste produced from a preparation of oats steeped in water.

In some of the remote parts of the Highlands, a candle would produce as much sensation as a Chinese lantern. On account of the difficulty and expense of procuring tallow, they substitute dry slips of the birch and fir tree, the stumps of which they find in the peat bogs when they cut for fuel. The care for attending to these rude tapers, which burn quickly and brightly, is confided to those of a family who are too aged or too young to perform any very serviceable labour.

The domestic distribution of labour in the little Highland farm is singularly interesting. The lesser boys take charge of the weaned lambs; the stronger attend the goats to the rocks and perilous precipices, upon which they love to browse; the young girls are employed at the distaff; the young men attend to the cattle upon the mountains, whilst their father cultivates his little patch of ground, repairs his hut, of which he is the designer and builder, and upon occasion the knife, the axe, and the augur are his simple materials ... At evening fall the children return home, the bearers of fish which they have caught in some neighbouring stream, and of alder-bark, and buds of heath and moss, with which their mother may stain her home-spun plaid. Amongst the Highlanders, both young and old, the season of "summer flitting" when they remove for the summer to the mountains with their flocks, is always hailed with a rapturous welcome. At this time they live in the mountains in shealings, or little huts constructed for the purpose, and sleep upon beds of heath, leading a life perfectly pastoral until the autumn is advanced, when they return to their glens.

The materials which they adapt to useful purposes are frequently very simple. In different parts of the Highlands, as in south-west Ireland, straw is found a convenient substitute for ropes. The horse-collar and crupper are frequently made of straw. Sticks of birch twisted together are also frequently used for halters and harness and are called woodies.

The hardiness of the Highlander is almost proverbial. He atrributes his health to the keenness of the air and the want of doctors. The Highlanders are accustomed to derive comfort from what would in all probability, occasion death to other men. It is well known that in cold dry windy weather, when these mountaineers are obliged to sleep amongst the hills to attend to their cattle, they soak their plaid in a burne or brook, in which having rolled themselves, they select a spot of heath upon the leeward side of some hill for their bed, where they are kept quite warm by the wet, which prevents the wind from penetrating the stuff.

The Highland dress is very manly and graceful, though it appears to be declining when I expected to have seen it entire, I found it yielding, as it were piecemeal, to the habitments of the south. Few gentlemen, except when they are sporting or farming, wear the kilt; the belted plaid is scarcely ever worn. The Scottish bonnet is also disappearing ... The undress of the gentlemen is generally a short coat of tartan and trowsers of the same stuff. The females of respectability dress precisely as our ladies do. The dress of the common people of both sexes, in most parts of the Highlands, is made of a thin coarse woollen cloth, which they make and dye in indigo colour blue. The men generally wear waistcoats and sometimes trowsers of the same stuff, or cloth, and beaver hats. They also frequently have a plaid in folds, part girt round the waist, to form a sort of short petticoat to reach half-way down the thighs, and the rest thrown over the shoulder, and fastened below the neck. Brogues and short tartan stockings are also much used. The very poor wear what are called mire-pipes, or stockings without feet, called also, in some parts of Scotland, huggers.

The women generally wear a petticoat and a sort of bedgown of the same stuff, and a cursche, or white mob cap, or a handkerchief worn over the head and tied under the chin. The married women wear lappits, and the unmarried have their hair turned up, and fastened with a comb; they wear no caps. The Highland dress of a chieftain is now seldom presented to the eye, unless in the island on a Sunday or in a family picture.

The Lairds house (Ulva) was about half a mile from the inn. The gates here, as in the isle of Mull ... The hinges are two curved sticks let into the wall, supporting the gate, than which nothing can be more rude and uncouth; the locks and keys are also frequently constructed of wood. The Laird of Ulva arranges all the lots of land upon his property in such a manner, that the holder of the smallest lot of land has his own two cows ... The bread generally made is of barley and oatmeal of which they also make porridge, which form their breakfast or supper, along with milk; and where there is any scarcity of that in the winter months, they take molasses with their porridge.

As every small tenant, or lot man has a garden attached to his house, he plants a quantity of cabbages, and of late turnip, which, with potatoes, are the principal vegetables; the latter are so much cultivated, and in such abundance, that they eat a great quantity of them with their fish, of which as I have mentioned, they have great variety, close to the shore of most of their respective lots; and in general every tenant has a row-boat for himself and family, with which they fish, make kelp etc.

The natives of the Highlands and the Hebrides still continue their dislike of eels as an article of food, and which they never touch. Their prejudice against pork has now subsided, and in general that species of food is as much made use of as any other ... The Highland honey is high in estimation, and is indebted for its peculiarly delicious flavour to the bloom of the heath. The Lowlanders call themelves the Land of Cakes, whilst the Highlander proudly boast of inhabiting a land of milk and honey.

To return to the plaid. The colours of the plaid harmonise so well with the russet and heathy colour of the Highland mountains, that they much facilitate the Highlander in the destruction of game.

Robertson: *General view of the agriculture of Inverness—1808*

On approaching the King's House inn, that steep accent, with its manifold travers, called the Devil's Staircase appears in full view of the west. This path is now deserted, and the public road is turned towards the left, down the valley of Glenco, which forms a long circuitous line to Fort William.

There is not perhaps a place in Britain more awfully wild than Glenco. This valley is narrow, naked, deep and gloomy, which the heights on both sides render more awfully striking. The mountains stand beside one another, like immense cones of bare and rugged rock, some of which are 3,000 feet high, with little verdure, and but few shrubs. The soil has been washed down by the deluges of thunder showers, which break on the summit; and where the soil is worn off by torrents the rocks themselves are loosened, and tumble down in fragments, which in some places cover several acres of the narrow flat top ...

After travelling some miles down the Glen, the eye is refreshed by the beauties of Inverco, which are no doubt heightened by contrast. The foot of this glen which had hitherto been dreary and frowning, all of a sudden assumes a pleasant aspect, by the winding limpid streams, the variety of wood which covers the verdant banks, the appearance of cultivation in the fields, the snugness of the laird's house, completely sheltered from the north, and situated at the extremity of a bay of the sea which opens to the meridian sun ...

The limestone of Ballachulish, which requires only to be carried across a narrow ferry, is extremely convenient for that district of Inverness-shire. The price of this lime is ninepence the boll in shells. Coals to burn the limestone are carried up Linne Loch by vessels, which come to the quarry to be loaded with slates for Glasgow and other markets on the west coast. Both the lime and the slate quarries seem inexhaustible. The lime is a bright white, having little sand in its composition, and much calcareous earth. The slate is of excellent quality, and has been long in request. The face of this quarry appears to be nearly two furlongs in length, and in most places eighty feet high. Fifty men were employed in Autumn 1804, and some vessels of considerable burden are generally lying at the quay, waiting for their cargo of slates ... Slates are not only found at Ballachulish, but also at Mamore. A quarry of grey slate opened at considerable expense by the late Mr Davidson of Cantray, at a place called Aultmore; but after houses had been covered with them, it was found that they were so porous as to admit rain.

To enumerate all the instances of these thrifty habits, would be endless. I shall mention only one or two as specimens of the rest. At a gentleman's house in Lochaber, I saw two hearth rugs of the most beautiful mixed colours; one dozen of chair covers and another dozen of chair covers woven, and another dozen sewed by a stitch called vigo (well known to ladies) having five different shades of green, four of red, three of purple, a black background with a yellow and white edging; all spun and dyed and sewed in the house. The whole drawingroom furniture, sofa and chair covers, was of the same kind; sixteen carpets of different patterns. The bed and table linen was countless; as also the blankets, which, in warm and fabric, were equal, and in firmness, superior to these sold in the great towns, under the name of being imported from the south. Shawls and gowns of twisted worsted, and tartan of the most lively colours, beautifully diversified and various articles all spun and dyed in the family under the inspection, and by direction of Mrs Cameron of Fasfern.

Lockhart: *Life of Scott from his diary—1814*

"1st August 1814—Last night went out like a lamb, but this morning came in like a lion, all roar and tumult. The wind shifted and became squally; the mingled and confused tides that run among the Hebrides got us among the eddies, and gave the cutter such concussions, that, besides reeling at every wave she trembled from head to stern, with a sort of very uncomfortable and ominous vibration. Turned out about three, and went on deck; the prospect dreary enough, as we are beating up a narrow channel between two dark and disconsolate-looking islands, in a gale of wind and rain, guided only by the twinkling glimmer of the light on an island called Ellan Glas.—Go to bed and sleep soundly, notwithstanding the rough rocking. Great bustle about four; the light-keeper having seen our flag, comes off to be our pilot, as in duty bound. Asleep again till eight. When I went on deck, I found we had anchored in the little harbour of Scalpa, upon the coast of Harris, a place dignified by the residence of Charles Edward in his hazardous attempt to escape in 1746. An old man, lately arrived here, called Donald Macleod, was his host and temporary protector, and could not, until his dying hour, mention the distresses of the Adventurer without tears. From this place, Charles attempted to go to Stornaway; but the people of the Lews had taken arms to secure him, under an idea that he was coming to plunder the country. And although his faithful attendant, Donald Macleod, induced them by fair words, to lay aside their purpose, yet they insisted upon his leaving the island. So the unfortunate Prince was obliged to return back to Scalpa. he afterwards escaped to South Uist, but was chased in the passage by Captain Fergusson's sloop of war ...

Ahead of us, in the mouth of Loch Linnhe, lies the low and fertile isle of Lismore, formerly the appange of the Bishop of the Isles, who as usual knew where to choose church patrimony. The coast of Mull, on the right hand of the Sound, has a black, rugged and unimproved character. Above Scallister are symptoms of improvement. Moonlight has risen upon us as we pass Duart Castle*, now an indistinct mass upon its projecting promontory. It was garrisoned for government so late as 1780, but is now ruinous ... The placid sea is very different from what I have seen it, when six stout rowers could scarce give a boat headway through the conflicting tides. These fits of violence so much surprised and offended a body of Camerons, who had been accustomed to the quietness of lake-navigation, that they drew their dirks, and began to stab the waves—from which popular tale this run of tide is called the men of Lochaber.

* Duart Castle is now restored and lived in by its owner, the Chief of Clan Maclean.

Ben Nevis.

Keats: *From the autobiography—1818*

July 1818 (Dumfries). We have now begun upon whisky, called here whuskey—very smart stuff it is. Mixed like our liquors, with sugar and water, 'tis called toddy; very pretty drink and much praised by Burns. Mr Abbey says we are Don Quixotes—but we are more generally taken for pedlars. All I hope is that we may not be taken for excisemen in this whiskey country . . .

(Mull) About 8 o'clock we arrived at a shepherd's hut, into which we could scarcely get for the smoke through a door lower than my shoulders. We found our way into a little compartment with the rafters and turf thatch blackened with smoke, the earth floor full of hills and dales. We had some white bread with us, made a good supper and slept in our clothes in some blankets; our guide snored on another little bed an arm's length off . . .

For some days now Brown has been enquiring out his geneology here—he thinks his grandfather came from the Long Island. He got a parcel of people about him at a cottage door last evening, chatted with one who had been a Miss Brown and who I think from a likeness, must have been a relation—he jawed with an old woman—flattered a young one—kissed a child who was afraid of his spectacles and finally drunk a pint of milk. They handle his spectacles as we do a sensitive leaf . . .

(Letter Findlay) Aug 30. We have made but poor progress lately, chiefly from bad weather, for my throat is in a fair way of getting quite well. Yesterday we went up Ben Nevis, the highest mountain in Great Britain. On that account I will never ascend another in this empire—Skiddaw is nothing to it either in height or in difficulty. It is above 4,300 feet from sea level and Fort William stands at the head of a salt water lake, consequently we took it completely from that level. I am heartily glad it is done—it is almost like a fly crawling up a wainscoat. Imagine the task of mounting ten Saint Paul's without the convenience of staircases?

We set out about five in the morning with a guide in the tartan and cap and soon arrived at the foot of the first ascent which we immediately began upon. After much fag and tug and a rest and a glass of whisky apiece, we gained the top of the first rise and then saw a tremendous crag above, which the guide said was still far from the top.

After our first rise our way lay along a heath valley in which there was a loch—after about a mile in this valley we began upon the next ascent, more formidable by far than the last and kept mounting with short intervals of rest until we got above all vegetation among nothing but loose stones which lasted us to the very top.

The guide said we had three miles of stony ascent—we gained the first tolerable level after the valley to the height of what in the valley we had thought the top and saw still above us another huge crag which still the guide said was not the top—so that we made an obstinate fag and having gained it, there came on a mist, so that from that part to the very top we walked in a mist.

The whole immense head of the mountain is composed of large loose stones—thousands of acres. Before we had got halfway up we passed large patches of snow and near the top there is a chasm some hundred feet deep completely glutted with it . . . After a little time the mist cleared away but still there were large clouds about attracted by old Ben to a certain distance so as to form, as it appeared, large dome curtains which kept sailing about, opening and shutting at intervals here and there and everywhere; so that although we did not see one vast wide extent of prospect all around we saw something perhaps finer—these cloud veils opening with a dissolving motion and showing us the mountainous region beneath as through a loophole—these cloudy loopholes ever varying and discovering fresh prospect west, north and south. Then it was misty again, and again it was fair—then puff came a cold breeze of wind and bared a craggy shape we had not yet seen though in close neighbourhood.

Daniel: *Voyage round Great Britain—1814–25*

Ballachulish gives its to a ferry over this loch, connecting with the great road to the capital of the Highlands. On either side of the ferry there is a good house for the accommodation of travellers. The channel to be passed is very narrow but the passage at times is so rough not to be unattended with peril, and is in general so inconvenient, that an intention is now entertained of avoiding it, by the formation of a circuitous road round the head of the Loch.

In reverting to the view it may be necessary to notice an object on the distance near the water's edge, which has somewhat of a castellated appearance and might be easily mistaken by a remote spectator for a ruin; this is the noted slate quarry of Ballachulish from which a very great quantity of excellent slate is supplied, not only to the west of Scotland but to distant parts of the kingdom. It affords occupation to a considerable number of workmen, who are distributed into classes of four each, called crews. It is calculated that a crew may be able to quarry one hundred and four thousand slates in a year. Other quarries of this useful material in architecture exist in the vicinity, but none have hitherto been found to produce slate equal in quality to that of Ballachulish.

(Thurso) It is noted as a resort of particularly fine salmon which if not interrupted will ascend to its head. The statistical account of Scotland contains an attested statement of an almost incredible draught which was taken here on the 23rd July O.S. 1743–44. The number of fish caught amounted to 2560 and they were taken in what is called the Cruive Pool, above the town of Thurso. The net was carried along by eighteen or twenty men furnished with poles to keep down the grond rope, and a similar net was employed to drag the fish to land. A great part of the salmon taken in the river is boiled and sent to London in kits; the rest is pickled, and exported in barrels.

The Isle of Skye has been long celebrated for its small breed of cattle, which are held in high estimation, and seldom fail to obtain considerable prices, when they are exported to the mainland for the purpose of being fattened in the southern pastures. Its breed of sheep is also very considerable, and the rearing of them has been found by no means prejudicial to the other description of stock, as the latter feed in the valleys, while the former derive abundant sustenance from the bleak mountain tracts, where the cattle would find no food. Thus, while the Highlands and isles sustain much more numerous flocks than they formerly did, the increase has not tended to diminish the herds of black cattle in a large proportion, as might be apprehended.

The marine plants from which kelp is made are forced up from the sea by the flux of the tides against the rocks, to which they adhere and grow, not infrequently covering them to a considerable depth. On account of their great value for the above purpose, as well as for manure, artificial means have been devised for propagating them. It has been recommended to roll stones upon the shores, which in many places may be done with little expense, and these in two years will be covered in crops of fucifit for gathering. Sandstone or basalt may be used, but preference is generally given to calcareous stones.

Botfield: *A tour of Scotland—1830*

Nairn . . . is so exactly the frontier of the Highlands, that the Gaelic language is spoken at one end of it, and the English or Lowland Scots at the other.

(Thurso) July 29. We had now attended the northernmost shore of the island, and traversed the land of the Gael, without having seen one individual clad in the peculiar and picturesque dress of the country, as his everyday wear. Loose blue trousers, with tartan coats, having superseded entirely the kilt and hose, so generally and pertinaciously worn only "Sixty years ago"

Tradition has recorded that coal was first discovered on the coast at Brora, and worked by the then Countess of Sutherland in pits, in which, from the impurity of the air, the workmen dared not use candles, but substituted for them the heads of fish strung together, from which the phospheric emanation enabled them to conduct their operations . . .

We were now about to enter the Great Caledonian Glen—Glen More nan Albin, that wonderful natural valley, whose surface is almost entirely occupied by magnificent lakes and arms of the sea, enclosed on each side by rugged and lofty mountains, and admirably adapted for the purpose to which it has been applied. Indeed it would appear, from the general tradition of the Highlands that some native seer, many centuries ago, predicted— what has actually taken place—the transit of white sailed vessels along the lonely glen of

There were three ferries across Loch Leven in the past. This is a picture of the one at Caolas-na-con

Loch Lochy.

lakes, foreseeing, by a mere exertion of the understanding, that advantage would ultimately be taken in that way of the natural configuration of the territory. Accordingly the Caledonian Canal was commenced in 1803–4, and opened from sea to sea upon its completion in 1822, after an expense of upwards of £800,000 upon the twenty-three miles of artificial cutting and locks, required to connect the lakes with each other and the arms of the sea ...

The gulf at the Point of Coran is much contracted, and the currents run extremely fierce and strong; so the "auld wyffies" of Gordonsburgh* are accustomed to say, that if they can but pass the point of Coran they account the greatest peril past, even of a voyage to the West Indies ... Continuing on our course we presently came upon the opening of Loch Leven, whose finely wooded and beautiful verdant sides so famous for the vast slate quarries, of Ballachulish, were sublime mountains of the dark valley of Glencoe which bore exactly the same striking and hyperboral appearance as the other mountains of Lochaber ... Proceeding forward, we passed the woods and houses of Ardsheal, where a mineral spring has recently been turned to some account by the proprietor (Stewart). Near this, a cave protected by a waterfall is still shown as the place of refuge of some of the fugitives from Culloden in 1746, the object of such severe and undeserved, because excessive persecution.

Note: The Highland seer who prophesied the coming of the Caledonian Canal 150 years before it came to pass was the Brahan Seer. Some one who was taking notes of the prophesies refused to write down that one day ships would sail round behind the back of Tomnahurich, a hill near Inverness to where the canal now goes.

Willis: *Pencillings by the way—1835*

I had just taken up a book while we were passing the locks at the junction of Loch Ness and Loch Oich, and was reading aloud to my friend the interesting description of Flora MacDonald's heroic devotion to Prince Charles Edward. A very lady-like girl, who sat next me, turned around as I laid down the book, and informed me, with a look of pleasant pride, that the heroine was her grandmother ...

We decided to leave the steamer at Fort William, and cross through the heart of Scotland to Loch Lomond ... We mounted our cart at eleven o'clock and with a bright sun, a clear vital air, a handsome and good humoured gallant for a driver, and the most renowned of Scottish scenery before us, the day looked very auspicious ... The boy sat on the shafts and talked Gaelic to his horse; the mountains and the lake, spread out before us, looked as if human eye had never profaned their solitary beauty ... We crossed the head of Loch Linnhe, and kept down its eastern bank, skirting the water by a winding road directly under the wall of the mountains. We were to dine at Ballachulish, and just before reaching it we passed the opening of a glen on the opposite side of the lake ... and, after hailing a fishing boat, I despatched my letters, which were sealed, across the loch, and we kept on to the inn. We dined here; and I just mention, for the information of scenery hunters, that the mountain opposite Ballachulish sweeps down to the lake with a curve which is even more exquisitely graceful than that of Vesuvius in its far-famed descent to Portici. That same inn off Ballachulish, by the way, stands in the midst of a scene, altogether, that does not pass easily from memory—a lonely and sweet spot that would recur to one in a moment of violent love or hate, when the heart shrinks from the intercourse and observation of men ... We had jolted sixteen miles behind our Highland horse but he came out fresh from the remaining twenty of our day's journey, and with cushions of dried and fragrant fern, gathered and put in by our considerate landlord, we crossed the ferry and turned eastward into the far-famed and much boasted valley of Glencoe.

* Gordonsburgh was at one time the name of Fort William.

121

Soon after passing Appin House, there are some enormous blocks of quartz lying close on the shore. A few miles further on, Loch Leven opens to view with great grandure sublimity; it is a branch of Loch Linnhe, and is nearly surrounded with lofty mountains. On riding a few miles along the banks of this loch you reach Ballachulish, where there is a ferry to Fort William.

Near this is the scene of the Massacre of Glencoe, remarkable in history. Should the traveller wish to see this glen, the road is along the banks of Loch Leven, by a slate quarry. The expectations of the tourist can hardly be disappointed. The steep and rugged mountains on whose sides the blue mist hangs, and which are worn down into deep furrows by the rapid currents that tumble over them, together with the fertile valley and the river winding through it,—render this glen awfully grand, and picturesque in an uncommon degree. On the right is Malmor, a mountain celebrated by Ossian; on the left, Con Fion, or the Hill of Fingal. The valley is closed by some other grotesque mountains, which are frequently covered with mist, and seem to shut the inhabitants of this spot completely from the world.

This celebrated glen was the birth-place of Ossian, as appears from several passages in his poems. Here the young bard inhaled those ideas of the sublime that prevails throughout his poems. He could see here nothing but grand and simple imagery,—the blue mist hanging on the hills,—the sun peeping through the clouds,—the raging of the storms,—the rocking of the thunder in his vallies,—with the turgid torrents rushing to their streamlets, and the streamlets roaring and chafing with their banks.

This glen was the frequent resort of Fingal and his party; indeed almost every glen tends to confirm the authenticity of Ossian; his description of places are so exact, that no fictitious imagery could delineate with so much truth the scenes alluded to in these poems.—The tourist who may feel inclined to take part in the controversy about Ossian may here have an opportunity of hearing many of the people repeat some of the most beautiful of his productions ... The tourist must return again from the glen to the ferry-house at Ballachulish, and crossing the loch, proceed along the banks of another arm to Fort William, distant about fourteen miles from the ferry. The road is extremely good, and being carried along the side of the loch, is, in a fine day remarkably pleasant ...

Today being Sunday, the road was full of country people going to church, in their best clothes. They were all clean and decent. About half the men wore the kilt, and tartan hose, and plaid, (the plaid is three yards long and one and a half broad, without seam) over their shoulders, and they looked best. The women by no means handsome, nor indeed the men, but healthy and active.

The rent of the worst huts, with a few roods of ground for potatoes, is often so low as 5s. a year. They have a tax, (hearth-money) of 4s. 6d. a year to pay, but it is not stricktly levied. The window-tax does not begin at a less number than seven windows,—which is quite beyond their mark. A horse under thirteen hands does not pay any tax, and one that size would pass in the Highlands, for a dromedary. We were often told that taxable horses, instead of 12s. 6d. are reduced to 2s. 6d. in favour of small farmers, whose rent is below L 10 sterling a year.

Rev. Lessingham Smith: *Excursions through the Highlands and Isles of Scotland—1835 and 1836*

Strolling along the banks of the loch (Fyne) I fell in with the man who rents the salomon fishing. He says that the fish come up in shoals, headed by a leader who may always be seen sporting at the surface of the water, or throwing himself out of it. I watched two or three of these adventurous admirals at the head of their squadrons, while I was walking with the lessee. When they reach the top of the loch, they usually turn and coast along the sides, so as to fall into the nets spread for them.

August 29. Set out with the stout young Scotsman to see the pass of Glencoe, celebrated for the abominable massacre committed by the Campbells on the MacDonalds in the reign of William. but we staid to see a large drove of black cattle "swum" across the loch. The animals were driven to the water's edge by the dogs and men, and appeared to enter, as if they were well accustomed to such exercise. There was some difficulty at first in making them start properly, as they attempted to come ashore again; but at last one of them struck right out, and they all followed him closely, the drove being kept in the right direction by men in boats behind them. The mass of heads and horns upon the surface of the water presented a curious appearance. They had great difficulty in landing, in consequence of the extreme slipperiness of the wetted rocks.

Having walked nine miles along the glen, I left my friend to proceed to Fort William, while I returned back again to Ballachulish. So much had I been fascinated with the sublimities of Highland scenery, that I did not feel the slightest fatigue though with by-excursions I had walked upwards of twenty miles.

Their smoking apparatus was very original. One of them took out of his pocket a roll of a skin, which proved to have belonged to an animal, the seal, which he had killed with his own gun. In this was most carefully deposited what appeared to me to be a small dark cord coiled together. From the coil he tore off a portion, and unrolling it, shewed me that it was tobacco leaf; dividing it into small pieces he crammed it into the bowl of his pipe. The stem of his pipe was not a whit longer than the bowl, each about an inch. He next extracted from his pocket a flinty stone, against which he laid some lint blackened with gunpowder water; then striking the stone with a piece of iron, he obtained a light instantly ...

The place was so dark that at first I could distinguish nothing. But as my eye became accustomed to the glimmer, I could scan the whole scene with precision. The seats were formed of coarse planks, on supporting blocks. Those who occupied them were chiefly shepherds, each wrapped up in his grey plaid, with a collie at his feet. The dogs proved to be rather unmanagable and sometimes even barked at those, who were entering. Some hens, also, on the rafters made a most audacious cackling. But the climax occurred when the minister, lifting up his eyes in the midst of one of his most cogent arguments, beheld a young red deer close to the Bible, staring him in the face. It was a truly Highland picture. Far less would have overturned the gravity of an English audience; but the Scotch are a serious people, and great decorum was preserved in spite of the interruptions.

Finlayson: *The observing farmer's travels through Scotland—1836*

It is a beautiful country from Inverness to Beuley, with some excellent farms; and as well farmed as any part in the south; some good horses also, and good stocks of cattle, but not large in the bone. I saw, near Beuley, in some of the glens, the people carrying off dung, from Beuley in carts, and no one ounce of iron about the car or cart; they call them cars in that place. They had a kreel made something like a mill-hopper, only it was round, and sat betwixt the axle-tree and a sheath, and when they turned or couped up the car, the kreel came out with the dung, and they lifted up the kreel, and set it in its place and off they went. The kreel would hold about two barrowfull of dung ... In Strathalladale the women carry the dung to the land, and the men fill it into a kreel something like a fish-kreel, and lift it on the women's backs; and when at the land, the women stoop down and turn all over and return with their empty kreel, singing a Highland pibroch.

The people in the Highlands of Scotland, in general, and in Ross and Black Isle, are an innocent looking people, and something anxious like in their appearance. Their dress is almost all of their own manufacturing, and neatly made. The young women wear prints on Sabbath, but nearly all uncovered; and their hair is most neatly made up. No art, but all nature. The old women have old fashioned caps. They answer the head better than straw hats, or bonnets, as they call them in the low country.

Mattieas D'Amour: *Memoirs—1838*

The first thing which struck me as singular in these islanders (Skye) was, that as soon as we were seated in their boat, and they had got fixed their oars, one of their number struck up asinging, in which the rest immediately joined. Although I did not understand their language, I could perceive their song was very simple; that it consisted of few words and of frequent chorusses. They took care continually to beat time with their oars in the water; and this was continued without interuption till we arrived at their island. Allowing for the simple customs of the place, and their apparently very stricken conditions, we were received with every mark of respect and towards my master affection too. But my readers may judge of what my luxuries were likely to consist of, where all the servants in the establishment without exception lived exclusively on two meals a day, and these meals composed of thick water porridge and barley bannocks! It is true ... I was allowed some extraordinary indulgences ... I had a room appropriated to my own use; the same being a large kind of chamber in one of the wings of the antique mansion; which chamber I can best describe by comparing it with a respectable hay loft. My bed was of loose long straw, with a rug to throw over me ...

For instance, I witnessed their manner of reaping barley in harvest time. The barley is obliged to be all shorn with a sickle, on account of the stony nature of the soil; and a group of reapers have universally a foreman whose business it is to lead the work and singing. The sickles keep time with the notes of the song; and the music never ceases from morn till night. If at any time the labour seems to lag the leader has only to give an extra impulse to the vocal strain and the work is impelled accordingly ...

It was a singular custom among these people that let them be labouring when or how they might, they had had nothing to eat till dinner time, which was eleven o'clock in the forenoon. They have nothing answering to our breakfast, nor have they even such a word in their language. As to dinner, in the instance of the reapers, their method was, when a number were at work in one field, to convey a tub of thick watery porridge mixed with chopped greens, upon a pole borne horisontally on the shoulders of two men. They were not each furnished with a seperate vessel (a noggin) but it was passed from one to another round the company.

Besides the gruel, there was always, according to the number of people employed, a hamper of their celebrated barley bannocks. These were a kind of unleavened cake, made of barley meal and water with a little salt. The cakes were about eight inches in diameter, and perhaps half an inch thick. They did not eat the cakes to the gruel, but afterwards as a kind of desert. And this was the chief meal of these cheerful and contented labourers! I sat cheerful and content for to see them return from their day's labour, all glee and merriment, anyone might have imagined them to have been engaged in nothing but festivity. I have known more than one instance of parties of them, after returning from the field, occuppying my room for the purpose of a dance. And with regard to the effect on them a person only need give them his hand to shake to be fully convinced of their muscular strength. They have nearly sometimes made my fingers stick together with their strong grasp, and when I got to know them better, I used to beg their pardon when they offered me the ceremony ...

With regard to meat it was very seldom that any was left from the first table, and that was so excessively lean that I did not care much for it. I commonly dined with a few of the other servants on kail, or the mixture of flour and greens without even salt; We never sat down to dinner, but universally stood around the table, and all ate out of one dish ...

But I must not omit to mention some of their marriage ceremonies, which I also witnessed. The day before the wedding a bucket of water is provided, and all the young women in the neighbourhood assembled together. The ring to be used is then thrown into the water and the girls scramble which can get it out first ... She who happens to be successful shall take precedence at the alter of Hymen.

Festivities of weddings were generally held in some large room or barn. On their return from the Kirk or Chapel, the party is met at the door by a person provided with a sievefull of shortbread; which he or she throws over the head of the bride as she enters the place; which is meant I suppose to prefigure the plenty which they desire she may always be supplied. After this the bride takes her seat at the head of the table—generally a long one no more than two feet wide. All the time she is so seated, she holds one arm round the waist of a girl who sits next her; but neither did I learn what this ceremony meant. The wedding dinner always consists of broth or soup, the meat being boiled down. The bridegroom's duty is to wait, and see that the dishes are refilled as they become empty. After dinner the bagpipes play, and dancing commences. A little whisky also goes round, and the merriment is continued till evening ...

This excursion to Skye Fair deserves a little notice ... On our arrival, myself and a companion soon seperated from the rest. The fair was chiefly for cattle, and was held in the wild open country, for as to towns, it is well known there is no such thing. Of assembled beasts there were thousands upon thousands ...

With regard to hospitality of these Islanders, it is, I think taking into consideration their scanty means, without parallel in the whole world. When a stranger comes among them if there happen to be three of four cottages, there is quite a strife amongst them as to who shall have the preference of giving him entertainment ... They are singularly honest; not a bolt or a bar or lock did they either use or need when I was among them. They were not without pride and to hear an insinuation of their poverty would have given them great offence, although they might not possess one farthing's value.

The manner in which the lairds of these Islands receive their rents, I thought very singular. Most of the householders, all around the neighbourhood occupied as much land under the laird as was valued at from twenty to forty shillings, but as for money it was out of the question they never saw any. Against the time when the laird intended to collect his rents, for it was not done at distinct and regular periods, the poor wretched looking head farmer or land steward was dispatched round to all the tennantry warning them of the event. When the time arrives suppose a man owes for two beasts, he perhaps brings with him a steer of two years old. If his beast is valued at forty shillings, his rent of course is paid; but if only at thirty shillings, he must either produce something more, or he must remain in arrears. As soon as the beast in question is taken into possession of the laird, either by himself or his domestics the front part of the dewlap is cut from the top downwards leaving a little skin at the bottom which suffers the part to dangle between the animals fore legs. These were the cattle annually assembled at the Isle of Skye, where a great number of Scotch graziers attended; and the beasts so marked used to be known by the butchers of Sheffield and even much further towards the south.

Telford: *Life of himself—1838*

From Ballachulish on Loch Leven (the boundary of Argyllshire) the military road to Inverary is reckoned fifty-eight miles, or indeed sixty-one if an intervening space of three miles of Perthshire military road be included. This occurs at Tyndrum, and divides the Argyllshire road into two sections; the one extending thirty-one miles from Ballachulish and called the Glencoe road, from passing through a rugged valley of that name, where it is liable to be obstructed in more places than one by stones, which in the stormy season rush down in torrents, and are deposited on the road and beyond it. This sort of damage to the road and to the valley is said to have been unknown, until the black cattle, formerly depastured thereabouts were supplanted by sheep, whose habit of ranging on higher ground disturbs and sets in motion the rocky rubbish of the summits before it is decomposed by the weather; moreover, the passage of the water down the steep side of the mountain being interupted by horizontal sheep tracts, it thereby acquires increased power of moving stones, which from these causes are so largely accumulated as finally to overflow and force their way down to the lowest ground, ... Thus Argyllshire military roads are reckoned at eighty miles, and have been very expensive hitherto, averaging at £14 6s. per miles per annum. But this includes the expense of rebuilding the Inveruran bridge, and of substituting covered cross drains for the shod-fords, of paving open drains, which heretofore at short intervals crossed the surface of all the military roads in a slanting direction much to the personal annoyance of the traveller, and very destructive to the springs of modern carriages ...

The difference of character between a Highland and a Lowland road is very considerable, and we have reason to think that this is not generally understood. In making a Highland road, the heaviest part of the expense is incurred in guarding against the effects of a stormy climate, and of an uneven surface, which imbibing little water, pours down upon the Highland road torrents by which they are inevitably and immediately destroyed, unless apertures are provided of sufficient dimensions to carry under the road all the water collected in the upper side drain, and in the preventitive drains above the line of the road, which convey the water directly to the covered cross drains and bridges; which last are of such frequent recurrence as to amount to eleven hundred in number on the roads made under our care ... From many considerations it will be obvious that the maintenance of Highland roads and bridges in a perfect state, requires unremitting attention; for although the passage of cattle, horses and light carts makes but a slight impression, the winter frosts and heavy rains sometimes inflict injuries which endanger a total interruption of intercourse ... This requires the unceasing watchfulness of six superintendents, each having about 200 miles under his charge; the general inspector moreover, visiting the whole in turn ... These military roads ... were constructed for military purposes in the Highlands between the years 1732 and 1750 and maintained at public expense ...

Upon Highland roads, the bridges etc I found it advisable to employ working masons as inspectors. These men being paid by very moderate weekly wage are encouraged to pass the greater part of their time in perambulating the roads, by a milage allowance for travel expense ... Luckily for these labourous men, who can scarcely be said to have a home, Mr Rickman (Secretary to the Board) saw several of them on the roads in the year 1819 and observed that they suffered from rhuematism, in consequence of their clothing being usually wet or damp, the smouldering fire of a Highland hut being of little efficency for drying it, and their duty compelled them to be always on the roads in stormy weather. On his return to London, he sent them a piece of stout water-proof woollen cloth, and materials for making it into garments, suitable to each man's own convenience; and thus was found to conduce so much to the health and efficency of the inspectors, that the Commissioners directed the same allowance of cloth to be distributed among them every August.

The discomfort attending the formation of new roads in a mountainous and thinly peopled district cannot be duly appreciated by persons accustomed to usual accommodation; the workmen ... were obliged to construct temporary huts, the frequent removal of which created trouble and expense ... To remedy military canvas tents were purchased ... but were found too hot when each was occupied by ten or twelve men so that in rainy weather they could not endure fires to cook their victuals and dry themselves ... Nor was it until the roads had been made generally passable by wheel carriages in 1824 that an effectual remedy could be introduced. This excellent contrivance (due to Mr John Mitchell) consists of a large caravan on wheels, capable of containing sixteen or eighteen men, with a fire place; it is movable from place to place by the Road Repair cart-horse, or even by the workmen themselves ...

Townsend: *Tour in Scotland—1846*

We crossed Loch Linnhe at Corran Ferry (our third trip by water this day) the distance about quarter of a mile, and proceeded to this place (Ballashulish) in a sort of cart, the only vehicle to be procured. It was near ten o'clock before we reached Ballashulish, having been 15 hours on the road from Aros. We are in a quiet, comfortable inn, close to Loch Leven and in the very heart of some of the finest scenery of the Highlands; but, as if to tantalise us, the mountains have put on their caps today, and rain is frequently falling. Occasionally, just to whet our curiosity, we catch glimpses of a fine pointed fellow opposite our windows; but our chief amusement is to watch the manovers of the ferry-boat that crosses the loch to an inn on the other side. The passage being just now a matter of difficulty, from the violence of the wind and the force of the tide, which is the consequence of the extreme narrowness of the loch, which sweeps along like what one can fancy of an American rapid ... We went, as we intended to see Glencoe yesterday. The day was fine, though there was a high keen wind, which I verily believe has continued to blow, through all weathers, ever since we came to Scotland. To one with a weak chest it is too much like breathing pins and needles, and I have sometimes longed to inhale a more milky air ... I think I was less struck with the individual grandure of Glencoe than the general beauty and magnificance of the scenery upon Loch Leven along whose shores lay our road thither.

Cocks and hens in Scotland occasionally pick up their own living on the wilds, in the most independent manner, being indebted to man for nothing in the world but a rude stone to shelter them in bad weather. Upon my word, Scotch poultry must be cleverer than ours. They must have a comfortable life of it, these denizens of the waste. I wonder what becomes of their eggs ...

Why did not some good angel, or our landlord, or our own divine spirit inform us that drovers love the braes where they pay no toll, and get good pasture for their sheep, better than the turnpike road? It was our luck, else we might have been forewarned; for, all yesterday their flocks were passing through Kenmore. Had we asked, "Whither bound?" However, regret was useless now, so I tried to pick out amusement and interest from out misfortune, by observing the curious scene that was passing before our eyes. Every drove was attended by two shepherds—picturesque figures in kilt and plaid, just such as Copley Fielding delights to place in his Highland landscape—and by two dogs, the sagacity and cleverness of which were something astounding. I marked one of them that made an observatory of a fragment of rock, on which he perched himself, high above the road, and glanced, like an general, over all his forces. Now he gravely moved his head from side to side, as if he were occupied in counting the sheep as they passed beneath him; now he lept down in a moment, from his commanding station to drive back some straggler into the proper line; and now, in another moment he was at the top of his watch-tower again. The multitudes of the great sheep-army winding away into perspective, were prodigious. I asked one shepherd how many there might be in his own drove, which looked a mere nothing, and he replied "six hundred". In all there must have been many thousands. Some of the dogs had enough to do to ferret out deserters from among the native flocks upon the braes, with whom they seemed to love to mingle, as if in hopes to be overlooked and left behind ...

The maternal command was thus issued; "Jamie, step west", considering that the boy had but a few paces to go, had sounded more strangely in our ears, had we not observed that the people in these parts use east and west as we do left and right ...

Hans Christian Andersen: *The fairy tale of my life—1847*

Travel is dear in England and Scotland, but one receives value for one's money. Everything is excellent; guests are looked after, and even the smallest village inn is comfortable; thus, at least I found it.—Callander is not much more than a hamlet, but I felt as though I were staying at a count's residence; there were soft carpets on the stairs and in the passages; the fire was blazing merrily and we were glad of that, although the sun was shining outside and all the Scots were going about with bare knees; and that is indeed also their winter dress. They wrapped themselves in their colourful plaids; even the poor boys had one, although it might only have been a rag ...

The Scottish women's dress was even more picturesque than that of the Danish women; a skirt with broad stripes was always fastened up in a charming manner, and the many coloured undershirt was always on view.

During my last stay in Naples I had bought a simple stick of palm; it had accompanied me on a few journeys, amongst others the one to Scotland ... When I was driving with Hambro's family across the heath between Loch Katerine and Loch Lomond one of the sons had it to play with ... The steamer came before we expected it and we were called on board in haste. "Where is my stick?" I asked. It had been forgotten in the inn. When? ... After I came to Edinburgh, the morning I was standing on the station to leave for London the train from Scotland arrived a few moments before our train was due to leave. The guard got out and came towards me; he seemed to know me, and then he gave me my walking stick, saying with a little smile, "it has travelled quite well alone". A little label had been attached to it with the inscription "The Danish poet, Hans Christian Anderson" and it had been handled with such order and care that it had been passed from hand to hand, first with the steamer on Loch Lomond, then with the omnibus driver, then by the steamer again, and then by the train, all with the help of its little address card. It was put into my hands just as the signal sounded to fly away from Scotland, I have still to tell of my stick's adventures; I hope I may do it one day just as well as it managed to travel all alone.

Dr. Carus: *The King of Saxony's journey—1846*

First for the comfort of all travellers the admirable roads must be mentioned with the highest commendation. What difficulties must a traveller have encountered in this country of inhospitable mountains, half a century ago! but now we travel with heavy carriages and excellent horses, if previously ordered, at a quick trot over the hills and along the valleys, and at every post station find an excellent inn. Secondly, with regard to the habitations and build of the people, it is to be observed, that every thing here is more and more characteristic (L Etive). For the first time on this journey particularly among boys and young men, we saw specimens of the naked legs and Scottish kilt, made of partly-coloured woollen stuff. This national dress has been prohibited in Scotland for several decennia, and at first the people were so little disposed to wear the ordinary nether garments of the south, that in order to comply with the letter of the law they often carried them on a stick, instead of wearing them on their person. In the poor districts, however the ancient customs as it appears, are preserved still.

After dinner, the landlord brought in a genuine Scotch-whiskey—that nectar of Scotland ... It is nothing but very strong corn brandy strongly impregnated however with the characteristic smell of turf, which is to be found in all Scotch dwellings and prepared in a somewhat peculiar way. A mixture of hot water, sugar, and some of this spirit forms an agreeable beverage, which, no doubt, is very pleasant and even beneficial, after a walk or any expedition in the misty moisture of these mountains.

I also heard much that was interesting concerning the difficulties which had been surmounted; as, for instance, the canal, in the neighbourhood of Inverness, passes through a soft sandy soil. To which it was found impossible to have any consistence or

Approach to Inverness.

firmness. At last Telford happened to notice one day, the manner in which the wife of a fisherman protected a hole which had been dug to draw water, from the intrusion of the sand, by means of a piece of woollen stuff, fastened by little sticks round the inside of the hole. The idea immediately occurred to him, of putting this plan into practice on a large scale; and, accordingly, this whole piece of canal was secured by a countless number of woollen sacks, made heavy with stones and clay—and so it remains.

(Inverness) The number of the inhabitants amounts to about 16000 and the principal commodities are woven Scotch stuffs in wool and silk. It was very interesting and yet at the same time a great temptation, when after supper an exhibition of some of the best woollen and silken stuffs was made in a neighbouring room for the inspection of his majesty. The soft plaids of various colours, the excellent heavy silk stuffa, the pretty Scotch plaid silken gloves for ladies, and the fine woollen veils, resembling the garments of nymphs, which are woven by the wives of fisherman in the Orkney Isles . . .

The company moved to another room, and several men immediately entered in full Highland costume, The piper commenced his enlivening strains, and a young man in Scottish garb first appeared with two naked swords. He laid them crosswise on the floor, and with a peculiar jerking motion of his legs and arms began to dance to the music of the bagpipes. With a certain rhythm, he stamped with both feet in the ground, quicker and quicker, trod now on this side and now on that, of the naked sword blades without ever touching them—threw up his arms in the air, and one while assumed the attitude of an attacking and at another of a defending warrior. At length he seized the swords again— swung them over his head and disappeared.

Gowrie: *Off the chain—1868*

Herrings are caught either in drift-nets or circle-nets, the latter being known as seines or trawls. To fit out a smack for drift-net fishing with nets and equipment costs about three hundred pounds, consequently such a boat is quite out of the reach of the poorer fishers. The drift nets are of considerable length, varying according to the size of the smack, some of them having twenty five barrels of nets of one hundred yards each barrel. One side is kept on the surface by a series of cork floats at regular intervals, with larger buoys at greater distances to mark its position. It is thus retained upright when the smack pays it out, as it goes slowly along with the wind, and then anchors at the other end. It is left lying through the night, and pulled up in the morning, with the fish sticking in the meshes by the gills. As will be seen from this, the only fish taken are those that may go into it, it being left to their option to enter or not and as it sometimes happens that they choose to take a different direction, the nets are often empty when the sea around is very full. Drifts are mostly employed by capitalists.

A trawl-net, on the other hand, is generally shared by the crews of four skiffs, with three to four men in each; the value of the skiffs varying from fifteen to five and twenty pounds. It is a net of two barrels, or a barrel and a half, in length; not very deep in the water, as the fish caught in the meshes are merely en passant and of no consideration in a haul.

In the centre of this net is a small bag, and at each end is a stout stick with a long rope attached; each rope being in a different boat, one of which having nearly completed a circle, they gradually approach, drawing in the net, with the fish in a dense mass in the middle. The companion boats now approach, drawing in the net, and lifting the fish into the bottoms of the skiffs with large baskets.

One word about the disposing of herring. To eat a herring in a civilised manner requires a knife, silver if possible, but a knife by all means. You first run the knife down the back of your fish—the head and tail removed—taking out all the small bones and fins, that would otherwise interfere with your operation. Then skip off the skin from the side lying uppermost, and take off the meat with the fork, outwards from the centre, towards the back and belly leaving the bones bare. The fish is then turned the other side similarly treated, nothing but the skeleton remaining. The sides towards the belly have to be skilfully manipulated, as the bones there become readily detached. To bring the herring prepared like white fish is a dreadful barbarity; a fresh herring brought in whole, and skilfully handled with silver, is indeed a delicacy ...

They are having their harvest home here today, if such a term can be applied to it. A few rugged acres, reclaimed from the heath and rocks, have yielded a scant supply of oats, still further deteriorated by months of rain. Having been spread out as long as any "drouth" can be hoped for to dry them, they are now being built into a stack. Let us join the workers.

A number of branches having been crossed as a ground-work, the gudewife carefully "wales" the driest sheaves, as a heart for the stack, while the gudeman, a freshlooking youngster of eighty, as gamesome as a colt places them in position. As it ascends, every tier is tied round with a rope formed from those everlasting old herring nets.

There are a number of bee "skeps" in the "Kaleyard" also providing pleasant reminiscences. These bees fill their homes with the famous heather-honey, for no flowers, so to speak of adorn this land of rock and sea. The gudewife tells me her bees never settle on the red clover either, leaving that to the wild bumblebees, contenting themselves with the white, the wee "sheepy maes" of our childhood.

On the west coast near this point is the miller of Gogh's place, whose sons were in Tarbert at the fishing—one of them having been musician at the late evening's dancing there. They own several smacks, and amuse themselves making fiddles in the winter evenings.

The drift net fishermen hang up their nets to dry whenever they return; and all require to mend them occasionally ... Their nets are of very beautiful workmanship, and are bought in "barrels" at four or five pounds each ...

That we might see to finish our evening repast, a wick was extemporised for the "cruisy" and a little girl stood by us picking it out with a pin as fast as it burnt down, which kept her constantly employed.

One morning I was awakened at the inn by a creaking noise, the continuance of which prevented me from sleeping; so dressing, and stepping out to learn the cause, I found it proceeded from a churning mill driven by a horse, where they prepared butter to forward to Glasgoe, and for the supply of their customers.

Robert Louis Stevenson: *Extracts from letters—1864*

Wick Friday September 11 1868. Dear Mother— ... Wick lies at the end or elbow of an open triangular bay, heemed on either side by shores, either cliff or steep earthbank, of no great height. The grey houses of Pulteney extend along the south almost to the cape; and it is about half-way down this shore ... The day when the boats put out to go home to the Hebrides, the girl here told me there was "a black wind"; and on going out I found the epithet as justifiable as it was picturesque. A cold black southerly wind, with occassional rising showers of rain; it was a fine sight to see the boats beat out a-teeth of it.

In Wick I have never heard any one greet his neighbour with the usual "Fine day" or "Good morning". Both come shaking their heads, and both say "Breezy breezy"! And such is the atrocious quality of the climate, that the remark is almost invariably justified by the fact ...

5th August At Oban, that night, it was delicious. Dr Stephenson's yatch lay in the bay, and a splendid band on board played delightfully. The waters of the bay were as smooth as a mill-pond; and, in the dusk, the black shadows of the hills stretched across to our very feet and the lights were reflected in long lines. At intervals, blue lights were burned on the water; and rockets were sent up. Sometimes great stars of clear fire fell from them, until the bay received and quelled them. I hired a boat and skulled round the yatch in the dark. When I came in, a very pleasant Englishman on the steps fell into talk with me, till it was time to go to bed.

Next morning I slept on, or I should have gone to Glencoe. As it was it was blazing hot; so I hired a boat, pulled all afternoon along the coast and had a delicious bathe on the beautiful white sands ...

Sixty One (The Rev G. H. H. Hutcheson): *Twenty years reminiscences of the*
Lews—1850–1870

Our notice was attracted by several boats appearing at the mouth of Loch Seaforth. Out went the prospects, and M'Aulay was summoned; after a long look through his glass he remarked, shutting it up, with emphasis and with that look of pleasure and determination on which gleams in his eye when he sees a good royal: "Its's just the Whalls". An electric shock seemed to pass through the whole party, and in less than no time every craft in the establishment was manned, and everybody seized every conceivable weapon of offence, and hurried in to the boats. The whale boat, our own particular conveyance across Loch

Seaforth, was manned by the best crew, under the special guidance of M'Aulay, who hoisted his flag on board it, and then took command on the whole squadron, to watch the movements. The whales had been descried off West Tarbert Loch, in Harris, when all the inhabitants got into their boats, and, followed them, "Put them" as it is termed, into Loch Seaforth". The reader is not to imagine that the whales I am describing are the great whales. They are what are called the "bottle-noses", from twelves to twenty feet long, and they consort together and go in shoals—for what purpose I don't pretend to say, nor am I sufficiently read in natural history to say what their birth, parentage or education may be. But they every now and again make a voyage of discovery to the Hebrides. When they come they produce great excitement, and their capture is a great object to the inhabitants, as each bottle-nose contains within himself a certain portion of very good oil. The method of capture adopted is, by following and flanking them at a very respectable distance, to get them into some sea loch, at the head of which lies some shoaling ground. An indented rockbound loch is no use. Having thus induced them to enter such a loch, you follow them up in the same manner, slowly and distantly, cautiously outflanking them but never pressing or disturbing them. Thus, as it were, left to themselves, they gradually advance up the loch, following their leader; and if the tide and all be propitious, he will of his own accord take the shoal water, even sometimes beach himself on the sandy spit, when the whole band will follow him like a flock of sheep, and strand themselves. But if you press them too hard, they will be apt to turn short round and make for sea again ...

Ladies and gentlemen, do you know what midges are? If you don't, pray go to the Lews.

All Stornaway was there dancing with that grim determination Scotchmen alone can put on such festive occasions. And how they do dance! In that very extraordinary, and when well done, beautiful dance, a Scotch reel—the dexterity and neatness which thick the evolutions and steps are performed, has oftentimes perfectly astonished me; so close-packed almost as herrings in a tub, they never jostle one another, or get into any mess. I have seen more confusion, more sprawling about, in a London ball-room, aye, and less manners too—than in many a Scotch dance in a barn. And not only in their own national dance is it that they so excel; but see them dance a French contre danse, walts, galop, or polka, and there is none of that rough horseplay work you so often see in England.

What is it in the Highlander that makes him generally so well-bred and civil-mannered a gentleman? It must be the remains of the clan education; for though, from the complete revolution of property that has been progressing for years, and still, alas! progresses, clanship is gone, or fast going—yet still a McKenzie claims kindred with high Kintail, and must not disgrace his name ... There is a quiet dignity about him that always sets him at his ease. He may be pompous—he may swell about his tartan hose and philibeg, as if the room were not large enough for him, but he is never vulgar ...

There is one very singular class of person attached to the fishing boats, and that is the fish cleaners, or rather gutters. They are mostly females. They do not live on board the boats, though some are attached to them; they never go out fishing with them. The fleet generally returns in the morning after fishing all night, and then begins the cleaner's work. There are along the different quays which are attached houses of some of the chief fish merchants, temporary sheds established, and in these the fish curing commences, and very expeditiously is it carried on. Herring gutting is no clean, pleasant or savory occupation; but it is very expeditious. With bare arms, feet, and legs, and not the greatest quantity of clothing these ladies set to work, and the expedition with which they prepare a herring for salting would rather astonish the most expert of London oyster openers when they have oysters to open.

Dr Beith: *Highland tour—1874*

I have already noted that before we started from home on our excursion, as it became one to whom the details of the arrangements were committed, I had corresponded with whom it was necessary ... Among other prearrangements I had ... secured two seats on top of the coach running to Inverness ... When we arrived at Fort William I immediately repaired to the coach office paid for our tickets ... It was now Friday ... This morning ... we had breakfast, and being all ready when the coach drew up we at once took our places, he (Dr Candish) on the box seat beside the driver, I on the one immediately behind, all snug, with our traps safely stowed in the box.

The day was beautiful. We had every prospect of a delightful journey ... The coach was soon occupied—inside outside, everyside. Why the coachman did not proceed. Someone was expected ... Dr Robert Lee of Edinburgh approached. Dr Lee did demand for himself and his friend the seats which he had, as he said, the previous evening paid for. I answered that they had been paid for by us at an earlier hour. We sat still I begged Dr Candish to be firm. The proprietor mounted the coach, and addressed himself to me. The engagement of the seats by me, which he admitted, had been of so long standing that the clerk at the coach office had by mistake let them last evening to Dr Lee ... He begged as a particular personal favour, that we would give up the seats, and engaged to put a chaise and pair at our disposal for ourselves to carry us to Invergarry Inn, without a moment's delay ... Certain disappointed personages attracted my notice, who appeared to be "hanging on" to whom I suspected the chaise had been promised as it had been to us. I hastened to the door of the conveyance; got it into my hand, held it, beckoned to my friend to hasten his step, turned my back on the intruding part, quietly resisted their attempts to possess themselves of the carriage, and felt confident of success. I had reckoned without my host. They rushed to the

Typical carriage of the time.

opposite side, opened the door there, and began to occupy the seats. I at once stepped in, endeavoured to hold two seats, but endeavoured to do so in vain. I took one however, and succeeded in getting my amazed travelling companion within the door ... Dr Candish and I alternated sitting and standing during the whole journey. (Editor Dr Beith had sent word ahead asking the Invergarry gig should be kept for him. He had offered to pay to Inverness though he wished to get off at Invergarry and from there visit other places.)

When two hours after time, we arrived at Invergarry Inn, we found that, despairing of our coming, the "machine" had been let to others ... MacKay, the innkeeper, was annoyed, and sincerely sympathised with us. We could ascribe no blame to him. He was willing to do everything to oblige us. He had a CART. he could nail a plank across and so make a seat for us. His only horse, besides the one which was away, was "in the hill". "It might take some time to find him". I too well knew what a wide word being "on the hill" was. An hour might suffice to discover, and to apprehend, the wanted quadruped, two might be required; or a whole day might be consumed in the enterprise. But what could we do? Scouts were dispatched to scour the hill.

"Have you seen the horse lately?" "In the morning early he was seen, but not since". "Can he be very far off?" "That we cannot tell".

Early dinner was ordered. The cart was got out and washed. The plank provided, and securely fastened on both sides, over the axletree. There was no support for the back. We dined comfortably, and felt quite equal, as we thought, to the labours which lay before us. Two hours had sufficed for finding the horse. In that space the "hill" had been successfully searched. By the time he was yoked in our extemporised carriage, the sun had begun to decline towards the west ... We made our first stage in wonderfully good time. At Tomandown, to our delight, we found a shaky, four-wheeled, tumble-down vehicle, in which we resolved to trust ourselves, for one stage, it might be for two. Our new carriage had springs—such as they were decidedly the worse for wear, but still we believed strong enough for our weight. They once had been springs. The sides and the floor of this worn-out thing were very delapidated, yet it offered upon the whole a fair prospect of holding together for our time ... We proceeded to encounter the formidable ascent from Tomandown on to Cluny ... The night was approaching; our horse-power was weak; whilst our equipage was neither promising nor imposing. Yet we went on. The lad who drove us was respectful and attentive, willing to save his horse by himself walking when he considered it necessary, which he did more frequently than we approved of ... When we arrived at Cluny it was bed-time. Some of the inmates of the so-called hostelry had retired to rest; and gladly should we have done so too had circumstances permitted. Two things forbade this indulgence. We learned, at once, there was no "entertainment" either for man or horse" ... With scarcely any delay, and scarcely any refreshment for man or beast, we proceeded on our way. The road was downhill, a circumstance on which we congratulated ourselves ... It was long past midnight when we arrived at Shieldhouse Inn, in the district of Kintail ... Very thankful I was when we drew, or rather crept up to the poor looking hostelry. The silence which reigned in and around it attracted our attention, and somewhat startled us ... Our driver rapped at the door. There was no response ... I knew the house well. I knew where the kitchen window was to be found. If matters were as they were want to be, I was sure the window was not fastened. I could enter by it and undo the bolts of the main door ... The secret of the unaccountable silence which had prevailed on our arrival was easily told. They had had a "gathering" for "spending the lambs" (separating them from their dams). For two nights in succession all the men, women and dogs—had been out of bed, watching the lambs. This was the third night. The lambs had settled at last, and the watchers had gone to bed. They were in their first sleep when we arrived; and no wonder that it was difficult to awake them. We had found it next to impossible.

A wonderfully short time sufficed for preparing ... a slight repast, and for "making down" the beds in the nice room upstairs.

130

Oban.

J. L. Richardson: *Cruise of the Elena—1877*

The hotels which line the bay (Oban) are handsome, beautifully fitted up, and the proprietors are looking forward to the 12th of August and the advent of the English. All the shops are doing a roaring trade, and as to eggs, not one has been seen in Oban these four days. Here come the coaches, something of a cross between omnibuses and wagonettes, which run to Glencoe and Fort William, and other spots more or less famed in Scottish story ...

We pass another old castle, that of Stalker, on a small island, a stronghold of the ancient and powerful Stewarts of Appin, who, though now extinct, anciently ruled over this region, and connected with the Royal family of that name, occupied a distinguished place in Scottish story. In the sunlight our trip is immensely enjoyable. The air has healing in its wings. You feel younger and lighter every mile. On the left are the splendid mountains of Kingairloch and Ardgour, and on the right those of Appin and Glencoe. The view of the pass is very fine, and to enjoy it more we land at Ballachulish, and take such a drive as I may never hope to enjoy again. Ballachulish itself is an interesting place. Here a son of a king of Denmark was drowned, and at the adjacent slate quarry some six hundred men are employed at wages averaging about three pounds a-week. It is their dinner hour as we pass, and I am struck with the fineness of their physique. Though they speak mostly Gaelic, and are shut out from English literature, they must, from their appearance, be a decent set. In an English mining village of the same size I should see a Wesleyan and a Primitive Methodist Chapel, and a goodly array of public-houses and beershops. Here I see neither the one nor the other. At this end of the village is an Episcopalian place of worship, with its graveyard filled with slate stones. At the other end is the Free Church, and then, separated from it by a rocky stream, are the Established Church and the Roman Catholic Chapel. The village street is, I fancy nearly a mile long, and the cottages, which are well built and whitewashed, seem to me crammed with children and poultry—the former, especially, very fine, with their unclad feet, and with hair streaming like that of Mr Gray's beard ... Late as the season is, a few women are haymaking. What sunburnt, weather-beaten, wrinkled faces they have! Plump and buxom at eighteen, they are old women when they reach twice that age.

As to Glencoe, what can I say of it that is not already recorded in the guidebooks and familiar to the reader of English history? The road is carried along the edge of Loch Leven, and is really romantic, with the rocks on one side, the winding glen in front, and the loch beneath. It is very narrow, and as we meet two four-horse cars returning with tourists we have scarce room to pass. Another inch would send us howling over into the loch below, but our steeds and our driver are trustworthy, and no such accident is to be feared. In the loch beneath we see St Mungo's Isle, marked by the ruins of a chapel, and long used as a burial-place, the Lochaber people at one end, the Glencoe people at the other, as their dust may no more intermingle than that of Churchmen and Dissenters in some parts of England. A little further on is the gable wall, still standing of the house of McIan the unfortunate chief, who was shot down by his own fireside on that memorable morning in February 1690 ...

As a Saxon, I am especially interested in the horned sheep in these parts, which at first sight naturally you take for goats ...

But I did see the churches filled, and all business suspended, and the sight of the Gaelic congregation was extremely interesting. The men in good warm home-spun frieze, the women with clean faces, and plaid shawls, and white caps, their younger ones with the last new thing in bonnets, looking as unlike the big, bare-footed damsels of the streets, and the old withered women whom you see coming in from the wide and dreary moors, as it is possible to imagine.

A cottage in the Hebrides is by no means a cottage orné. Its walls are made of stone and clay of a tremendous thickness. On this wall, on a framework of old oars or old wood, are laid large turfs and a roof of thatch. In this roof the fowls nestle, and lay an infinite number of eggs; but all things inside and out are tainted with turf in a way to make them disagreeable. There is no chimney, and but one door, and the floor is the bare earth, with a bench for the family formed of earth or peat or stone. Beds and bedding are unknown ... Every cotter has a portion of the adjacent moor in which to cut peat sufficient to supply his wants. But of the homespun wool the women make good warm garments—and they need them. Fish and porridge seem their principal diet, and it agrees with them. The girls are wonderfully fat and healthy; and consumption is utterly unknown ... As to agricultural operations, they are conducted on a most primitive scale. A few potatoes may here and there be seen struggling for dear life; and as the hay is cut when the sun shines, it is often in August or September that the farmer reaps his scanty harvest.

Editor's note: The family of the Stewarts of Appin has not died out. The Island used for burial in Ballachulish is St. Munda's Isle after a Saint of that area. Quite a different Saint from St. Mungo. The date of the Massacre is 1692.

Dunstaffnage (right) and beside it Dunolly, two castles near Oban. Dunolly is at the end of the town while Dunstaffnage is a few miles distant

The Rev. Donaldson: *A minister's week in Argyll—August 1879*

As we drew near to Ballachulish the curtain of mist which has shrouded mountain and glen from our view rose gradually and passed imperceptibly away. The beautiful Loch Leven shone like a silver glass, and reflected on its fair bosom the rugged peaks of Glencoe! ... It was a sublime spectacle there as I stood alone by the rushing waters of the Cona and saw far above me the dark canopy of clouds, and the sun casting at times a lurid gleam over the peaks and athwart the waters of the lake.

The sail from Ballachulish to Corpach was delightful. There was a transparency in the air and a light upon the sea and land such as I have rarely seen in all my wanderings.

At Fort William: In 1825 I more than once conversed with a very aged women then 98, who eighty years before had waited upon the Prince and his suite when they passed their first night on the English ground at a small cottage which was standing 50 years ago at the side of the Liddal, across from Canonbie Lee, but which has long been swept away by that spirit of "destructive reform" which is me judice too leading a tendency of this age. There was a company of Highlanders with the Lochaber axes she said who kept guard round the cottage through the night. The Prince, she said was far the "bonniest of the hale companie" though "there were other braw men there". The Prince gave her a gold piece, a "Carolus" which she long preserved, but had lost at last after George III had died. The main army, if it could be so called, bivouacked at Kirkandrewa, on the English side of the Scots Dyke, and had thus to ford the Esk above Longtown. The river was rather flooded, and the horsemen, who were but few in number, broke as best they could the force of the stream for the poor kilted men on foot.

Miller: *The cruise of the Betsy—1879*

Among the various things brought aboard this morning, there was a pair of island shoes for the minister's cabin use, that struck my fancy not a little. They were all around of a deep madder-red colour, soles, welts, and uppers; and, though somewhat resembling in form the little yawl of the Betsy, were sewed not unskilfully with thongs; and of their peculiar style of tie seemed suited to furnish with new idea a fashionable shoemaker of the metropolis. They were altogether the production of Eigg, from the skin out of which they had been cut, with the lime that had prepared it for the tan, and the root by which the tan had been furnished, down to the last on which they had been moulded, and the artisan that had cast them off, a pair of finished shoes. There are few trees, and, of course, no bark to spare, in the island; but the islanders find a substitute in the astringent lobiferous root of the tormentilla erecta, which they dig out for the purpose among the heath, at no inconsiderable expense of time and trouble. I was informed by John Stewart, an adept in all the multifarious arts of the island, from the tanning of leather and the tilling of the land, to the building of a house or the working of a ship, that the infusion of root had to be thrice changed for every skin, and that it took a man nearly a day to gather roots enough for a single infusion. I was further informed that it was not unusual for the owner of a skin to give it to some neighbour to tan, and that, the process finished, it was divided equally between them, the time and trouble bestowed on it by the one being deemed equivalent to the property held in it by the other ...

We descended the Scuir together for the place of meeting, and entered, by the way, the cottage of a worthy islander much attached to his minister. "We are both very hungry" said my friend; "We have been out among the rocks since breakfast-time, and are wonderfully disposed to eat. Do not put yourself about, but give us anything you have at hand". There was a bowl of rich milk brought us, and a splendid platter of mashed potatoes, and we dined like princes. I observed for the first time in the interior of the cottage, what I had frequently occasion to remark afterwards, that much of the wood used in buildings in the smaller and outer islands of the Hebrides must have drifted across the Atlantic, born eastwards and northwards by the great gulf-stream. Many of the beams and boards, sorely drilled by the Teredo navalis, are of American timber, that from time to time has been cast upon the shore,—a portion of it apparently from timber laden vessels unfortunate in their voyage, but a portion of it also, with root and branch still attached, bearing mark of having been swept to the sea by Transatlantic rivers. Nuts and seeds of tropical plants are occasionally picked up on the beach. My friend gave me a bean or nut of the Dolichos urens, or cow-itch shrub of the West Indies, which an Islander had found on the shore some time in the previous year, and given to one of the children as a toy; and I attach some little interest to it, as a curiosity of the same class with the large canes and fragments of carved wood found floating near the shores of Madeira by the brother-in-law of Columbus, and which among other similar pieces of circumstantial evidence, led the great navigator to infer the existence of a Western Continent. Curiosities of this kind seem still more common in the northern than the western islands of Scotland. "Large exotic nuts or seeds", says Dr Patrick Neil, in his interesting "Tour", quoted in a former chapter "which in Orkney are known by the name of Molucca beans, are occasionally found among the rejectamenta of the sea, especially after westerly winds. There are two kinds commonly found; the large of which the fishermen, very generally, make snuff-boxed seem to be seeds from the great pod of the Mimosa scandens of the West Indies; the smaller seeds from the pod of the Dolichos urens, also a native of the same region. It is probable that the currents of the ocean, and particularly the great current which issues from the gulf of Florida, and is hence denominated the Gulf Stream, aid very much in transporting across the mighty Atlantic these entire, and afford an additional proof how impervious to moisture, and how imperishable, nuts and seeds generally are".

Kearton: *With nature and a camera—1897*

In the late spring of 1895 my brother and I left Oban in a steamer plying amongst the Western Isles of Scotland. The passengers we met on board were a rather mixed order—tourists, missionaries, Highland servants of both sexes on their way to or from engagements, commercial travellers, pedlars and migrants.

One hearty old Highland woman and her buxom daughter were moving to the bleak and lonely Isle of Rum, with their few sticks of household furniture, a cow, yearling calf, and half a dozen domestic fowls. The cow had not been milked on the morning she was put on board, and as the day wore on the poor creature's udder became distended, and she lowed as cows will under similar circumstances for relief. I noted this, and asked the owner's daughter whether I might milk the animal. At this she laughed until the tears shone upon her brown healthy-looking cheeks. The mere incongruity of a Heeland Coo being milked by what she no doubt took to be a Cockney tourist, struck her as being altogether too funny for resistance. A great hulking Highland lad, with a red head and a supercilious affectation of wisdom on his countenance, had a deal to say, mostly in Gaelic, upon the matter; and just to see how far he would allow his assumption of knowledge to get the upper hand of his native caution, I offered to wager him a shilling that I would milk the cow dry inside ten minutes. Although the stake was small, his discretion saved him. The old woman to whom the cow belonged readily gave her assent, and borrowing a bucket from the chief steward, I sat down to my task. Some of my fellow-passengers looked on in amused curiosity, no doubt expecting to see me sent sprawling along the cargo deck by the resentful cow, whilst others of the superior order appeared shocked but I did not mind as long as there was some fun and good new milk to be got out on the transaction, besides relieving a suffering dumb animal. When I started to milk, the cow turned her head and looked at me in great amazement. She sniffed the scent upon my clothes, and rolled up the whites of her eyes in such a wicked way as made it quite plain to me that under different conditions she would not, without effective protest, have suffered the indignity of being milked by a man who carried not the aroma of peat smoke about him. I milked the flood of thin milk away into the bucket and calling for a drinking glass, drew the rich remainder for a Highland railway manager, a missionary, my brother, and myself. This piece of practical sagacity, proving that I knew a cow's richest milk is always given last, raised the red-headed Highlander's opinion of me considerably.

Many travellers passed through this part of the country.

Chapter 15   The Highland way of life

Pennant: *Tour of Scotland—1771*

It will be fit here to mention the method that the Chieftains took formerly to
assemble the Clans for any military expedition. In every clan there is a known
place of rendezvous, styled Carn a whin, to which they must report at this signal. A person
is sent out full speed with a pole burnt at one end and bloody at the other and with a cross
at the top, which is called Crosh-tàrie, the cross of shame or the fiery cross; the first
disgrace they would undergo if they declined appearing; the second from the penalty of
having fire and sword carried through their country in the case of refusal. The first bearer
delivers it to the next person he meets he running at full speed to the third, and so on. In
every clan the bearer had a peculiar cry of war; that of the MacDonalds was Freich or
heath; that of the Grants, Craig-Elachie; of the MacKenzies, Tullickard. In the late
rebellion it was sent by some unknown disafected hand through the country of
Breadalbane, and passed through a tract of thirty-two miles in three hours, but without
effect.

The old Highlanders were so remarkable for their hospitality that their doors were
always left open, as if it were to invite the hungry travellers to walk in and partake of their
meals. But if two crossed sticks were seen at the door, it was a sign that the family were at
dinner, and did not desire more guests. In this case the churl was held in the highest
contempt; nor would the most pressing necessity induce the passenger to turn in. Great
hospitality is still preserved through all parts of the country to the stranger, whose
character or recommendations claim the most distant pretentions.

On the death of a Highlander, the corpse being stretched on a board, and covered with
coarse linnen wrapper, the friends lay on the breast of the deceased a wooden platter,
containing small quantity of salt and earth, separate and unmixed: the earth an emblem of
the corruptible body; the salt an emblem of the immortal spirit. All fire is extinguished
where a corpse is kept; and it is reckoned so ominius for a dog or cat to pass over it, that the
poor animal is killed without mercy.

The Late-wake is a ceremony used at funerals. The evening after the death of any person
the relations and friends of the deceased meet at the house attended by bagpipes or fiddle;
the nearest of kin, be it wife, son, or daughter, opens a melancholy ball, dancing and
greeting, i.e. crying violently at the same time; and this continues till day-light; but with
such gambols and frolics among the younger part of the company, that the loss which
occasioned them is often more than supplied by the consequences of that night. If the
corpse remains unburied for two nights, the same rites are renewed. Thus, Scythian-like
they rejoice at the deliverence of their friends out of this life of misery ... The Coranich, or
singing at funerals, is still in use in some places; the songs are generally in praise of the
deceased, or a recital of the valiant deeds of him or his ancestors.

Matrimony is avoided in the month of January, which is called in the Erse the cold
month; but, what is more singular the ceremony is avoided even in the enlivining month of
May; ... After baptism, the first meat that the company takes, is crowdie a mixture of meal
and water, or meal and ale thoroughly mixed. Of this every person takes three spoonfuls.

The mother never sets about any work till she has been kirked. In the Church of
Scotland there is no ceremony on this occasion; but the woman, attended by some of her
neighbours, goes into the church, sometimes in service time, but oftener when it is empty;
goes out again, surrounds it, refreshes herself at some public house, and then returns
home. Before this ceremony she is looked on as unclean, never is permitted to eat with the
family; nor will any one eat of the victuals she has dressed.

It has happened that, after baptism, the father has placed a basket, filled with bread and
cheese, on the pot-hook that impended over the fire in the middle of the room, which the
company sit around; and the child is thrice handed across the fire, with the design to
frustrate all attempts of evil spirits, or evil eye.

The method of letting a farm is very singular; each is commonly possessed by a number
of small tenants; thus a farm of forty pounds a year is occupied by eighteen different
people, who by their leases are bound, conjunctly and severally for the payment of the rent
to the proprietor. These live in the farm in houses clustered together, so that each farm
appears like a little village. The tenants annually divide the arable land by lot: each has his
ridge of land, to which he puts his mark, such as he would do to any writing; and this
species of farm is called runrig i.e. ridge. They join in ploughing; everyone keeps a horse or
more; and the number of those animals consume so much corn as often to occasion a
scarcity; the corn and peas raised being (much of it) designed for their subsistance, and
that of the cattle, during the long Winter. The pasture and moor-land annexed to the farm
is common to all the possessors.

The common diseases of the country (I may say of the Highlands in general) are fevers and colds. The putrid fever makes great ravages. Among the nova cohons febrium which have visited the earth, the ague was till of late a stranger here. Common colds are cured by Brochan, or water gruel, sweetened with honey; or by a dose of butter and honey melted in spirits, and administered as hot as possible. Adult persons freed themselves from colds, in the dead of winter, by plunging into the river: immediately going to bed under a load of cloaths, and sweating away their complaint. Warm cow's milk in the morning, or two parts milk and one of water, a little treacle and vinegar made into whey, and drank warm, freed the highlander from an inveterate cough.

The chincough was cured by a decoction of apples, and of mountain ash, sweetened with brown sugar. Consumptions, and all disorders of the liver, found a simple remedy in drinking buttermilk. Fluxes were cured by the use of meadow sweet, or jelly of bilberry, or poultice of flour and suet; or new churned butter; or strong cream and fresh suet boiled, and drank plentifully morning and evening. Formerly the wild carrot boiled, at present the garden carrot, proved a relief in cancerous, or ulcerous cases. Even the faculty admit the salutary effect of the carrot-poultice in sweetening the intolerable foetor of the cancer, a property till lately neglected or unknown. How reasonable it would be therefore, to make tryal of these other remedies, founded in all probability, on rational observation and judicious attention to nature. Persons affected with scrophula imagined they found benefit by exposing the part every day to a stream of cold water.

Flowers of daisies, and narrow and broad leaved plantane were thought to be remedies for ophthalmia. Scabious root, or the bark of ash tree burnt was administered for toothache. The water ranunculus is used instead of cantharides to raise blisters. . . . The corr or cor-meille must not be omitted, whose roots are the support of the Highlanders in long journeys. A small quantity . . . repels attacks of hunger.

Fern ashes bring in about a hundred pounds a year: (Jura) . . . Sloes are the only fruits of the island. An acid for punch is made of the berries of the mountain ash; and a kind of spirit is also distilled from them.

Corcar, or Lichen omphaloides, is an article of commerce; great quantities have been scraped from the rocks, and exported for the use of the dyers, at the price of a shilling or sixteen pence a stone.

Necessity hath instructed the inhabitants in the use of native dyes. Thus the juice of the tops of heath boiled supplies them with a yellow; the roots of white water lily with a dark brown. Those of the yellow water iris with a black; and the Galium verumru of the islanders with a very fine red, not inferior to that from madder . . . The Fillan a little worm of Jura, small as a thread and not an inch in length . . . insinuates itself under the skin, causes a redness and great pain, flies swiftly from part to part; but is curable by a poultice of cheese and honey. In burning fevers a tea of wood sorrel is used with success to allay the heat. An infusion of ramsons or allium ursinum in brandy is esteemed here a good remedy for the gravel . . . Below this town (Kinghorn) on the rocks grows the ligusicum Scoticum or Scotch parsley the shunus of the Hebrides; where it is often eaten raw as a salad or boiled instead of green. The root is esteemed a good carminative; and an infusion of the leaves in whey is used there as a purge for calves.

All the cloathing is manufactured at home; the women not only spin the wool, but weave the cloth; the men make their own shoes tan the leather with the bark of willow, or the roots of tormentilla ereta, or tormentil, and in defect of wax thread, use split thongs . . . Their diet is chiefly potatoes and meal; and during the winter some dried mutton or goat is added to their hard fare.

I saw also here a true Highland gre-hound, which is now become very scarce; it was of a very large size, strong, deep chested, and covered with very long and rough hair. This kind was in great vogue in former days, and used in vast numbers at the magnificent stag-chases, by the powerful Chieftains.

Dr Johnson: *A journey to the Western Islands—1773*

At Nairn we may fix the verge of the Highlands; for here I first saw peat fires, and first heard the Erse Language.

Here the appearance of life began to alter. I had seen a few women with plaids at Aberdeen; but at Inverness the Highland manners are common. There I think is a kirk in which only the Erse language is used. Near the way, by the water side, we espied a cottage. This was the first Highland Hut that I had seen: and as our business was with the life and manners, we were willing to visit it. . . . A hut is constructed with loose stones ranged for the most part with some tendency to circularity. It must be placed where the wind cannot act upon it with violence, because it has no cement; and where the water will run easily away, because it has no floor but the naked ground. The wall, which is commonly about six feet high, declines from the perpendicular a little inward. Such rafters as can be procured are then raised for a roof, and covered with heath, which makes a strong and warm thatch, kept from flying off by ropes of twisted heath, of which the ends reaching from the centre of the thatch to the top of the wall, are held firm by the weight of a large stone. No light is admitted but at the entrance, and through a hole in the thatch, which gives vent to the smoke. The hole is not directly over the fire, lest the rain should extinguish it; and the smoke naturally fills the place before it escapes . . . When we entered we found an old woman boiling goat flesh in a kettle . . . I never was in any house of the Islands, where I did not find books in more languages than one.

Castle Urquhart on Loch Ness.

Their native bread is made of oats, or barley. Of oatmeal they spread very thin cakes, coarse and hard, to which unaccustomed palates are not easily reconciled. The barley cakes are thicker and softer: I began to eat them without unwillingness; the blackness of their colour raises some dislike, but their taste is not disagreeable. In most houses there is wheat flour with which we were sure to be treated, if we staid long enough to have it kneeded and baked. As neither yeast nor leaven are used among them, their bread of every kind is unfermented. They make only cakes, and never mould a loaf.

Their suppers are, like their dinners various and plentiful. The table is always covered with elegant linen. Their plates for common use are often of that kind of manufacture which is called cream coloured, or queen's ware. They use silver on all occasions ... The knives are not often either very bright or very sharp. They are indeed instruments of which the Highlanders have not long been acquainted with the general use. They were not regularly laid on the table, before the prohibition of arms and the change of dress. Thirty years ago the Highlander wore his knife as a companion to his dirk or dagger, and when the company sat down to meat, the men who had knives, cut the flesh into small pieces for the women who with their fingers conveyed it to their mouths.

Our reception exceeded our expectations. We found nothing but civility, elegance, and plenty. After the usual refreshments, and the usual conversation, the evening came upon us. The carpet was then rolled off the floor: the musician was called and the whole company was invited to dance, nor did fairies trip with greater alacrity. The general air of festivity, which predominated in this place, so far remote ... (Raasay).

The corn of this island is but little. I saw the harvest of a small field. The women reaped the corn, and the men bound up the sheaves. The strokes of the sickle were timed by the modulation of the harvest song, in which all there were united. They accompany in the Highlands every action, which can be done in equall time ...

The cuddy is a fish of which I know not the philosophical name. It is not much bigger than a gudgeon, but is of great use in these Islands, as it affords the lower people both food and oil for their lamps.

Their corn grounds often lie in such intricies among craggs, that there is no room for the action of a team and plough. The soil is then turned up by manuel labour, with an instrument called a crooked spade, of a form and weight which to me appeared very incommodious, and would perhaps be soon improved in a country where workmen could easily be found and easily be paid. It has a narrow blade of iron fixed to a long and heavy piece of wood, which must have, about a foot and a half above the iron a knee or flexture with the angle downwards. When the farmer encounters a stone which is the great impediment of his operations, he drives the blade under it, and bringing the knee or angle to the ground, has in the long handle a very forcible lever.

In Skye there are two grammer schools, where boarders are taken to be regularly educated. The price of board is from three pounds, to four pounds ten shillings a year, and that of instruction is half a crown a quarter. But the scholars are birds of passage, who live at school only in the summer; for in the winter provisions cannot be made for any considerable number in one place. This periodic dispersion impresses strongly the scarcity of the countries.

Interior of a cottage.

The wall of a common hut is always built without mortar, by a skilful adaptation of loose stones. Sometimes perhaps a double wall of stones is raised and intermediate space filled with earth. The air is thus completely excluded. Some walls are I think, formed of turfs, held together by a wattle, or texture of twigs. Of the meanest huts, the first room is lightened by the entrance, and the second by the smoke-hole. The fire is usually made in the middle. But there are huts, or dwellings of only one story, inhabited by gentlemen, which have walls cemented with mortar, glass windows, and boarded floors. Of these all have chimneys and some chimneys and grates.

The house and furniture are not always nicely suited. We were driven once, by missing a passage, to the hut of a gentleman, where, after a very liberal supper, when I was conducted to my chamber, I found an elegant bed of Indian cotton, spread with fine sheets. The accommodation was flattering; I undressed myself, and felt my feet in the mire. The bed stood upon bare earth, which a long course of rain had softened to a puddle.

There still remains in the islands though it is passing fast away, the custom of fosterage. A Laird, a man of wealth and eminence, sends his child, either male or female, to a tacksman, or tenant to be fostered. It is not always his own tenant, but some distant friend that obtains this honour for honour such a trust is very reasonably thought. The terms of fosterage seem to vary in different islands. In Mull the father sends his child with a certain number of cows, to which the same number is added by the fosterer. The appropriates aproportionable extent of groud, without rent for their pasturage. If every cow brings a calf, half belongs to the fosterer and half to the child; but if there be only one calf between two cows, it is the child's, and when the child returns to the parents, it is accompanied by all the cows given, both by the father and by the fosterer, with half of the increase of the flock by propagation. These beasts are considered as a portion, and called Macalive cattle, of which the father has the produce, but is supposed not to have the full property, but to owe the same number to the child, as a portion to the daughter or a flock for the son.

Children continue with the fosterer perhaps six years, and cannot, where this is the practice be considered burdonsome. The fosterer if he gives four cows, receives likewise four, and has while the child continues with him, grass for eight without rent, with half the calves, and all the milk, for which he pays only four cows when he dismisses his Dalt for that is the name for the fosterchild.

The only fewel of the Islands is peat. Peat is dug out of the marshes, from the depth of one foot to that of six. That is accounted the best which is nearest the surface. It appears to be a mass of black earth held together by vegetable fibers. The heat is not very strong nor lasting. The ashes are yellowish, and in a large quantity. When they dig the peat, they cut it up to dry beside the house. In some places it has an offensive smell. It is like wood charked for the smith. The common method of making peat fires, is by heaping it on the hearth; but it burns well in grates, and in the best houses is so used.

As it is, the Islanders are obliged to content themselves with such a succedaneous means for many common purposes. I have seen the chief man of a very wide district riding with a halter for a bridle, and governing his hobby with a wooden curb. In every house candles are made, both moulded and dipped. Their wicks are small shreds of linen cloth. They all know how to extract from the Cuddy, oil for their lamps. They all tan skins, and make brogues.

James Boswell: *Journal of a tour to the Hebrides—1773*

(Coll) The people are very industrious. Every man can tan. They get oak and birchbark, and lime from the mainland. Some have pits; but they commonly use tubs. I saw brogues very well tanned; and every man can make them. They all make candles of the tallow of their beasts, both moulded and dropped: and they all make oil of the livers of fish.

There are no carpenters in Coll but most of the inhabitants can do something as boat carpenters. They can all dye. Heath is used for yellow; and for red, a moss which grows on the stones. They make broad-cloth, and tartan, and linen of their own wool and flax, sufficient for their own use; and also stockings. Their bonnets come from the mainland.

We were entertained here with a primitive heartiness. Whisky was served round in a shell, according to the ancient Highland custom.

The walls of the cottages of Sky, instead of being one compacted mass of stones, are often formed by two exterior surfaces of stone, filled up with earth in the middle, which makes them very warm. The roof is generally bad. They are thatched sometimes with straw, sometimes with heath, sometimes with fern. The thatch is secured by ropes of straw, or of heath; and, to fix the ropes there is a stone tied to the end of each. These stones hang round the bottom of the roof, and make it look like a lady's hair in papers: but I should think when there is a wind they would come down and knock people on the head.

Our money being nearly exhausted we sent a bill for thirty pounds, drawn on Sir William Forbes and Co to Loch Braccadale, but our messenger found it very difficult to procure cash for it; at length however he got us value from the master of a vessel which was to carry away some emegrants. There is a great scarity of specie in Sky. Mr M'Queen said that he had the utmost difficulty to pay his servants wages or to pay for any little thing which he was obliged to buy.

Lettice: *A tour through various parts of Scotland—1783*

All round Ecclesfechan, and for some miles indeed before we reached, as well as after we had passed it, we saw numerless large herds of black cattle and galloways, which at this season continually descend from the northern mountains, occupying the pastures on our road's side, and snatching their hasty meal, as they journey to the fairs of South Britain. Each herd is conducted by a Highlander completely dressed in his national garb, accompanied by his brindle dog, of the true shepherd race; as sagacious, docile, and adroit an animal, as retains to the service of man. It is amusing to see something of order and discipline of movement of eighty, or a hundred head of cattle, under the skillful manoeuvres of a single herdsman and his dog.

The men in this country are not accustomed to reap, or shear the corn, as they call that operation; the women always do it, and every species of corn, is reaped. The men, however, bind and set up the shocks. Their name for them is stooks. Reaping and other harvest work are commonly paid not in money, but by the allowance of a cow's grass: the farmer finding pasture for the peasant's cow during a certain portion of the year.

Upon stones and pebbles mingled together, and reared, outwardly, without cement of plaister, into four rough walls, about five feet and a half high, some rude unhewn poles, often about the same height, are placed parallel to each other, and reach, angularly one transverse beam, or rafter, at the ridge. A few light pieces, upright or horizontal, are nailed at the sides. A quantity of oat straw, not very artistically laid upon split sticks, nailed over these poles, substitutes the roof. The thatch is secured against the wind, by heath or hay bands staked upon it, and running all over in small squares. A couple of holes, about a foot square, are left in the walls for windows, and another for the doorway; the former near Tyndrum, commonly occupied by a glazed casement, of four panes, or a large single one, and oftener elsewhere, by nothing but a wooden shutter, kept open in the day, and closed at night. The door seldom about five feet high, is generally of board; but I have often seen a kind of willow, or osier-hurdle pretty closely wattled, serve for the same purpose. When the smoke is allowed any other issue than at the door, or windows, four stout sticks set upright, and square, with a few others, running transversly, to frame them, the whole bound round with heather-bands, and plaistered with mortar on the inside, form the chimney. But as these chimneys are seldom so constructed as to exclude the rain, a serious inconvenience in a wet climate, these apertures, in the roof, are often dispensed with, to avoid it. The floor is bare earth, sometimes made even, and tolerably smooth, but oftener left rough. Where the inside of the walls are not plaistered with mortar, the peat, or turf, is so piled up the room, in double, triple, and quadruple rows, as to serve till its consumption, as fewel reaches the wainscot of the house ...

The men wear the short coat, the feilabeg and the short hose, with bonnets sewed with black ribbon around their rims, and a slit behind with the same ribbon in a knot. Their coats are commonly tartan, striped with black, red, or some other colour, after a pattern made, upon a stick, of the yarn, by themselves, or some other ingenious contriver. Their waistcoats are either of the same, or some such stuff; but the feilabegs are commonly of breacan, or fine Stirling plaids, if their money can afford them.

At common work they use either short or long coats and breeches made of striped cloth, and many of them very coarse, according to their work. Their shirts are commonly made of wool; and however coarse they may appear to strangers, they are allowed to conduce much to the health and longlivity for which this country is famous; as I have known them eighty ninety and some even a hundred years old, in these islands, and able to do their daily work.

When they go in quest of the herring, they dress something like the sailors, but of coarser cloth, with hats over their eyes to mark the fish better. They are careful about drying their nets, and other fishing tackle.

Their brogues (shoes) are made of cow or horse leather and often of seals skins that are commonly well tanned by the roots of tormentile which they dig out from hillocks and uncultivated lands about the seaside ... The women wear long or short gowns, with a waistcoat and two petticoats, mostly of the stripes or tartan, as already described, except the lower coat which is white. The married wives wear linen mutches, or caps, either fastened with ribbons of various colours, or with tape straps if they cannot afford ribbons. All of them wear a small plaid, a yard broad, called guilechan, about their shoulders, fastened by a large broach. The broaches are generally round, and of silver, if the wearer be in tolerable circumstances; if poor, the broaches, being either circular or triangular, are of baser metal and modern date. The first kind has been worn time immemorial even by the ladies. The arrisats are quite laid aside in all this country, by the different ranks of women; being the most ancient dress used by that class. It consisted of one large piece of flannel that reached down to the shoe, and fastened with clasps below, and the large silver broach at the breast, while the whole arm was entirely naked. The ladies made use of the finer, while common women used coarser kinds of flannel, or white woolen cloths. The married women bind up their hair with a large pin into a knot on the crown of their heads, below their linens; and the unmarried frequently go bareheaded, with their hair bound with ribbons, or garters. They often wear linen caps, called mutches, particularly on Sabbaths. Many of the more wealthy appear at church with a profusion of ribbons and head-dresses, with cloaks, and high-healed shoes. Those whose circumstances cannot admit of that, must appear with one of their petticoats either tartan or of one colour, around their shoulders, on Sundays as well as on weekdays. They seldom travel anywhere without this appendage ... Most of them wear napkins, or handkerchiefs, on their necks; and many of the richest of them use silk ones, whether black or spotted, as suits their fancies.

Frequently the old women wear little guilechans, (small plaids) about their shoulders and woolen hoods about their heads, with very coarse linen under them fastened with a pin below their chins. The breeid, or curtah, a fine linen handkerchief fastened about married women's heads, with a flap hanging behind their backs, above the guilechan is mostly laid aside.

Every subtenant must have his own beams and other side timbers. Four or five couples, with their compliment of side timbers, are reckoned a good sufficience for a hut. The walls of them are six feet thick, packed with moss or earth in the middle, with a facing of rough stones built on both sides. This is called a stall, and commonly belongs to the master: upon this the timbers are erected as follows.

First, the beams and spars are bound together by ropes made of heather or bent, and placed standing on these stalls. Then the side rafters are fastened with ropes to those beams pretty fast, and the rows of ropes wrought very close, so as to keep the stubble with which the houses are thatched from falling through. For the beams and roof tree, with the side timbers, could not bear the weight of divats above them, and therefore the ropes must be the thicker plaited over them.

Their cakes are made of barley meal, and toasted against a stone placed upright before a good fire, and sometimes, when either haste or hunger impels them, they are laid on the ashes, with more ashes above, to bake them more quickly. The men keep their tobacco in leather bags made of seal skins, called spleuchans which keep the tobacco soft and tastely. They make very neat wooden locks, both for their doors and chests. They are made of the same materials: and I have seen pieces of wooden workmanship such as trunks chests, and tobacco pipes, so well made, and elegantly engraved, as would not disgrace the most capital artist.

This ware (kemp) is cut with sickles every third year, for kelp, and the immense quantity of cast ware which hurls daily on the shore for the same use, bring very rich returns from the markets to the owners yearly ... The Kelp Kilns are from eight to twelve feet long, and three feet broad. After one floor full is burnt of the kelp, or ware, two men work the red-hot liquid with irons made for the purpose, until that also is hard; and then they burn another stratum above, and the same operation is gone through, until that also is hardened into a solid body, and so on from one stratum to another, and then it is well covered with turfs, to keep out the rain, until a vessel arrives to carry it to the markets.

In many parts of Scotland a practice prevails, which not only lessens the expense of the weddings, but even makes them so profitable as to enrich the young couple. That is what is called penny weddings, at which the bridegroom prepares a feast, and invites the whole country. Everyman, and every woman, pays a shilling, which voracious as they may be, is twice as much as the value of what they eat. The men drink four or five shillings a-piece, so that (to such poor people) a great sum is collected. These penny weddings, and all promiscuous meetings it is said contribute much to the population.

Saint Fond: *Travel in England and Scotland—1784*

A peat fire, on a large round stone, raised ten inches above the floor, and placed in the middle of the room, served to warm it. The smoke rose vertically through an aperture in the middle of the roof. A rustic wainscot, in shape like an inverted mill-hopper, starting at their aperture and gradually widening downwards, descends to within four feet of the ground, at the distance of three feet from the wall of the hut. It is therefore necessary to stoop on entering this room or rather this chimney . . . This construction is well adapted to preserve the inmates both from smoke and cold; . . . When we were seated, a young man shut the window, a second lighted a lamp, of a peculiar form which gave a large flame accompanied by resinous smoke. This economical lamp consisted of a kind of iron shovel, bent towards the bottom into a knee shape, and hung by a long handle in an angle of the chimney within reach of the spectators. On this were lighted some pieces of resinous wood chiefly cut from pinus taeda, and well dried, which gave a very bright flame intermixed, however with a great deal of smoke. The person in charge of the lamp, has beside him a supply of this wood cut into small bits with which he constantly replaces what is consumed. [Footnote by Ford. Though wood is now extremely scarce in the country and there is not a pine of this kind to be seen, nevertheless old stumps of it are found at the depth of several feet in the peat mosses.]

The hamlet of Tyndrum consists of only a few houses almost all detached it stands upon a low marshy piece of ground; a humid and unwholesome vapour renders the site disagreeable.

The place where the lead-ore is found is not far from the inn in actual distance, but a good deal in height, for the galleries have to be sought on a pretty high mountain difficult of access. They are cut through a grey micaceous schistose rock, with much white quartz: the vein of lead is found in a vein of the later substance. The ore is usually accompanied by pyrites or blende, and is fairly abundant. It is sometimes covered with pretty crystals of calcareous spar. The galleries in general are very badly kept up, an the works are negligently managed.

The pieces of ore are sorted out, broken with hammers, and then washed to separate the ore from foreign substances. Thus prepared the ore is sent to the foundry in the valley at the bottom of the mountain and cast into the melting furnace. Charcoal and turf are being used, but I do not know in what proportion . . . I observed under large sheds considerable piles of peat and near them a heap of pit coal . . . It appears that the lead-mines of Tyndrum have formerly been more productive and valuable.

John Knox: *The Highlands and Hebrides—1786*

Near this Lake (Loch Lubnich) are some natural woods, consisting chiefly of dwarf-oak, now a valuable article on account of the bark, which sells at one shilling a stone. (Near Dalmally) A commodious inn at this place is rented at £6. and the window-tax amounts to £4. 10s. This disproportion arises from the well-judged munificence of the proprietor, who thus almost at his own expense, accommodates travellers with decent lodging.

In order to preserve the trifling crops of grain that are raised here, (West Coast) the corn is carried, in wet weather, and as soon as it is cut down, into barns where it is dried by means of sifting air.

He declares that the greatest bar in the way of every exertion in these islands, is the high duty on, and the vexatious trouble attending the purchase of salt and coals. As an instance of the inconvenience the inhabitants undergoe with regard to the latter, he stated the following fact. "I sent a sloop loaded with coals from Greenock to this place; I offered to pay duty at the custom-house of Greenock, but it was refused. The sloop sprung a leak on the passage, and the factor on her arrival thought it advisable to unload the coals, but at the same time wrote to the collector at Stornaway, in Lewis, mentioning the circumstances, and requesting he would send an officer to see the coals measured, that the bond might be relieved and the duty paid, and that he (the factor) would defray any expense attending his journey. The collector returned for an answer that he would not comply with the request, as it was absolutely necessary that the sloop should be sent to Stornaway from the port of Rowdil, where she had in the meantime arrived, and had discharged the coals.

The factor was obliged to ship the coals a second time, and send the vessel to Stornaway, where they were landed, reshipped a third time, and brought back to Rowdil, not only attended with great expense, but with the mortifying delay of every work then on hand. This, and like circumstances, says he, are found more grating, as government reaps no benefit from the tax, as it almost totally prevents any coals from being brought into this country. Were it otherwise, not only the proprietors of coal pits would be benefited, but all improvements here would be facilitated, the fuel of this country not being near to proper."

My course being northward, I had an agreeable passage through that part of the channel, called Kyle Ree, which though no more than a quarter of a mile wide, has a depth of water sufficient for the largest ships. Here the flood tide runs at seven miles an hour; but at the lowest ebb, this straight is the usual passage where horses, and black cattle, are swam across, between Sky and the mainland; for though this is the principal passage to that great island, it is not accommodated with a horse-ferry. When horses are to be taken over, they are pushed off the rock into the water. A small boat with five men attends, four of them holding the halters of a pair on each side of the boat. When the black cattle are to cross the Kyle, one is tied by the horn to the boat, a second is tied to the first; and a third to the second; and so on, to eight, ten or twelve.

Hon Mrs Murray: *A companion and useful guide to the beauties of Scotland—1799*

In most of the sequested parts of the Highlands the substitute for tallow candles are the stumps of birch and fir trees, which the Highlanders dig out of the peat mosses when they cut that fuel. These stumps appear to have lain buried in bogs for a vast time; and when prepared for candles, they really give a charming light, but of short duration. After drying these stumps thoroughly they cut them into slips like long matches, which are burned singly, or in a bundle, according to the light required. It falls to the lot of whatever useless being there is in a hut (old folks or children), to hold this torch, and renew it; for it burns out very fast. It is a pleasant sight to see an old woman of seventy or eighty, dressed in her snow-white cursche, sitting by a cosy (snug) fire, holding this clear taper for daughter and grandchildren while they are some spinning, others singing and dancing and a group of youngsters playing on the ground with each other, and their faithful sheep dog.

Beauties of Scotland—1805

This river, particularly about Callander, considerable quantities of muscles, which some years ago afforded great profit to those who fished them, by the pearls they contained, which sold at high prices. Some of the country people made £100 in a season by that employment ... They are fished with a kind of spear, consisting of a long shaft, and terminated by two iron spoons, forming a kind of forceps. The handles of these spoons are long and elastic, which keeps the mouth closed, but they open upon being pressed against anything. With this machine in his hand, by way of a staff, the fisher being up to the chin in water gropes with his feet for mussels, which are fixed by one end in mud or sand; he presses down the forceps, which opens and grasps the shell, and enables him to pull it to the surface. He has a net-bag hanging by his side to carry the muscles till he comes ashore where they are opened.

Rev Hall: *Travels in Scotland—1807*

It was now time to call for what I had to pay. The landlord said, that his "gude wife managed these things". Being sent for, she came smiling into the room, and was prevailed on to sit down, and take a glass of wine. Instead of presenting a bill, she said with hesitation, "I am sure I dinna ken weel to say what the skaith (loss or expenditure) has been, I wot weel, it has nae been muckle". I reminded her, that I had both breakfasted and supped the day before, of my bed, my horse etc. She proposed, rather than charged a small sum for each article; stating at the same time, the grounds for each. For example, for the whisky-punch after supper—"I canna charge mair than a shilling, for the mutchkin (an English pint) for my aqua vita", pronounced akka vytie. "I didna think you used mair nor an ounce or twa of sugar. For the hen you have had hens are now very dear, nane under eighteenpence at the lowest; but the half of the hen is to the fore, and it winna be lost". Here I interupted my simple hostess "My dear and good lady, I pray do not reckon up the value of the remains I have been wandering about, as hungry as a hawk, and have ate like a highland drover"—"Waes me, Sir, you have ate nothing". The result was, as I stated in the account, which I took down with my pencil from the mouth of my landlady.

	£	s.	d.
Breakfast or luncheon or both. Tea, eggs ham etc	0	0	8
Supper, including whisky-punch	0	1	8
Breakfast again, in the style of the former	0	0	8
Dinner	0	1	0
A bottle of wine, and a bottle of English porter	0	3	6
Corn hay for my horse	0	2	0
	0	9	6

I reminded mine hostess that I had had a dram of ferintosh after the trouts. "Oh," said she "that was out of our bottle" I put her in mind that I had had a bed, and that a very good one. "Oh" said she and in the same breath the landlord, "We have never thank God, charged anything for a bed, and I hope never will need to do sick an unchristian-like thing". (This from Perthshire)

Ragwort ... when young besides being good for sheep is found to contain an excellent dye stuff, it is a fact that from the bark of the elder or arn tree, as the common people call it, the juice of ragweed, and a few other productions of the country, the women of the interior even at this day, as has been done in all ages, produce in their tartans etc as various and vivid colours as the dyers in England can do with their foreign drugs; and, however much the tanners may call the fact in question, certain it is, that besides producing an excellent die, the bark of the alder, as well as that of the birch tree, contains an excellent tawn; and they are often employed for that purpose by the country people, many of whom make, even yet, their own shoes; and, as their forefathers did, to avoid the tax on leather, privately tawn hides with the bark of birch and alder.

Garnett: *Tour of Scotland—1811*

Shoals of herring frequent this Loch (Loung now spelled Long) and afford occupation to a number of fishermen; at present there were few boats, and those were preparing to set out for Loch Fyne, where the herring fishery was just beginning. The other fish which frequent Loch Loung, are cod, haddocks, whitings, flounders, mackarel, trout, and sometimes salmon; but no person in the neighbourhood except a very few individuals, pays attention to any other fishery than that of herrings. Each man employed in the herring fishery on this loch, clears on an average £8 or £10 between the month of September and the first of January, besides laying up a sufficient quantity of herring for their winter food.

The shepherds as I observed before, are the servants of the tenants; their allowance is a cottage, fifty stones of oatmeal, grass for two cows, a little ground for potatoes, and the liberty of pasturing a few sheep with their master's flock. The value of all these advantages may be equal to about £14 or £15 sterling per annum.

Drying barns have been found very useful in so wet a climate, for by means of them hay may be made, or corn dried, during the heaviest rains. The building stands across the valley, and is of a circular form, and so contrived as to cause a draught of air even in calm weather, there being open arches, opposite to each other, through the whole building. It is divided into two stories, and the upper one is used for drying; the lower consisting of cow-houses and other conveniences. The floor of the upper story is made of small boards or battens, about an inch distant from each other to receive the benefit of the air below. There are likewise openings, in the sides of the walls at convenient heights, to receive the hay and corn from the carts. On this floor the grass is laid soon after it is cut, a few hands serve to turn it over for two or three days, when it is found perfectly dry, and of a much finer flavour than hay dried by the hot sun. In this story are jointed frames of wood, suspended from the roof, at convenient distances from each other. These frames have a number of sharp pointed pegs on each side of them, inclining upwards; upon each of which a sheaf of corn is hung to dry. The frames by means of joints, are lowered down to receive the corn; and when the drying is finished they are moved up again out of the way. (Argyll)

The Quern consists of two circular pieces of stone, generally of grit or granite, about twenty inches in diameter. In the lower stone is a wooden peg rounded at the top; on this the upper stone is nicely balanced, so as just to touch the lower one, by means of a piece of wood fixed in a large hole in this upper piece, but which does not fill the hole, room for feeding the mill being left on each side; it is so nicely balanced, that though there is some friction from the contact of the two stones, yet a very small momentum will make it revolve several times, when it has no corn in it. The corn being dried, two women sit down on the ground, having the Quern between them; one feeds it, while the other turns it round, relieving each other occasionally, and singing some Celtic songs all the time.

Larkin: *Sketches of a tour in the Highlands of Scotland—1817*

Many of the men and women went to the low countries and were employed there in the harvest labour, which is usually finished before the Highland harvest began.

Torrents of smuggled whiskey, increasing as they proceed, descend from both sides of the ridge ... The illicit manufacture of this article is almost universal over all the Highlands and Islands; and whiskey is to the full as much a staple commodity as black cattle, sheep and wool. The people, anxious to remain among their native straths and mountains, outbid the great capitalists for their possessions; and the smuggling of whiskey is the only resource for the regular payment of their rents ... In the middle of the darkest and most stormy nights the whiskey is sent down towards the low country on horseback, or in carts along the great roads, in bladders carried on men's shoulders along the pathless wilds, or in boats along the lakes and rivers; the smugglers sometimes proceed trusting to the better opportunity of concealment, at other times uniting in considerable parties, and placing their security on their formidable appearance and numbers. Journeying by night, and hiding by day, they usually convey their commodity to its destination and the day-light traveller then sees them returning joyfully with their empty casks. When united in large parties, they sometimes travel with their whiskey by day; and the excise officers although they meet them on the road, feel it necessary to allow them to pass without asking questions, or find reason to repent their useless interference.

Cobbett: *Tour in Scotland—1832*

That all the beef I have tasted in Scotland has been excellent. It appears to come from the little oxen which the Highlanders send down in such droves; and a score of which, please God give me life, I will have next year in Surrey. I should suppose that these little oxen, when fatted, weigh about twenty score which is about the weight of a Hampshire hog eighteen months or two years. The joints are of course, small compared with the general run of beef in London. A sirloin appears not to be a very great deal larger than a loin of large veal rump and all. The meat is exceedingly fine in the grain; and these little creatures will fat where a Devonshire or Lincolnshire ox would starve.

Lord Teigmouth: *Sketches of the coasts of Scotland—1834*

Cod-smacks are capital sailing vessels, well manned, and well appointed; they vary in size, from fifty to sixty tons, and are rigged as sloops, and the crew are well accommodated on board. Each vessel contains a well for the reception of live fish, of which the cargo sometimes amounts to ninety score. To secure a current of water for the preservation of the fish, the vessel keeps the sea as much as possible, and even when in harbour, is usually under sail, the large Lochs of Eribol and Laxford affording ample room for cruising. The character of the skippers of these smacks, as seamen, stands very high in the estimation of the coasters. They are said to be better acquainted with the headlands and landmarks than any other navigators, and yield to none in skill and intrepidity.

Ballachroy affords a pleasing specimen of a Highland village; it consists of a single street, composed of neat but small houses; a good schoolhouse a public house, and the church rising on an adjacent eminence. The houses belong to crofters, there being attached to each a small piece of ground, called a croft, on which vegetables are raised for the use of the family. The numerous little patches in the neighbourhood of the village, belonging to these people and the herd of cows, each keeping one or two, ranging the adjoining hill under the charge of a single lad, awaiting the pleasing conviction of independence and comfort ...

On Sunday, we attended Divine service in the parish church of Ballanchroy. The dress and general appearance of the congregation were highly respectable. The minister officiated in the Gaelic language; but another, who was of our party, supplied afterwards a service in the English; and the congregation, though the greater part understood not the language, remained till its conclusion. The clergy in the Highlands are obliged by an act of the General Assembly, to preach an English sermon on every Sabbath-day, should there be but one hearer incapable of understanding Gaelic.

The stake consists of netting extended upon upright stakes, fixed in the beach or sand-banks, which are left uncovered when the tide ebbs. These stakes run in a line nearly at right angles with the current of the tide, extending from the highwater mark to low-water mark. They are placed at two or three yards distance from each other, or at such other distances as the fishermen find necessary for strength. The netting is stretched tight along the stakes from the ground up to the full height to which the tide rises; the meshes of the net are very large, generally three inches from knot to knot, or twelve inches in circumference, and they are always open. There is thus, as it were a hedge of fence constructed, sufficient to intercept the salmon, but through which the water and all small fish pass freely.

When salmon, running with the tide, come against a stake-net, they swim along the side, seeking an opening through which to pass. To receive them when thus swimming along, an entrance is formed, which leads into a chamber of labyrinth, constructed also by netting, stretched on upright stakes. Into this labyrinth fish pass freely with the tide; but, from its construction, it is hardly possible for them to find their way out; thus they are detained until the tide retires, when they are taken by the fishermen. These chambers have their openings or entrances so placed as to receive the fish going upwards with the flood-tide, or those going downwards with the ebb, according to the set of the tide on the coast happens to lead the fish on the station, in the ebb or in the flood. Frequently there are more chambers than one; and when it is suitable, there are chambers both for the ebb and the flood in the same net.

The tanning of leather has been much prevented by the Excise. The fishermen of Tarbert still avail themselves of the exemption in their favour, granted with a view to the encouragement of the fishery in tanning their nets, using the bark of oak or beech for the practice, though tanneries have been established at both Campbletown and Rothsay. The whole process of shoe or brogue making is performed by the people. The brogue is stitched with wang i.e. thongs of calf leather, instead of hemp, and as the ligament is less tight, admits water freely, but the brogue is also fortified at the toe with an additional covering of leather, to protect it from cutting of the heath. The cow leather is first steeped in water impregnated with lime to consume the hair, which is never retained in the Highland brogue, and then tanned by being steeped in bark water. Brogues are finished in half the time required for shoes; and the difference of the price of the article when purchased is 7s. or 7s. 6d. of the former, and 8s. and 8s. 6d of the later. The cost of the brogue to the shepherd is merely 1s. 3d. the price of the work.

The common household work of repairs & etc is executed by travelling bands of tinkers, (Highlanders), usually consisting of about fifteen or twenty persons, men women and children, who wander about the country living a gipsy life, and are very usefully employed in making lamps, mending pots and pans, and performing other work of this description . . .

I returned to Tarbert . . . They do not carry their fish to market, but adopt the more profitable and expeditious method of selling them in vessels, in which they are cured and conveyed to various parts. They are also barrelled both at Tarbert and Inverary. The outfit of a boat is expensive; the cost of it, including rigging, varies from £30 to £50 and upwards, and may be estimated on average to £40 and the price of a set of nets is £30, or £5 to a piece or barrel, of which six form a net. The usual length of the boat is twenty feet; it is built at Tarbert, Greenock, or Rothsay. It is furnished with three masts, a mainsail, a foresail, and a jib; and part of the bow of the boat is covered by boarding or an awning, in which bedding is placed. When the awning occurs, it is occasionally removed, and instead of bedding a pan of coals is placed, on which the fisherman cooks his provisions when in harbour, or at sea, when the weather permits. Each boat is usually furnished with three men, one of whom is the master, who defrays the whole cost, and receives a double share of the profit of the fishery. He is also exempted by the law from impressment . . . The measure used is called a maize, containing 500 herrings the greatest number I have heard being taken at one time was forty-one maize, the maize then selling at 10s.

The old fashioned kiln for drying corn, in this and the neighbouring islands is of simple construction; a turf-built cone, covering a hole dug in the ground, the sides of which are walled with stones, admitting below an aperture like that in a kiln. The hole is covered with layers of wood and twigs, on which is placed a stone, and in this the grain is deposited for the purpose of being dried after being thrashed in the small bar. The instrument used for this later purpose is metalic.

Wool is also carded and spun by the women and girls, and woven at the loom into plaiding, blankets & etc. The looms are erected in cottages appropriated to the purpose; and supply twenty or more neighbouring farmers with what is called customary work, or work done for customers. The men employed at these looms earn from 2s. to 2s. 6d. per day, wrights, smiths, tailors, shoemakers, & etc are similarly maintained by a cluster of farms; each customer chars his peat and provides the timber, and pays for the work done; sometimes the mechanic is allowed, in lieu of pecuniary compensation, a portion of land. The cloth when woven is dyed by the people; the black colour, which is generally used, is produced from the bark of the elder-tree steeped in a caldron, and called Scotch mahogany. Indigo is purchased, to supply the blue colour, which is preferred near the towns, and where the people are better dressed. The tailor receives a day's wages for making up a coat.

Wilson: *A voyage round the coast of Scotland and the Isles—1842*

(Stornaway) Another fishing of a more peculiar nature likewise occurs here. In the clear weather (should such occur) in the month of October, the people repair at night to those portions of the shore where the stream debouches into the sea, and shallow fords occur. They take chains of blankets which they drag against the stream, at the same time beating the waters above so as to frighten the countless congregations of cuddies or young coal-fish (sethe) into this unusual bedding, and so drag and drive the fish upon the sandy beach. In this way in one night, by a couple of hauls of six blankets, twenty four barrels of cuddies have been captured so vast are the numbers which come up the little firths and freshlets towards the conclusion of the harvest. The fish are both sweet and fat. They are sold at 4d. per peck, and the livers produce an oil which when the article is scarce, brings about a shilling a pint.

Kohl: *Travels in Scotland—1849*

The Scottish bagpipes sound louder and sharper than the Irish pipes particularly because they are intended to sound above the thunder of battle. They are also made differently from Irish pipes. Those used in the army are usually very elegant.

The mull (snuff) is a long winding ram's horn. The horn terminates in a spiral, which is commonly ornamented with a silver thistle, made by some of the famous goldsmiths of Perth, and the lid in most cases adorned with a beautiful cairngorm. As its form is one of the most inconvenient imaginable for the finger a few little silver instruments, attached to the mull by a silver chain, performs its offices, a little hammer, to knock the mull to loosen snuff that may be sticking to the sides, a little spoon to take it out withal, a little scraper to be used occasionally, a little silver mounted hare's foot to be used as a brush and other articles of a similar nature. The whole is attached to the person with silver chains.

We entered the last hut, in order to be instructed once more as to our right direction. A few people were sitting about the fire, and behind the fire was placed a great stone, blackened by the smoke from the turf. On the stone again stood the great Scottish salt-box (saut backet) already alluded to. It looked almost like a little dog's kennel, for, like this it had a small round hole in it. This hole however, is only intended for the arm of the cook. I asked the people why, in Scotland the salt-box always occupies so prominent a place? They replied, that it was partly to have the salt handy for cooking, and partly to keep it dry. "Does not the Bible say 'ye are the salt of the earth'?" said an old man "and according to this text is not salt in a certain manner sacred, and is it not thereby intended that it is one of the best things for our use?" "That is why we hang the salt-box over our hearths."

The two principal and most esteemed national games in Scotland are curling and golf. The former is, of the two the most distinguished and interesting. The beautiful, smooth ice formed upon the smaller Scottish lochs, and upon the inundated banks of rivers, gave rise to the invention of this glorious game, which consists in hurling a round smooth-faced stone at a certain mark on the ice, and not only exercises the strength of the players, but warms and rejoices the heart with all its attendant scenes and circumstances.

Weld: *Two months in the Highlands—1860*

You are indebted for many of the frequent stoppages to the wool trade, which has long been carried on in the Hebrides. This trade has formed a considerable feature in the commerce of Scotland since the period when a commission appointed by James VI in 1616 reported against the exportation of wool, and in favour of manufacturing it into plaids, stuffs, and kerseys. Previous to that time it was shipped to the Low Countries and elsewhere.

We learn some curious particulars respecting this foreign wool trade from the ledger of a Scotch merchant, named Andrew Haliburton, who resided at Middleburgh and carried on business with Bruges and Antwerp, in the later part of the fifteenth century. His books show that he sold wool on commission, for thirty one marks per sack, equal to £61 18s.; and that the usual commodities shipped back to Scotland were Claret, Rhenish, vinegar, Maloise, canvas, fustian, velvet, damask, satin, pepper, ginger, mace, cloves, and soap.

In the drover days, when the sheep and cattle tramped wearily day after day to London, in order to be eaten when they got there, instead of travelling in their open carriages, as they do now, upon the great iron roads of the land, the dog was often summarily dismissed as soon as he had escorted his charges safe to their doom. Master went home on top of the coach; but Laddie must find his way back alone and on foot. And how about his rations by the way? Ah; that was all an understood thing. Laddie, alas knew every public house on the road, knew perfectly well where his master baited and lodged, and was himself well known in the accustomed haunts. "Oh, here's the drover's dog come back; very well, give him his feed"; and the expected bowl of porridge, sometimes varied by the luxury of a bone was forthwith supplied. A short siesta followed; and then, stretching his tired limbs, Laddie was off again for his distant home.

The Market (Aberdeen) was filled to overflowing (it was market day) with a profusion of fish, flesh, fowls, fruit, and vegetables. There were heaps of delicious strawberries, not sold in attenuated pottles tapering to nothingness, but in capacious cabbage leaves at prices astonishing to a Londoner. Serried ranks of baskets filled with golden hued fresh butter, resting on snow white cloths—and hear it, ye cockney housewives only 11d. a pound. Piles of fish, among them salmon were very conspicuous,—the best cuts 9d. a pound—and a prodigious number of fowls whose decease must have reduced the harems of many chanticleers to the condition of single-wife man.

The sea was literally covered by boats, all similar in size and rig, and differing only by numberals on the bows beneath a huge W. (Wick) As we drew near the harbour, the boats were closer packed, until at its entrance, we were obliged to go at quarter speed to guard against frequent collisions. At length the steamer reached her moorings, and after more than usual confusion, occasioned by disembarking in boats, we landed.

The bustle was amazing. You had to keep a sharp lookout to avoid being tripped up by ropes, or caught in the wet nets which were being hauled out of the newly arrived boats. Besides these, the narrow quay was encumbered by hundreds of carts in readiness to carry the herrings to the gutting troughs. And the herrings—there had been a great take on the previous night, and in every boat were silvery heaps glistening in the rays of the rising sun. Now, indeed, you are enabled to form some idea of the deep, and how inexhaustible is that storehouse. The Wick boats are provided with sets of nets 850 yards long and manned by four men and a boy. The cost of each boat fully equipped for fishing is about £150, the profit estimated at 1s. per barrel.

Let us watch the operation. First, the herrings are carried as fast as possible in baskets from the boats to the gutting-troughs until the boats are emptied of their scaly treasures. Then, the women, familiarly called gutters, pounce upon the herrings like birds of prey, seize their victims, and, with a rapidity of motion which baffles your eye, deprives the fish of its viscera. The operation, which a damsel, not quite so repulsive as her companions obligingly performed for me in slow time, is thus effected. The herring is seized in the left hand, and by two dexterous cuts made with a sharp short knife in the neck an opening is effected sufficiently large to enable the viscera and liver to be extracted. These with the gills are thrown into a barrel, and the gutted fish cast among his eviscerated companions. I timed the Wick gutters an average twenty-six herrings a minute.—The herrings undergo successive packings at various intervals of time before the barrels are finally closed. At each packing more salt is added, and at the final packing great care is taken to dispose the herrings in even layers.

The viscera is deposited in barrels and sold to farmers for manuring purposes, at the average price of 1d. per barrel.

Alexander Smith: *A summer in Skye—1865*

When Peter came in with his violin the kitchen was cleared after nightfall; the forms were taken away, candles stuck into the battered tin sconces, the dogs unceremoniously kicked out, and a somewhat ample ballroom was the result. Then in came the girls, with black shoes and white stockings, newly-washed faces and nicely-smoothed hair; and with them came the shepherds and menservants, more carefully attired than usual. Peter took his seat near the fire; M'Ian gave the signal by clapping his hands; up went the dancers, man and maid facing each other, the girl's feet twinkling beneath her petticoat, not like two mice, but rather like a dozen; her kilted partner pounding the flag-floor unmercifully; then man and maid changed step, and following each other through loops and chains; then they facd each other again, the man whooping, the girl's hair coming down with her exertions; then suddenly the fiddle changed time, and with a cry the dancers rushed at each other, each pair getting linked arm in arm, and away the whole floor dashed into the whirlwind of the reel of Hoolichan.

... In a little while the road was filled with cattle, driven forward with oath and shout. Every now and then a dog-cart came skirring along, and infinite was the confusion, and dire clamour of tongues, when it plunged into a herd of sheep or skittish "three year olds". At the entrance to the fair the horses were taken out of the vehicles, and left, with a leather thong fastened round their fore-legs, to limp about in search of breakfast. On either side of the road stood hordes of cattle the wildest looking creatures, with fells of hair hanging over their eyes, and tossing horns of preposturous dimensions. On knolls apart women with white caps and wrapped in scarlet tartan plaids, sat beside a staked cow or poney, or perhaps a dozen sheep, patiently waiting the advances of a customer.

Troops of horses neighed from stakes. Sheep were there, too, in restless throngs and masses, continually changing their shapes scattering hither and thither like quicksilver, insane dogs and men flying along their edges. What a hubbub of sound! what lowing and neighing! what bleating and barking!

Down in the hollow ground tents had been knocked up since dawn; there potatoes were being cooked for drovers who had been travelling all night, there also liquor could be had. To these places I observed contracting parties invariably repaired to solemnise a bargain.

At last we reached the fair ... Picking my steps through the fair—avoiding a flock of sheep on the one side, and a column of big horned black cattle on the other, with some difficulty getting out of the way of an infuriated bull that came charging up the road scattering everything right and left, a dozen blown drovers panting at its heels—I soon quit the turmoil—When I got back to the fair about noon it was evident that a considerable stroke of business had been done. Hordes of bellowing cattle were being driven towards Broadford, and drovers were rushing about in a wonderful manner, armed with tar-pot and stick, and smearing their peculiar mark on the shaggy hides of their purchases ... As I advanced, the booths ranged along the side of the road—empty when I passed them several hours ago were plentifully furnished with confections, ribbons and cheap jewellery, and around these fair-headed and scarlet-plaided girls swarmed thickly as bees round summer flowers.

A group of many-coloured rough Highland cattle had wandered down from the green hills, and were cooling themselves in the sea, and nibbling sea-weed; which I believe in winter time when other pasture is buried in snow, afford a livelihood to cattle and sheep, and sometimes even to deer.

Little carts, drawn by shaggy ponies, whose harness was the most primitive combination of bits of old rope, connected by twists of the strong wiry grass of the sandhills (bent, we call it on the east coast). Now the carts were tilted up and watched over by wise collie-dogs while the ponies were turned loose to graze on the heather ...

... The large seeds of Western forest trees, ... are esteemed great treasures, and are worn as charms, especially by women whose progeny is not as numerous as they might wish ... The commoner seeds are of two sorts, a large purplish brown bean with a black band, and a round grey one ...

The lilies are very precious to the islanders, who use their roots for dyeing wool. Another rich brown dye is obtained from some of the dark mosses and lichens that make such kindly coverings for the cold rocks. Heather yields a yellow colour, and a warm red is extracted from the common bramble.

Queen Victoria: *Leaves from the journal of our life in the Highlands from 1848–61, pub. 1868, also, More leaves from the journal of a life in the Highlands, 1883—12 September 1850*

We lunched early, and then went at half-past two o'clock, with the children and all our party, except Lady Douro, to the Gathering at the Castle of Braemar, as we did last year. ... There were the usual games of "putting the stone", "throwing the hammer" and "caber" and racing up the hill of Craig Cheunnich, which was accomplished in less than six minutes and a half.

10 September 1852
We dined at a quarter-past six o'clock in morning gowns, (not ordinary ones, but such as are worn at a "breakfast") and at seven started for Dorriemulzie, for a torch-light ball in

147

the open air. I wore a white bonnet, a grey watered silk, and (according to Highland fashion) my plaid scarf over my shoulder.

20 September 1861
... We crossed the burn at the bottom, where a picturesque group of "shearers" were seated, chiefly women, the older ones smoking. They were returning from the south to the north, whence they came.

11 October 1861
Another wretchedly wet morning. Was much distressed at breakfast to find that poor Brown's legs had been dreadfully cut by the edge of his wet kilt on Monday, just at the back of the knee, and he said nothing about it; but today one became so inflamed, and swelled so much, that he could hardly move.

31 October 1886
While we were at Mrs Grant's we saw the commencement of the keeping of Halloween. All the children came out with burning torches, shouting and jumping. The Protestants generally keep Halloween on the old day, November and the Catholics on this day; but hearing I had wished to see it two years ago, they all decided to keep it to-day. When we drove home we saw all the gillies coming along with burning torches, and torches and bonfires appeared also on the opposite side of the water.

1868
At a quarter to twelve I drove off ... to see them "juice the sheep". This is a practice pursued all over the Highlands before the sheep are sent down to the low country for the winter. It is done to preserve the wool. Not far from the burnside where there are a few hillocks, was a pen in which the sheep were placed, and then, just outside it, a large sort of trough filled with liquid tobacco and soap, and into this the sheep were dipped one after the other; one man ... took the sheep one by one out of the pen and turned them on their backs; and then William and he, holding them by their legs, dipped them well in, after which they were let into another pen into which this trough opened, and here they had to remain to dry. To the left, a little lower down, was a cauldron boiling over a fire and containing the tobacco with water and soap; this was then emptied into a tub from which it was transferred into the trough. A very rosie-faced lassie, with a plaid over her head was superintending this part of the work, and helped to fetch the water from the burn, while children and many collie dogs were grouped about, and several men and shepherds were helping. It was a very curious and picturesque.

13 June 1870
... Here, in the nearest adjoining field, close to the wall, all the sheep (mine) were in a pen and James Brown, the shepherd, and Morrison my grieve at Invergelder assisted by others ... took them out one by one, tied their legs together, and then placed them on the laps of the women who were seated on the ground, and who clipped them one after the other, wonderfully well, with huge scissors or clippers. Four were seated in a sort of half-circle ... of whom three were Mrs Durran, Mrs Leys (both these did their work admirably) and Mrs Morrison, who seemed rather new to it, and had some difficulty with these great heavy sheep, which kick a good deal. The clippers must take them between their knees, and it is very hard work. Four other women were sitting close under the wall, also clipping. Then the sheep were all marked; and some, before being clipped, had to have their horns sawn off the prevent them growing into their heads. It was a very picturesque sight and quite curious to see the splendind thick wool peel off like a regular coat.

Buchanan: *The Land of Lorne—1871*

On a summer afternoon, while we are wandering in the road near the shore, we see the cattle beginning to flock from the pastures, headed by two gentle bulls, and gathering round the dairy house, where, in "short-gowns", white as snow, the two head dairymaids sit on their stools. The kine low softly, as the milk is drawn from the swelling udder, and now and then a calf, desperate with thirst, makes a plunge at his mother and drinks eagerly with closed eyes till he is driven away.

We visit many of their houses, and hold many of their hands. Kindly, gentle open-handed as melting charity, we find them all; the poorest of them as hospitable as the proudest chieftan of their race. There is a gift everywhere for the stranger, and a blessing to follow, for they know that after all he is bound for the same bourne.

A busy sight indeed is Loch Boisdale or Stornoway in the herring season. Smacks, open boats, skiffs, wherries, make the narrow waters shady; not a creek, however small, but holds some boat in shelter. A fleet, indeed! the Lochleven boat from the east coast, with its three masts, and three huge lugsails; the Newhaven boat with its two lugsails; the Isle of Man "Jigger"; the beautiful Guernsey runner, handsome as a racing yacht, and powerful as a revenue-cutter; besides all the numberless fry of less noticeable vessels, from the fat west-country smack with its comfortable fittings down to the miserable Arran wherry. (The Arran, now nearly extinct is a wretched-looking thing without a bowsprit, but with two strong masts. Across the foremast is a bulkhead, and there is a small locker for blankets and bread. In the open space between bulkhead and locker birch tops are thickly strewn for a bed, and for coverings there is a huge woollen waterproof blanket ready to be stretched out on spars. Close to the mast lies a huge stone, and thereon a stove. The cable is of heather rope, the anchor wooden, and the stock a stone. Rude and ill-found as these boats are, they face weather before which any ordinary yachtman would quail.) Swarms of seagulls float everywhere, and the loch is so oily with fishy deposit that it requires a strong wind to ruffle its surface.

The boat's head is brought up to the wind, and the sails are lowered in an instant. One man grips the helm, another seizes the back rope of the net, a third the "skunk" or body, a fourth is placed to see the buoy clear and heave them out, the rest attend forward, keeping a sharp look-out for other nets, ready, in case the boats should run too fast, to steady her by dropping the anchor a few fathoms into the sea. When all the nets are out, the boat is brought bow on to the net, the "swing" (as they call the rope attached to the net) secured to the smack's "bits", and all hands then lower the mast as quickly as possible. The mast lowered, secured, and made all clear for the hoisting at a moment's notice, and the candle lantern set up in the iron stand made for the purpose of holding it, the crew leave one look-out on deck with instructions to call them at a fixed hour, and turn in for a nap in their clothes.

Day breaks and every man is on deck. All hands are busy at work, taking the net in over the bow, two supporting the body, the rest hauling the back rope, save one who draws the net into the hold, and another who arranges it from side to side in the hold to keep the vessel even. Tweet! Tweet! that thin cheeping sound resembling the razor-like call of the bat, is made by the dying herrings at the bottom of the boat. The sea to leeward, the smack's hold, the hands and arms of the men, are gleaming like silver. As many of the fish as possible are shaken loose during the process of hauling in, but the rest are left in the net until the smack gets to shore. Three or four hours pass away in this wet and tiresome work. At last however the nets are all drawn in, the mast is hoisted, the sail set, and while the cook plunges below to prepare breakfast, the boat makes for Loch Boisdale.

Even when the anchorage is reached, the work is not quite finished; for the fish has to be measured out in "cran" baskets and delivered to the curing station. A cran holds rather more than a herring barrel, and the average value of a cran measure of herrings is about one pound sterling. By the time the crew have got their morning dram, having arranged the nets snugly in the stern, and have had some herrings for dinner, it is time to be off again to the harvest field. Half the crew turn in for sleep, while the other half hoist sail and conduct the vessel out to sea.

. . . Tormentil, properly pounded and prepared furnishes a first-rate tan for cow or horse leather, of which the people make shoes.

The rafters of most of the dwellings on the sea shore are composed of the great logs of driftwood which find their way over the ocean to the western coasts—mighty trees, with stumps of roots and branches still remaining, wafted from the western continents. Many of these trunks are covered with the foliage of seaweed, and adorned with barnacles.

In hard times the people subsist almost entirely on shell-fish such as cockles and mussels, which abound on the endless sea-coast. At certain seasons of the year, they reap an excellent harvest out of the cuddies or young lithe which appear on the coast in numbers nearly as great as the herring fry.

Cumming: *In the Hebrides—1883*

I have sat sometimes at this spot throughout the beautiful long day without seeing a living creature save a group of picturesque lassies, in the usual short petticoat and white bed-gown, with bare feet and bright scarlet or white handkerchief on their glossy hair, half hidden by the huge bundle of heather which they would have to carry six or eight miles, that the men might rethatch their bothies . . .

. . . The small flies, alias midges, was a sure bond of sympathy, for these little miscreants are the very torture of life in Skye. You have only to brush over the heather, and even if by accident they were at rest, up they start in ravenous myriads, making work literally impossible till at last, with fevered blood, and face and hands literally swollen by their attacks, you probably have to leave the spot to which you had attained with such toil and trouble, and make for home or the seashore as fast as you can . . . We tried every conceivable mixture to drive them away, and even sent to a London physician for special antidotes for our tormentors, but all prescriptions failed, and we found that the only thing approaching to relief was always to carry a small bottle of essential oil of lavender, with which to rub our face and hands . . .

So apparently does the kindly-looking old crone in the large clean white cap bound round her head with a rusty black ribbon, who bends over the peat fire turning the well-browned oat-cakes on the flat iron girdle which hangs from a heavy chain, suspended from the open chimney, down which streams a ray of light which perchance glances on the blue bonnet and silvery hair of the old grand-father, who sits in the corner quietly knitting his stout blue stockings, and perhaps indulging in a pipe at the same time. A tidy woman dressed, like all the family, in warm thick homespun, is spinning at her wheel, the most picturesque of all occupations, and the most soothing of sounds. Possibly the home also owns a loom in which she can weave the yarn of her own spinning, and so indeed clothe her household in the work of her own hands.

Probably the baby is in a rough wooded cradle at her side, the bigger bairns being away at school; ... Near the fire are a heap of peats, drying for future use and perhaps some tarry wool, and a coil of rope, and fishing nets, proving here that farming and fishing are combined professions.

A few plates and bowls, spoons and wooden porringers, stand on the rude dresser. A rickety table, a few stools and benches (all probably made of worm-eaten driftwood), complete the furniture, always excepting the kist, or seaman's chest, which contains all the Sunday garments of the family, then and perhaps, too, the carefully treasured winding-sheets, prepared by the good-wife for herself and her husband against the day when they will surely be required ...

Many of the houses are most picturesque. In old age the thatch acquires a canopy of gold and brown velvety moss, and is perhaps also adorned with so rich a crop of grass as is positively valuable to the thrifty gude-wife, who, mounting on the roof with her rusty sickle, carefully cuts it all for her cow, should she be so fortunate as to possess one.

Anderson Smith: *Lewsiana life in the Outer Hebrides—1874*

The herring fleet, "All in a bunch" to be covered by a blanket if it were big enough, is entering the harbour, and skimming along under a five knot breeze. The sun is going down behind the Lews as the vessels slip quietly to berth.

Meantime there have been "Mustering in hot haste" for the Stornoway fish are no longer for the most part rudely salted in barrels and despatched to market. These large new erections are all for preparations of the famous Stornaway kipper, and to one of them we will now hasten. Well built of concrete with clean floors and surrounding benches, the girls come trooping into it, tumble into waterproof petticoats of the most nondescript character, and struggle for their knives, while they bind their left thumbs with a bandage to prevent injury. Merrily they prepare for their work and soon the herring, now arriving in silvery crans from the boats, are being whipped open down the back and gutted with marvelous speed and dexterity. A strong wickerwork basket receives the gutted fish, and by a few dexterous swirls in the vat the contents are thourghly cleansed without handling the fish, which are now tossed into baskets for the pickling vats. In these the brine is tested in the old fashioned way by means of a potato, and after a certain time of immersion—generally a moderate time, as they are not meant to keep for long—the herring are removed hung up upon hooks along strips of wood, and transferred to the smoking huse. This is built high with ventilator on the top, and rows of supporting frames ascending to the summit. On these, rows of fish are placed until the whole filled, when a fire of hardwood shavings with perhaps a little turf or other material as a delicate adjunct is lit on the floor and the contents smoked for a period varying with the market.

... Let us suppose there has been a good year for potatoes, what a work there is for the clergyman! The whole country-side is marrying and giving in marriage. In the year '71, not an unmarried girl over eighteen was left in Shaddar, and everywhere else it was on the same scale. The potato crop did it. But before a Lews young man can hope to make a good matrimonial bargain he must go to the Wick fishing. Once he has proved his manhood by bringing back a few pounds from the everlasting Northern herring harvest, he can calmly look round for the girl that can carry the heaviest creel of peat across the moor, or the heaviest creel of seaweed from the shore beach. Let him add to this a scrap of a lot from the laird, or from the lot of his father, and as soon as he has knocked up a hut, he is a remarkably marriageable young man.

... They say the cows like to have their company and see the fire, and as these are their main stay they pet them accordingly; spoil them with fish bones for sweetmeats and treat them with great familiarity generally.

... The furniture consists of a large chest or two, and sometimes a half-box bed; very little further, excepting the pots in which every article of food in Lewis is conscientiously boiled, and a few necessary dishes for porridge fish and potatoes.

... Amongst the dyes still in use is the grey moss called "crotul" which covers the surface of the outcropping rocks throughout the country. It yields a fine, rich brown dye, much used for stockings and other such articles, seeing it is so easily obtained and always at hand. Soot, more especially that scraped from the iron pot suspender gives a capital maroon colour, and the wives of those farmers who still indulge in home-made clothes often make a good lasting mixture of these two colours. A first-rate black is extracted from the root of the water lily, with which plant many of the small lochs are overgrown; heather, that rare plant becoming the Lews, yields a good yellow; goatsbeard, a green, the root of a small yellow plant growing in the "macher" a fawn colour. It is called rue and is said to be a specious of madder. The root of a small yellow species of cinquefoil or potentilla, abundant all over the country, was formerly generally employed in barking nets, and lines, and is also used as a yellow dye. It is said to be superior to cutch, but the latter has almost entirely superseded it.

Thus any crofter is really independent of civilisation for his clothes, the wool coming from his own sheep, spun by the women of his house; dyes are good, and easily procured; and the yarn is woven into cloth by his neighbour or himself. Besides the common mordant, they use "sooriks" (wood sorrel) with blue and black alum with yellow; while common salt and sea water are sufficient for others. Dulse is used to give a fine purple colour to blue, and otherwise improve it and make it clearer. You often see newly made clothes of capital quality held together by wooden skewers or nails in place of buttons.

We will introduce the reader to a favorite bonne bouche. Take two eggs, together with a little butter and meals, whip them all well up together, and place on the top of a hot barley bannock. Spread evenly over, and hold a live peat above until it firms sufficiently to allow the cake to be toasted before the fire.

It may be observed here that, as the white oats do not grow well in most parts of the Lews, the old native black oats is still cultivated; it has a much smaller grain and smaller yield generally, and is too dark for porridge. This, then, they principally consume in the form of sowans, made thus—as the meal comes from the mill it is steeped in water, until the grain dissolves and the whole sours: this takes from three days to a week. The mixture is then strained, and the fine allowed to settle while water is added regularly to keep it the right consistence. This is kept for making a kind of pudding called sowans, which, when well strained and not allowed to become too sour, is a most agreeable and exceedingly nourishing food. Eaten with milk, it is a favorite supper both among the natives of the Hebrides and many parts of the mainland of Scotland. Ocassionally they slaughter one of their small sheep or some of their chickens, and therewith make soup, adding a few cabbages from their gardens.

When in urgent need of meal the grain is sometimes dried in an iron pot on the fire, and then taken to the quern or handmill, where, however a great quantity is necessarily lost, from the difficulty of collecting it as it issues from between the stones. This meal is called "gratanach" is much liked by some people who could not well digest the common meal, and is the ancient way of preparing it. In olden times also, the barley heads were taken and the grain "switched" out of them, as is done ocassionally in some parts even now, and kiln dried in the husks. Today however the most usual way is by the flail, when the grain is winnowed in the breeze that is always ready for it and then taken to the kiln. Every six or eight crofters join together and build one of these little huts for their mutual benefit. A hole is dug in the centre, with a trench leading to it. This is covered over so as to support a quantity of straw on which the grain is laid. The heat from a peat fire is lead under the straw along the trench, and the grain is thus dried. After this the grain is taken to one of the little mills, also erected by the joint efforts of a portion of the crofters.

Following of the narrow mill-lades from some stream and you will arrive at a little Esquimaux-looking hut. Crawl into this, and you will find two good granite stones; suspended over the centre is a stout bag of woven rushes; through one corner of this the grain trickles into a wooden shoe. As the stone revolves a projecting stick strikes this shoe and tilts the contents into the hole in the stone, the shoe being refilled by the next revolution. The grain is deposited in a hole in the stonework on which the millstone rests, the hut itself being in most cases built of turf. The stones are cut with great labour and patience out of the granite rock by the village mason or blacksmith.

F. Murray: *Summer in the Hebrides—1887*

When Neil Darroch, the lobster fisher and cotter, discovered two years ago that his family of eight or ten children were something cramped for room in his unplastered hut, he gathered some stones which were lying not twenty paces away, sent a message to the neighbours, laid in two bottles of whisky and a few loaves of bread, and in one day the addition was ready for thatching. At the going down of the sun the next day, the bent was roped and made fast with stones, and the family installed under the new gable ...

M. Ferguson: *A visit to Staff and Iona—1894*

A marriage, as a general rule, takes place on a Thursday, and on the evening of the proceeding Monday the invitations are given in person by the bride and her bridesmaid. After dusk they set off together, and commence at the one end of the island—i.e., at the extreme end of the houses—calling at every dwelling, inviting both old and young to the wedding, until they reach the other end. The bridegroom and his best man begin at the opposite end, and go through the same routine as the bride and her maid had done; so that there are none of the inhabitants left without a double invitation to the wedding. On the Tuesday after the invitations all the housewives proceed to the bride's house loaded with nice, plump, nine-month-old chickens, big kebbucks of sweet milk cheese, mutton, hams, and innumerable other dainties for the marriage feast. On the wedding day the friends and relatives of the bride assemble at her father's house, and the bridegroom's friends and relatives assemble at his house. In the respective houses the company sit down and partake of a substantial lunch, usually consisting of bread and biscuits, butter and cheese, & etc and a dram—"maybe twa; wha kens" After lunch the separate parties start from their respective dwellings in procession proceeded by a piper in full Highland costume, the gaudy ribbons of his braw piop waving hither and thither in the breeze, to meet the other party—as previously arranged—at the church. After the solemn marriage ceremony is over ... on leaving the church the two parties join ... The whole company then return in procession, headed by the two pipers, to the place previously prepared—usually a barn— to have a dance, "which is continued until the company are summoned about ten o'clock

Staffa's Fingal's Cave.

to the bride's house where they all sit down to a sumptious supper, the tables groaning with the good things of this life. The tables are always set in a barn for the occasion, there being no room large enough in any of the dwellings to accommodate all the guests. After a good while spent at the wedding feast with toasts and favorite Gaelic songs the company return again to the dance, which is kept up with spirit and joyous glee until break of day, when the company separate and return to their respective homes.

This is another noted Hebridean island, Iona. It was visited by many travellers. Dr. Johnson said of it "that man is little to be envied, whose patriotism would not gain force upon the plains of Marathon, or whose piety would not would not grow warmer among the ruins of Iona."

Chapter 16 The view of the traveller

John Ray: *Selected remains of the learned John Ray—1661 published 1760*

The Scots generally (that is the poorer sort) wear, the men blue bonnets on their heads, and some russet; the women only white linen, which hangs down their backs as if a napkin were pinned about them. When they go abroad none of them wear hats but a party-coloured blanket which they call a plad, over their heads and shoulders. The women generally to us seemed none of the handsomest ... They use much pottage made of coalwort, which they call keal (kale) sometimes broth of decorticated barley. The ordinary country houses are pitiful cots, built of stone, and covered with turves having in them but one small room, many of them no chimneys, the windows very small holes, and not glazed ... In the most stately and fashionable houses, in great towns, instead of ceiling, they cover the chambers with firr boards, nailed on the roof within side. They have rarely any bellows, or warming pans. It is the manner in some places there, to lay on but one sheet as large as two, turned up from the feet upwards. The ground in the valleys and plains bears good corn, but especially beer-barley or bigge and oats, but rarely wheat and rye. We observed little or no fallow grounds in Scotland; some layed ground (i.e. unploughed) we saw, which they manure with sea wrack. The people seem to be very lazy, at least the men, and may be frequently observed to plow in their cloaks. It is the fashion of them to wear cloaks when they go abroad, but especially on Sundays. They lay out most they are worth in cloaths, and a fellow that hath scarce ten groats besides to help himselfe with, you shall see come out of his smoaky cottage clad like a gentleman ... We passed by the Basse Island where we saw, on the rocks innumerable soland geese ... It feeds upon mackrel and herring and the flesh of the young birds smells and tastes strong of these fish ... The laird of this island makes a great profit yearly of the solen geese taken, as I remember they told us £130 sterling ... By the way also we saw glasses made of kelp and sand mixed together, and calcinated in an oven. The crucibles which contained the melted glass, they told us, were made of tobacco-pipe clay ... Their money they reckon after the French manner. A bodel (which is the sixth part of our penny) they call tway-pennies, that is with them two-pence; so that, upon this ground, 12 pennies or a Scotch shilling (that is, six bodels) is a penny sterling. The Scotch piece mark'd with XX, which we are wont to call a Scotch two-pence, is twenty-pence Scotch, that is, two-pence sterling, wanting two bodels, or four pennies Scotch; The piece with XL is four-pence sterling—4 bodels; and so one shilling sterling is 12 shillings Scotch. Thirteen pence half-penny English, a mark Scotch. One pound Scotch, 20d sterling. One bodel they call tway-pennies, (as above) 2 bodels a plack, 3 bodels a baubee 4 bodels 8 pennies, 6 bodels 1 shilling Scotch ...

The people here frequent their churches much better than in England, and have their ministers in more esteem and veneration. They seem to perform their devotions with much alacrity.

Martin Martin: *A description of the Western Islands of Scotland—1703*

Lewis
The cattle produced here are cows, horses, sheep, goats, hogs. These cows are little, but very fruitful, and their beef very sweet and tender. The horses are considerably less here, than in the opposite Continent, yet they plough and harrow as well as bigger horses, though in spring-time they have nothing to feed upon but sea-ware. There are abundance of deer in the Chase of Oservaul, which is 15 miles in compass, consisting in mountains, and valleys between them; this affords good pasturage for the deer, black cattle, and sheep. This forest for so they call it, is surrounded with the sea, except about one mile upon the west side; the deer are forced to feed on sea-ware, when the snow and frost continue long, having no wood to shelter in, and are so exposed to the rigour of the season.

There are a great many fresh-water lakes in this island, which abound with trouts and eels. The common bait used for catching them is earthworms, but a handful of parboiled mussels thrown into the water attracts the trouts and eels to the place; the fittest for catching them is when the wind blows from the southwest. There are several rivers on each side of this island which affords salmons, as also black mussels, in which many times pearl is found.

Harris
The natives make use of the seeds of a white carrot, instead of hops, for brewing their beer; and they say that it answers the end sufficiently well, and gives the drink a good relish besides ... Allium latisolium, a kind of wild garlic is much used by the natives, as a remedy against the stone: they boil it in water, and drink the infusion, and it expels sand powerfully with great ease.

I have seen a great many rats in the village Rowdil, which became very troublesome to the natives, and destroyed all their corn, milk, butter, cheese, and they could not extirpate these vermin for some time by all their endeavours. A considerable number of cats were employed for this end, but were still worsted, and became perfectly faint because overpowered by the rats, who were twenty to one. At length one of the natives, of more sagacity than his neighbours, found an expedient to renew his cat's strength and courage, which was by giving it warm milk after every encounter with the rats; and the like being given to all the other cats after every battle, succeeded so well, that they left not one rat alive, notwithstanding the great number of them in the place ...

North Uist

The arable ground hath a mixture of clay in some places; and it is covered all over in summer time and harvest with clover, daisy, and a variety of other plants, pleasant to the sight, and of a very fragrant smell; and abounds with black cattle and sheep. The soil is very grateful to the husbandman, yielding a produce of barley from ten to thirty fold in a plentiful year, provided the ground be manured with sea-ware and that it have rain proportionable to the soil ... The way of tillage here is commonly by ploughing, and some digging. The ordinary plough is drawn by four horses, and they have a little plough also called ristle, i.e. a thing that cleaves, the cutter of which is in the form of a sickle; and it is drawn sometimes by one and sometimes by two horses, according as the ground is. The design of this little plough a deep line in the ground to make it the more easy for the big plough to follow, which otherwise would be retarded by the strong roots of bent lying deep in the ground, that are cut by the little plough. When they dig with spades it produceth more increase. The little plough is likewise used to facilitate digging as well as ploughing ...

South Uist

The cattle produced here are horses, cows sheep and hogs generally of a low statue. The horses are very strong, and fit for pads, though exposed to the rigour of the weather all the winter and spring in the open fields. Their cows are also in the fields all the spring, and their beef is sweet and tender as any can be. They live upon sea-ware in the winter and spring, and are fattened by it, nor are they slaughtered before they eat plentifully of it in December. The natives are accustomed to salt their beef in a cow's hide, which keeps it close from air, and preserves it as well, if not better, than barrels, and tastes, they say best when way is used. This beef is transported to Glasgoe, a city in the west of Scotland, and from hence (being put into barrels there) exported to the Indies in good condition. Some of the natives wear a girdle of seal-skin about the middle, for removing the sciatica, as those of the shire of Aberdeen wear it to remove the chincough ... The skin is by the natives cut in long pieces, and then made use of instead of ropes to fix the plough to their horses, when they till the ground ... Their common cure for coughs is brochan, formerly mentioned ... The broth of a lamb, in which the plants Shunnish and Alexander have been boiled, is found by experience to be good against consumption.

There is good wool in most of the isles and very cheap; some are at the charge of carrying it on horseback, about seventy miles, to the shires of Moray and Aberdeen.

Barra

The rivers on the east side afford salmon, some of which are speckled. The natives go with three several herring nets, and lay them crossways in the river where the salmon are most numerous, and betwixt them and the sea. These salmon at the sight of shadow of the people make towards the sea, and feeling the net from the surface of the ground, jump over the first, then the second, but being weakened, cannot get over the third net, and are so caught ...

St Kilda

This isle produces the finest hawks in the Western Isles, for they go many leagues for their prey, there being no land fowl in St Kilda for them to eat except pigeons and plover.

The little commonwealth hath two ropes of about twentyfour fathoms length each, for climbing rocks, which they do by turns; the ropes are secured all round with cow's hides, salted for the use, and which preserves them from being cut by the edge of the rocks. By the assistance of these ropes they purchase a great number of eggs and fowl. I have seen them bring home in a morning twenty-nine large baskets all full of eggs. The least of the baskets contained four hundred big eggs, and the rest eight hundred and above of lesser eggs. They had with them at the same time about two thousand sea fowl, and some fish, together with limpets, called patella, the biggest I ever saw. They catch many fowls likewise by laying their gins, which are made of horse hair, having a noose at the distance of two feet each; the ends of the rope at which the noose hangs are secured by stone.

Thomas Morer: *A short account of Scotland—1715*

Scotland is distinguished into High-lands and Low-lands. The people of the first were anciently called Brigantes a name the Irish sometimes go by, of whom they are supposed to be descended from Briga or Bria, a Bray, a word still in use with 'em to signifie an high place; as they would say the Bray of Athol, they mean the mountainous part of that country ...

The High-landers are not without considerable quantities of corn, yet have not enough to satisfie their numbers, and therefore yearly come down with their cattle, off which they have greater plenty, and so traffick with the Low-landers for such proportions of oats and barley as their families or necessities call for ...

They are constant in their habit or way of clothing; pladds are most in use with 'em, which tho' we English thought inconvenient, especially for swordsmen in time of action, and in the heat of summer, as when we saw 'em; yet they excused themselves on these accounts, that they not only served them for cloaths by day, in case of necessity, but were pallets or beds in the night at such times as they travelled and had not opportunities for better accommodation, and for that reason in campaigns were not unuseful: the Low-landers add, that being too often men of prey, by this means they cover their booty the better, and carry it off without the owner's knowledge. These pladds are about seven or eight yards long, differing in firmness according to the abilities or fancy of the weavers. They cover the whole body with 'em from neck to the knees, excepting the right arm, which they mostly keep at liberty. Many of 'em have nothing under these garments besides waistcoats and shirts, which descend no lower than the knees, and they so gird 'em about the middle as to give 'em the same length as the linen under 'em and thereby supply the defect of drawers and breeches. (Note this describes the old philliemor or belted plaid not the short modern kilt.)

Those who have stockings make 'em generally of the same piece with their pladds, not knit or weaved, but sow'd together, and they tie 'em below the knee with tufted garters ... In war, they had formerly bows and such kind of arrows as once entered the body could not be drawn out without tearing away the flesh with 'em: but now carry muskets and other firearms; and when they are on the defensive part, they depend much on the targes or targets, which are shields of that form that the Latines call by the name of Xlypeus, round and acquidistant from the center, and are made of the toughest wood they can get, lined within and covered without with skins, fenced with brass nails, and made so serviceable that no ordinary bullet, much less a sword, can penetrate to injure them or their masters, who have such an artificial way of twisting themselves within the compass of these shields, that 'tis almost a vain attempt for their enemy to seek to annoy 'em. And indeed they fight with too much odds, when they come so near us, because they not only have the protection of their bucklers, but are withal very expert at their swords, which consist of the best blades now in being and were therefore much sought after by our officers and souldiers who were very well furnished with 'em before wee left the High-lands.

Their ordinary women go barefoot, especially in the summer. Yet the husbands have shoes. Their children fare no better, but what surprised me most some of the better sort, lay and clergy made their little ones go in the same manner which I thought a piece of cruelty in them, that I imputed to the others poverty. But their apology was, the custom of the country founded on an ancient law, that no males were to use shoes till fourteen years of age that they might be hardened for the wars when their Prince had ocassion for their service.

Their bread, for the most part, is of oat-meal, which, if thin and well baked upon broad irons or stones for that purpose, is palatable enough, and often brought to gentlemen's tables. But the vulgar are not so curious, for they only water and meal into a convenient consistence, and they make 'em into thick cakes called bannocks, they set 'em before the fire to be hardened or toasted for their use. These people prepare the oats after this manner—they take several sheaves, and setting fire to 'em consume the straw and chaff to ashes, which, after a convenient time they blow away, then gather up the grain sufficiently parched, they bruise it into meal.

Their flesh is good enough, yet I confess it will not keep as long as that in England which they say proceeds from the largeness of the pores exposing it more than elsewhere to the air and weather. Their cheese is not the best, nor butter, made in parts of ewes-milk which did not relish with us, yet we could not tempt 'em to forebear that mixture. Their drink is beer, sometimes so new that it is scarce cold when brought to the table. But their gentry are better provided, and give it age: yet think not so well of it as to let it alone and therefor add brandy and sugar, and it is the nectar of this country at their feasts and entertainments, and carries with it a mark of great esteem and aggestion. Sometimes they have wine (a thin bodied claret) at 10d. the muskin, which answers our quart, but is no more than half of the Scotch pint; and therefore they tell us, that if their drink be not as good as ours yet their measure is better ... They have poultry and fowls in convenient plenty. Among the rest there is the solen goose, a large bird, but tastes more of fish than flesh, because accustomed to the sea and feeds there oftener than in other places ... Orchards they have few. And their apples pears, and plumbs are not of the best kind, their cherries are tolerably good. They have one sort of pear, large and well tasted, but seldom had. Wall fruit is very scarce. But gooseberries, currants, strawberries, and the like, they have of each; but growing in gentlemen's gardens, and yet from hence we sometimes meet with 'em in the markets of their boroughs.

They have excellent pit-coal, so bitumous and pitchy that it burns like a candle, and is both pleasant and useful. But it is chiefly for their gentry and boroughs; the common people deal in peat and turf, cut and dried in the summer, and would be no bad fuel, but that at first kindling it makes a very thick and offensive smother.

They are fond of tobacco but more from the snush-box than pipe ... it consists of the coarsest tobacco dried by the fire, and powdered in a little enguine after the form of a tap, which they carry in their pockets and is both mill to grind and a box to keep it in.

Note: Research has not discovered any evidence of the law referred to about shoes being forbidden to children.

Daniel Defoe: *A Tour through the whole island of Great Britain—1724–26*

On this coast is the Isle of Skye, lying from west north west ... We left this on our right, and crossing the mountains came with as little stay as we could do to the lough of Abre, that is, the water which assists with Lough Ness, to separate the north land of Scotland from the middle part.

From this river or water of Abre, all that mountainous barren and frightful country which lies south is called Loquabre. It is indeed a frightful country full of hideous desert mountains and unpassable, except to the Highlanders who posses the precipices. Here in spite of the most vigerous pursuit, the Highland robbers, such as the famous Rob Roy in the late disturbances find such retreats as none can pretend to follow them into, nor could he ever be taken.

On this water of Abre, just at the entrance of the loch, was anciently a fort built to curb the Highlanders, on either side ...

The Western Highlands are the only remaining part of Scotland which as yet I have not touched upon ... in the north Highlands, there are such great woods of fir-trees, which I have taken notice of there, and which we do not see the like here. Nor did we see so many or so large eagles in these western mountains as in the north, though the people assure us there are such too.

The quantity of deer are much the same, and the kinds too, and the black cattle are of the same kind, and rather more numerous; the people also dress after the same manner, in the plaid and the trews, go naked from below the knee to the mid thighs, wear the dirk and the pistol at their girdle and the targe or target at their shoulder.

Some reckon the shire of Braidalbin to belong to these Western Highlands, all the reason that I could find they give for reckoning this country among the Western Highlands, is because they say one part of it is inhabited by the Campbells, whose clan as I have observed, generally possess all the West Highlands ...

We went away west but were presently interrupted by a vast inland sea, rather than a lake called Loch Lomond. It is indeed a sea, and looked like it from the hills from whence we first descried it; and its being a tempestuous day, I assure you it appeared all in a breach rough and raging, like the sea in a storm. There are several islands on it which from the hills we could plainly perceive were islands, but that they are adrift, and float about the lake, that I take as I find it, for a story, namely, a story called a F--- as I do also that of the water of this loch turning wood into stone.

Rowardenan, Loch Lomond.

This lake or loch is, without comparison, the greatest in Scotland, no other can be called half so big; for it is more than twenty miles long, and generally eight miles in breadth, though to the north end of it, 'tis not so broad by far. It receives many rivers into it, but empties itself into the Firth of Clyde, at one mouth; near the entrance of it into the Clyde stands the famous Dunbarton Castle the most ancient as well as the most important castle in Scotland; and the gate, as it is called of the Highlands.

Burt: *Letters from a gentleman in the north of Scotland to his friend in London—1726*

The poor Men are seldom barefoot in the Town of Inverness but wear Brogues, a Sort of Pumps without Heels which keep them little more from the Wet and Dirt than if they had none, but they serve to defend their Feet from the Gravel and Stones.

They have several Sorts of Carts, of which that Species wherein they carry their Peats (being a light Kind of Loading is the largest;) but as they too, are small, their Numbers are sometimes so great, that they fill up one of the Streets (which is the Market for Fuel) in such a Manner, it is impossible to pass by them on Horseback and difficult to on Foot ...

156

Some of these Carts are led by Women, who are generally bare-foot with a Blanket for the covering of their Bodies, and in cold or wet Weather they bring it quite over them. At other times they wear a Piece of Linen upon their Heads, made up like a Nap-cap in an inn, only not tied at top, but hanging down behind.

Instead of Ropes for Halters and Harness, they generally make use of Sticks of Birch twisted and knotted together; these are called Woodies; but some few have Ropes made of the Manes and Tails of their Horses, which are shorn in the spring for that purpose.

The Horse-Collar and Crupper are made of Straw-bands; and, to save the Horse's Back, they put under the Cart-Saddle a parcel of old rags ... Their Horses are never dressed or shod, and appear, as we say, as ragged as Colts ... If the Horse carries any Burden upon his Back a Stick of a Yard long goes across, under his Tail, for a Crupper ...

The Wheels, when new, are about a Foot and a half high, but are soon worn very small: they are made of three pieces of Plank, pinned together at the Edges like the Head of a Butter-Firkin, and the Axle-tree goes round with the Wheel; which have some part of the Circumference with the Grain and other Parts not, it wears unequally, and on a little Time is rather angular than round, which causes a disagreeable Noise as it moves upon the Stones ...

It is a common Thing for the Poorest Sort hereabouts to lead their Horses out in Summer, when they have done their Work, and attend them while they graze by the Sides of the Roads and Edges of the Corn fields, where there is any little Grass to be had without a Trespass; and generally they hold them all the while by the Halter, for they are certainly punished if it be known they encroached ever so little upon a Field, of which none are enclosed. In a like Manner, you may see a Man tending a single cow for the greatest Part of the Day ...

The Plaid is the Undress of the Ladies; and to a genteel Woman, who adjusts it with a good Air, is a becoming Veil ... It is made of Silk or fine Worsted, chequered with various lively colours, two Breadths wide, and three Yards in Length; it is brought over the Head, and may hide or discover the Face according to the Wearer's Fancy or Occassion: it reaches to the Waist behind; one Corner falls as low as the Ankle on one side; and the other Part, in Folds hangs down from the opposite arm.

Our principal Diet, then, consists of such Things as you in London esteem to be the greatest rarities, viz, Salmon and Trout just taken from the River, and both very good in their Kind: Partridge, Grouse, Hare, Duck, and Mallard, Woodcock Snipes each in its proper Season. And yet ... we are hankering after Beef Mutton Veal Lamb and ... There is hardly any such Thing as Mutton to be had till August or Beef till September,—that is to say in Quality fit to be eaten; and both go out about Christmas. And therefore, at or about Martinmas (the 11th November) such of the Inhabitants who are any Thing beforehand with the World, salt up a Quantity of Beef, as if they were going a Voyage. And this is common in all Parts of Scotland where I have been ... Mutton and Beef are about a Penny a Pound; Salmon which was at the same price is, by a late regulation of the Magistrates, raised to Two-pence a Pound, which is thought by many to be an exorbitant Price. A Fowl which they generally call a Hen, may be had at Market for Two-pence or Two-pence Halfpenny, but so lean they are good for little.

The little Highland Mutton, when fat, is delicious, and certainly the greatest of Luxuries. And the small Beef, when fresh, is very sweet and succulent, but it wants that Substance which should preserve it long when salted. The meanest Servants, who are not at Boardwages, will not make a Meal upon Salmon if they can get anything else to eat ... French Brandy, very good is about three Shillings and Sixpence or four Shillings a Gallon, but in Quantities from hovering Ships on the Coast, it has been bought for Twenty-pence ... Lemons are seldom wanting here; so that Punch for those that like it, is very reasonable ...

Their Huts are mostly built on some rising rocky Spot at the Foot of a Hill, secure from any Bourne or Springs that might descend upon them from the Mountains; ... The Walls were about four Feet high, lined with Sticks wattled like a hurdle, built on the Outside with Turf; and thinner Slices of the same served for Tiling. The last they call Divet ... When the Hut has been Built some Time it is covered with Weeds and Grass; and I do assure you, I have seen Sheep, that got up from the Foot of an adjoining Hill feeding upon the Top of the House ...

To supply the Want of Candles, when they have Occasion for more Light than is given by the Fire, they provide themselves with a Quantity of Sticks of Fir, the most resinous that can be procured: some of these are lighted and laid upon a Stone; and as the light decays they revive it with fresh Fuel But when they happen to be destitute of Fire and none is to be got in the Neighbourhood, they produce it by rubbing Sticks together; but I do not recollect what Kind of Wood is fittest for that Purpose ...

About the latter end of August, or the Begining of September, the Cattle are brought into good Order by their Summer Feed, and the Beef is extremely sweet and succulent, which, I suppose, is owing, in good Part, to their being reduced to such poverty in the Spring, and made up again with new Flesh.

Now the Drovers collect their herds and drive them to Fairs and Markets on the Borders of the Lowlands, and sometimes to the North of England; and in their passage they pay a certain Tribute, proportional to the number of Cattle, to the Owner of the Territory they pass through, which is in lieu of all Reckonings for Grazing.

I have several times seen them driving great Numbers of Cattle along the Sides of the Mountains at a great Distance, but never except once was near them. This was in a time of

Rain, by a wide River, where there was a Boat to Ferry over the Drovers. The Cows were about fifty in Number, and took the Water like Spaniels; and when they were in, their Drovers made a hidious Cry to urge them forwards; this, they told me, they did to keep the Foremost of them from turning about; for, in that Case the rest would do the like, and then they would be in Danger, especially the weakest of them to be driven away and drowned by the Torrent. I thought it a very odd Sight to see so many Noses and Eyes just above the Water, and nothing more of them to be seen, for they had no Horns, and upon landing they appeared in Size and Shape like so many large Lincolnshire Calves.

The Soil of the Corn-lands is in some Places so shallow with rocky Ground beneath it, that a Plough is of no manner of use. This they dig up with a wooden Spade; for almost all their Impliments of Husbandry, which in other countries are made of Iron, or partly of that Metal, are, in some Parts of the Highlands entirely made of Wood,—such as the Spade, Plough-share, Harrows, Harness, and Bolts; and even Locks for Doors are made of Wood. By the Way, these Locks are contrived so artfully, by Notches, made at unequal Distances within-side, that it is Impossible to open them with any Thing but the wooden Keys that belong to them.

By the Cannon Law of Scotland all Kind of Usury is prohibited; but as the forbiding is very incommodious to a Country, on Account of Trade and Husbandry, as well as to particular persons, and besides, a Law most easily evaded; there was a Method contrived by the People, whereby to sell their Estates, with a conditional Right of Redemption. This is called a proper Wadsett, where the Morgagee takes into Possession so much Land as will secure the Principal and Interest of the Money lent, and sometimes more; for which he is ever to give Account, though there should be a Surplus, but only to return the Lands to the former Proprietor when the principal Sum is paid off.

They have a Penny-Weding; that is, when a Servant-Maid has served faithfully, and gained the Good-will of her Master and Mistress, they invite their Relations and friends, and there is a Dinner or Supper on the day the Servant is married, and Music and Dancing follow to complete the Evening.

The Bride must go about the Room and kiss every Man in the Company, and in the End every Body puts Money into a Dish, according to their Inclination and Ability. By this means a Family in good circumstances, and respected by those they invite, have procured for the new Couple where-withal to begin the World pretty comfortably for People of their low Condition. But I should have told you, that the whole Expense of the Feast and Fiddlers is paid out of the Contributions ...

The Highland Dress consists of a Bonnet made of Thrum without a Brim, a short coat a waist-coat, longer by five or six inches, short stockings and Brogues, or Pumps without Heels. By the way they cut Holes in their Brogues, though new made, to let out the water, when they have far to go and Rivers to pass; this they do to preserve their feet from galling.

Ray: *A compleat history of the rebellion printed—1755 (Ray served under Cumberland)*

The weekly Markets being now supplyed with Flesh fresh or salted in the Hide of the beast, and extream bad Goats-Milk-Cheese. Here you may have Butter of several Colours, which is brought to the Market in the Membranes that hold the Calves: Further in the Country, when the cow-cleaning is scarce, they have an artful Way of making it up in Rolls or Balls, bound in Straw ropes; For the Quality it is salted up in little Dishes that hold about two or three Pounds; if fresh it is entirely so, and called Sweet Butter then the Salt is brought with it to the Table, where you may season it to your Palate; you may likewise have a fresh Hung-Beef; for it is customary in the Highlands when the Cattle die to hang the Hind-Quarters, (I cannot say in the Chimney, because there is none) in the Smoak near the Fire, without Salt. As the weather became warm, it brought still greater Plenty; for you might see the Highlandmen coming over the Hills, with Milk of several Sorts, as Sheep, Goats, Cows, which they carry on their Backs in a Goat-Skin, with the Hinder-feet over each Shoulder, held in their Hands and a small Wooden Piggen, that floats in the Milk, with which they measure it out to their Customers. Then the nicer of them has a more ingenious Way of carrying the Goat-Skin, by the two Fore legs; and as there is naturally a Hole at the other End in which they affix a Tap, it is followed by a Caudy, i.e. a Boy with his Piggen, who draws the Milk off as the Occasion requires.

I shall only at present mention one other Piece of their Ingenuity; which is, that they can boil a Quarter of Flesh, whether Mutton, Veal, Goat, or Deer, in the Paunch of the Beast, which is prepared by cutting it open and turning it in-side out; by this Method it is made clean; then they affix it with Scuers on a Hoop; to this they tie a String or a Thong, cut from the Skin of the Beast, and by this Thong they hang it over the Fire.

The Highlanders have been reckoned an indolent People; although, by what I have said it may appear that they are ingenious and industrious; for the Truth of which I appeal to any of our Military Gentlemen, who have had the Honour to serve the Government in that Part of the World.

Their Cattle are exceeding small but very sweet Meat when in good Order; A full grown Ox is not much bigger than one of our Calves of a year old ...

Loch Ness is a most remarkable and beautiful Loch 24 Miles long, and two broad; on each Side of this Loch is a Ridge of most terrible barren woody Mountains; you travel along the Banks, which makes the Foot of these Mountains for about 12 miles, and through a Road made with the greatest difficulty, by blowing up very large Rocks which in many Places hang declining over the Passengers, and higher than Houses, so that it is frightful to pass them; you then come to a poor small House of Entertainment (yet the only one on the Road) called the General's Hut, from General Wade, who once lived there when he commanded the Force in making those surprising and useful Roads through the Highlands of Scotland.

John MacDonald: *Memories of an XVIII century footman—1790*

I was born in the begining of the year 1741; and, about two years after, my mother had another son, of whom she died in child-bed. On this my father was almost distracted, . . . and when the Rebellion began, in 1745, he raised a number of men of his own name, whom he employed as his drovers, and marched them up to Prince Charles, whose first camp was about twenty miles off my father's house. The Prince received him very kindly, and made him a captain of the Macdonald's clan . . . We four were left with the maid . . . who soon went off. We were now left alone; . . . having read a letter dated from my father, Captain Macdonald, at Goolen's Inn and Livery Stables, Head of the Canongate Edinburgh, an answer was returned; but I believe all letters to the Prince's camp were intercepted, for we never saw or heard from our father more.

After the letter came from our father, my sister was never easy, but going from one town to another, on foot, sometimes to Inverness, then to see my brother out and in, to and fro. This made the people take notice and say she had something extraordinary to go through. Now we had no person with us in the house; but the neighbours came to see us now and then. My sister had it in her head to go to Edinburgh, to see my father. She got all the money she could get together which was fourteen pounds Scots, or twenty-three shillings and four pence English. With this, the letter from my father in her bosom, and her three brothers in her hand, out she sets for Edinburgh, from the parish of Urquart, about the middle of September 1745. Now our ages were as follows: Kitty, fourteen, Duncan, that was left with Boyd, betwen ten and eleven; Daniel, seven I, four and a half; and my brother, Alexander, two and a half. She chose for her departure a moonlight night, that the people should not stop her; and so she got to Inverness about breakfast, having travelled nine miles. My sister carried the child on her back, Daniel carried the bundle, and I ran along side of both. In this manner we travelled from Inverness to Edinburgh, which is one hundred and fifty measured miles, in the space of two months.

Now you shall see the provision of God towards helpless orphans that are left to his care alone. As we travelled, we were surprised of everyone, as we were so young. Our money being expended, we were obliged to beg our bread. We were kindly used by some and harshly by others that were against the Prince, One kind woman equipped us with a little bag for oatmeal, for people that would not take us in would give us a handful of meal. She gave us a round wooden dish also, which my sister put our pottage in when she met with good people that would let her bake it or bake cakes of oatmeal on their gridiron. The chief of our food was pottage and milk, or cakes and milk; and sometimes, if we met with good friends at a farmhouse, we got a bit of meat. If it rained, we waited at a farmhouse sometimes for two or three days. On the journey we had two things to recommend us, although begging from house to house; the things we had on were all plaid, and of the finest kind, for an extravagant father cares not what he buys. Our apparel looked like that of a gentleman's children, and we had a great share of beauty . . . We never marched when it rained, if it had been two or three days and, on a fine sunshining day, we played on the road till near night, when we continued to shuffle forward. If we could not reach a house, my sister would cover us with our plaids, and cut the tops of brooms with her knife to lay on top and cover our plaids. In this manner we lay at nights for weeks, and always set off in the morning. When we had any brook to cross, or small river, my sister would carry over my young brother, then come for me, and afterwards come back to take my brother's hand. One time as she was wading a river with Alexander, when she came to the otherside, the water overpowered her and carried her and my brother into a whirlpool, where they floated, till a man who was digging potatoes at a little distance saw her distress and ran to her relief. He took her and the boy out of the pool, and carried my brother and me also. He then took us to a farmhouse where we had victuals and drink, and our clothes dried; and at night we were put into a barn amongst the straw. If at any time we happened to be benighted, and could not get quarters, we sometimes lay in an old house without a roof or any house near it; another time, if the weather was fine, near the road-side, amongst some fine broom . . . When we came to Dundee, not far from the town, on the side of the river there was an old castle where there was a blacksmith's shop. The blacksmith's wife was as good a woman as ever lived; she put hay in one corner of the castle where the rain didnot come in, and there at night we lay. In the day we went a-begging to Dundee, and at night we came home. She let my sister dress our pottage and bake cakes; so we staid here three weeks, after which we set out again on our journey. When it was fine weather and we came to a rivulet, my sister washed our second shirt and stockings, for we either had no more at first, or else she did not chuse to bring any more with her. When we came to a river where there was a ferry-boat, we begged our passage over. Then we came to Perth, where we stayed a week or two. The letter from my father was now so worn, with fretting and chaffing, that it was scarce legible; but a gentleman made shift to copy it for us afresh. From Perth we travelled to Kinghorn, where we staid a few days till we could get our passage to Leith. A gentleman who was a passenger in the same boat with us, paid our fare. Before we left the boat the same gentleman made a collection for us. He raised a half-a-crown. As we passed through Leith we went into an eating house, and had plenty of bread, meat and broth, for five-pence. In those days a working-man could dine well for two-pence. After dinner, we set out for Edinburgh on a fine walk, a mile and a half in 1 length.

Now, my readers, let me tell you, that for what I have wrote hitherto, I have been obliged to my sister; for I was too young to remember it.

Garnett: *Tour of Scotland—1811*

Mull

Potatoes grow extremely well; they are sown in lazy-beds by the spade, and are the chief substance of the poor people for three-quarters of the year ... The Chief manure made use of in this island, is sea-ware, and in some parts shell-sand. The dung of horned cattle will go but little way, as the convenience for housing them is so small; but the cattle are generally folded on some part of the ground, during the night, in summer and harvest; this is called teathing, and is one way in which the ground is manured. As there are few cart roads, the manure, whether sea-ware, shell-sand, or dung, is carried on the backs of horses, in baskets or creels which wastes a great deal of time. The plough commonly made use of in this island is very rude, and ... it is drawn by four horses a-breast ... There are no ploughmakers, so each farmer is obliged to make his own.

The first introduction of the kelp manufacture, was into the island of Uist, about the year 1730, by a Mr MacLeod, who brought it from Ireland, where it had been carried on for several years ...

Iona

Their method of sowing barley is singular: the seed is sown before the ground is ploughed, and they plough the ground over it. This prevents the grain from being bared by high winds, which was undoubtedly introduced by necessity answers very well ...

Perthshire

The Duke (of Athol) has been very successful in the cultivation of rhubarb (Rheum palstum) which grows here in as great luxuriance as in any part of the world. The quantities raised have not been exceeded in Britain, and evidently show that with a very little attention, we need have no recourse to Turkey or India for this drug ... The salmon fishery on the Tay is very extensive ... The fishing begins on the 11th of December, and ends on the 26th August. The spring and part of the summer fish go fresh, packed in ice to the London market and when they are plentiful in warm weather, they are pickled, and sent to the same place. A man is stationed constantly on the bridge, both day and night, when the latter is not very dark. When he sees a fish go up the river, he makes a signal to some fishermen in a hut about 200 yards above, who immediately take to their boat and intercept it. (The Falls of Tummel) Great quantities of salmon were formerly caught here in wicker baskets, by men who hung on to the face of the slippery rocks, in ropes made of birch twigs ...

(Kenmore) The Highland dress is more common here than in any part of the country through which we passed. This dress bears a considerable resemblance to that of the Romans, from which it may perhaps have been derived. It consists of a short jacket of tartan of woollen cloth, woven in squares of the most vivid colours, in which green and red are however predominant; the Philabeg, or kilt, which is a sort of short petticoat reaching to the middle of the thigh, of the same stuff; of hose or half stockings, which do not reach the knee, knit or wove in diamonds of red and white. They have generally when dressed, a pouch made of the skin of the badger fox or some other animal, hanging before, in which they keep their tobacco and money. They wear a mantle, or plaid of tartan, which is folded in a graceful manner over the shoulder, but covers the whole body when it rains. Instead of a hat they wear a blue bonnet with a border of red and white. This dress, which is much more picturesque than the modern, is fast wearing out in the Highlands; many dress in the English manner, and still more have a mixture of the Highland and English; for instance many have a hat and short coat, with kilt and hose, while others have no other part of this dress than the hose and bonnet.

Perth

A manufacture of gloves has been carried on here to a considerable extent for a long time; the vicinity of Perth to the Highlands and consequently the ease with which the skins of deer and other animals are procured, probably at first gave the origin to it. From two to three thousand dozen pairs of gloves are manufactured yearly. The glovers are incorporated along with the skinners, and this corporation is the richest in Perth. The skinners dress about thirty thousand sheep and slaughtered lambskins annually, more than twenty thousand of these are of sheep killed in Perth; the rest are brought from the neighbouring country and the Highlands. Most of the skins are sent to the London markets, and are much esteemed for their cleanness from grease, and fine grain.

Bonaw

This place is called Bonaw. About 1753 a company from Lancashire erected a furnace for casting pig iron here, and obtained a long lease of several farms, for rearing wood, and grazing their work-horses. A part of the wood is cut down every year and converted into

Kenmore.

charcoal, with which they are enabled to make extremely pure iron the charcoal deoxydating the metal, and freeing it from impurities much better than fossil coal. The iron is imported from the west coast of England and other places.

The Highland canals, like the highland roads, ought to be public works. Were the roads in the Highlands supported by a toll, I should suppose that half-a-crown, or five shillings a horse, would be necessary to pay the interest of the money laid out in forming them, so few are the travellers, and yet good roads are absolutely necessary. Some idea of the very few travellers, on these roads may be formed, which it is mentioned, that, during the first three weeks of our tour in the Highlands, we did not meet a single traveller, either on horseback or in a carriage . . .

Mrs. Grant of Laggan: *Letters from the mountains—1813*

Do you know the Highlanders resemble the French, in being poor with a better grace than other people. If they want certain luxuries or conveniences, they do not look embarrassed, or disconcerted, and make you feel awkward by paltry apologies which you don't know how to answer; they rather dismiss any sentiment of that kind by a kind of playful raillery, for which they seem to have a talent. Our visit was if not a pleasant one was at least a merry one. The moment tea was done, dancing began. Excellent dancers they are, and in music of various kinds they certainly excel. The floor is not yet laid, but that was no impediment . . .

This is certainly a fine country to grow old in; (S Kilmore near Oban) I could not spare a look to the young people, so much was I engrossed in contemplating their grandmothers. They preserve the form of dress worn some hundred years ago. Stately, erect, and self-satisfied, without a trace of the lanquor or coldness of age, they march up the area, with gaudy coloured plaids fastened about their breasts with a silver broach, like the full moon in size and shape. They have a peculiar lively blue eye, and a fair fresh complection. Round their head is tied the very plain handkerchief Mrs Page alludes to, when Falstaff tells her how well she would become a Venitian tire; and on each cheeck depands a silver lock, which is always cherished and considered, not improperly, as a kind of decoration. These you must observe were the common people; the old ladies were habited in the costume of the year one . . .

We landed on the west side, and to save sailing round the long point resolved to walk to Ballacheulish by the light of the moon: it was a bleak evening, and the wind whistled dolefully while we were passing, in utter darkness, through a small wood; the moon broke through a cloud, and the owl began to hoot most opportunely. I started and was shown the cairn (or rude monument of loose stones) where Campbell of Glenure had been murdered, and where every passenger throws a stone. I can't convey to you the impression which this assemlage of gloomy images made at once on my mind, aided by the recollection that a worthy and innocent gentleman, related to my mother suffered death in consequence . . .

Roups (Sales) then, are a source of great amusement here, and a very expensive one to the roup-makers. At the dissolution of any family, by the death or removal of its head, it is customary here to send letters of invitation to all the connections, which inter-marriages have created to the defunct for a century past in the neighbouring counties, inviting them to countenance the ceremony by their presence. This invitation tacicly includes an expectation, warranted by old custom, that these allies, as they call them, will purchase things rather beyond their value. The wealth of the family consisting in the number of their cattle, and their pride in the number of their connections, the one come to purchase the other, and both are displayed in their full extent. Whether it can be afforded or not, there is always a plentiful dinner, and very plentiful drink on these occasions, which the friendly greetings of so many people bound by a common tie, frank and lively . . . Besides the entertainment for the superior class, there is always a plentiful distribution of bread the cheese and whisky to the peasantry whose cheerfulness never exceeds the bounds of respect and decorum. The general good humour diffused by this meeting of numbers who know and like each other, though they do not often mingle and the emulation of good will to the entertainers, generally raise things to a great price.

You Lowlanders have no idea of the complicated nature of Highland Farming, and of the old customs which prevail here. Formerly, from the wild and warlike nature of the men, and their haughty indolence, they thought no rural employment compatible with their dignity unless, indeed, the plough . . . This naturally extended the women's province both of labour and management. The care of the cattle was peculiarly theirs. Changing their residence so often as they did in summer, from one bothy or glen to another, gave a romantic peculiarity to their turn of thought and language. Yet as they must carry their beds, food, and utensils, the housewife who furnishes and divides these matters, has enough to do when her shepherd is in one glen, and her dairymaid in another with her milk-cattle. Not to mention some of the children, who are marched off to the glen as a discipline, to inure them early to hardiness and simplicity of life. Meanwhile, his reverence, with my kitchen damsel and the ploughman, constitute another family at home, from which all the rest are flying detachments, occasionally sent out and recalled, and regularly furnished with provisions and forage . . . I shall, between fancy and memory sketch out the diary of one July Monday. I mention Monday, being the day that all dwellers in glens come down for supplies. Item, at four o'clock, Donald arrives with a horse loaded with butter, cheese, and milk. The former I must weigh instantly. He only asks an additional blanket for the children, a covering for himself; two milk tubs, a cog, and another spoon, because little Peter threw one of the set in the burn; two stone of meal, a quart of salt; two pounds of flax for the spinners, for the grass continues so good that they will stay a week longer. He brings the inteligence of the old sow's being the joyful mother of a dozen pigs, and requests something to feed her with. All this must be ready in an hour; before the conclusion of which comes Ronald, from the high hills, where our sheep and young horses are all summer, only desires meat, salt, and women with shears, to clip the lambs, and tar to smear them. He informs me that the black mare has a foal, a very fine one; but she is very low, and I must instantly send one to bring her to the meadows. Before he departs, the tenants who do us service come; they are going to stay two days in the oak wood, cutting timber for our new byre, and must have a competent provision of bread, cheese, and ale for the time they stay. Then I have Caro's breakfast to get, Janet's hank to reel, and a basket of clothes to dispatch to the weaver. K—'s lesson to hear, her sampler to rectify; an all must be over before eleven ... One of the great concerns of life here is, settling the time and manner of these removals. Viewing the procession pass, is always very gratifying to my pastoral imagination. I rise early for that purpose. The people look so glad and contented, for they rejoice at going up; but, by the time the cattle have eat all the grass, and the time arrives when they dare no longer fish and shoot, they find their old home a better place, and return with nearly as much alacrity as they went ...

The only cause for complaint in Scotland is the rage for sheep-farming. The families removed on that account, are often as numerous as our own. The poor people have neither language, money nor education, to push their way any where else; though they often possess feelings and principles, that might almost rescue human nature from reproach which false philosophy and false refinement have brought upon it. Though the poor Ross shire people were driven to desperation, they even then acted under a sense of rectitude, touched no property, and injured no creature ...

My next care was, to prepare for Sandy's wedding, which proved in his own way, a very splendid one. The day before the marriage, we had the bride's friends, with all the servants, dancing all evening. The wedding day he had the same party at dinner, in the nursery. You are to understand, the bride served us eight years, and her swain seven, at a former period; so we could not with-hold our countenance. The sheriff (a nickname) is rich, according to Anne's estimate of wealth and excels in strong sense. You know that he is our tenant in the glebe, which forms an additional tie. He is counted penurious, but shone on this occasion. Four fat sheep, and abundance of game and poultry, were slain for the supper and following breakfast, which was only served in the Chinese manner to the inferior class. At this feast above a hundred persons assisted, three-score of which consisted of our children and rustics, our tenants and servants, and the teachers of arts and sciences from neighbouring hamlets ... The music and dancing were very superior to any thing you could imagine. Don't whisper any thing so treasonable, but both were superior to many fashionable performers in each way ... The wedding was in a large barn. After breakfast, they danced a while on the green, and the scene closed with the young couple going home ...

The contrast of Scotland as it was in the year 1745 and since in the year 1819 published 1825

Aberdeen

Their manufacture is chiefly in stockings, of which they make vast quantities all around the adjacent country: and every morning the poor bring in loads to sell about the town to merchants who export them, some to London but the most part go to Hamburgh or Holland; they are generally white when they bring them in, and exceedingly cheap; and the maid servant scours them by treading them in lye on a large tub which gives the strangers great diversion, for by doing so they are obliged to expose their legs and thighs, by holding up their coats sometimes rather too high. It is great earning when these poor wretches get two-pence per day that make them; so the merchant told me with whom I quartered.

They knit them all with wires, the most part plain, some ribbed and vast quantities in squares, and with flourishes, which greatly please the Dutch; they have stockings here, in common for a shilling the pair to a guinea and a-half; and stockings have been made here to five guineas the pair.

They have also a particular export here of pork, pickled and packed up in barrels which they sell chiefly to the Dutch, for victualling their East India ships, and their men of war. The Aberdeen pork having the reputation of being the best cured in Europe for keeping on very long voyages ...

Inverness

The manufacture here is chiefly in linen and plaids; and the market once a week, is well supplied by the country people with extreme bad goat's milk cheese and fresh butter of several colours full of hairs; but the salt butter is brought to market in wooden dishes that hold about three pounds each, covered over with membrains that hold the calves, and within-side is full of large grains of salt ...

Their drink is the broth of the boiled meat, or whey kept for some years, which they quaff plentifully at their entertainments; but most of them drink water. They also brew ale now ... Their bread is of oats and barley, the only grains their country yields, which they prepare after various forms, boiling it with water; they eat a little of it in the morning, and content themselves with that, through necessity, hunt or go about their business without eating any more till eight. They delight most in cloaths, of several colours, especially striped; the colours they effect most are purple and blue. Their ancestors, as most of them still make use of plaids, very much variegated; but now they make them rather of dark colours, resembling that of the crops of heath, that they may not be discovered, while they lie in the heaths waiting for their game; being wrapped up, than covered with their plaids they endure all the rigours of the seasons, and sometimes sleep covered with snow.

Highland whisky is in great repute, but the common kind obtained by the usual process from fermented grain, finds a copious and ready sale. In walking ... we stopped at a distillery ... The engine employed in grinding the grain is a machine of forty seven horse power, and moves five pair of stones. The fermented liquor is distilled by the old fashioned boiler and condenser but these are so large a size that the spirit ran from the worm in a large stream ... the grain is chiefly barley.

Chambers: *The picture of Scotland—1828*

On arriving at Inverness, the southern stranger finds himself all at once transplanted into a population quite different, in appearance and language, from any thing to which he has been accustomed. The women of the lower rank walk the street, and even to church, the wives without bonnets, and the maidens without caps; while the extreme simplicity of the rest of their attire is quite consistent with this strange and primeval fashion. The men of the same condition, at least the peasantry, wear garments of the coarsest materials, as homespun blue short coats rig-and-fur stockings, and small blue bonnets; some have plaids, but all of their garments display more or less the Celtic fashion ...

One of the most remarkable objects of antiquarian interest connected with Inverness, is a strange blue lozenge-shaped stone, which formerly stood in the middle of the High Street, but is now transtered to the front of the Town House, where it is fixed or set into a circle of sandstones for preservation. This is called the Clach-na-Cidin, from its serving as a resting-place for the women of Inverness, who carrying water in deep tubs, slung upon a pole like a dray, used to set the same upon this stone on passing from the river, in order to give a temporary ease to their shoulders. The Clach-na-Cudin however, had in reality a nobler use than this. It was in some measure the palladium of the town, as the Stone of Scone was considered that of the kingdom. It was to Inverness what market crosses are to other towns and used in that capacity for proclamations ...

Comrie, a respectable-looking parish town of above a thousand inhabitants, affects a terrible kind of interest in the eyes of strangers, on account of earthquakes with which it is occasionally visited. Its earthquakes are, indeed like those of Inverness more frequent than mischievious, but it is said to have got up a shock of considerable merit on the 5th of November 1789.

Dunsinnan is about eight miles directly north of Perth. It is all but proved that Shakespeare was one of the company of players sent by Queen Elizabeth, in 1598, to amuse James VI at Perth, and that the immortal bard thus became personally acquainted with the localities of the tragedy which he afterwards wrote upon the story of Macbeth.

The Highlanders are remarkable for their attachment to this excellent beverage (whisky) which, with snuff may be said to be the chain which binds them to existence ... An aged Highlander, who had followed Prince Charlie with heart in hand in the campaign of 1745–6, being asked by a curious modern what sort of a man he was, could find no way of expressing his admiration and esteem of that individual but by exclaiming with an emphatic earnestness which almost precluded laughter "Och he was just like a cool sneeshin or a good dram o' whisky".

Glencoe is a singularly wild vale in the north of Argyllshire, usually transversed by persons travelling between Fort William and Tyndrum. It opens a little to the north of a solitary inn called the King's House, and extends about ten miles in a north-westerly direction to Ballachulish, a place on Loch Linnhe, noted for its prodigious quarry of slate ... The military road sweeps along the right side of the glen. From the sides of the hills an immense quantity of torrents descends sometimes sweeping over and spoiling the road, which is therefore always in a very precarious state; the goats scramble among the rocks and the wild eagle hovering about the tops ... are usually the only living objects in sight.

Anon.: *Back to Scotland—The temple bar of 1861*

I bid good-by to Edinburgh early next morning, and hurry towards Perth and Aberdeen by the "Great North of Scotland", the most pleasant and best-appointed line of railway I ever travelled by. The carriages are roomy, well-built, and clean; those of the second class have stuffed seats and padded backs, and even the third-class are provided with something in the shape of cushions, to mitigate the hardness of the elm seats ... Every station is clustered about with flowers and each succeeding one seems to be more trim and more resplendent than the last. You see no gardens like those at the railway-stations in England. I ascribed it to the national prediction and aptitude of the Scotch for gardening. But I learnt that there is a special incentive in the case. The directors of the line furnish the seeds and plants at their cost, and every year prizes are given for the best-kept gardens, English directors might take a leaf out of the Scotch book. These gorgeous flowerbeds are far more pleasing to the eye, and far less expensive to the share-holders, than the huge useless hotels, and refreshment-saloons with which directors adorn the stations of English lines. But the Great North of Scotland has refreshment-saloons, and very comfortable ones too, with an infinite variety of things to eat on the counters, including hot mutton-pies, and an abundance of things to drink, not forgetting whisky-toddy served with tumbler, wine glass, and silver ladle; And what do you think, they sell besides at Scotch stations? Why cigars with fuzees and the latest article in Vesuvians to light them withal... One of them (a newsboy) came into my carriage at Dunblane while I was reading the Times. I had a copy of Punch also by me. My youthful friend nearly turned himself upside down to see what paper I was persuing; and when he ascertained that it was the Times he related to me, with a naivete of tone and a power of Lothian dialect which I have never heard equalled, the following little story "Thir wis a gentleman in the train yisterday that sold me the Times and Punch for tippence-hepney, and I sold them again to anither gentlemen at the next station for the full price".

Further North by an innocent steady going railway where the engine driver will stop between stations to set a friend down convenient to his house, and I am in a region where even the trees and stone dykes and the styles are familiar to me. The warm-hearted hospitality extended to me is quite over-powering in this land we wish well, whisky-toddy with hare soup, with cock-a-leekie, with flour scone, with marmalade, with haggis, with whisky toddy! I mentioned the last item before but it deserves repetition for it came in often ... In the course of a fortnight I drank more whisky-toddy and went to church oftener that I could have conceived my constitution, whether physical or spiritual, capable of withstanding. My impartiality as regards toddy was more strict and complete than as regards my church going. I partook of Kirth, Ben Nevis, Fairntosh, and Islay and I listened to sermons in all the kirks; The Established, the Free, the Dissenting, and the Revival. If I might compare the doctrine with whisky, I would place the Revival sermon in the position of the liquor when it comes out from the still — hot and fiery, and take the Established kirk as representing the mellow and matured article after passing through the other two stages.

W. MacIntosh: *A holiday in North Uist—1865*

After sailing up the loch for several miles, a sudden bend disclosed a sight of considerable interest even to a pleasure-seeker. The little bay which has just before us is one mass of small ships — smacks, schooners, and sloops, fishing boats and water craft of every size downwards. Flags flaunt gaily from the masts of the larger vessels, and the decks of all are alive with busy fishermen (some of them scarcely professional in appearance, yet none the less bustling), who prepare to transfer their little cargoes to the hold of the giant steamer. There are numerous huts on shore, screened by a massive drapery of herring nets suspended on poles; while the smoke from many fires along the beech, each with a busy cluster of men, gives a liveliness to the scene that is refreshing after the weary waste of hill and heath, rock and surf, that have greeted the traveller all along the loch. The crews of the smaller boats cannot cook their food on board, and hence the necessity of resorting to the beach for a kitchen.

The steamer has now come to a stand within eighty yards of the fleet, and there is a general rush amongst the boats for the side of the vessel. When they approach, the shouting of the eager crews as to who shall be first opposite the crane, and the collision of oars and timber create some amusement. Then comes another hubbub as the emptied one departs, and so on until the entire field is exhausted ...

In the outward trip are to be seen endless furnishings—from drawing-room loo tables and pianos to coarse cast iron vessels for the kitchen and hovel. Bales, boxes, barrels, and packages of every conceivable size are mixed with bags of flour, rice, and peas. A return journey again, has a totally different cargo. Hundreds of black-faced or Cheviot sheep stand in meek silence in the forepart of the vessel, and it is one of the amusements of the passengers to witness the transfer of these into the steamer from boats that issue from various islands. The shipping of the horses (Galways) from a Saline or Aros market however is more attractive. A group of thirty or more unkempt ponies and colts of various size are driven together between fences that conduct to the steamer ... it is only by haltering each individual, and apportioning it a special castigation, that progress in shipping can be made. Thus each is led, willingly or unwillingly, off terra firma. Even after this is done, several seat themselves in the middle of the gangway apparently preferring to have the necessary assistance at head and tail to performing the journey themselves. Once fairly on deck they are quiet enough ... Of the other live and dead stock on board there are some shaggy north highland cattle in the stalls, numerous sacks of perriwinkles, and hundreds of splendid lobsters packed in large boxes ... Salmon from Skye and other islands are also well represented. A few hampers of unlucky fowls personate the feathered tribes (if we omit some grouse and black-cock belonging to passengers).

Of the two sexes the females certainly seem the most industrious, and they have a full share of the duties of everyday life. They attend to the cattle, carry home the peats on their own backs, or by means of panniers on those of their ponies, gather whelks, spin weave, and assist in rowing boats as the ocassion may require ... They are seldom or never seen with stockings or shoes on their feet, except perhaps in a few cases on Sundays ... When gathering shell-fish the females wade amongst the Fuci at ebb-tide lifting up the blades most nimbly, and collecting the perriwinkles with the right hand, depositing them in the left, and when that is filled transferring them to a kind of pouch made be fastening up their dress in front ... The potatoes are irregularly planted in spaces three feet broad, which spaces run the entire length of the field or patch, each separated from the adjoining one by a small trench. This is done with a view to render the soil thicker and the crops somewhat drier ... The impliments used in this agricultural proceeding are of an orignal description, and consists of a spade-plough which is pressed into the ground by placing the foot on the transversal bar at the base of the shaft; by a slight rotation of the instrument the cut portion of the turf turnes over; a dibble of unusual length, for making the potato holes in the erect posture by aid of the foot on the ledge; and a small, heavy rake with wooden teeth, for covering the tubers when planted. Before introducing their crops a coating of seaweed is laid on the surface of the soil ... The pith of the rush is burned in a little oil lamps: the oil of the porpoise being considered very suitable for this purpose ... The mortar was formerly made from burnt shells gathered on the western shore of the island ... In erecting a stone house, a massive, dry stone, wall is built all around, no mortar being used in the common houses at all, in others only when this is done. The stones in most of the houses on the east side are rough, undressed, gneiss boulders, that have been unearthed in digging peats, or carried from a neighbouring creek ... The roof is formed in the same manner as the turf houses, and bound down with heather ropes. The latter are twisted when the shrubs are fresh, so that when dry the strands retain the curves of their own accord. Large coils, about two feet in diameter, may be seen at the new houses in readiness for roofing purposes. The houses on the western coast of the island ... assume a better aspect, many having walls of stone and lime, and roof neatly thatched with bent grass.

Of the domestic animals the horses are universally small, but look hardy and active. They do not prepossess the beholder by neatness of form, for their heads are coarse and bodies large for their slender haunches and thin limbs ... Their harness has in general a very primitive aspect. The carts are small, and so are the loads, the cost of a horse, at three years of age, is from £3 to £3. 10s. The cows are small long horned, shaggy animals, like the north highland cattle; they give excellent milk, and their butter is rich, firm, and finely tasted.

Walker Fraser: *Magazine rambles—1871*

But meanwhile dusk has spread, and a heavy shower of rain comes on, in the midst of which we pull up at our goal, the Trossacks Hotel, to find it crammed full from roof to cellar. What to do? The host is very sorry—will send our luckless nine back free to Callander in the coach. Only three go back (so nauseous to human nature is force retrogression) two ladies are "crowded in" somehow; three young men will sleep on chairs in the billiard room. For my part, making rapid enquiries among some bystanders, I hear of a cottage a mile and a half distant, where there is a good chance of a bed. "It's a poor place", said my informant "but clean ye ken. Artists and such-like stops there whiles". The rain had ceased. I go, enter the open door of a low thatched cottage by the roadside, and after a word or two find myself familiarly seated in good old Mrs Macfarlane's chimney-corner, by a great fire, over which hangs a large black pot. The good granny, with fresh coloured shrewed face full of wrinkles and intelligent grey eyes under the large borders of her cap, busies herself in quitely arranging the hearth; her son, a grave handsome dark man of thirty sits opposite, while her granddaughter, who stays with her grandmother a comely well-grown lass of fifteen, with flowing black hair, short blue petticoat, and bare legs, after sweeping up the earthen floor stands shyly in the background. They speak Gaelic to each other, and my smattering of that language in the Irish form interests them much. Their manners were excellent, showing a respectful ease and curiosity without impertenance ... The old lady was never so far as Edinburgh; she is now some years over seventy; her husband died about fifteen years ago and her granddaughter Maggie stops with her and helps to mind the cow and two or three pigs and the fowls. Her unmarried son comes now and again to work the patch of ground on the hill-slope behind; he is here now for the potato-digging ... The old lady's sleeping place was a big bed in the wall of the "spence" or kitchen, where we sat with the smoky rafters over head ... I had a capital breakfast, better than I ever got in an English hotel, and two new laid eggs boiled to perfection. While I ate them the hens ran about the floor picking up the crumbs, which was only fair. Jam was not wanting; and there was cheese, which in agreement with Mr Boswell "I cannot help disliking it at breakfast" ...

Next day I went eleven miles by rail to Mauchline, a rather straggling village of small houses, whose industry now is making fancy articles of wood, boxes paper knives. Many are adorned with tartan patterns, which are printed on paper, firmly pasted or glued on, and covered with a thick varnish. Most of the village girls of Mauchline are employed thus. It seems a light and pleasant occupation, with a touch of the artistic. In a work shop which I visited numerous engravings and coloured sketches hung on the walls, to be copied by hand on the more costly boxes; portraits of Garibaldi, Burns, Princess Louise, Empress Eugenie (a star in the ascendant a star in the eclipse) Scottish landscape and buildings and so on.

Shieling.

Walter Carruthers: *Transactions of Inverness scientific & field club—1880*

There is another curiosity still to be met with in the Lews that may soon become extinct—namely, what are called the bee-hive houses. From time immemorial it has been the practise in the fishing villages of the Hebrides to send away the cattle from the crofts when the crops are put down. The people have a bit of grazing among the hills, on which the cattle find a pleasant bite of early summer grass, and while they are away the crops of corn has a chance of growing, without the necessity for a fence and the shift under grass comes to maturity for the cows against autumn. One or two girls go with the cows to the sheiling and make the winter supply of butter and cheese. A boy visits them periodically from the hamlet, taking supplies of provisions, and generally also a creel of grass and a quantity of fish bones for the cows to munch while the milking is going on. The bee-hive houses are bothies occupied by these crofter girls during the summer excursion. They can be distinguished miles away by the emerald green of the grass about the doors—almost the only green spots to be seen in this wilderness of peat bog and mossy lakes. The houses are just the shape of bee-hives; they are built entirely of stone; one tier of flat stones overlapping the other until they culminate in a dome which is surmounted by a flat stone, easily removed to admit light or let out smoke. The exterior is heavily covered with turf, so that the building is wind and water-tight. The entrance is quite bee-hive like; it is a little apperture at the base through which one has to crawl on hands and knees. For the most part these houses are about eight feet in diameter; they have little recesses made in them for storing milk and provisions, and a couple of rude stones to hold a peat-fire together, but beyond this there is no attempt at furnishing. They are simply tents of stone and turf, in which, on a bed of heather gathered from the moor outside, one may find shelter from the blast and be thankful for a cosy bigging. The natives are chary of admitting that these houses are still in use.

Nauticus: *In Scotland—1882*

I noted that we heard the Gaelic language for the first time at Killin ... I was thankful to find smooth water and a slack tide, which enabled me to cross to Skye in a small boat, my tricycle being carefully placed amidships (fare 1s.) ...

Calling for my share of the bill I read the following

	S	D
Tea	2	6
Washing hands		6
Total for one tea	3/-	

View from Killin.

Although the weather had settled into a real Scotch mist I decided to make a move and tear myself away from Mrs MacKenzie, who presented me with an envelope full of a kind of cowrie shell peculiar to this place, called Groate buckies (Duncansbay Head).

The Dutch first turned their attention to the importance of herring fishery. Britain took it up in 1749, and a Fishery Board was established in 1808. The different classes employed in the trade are; Fishermen, fish-curers, gutters, packers, coopers. The nets are 50 yards long and 14 deep, with an inch mesh. It is usual to join twenty-six of these together, thus making the net 1,300 yards in length; to this is attached a rope of 120 yards, causing the total length to be about four-fifths of a mile. In the evening the boats proceed to the fishing ground (at Wick a tug is hired for this purpose) pay out their nets, and drift all night. The fish run their heads into the mesh, and the gills, acting like the barb of a hook, prevent their retreat.

At daylight, the crew—four men and a boy—begin to haul in; an exciting time, for the silvery prize is almost as uncertain as that of a lottery. Great care is taken to shake the fish clear of the net into the boat, or they would become bruised and worthless.

On landing the herring are measured by the cran—four baskets of thirty-six gallons—gutted, sorted, and placed in separate tubs.

Matties have the roe and milts moderately developed, and are the best eating. Full fish are large, but not so well-flavoured.

Spent fish are lean and unpalatable, having just performed the function of spawning.

After the process of gutting, they are worked to and fro in salt until a proper quantity has adhered to each; this is done as soon as possible, to preserve the scales and appearance. They are then carefully packed in barrels with salt, being stowed on their backs for the Continent, and on their sides for the Irish market. After a few days the casks are opened, and most of the pickle which has been forming is poured off, and the barrels filled up by adding more fish of the same date. In about a fortnight they are finally headed up and shipped off to Stettin, Ireland or other Roman Catholic countries.

Smoked or red Herrings—the fish are at once salted in barrels for two or three days, then put on spits and repeatedly plunged into cold water, and after having been dried in the open air, they are suspended in rows in the smoking house and exposed to the smoke of oak billets for ten or twelve days. The bright yellow colour is given by burning sawdust, and those intended for exportation are smoked from fourteen to twenty-one days.

Bloaters are cured by a more rapid process being first put in a strong pickle for six–eight hours then spitted, washed, and smoked from six to ten hours; when cooled and packed they are ready for sale. Kippered herrings are partially salted in pickle, then cut open and slightly smoked.

Falls of Foyers.

On hearing that the road beyond Foyers was very bad, I decided to cut off the lower part by crossing the ferry there. "How about the ferry?" said I to the hotel people on my return; "Can the man be relied upon for, it is too late to waste time?" "Oh yes, if you make a smoke he is sure to come over", was the reply. I took a box of matches, and amused the ostlers by going off on my tricycle with my arms full of straw. On my way down I passed a score of yelling tourists who had just landed from the steamer, and I felt thankful that I had been beforehand with them at the Falls. I took my machine across a field to the beach, the ferry house being opposite at the distance of half a mile. After collecting some wood, wet and dry, large and small, I laid my fire on the most scientific principles, and, having applied the match, soon had the satisfaction of seeing a dense column of smoke arise from it. As there appeared to be no sign of a move on the other side of the water, I sounded my

167

whistle, shouted piled on wet wood, whistled again, waved frantically executed a war dance, hailed loudly, in strickly parliamentary language, all to no purpose.

I went on board the celebrated whaler, "Eclipse" which had just returned from a most successful cruise. She was barque-rigged, with auxiliary steam power, but a smaller vessel that I had expected to see. I was allowed to go below and examine the manner in which she had been strengthened with wood and iron beams, in order to resist the fatal embrace of ice floes.

In the hold were a number of large iron tanks, used in the first place for storing coal but their contents were now infinately more valuable than "black diamonds" viz., sea oil. The men were at work whipping it up in buckets and pouring it into casks, and I was struck by its clear colourless appearance. One of the crew informed me that the fresh skins of the seals are thrown into the tanks and left there until the end of the voyage, when they are found to be floating in the oil which has exuded from the fleshy parts. On this occasion they had brought home a prize of three thousand skins, and I visited the shed where they were being sorted, salted, and stowed in different parts of the building ready for sale. The shade of colour varied from nearly black to light brown; the latter being from young animals, were the most valuable, and now fetch from eight to nine shillings each, in their raw state but their market value was far higher in former days.

... And reached Invercauldy Arms at 8.30 p.m. I felt curious to know what kind of quarters I was going to have. The woman said that the tourist apartment was engaged, but if I didn't mind she could let me have a cupboard bed in another part of the house ... My cupboard bed with its chaff mattress was very comfortable, and I should no doubt have slept like a top, had not my slumbers been disturbed first by a fellow who played the bagpipes until one or two a.m. and afterwards by the mail cart man who came thundering at the door at four.

J. Anderson: *Sprig of heather—1884*

Forty odd years ago I found myself, on a fine summer afternoon, standing upon the pier at Oban, a dusty, weary, footsore boy of sixteen. I had tramped every inch of the way from the banks of the "lordly Tay" to the fairy-like bay, that seems to enjoy a perpetual calm, and is only lulled into a slumberous repose by the music of the billows that race gaily down the Sound of Mull, and break dreamily on the rocky shores of the green-carpeted Kerrara. Then Oban was nothing more than a little fishing hamlet by the sea, with a few coasting vessels of small tonnage, and the echoes of its heath-clad hills, now and then awakened by the rushing steam of some boat from the Clyde or the "Isles". It boasted at that time of moderately sized inn—now its bay is cinctured by more than a score of palatial hotels, and sits enthroned among its cliffs, the crowned Cybele of the western seas. The waters of its quiet roadstead, are now ploughed by the keels of countless white sails, or red black, and yellow funnels, make a pleasant picture, and whose twinkling lights in the stillness of the sombre evening seem like a swarm of fire-flies, dancing in the radiance of their own golden light ...

From Callander the drive is splendidly panoramic—past Lubnaig, "The Loch of the bends" and into Strathyre, past which the fiery cross "glanced like lightening".

There are still fiery things here? A pedestrian once stumped the Pass, and found himself at the little Highland village. Fond of our "mountain dew", he halted at the first house or "public". So refreshing was the dew that he stayed all night. Next day, shouldering his knapsack he started, but found another "public" about the middle of the "clachan", and turned in out of pure innocence, just to compare notes. "Struck Ile" again, and, out of pure gratitude for the mercies, put up for the night. Once more next morning, made off, much delighted—but behold! at the extreme end another "ministering angel" whose wings consisted of a flaming sign swinging in the breeze. Turned in to test the entertainment. Beat the two last experiments hollow, and again he set up his tent. Curiosity prevailed and he enquired the name of this barley-corn oasis. "Sir, it is called Strathyre". "Stuff! its proper name is Nineveh, a city of three day's journey" ...

Got to the end of the lovely lake—discovered a small dog-kennel of a place with the thatch-roof of a sanded parlour, a box-bed, and therein, snugly-ensconced, a pair of drovers performing a nasal duet with laudable energy, if not with pleasing melody. Sumptuous repast at "the wee short hour" of oatcakes, which seem to have been toasted on the hearth-stone, judging from the quantity of gritty sand which had got engrained among the meal, some very questionable, high-smelling butter, and a noggin of "whisky", which bowed not to the authorities of the land ...

A certain Mr Stuart went "out" on a most uncertain venture—the luckless '45. I am not going to drag the reader through the mazes of the old sad story that ended at "bloody Culloden". My purpose is with the "Auld House" of Gask. When their lords were away on their adventurous campaign, several of their ladies took refuge with the hospitable Oliphants. The dismal tale of Culloden found its way to them, like all bad things, with woeful celerity, and in down-heartedness they awaited the sequel. By and by some "broken men" came hurrying to the house, bearing proudly along with them the rescued "colours", red with more than one drop of their patriotic blood. But the sleugh-hounds of Cumberland were on their track—the "Auld House" was in no state to stand a siege—and where to hide the battle-rent colours, became the anxious question. "Give them to me", said Mrs Stuart, with a spirit worthy of Duncraggan's Dame", and with ready-resource she hid them down the shaft of the moss grown pump, where they remained secure. The pursuers came, the house was ramsacked from floor to roof-tree, the men were roughly handled and the ladies insulted; but the precious relic of olden fights was never found. Meanwhile, what about the fugitive Prince, and seven companions in arms who stuck to him through good report and through bad report? Stuart was of the number, and they wandered from moor to mountain, hiding in cold damp caves and never, for safety remaining long in one place . . . Long after those vagrant days, Stuart was wont to tell how he often made "crowdie"—oatmeal and cold water, and a little salt—in the heel of an old shoe for the half-starved Prince, and how he lulled him to sleep like David with gloomy Saul by playing on an old Jew's harp, which was then a commonly-used instrument among the Scotch. We all know—to the honour of the devoted Celts—how the bribe of £30,000 could not sap the fidelity of even one bare-legged Highland gillie . . . A strange magic still hangs around the story of "Bonnie Prince Charlie". His was once a "name to conjure with" and has still the power to stir the hearts that love the heather and beats beneath the tartan. Although our justly-respected Queen has no more loyal subject than the author of these reminiscences, I at once confess to the spell of the Stuart name, the very mention of which sends a tingling through my veins. I cannot explain it. I simply state a fact . . .

Not far from the beautiful situated mansion of Invercoe, the property of my kind friend Mrs McDonald, the descendant of the murdered Chief, a stately cross is raised, marking the bloody spot where the atrocious massacre began. It is in the style of the famous crosses of Iona, the upper portion of red granite the lower of grey granite, resting on a rugged rock-work.

Ferguson: *Rambles in Skye—1887*

Monday 29th Left Strome by steamer Lochiel about 3 p.m., half an hour behind advertised time. A pretty large number of passengers had come from the south by rail and joined the steamer, the large majority being farmers, cattle dealers, drovers and, going to attend the Portree Cattle Market on the following day (Tuesday 30th May). Our first place of call was at Plockton, where a considerable number of people joined the steamer. We next passed on our left the picturesque looking village of Kyle Akin . . . Our next call was at Broadford, where we got a large addition to the number of our passengers, two large-sized ferry boats packed with people were waiting the arrival of the steamer in the bay, the large majority being farmers and shepherds, accompanied by a regiment of collie dogs . . . We arrived at Portree, the Capital of Skye about 8 o'clock, and went to the Marine hotel . . . Straight before us was a wide, circular sloping heath and heather-clad valley, dotted all over for miles on either side of the road, and all in commotion, with people, and lowing, bellowing cattle, and dogs, slowly advancing from all the airts of the compass towards the market stance situated a mile or two west from Portree. We were much surprised to see such a large number of cattle, and almost exclusively the Highland breed, many of them excellent specimens of the well-formed, shaggy-haired, long and finely shaped horned hardy old Highland stock, for which Skye has for long been widely famed. We were much amused to see a large number of females of varied ages, from the smart barefooted girl in her teens to the withered, dark visaged old dame of threescore or more, leading one animal by a rope tied round the horns, and also of various ages, from the gambolling frisky, plump, curly-coated calf of a few months, to the lean, dry-haired aged crummy, with a dozen nicks in her long well-place shaped horns. There were also a good many aged men leading just one beast, probably all the overplus from their scanty stock they had to dispose of. Here and there we observed men rolled up in their plaids lying on the roadside among the heather apparently asleep, having probably travelled all night with their cattle; their faithful and trusty collies, curled up with their eyes half-open, lying close to their master's side . . . For several miles we continued to meet droves of cattle, and a few horses, people driving gigs and carts of all sorts and sizes, all on their way to the market.

After crossing a narrow hill ridge, we came suddenly face to face with a big, dark-brindled Highland bull, with a long, finely formed, sharp-pointed head of horns shaggy mane, short-set legs, deep chest, fine straight back, a long bushy tail and powerful well formed frame. The day being hot I had my coat off, and was carrying it over my arm with a good oak cudgel in my hand. The proud haughty Highlander on seeing us, raised his head aloft, giving us a surprising stare and uttering a suppressed bellowing roar, began to scrape the ground with his forefeet.

We were much pleased and interested with all we saw at the woollen Mills. The proprietor by us "tarry-oo," and sells the cloths finished—chiefly "gude rouch teuch" tweeds—for which I believe there is a great demand . . .

As a general rule every crofter keeps a cow, or two or three as the case may be, and I believe that almost every calf that sees daylight is reared with every care and attention. A large number of cattle are exported annually from the island. Cattle is about the only stock that crofters have to dispose of, from their smallholdings, to pay rent, and so there is great attention and care bestowed on the rearing of them. Small cattle dealers are often met travelling through the country picking up any odd beast that crofters may have for sale. It is very common to see horses and cattle tethered on some odd neuks between the plots of corn, green crops, and I was amused occasionally to see even some hens tethered, just a small string tied to one of their feet, the other end to some twig . . .

Of late, the usual mode of sea-fishing about Dunvegan is by trolling. There are generally three lines out from each boat, with indisrubber bait about 5 or 6 inches long, representing

Above: Old Man of Storr, Skye.

Above right: Glamaig, Skye.

a small sand eel. Three different colours are used—black, brown, and white. I observed that as a rule the black was the favourite, but a good deal depends on the weather, colour of sky, and I had never seen that style of bait used before. It is very handy, as it lasts for almost any length of time, barring accidents, catching on the bottom, and the hook is fixed to the one end of several yards of fine copper wire, and is enclosed in the tube, except the barbed point which is about the middle of the small tube. There is a small swivel in the wire close to the bait spins and as the boat is rowed at a certain rate of speed the bait spins rapidly round in the water, and looks very like one of the small sand eels . . .

I tramped a considerable distance off my way to have a near view of a large drove—more than a hundred browsing on a green hill side, and nearly all Highland cows with their calf at foot—finely formed, plump, shaggy, curly-coated, little fellows, of varied shades of colour, from light dun to the jet black. Several groups of them were congregated here and there, busy at play, some couples pretending to be fighting with their curly heads down, their two pair of sturdy legs well set for a punishing tussle . . .

On Fast-day (Thursday) divine service was held in the three places of worship . . . The following day (Friday) is called Latha na Bodach, or "Speaking to the Question Day," and is looked forward to with special interest, not only by the regular congregation, but by the large majority of the Free Kirk folks throughout the Island. The Communion, which is held only once a year, seems to be considered the great annual event in Skye, and any one residing in any of the populous districts will readily observe the unusual stir and preparations for the occasion—extra washings, scouring of blankets, redding up, and decorating with newspapers (illustrated and otherwise) the black houses, putting in an extra store of provisions and other dainties to regale the many friends and visitors expected from the most distant neuk and corner of Skye, in many cases seen only once a year at the Communion. I was informed by several parties on whose veracity I could fully rely, that no fewer than sixteen visitors had dined in one of the black thatched cabins, near the church on the Friday.

Having heard so much about the Friday's meeting I resolved to go and see it . . . As is customary at the Communion time, divine service was to be conducted in the open air, as the church a very plain, ordinary sized edifice would not hold a fourth of the congregation assembled. The tent, a very plain erection, was placed on a small circular green, grassy lawn, formed by a sudden bend of link of a mountain stream of considerable volume. The back of the tent was quite close to the bank of the purling murmuring stream . . . Beyond the green plot in front of the pulpit rose a sloping, crescent shaped mound, clothed with heather. The congregation was to be seen slowly advancing from all the airts of the compass some along three converging roads, others coming over the moor wading knee deep among the long heather. A large number had come from a distance in vehicles of various descriptions, which were left along the roadside in a long row. The horses—many of them were mares with their foals following them—after being unyoked and unharnessed, the forefeet tied together with a piece of rope were left to feed among the blooming heather. I was amused to see a considerable number of frail aged folks of both sexes sitting in their little "carties" some in old arm chairs, others on four legged stools of the plainest and most primitive description imaginable . . . When wending our way along the bridge towards the tent which was on the opposite side of the river from the church . . . I observed a lot of plain delf plates placed here and there on a stone or dumple of turf to hold the "bawbees" collection . . . Prompt at 12 o'clock the service commenced by praise and prayer . . . At the close of the sermon the clergyman . . . invited any member of the flock to stand up, select a passage of scripture and give his views or expound it to the best of his ability. A big towsyheaded elderly man rose up close to the tent and read . . . and discoursed very fluently for 20 minutes or more. After he sat down five other members of the congregation stood up one after another and discoursed on the same passage ... On Saturday as on the two previous and following days there was a prayer meeting in the Church at 7 a.m. and in the evening ... On Sunday the service commenced at 11.30 and except for a short interval after the tables were served which was late in the afternoon, they continued till 9 o'clock at night ... The characteristic features of many of the regular attenders became quite familiar to me ... As a rule they appeared a strong, healthy hardy-looking race, and all fairly well dressed. The females especially the younger portion, were even gaily rigged out, particularly in the bonnet department, many of which were evidently splitnew and got for the occasion, decked with gaudy ribbons and flowers. Generally the men sat the whole time during service with their heads uncovered ... Several of the elders had a white shawl or some cloth round their heads whilst serving the tables ... A goodly number of elderly women had a white cloth, evidently made for the purpose tied round their head. This particular style of head dress is very common in Skye and is usually worn by women, old and young, while working outside making peats and hay ...

A. Goodrich Freer: *Outer Isles—1902*

The growing of flax continued in the islands ... till the middle of the 19th century.

The loose sandy soil of the south and east parts of the island (Tiree) was excellently adapted for the purpose, and sown with grasses which are a common succession crop after flax would flourish admirably in Tyree, so that spinning dressing and weaving the linen mainly it is said, for home use, occupied a great deal of time among the women.

A few looms are left in the island, mainly used for weaving blankets and a strong striped cloth which is quite a speciality in Tyree; and is worn by all the women, except those who, through some unfortunate circumstance of having been in relation with the mainland, have come to prefer shoddy material and aniline dyes ...

Even the "black houses" i.e. those thatched with turf or heather, can be made exceedingly comfortable, and in one case we know well even elegant. The whitewash used here round the outside of doors and windows gives an air of brightness to the rough grey stone, and the ingenuity of the patterns drawn upon the flagged flooring often found in the island testifies not only to the industry but to the skill and artistic taste of the artist. They are often of the true Celtic type, accurately drawn in rough outlined squares and renewed everyday. Inside the houses are warm and comfortable, the system of double walls, is somewhat clumsy, being probably warmer than that of mortar and hewn stones in a climate which, though not cold, is as boisterous and humid as one might expect upon a treeless sandbank in mid-Atlantic.

There is a Gaelic proverb, "Am fear bhitheas trocaireach ri anam, Cha bhi e mi-throcaireach ri bhruid"—He who is merciful to his soul will not be unmerciful to his beast", and I think we may fairly say that we have never met with a single case of intentional unkindness to any animal in the Hebrides.

A curious sight, in certain places is to meet the cats of the island coming down to the landing-places at the time when the fishermen are sorting and cleaning the fish ... One of the duties of the constabal baile, a voluntary officer, elected by the people themselves ... was to see that in the hard labour of carting peats and tangles the brave little horses should not be over-worked, but that the various crofters should contribute a share of the labour both of man and beast in just proportion.

Barra

Always in these islands the men among the Church-goers were in excess of the women. They were evidently fishermen, and all old and young, were clad in their best blue jerseys or sleeved waistcoats. Among the women the Macneill tartan was conspicuous. The younger women wore little kerchiefs falling back from their hair, sometimes held in place by foreign-looking combs or pins. Their dress was generally a blouse and skirt, and the lineal successor, differently worn, of the jacket and petticoat of the older women who moreover, wore a shawl which covered head and shoulders. All were neat and looked more picturesque than some half dozen who wore hats generally of a startling variety imported from Glasgow. The occasion was obviously a special one, as we soon discovered was the farewell service for the men going off to the "loch fishing".

South Uist

Many of the common-place affairs of everyday life used to be conducted in the most picturesque manner. In every township, even if only half a dozen houses, there was formerly a constabal baile (constable of the hamlet) whose business it was to direct and distribute the work of gathering peats, to select new peat grounds when the old were exhausted, to see to the repair of the mountain paths by which the peat was brought down in creels, to direct the reclaiming of land, to represent the crofters in their dealings with the factor, and in much else. He was elected yearly, or for longer periods or even for life according to the custom of his district. When he accepted office he would take off his shoes and stockings—to show that he was in contact with the earth of which he was made and to which he would return, and then raising his bonnet, and lifting up his eyes to heaven he would declare that upon his honour ... he would be faithful to his trust ...

When Eriskay was first inhabited, separate spots in the island were marked off for certain families, for collecting wild spinach. It is still found where sea-weed has been lying on the land, but is not eaten now ... The goose-foot, wild mustard, and young nettles were boiled for food. Then there were certain kinds of sea-weed: the dulse is still used, raw, or boiled, also a sea-weed which grows on the rocks called Sloak, which is boiled with butter, so too another called Gruaigean probably identical with Iceland moss ...

The "lazy bed" system which has been largely used in Eriskay as it is in all the peat islands, may as well be described. Imagine a strip of soil, about three feet wide upon which is spread a thick layer of decomposed sea-weed. At either side a deep trench is dug, the soil from which is thrown up on to the top of the sea-weed, thus forming a sandwich of soil with the sea-weed between. The bed so constructed has two advantages—that of artificial depth, seldom to be acquired otherwise on the islands where the rock is very near the surface, and that of artificial drainage ...

... In the Northern Hebrides where looms are common, most weavers undertake the entire work. This includes washing the wool, drying it (often on the roof) dyeing carding, spinning running on to the spindles, setting the warp, weaving, washing, drying, fulling (or waulking) baling, and delivering the goods to merchant, often carried in a creel, perhaps on the weaver's back for miles.

As a rule the cloth is woven in lengths of from thirty to forty yards,—the shorter the length the greater the multiplication of labour in setting the warp, which from personal experiment is, I can testify a somewhat tedious process, and trying to the sight. Cloth of good quality weighs, when finished, and dried, very nearly a 1 lb per yard, say 28 lbs to a length of thirty yards. The loss in carding and washing wool is at least thirty per cent, so that about 8½ lbs be allowed for waste. This does not include the loss in process of fulling, when the cloth shrinks about an inch to every foot of length, so that for a web intended to be thirty yards long when finished about two yards and three-quarters extra have to be allowed. The pieces will therefore require at least 38 lbs of wool, which costs at present value October 1891 about ten shillings a stone of 14 lbs for black-faced sheep, and about fifteen shillings for the superior Cheviot; the cost of raw material therefore is in itself considerable.

The intrinsic value of the dye is trifling, as it is generally some local product—sea-weed, undew, lichen, dandelion, iris, heather, blaeberries, tormentil, bogmyrtle, and various other simple herbs ... A recent article in the Celtic Monthly gives the cost of carding and spinning at 8d. per lb (raw, material) and 7d. per yard for weaving thus adding another thirty-five shillings to the cost of the web. Elsewhere we heard of a shilling per Highland yard of eight feet, and were told that this was about a day's work, though sometimes a good weaver might earn as much as 1s. 6d. ...

The visitor to Barvas should not omit to see the manufacture of the crogans or bollachans still made by the old women of the district for domestic use. They are pots or jars with a wide mouth not ungraceful in shape, moulded in the hand without tools from the local red clay, and hardened in the sun. Then warm milk is put into them, and boiled slowly over a peat fire, which produces a fairly good glaze ... roughly decorated with patterns drawn with a pin.

The oldest implement in the Islands ... is the cas-chrom, the crooked spade (literally crooked foot) ... is said to be far more effective than the plough, besides being suitable in positions practically inaccessible for horse-labour, for many an Island plot is too small for a plough to turn in.

The cas-chrom is extremely strong. The right foot is placed upon the sidepin, and the head, which is about 2ft 9in long, jerked into the ground with the entire weight of the labourer, who rests upon the long shaft or handle which measures between 5 and 6 feet. He works from right to left, walking backwards ... Then there is the racan or clod-breaker so primitive but withal so useful an implement that one may suppose it to have been unaltered from the earliest days of tillage. It is primarily used as a mallet, and the teeth are only called into requisition on occasion.

The treisger and the pleitheag are used in cutting peats, and how ever primitive are admitted to be very effective for their purpose. The head is shod with iron, and the labourer cuts the peats the size intended at one push while a second man casts them out on to the nearest plot of dry ground ready for drying and subsequent stacking.

The brath (two stones revolving one upon the other) is by some thought to be the oldest form of handmill in existence; the cnotag is a very simple instrument for bruising grain for immediate use, and consists of a solid piece of rock, ofter merely rough hewn, with a hollow for receiving the grain.

The buck-bean lus nan laogh is good for headache, a handful to be boiled in a quart of water till half evaporates, a glassful to be taken every morning. The centaury, and teantruidh is good for colic; one "fistful" to be boiled in a quart and a half of water with three teaspoonfuls of sugar till half a quart evaporates; a glass every two hours; this is good for haemorrhage. A common fungus maolconain cut up and soaked in warm water makes a valuable poltice for festering wounds ... The ribwort plantain, snath lus mixed with butter, is used for poultices ... A decoction of burdock is used for jaundice.

Chapter 17 Highland journeys

Wesley: *Extracts from journal—1760*

Descriptions of Scottish scenes.

After Edinburgh, Glasgoe and Aberdeen, I think Inverness is the largest town I have seen in Scotland. The main streets are broad and straight, the houses mostly old, but not very bad or very good. It stands in a pleasant fruitful country, and has all the things needful for life and godliness. The people in general speak remarkably good English, and are of a friendly courteous behaviour ... Doubting whether Mr Grant was come home, Mr Kershaw called at the Grange-Green near Forres, while I rode forward; but Mr Grant soon called me back. I have seldom seen a more agreeable place. The house is an old castle, which stands on a little hill, with a delightful prospect all four ways; and the hospitable master left nothing undone to make it still more agreeable. He showed us his improvements, which are very considerable, in every branch of husbandry. In his gardens many things were more forward than at Aberdeen, yea, or Newcastle. And how is it that none but one Highland gentleman has discovered that we have a tree in Britain, as easily raised as an ash, the wood of which is of full as fine a red as mahogany, namely the Liburnum? I defy any mahogany to exceed the chairs which he has lately made of this ...

Thurs. 12 We rode through the pleasant and fertile country of Murray to Elgin. I never suspected before that there was any such country as this near a hundred and fifty miles beyond Edinburgh; a country which is supposed to have generally six weeks more sunshine in a year than any part of Great Britain.

At Elgin are the ruins of a noble cathedral, the largest that I remember to have seen in the kingdom. We rode hence to the Spey, the most rapid river, next the Rhine that I ever saw. Though the water was not breast high to our horses, they could very hardly keep their feet. We dined at Keith, and rode on to Strathbogie much improved by the linen manufacture ...

Wed 25 Taking horse at five, we rode to Dunkeld, the first considerable town in the Highlands. We were agreeably surprised: a pleasanter situation cannot be easily imagined. Afterwards we went some miles on a smooth delightful road, hanging over the river Tay, and then went on, winding through the mountains, to the Castle of Blair. The mountains for the next twenty miles were much higher, and covered with snow. In the evening we came to Dalwhinny, the dearest inn I have met with in North-Britain. In the morning we

Dunkeld.

were informed so much snow had fallen in the night, that we could get no farther. And indeed three young women, attempting to cross the mountain to Blair, were swallowed up in the snow. However we resolved, with God's help to go as far as we could. But about noon we were at a full stop; the snow driving together on the top of the mountain, had quite blocked up the road. We dismounted, and striking out of the road warily sometimes to the left, with many stumbles, but no hurt, we got on to Dalmagarry, and before sunset to Inverness ...

Mon 16 I took a view of one of the greatest natural curiosities in the kingdom: what is called Arthur's Seat, a small rocky eminence, six or seven yards across, on the top of an exceeding high mountain, not far from Edinburgh. The prospect from the top of the castle is large, but it is nothing in comparison to this ...

Inverness; In the afternoon we took a walk over the bridge into one of the pleasntest countries I have seen. It runs along by the side of the clear river, and is well cultivated and well wooded. And here first we heard abundance of birds, welcoming the return of spring ...

We travelled through a delightful country by Stirling and Kilsythe to Glasgow. The congregation was miserably small, verifying what I had often heard before, "that the Scots dearly love the word of the Lord,—on the Lord's Day". If I live to come again I will take care to spend only the Lord's day at Glasgow ...

The '45 from a whig point of view

Wed 18. About five we came to Newcastle, in an acceptable time. We found the generality of the inhabitants in the utmost consternation; news being just arrived that, the morning before, at two o'clock, the Pretender had entered Edinburgh. A great concourse of people were with us in the evening ... Thurs 19 The Mayor (Mr Ridley) summoned all the householders of the town to meet him at the town-hall; and desired as many of them as were willing to set their hands to a paper, importing that they would, at the hazard of their goods and lives, defend the town against the common enemy. Fear and darkness were on every side ... Fri 20 The Mayor ordered the townsmen to be under arms, and to mount guard in their turns, over and above the guard of soldiers; a few companies of whom had been drawn into the town on the first alarm. Now, also, Pilgrim-Street Gate was ordered to be walled up. ... Sat 21 The same day the action was, came the news of General Cope's defeat. Orders were now given for the doubling of the guard, and for walling up Pandon and Sally-Port Gates. Sun 22 The walls were mounted with cannon, and all things prepared for sustaining an assault. Meanwhile our poor neighbours on either hand were busy in removing their goods; and most of the best houses in our street were left without either furniture or inhabitants. Those within the walls were almost equally busy in carrying away their money and goods, and more and more of the gentry every hour rode southward as fast as they could ... Sun 29 Advice came that they were in full march southward so that it was supposed they would reach Newcastle by Monday evening ... Among those who came from the North, was one whom the Mayor ordered to be apprehanded on suspicion of his being a spy. As soon as he was left alone he cut his own throat; but a surgeon coming quickly, sewed up the wound; so that he lived to discover those designs of the rebels which were thereby effectually prevented ... Mr Nixon (the gentleman ... cut his throat) being still unable to speak, wrote as well as he could "That the design of the Prince (as they call him) was to seize on Tinmouth Castle which he knew was well provided both with cannon and ammunition; and hence to march to the hill the east side of Newcastle which entirely commands the town".

Mary Hanway: *Journey to the Highlands of Scotland—1776*

Thursday, after breakfast we set out for Crief, where one the horses fell sick, and we were forced to stay.—Friday proved a day of misfortunes. Indeed, we had scarce quitted the house when the horse appeared almost too bad to go on. The road was rather disagreeable, laying between immense "cloud-topt" hills ... When we arrived within three miles of our stage, the horses would not go any farthur; there was no resource, but to unharness and bait them, while we took up our abode in a hovel filled with hay ... Here we sat an hour and a half; till, being quite frozen with cold, I was obliged to take the shelter of a little hut, the inhabitants of which made me a fire, and treated me with untaught good-manners nature and hospitality ...

We left the dreary place to meet with worse misadventures than before. We had not proceeded a mile when the horses run back, and instead of ascending the hill, and broke the pole, which luckily hindered the chase from running back. We got out, and walked up; but neither ill or good usage could prevail on them to follow: we now found their only disease was being restive; With a great deal of trouble they were persuaded to go two miles farther; when, on the appearance of another hill, they performed the same trick, with some considerable additions, for they would not move a foot. What was to be done? there were no horses at the place we had left, and it was twelve miles to Taybridge, where if we had sent it was very unlikely we should be better supplied, there being no post-horses kept on the Highland roads. ... In this terrible dilemma—chance ... sent us help ... a return post-chaise ...

I was last Sunday, for the first time, at a Highland kirk, or church; and such a strange appearance as the lower sort of women make would amaze you. The married ones wear a handkerchief croffed over their heads, with two ends pinned under their chin, and the third flying behind; the young ones wear nothing but a ribband on their hair; the other parts of their dress are like those of the common people with us; only over all, they wear a plaid, which reaches to their feet, and is wrapped over their head, so that nothing is left to be seen but their noses—The poorest sort of all, who cannot afford a plaid, rather than not be ornamented, walk forth arrayed in their blankets; so that when all are assembled in this strange fashion they really have just the appearance of a set of lunaticks. All here sung psalms; ...

There is hardly ever such a thing heard of, as a Highland highway robber; their roads are not like ours infested by those pests to society. Your purse and your person are here equally secure; nor do their newspapers, like ours, shock humanity every month with an account of five or six and twenty poor wretches condemned to an ignominious death ... Their laws are too wisely calculated for the good of the community in general, and their church is under most excellent regulations; their livings are from forty pounds a year to one hundred and fifty, with a decent house and some land. Not as with us, a vicar, with eight hundred or a thousand pounds a year, who will give thirty pounds to a poor curate to do the duty of three parishes, and maintain his wife and ten children.

William Gilpin: *Observations, relative chiefly to picturesque beauty made in the year 1776 on several parts of Great Britain; particularly the High-Lands of Scotland*

We did not see the valley of Glencoe; as it would have carried us too far out of our road; but it is described as one of the most interesting scenes in the whole country; hung with rock, and wood; and abounding with beauties of the most romantic kind. This valley is famous also for being the birth place of Ossian. In its wild scenes that bard is said to have caught his first poetic raptures. Near it lies the country of Morven; which Fingal hath turned into classic ground by his huntings, and his wars.

At Killin, we heard of the little history of a Highland migration. Several expeditions of this kind to America, from different parts of Scotland (which were supposed to have been attended with success) began to make a noise in the country; and a discontented spirit got abroad, even in those parts, where no oppression could be complained of; ... The Word Was Given, as it was phased, in the beginning of March 1775; and a rendezvous was appointed at Killin, on the first of the ensuing May. Here convened about thirty families, making above three hundred people. The first night they spent at Killin, in barns, and other outhouses, which they had previously engaged. Early the next morning the whole company was called together by the sound of bag-pipes, and the order of their march was settled. Men, Women, and children, had all their proper stations assigned. They were all dressed in their best attire; and the men armed in the Highland fashion. They who were able, hired carts for their baggage: the rest distributed it in proper proportions, among the several members of their little families: each of them, in a patriarchal style, carrying provisions for the way. Then taking a long adieu of their friends, and relations, who gathered round them, the music began to play, and in the midst of a thousand good wishes mutually distributed, the whole train moved on ... But these emigrants were of a different stamp. Many of them were possessed of two or three hundred pounds, and few of them less than thirty or forty; which at least shewed, they had not starved upon their farms. They were a jocund crew, and set out, not like people flying in the face of poverty; but like men who were about to carry their health, their strength, and little property, to a better market. The first day's march brought them to Loch-Lomond, which is about twenty-five or thirty miles from Killin. At the head of this lake they had provided vessels, in which the greater part of them embarked; and were carried by water twenty-four miles further, into the neighbourhood of Dunbarton; where they cantoned themselves, till their transport vessel was ready at Greenock.

Loch-Fyne is a salt lake, communicating with the sea, at a distance of about twenty-five miles from Inveraray Castle ... It is one of the favorite haunts of the herring; and at certain seasons of the year is frequented by innumerable shoals. The country-people express the quantities of the fish in strong language. At those seasons, they say, the lake contains one part water, and two parts fish. In this single bay of the lake, we were told that above six hundred boats are sometimes employed in taking them. The groups of these little fishing vessels with their circling nets make a beautiful moving picture; while it is frequently varied by vessels of a larger size, shooting athwart; threading the several little knots of anchoring barks; and making their tacks in every direction.

The herring-boats commonly take their station on the lake, as evening comes on; ... The crews of these boats seem generally to be a cheerful, happy, race. Among the impliments of each boat, the bagpipe is rarely forgotten; the shrill melody of which you hear constantly resounding from every part; except when all hands are at work. On Sunday, the mirth of the several crews is changed to devotion: as you walk by the side of the lake, if the evening be still, you will hear them singing psalms, instead of playing on the bagpipe.

But notwithstanding the proness of the Scotch Highlander to acts of revenge, and rapine, he was, in other respects, in the worst of times, a virtuous character. He was faithful, hospitable, temperate, and brave; and if he is not slow to forget an injury he was always esteemed grateful for a benefit. How strict he was where confidence was reposed, appears in a very strong light from that universal protection and fidelity, which the Pretender experienced after the battle of Culloden. Tho the penalty for concealing him was so great; and the reward for giving him up so tempting but there was not a single man found among them such numbers as he was obliged to trust, who did not contribute all he could to conceal, and succour him ... To this virtuous disposition of the highlander may be added ... an independent spirit. There are no poor-rates in Scotland ... the Scotch highlander, even in his real distresses will make his last effort, and submit to any inconvenience, before he will complain.

There is another reason however given for burying in islands; which is practiced also in other parts of Scotland. When the country abounded with wolves, it is said, these animals would often attack church-yards; against which the people guarded by insular graves.

(Loch Lomond) In an opposite direction lies Inch-Galbreith. This island the osprey-eagle inhabits, in preference to any other on the lake, but for what particular advantage the naturalist is ignorant. From his residence here he sends out his rapacious colonies. Fish is his prey: but nature hath neither given him power to swim nor the art to dive. She has furnished him however with powers equally destructive. With a keen eye he hovers the lake; and seeing from a great height, some inadvertant fish near the surface, he darts rapidly upon it; and plunging his talons, and breast if need be, into the water, keeps his pinions aloof in the air, undipped; on the strength of which he springs upwards with his prey, tho it is sometimes very bulky. The osprey differs little from the sea-eagle; only he is more, what is commonly termed, a fresh-water-pirate.

In one of his parks, (the Duke of Queensbury? Hamilton?) we were informed, the Duke had preserved a breed of the old Scottish buffalo, which we were very desirous to see ... As we approached, they rose and retired gently into the wood; but gave us sufficient opportunity to examine them. There were two bulls, and several cows, and some calves. They were milk white, except their noses, ears, and the orbits of eyes which were black.

The Scotch fir, which generally makes a distinguished part of these plantations, is naturally a beautiful tree ... Besides the Scotch fir, the spruce seems also a native of this country: at least it flourishes here very happily.

These groups of cattle were picturesque, wherever we found them; the cattle themselves as individuals, are in general homely. Their colour is commonly black, with patches of white; which makes together the most inharmonious of all mixures. They are small: their countenances usually sour; and their horns wide—very unlike the small, curled beautiful horn of the Alderney, and the French cow. But these deformities are of little consequence in a group.—The sheep are also diminutive and ordinary; but in their tattered rough attire, exceedingly picturesque.—These scenes are often enlivened by a species of little, wild horses; which tho not absolutely in a state of nature, are perfectly fui juris, for the first three or four years of their lives. Some of these however are very beautiful.

Nor are the cattle of this wild country more picturesque, than its human inhabitants. The highland dress (which, notwithstanding an act of parliament, is still in general use) is greatly more ornamental than the English. I speak of it's form; not it's colour; which is checked, of different hues, and has a disagreeable appearance. The plaid consists of a simple piece of cloth, three yards in length, and half that measure in breadth. A common one sells for about ten shillings. The highlander wears it in two forms. In fine weather he throws it loosely round him; and the greater part of it hangs over his shoulder. In rain he wraps the whole close to his body. In both forms it makes elegant drapery; and when he is armed with his pistols and Ferrara has a good effect. Oftener than once we amused ourselves with desiring some highlander, whom we accidentally met, to perform the exercise of his plaid by changing it from one form to the other. Trifling as the operation seems, it would puzzle any man, who had not been long used to it.—But to see the plaid in perfection, you must see the highland gentleman on horse-back. Such a figure carries you into Roman times ... The bonnet is commonly made in the form of a beef-eater's cap which is very ugly. I have sometimes seen the bonnet sit snugger to the head, and adorned with a plume of feathers. It is then extremely picturesque.—When the common people take a journey on horse-back they often gather up the plaid in a few plaits; and so form it into a cloak. In this shape it is scanty, and unpicturesque.

J Robertson: *Jaunt between Edinburgh and the West Country in 1781*

... Stop at Bucklivie, 15 miles from Stirling, a poor insignificant village and miserable inn, where we could get no hay to our horses nor entertainment for ourselves. Here, however we were obliged to stay an hour and a half or two hours, for a sake of a rest to the horses. To compensate for the want of hay they got a double feed of oats, and we proceeded in our journey.

The inn at Dumbarton is far from being good. We, however got pretty comfortable beds, and start by 6 O'clock in the morning, and sett out for Luss. A pleasanter ride could not be wished for than betwixt Dumbarton and that place. In our way to Dumbarton it has been observed we came along the banks of that beautiful and rapid river Leven which, issuing from Loch Lomond after a course of five or six miles empties itself into the Clyde. We now cross it at Dumbarton Bridge and proceed directly up the opposite side. About two miles from Dumbarton we see a very handsome monument with a Latin epitaph erected immediately upon the road side by the late Commissary Smollet, to the memory of his friend Dr Tobias Smollet, a gentleman well known and much respected in the literary world. There are a great many excellent bleachfields and several very handsome country seats upon the side of the Leven ... Breakfast being over, we hired a boat and take a sail upon the loch ... We had the good fortune in our peregrinations upon the loch to fall in

Fascally.

with the fishermen, and landing upon another island, we saw them draw their nets full of great variety of fish, but particularly a great many very fine large trout. The small sum of threepence procured us the pick of the perches, powans, and a very large pike, which we purchased as a regale for ourselves at Glasgow in the evening. Upon Loch Lomond and the river of Leven are most excellent salmon fishing; ... In this part of the country the Erse language begins to be pretty generally spoken. ... We dine at Dumbarton, and in the afternoon sett out for Glasgow, and have a most agreeable ride along the north banks of the Clyde, a beautiful river, yet of little service in the way of navigation, in respect of its shallowness, but of late the channel has been considerably deepened, and the river consequently rendered more useful.

Chambers: *Burns' life and works*

Trip in the West Highlands—1787

We light upon him first with certainty at Inveraray ... Hereupon he penned an epigram ...

On incivility shewn him at Inverary

Whoo'er he be that sojourns here,
I pity much his case,
Unless he come to wait upon
The Lord their God—his Grace.

Ther's naething here but Highland pride,
And Highland scab and hunger;
If Providence has sent me here,
'Twas surely in an anger.

To Mr Robert Ainslie, Arrochar by Lochlong June 23 1787,

I write you this on my tour through a country where savage streams tumble over savage mountains, thinly overspread with savage flocks, which starvingly support as savage inhabitants. My last stage was Inverary, to-morrow night's stage Dumbarton. I ought sooner to have answered your kind letter, but you know I am a man of many sins.

To Mr James Smith—June 30 1787

On our return at a Highland gentleman's hospitable mansion, we fell in with a merry party, and danced till the ladies left us, at three in the morning. Our dancing was none of the French or English insipid formal movements; the ladies sang Scotch songs like angels, at intervals; then we flew at "Bab at the Bowster" "Tullochgorum", "Loch Erroch side" & like midges sporting in mottie sun, or craws prognosticating a storm in hairst day ...

Composed on leaving a place in the Highlands where he had been kindly entertained.

When Death's dark stream I ferry o'er—
A time that surely shall come—
In Heaven itself I'll ask no more
Than just a Highland welcome.

Burns' Tour of the Highlands 1787. (from his own journal & visiting the N and central H. Friday 31st August. Walk with Mrs Stewart and Beard to Birnam top—fine prospect down Tay—Craigiebarns hills—hermitage on the Bran water, with a picture of Ossian—Breakfast with Dr Stuart—Neil Gow plays—a short stout-built, honest Highland figure, with his grayish hair shed on his honest social brow—an interesting face, marking strong sense, kind openheartedness mixed with unmistrusting simplicity—visit his house—Margaret Gow.

Ride up the Tummel river to Blair-Faskally, a beautiful romantic nest—wild grandure of the pass of Killiecrankie—visit the gallant Lord Dundee's stone ... Friday 7th September Cross the Findhorn to Forres—Famous stone at Forres—Mr Brodie tellt the muir where Shakespeare lat's Mcbeth's witch meeting is still haunted—that country folks won't pass it by night—.

W.A.: *A journal of a short tour from Edinburgh—1787*

(Dundee) We dine about two, on beef-stakes and Mutton pyes, after which we drink some delicious strong ale, for which Dundee is celebrated being furnished with plenty of Rich Corn from Angus Shire of wch it is the Capital.

(Perth) The town consists of three or four streets, all of them much of the same size, and compossed of very handsome houses, tho' pretty old; they are kept amazingly clean being constantly washed with a number of little Wells which are placed in rows along both sides of the streets, so that instead of being filled with dirt, the kennels are perpetually running with ye. cleanest water. The Wells are about three foot high, and besides cleaning the streets and serving the inhabitants with water, form a very good Bulwark for the pavement, on the sides, against horses and carriages.

The Tay affords as great quantities of Salmon as any river in Scotland and there are great Fisheries all along its banks above the Town; but wonderful to tell, every one of the Fish are shipped off for the Metropolis of England, and, whereas formerly the poor of the

Country round about were plentifully and cheaply supplied with excellent food, at present even the most opulent inhabitants esteem their native Fish a very great rarity. But this is partly owing to the mal-administration of the magistrates, who are bound to compell the Tacksmen of the Fisheries abundantly to supply the Town Markets at a resonable price.

In about an hour's walk, after drinking some good Highland Whisky, we reach a Ferry, cross the River, which is here Broad, Deep, and Rapid. A little Boy, with a pair of oars, rowed us safely over fourpence a piece, ... We dine upon Salmon, & which is so dear as sixpence pr Lb. tho' great quantities of it are taken just at the door.

After this we walk north along the Tay on a smooth mossy bank. We here see a Boy fishing pars, a little fish, though generated between a trout and a salmon; but I have heard some people say that they have seen them weigh upwards of sixteen pounds ... they are much more delicate than a trout and are very plentiful in every River where there are Salmon.

We this evening sup upon Kidstakes, a delicious sort of meat, which had a better relish because dressed with a fire of Peats: which, with wood, is the only fuel the Country produces. After supper, while drinking our Bottle of Wine as we usually did, we were very well entertained by the Music of a Highland Fidler in the next room ...

We repass the Bridge of Dochart ... We spent some time in viewing Tombstones; and a man fishing in a manner peculiar to himself engaged our attention for a long time. He had a strong rod about 4 fathoms in length. His line was wound on a wooden reel, being a Rope somewhat thicker than a penny cord. To this was attatched an Iron Hook as big as one's hand, and he used more than a pound of lead as a plummet to sink his hook in the water. His tackling being thus prepared without bait of any sort, he threw his line into a deep tumultuous pool a little way under the Bridge; after he perceived by his plummet that the hook had reached the bottom he drew it forth again with a sudden jerk. This he repeated till he hooked a Salmon, and he told us he seldom drop'd a dozen times without catching one.

The day being as yet exceedingly tempestuous we resolved to stay here all night, and having expressed a desire for a fiddler we are instantly furnished, for the Highlanders delight much in music.

The Country people here have a horrid aversion at the thought of listing in the army. As we were coming along a poor old Countryman imagined that we were going to turn Soldiers. He came running after us, and greatly surprised us when he cried out "Stay, Laddies, dinna list, stay for ony sake. Stay and I'll gee ye a bottle of Ale". So much would he have given from his penury to enjoy the satisfaction of having saved us from Ruin. When he came up we told him we did not mean to list, and he went off contented.

Rev. William Macritchie: *Diary of a tour through Great Britain—1795*

Next morning, Tuesday the 23rd, set out for the waterside. At Kelty-bridge meet a vast number of coal-drivers, who inform me they have them at the pits there at the rate of sixpence and eight-pence every eighteen stone-weight. Saw, with some surprise indeed, a shepherd reclining on a green hill by the side of the way, busied in reading a newspaper. "Curse on French politics!" said I, "for they will ruin our country. This fellow would be better employed gathering plants as I am, and at the same time taking care of his sheep. What connection has French cruelty with the happiness of this poor fellow's situation? If he has not the felicity at this moment to congratulate himself on his having been born a Scots herd, I both pity and despise him. But what business has he with that newspaper? I don't like to be uncharitable, but I cannot help thinking he puts me too much in mind of too many fine giddy girls who set their heads agog by reading romances that ought to be made a bonfire of. I like liberty as much as any man: the liberty of the press is certainly a great blessing; but alas! the very best of blessings are too often abused."

The Borderers seem to be fond of rhiming. Such trifles as these sometimes catch the eye of a solitary traveller. Have a fine view of Mossknowe, the seat of Captain Graeme of Dumfries, on the left hand. Arrive at the famous Gretna-green (Mrs. Howe), and dine sumptuously in one of the pleasantest inns in the kingdom, where so many fond lovers have had their hearts and their fortunes united by Pasley, of whom I here find the following lines pencilled on one of the window-shutters in the room where I dine:

"Old Pasley the priest, who does lovers unite,
Is stiled by the wise ones an old Gretna Bite;
To be sure 'tis for money he follows the trade;
No woman possessing it should die an old maid."

A peasant here told me he had in his house a cannon-ball, found in his wife's father's time under the furrow of the plough, near the scene of the battle. He told me the bullet weighs about eighteen pound. Many weapons of war were dug up hereabouts at different times.

"This gate hangs well and hinders none;
Refresh and pay, and travel on."

"Bread, beer,
Sold here".

"Gentlemen here take a guide
To either Scotch or English side,
And have no cause to fear the tide".

Lochleven East Coast abounds with fish; all the different species of the hill, and the burn or muir trout, known in Scotland, are to be found in it. The silver grey trout, for which this lake is famed, is said to be the original native, and is, in every respect, the richest and finest. All these kinds of trout are white in the flesh, till their third year; then they become red. Char are, also, found in this loch, in greater plenty, than in any other place in Scotland; often as large as to weigh two pounds.

Return to Inver, which is the birth place and residence of Mr. Neil Gow, the celebrated self-taught violin player. As if inspired by the genius of his native mountains, the "Strathspeys" and "Laments" of this reverend Knight of Cremona, are here given with double energy and enthusiasm. Few occurrences in your tour will afford you more satisfaction than hearing him perform.

In the year 1784 Lochtay experienced a very unusual agitation. At the extremity of a bay at the South side of the village of Kenmore, the waters suddenly retired five yards within their usual boundary, and in a few minutes returned; continuing thus, alternately, to ebb and flow, for about a quarter of an hour. Then rushing, suddenly, in opposing currents, from east and west, they roaring met, and foaming rose into a billow of considerable magnitude; which, driven westward by the overwhelming impetus of the waters from the bay, slowly decreased as it proceeded, and at length totally disappeared. About five minutes afterwards, the waters rushed back into the bay, and continued, at certain intervals, to ebb and flow for about two hours, lessening gradually in violence, till they finally resumed their wonted tranquillity.

On the next and four following days, however, they suffered fresh, though not so violent, commotions; and it was not till a month had elapsed, that they totally subsided.

While the waters in the lake were thus agitated, the river Tay, which issues from it on the north side of the village, ran backwards into the lake, with such velocity as to leave its shores and many parts of its bed entirely dry.

In the year 1794, the waters in the lake were again disturbed, but neither so long nor so forcibly.

Lochaw abounds with salmon, char, trout and eel, the last of which are abhorred by the country people, who consider them as water serpents, and unfit for the use of man.

On the first of November 1755, when the city of Lisbon was destroyed by an earthquake, Lochlomond was very much agitated. The day was perfectly calm; and the surface of the lake still and serene; when, all at once, its waters rose, in large undulations, to the height of many feet; then, suddenly retiring, they sunk as much below their usual level. Their next flow and ebb, though still considerable, were less than the first; and, gradually diminishing, after some hours, the fluctuation entirely subsided. A boat was found on the dry land forty yards from its station in the lake; and, where the banks of the lake were low, the country was overflowed to a considerable extent.

D.B. Crailing (Rev. David Brown of Crailing): *A tour in Scotland in 1802—published 1902, Scottish Antiquary*

We had been entertained viewing the coasts on both sides—which are hilly, particularly the coast of Argleshire, on which there is very little arable land, and nothing appearing green, even at that advanced time of year (May). The soil is so light in the colour as to give the plowed fields the look of autumn when the crops are taken off. On the Renfrew coast there is also but little extent of arable ground—the country on that side also becoming mountainous short way from the shore; but here and there are to be seen gentlemen's country seats with the lands considerably improved around. The grounds in view seem much inclined to produce whins, which have over-run many of the fields lately in tillage, ... The ship ... was hired to carry emigrants from the West Highlands to Cape Breton in North America ...

Mr Grant, a young gentleman from the house to which the ship belonged, was along with us going to see the Highlanders embarked.

In the afternoon we came to anchor off the island of Shona, at the mouth of Loch Moidart, having been eleven nights and twelve days at sea. We were this night at the house of Mr Andrew M'Donald, of Shona, from whom we met with great civility, and who next morning procured a boat with four men at the rate of two and a half guineas to carry us to Auchtertyre ...

We entered the Canal of Crenan about eight in the evening ...

Next morning (July 3rd) we were early in motion—breakfasted and continued on board till the vessel passed several locks we then took leave of our mariners, moved our luggage to a cart which was hired to convey us to Lochgilphead, there being no better carriage to be got in the country ... Next morning July 4th it cleared up to a fine day. We all breakfasted with Mr Paterson, writer, son in law to Dr Frazer—were kindly entertained and were favoured with a dish of fresh herrings, the first of the season. Besides this dish, there were plenty of eggs, butter, and ham, ... About a mile distant a neat farmstead and pleasant pastures attracted our notice. Our boatman informed us that the tenant is bound by his lease always to maintain a certain number of cows whose milk must be sold twice a day at Inveraray, sweet and good as it comes from the cows, and at a stated and moderate price; which is a very valuable accommodation to the Inhabitants . . . We reached Dalmaly about three o'clock . . . The Inn was built twenty years ago, and is considered large and commodious. We got a tolerable dinner, and our English fellow travellers were, here, for the first time obliged to content themselves with barley bread . . . The fuel consists wholly of peat and not of the driest, which was also a novelty . . . It is proper to mention that we here (*Dunkeld*) visited the deservedly celebrated fiddler Neil Gow, the father of several of the most noted musicians at present in Great Britain. He is an aged and venerable figure, clad in blue bonnet and blue coat, with waistcoat breeches and hose of tartan: and though he is said to be worth about £8000, he still lives in the same turf-covered hut in which he reared his family. He received us kindly and soon roused us to dance to his music.

North British Magazine: *Topographical account of some parts of the West Coast of Scotland—1804*

We sailed from Greenock to Sky, for the purpose of taking in emigrants for America. Before taking them on board of the vessel in which I myself was to accompany these people to the western world, it may be interesting for you to know how the actual conditions in which I beheld them on their native heaths and mountains.

The first thing that presents itself to a stranger, is the exterior appearance of the inhabitants. You have all observed their modes of dressing; perhaps except in their partiality for tartan, there is no essential difference from people in the lowlands farther than poverty occasions . . .

Marriage does not take place among these people from any opinion of the female perfection but almost altogether this affair is managed by the father and intended bridegroom, the later chuses a wife where he gets most cattle or money. This is so common, that on asking a man who had several daughters, how they were not married, as they were of age? he told me, he had been only able to marry the oldest, but he would do his best to get husbands for the others. To have a number of daughters in Sky is no blessing to the parents; they look on themselves as bound to procure them husbands, and it is no easy matter, in a country such as it is, to find the means. The people are very hospitable the poorest person will produce his best to serve the stranger. Till very lately, they would have looked on it as an insult, to have passed their house without receiving some kindness. Frequent imposition, however, has made them more cautious whom they entertain. Still the slightest introduction is sufficient. I have often, with pleasure taken a potatoe and herring with them: I thought it had relish, from the goodwill with which it was bestowed. On being simply told who I was, that I belonged to the ship come to take the people to America, I have been supplied with guide, horses, lodging, and ferried over a dangerous sound of ten miles, free of expense, by a people, whose appearance by no means bespoke the power; when I offered the money, they were much hurt . . .

All the songs I heard had choruses; many of them are a sort of duets. When they begin to sing, one person takes the lead. I think, as far as I could judge many of the choruses are similar to the tol, lol, fal, lal & etc. of our songs, but the sounds very different. Each takes hold of the corner of a handkerchief, or another's hands; but whatever way, all must be connected during the song. The hands and heads of the company move backwards and forwards, in unison to the tune, which is generally in a moderate key; but, on the leading singer increasing the pitch of the voice, those who take up the chorus must do it also; and before it is finished it is generally sufficiently high for ears of common structure. I have been frequently delighted to see old women, men and children, moving in great harmony and seriousness . . .

The people in Sky live on almost nothing. They have not so much butter and cheese among them as you would imagine in a country almost solely dedicated to feeding cattle. The chief part of the corn made use of is imported; what grows on the island is not sufficient for feeding the cattle in winter. There is scarcely such a thing as a road. All their goods are carried on horse back, or in creels suspended on each side of the animal. But the poor people live chiefly on potatoes and herring. There are fine hadocks in the sound, but they have no market even if they would catch them.

J. Mawman: *Excursion to the Highlands of Scotland and the English lakes— 1805*

In a walk to the Green (Glasgow) a spacious piece of ground appropriated to the use of the inhabitants, we observed a great number of women washing linen, by trampling upon it in tubs of water with their naked feet. Here the gentlemen of the town amuse themselves by playing at goff, a game in which they are said to excel . . .

We soon however quitted these scenes of cultivation, and advanced into a bold-featured, majestic, desolate country, where we first beheld the Highlands, sweeping along in that wild state of nature which produces an impression perfectly new to an untravelled Englishman. Here the tourist forcibly seizes their true character. Mountain after mountain destitute of trees, contiguous in position, but irregularly rolling without intermission or apparent termination; and the wide lakes stretching boldly up the country, amidst the branching chains of naked hills; . . . In this wild romantic scenery the eye wanders in vain to discover a solitary cottage, or even a spot of cultivated earth; and till our arrival at the inn of Arroquhar, nothing was to be seen but a few mean huts, here and there a half-naked human being, and at intervals a boat on the lake with a fisherman and a boy.

A drizzling rain gave a thick darkness to the natural dinginess of the lake, the effect of which was still farther augmented by the sea-weed that clung to the shores and rocks, and rode on the surface of the mournfully dashing waves and by the lowering clouds which enveloped in obscurity the tops of the hills, and threw awful majesty over this dreary region. The sides of the lake stretched along without the intervention of trees, or the relief of any vegitation upon its banks ... While, from the front of Arroquhar-inn we were admiring the desolate and magnificent scenery of the opposite mountains, a traveller just returned from the west excited our laughter, by telling us that these were but mole-hills, in comparions with those which he had left behind.

It cannot be doubted that elegance of dress and manners gives a luster to beauty, and excites the senses through the medium of the imagination; it has even been observed, that were it the fashion to go naked, the face would hardly be noticed; certain it is, that the bare feet very much attracted our attention. The conspicuously-active spring of the ball of the foot, and the powerful grasp of the toes, increase our knowledge by exhibiting the beauty and utility of that member. All Highlanders walk with firmness and agility. We saw not a single instance even of a female turning in her tows, or stepping with a stiff bent knee.

We remarked that, north of Glasgoe, we had not beheld one individual, man, woman, or child, crooked; and that, though their feet were freely applied to rugged roads and gravelly shores, they yet did not appear to have received any injury. ... We naturally expected to have seen the tartan-plaid much worn, but we did not meet any one in this highland dress; in the philibeg and bonnet very seldom; and the ancient costume seems here to be entirely laid aside.

We observed that all the people in the highlands had linen next their skins ... The young women let their hair grow long behind, and twist and fasten it on the top of the head with a comb, and thus wear it without caps. They, as well as the men, are uniformly short in statue, unencumbered with flesh, and very active, but their faces are rarely handsome, and generally as we thought, indicated the appearance of premature old age. Their features are probably hardened by exposure to the severe blasts of winter ...

The manners of the people however are easy, respectful, and agreeable, showing simplicity mingled with inteligence, and an openness of manner and behaviour superior to disguise of artifice; and possessing great presence of mind and ready wit ... The Highlander, on long journeys over hills, destute of human support, will for a long time repel the attacks of hunger by eating dried roots ... While our horses were feeding and resting, we amused ourselves with walking about the village, and along the shores of the Lake. One of the houses, built like that in Glen-Croe, we entered. The fire was here also in the middle of the floor, and the smoke was left to find its way out at the door, and through the holes which admitted the light. ... We were not sparing of our compliments to their country, of which those at least relative to their hospitality were most sincere; for never was a nation more courteous in their reception of strangers, or more solicitous to conciliate by their kindness those whom they enlighten by their intelligence ...

On the road to Lanark we entered into conversation with two well-dressed girls, of about eighteen, who were as usual without shoes and stockings. They had walked (they told us) from Glasgow, and were going five miles west of Lanark to see their aged parents. On our expressing surprise that they should have travelled upwards of thirty miles in the course of the day, one of them observed that they had not left Glasgow till after twelve o'clock at noon. We told them, that our English girls would not be able to walk so far in twice the time; upon which one of them smartly remarked "then they are not good for muckle".

About the middle of the glen, near the road, we had the curiosity to inspect a shepherd's hut. It is hardly possible to describe the wretchedness of this miserable habitation, built of slate, that had shivered and slid down the sides of the mountains. It was about nine yards long, and four or five wide; the door faced the road, at which entered promiscuously the shepherd, his wife, his children, and his cattle. Of the two unequal compartments, into which it was divided, the first and largest is principally intended for the cattle, the other for the family. In the former, however, we found lying on a hurdle three children, close to the door, with their feet almost against the tails of the cows; on the floor was a quantity of fern, which had long lain steeped in their evacuation. At the further side the ground being somewhat more elevated, we could with due care avoid sticking fast in soft and wet dirt, in our progress to the inner division. Here we found a blazing fire in the midst of the apartment, with a large pot hanging over it, containing some coarse and meagre fair little calculated to sustain vigerous life; and the smoke freely making its way through the door and the crevices of the building. Near the fire, in the depth of the smoke and covered with heavy rugs, lay three "children of larger growth".

Emerging from a hut which we never desired again to enter, we looked upon the children who were by the door, and observed that though their dwelling among cows is agreeable to the advice of an eminent physician, they had yet not that fine bloom upon their cheeks, which his theory would have led us to expect.

The mother of this large family was busily employed at a rivulet near the hut in washing coarse woolen clothes, and came up on our approach to her habitation. She readily gratified our curiosity, and was very thankful for the pittance which we gave her in return. Her husband, she said, was, "far awa" amongst the sheep.

J. R. Robertson: *General view of the agriculture of Inverness—1808*

Into that arm of the sea, which divides the county of Inverness from Argyllshire, several small vessels come to the quarry at Ballachulish, for slate and wool, which they carry to the towns situated on the banks of the Clyde, to England and elsewhere. These vessels import coals, metal, and other articles into that part of the Highlands. At the Port of Fort William, eight sloops are employed in the trade of Lochaber. The imports are chiefly coals and meal, and tar for smearing sheep. The exports are wool, and some oak timber, and bark. A few coasting vessels, carrying from fifteen to twenty tons, are employed from Arisaig to Skye, and the other Islands. These frequently import shell-sand from the Long Island to the mainland, as ballast. . . .

The road entering the county by the Black Mount, has got a different direction from what it had at first, in various places, and particularly by turning to the left, at the place called the Stairs, down through the valley of Glenco. But neither of these lines is the proper one; the road should have been conducted, not by the left, but north of the Stairs, through an opening called Mamghrianan, round the head of Loch Leven, where the ascents and distance to Fort William are less than by Glenco or the Staircase, besides avoiding the Ferry. In Glenco, the principal road is often choked by the stones which are loosened by the rains and tumbled down from the face of the rocks, that tower on eiter side aloft to the skies, and seem to close on the traveller's head. In one place I travelled over a field of these stones, whose depth was at least five feet, as appeared by a wall at its extremity, and whose breadth covered some acres of ground. If the frittered rocks, were in the act of falling during a thundershower, one might as well have been an inhabitant of the ancient Heraculancum at the foot of Vesuvious. In this, and in similar places, the larger fragments are carefully removed every year, otherwise the road would soon be impassable; but notwithstanding all this attention, the remaining stones have such sharp points and edges, as to endanger the hoofs of horses, unless they be uncommonly hardy.

John Walker D.D.: *An economical history of the Hebrides and Highlands of Scotland—1808*

The following work was the result of six journies made into the Highlands and Hebrides from the year 1760, to the year 1786, during which, a greater extent of these distant parts of the kingdom was surveyed, than what had probably ever been traversed by any former traveller . . .

It was long ago a general practice in Scotland to have part of the rent of every farm, and sometimes the whole, paid in grain, which is called payment in kind. This custom still prevails in many places, and especially in the north, where two-thirds of the rent are often paid in grain and other articles, and one-third in money. Sometimes the money rent makes but one-fifth of the whole. . . .

At no very remote period, the common production of the kitchen garden were unknown in the Highlands. Lochiel, on returning from abroad, with excellent intentions to improve his country, established a kitchen garden at his seat at Achnacary; and in August 1734 entertained his guests with hotch-potch, containing pease, turnip, and carrot; which was the first time these vegetables had been produced in that part of the world. . . .

The land dug with a cascrome, always affords a more considerable increase than that which is laboured with the plough. If a boll of bear, raised with the plough on good land, yields ten bolls; raised by the spade, it would produce better than thirteen; and on poorer land, the proportion in favour of the spade is still larger . . .

The island of Lismore is of a very peculiar soil, and different from that of all the other Hebrides. The island is composed almost entirely of black limestone. The soil above this rock is thin, of a black colour, and very full of calcareius earth. In consequence of this, the corn fields are over run with several very rank and hurtful weeds; particularly the Spear-thistle, the Hemp Agrimony, and especially by the wayside thistle. This has led the inhabitants to a contrivance very well adapted for destroying them. It is a pair of large strong wooden pincers: their jaws are ten inches, and their handles two feet ten inches long; the whole instrument being three feet ten inches in length. The handles, when expanded, are at the extremity two feet asunder. It is called in Gaelic the clou-mait, or timber tongs. When the thistles are of a proper age to be destroyed, a man transverses the field with this instrument, and draws them out by the root, more expeditiously and with less detriment to the crop, than when pulled by the hand, covered with a thick glove, which is the practice in other parts of Scotland . . .

The old Scotch tillage was all confined to one season. Ploughing did not begin till after old Candlemas, the 13th of February, and concluded in May. This is still the case in many parts of the country. In the Highlands they so not in general begin to plough till March. Since the introduction of potatoes, they begin in some places more early: but not untill the month of January . . .

In Lochbroom and Gareloch, the oats which were sown on the 10th of April were ripe on the 8th of September. In the year 1762, in the island of Tirey, the common bear, or square barley, produced a crop in eighty-five days; being sown the 28th of April, and reaped the 23rd of July. . . .

The advantages that arise from rabbits regularly colonised, are very considerable. They afford, in a country, a great stock of cheap and wholesome provision, from the month of

October till March, peculiarly useful, where the inhabitants, during that period, live chiefly on salted meats; their skin is valuable, and supports the hat manufacture. Whereever they are settled, they improve the pasturre and the soil; and are capable in many situations of affording more profit than the land could otherwise yield ... The only instance of the utility of rabbits that occurred in the Highlands, was in the island of Colonsay. On the north side of that island there are several hills of sand, and an extent of sandy downs which were stocked with rabbits by the late Mr MacNeil of Colonsay. In the year 1764 this very barren tract afforded one hundred and thirty dozen odd skins, which sold at Glasgoe at the low price of five shillings the dozen; the meat of these rabbits supplied the people of the island with fresh wholesome provision; and the very skins, which brought in thirty-two pounds ten shillings, amounted to ten times more than what this piece of sandy desert could otherwise produce. ...

In the Highlands and Islands there are varieties of soil, fit for raising all the barren trees which afford us with the most useful sorts of timber ...

There is a peculiar property in the bark of the birch tree, which well deserves to be noticed in this place. In winter and spring, the buds of the birch are covered with a gum of a very agreeable smell; when the young leaves expand, they are in some degree besmeared with this clammy substance which gives them that fragrance so generally admired. This gummy matter is high inflammable. The bark of the tree is so replete with it, that when dried it is capable of burning like a taper ...

One fir tree cut in Glen Etive in Argyllshire, and which grew very high on the mountain, was examined, and found to be three feet three inches in diameter ...

Before the year 1756, there was no post-office in the Hebrides, nor in all the West Highlands, beyond the Chain. ...

Heather, upon the whole is the plant with us that forms the best thatched roof, and of this, also there is no scarcity in the Highlands ... and it has been known to last forty to sixty years without any reparation. For this end, it requires only to be laid on green and fresh; its different layers to be disposed like so many slates, to be firmly compacted, and of a sufficient thickness; and to be strongly tied down with thick tarred rope ...

The quern was the original corn mill of Scotland; though a very imperfect machine, the Highlanders were, with great difficulty, induced to give it up, even in our own times and to accept the superior advantages of a water mill.

Stranger: *Through Scotland and the steamboat companion—1811*

Bute
About 8,070 barrels of herring, were cured here in the year 1822. Caledonian Canal: The difficulties attending the formation of this canal, were very considerable. One artificial embankment, is 1,000 yards long and 12 feet high. The locks are 25, and the lock-gates 38. Near Inverness too, the soil was so porous by reason of sand and gravel, that in pits sunk for trial, the water rose and fell with the tide ... it was successfully completed and opened on the 30th day of October 1822. On that day, the Loch-Ness steam-boat, accompanied by two smacks, left the locks at Muirtown, and proceeded on the first voyage through the canal, amidst the firing of cannon, and the cheerings of an immense assemblage of spectators ... The number of miles paid for by a trading vessel is 62, and the rate is about one farthing a mile registered tonnage. The Loch-Ness steam-boat which confines her voyages solely to the canal, was in the first year, it is said, highly successful, having divided 12½ per cent besides paying off her debts.

Argyllshire
On the mountainous and barren districts are reared a blackfaced breed of sheep, with coarse wool, lately introduced from some of the lowland counties; the richer hills are stocked with black cattle of a native breed, highly prized by cattle dealers, as combining a greater number of valuable qualities than any other in Britain. Both these species of cattle are annually exported in great numbers to the English pastures ...

Argyllshire cannot boast of any important manufactures. The principal are the making of salt from sea water, near Campbelltown; the spinning of woollen yarn by machinery, near Inveraray; tanning of leather at Oban; and the manufacture of pig-iron at the furnace of Bunaw. The ore employed at Bunaw is conveyed by sea from England, and after being smelted by charcoal is returned to the English manufacturers ...

The inhabitants of the Highlands did not live either in plenty or in elegance, yet they were happy. They piqued themselves on their capacity to endure hunger and fatigue. They were passionately fond of music and of poetry. The song and the dance soon made them forget their toils. At present the change is so considerable; now the sound of the bagpipe is seldom heard. With the modes of life that nourished it, the vein of poetry has also disappeared. The deer have fled from the mountains. Extensive forests are now turned into sheep walks.

Lismore and Appin
The districts of Lismore, Airds, Appin, Duror, Glenmorenen, Glencoe, and Kingerloch. By far the greater part is hilly and mountainous. The best soil is in Appin; it is equally capable of bearing corn as grass. There is one farm 18 Scots Miles long ... Formerly a lead mine was wrought in Appin but it was given up several years ago. The quarry of Ballichulish produces slate of a good quality, and is wrought with much spirit and success ...

County of Perth

The inhabitants of the Highlands of Perthshire speak the Erse language, though most of them now speak the English also; their dress is the ancient garb of the country, the bonnet, short coat, philibeg, and tartan hose ... The inhabitants however are inquisitive, intelligent, and hospitable, but rather superstitious, and very tenacious of old customs ...

MacCulloch: *The Highlands and Western Islands of Scotland—1811–12*

There are few parts of the Western Highlands more beautiful than the district of Appin and travellers particularly the gentlemen and ladies who drive gigs and barouches have only to lament that the two ferries of Connel and Shian are not only wide and boisterous, but not so convenient for exit and entrance as a few pounds spent on landing places might make them. The former is in fact abominable. Are ferries always to be bad because it is classical? Because there is a villainous one across the Styx must there be a bad one at Shian? and because the gentlemen whom Achilles dismisses to this navigation were obliged to wait shivering in the cold till Charon chose to admit them, must we wait in a Highland shower on a naked rock till he of the Connel chooses to see or hear ... The scenery is beautiful but everything is beautiful between these two ferries. There are but five miles; yet it is a day's journey to a wise man. The road from Shian ferry to Ballachulish is throughout interesting and presents much landscape scenery. It is perhaps most so where it skirts the margin of the water displaying a lively and moving picture produced by the crowd of vessels and boats which navigate the Linnhe Loch. It is with justice that Glenco is celebrated as one of the wildest and most romantic specimens of Scottish scenery; but those who have written about Glenco forget to write about Loch Leven and those who occupy a day in wandering from the inns at Ballachulish through its strange and rocky valley forget to open their eyes upon those beautiful landscapes which surround them on all sides and which render Loch Leven a spot that Scotland does not often exceed either in its interior lakes or its maritime inlets ... St Mungo's Island is an interesting spot no less on account of the various views it affords than because of its burial ground crowded with gravestones and ornaments and with sculptures which in a place so remote and unexpected attract an attention that more splendid works could hardly command in the midst of civilisation ... The slate quarries of Ballachulish have generated a considerable village: and the workmen, the noise, the shipping, the women and children and the confusion of all kinds form a strange contrast with the dark and dreary solitude of Glenco itself, scarcely a mile removed.

This is true Highland hospitality never boasted of, yet never failing. In all the wilds, I ever visited I never yet entered the blackest hut without having what was to be given, the best place at the fire, the milk tub, the oat-cake, the potato, the eggs if it was possible to persuade the hens to do such a deed, and a glass of whisky if it was to be found. All this too seems quite matter of right not of favour.

It is meant to be quaintly remarked when it is said that domestic or personal theft is rare in the Highlands because there is nothing to steal ... It is sufficient answer indeed to the piece of the above quoted that clothes and new linens are exposed to bleach for days or even weeks in situations where they cannot be watched and with perfect security. The same remark is true of the stacks of salt fish which remain piled up on the shores in safety even among a people, who, in our sense of the word would be considered starving. There is nothing to prevent a bold Highlander from stopping a monied Englishman traveller in the secluded roads or wild passes of this country. But such acts are unknown.

Jameson: *Mineralogical travels through Scotland—1813*

As the weather continued very pleasant, we preferred going to Oban by sea, in place of the circuitous rout by land. Having procured a boat, we left Seil, with a fine breeze; our voyage was agreeable, with scenery often striking, on one hand was the lofty coast of Mull, extending from Loch Bay to Crogan all apparently basaltic ... Having passed the isle of Kerrera, which lies across the bay of Oban; in a short time afterwards we landed at the village. The bay of Oban is of a semicircular form; it is from 12 to 14 fathom deep with good anchoring ground and will contain 500 sail of merchant ships. The village is pleasantly situated at the upper part of the bay, a station excellently adapted for the fishing. The decline of this branch of trade has indeed been unfavorable to the rise of Oban; but it is notwithstanding, the most considerable village on this part of the coast, containing 587 inhabitants. It is to the exertions of the two brothers, the Messrs Stevensons, who settled here in 1778 that Oban is chiefly indebted for its present flourishing condition.

Coll. The shore upon the east side, is generally low and rocky on the west it rises into considerable cliffs, and, in many places of this side, great sandbanks extend for a considerable way ... These banks ... are sometimes covered with Arundo arenarie, Galium verum &. but most frequently they present only a dreary waste ... The inhabitants have themselves partly to blame for the continuence of this evil, by their obstinacy in rooting up certain plants which prevent the blowing of sand; this, it is a common practice to use Arundo arenaria as a substitute for ropes, and the Galium verum as a yellow dye; two plants which are very remarkable for their powers in binding the sand.

A cottage in Islay.

Skye. The old house, in which Mr Campbell at this time lodges, is remarkable for having afforded shelter to Prince Charles, when pursued by the king's troops; and the shore is noted in history as the place where King James V landed when he was making the tour of his kingdom. After leaving Kingsburgh we walked for a mile or two along the side of Loch Snizort ... until we reached the mill which is situated upon a stream of water at the head of Loch Uig. A considerable way above this mill there is a pretty large cascade ... and near it we observed appearances of coal.

(On Kelp) The method of manufactureing, though rude, is sufficiently simple. The different species of fuci, particularly the vesiculus ferratus, and nodofus, are cut from the rocks in the months of May, June, and July, and spread out and dried so as to enable them to burn more easily. In drying the ware, they are very cautious to prevent any fermentation from taking place, or to suffer it to be exposed to rain; as kelp, made from such damaged ware, is necessarily of a very inferior quality.

The ware being well dried, a small quantity is kindled in a pit dug in the sand, or upon a piece of ground which is surrounded with loose stones, so as to form what is called a kiln. They continue adding fresh quantities, until the pit or kiln is nearly filled. When the whole is frequently stirred towards the evening, when it gets into a semifluid state; it is allowed to cool, and afterwards taken out of the pit ready for the market.

Spencer: *Journal of a tour in Scotland—1816*

It is impossible to do justice to the sort of roughness and inequality which characterizes the roads in the western islands. They are in fact, nothing more than incisions cut through rocks otherwise inaccessible, with about as much nicety as a common pick-axe can be supposed to attain. Nothing is more common than for the luckless traveller to set his foot upon a piece of rock, so sharp as to give him considerable pain, to relieve himself from which he steps further, and suddenly sinks to his middle in a morass ... This morning we rose at five. It was a fine calm day, and we resolved to start for Staffa as soon as possible: with this view we breakfasted, hastily, gave provisions to the boatmen (who were in readiness) to be conveyed to the boat, and were off by half past six ... The objects which now presented themselves to our view were two insulated rocks close to the south-west side of the island, of a most singular shape, and composed of basaltic columns, perhaps more regular and beautiful than any of those on Staffa itself ...

The native bread, both of the highlands and the Hebrides, is made of oats or barley. Of oatmeal they spread very thin cakes, coarse and hard, to which unaccustomed palates are not easily reconciled. The barley cakes are not disagreeable.

Not long after the morning dram, of which every islander partakes, may be expected the breakfast; a meal in which the Scotch, whether of the lowlands or mountains, must be confessed to excel us. The tea and coffee are accompanied not only with excellent butter, but with marmalades and conserves.

A dinner in the western islands differs very little from a dinner in England, except that in the place of tarts, there are generally set different preparations of milk. Their gardens afford them no great variety, but there are always some vegetables on the table. Potatoes are never wanting. I have been given to understand that knives, of which the use in the islands in now general, were not regularly laid on the table, before the prohibition of arms, and the change of dress. Seventy years ago the highlander wore his knife as a companion to his dirk or dagger, and when the company sat down to meat, the men who had knives, cut the flesh into small pieces for the women, who with their fingers conveyed it to their mouths.

The agriculture of the Hebridians is laborious, and rather feeble than unskillful. Their chief manure is seaweed, which, then they lay it to rot upon the field, gives them a better crop than those of the highlands. The soil, as in other countries has its diversities. In some parts there is only a thin layer of earth spread upon a rock, which bears nothing but short

185

brown heath, (called in Scotland heather) and perhaps is not generally capable of any better product.

Of their gardens I can judge only by their tables. I did not observe that the common greens were wanting, and suppose that besides potatoes which I have before mentioned they can raise all the hardy esculent plants.

The huts here are of many gradations; from murky dens, to commodious dwellings. A common hut is constructed with loose stones, ranged for the most part with some tendency to a circular form. It must be placed where the wind cannot act upon it with violence as it has no cement; and where the water will run easily away, because it has no floor but the naked ground. The wall, which is commonly about six feet high, declines from the perpendicular a little inward. Such rafters as can be procured are then raised for a roof, and covered with heath, which makes a strong and warm thatch, kept from flying off by ropes of twisted heath of which the ends, reaching from the centre of the thatch to the top of the wall, are held firm by the weight of a large stone. No light is admitted but by the entrance, and through a hole in the thatch, which gives vent to the smoke. The hole is not directly over the fire, lest the rain should extinguish it; and the smoke therefore naturally fills the place before it escapes. But there are huts or dwellings, of only one story, inhabited by gentlemen which have walls cemented with mortar, glass windows, and boarded floors. Of these all have chimnies, and some chimnies have grates.

An English commercial traveller: *Letters from Scotland—1817*

We crossed the Clyde to Helensburgh in an open boat, and were amused on our passage by the unwieldy gambols of the porpoises ... We did not stop at Helensburgh, but immediately commenced our pedestrian excursion, and soon arrived at Gairloch, an arm of the clyde, which, expanding into a lake, appeared to me very beautiful, but which I was told I should think tame, when I had seen more of Highland scenery ... The Scotch ladies have a good deal of the characteristic prudence of their country, which makes them reserved in mixed society, but when in the company of their intimate friends their naivety and grace is charming. We had not been long together when someone expressed a regret that we had no music for a dance. It was proposed to send for a performer on the bagpipes, which of all the instruments in the world produces the most execrable sounds, when as good luck would have it, an itinerant fiddler was heard torturing his cat-gut in the kitchen. Soon obtained his instrument, and produced such animating sounds, that we started up by a simultanious movement ...

When the ladies retired, the gentlemen paid their respects most heartily to the national drink ... But I could not be prevailed on next morning to follow their example by taking a large bumper of this potent liquor as soon as we got up. It is the custom in the Highlands, and a guest who does not take a couple of glasses when he departs before breakfast, is thought not to honour the hospitality of his host. ... On our way along a valley, which extends from Loch Long to Loch Lomond, we perceived proofs of depopulation, in several ruinous cottages, and of the poverty of the wretched huts which formed their dwelling ... The Highlanders when they emigrate to the south, are industrious, and to an extreme degree economical. There are in the Highlands fertile vallies, which, with proper cultivation would raise food enough for twice the population they have ever contained. The sea throws out in abundance marine plants, easily convertible into kelp, or which laid upon the land, forms a most fertilizing manure, and the numerous salt water lochs which indent the countey abound in fish. Yet one half of the Highland population has emigrated, and the remaining inhabitants are in a state so wretched, that they also would seek a happier land, but that they want the means of removal ...

I have already remarked to you that the poor are comparatively comfortable, where it is the custom to let them have grass for a cow, and as much land for potatoes as they can manure.

... A good natured lady wishing to undeceive him, said that cheese was made from milk. "Come" said he "that's a good one old lady; cheese made from milk. nay that won't do, I can't swallow that" "But you can swallow the Dunlop't cheese" said the Glasgow man.

Austen: *Light and shadow of Scottish life—1822*

Two cottagers, husband and wife, were sitting by their cheerful peat-fire one winter evening, in a small lonely hut in the edge of a wide moor, at some distance from any other habitation. ... The affairs of the small household were all arranged for the night. The little rough poney that had drawn the sledge, from the heart of the Black Moss, the fuel by whose blaze the cotters were now sitting cheerily, and the little Highland cow, whose milk enabled them to live, were standing amicably together, under cover of a rude shed, of which one side was formed by the peat-stack, and which was at once byre, and stable, and henroost. Within, the clock ticked cheerfully as the fire-light reached its old oak-wood case across the yellow-sanded floor—and a small round table stood between, covered with a snowwhite cloth, on which were milk and oatcakes, the morning, mid day, and evening meal of these frugal and contented cotters. The spades and the mattocks of the labourer were collected into one corner, and showed that the next day was the blessed Sabbath— while on the wooden chimney piece was seen lying an open Bible ready for family worship. ...

Miller: *My schools and schoolmasters—1830(?)*

My aunt ... urgently besought my mother ... to visit and assist her. The place was not much above thirty miles from Cromarty; but then it was in the true Highlands, which I had never before seen, save on the distant horizon; and, to a boy who had to walk all the way, even thirty miles, in an age when railways were not, and ere even mail gigs had penetrated so far, represented a journey of no inconsiderable distance. My mother, though rather a delicate-looking woman, walked remarkably well; and early on the evening of the second day, we reached my aunt's cottage, in the ancient Barony of Gruids. It was a low, long dingy, edifice of turf, four or five rooms in length, but only one in height, that lying along a gentle acclivity, somewhat resembled at a distance a huge black snail creeping up the hill. As the lower apartment was occupied by my uncle's half-dozen milk-cows, the declination of the floor, consequent on the nature of the site, proved of signal importance, from the free drainage which it secured; the second apartment, reckoning upwards, which was of considerable size, formed the sittingroom of the family, and had in the old Highland style, its fire full in the middle of the floor, without back or sides; so that like a bon fire kindled in the open air, all the inmates could sit around it in a wide circle—the women invariably ranged on the one side, and the men on the other; the apartment beyond was partitioned into small and very dark bed-rooms; while further on still, there was a closet with a little window in it, which was assigned to my mother and me; and beyond all lay what was emphatically "the Room" as it was built of stone, and had both windows and chimney, with chairs, and table, and chest of drawers, a large box-bed and a small but well-filled bookcase. And "The room" was of course, for the time my cousin the merchant's apartment—his dormitiry at night, and the hospitable refractory in which he entertained his friends by day. ...

... There was a little solitary shieling: ... a heath-bed occupied one of the corners; a few grey embers were smouldering in the middle of the floor; a pot lay beside them, ready for use, half-filled with cockles and razor-fish, the spoils of the morning ebb; and a cog of milk occupied a small shelf that projected from the gable above. Its only inmate a lively little old man, sat outside, at once tending a few cows grouped on the moor, and employed in stripping with a pocket knife long slender filaments from off a piece of moss-fir; and as he wrought and watched, he crooned a Gaelic song, not very musically perhaps, but, like the happy song of the humble-bee there was perfect content in every tone. ... He was employed in preparing these ligneous fibres for the manufacture of a primitive kind of cordage, in large use among fishermen, and which possed a strength and flexibility that could scarce have been expected from materials of such venerable age and rigidity as the roots and trunks of ancient trees, that had been locked up in the peat-mosses of the district for mayhap a thousand years. Like the ordinary cordage of the rope-maker, it consisted of three strands, and was employed for haulsters, the cork-bauks of herring-nets, and the lacing of sails. Most of the sails themselves were made, not of canvas, but of a woolen stuff, the thread of which greatly harder and stouter than that of common plaid, had been spun on the distaff and spindle.

On visiting however a boat-yard at Gairloch, I found the Highland builder engaged in laying a layer of dried moss, steeped in tar, along one of his seams, and learned that such had been the practice of boat-carpenters in that locality from time immemorial.

Griffin: *Remains—1831*

The drawingroom is always on the second story, and occupies the whole front or depth of the house. Adjoining is a small parlour, closed by a folding door, or left entirely open, and constituting a part of the drawingroom. The dining-room is always below, and the library beside it. The furniture is much plainer than ours, but far more tasteful. No flaring mirrors or gilt-pier-table are to be seen; the most striking objects are an ottoman in the middle of the room, and a chandelier above it. As few as possible of those awkward articles, called chairs are admitted; their place is supplied by sofas, and in some instances by cushioned benches placed along in the recesses of the windows. The dining-room is very plain. The dresses of the ladies are remarkably simple. I have seen the daughter of a baronet dressed in something that looked very much like calico, at a large musical party at home ... The conversation among both ladies and gentlemen is of a far more literary cast, I am sorry to say than with us. Without being downright blue or pedantic it is sensible and instructive without marching always upon stilts, it yet manages to get over the mud of scandle and the dust of frivolity without soiling a shoe ...

The Scotch ladies dress with good sense and good taste, warmly as becomes the season, and plainly and in dark colours, as becomes the place ... The weather has been just cold enough to freeze over Duddington Loch, and make it capable of bearing. Such an occasion is eagerly embraced, not only by the boys and youth, but by men of advanced years and dignified character ... By the by, it is a marked distinction between the manners of our country and this, that sports, which with us are abandoned on leaving school, or at farthest on quitting college, are here persisted in with increaseing ardour, to the very verge of old age. The active game of goff, skating, curling, have the same attraction for a man of fifty, as they had for the boy of ten ...

Yet, cheerful as is the spirit which circumstances would seem to indicate, the Christmas holidays are not kept here with any show of festivity. Except on the Episcopal chapels, there are no religious services on either Christmas or New Year's day. On both days the

187

shops are all open; ... One singular exception, however to this general rule, is presented on New Year's Eve. On this occasion, the ancient Saturnalia seems to be revived ... I would with great satisfaction remain at Edinburgh the whole winter, instead of going to London. The Scotch are the kindest, the most hospitable, and most agreeable people in the world.

Harriet Martineau: *Autobiography—1838*

... I therefore agreed to join a party of friends, to attend the meeting of the British Association ... and into Scotland, visiting both Western and Northern Highlands. It is always pleasant I find to have some object in view, even in the direction of a journey of pleasure: and this was supplied to me by Mr Knight's request that I would explore the topography of Shakespere's Scotch play now; When we were at Lord Murray's, at Strachur, his brother gave us a letter of introduction which opened to us all the known recesses of Glamis Castle. We sat down and lingered on the Witches' Heath, between Nairn and Forres, and examined Cawdor Castle. Best of all, we went to Iona, and saw Macbeth's grave in the line of those of the Scottish kings. I have seen many wonders and beauties in many lands; but no one scene remains so deeply impressed on my very heart as that sacred Iona, as we saw it, with its Cathedral standing up against a bar of yellow western sky, while the myrtle-green tumbling sea seemed to show it to be unattainable. We had reached it however; and examined its relics with speechless interest ...

While at Strachur, Lord Murray's seat in Argyleshire, we found ourselves treated with singular hospitality. Lord Murray placed the little Loch Fyne steamer at our disposal. He and Lady Murray insisted on receiving our entire party; and every facility was afforded for all of us seeing everything. Every Highland production, in the form of fish, flesh and fowl, was carefully collected: salmon and Loch herrings, grouse pies, and red-deer soup and so forth. What I best remember, however, is a conversation with Lord Murray by the Loch side ... He wished to know my opinion in a subject which was more talked of than almost any other;—our probable relations with Russia. I hardly know how the notion came to spread as it did that the Czar had a mind to annex us: but it was talked over in all drawing-rooms, and, as I now found in the cabinet ... I could only say that the idea of our ever submitting to Russia seemed too monstrous to be entertained ... Lord Murray ... offered as a speculation,—just as a ground for speculation—the fact that for centuries no quarter of a century had passed without the incorporation of some country with Russia; some country which no doubt once regarded its absorbsion by Russia as the same unimaginable thing that our own appeared to us now.

C. Ployen, translated Spense: *Reminiscences of a voyage to Shetland, Orkney, & Scotland—1839, published 1894*

What most arrested my attention at the cross was a party of non-commissioned officers who were stationed at Aberdeen for the purpose of enlisting recruits, and who were standing there dressed out in their most dazzling uniform; and among them was a Highlander in the full costume of his country, with bonnet, plaid, military jacket, kilt, spleuchan or purse of otter skin which is worn in front, dirk and sword. The kilt reaches to about the middle of the thigh, and the stockings, which are red tartan with a red garter, come to the middle of the leg, so that part of the leg beyond the kilt and the stocking is left naked.

Even my Faroese readers have doubtless heard or read, that in modern times, in England and more recently in other countries, iron railroads have been constructed on which an enguine driven by steam can run drawing after it carriages with passengers and goods. I shall therefore only briefly observe, that the road must be perfectly level, for which reason bridges are built across those natural inequalitites found everywhere, and a passage is tunnelled through higher acclivities, when this is found easier than to level them. This road is fenced on each side by a parapet to prevent persons in ignorance attempting to cross it, two rails of cast iron are fixed on the way, and the enguines as well as the vehicles that are to run on it have their wheels hollowed out like a spinning wheel in order to grasp the rails. In England, there are railways traversing the entire country from Liverpool to London, whilst that which I was about to make proof of was only 16 English miles, or between 3 and 4 Danish miles in length. The extent of the road, however was of small importance to me, as it gave me an opportunity, of which I was extremely glad, of trying this new mode of travelling.

The enguine stood in a long shed made of boards, and had 7 carriages attached to it, each fastened to the one behind it by an iron chain. The first three were open vehicles called trucks, the other four carriages. I took my seat in one of the first-class carriages, and sat, watch in hand, to note the moment of starting, eagerly awaiting this new experience. At last the guard gave the signal to start with his horn, and motion began, at first slow, but soon increasing to a speed of which I had never before had any conception. The perfect smoothness of the road and the rails on which the carriage move, makes the furious swiftness of the pace by no means unpleasant; the noise, too, caused by the rapid progress of the train, is not nearly so loud as I had anticipated. I could, without straining my voice, converse with my neighbour. I could read the most minute name on a traveling map, that I carried in my pocket; I could, if I had chosen, have written. I have also a very distinct idea of the country through which we passed; individual places so vividly impressed my memory by their beauty, that, I believe I should recognise them, were I suddenly transported thither. Only the objects in close proximity flew past the view in wild rapidity; for instance, the walls on each side of the railroad, seemed to be a confused line, but everything at the distance of from twenty to thirty yards was, as I have said, perfectly distinct. I often observed that we passed under an arch, or over a bridge, under which was a road of the usual kind, but this perception was but momentary; new objects immediately presented themselves to my sight, which again also rapidly gave place to others. We stopped four times on the way to take in passengers and fuel, and these slight interruptions included, we travelled the distance of 16 miles in scarcely quarters of an hour, an astonishing rapidity, though the larger enguines in England fly at even greater speed.

On the 21st of June I set off in the morning by the mail coach from Aberdeen to Arbroath, a small town on the east coast of Scotland. The Royal Mail is always a coach of imposing appearance with four horses, and the coachman a perfect gentleman. On the back of the coach is a comfortable seat for a man who is called the guard. He wears a fine red coat, and is provided with a long horn or trumpet, on which he blows to give notice to other vehicles to make way for the mail. The whole elegant appointment of a Scotch mail coach would have astonished me, if I had not had an opportunity in the year 1836 of rejoicing over the remarkable improvements in the facilities of travelling made recently in Denmark ... On the other hand, we have one great superiority over the Scotch in the comfort of travelling by mail coach—with us drinking money is abolished, whilst in Scotland, one is plagued by both coachman and guard. Not to give something is considered mean, and when one must give it is not a trifle that will serve. They are too civil and well dressed for that. ... In our diligeces, I never saw any contrivance by which the passengers could sit outside, or more correctly on the top of the coach, which is always the case in Scotland, and it is unquestionably more agreeable and more airy in fine weather to travel outside than inside the coach. Though the difference in fare is very light, most gentlemen prefer the outside, and it was there I had taken my place.

Precisely as the clock on the neighbouring steeple struck seven, the guard blew his horn and we left the town to visit places entirely unknown to me, and which I approached with the keenest curiosity. Once off the pavement the horses began to go in earnest, the leaders at a gallop, the larger and stronger pole horses at a very hard trot. The morning was cold and raw, a man at my side had wrapped himself up in cloaks and cravats till hardly the tip of his nose could be seen ... The first thing I observed was I was driven at a furious rate, and I am not ashamed to own I was frightened ... But here I found myself on the top of a coach swung at a gallop down heights and over hollows, so that I thought I could perceive our vehicle sometimes rested on two only of its four wheels, which may perhaps have been only the force of imagination. ...

At last, on the 1st of July, I found myself on board of a boat which plies on a canal between Edinburgh and Glasgow, being drawn by horses that run on a path constructed at the edge of the bank. The boat is 90 feet long, and 7½ broad, lightly and elegantly built and roofed with an awning of painted sail cloth. Inside there are two long benches, and when these are both filled with passengers, there is scant space for one person to move from one end to the other of the vessel. When you take your seat, there you must remain, and allow yourself to be conveyed sideways through the country. The horses are fastened by at the forepart of the boat, and generally go at a gallop, but the boat would be drawn out of its direct course, and soon head to the shore, if the steersman did not continually counteract this motion by means of the rudder, and so keep it steadily in position. Two horses, which are often changed, draw the boat, and a boy rides the hindmost one.

Carrothers: *The Highland note book—1843*

For upwards of a century Doune was distinguished for its manufacture of pistols. About thirty years ago the last of the old pistol makers died, and the trade here died with him. One of the greatest of the Scottish cattle markets is held at Doune. On one occasion, the drovers and dealers drank the innkeeper dry, and tempted him to broach some excellent clarit which the country gentlemen kept for their meetings as an agricultural club. The deficiency was not supplied when the heritors next assembled, and there was the want of wine. The cause was explained; it was a damper but the old laird of Blair Drummond cut short the matter by exclaiming "Weel, if the drovers have ta'en to our drink, we must take to theirs"; and the party got very merry on whisky punch.

The salmon fishing on the Teith and Forth were also a source of anxiety; but Earl Moray and the other proprietors were exceedingly liberal, and offered no opposition (for industrial use of the river). In order to protect the interests of fishing care was taken in the construction of the dam, to provide for the easy passage of the salmon, by forming a sloping channel at one side of the river, having a rise of about one foot in ten. It was found however, that the water gained so much velocity in flowing down this channel, and over the surface of the dam-dike generally, that, when there was any body of water in the river, few fish could stem it. It was at last found, that by placing bars or steps across the channel, at successive distances of from eight to ten feet, from bottom to top, the object was secured.

Dear are the homes and warm the hearts, hid among these wild fastnesses! You look, and at the foot of a crag, on the moorland, from which it can scarcely be distinguished, you discern a hut: its walls are of black turf; window, or chimney, it has none, save rude apertures; yet, pervious to all the blasts that blow, like hurricanes, in the trough of these mountain ranges, the hut stands, and the peasants live, and bring forth in safety. You enter, and find the grandmother, bent double with age, or the grey-haired sire, the only inmate of the house. The husband has gone to dig turf, or to perform some other out-of-doors occupation; the children are over the hill, barefoot to school; and the wife or daughter is at the shealing—a fertile valley among the mountains, where all neighbours take their cattle, in the summer to graze. Poor is the hut in which the stranger is not offered some refreshment, and is greeted, in a few words of broken English, with a cordial welcome. In cottages like these, amidst the veriest gloom and poverty, still subsist a high-souled generosity, stainless faith, and feudal politeness, spontaneous and unbought; and from these huts have sprung brave and chivalrous men, who have carried their country's renown into many a foreign land.

There is a tradition that the first hats ever worn by the Town Council of Inverness, in place of the old blue bonnets, were presented to them by President Forbes one day after dinner, at Bunchrew!

Darnaway Forest: Another picturesque point here is formed by what are termed the Esses, or salmon leaps, where the rocks in the bed of the river suddenly converge, leaving narrow passes and falls, up which the fish try to ascend. Numbers are caught by a process which we have not seen elsewhere. Men sit on the crags, each with a long pole, to which is attached a hook. The vibration of the pole tells when a fish is caught, and in a moment it is snatched out of the water, and deposited in the basket. This mode of fishing, with the peculiar sort of hook used, has been practised for centuries in the river Findhorn ...

The goat does not, in Great Britain hold that rank among quadrupeds that its many good qualities seem fairly to entitle it. ... Yet the animal is really valuable; in milking qualities it far surpasses even the best Ayrshire cow; and it will feed on herbage inaccessible and unpalatable to almost every other herbivorous animal. Cobbett—a high authority on these matters—says that the goat will make a hearty meal on paper, white and brown, written or unwritten; and the statement is correct. Retired lawyers and merchants who have betaken themselves to the delightful occupation of pastoral farming, will have a large supply of goats, keep in their old law papers, day-books and ledgers.

Christina Brooks Stewart: *The loiterer in Argyllshire—published 1848*

Exactly two hundred years ago, the Marquis of Montrose, when meditating a descent upon Argyll asked one of the M'Donalds of Glencoe whether he would find means for the support and accommodation of his rather belligerent troops, were he to make that county his winter quarters. To this interrogation the bold and blunt Highlander replied, "that though in Argyll there was not a town, nor half a town, yet would he find plenty of houses to live in, and plenty of fat cattle to feed upon" ... The cheerful harbour, filled with the wealth of the fisher man, the herring boats—the stillness which prevails, alone broken by the splash of oars, or the harsh guttural Gaelic of the rowers, and the curling smoke which appearing like a wreath of mist in the distant horizon, announces that a steamer is approaching—conspire to form a picture full of life and not devoid of beauty (*Lochgilphead*).

(Talking of the Crinan Canal) It saves, however, a stormy and lengthened route of navigation, and, since the time it was opened, has proved of infinite service. But the price of its shares has fallen very much. In the year 1805, when it was formed, the cost of each share was £50; twenty-six years thereafter it fell to £2.

But the passengers for whom we are waiting are now making their appearance. They are not nearly so numerous as those who left the steamer, nor do they present such a motley group. From the number of plaids thrown across their shoulders, the rattling of sneeshn mulls, and the friendly interchange of Gaelic salutations, one is convinced that these hardy mountaineers are indigenous to the soil. And now see the old wives carrying their baskets, eggs and fowls. How grotesque is their appearance, and that of their feathered companions, who are peering with eyes of wonderment on a scene so foreign to the barnyard! But all are safely stowed into the vessel, and again she bounds along ...

Our route lay contiguous to a number of small Highland farms; and while passing them I was highly amused to perceive the extremely novel manner in which the work of harvest was carried on. Would you believe, dear Mrs H-, that in one field, the reapers were using what kind of scythes think you?—their own fingers!* and these digital implements they employed in pulling up the stalks of grain. Had the season been a sultry one, or had the short, parched grain left the reaper no other alternative of gathering it, I would have regarded this Portuguesan scene without any feeling of astonishment; since I have been told that this method was resorted to during the parched season of 1826. But 1845, so far from being a sultry season, was totally the reverse, that on the 28th of June the summit of Cruachan was actually covered with snow. (Dalmally) ... and long may the worthy roof-trees of those happy Highland homes gladden and support their ancestral dwellings.

J. Coquhoun: *Rocks & rivers of Highland wanderings—1849*

... Had an account of a Loch Fine herring-fisher's life, from Angus, a frank athletic young man. The skipper and part owner of a boat. The fleet of skows, which are always hauled up, high and dry to refit after the season is over, were all launching at present and Angus

* Likely it was flax which is *always* pulled by hand.)

meant to set sail in ten days. When shooting their nets, they had their choice of the best herrings to eat, for when they sold them "by the dizen/the warst made up the count, and fetched the same price as the best". In the creeks and lochs where they anchored, they could always get milk from the shepherds' shealings and bothies scattered along the banks, which the milk from the little Highland cattle, grazed in the sheltered straths and glens, was "as rich as cream every drap o' 't". "Some fishermen", he said "indulged in dirt" which luxury, however, he strictly prohibited in his boat. ...

The young gulls are very fond of slugs, and two kept in my father's kitchen garden were of great use in destroying such reptiles. They require more solid food, however, but these dainties appear to come in as a dessert.

A tame white owl supersedes the necessity of a cat. My little boy had one a few years ago kept in the kitchen. Its dexterity in catching mice was the wonder of all who saw it. Once, when a mouse had been troublesome in the night, he darkened the window next morning, and brought up his owl. In a very short time there was a crash, a faint squeak, and the mouse was never heard again.

Anon: *Notes of a Highland tour—1852*

... Reached Edinburgh, and preceeded by Queensferry road to the ferry. This we reached at ten minutes to two. Were told that the steam boat would not be over until three, but that if we wished (as we had a carriage and pair), it could be signalled. We consented to this, and were all inquisitive to know what sort of signals were used in these localities, whether a cannon would be fired, or a blue light used, or a rocket sent up. Presently Davie was called, who came with an assistant, and under the superintendence of the landlord, some dirty straw was laid on top of a wall, and hot ashes thrown on it. Some smoke arose; but the steam-boat not appearing one of our party said that the landlord might as well get on the wall and smoke his pipe for a signal. In the meantime we comforted ourselves with biscuits and port wine. At last, when we began to think that our signal would end in smoke, the boat made her appearance; and having disembarked some cattle, took us on board. The smoke cost sixpence ...

Visited the gardens of the Marquis of Breadalbane ... Two undergardeners acted as our guides ... He showed us their method of cultivating the pine-apple. A pit is prepared, into which dry leaves are put, to the depth of six feet. These, being made thoroughly wet with cold water, generate heat sufficient for the growth of the pines. Glass sashes cover the pit; and the pots containing the plants are placed in the moistened leaves. When the sun shines with intense heat on the glass, a piece of gauze is thrown over the sashes. The plants looked remarkably healthy.

Korner: *Rambles round Crieff—1852*

The gallows are probably the most notorious relics of the past history of Crieff. ... A portion of it, too, was used, not so very many years ago, as a supporter for the roof of an old smithy, at the door of which Prince Charlie had his horse shod in 1745 ... We have already remarked that Drummond Castle has been the scene of stirring events. It has also, both in peace and war, received guests of distinguished name. Prince Charles Stuart supped here with the Duchess of Perth, on the Friday night preceeding the Sunday he spent at Fairnton or Ferntower, mentioned in our last ramble. A century later Queen Victoria was delighted with the castle.

Scattered along the bottom path a moist grassy bank, which in April was decked with primroses, we find in June the slender-stalked yellow pimpernel, with spreading stem and egg-shaped leaves. Its scarlet sister is "The poor man's weather glass" for the petals expand in sunshine only: in damp days they close up like the spiral-folding convolvuous. But as we wish to extract something more than mere names and appearances and mythological stories out of our ramble, let us state some properties and uses of these interesting objects. That little creeping thing at your feet, with shrubby stem and cruciferous-looking corolla, borne upon an eight-leaved calyx and named tormentil possesses healing qualities. An infusion of its leaves is an excellent remedy in cases of diarrhoea, and the root is much used in the Hebrides for tanning. It is a powerful astringent. These crowfoots too, of which we have seen so many, may be turned to practical account. The cottager's wife, when her supply of rennet is exhausted knows how to curdle milk with its juice. Their use is sometimes abused. Strolling vagabonds puncture the skin of their legs or arms, apply the poisonous liquid of the lesser spear-wort by raising blisters and try to gall the public with wicked lies about burns and scalds and frightful accidents. Bees are never seen to rest upon this poisonous class of plants; yet the unexpanded buds of marsh marigold are sometimes plucked by country people and pickled like capers. Moreover, the distilled water of the lesser spear-wort has been recommended by eminent physicians as an instant emetic in case of poisoning.

In Glencoe one is scared from looking on the immense and almost perpendicular black rocks, which rise on each side, more than 2,000 feet ... with wild and terrific summits shoot into lofty spires and cones wrapt in grey mist, which gives them all the appearance of gigantic spectres.

Our highest expectation now was Glencoe, but the Black Mount Forest—a day's journey in itself—intervened. After walking seven miles, the small Kirk of Urchay stood, like "a lodge in some vast wilderness" on our left. Five miles more brought us to Inverourain Inn, Loch Tulla, and the Marquis of Bardalbane's shooting lodge, on the confines of the dreary Moor of Rannoch. This moor, which stretches west from Loch Rannoch, is the largest extent of heath, covered with rocks and morass, in Scotland: it is not merely the picture of desolation and bareness,—it is wild sterility itself. The tourist has fifteen miles now before him, with monotony clothed in desert-loneliness on his right, while on his left, stand sharp weather worn mountain ridges, whose sides are cut in zigzag furrows by the frosts and snows and storms of winter. Then he enters, enveloped in haze and mist, the vale of weeping. It is several miles in extent, with only one residence from one end to the other. The tourist who proceeds by this route should, by all means rest a while at Kings House Inn before entering the pass. The lonely moor which he has just crossed is apt to induce a langour, which it would be well to throw off before encountering the further loneliness of the glen, with dread-inspiring frown super-added. In the centre of the glen is a small sheet of water, from which Ossian's Cona meanders through the vale, lying below the mountain of Malmor on the south, and Dun Fion or Fingal's hill, on the north ... The granite of Ballachulish is of a light grey colour, quite different from Ben Cruachan. At Ballachulish upwards of two hundred men quarry annually several millions of roofing slates. The slate-quarry here we were very desirous to see, and the boys and girls of the village were anxious to sell us specimens of beautiful calcareous spar and pyrites. A delightful landscape was now before us on the shore of Loch Leven.

Hicks: *Wanderings by loch and stream—1855*

To walk along the banks of the Ness, one would suppose that the principle occupation of the inhabitants of the town was the washing of linen. The banks are spread with under garments of every description; while the laundresses are dancing in the river, their dresses being tucked above the knee, and held securely between tier legs, while with their feet they are scouring the linen under the water. ...

Having refreshed myself with a glass of excellent milk, at a neighbouring cottage, I returned to Inverness. On my way back I passed a farm house to which a young Highlander was conveyed a corpse after the battle of Culloden. The body was wrapped in a plaid. The farmer's wife remarked that some mother was bereft of her child. The mourning became her own when, on unfolding the Tartan covering, she beheld the body of her own son, whom she supposed to be in safety at a distance.

We found most comfortable quarters at the inn at Lairg, the best in the county of Sutherland. The culinary department at this house is very well conducted, and the liberality and profusion displayed at dinner, and still more at breakfast, is far beyond expectation. At the last named meal I never beheld such an assortment of dishes or abundance of food. The charges here, as at all inns in Sutherlandshire, are extremely moderate—bed, one shilling; breakfast fifteenpence, dinner, eighteenpence. Our breakfast here comprised the following edibles: cold lamb and beef, broiled salmon and trout, the same fish pickled, besides marmalade, jams, and jellies, an abundance of eggs, cakes, oatmeal cakes, bread, toast, and most excellent cream and butter.

In the rocks over which the water here ascends (river Oikel) are several large holes termed "traps" into which ascending salmon and grilse are constantly falling, as they attempt to leap the cataract, which many accomplish, while the more unsuccessful drop into these traps, from which they cannot extricate themselves. In the course of quarter of an hour, we saw five ill-fated fish fall into these holes. Two men soon arrived on the opposite side of the river, one of whom having a large hoop-net on the end of a long pole, resembling a landing net on a large scale, walked steadily over the slippery rocks, knee-deep in the descending water, and proceeded to thrust the net into the traps, from which he took nine grilses and two good-sized salmon, returning with one individual at a time to his companion, who stood on a rock with a thick stick ready to fell each new comer.

A frequent mode of the conveyance of baggage, especially merchandize, is by a pack horse, a man walking beside him. The manner in which the rude packsaddle which, however, answers the purpose extremely well, is put upon the horse's back, and retained in its position, is both primitive and ingenious. The saddle which is formed of wood, has an arch behind, which is cleft in two, a portion of wood being removed forms a kind of hook on each side, from each of which is suspended a large sack, or bag, containing the goods; an old plaid or two placed on the beast's back, under the saddle, prevents galling. A couple of holes are bored on each side of the wooden saddle, through which ropes are passed, and tied underneath the belly of the horse, the ends are prevented from slipping through the holes of the saddle by knots. Thus the plaid forms a horse cloth, and the ropes a roller, which are well suited to the purpose, although they would appear strange at Newport ... The remaining portion of the harness is of equally rude construction. The head-stall or bridle, is formed of wicker, while the same substance being attached to the back of the saddle secures it to the ends of a stick, which is placed under the horse's tail, thus forming a cheap and curious crupper. ...

I was ushered into an apartment (a kind of kitchen without a fire place) whose furniture consisted of a bedstead, a wooden form, one chair, a small table, and a large barrel of herrings. Rafters, here and there, served the purpose of a ceiling, while the sides of the room were composed of similar materials, rather more closely compacted, but still admitting a free ventilation through the numerous clefts and crevices. The walls and roof

Cottage interior.

presented the same hue, for which they were indebted to peat-smoke. Two lambs which had taken shelter from the rain, accompanied by sundry chickens, occupied the room previous to our entrance, and remain undisturbed by our presence. The landlord whose manner and appearance were somewhat singular, stood for a few minutes in silence, and after gazing at me in apparent astonishment ventures to express his opinion that I might possibly be wet and require some food. ...

This woman, after arising from sleep, afforded a fine study for an artist wishing to introduce into a picture a true portrait of a Highland wife. Let the painter imagine a remarkably good-looking woman, with a clear and healthy complection, dark hair, good teath, sparkling eyes, cheerful smile, coupled with a figure by no means devoid of grace although decidedly stout; dressed in a dark stuff petticoat, surmounted by a short, loose jacket of white linen, leaving the arm partially bare, as suited to the offices which is required to perform such as baking bannocks, or washing the linen of the household; and he will not err in his representation—which will become still more faithful if he can portray upon the countenance that peculiar and delightful matronly innocence and contentment, which those bred in towns so seldom behold.

I found the inn (Fort William) much crowded, as the Highland meeting was to be holden here on the following day, when the town was enlivened by kilts, displaying the tartan of various clans. It was half-past twelve when I reached the inn, with a tolerable appetite, which the waiter informed me could not be appeased till the morning, as the cook had gone to bed. After declaring that unless I could have something to eat, I should go to another house, I succeeded in obtaining some excellent cold mutton and pickles, which together with a bottle of bitter ale, induced me to retire to rest, satisfied till the following day.

After breakfast, I passed a short time in witnessing the Highland games of running, putting the stone, throwing the hammer, and after which I took my departure for Ballachulish, a distance of thirteen miles. I have endeavoured throughout the recital of my tour, to give a true and just account of the inns which I visited, and cannot proceed further without remarking that while I have no reason to complain of the provisions or accommodation to be met with at the Caledonian hotel, I consider the charges very exorbitant, and a demand of four shillings for a room in which I took my breakfast and remained for two hours was a gross imposition. ... The road from Fort William is very level, skirting the south side of Loch Linnhe, an arm of the sea, on the opposite side of which rise the mountains of Argyllshire. This lake is enlivened by a number of boats employed for the purpose of fishing. At the distance of nine miles I halted for a short time at Coran ferry, watching the extraordinary rapid current as it boiled in its progress, carrying boats that were crossing a considerable distance beyond a straight course, from which cause the distance as well as the labour of the rowers is wonderfully increased.

Soon after passing this ferry the road continues for a short distance along the north side of Loch Leven, which is a branch of Loch Linnhe, pursuing a straight course between the counties of Inverness-shire and Argyllshire. The road becomes more wooded and picturesque for the last mile before reaching Ballachulish, where there is a ferry across Loch Leven, on either side of which there is an inn.

I took up my quarters tonight at the house on the north side, the larger and more frequented tourist's hotel displaying a number of lights which argued a pretty full compliment of visitors. I found this house, though of more moderate pretensions than its southern rival, extremely clean and comfortable. ...

This ferry (Ballachulish) presents something of the rapidity of stream obserable at Coran, and it was by no means a straight passage ...

Having crossed the ferry, and arrived on the south bank ... I proceeded along the side of Loch Leven for a distance of two miles, when I reached the celebrated slate quarries which, while they give employment to a number of people, are decidedly eye sores in this lovely scene. I could not help being struck with the pale and puny appearance of the numerous offspring of the quarrymen, as I passed through this long line of cottages and works, which seemed interminable. I was glad to hurry through this place ... After pursueing my course for two or three miles, I entered the magnificent "Pass of Glencoe" which has been too frequently described and extolled to need any remarks from me ... From one end to the other of this wild and savage glen, but one solitary farm house is to be seen. The sides of this pass are grand in the extreme, being composed of steep rocks and precipices, which rise to an immense height, while the Cona which issues from a small lake in the glen pours its crystal waters over a rocky bed at their base.

At a considerable height, is discerned the Cave of Ossian, which appears like a narrow window, or niche. On issuing from the pass, a wild barren tract of moorland presents itself, while an endless number of mountains arise on all sides. After pursuing this road for about three miles further, I arrived at the solitary Inn called the King's House, the situation of which, is bleak and desolate in the extreme. ...

I slept here to-night, and found the accommodation very clean and comfortable, and was supplied at tea with some of the largest and finest flavoured herrings I ever tasted.

... At a quarter of a mile from the inn, I commenced a long and steep ascent over what is called the Black Mount. At this point besides Loch Lydoch, an immense number of small lakes lie stretched over the dreary moorland in the direction of Loch Rannoch ...

A plaid to be really serviceable, should be composed wholly of wool, without any intermixture of cotton. It should not be overfine; neither should it be open and porous but rather close in texture ... Plaids are manufactures of all sizes and degrees of thickness some being so large and heavy as to form sufficient bedding for a shooter, when sleeping on the hillside. Whilst however, these offer peculiar advantages by night, they are far too cumbersome for daily wear; and are generally conveyed on the back of a shooting pony, to the moors.

It is a great mistake to run to the opposite extreme, by selecting a covering of such fine and thin texture, that while it may be very portable and convenient in bright sunshine becomes worse than useless in a drenching rain. My own plaid which is a full sized one composed entirely of Highland wool, weighs exactly four pounds; and from experience I would recommend one of the same kind as being the best for general use. I purchased this excellent piece of stuff at Inverness for thirteen shillings and six pence; this is a cheap one, of course far more expensive articles may be procured, the extra price being occasioned by fineness of texture.

I shall now mention the few instances in which this useful article is less conveniant than a great coat, or water proof garment, made with sleaves. The first instance is riding on horseback in which case a coat is decidedly more comfortable. The second is fishing during heavy rain when the arms must be either unprotected or to a certain extent deprived of free action ...

Another and most useful important advantage which the plaid has over all other wraps, is the quickness and facility with which it is dried ... I must in conclusion give a few hints as to the modes of wearing it.

When the plaid is not required to protect the wearer from storm or tempest, he may take his choice of the following modes:

First—throw it fourfold over the left shoulder, allowing it to hang nearly to the knee; pass the plaid under the right arm, across the chest, and again over the left shoulder. This is the most ordinary method of wearing the garment; it is not however the most convenient one, when a high wind is blowing behind the wearer. ...

Second—fold the plaid in the same manner over the left shoulder, allowing it to hang a little below the waist, bring the other end under the right arm, but instead of proceeding as in the last instance, bring it round the body, passing it over the short end, under the left arm across the back, over the right shoulder, and under the fold previously passed over the chest. The plaid is thus crossed upon the back, whilst the two ends are tightly secured beneath the fold across the body.

Third—... I am supposing the reader to have a scarf plaid, i.e. one open at both ends—there are what are termed poke plaids, which have one extremity sewed up, to form a pocket. These are frequently worn by shepherds and others for the convenience of carrying lambs or other articles; they cannot however be applied to the purpose I am about to name. ... Open the plaid, and put it singly across the shoulders, permitting its extremities to hang down of equal length in front. Now tie the two uppermost corners in a tight knot, which throw over the head leaving it close to the nape of the neck; bring the arms forward, and you will find yourself enveloped in a very comfortable cloak.

There is another way ... Open the plaid singly out, take one end and fold it down lengthwise to within half-a-yard or so of the other end; now put the plaid lengthwise over your shoulders, bringing the folded part well over your head, then passing a piece of string, or your pocket handkerchief over the plaid, gather it closely round the neck, tying the cord under the chin. Thus a hood is formed, which on being thrown back form a four-fold covering for the shoulders; whilst the lower part of the person is also well protected.

Ossoli: *At home and abroad—1856*

We left Edinburgh by coach for Perth, and arrived there about three in the afternoon. I have reason to be very glad that I visited this island before the reign of the stage-coach is quite over. I have been constantly on the top of the coach, even one day of drenching rain, and enjoyed it highly. Nothing can be more inspiring than this swift, steady progress over such smooth roads, and placed so high as to overlook the country freely, with the lively flourish of the horn preluding every pause. Travelling by railroad is, in my opinion, the most stupid process on earth; it is sleep without the refreshment of sleep, for the noise the train makes it impossible either to read, talk, or sleep to advantage. But here the advantages are immense; you can fly through this dull trance from one beautiful place to another, and stay at each during the time that would otherwise be spent on the road ...

We came by a row-boat up Loch Katrine, though both on that and Loch Lomond you may go in a hateful little steamer with a squeaking fiddle to play Rob Roy MacGregory O. I walked almost all the way through the pass from Loch Katrine to Loch Lomond; it was a distance of six miles; but you feel as if you could walk sixty in that pure, exhilarating air. At Inversnaid we took boat again to go down Loch Lomond to the little inn at Rowardenan, from which the ascent is made of Ben Lomond, the greatest elevation in these parts. The boatmen are fine, athletic men; one of these with us this evening a handsome young man of two or three and twenty, sang to us some Gaelic songs ...

Passing from Tarbet, we entered the grand and beautiful pass of Glencoe;—sublime with purple shadows and bright lights between, and in one place showing an exquisitely silent and lonely little lake. The wildness of the scene was heightened by the black Highland cattle here and there ...

Dendy: *The wild Hebrides—1859*

(Jura) The zoology is not highly interesting, but there is a worm that, like the chigoe of Guinea, penetrates and inflames the skin—the Fillan, or worm of Jura ... Coll is a very fair field garden ... In the pools springs rare eriocaulon. On the western side sea-kale is indigenous and most luxuriant; and in spring the islets are gemmed with blossoms ... We may chance to get buttermilk, or what is called by Martim "oon troth" curds and whey; sweet milk "lac blighe or easoc" meal butter and treacle, and a bannock we must hail as a feast for an emperor in Skye ... but there are relics of the Highland sandal—the brogue; the white plaid tied by a belt round waists of the peasant girls, is it not the arisad in the olden times worn by the proud laird's lady ...

William Keddie: *Staffa described and illustrated—c. 1860*

The shell used for a drinking cup in the days when Ossian sang and Fingal fought was the hollow valve of the scallop or clam-shell of our seas (Pecten maximus). The flat valve, in a like manner, served the heroes for a plate, before the invention of forks ... The shell becomes, therefore the symbol of the rude hospitality of the age; and it is still occasionally used in drinking strong liquors at the tables of gentlemen desirous of preserving the usage of their ancestors. "We were entertained in the Island of Coll", says Boswell, in the account of his tour with Johnson to the Hebrides "with a primitive heartiness. Whisky was carried round in a shell, according to the ancient Highland custom. Dr Johnson would not partake of it; but, being desirous of doing honour to the modes of other times, drank some water out of the shell".

The people make most of their own clothing (Iona). As soon as the wool is cut off the sheep's back, it is put into the hands of the female members of the family, who speedily pass it through the processes of carding, dyeing and spinning. It is then transferred to the loom; after which it returns to the females, to waulked or fulled ... In dyeing cloth, in addition to indigo, which is in general use, heather tops, and flowers (Erica cinerea) are employed for green and yellow; and a reddish brown is obtained from a lichen gathered on the rocks (parmelia saxatilis), and probably also P. omphalodes. The natives weave a Culdee tartan plaid, the purchase of which by visitors would give a profitable direction to the industry of the people. They have an ancient practice, also, of forming a milk jug, of antique appearance, out of clay found in the island; and no doubt, were these specimens of Ionian pottery of a primitive description offered for sale, they would find ready purchasers.

There is no corn-mill in the island; and the grain is conveyed eight miles by water, to Bunessan, in Mull, to be ground. When the mill there is out of gear, or the stream fails, which is no uncommon occurrence, the islanders resort to the use of the quern, or ancient hand mill ...

Alexander Smith: *Rambling about the Hebrides—Temple Bar, 1862*

The Highlander is a distinct class amongst the British people. For generations his land was shut against civilisation by mountain and forest and intricate pass ... He was, and is, a proud, loving and punctilios being, full of loyalty, careful of social degree; with a bared head for his chief, a jealous eye for his equal, and an armed heel for his inferior. His sense of family relationship was strong, and around every individual the widening rings of cousinship extended to the very verges of the clan. He is song-loving, "of imagination all compact", and out of the natural phenomena of his mountain region,—his mist and rain-cloud, wan sea—setting of the moon, keen stars glancing through rifts of murky vapour,—he has drawn his superstition of death—lights on the sea, and the boding shroud drawn high on the living heart. To a great extent his climate has made him what he is. He is a child of the mist. His songs are melancholy for the most part; and the monotomy of the moor, the sob of the wave on the rock, the sigh of the wind in the long grass of the deserted churchyard may be discovered in his music. The musical instrument in which he chiefly delights renders most successfully the battle-march and the coronach.

Marshal MacDonald had Hebridian blood in his veins; and my friend M'Ian remembers meeting him at Armadale Castle, and tells me that he looked like a Jesuit in his long coat.

Some thirty miles north of Corrichatschin, on the shores of Loch Snizort,—waters shadowed by King Haco's galleys, as they passed to defeat at Largs—we stumble on the ruins of the old house of Kingsburgh. The site is marked by a mere protuberance on the grassy turf, and in the space where fires burned, and little feet pattered, the men and women eat and drank, and the cheerful bowl smoked, great trees are growing. To this place did Flora MacDonald come, and the Prince dressed in woman's clothes; there they rested for the night, and departed next morning. And the sheets in which the wanderer slept were carefully put aside, and, years after, they became a shroud for the lady of the house. And the old shoes the Prince wore were kept by Kingsburgh till his dying day, and after that a "zealous Jacobite gentleman" paid twenty guineas for the treasure. That love for young Ascanius!—the carnage of Culloden, and the noble blood reddening many scaffolds, could not wash it out.

Across Ross-Shire (by the author of three weeks in Skye)—Chambers Journal, 1864

The magnificant area of Strath Bran furnishes a rich pasture ground for sheep, an animal that has of late years proved a source of wealth to the Highlands, every fleece being literally "golden" being frequently sold as raw material in the market at as high a rate per pound as tea. ... For some years back sheep have been more esteemed than men in the Highlands, a fact which was ludicrously hit off at the last election in Inverness, when an independant elector asked Mr Baillie, if in the event of his being returned, he would be willing to "give the sheep a vote", a joke intensely exquisite to the ears of the wool-producing community. If the tourist pass along the Highland Straths during the months of June and July, he may observe the wool-clipping going on in various districts. Just before the clipping time, the distress evinced by the "simple sheep", under its heavy coating of wool, is often ludicrous in the extreme while here and there a few unfortunate members of the fold may be seen running about with their fleeces dangling over their backs, the result of mishaps they have sustained in scrambling through the fences. The old fleece is never shorn till the new one has raised it sufficiently above the skin to enable the shears to sever the two fleeces without injury to the animal. On inquiry, I found that the ancient custom of milking the ewes, in order to make cheese from the milk has almost entirely died out. In the old Scottish song called the "Ewe Brights" the lover sings

"I've nine milk ewes, my Marian
A cow, and a brawny quey".

and in the beautiful and pathetic ballad, the "Flowers of the Forest" we have the well known line,

"I've heard the lilting at the ewe-milking".

both passages clearly showing that cheese was considered as valuable a product as wool in the days when ballads were written.

Close to Achnasheen is a little clachan of the true Highland type, whose every door and window are filled with faces, human, bovine, and swine, at the sound of approaching wheels, all eager to see the "Englishman" as all Southerners are called in Rossshire.

... On entering the throat of Loch Carron we met a second, and much larger, band of Skye fishermen, numbering between fifty and sixty, all on their way to Inverness or the Lowlands; for besides letting themselves out as fishermen, they go as far south as the Lothians, to find employment at harvest-work. Truely these poor Celts are, in respect of their self-denying, self-sacrificing, habits of life, worthy of admiration. How many of the "gentlemen of England" who live at home at ease, "would like to leave the comforts of their own homes, and endearing companionship of their families, and go into cold comfortless lodgings among strangers, for four or five months in the year, that the mouths of their children might be filled, and the backs of their aged grandmothers be duely clad.

Three weeks in Skye—St James Magazine, 1866

At Broadford the mail waits for nearly an hour, during which we enjoyed a hearty tea at the inn, one of those half-dinner teas which the Scotch call "tousee", to which you have cold salmon, mutton or lamb, and which are so pleasant after an appetizing drive of three or four hours' length in the pure Highland air. By the way, the lamb and mutton which one gets in Skye are both edible and digestible, recommendation which cannot as a rule be given to the same article in Inverness, where they are far too fat to be agreeable at least to delicate stomaches ...

Deerstalking is, perhaps the most highly fashionable amusement of the present day, but one which only the very wealthy can afford. In one forest, the rental of which is £1,200 a year, the lease is limited to sixty head in the season, which makes each deer cost £20; and when one adds the cost of the lodge, gillies, and attendant expenses the entire value of each animal must be close on £40. They must be shot too in a sportsmanlike fashion and not in battue ...

Both being interested in education we paid a short visit to the parish school, which looks like an ordinary dwelling house, and is entered without porch or lobby from the pavement of the chief street. Within were a score of boys, taught by a massive-browed intelligent, elderly man, who is, we were informed, an able schoolmaster. Some of his pupils have at sundry times carried off high prizes at the university of Edinburgh. Some schools as this have from time immemorial proved feeders to the Scottish pulpit and bar, and it is to be hoped that the present Commission on Education will found on a broader basis still, a national system that will continue to the children of the poor man the privilege which in Scotland they have so long enjoyed of obtaining at the parish school the groundwork of a liberal education. ... Most of the scholers are absent from April till October, herding cows or hoeing potatoes.

On the north side of Uig Bay is a long row of crofters' houses of the poorer class, a tenant paying perhaps a rental of only three or four pounds a year, and raising with the spade and cas-crom a small crop of potatoes and oats, which, with what fish he can catch in the bay, form the chief support of his family during the winter. In summer a good proportion of the able-bodied male members of the different families emigrate to the lowlands, and there hire themselves out to large farmers for a few months, or take part in the herring fishery along the east coast from Dunnet Head to Aberdeen. On our way through Ross-shire we had met large band of those Skye men bound for the fisheries, from which they return at the end of the season with a harvest of from twelve to twenty pounds a head. ...

Most Englishmen would be puzzled by the following account sent to a gentleman of my acquaintance by a village saddler "March 8th 1863, To repairing horse's trousers 2/6." The part of the harness repaired was the "breechin" ...

Black cattle there were also in abundance, some of them magnificent animals, one of the bulls especially being as fat Bashan, and a true type of the ancient urus. ...

About halfway between Kilmuir and Uig stands the large farmhouse of Monkstadt, also memorable in the wanderings of Prince Charles. Here he succeeded in effecting a landing, after being driven from Waternish by hostile bullets, and tossed about in a storm in the Minch, and from hence he went along to Kingsburgh, where he rested his weary limbs under warm shelter for a day or two. When we had reached Uig we found the bay dotted with dozens of smacks that had arrived from Harris during the night, freighted with cattle for Portree market. The little inn was crowded as before, and such a scene. Twenty genuine Celts smelling of herring and heather and jabbering in Gaelic. All as proud as pipers, many of the real old Highland blood—cousins, nephews and grandsons of chiefs. ...

Our hostess had been expecting us for a day or two, and had lots of delicacies prepared for us,—venison soup, salmon, burn trout, cod, and other fish of various kinds; roast mutton, venison, rhubarb tarts and magnificent curds and cream, all the produce of Waternish.

The houses are built usually of ordinary-sized boulders wedged closely together without mortar or cement of any kind; the walls being what is called in Scotland "dry stane dykes". Their thickness and compactness serve effectually to keep out the cold, though a layer of earth is often placed in the middle to secure greater warmth. The roofing is generally straw-thatch, which being laid on pretty thickly keeps the interior as warm as a beehive. This thatching is secured to the rafters by ropes of heather, to the ends of which stones are sometimes tied, causing the roof to look like "a lady's hair in curl papers". The better class of huts had rude chimneys, often an old barrel or wooden box; but in general the smoke is left to its own resources to secure an exit, which it must do by a hole in the roof or by the door or window. But the later aperture is in many cases a luxury, and often consists of a mere skylight or single pane through the roof. The first or outer apartment is in general reserved for the horse, cow, or stirk, which salutes strangers, if well dressed with a loud "boo" indicative of welcome or intrusion. The next or inner apartment is the kitchen and sittingroom of the family ... The light is generally subdued and dim, from the scarcity of window and abundance of smoke. Truely there is no need for a smoke-inspector in Skye for the good folks invariably consume their own smoke. In the centre of the floor is the fireplace, which is slightly raised from the level of the ground beside it, and sends its cloud of smoke and flame into the midst of the apartment. Peat reek is not so disagreeable as the smoke from coal however. Indeed many folks rather like the smell of it. I should prefer a homoepathic dose of it, notwithstanding, in preference to the copious and constant use of it so prevalent by the cottars. At this fire all the cooking of the household is done, a pot or kettle being usually seen suspended over it by a chain from the ceiling. The furniture is of the plainest kind. A small dresser, sparely filled with the plainest delf, stands along the wall; in one corner may be seen a deal table and in another a spinning wheel. A rude bench for sitting on lines one or two sides of the apartment. Fishing lines, nets, and baskets, hanging from the ceiling, complete the household gear. There is often a third apartment or inner sleeping room leading off the common kitchen and sittingroom. In many cases this third apartment however, cannot lay claim to being so called; for there is no partition save a coarse curtain or boarding between them. Indeed the partition between the quadripeds and humans being in general only half the height of the ceiling, so that the breath of the cow or pony mingles freely with the breath of the other inmates. In every cot one usually meets with at least three generations, a fact which clearly shows that the people increase in a greater proportion than the house-accommodation. Close to the fire sits the grandfather or grandmother, as the case may be, while the married daughter or son's wife bustles about the apartment in the course of her domestic duties. From behind some inner boarding or curtain, again peeps the little granddaughter afraid of the presence of strangers and Englishmen. In general the people are affectionate and kind-hearted, and seem quite happy and content with their lot. They have not the florid look of health, however, so common among lowland cottars; but on the contrary they are in general pale and careworn.

In our visits, we came upon two ancient agricultural impliments. One was the quern or hand-millstone, at which two women sit and grind as in the days of our Saviour. "Two women shall be grinding together; the one shall be taken, and the other left." The other was the "cas crom", a very old Celtic impliment, intermediate between a spade and the plough. The word means literally the "crooked leg or foot". It is used for layering over, in a rough way the rigs set apart for oats and potatoes. We saw in some houses, too, the old spinning wheel, at which the women sit in the long winter evenings spinning wool and flax and "working diligently with their hands". Songs are sung, stories told of bygone days are told for the hundredth time, news related and the evening beguiled cheerily around the fire of peats, which is the chief and in some places the only fuel consumed. The cost of the peats is not great, the cottars being allowed to cut them free, and in a few others for the rendering of ten or fifteen days service to the laird in the course of the year. In Skye the cottars generally cut the peat-moss perpendicularly into cakes of the same size and shape of ordinary bricks. These bricks of moss when sufficiently hardened and dried, are piled up into little stacks on the ground where they were cut, and are usually left there throughout the year. When required for use they are carried home by women or boys. Those who have no pony generally carry the peats home in creelfuls on their backs, and those who have, bring them in panniers strung to the pony flanks. It is a picturesque sight to see two or three bare-legged bare-headed Highland boys cantering over the green hills on the backs of Shelties going out to the peat-grounds. In one of these peat-bogs, we came upon an elderly man loading his cart and entered into conversation.

In my intercourse with the people the only thing that positively pained me was their excessive bigotry. The Free Church, like the Jews of old has no dealings with the Samaritans of the Establishment. "Thank God" said an old grey-haired Highlander, "I have never entered an Established church since the Disruption," whether the pastors or the people are to blame for this sad state of matters, I cannot say, for both seem equally responsible for it. A Free Church clergyman dares not move hand or foot towards a free exercise of Christian liberty, being obliged to regulate this conscience by the opinion of his flock. This humiliation is painfully apparent in the most trivial concerns of the mansehousehold. When he wishes to indulge in a little ale, wine or porter "for his stomach sake" he must have the cask sent to the manse, labelled "parafin oil" or "molasses". If such a cask should come with the true brand on it, there would be an end to his peace for ever. There was no end to the congregational uproar when, by an unlucky mistake, porter was handed round instead of wine in the communion cups in a certain Free Church in Skye.

Sir R. Roberts: *Glenmahra or the Western Highlands—1870*

The breakfast bell cut short the discussion, and summond us to lay in provender for the day. A really jolly Scotch breakfast, with steaming bowls of porridge (a mistake, by the bye—they ought to be cooled; the uninitiated are apt to burn their throats, whilst the more wary are reduced to make rivers and lakes of milks with their spoons upon it until it is cool, which is somewhat a waste of time), placed on the sideboard at the head of the table. Literally immensed in tea cups sits Mrs Jones, gravely discussing with my young friend Smith . . . the propriety of slicing beetroot into the sandwiches, to keep them fresh, Smith advocated watercresses. Let me recommend both these to my readers; it keeps the sandwiches fresh, and they taste less like blotting paper . . . Our good friend and host is busy in the mysteries of "kedgeree", i.e. fish, eggs, and rice, with pepper, salt, and butter, mixed together and warmed up—a capital thing for breakfast. Then there are fried flounders, codling, ham and eggs, kidneys, and a perfect pyramid of scones, curious little rolls, and wheaten-meal cakes; the spaces on the table being filled up by jams, marmalade, and honey.

For the information of those of my readers to whom the terms "cuddy" and "lythe" may not be familiar, let me say that the former is the young of the coal fish, who when they are about 6 inches or 8 inches long are called on the western coast "cuddies"; when they attain about the size of a good herring are called "saythe", and when full grown, "stane lochs" of coal fish whilst the latter represent what is called in the south pollack, or whiting pollack. The cuddy is an excellent little fish, but the bigger he grows the more coarse does he become in the flesh, until he arrives at the stane loch size, when he is almost next to useless for food. The fishermen of Lochfyne, however, where large numbers of these stane loch are taken, split then open, salt and dry them, when after having undergone this process they are perhaps more palatable. The lythe, on the contrary, is a most delicious fish; it attains great size, is caught in considerable quantities, and affords great sport to the fishermen. At this season of the year (October) cuddies are to be found in considerable quantities in any of the rocky bays, where they come in to feed on the herring fry. Lythe, however are to be found in deeper waters, and in the neighbourhood of sunken rocks. . . . The skiff is launched . . . the rods are light bamboos, about 16 feet in length, to the top of which your line is made fast, which consists of 8 feet or 9 feet of light twist or silk. To this is attached a collar of strong salmon gut. We used two flies on each rod, and varied them according to our fancy. The flies we used and seemed to be most successful with were Nol, a white wing made from the fibres taken from the pinion feather of a Solan goose, no body the wings being put on to the shank of the hook with two or three half hitches. . . .

The skiff, a boat about 15 feet keel, and 6 feet beam, with stem and stern alike, lay moored at the quay with the scringe-net in the stern-sheets. A scringe-net is nothing more than a sein with a long bag, the cork line being about 50 to 60 fathoms in length, the mode of using it is by sending two hands on shore with the tail rope, the boat then pulls oars, and the net is shot in a large curve, whilst the other end or trail rope is put on shore also; one hand then remains in the boat, he runs along the cork-line with his hands, until he gets to the centre of the net, where he hangs on, directing the movements of those on shore, in order that both ropes may be evenly hauled upon; he is also useful in holding up the cork-line, for in many instances when the body of the net is full of fish they come to the surface, and many a good one springs over it and escapes . . . On certain nights the water is so disturbed by the movement in it of the shoals of herring, mackeral, or coalfish, that it is lighted up by brilliant phospherescence lights, this is what they call the water burning . . . The boat scarcely touched the beach when my friends sprang out, seizing the rope, and hauling together with a will. I seized the cork-line, and run the boat round to the centre of the net, shouting to either side to ease or haul as the case required; meantime the bag of the net seemed like one mass of molten silver below the bows of the boat, the darkness of the night making this more apparent.

Seizing the lead-line in one hand and the cork in another, the two ends of the net were brought together on the beach, and the heavy bag drawn on the shore.

. . . I was fortunate enough to obtain four large conger eels and some fresh herring, enough to bait five hundred hooks. With this I returned on board, and after supper the crew turned to bait the lines. A long line, or as it is called in England a "trot" and in Ireland a "spiller", is of very simple construction, and is generally used in deep water for cod, ling, halibut, turbot, skate. and conger—smaller lines on the same principle being used for flounders, whiting, and codlings. The lines we had were dressed with large hooks for cod and ling, each tray or basket containing about 200 hooks, with a fathom distance between each hook—the length of the foot-line being 250 fathoms and the buoy-lines 40 fathoms each. . . . The best bait for the large lines are buckies or whilks, fresh herring and conger. When fishing with small lines, muscles and lugworm, with bits of crab, are excellent, especially the small soft crab found in the fissures of the rocks. These are an almost irresistible attraction to flounders and whiting . . . The best time to shoot long lines is at about half-tide, and to let them fish for two hours . . . We put 500 hooks into the gig and pulled out to a bank . . . the line is very easily shot, but care must be taken in paying it out to prevent the hooks fouling one another. The man who shoots stands at the stern sheets, whilst the men rest on their oars paddle gentle. The buoy-line with the stone attached is first hove overboard to leeward, and the men rest on their oars until the stone touches bottom . . . the foot line paid out over the leeward side . . . the other buoy line is attached, and the stone sunk to the bottom. The buoys are generally made of inflated dog or sheep skins and the advantage of having two buoys is that in case one gives way there is always the other to mark the end of the line.

Several instances of tame seals have also occurred in the Highlands, where they have been caught when young, and have lived in the cabins, going every now and then to the sea. Extraordinary to say, also, they seem particularly partial to lying as close to the fire as possible and when they have been removed invariably wriggling themselves back to the heat.

Ferguson: *A tour through the Highlands of Perthshire—1870*

Balloch. When there a few weeks previously, I observed a large hole which, having decayed in one of the trunks, had been neatly stuffed—like a decayed tooth—with bricks and Roman cement, and now seemingly as strong and vigorous as ever . . .

On the "big" Cumrae, in a crescent shaped bay looking out on the Atlantic, is the favourite saut water toon of Millport, where a late parish minister used to offer up a prayer regularly every Sabbath morning from his pulpit for the safety and prosperity of the "big" and "wee" Cumbraes, and the adjacent islands of Great Britain and Ireland. . . .

Janet was at the front of her cottage feeding her hens, half-a-dozen in number; and really very braw hens they were; four of them all speckled sky-blue colour, with smart, tidy "kames" descendants of the real Scotch hen. The other two were jet-black, with very red, flabby overhanging combs, and evidently closely related to the Spanish breed. The lot seemed in excellent fettle, and apparently either old maids or widows, as I saw no sign of a cock or mate.

Behind the planting, on a level lawn near the base of a gentle slope, stands the Fank or sheep-pen, and close to it the place where the sheep are annually washed, which I examined with considerable interest, as I had never seen one of them before, the practice of washing sheep being comparatively modern. In my young days nothing of the kind was attempted, with the exception of smearing them with tar, mixed wih a certain proportion of butter, at the end of the season, as a protection against the cold winter blasts and snow to which they are so much exposed in the Highland districts. I believe there are several kinds of wash used. Many farmers use tobacco juice; others some patented chemical stuffs, sold in a solid state in small casks, and when being used diluted with a large quantity of water. The washing process is quite a simple affair. Near the pen gate is an oblong wooden trough, somewhat the shape and form of a common bath, but larger, plumb at the end next the pen gate, with a gentle slope at the opposite end. Up this slope there is a neat wooden stair. The sheep are first put into the Fank or pen, and then caught by the horns, by a number of hardy, "swanky shepherd chaps" and taken out one by one, and popped into the trough, and after being well soused, are allowed to bolt up the small stair, and enter a circular wooden enclosure, floored with stout planks, which are grooved and made watertight, and formed with an incline towards the centre. From this point a small groove runs direct to the bath. After getting their "dook", the sheep are kept in the circular wooden pen to "shake theirsels" and dreep the dreepings, which run direct to the trough, to do their duty over again ...

There are few things have ever amused me more than a sheep-shearing, the fun of which continues the whole day. The whole flock are put into a pen or fold; the lambs sent out to the hills, and after them the ewes, one by one as they are shorn. The moment a lamb hears its mither's voice it rushes from the bleating crowd to meet her. But, instead of finding the rough, well-clad, and comfortable-looking mamma which it left an hour or so ago, it meets a poor, naked shrivelling, most deplorable-looking creature. It suddenly wheels, and, uttering a loud, tremulous bleat of perfect despair, flies from the frightful vision. "Mamma" cries after it saying "come to your ain mammy, my wee pet"! It returns, flies again, saying "Mae mae! nae, nae! you canna be my braw, sonsie mamma, you skinny, ugly-looking wretch!" returns again and again. Perhaps a dozen times before reconcilement is fairly made up.

The lambing season in the Highlands of Perthshire is generally about the middle or end of April; about the second week of August the lambs are separated from thier dams, and on Halloween drop their baby name, and are called "hoggs". About that time a large number of them are sent off to some sheltered and grassy district in the Lowlands, and are brought back home again about the end of March or beginning of April. On their return their name is changed again; the ewe-hoggs are now called "gimmers", the male hoggs "year-old-wethers" ...

J and I were examining with keen interest a prodigious-sized "sneeshin mull", placed on the table, gorgeously mounted in glittering silver, and all the necessary "impliments". The big spoon to lift the "sneeshin" to the nose—the hammer to chap the mull—the spade to delve the snuff—the rake—the brush (a hare's shank)—all attached to the big mull by pretty silver chains. ...

The game usually commenced with a competition of pipers; athletic competitions followed, such as throwing the hammer, putting the stone, tossing the caber, leaping, dancing, and racing, both on foot and in boats. After the games were concluded the members marched in order, with perhaps twenty or more pipers at their head, to the Hall of the Society in the village where the members dined together.

John Pacy: *The reminiscenses of a Gauger Imperium. Taxation past and present compared—1873*

It will not be out of place, I consider, if I enumerate the articles subject to taxation at that period, 1827. They were Beer, Calico, Glass, Leather, Hops, Malt, Paper, Soap, Starch, Sugar, Vinegar. The odious tax on Salt was repealed just before that date. Some of these taxes were so enormously high that dishonest persons were tempted to evade them by some ingenious device or other, and as a necessity, very severe and stringent laws were enacted to prevent imposition on the revenue. A Gauger at that period, when the Excise bristled with so many taxes, might be looked upon as an Ishmelite whose hand was against every man, and every man's hand against him.

Unlocking chandlers' utensils and visiting malt houses occupied my Instructor's time to breakfast hour. That meal hastily dispatched, he would proceed to visit innkeepers, to ascertain who of them was brewing. He would again visit the candle makers, which he had to do every four hours while they might be at work; and attend at the tanners it might be to weigh and stamp leather; which occupied his time till dinner. After that until tea time, he was employed measuring and weighing the stocks of spirits, tea, and tobacco, at the dealers and retailers of such articles. From tea time to bed time was taken up with what was termed "in-door work". In addition, he would make his last visit to the chandlers, to weigh off candles and to lock up utensils, which would at times be as late as midnight. Jaded and tired, he would retire to rest only to rise in the morning to pursue the same round of duties.

The Sabbath was not a day of rest to the Gauger as with most other people. It was no unusual thing to see him pass along the streets, when others were on their way to church or chapel, dressed in his everyday clothes. A capacious coat with large pockets he would be sure to wear. A gauging stick in one hand, in the other keys, gave him the appearance of the turnkey of a prison ...

My duty there was simply to give attendance at soap boilers when they were at work, to see that the soap was not clandestinely removed to evade tax. It was not by any means an exhilarating duty, watching for twelve hours together—often more—soap coopers with their boiling, bubbling, frothy stuff, as it advanced to the perfection of soap proper.

Excise restrictions were in full force as applied to soap makers, the same as to candle makers. Their coppers were kept strictly under lock and key, except when an assistant was in attendance. It was his duty to unlock or lock them as they were wanted. The soap when it was gauged and charged with duty by the proper Gauger in charge, or by the supervisor the assistant merely looked on.

The following anecdote, which was told me about Burns, when he was Gauger. The poet received information from some quarter that an old woman who kept a toll-house in a remote quiet place was selling whiskey without the necessary authority. He made a purposed visit to her, stepped into the house, and in an off-hand way asked for bread and cheese and a gill of whiskey, which were instantly served to him. Having finished his repast he asked what there was to pay, "Six pence for the bread and cheese" the woman cautiously replied. "What for the whiskey?" Burns cautiously asked. "Nothing at all for the whiskey" replied the old woman. It is said that the poet was amused at her cunning and admitted he had been fairly outwitted by her.

Campbletown whiskey was somewhat celebrated, and was in great request both in the home and in foreign markets. Distilled on still of small size and made from peat-dried malt, there was a flavour about it peculiar to itself, and which was much relished by consumers of that kind of spirit.

The peat-dried malt from which whiskey was produced was made from grain designated in Scotland "Bere or Bigg", a small kind of barley grown on the light sandy soil of that country. The tax on that description of malt was something like one-fifth less than on malt made from barley, a kind of boom or protection to the grower of this lighter kind of grain ...

If there was one thing more disagreeable than another to a Gauger it was charging duty on candles. The early morning visit to unlock utensils, and the late evening visit to weigh the candles that had been made during the day, and to lock up the utensils again, were very harassing duties.

Note: Whisky is spelt Irish fashion in the book and this spelling is retained.

Moffat: *A summer ramble in Scotland—1874*

At Ballachulish, on Loch Leven, we landed, and went up to Glencoe, interesting for its own savage grandure; for its river, said to be the Cona of Ossian; and for the terrible massacre of its population, a sept of the clan MacDonald, about one hundred and eighty years ago. The last has been touched by many a poet, but none more feelingly than one bearing the name Campbell, on which rests the charge of the crime:

> "They lay down to rest with their thoughts on the morrow,
> Nor dreamt that life's visions were melting like the snow,
> But daylight had dawned in the silence of sorrow,
> And ne'er shall awaken the sons of Glencoe".

From the point where Loch Leven sets off to the east, Loch Linnhe gives way to Loch Eil, which follows the same northeastward direction, and between the same mountainous embankments. Upon reaching its extremity, one looks forward over a low, dreary, flat, moorland of a least ten miles in length, increasing a little in elevation as its recedes from the sea, and extending by an opening among the hills indefinately. On its eastern side the mountains rise suddenly to a great altitude. For there is Ben Nevis, whose foot is on the flat, and his summit in the heavens more than forty-four hundred feet immediately above.

A. A. Becket & L. Sambourne: *Our holiday in the Scottish Highlands—1876*

Glencoe. The next morning we started for Glencoe. Our party consisted of tourists. An old lady was seated on the box with an immense guide book, from which she gave occasional extracts. The coach was a cousin to the conveyance in which we had ridden over to Gairloch. It was slightly better about the springs, but the seats were more uncomfortable. The horses were high-spirited, and dashed along at a grand rate. My friend and myself were seated on the outside of a bench, and had to hold on as we turned corners. We raced down hill at a gallop, and performed other feats of skill and daring.

'Glencoe" said the old lady on the box, "Means the glen of weeping".

Then she was silent, and once more studies the work she was reading. As we passed through many an interesting village the old lady kept her eyes glued to her book. She was so anxious to obtain information that she neglected to look at the places we were passing.

"The lower part of the glen consists of mica slate," she observed after a pause of five minutes, and then she disappeared once again into the recess of her guide book. When we had left Ballachulish about a quarter of an hour, she exclaimed—

"The mournful story of the Massacre of Glencoe has been related by Sir Walter Scott in the 'Tales of a Grandfather ...' "

We now found ourselves in a slate country. Everything was made of slate; cottages, churches, and tomb-stones. The divisions between the little kitchen gardens, the boundaries of fields, the substitute for the hedges, were all furnished by the same material. Huge slabs of slate met our gaze. ...

"The massacre commenced at four in the morning on the 13th of February 1692" read the old lady on the box. Yes, we were in the Pass of Glencoe. ... We were now at our journey's end. ... We stood on a desolate road, rudely hewn out of the rock. On either side of us were hills reachings to the clouds, steep and sterile ... And yet in the midst of all this desolation civilisation was represented. As we got down from the coach we found an old woman waiting to sell us whisky!

The horses were soon baited, and then we returned home. The old lady on the box once more opened her guide book, but now she seemed to be testing the veracity of its statements rather than to be imparting its information to the ears of her fellow passengers.

"This book informs me", said she, with a glance round, directed to all of us collectively and individually, "this book informs me that eagles hover over Glencoe. Can you tell me, please, when they can be seen?"

There was a silence. We none of us liked to be the first to answer. At last a mild young man, who had made several remarks of a jocular character ... "The eagles ma'am invariably come down to the pass at four o'clock daily—to be fed!"

The old lady produced a pencil and gravely added this fact to the other statements contained in her guide book.

The Outer Hebrides all the year round—1883

The Tarbert of Harris is so narrow that less than five minutes' walk from our anchorage brought us to the shore on the other side of the isle. Much we marvelled at the primitive methods of cultivating the tiny fields—mere patches sprinkled over the face of morass and peat-moss wherever the soil seems to promise any response to the toil bestowed upon it.

We found that the little inn owned a dog-cart—a wonderful old trap, mended at all points, but still capable of carrying us without undue danger; so we hired, and started on a long drive to the interior of the island. Our way lay through most beautiful scenery glorified by floods of sunshine which gleamed on the yellow sands of Laskantyre, transforming them to fields of gold. Scarcely a ripple disturbed the broad surface of the calm ocean, which broke lazily on the shore in tiny wavelets, while the moorland revealed tints of golden-brown, and green, and purple, such as no one could deem possible who only saw such scenes on the dull, monotonous grey days so common to our northern skies.

We passed by the dark waters of the Bonavets Loch, and halted in Glen Mevig to secure a rapid sketch of the grand hill which rises to precipitously from the head of the valley, then on to Fincastle, a modern castle built on a site apparently selected as being the rockiest and noisiest that could be found in all the district. ...

Ere we started to retrace our way to Tarbert the scene had utterly changed. Leaden-hued clouds rested on the summits of the dark hills, and soon rolled down their sides, shutting out the last gleam of sunlight ... A scene of more animated interest invited us southward, to North Uist, where a great cattle-market was to be held on the low flat shores of Loch Maddy—a strange sea-loch, to which the entrance is by a narrow opening, guarded as it were, by great masses of basalt, which jut up from the sea and are remarkable as being the only basalt within many hours sail. These are called the Maddies, or watch-dogs ...

It was no easy matter to find a piece of sufficiently connected land to form a suitable site for the great cattle-market, and even that selected was a strangely blended bit of land and sea. I doubt if any other spot could show so picturesque a cattle fair.

In the first place, all the cattle had to be brought from neighbouring isles to this common centre, and, as each boat arrived, with its rich brown sails and living cargo of wild rough Highland cattle of all possible colours, the unloading was summarily accomplished by just throwing them overboard and leaving them to swim ashore.

These Island beasties take kindly to the salt water, and seemed to rejoice in finding cool-bathing places on every side. All day long there were groups of them standing in the water or on the shore—such attractive combinations of rich warm colours, silvery-greys and reds, browns and blacks, rich sienna and pale sand-colour, all reflected in the pale aquamarine water. In the whole market there was not a beast that was individually a study for the artist, with its wide-spreading horns, and rough shaggy coat, and its large, soft, heavily-fringed eyes that seemed to look so wonderingly on the unwonted assemblage around them.

Besides the fishers'—brown-sailed boats, several tiny white-wings yachts had brought customers to the market and added to the general stir—a stir which must have so amazed the quiet seals and lone sea-birds, which are wont to claim these waters as their own.

An incredible number of islanders had assembled. It seemed a fair matter for wonder where they could all have come from, but a tidier, more respectable lot of people, I have never seen. These people of North Uist—now alas! like their neighbours, so sorely oppressed by downright famine—generally rank among the most prosperous of the Outer Islesmen, their patient industry being proverbial.

Most of the four thousand inhabitants of North Uist live on the further side of the isle, and had come across in the rudest of little carts, drawn by shaggy ponies, whose harness was the most primitive combination of bits of old rope, connected by twists of the strong wiry grass of the sand-hills ("bent" we call it on the east coast). Now the carts were tilted up, and watched over by wise collie-dogs, while the ponies were turned loose to graze on the heather. Indeed, the number of these was a noteworthy feature of the scene, for these rough little creatures find their own living on the moor, whence their owners must cut, and the ponies must carry, the peats which are the sole fuel of the isles.

Most fortunately for us all, the weather was glorious; indeed, the blazing sun, reflected by the still waters, made us long for shelter, but not a rock or a bush was there to break the monotony of the flat shore. The only morsels of shade lay beneath the few white booths set up by itinerant merchants, that lads and lasses might buy their fairings, and that the drovers might get their dram—the latter being a very important item in the day's pleasure, for the Blue Ribbon Army has not yet weaned the islesmen from their love of mountain-dew, and of the only two manufactories established in the isles, one a good woollen factory at Portree, and the other is a distillery at Tallisker, in the Isle of Skye, which turns out forty-five thousand gallons of whisky per annum, of which about twenty thouand are consumed on the Isle of Skye itself.

Naturally, there was a liberal consumption of "the barley bree" at the market, but, the consumers being all hardened vessels, no one appeared any the worse, nor even any livelier—liveliness, indeed, is by no means a characteristic of these gentle, quiet folk, most of whom seem to be naturally of a somewhat melancholy temperament.

The only sensible folk who had made provision against sun or rain were some wise old women, possessed of large bright blue umbrellas, beneath the shadow of which they sat on the parched grass. They were comfortably dressed in dark-blue homespun, with scarlet plaids and white mutches, and near the grazed several sand-coloured ponies, forming a pretty bit of colour. Behind them in groups of bright healthy-looking lads and lasses were assembled round the white booths, and all along the yellow shore faint wreaths of white smoke from the kelp-fires seemed to blend the blue of the sea and sky; for the blessed boom of sunshine is too precious to be wasted even in a holiday to Loch Maddy Fair, and the kelp burners dare not risk the loss of one sunny day. Here, in North Uist, the industry of kelp-burning is still continued—that toiling harvest, whose returns are now so small, and always so uncertain, that the men of Skye have altogether abandoned it. This difference is, however, partly due to the fact that the seaweed of Skye contain a much smaller proportion of the precious salts which give it value than does the weed on some other isles. For instance, in the Orkney group, the kelp is used in the manufacture of plate-glass, whereas that made in the Hebrides is only fit for soap.

They say "It's an ill wind that blows no man good", and, without referring to the precious driftwood and other treasures cast up by the sea after wild storms the kelp-burners know that such tumults of ocean will assuredly bring them riches from the submarine forests, so they anxiously follow the tide-line to collect from among the masses of sea-ware every branch of the small brown tangle covered with little bladders, which yields the richest store of carbonate of soda, iodine and other precious salts for which they toil. They pass carelessly by the broad fronds of brown wrack which strew the shore so thickly—those may help to manure the soil, but their search is chiefly for the one plant.

At low tides they go out to the furthest rocks to cut all they can find growing on the rocks, such fresh weed being far more valuable than that which is cast up by the sea. This they collect in the creel which they carry on their shoulders; or accumulate in larger creels slung on either side of sturdy little ponies; and again and again they toil to and fro across the west sands and slipper rocks, bearing their burden of heavy, wet weed to some safe spot above high-water mark, where they spread it over the sand or grass, and leave it for several days to dry.

This is the most anxious stage in the kelp harvest, for one heavy shower of rain will wash away all the salts which give it value and leave only worthless seed. So the moment it is dried, the weed is collected in little heaps, like haycocks, and so remains till the moment when the furnace is ready to burn it.

The furnace or kiln is a large deep grave, lined with large stones. Over these is laid a thin covering of dry weed, and this is first patiently ignited, for it does not burn very readily, but needs careful kindling. Then a handful at a time is added till the grave is filled and heaped up, and the kelp becomes a semi-fluid mass, which is stirred incessantly with a long iron bar, a labour which must be continued for hours.

Very picturesque is such a group of workers, surrounded by their piles of dried brown weed, and half veiled by the volumes of white, opal smoke, with its pungent marine scent.

When all the tangle has been burnt, the kiln is allowed partially to cool, and the kelp is then cut into solid blocks of a dark blueish-grey material. These very soon become as hard and as heavy as iron, and are then ready for market. From this material much carbonate of soda and various salts are obtained. But its most valued product is iodine, which is only to be obtained from the ash of dried seaweed, and is precious alike to the physician and the photographer. In former times the manufacture was highly remunerative, but the removal of the duty on Spanish barilla greatly decreased its value, which has further diminished by the large amount of potass which is now imported. Moreover, it is now found that crude carbonate of soda of better quality and cheaper, can be obtained from sea-salt. The iodine, however is a comparitively recent discovery, and one which must give a renewed impetus to the kelp trade.

Kelp-making does not appear to have been one of the industries of the Isles till about the middle of the last century, when it became a distinctive feature, and so lucrative that some small farms paid their whole rent from the product of the rocks.

The price of kelp has been subject to serious fluctuations, at one time falling as low as two pounds per ton, at another rising to twenty pounds. ... Now the price of kelp in the Hebrides averages about four pounds per ton, and when you consider that twenty-four tons of certain seaweeds must be collected, dried, and burnt, in order to produce one ton of kelp, you will readily perceive that the kelp-burners do not eat the bread of idleness ... One ton of kelp should yield an average of about eight pounds of iodine, and certain quantities of chloride of sodium, chloride of potassium, carbonate of soda etc. When subject to certain treatment and to distillation, it can also be made to yield two or three hundredweight of suphate of ammonia, and several gallons of naphtha, of paraffin oil and of volatile oil. ... These lochs have sedgy shores and are covered with white and yellow water-lilies, dear to the radiant dragon-flies, which skim among the blossoms. The islanders however, prize the lilies chiefly for the sake of their roots, which are used in dyeing wool. They also extract a rich brown dye from certain lichens which grow on the rocks, and a warm red dye from the common bramble, while heather yields a yellow dye. Another much prized red dye is obtained from a kind of rue which grows on the sandy shores, but such is the danger of uprooting any kindly weed which helps to bind those light sands, that it is illegal to gather it ... These nuchars are partially overgrown by wiry bent-grass which is most carefully preserved by the islanders, because it binds the sand with its network of long clinging roots, and eventually forms the ground work for a thin crust of soil, on which grasses fit for pasturage may be cultivated. ...

But the distinctive feature of St Kilda is its bird-life ... For the birds represent their harvest and their work—a work enlivened by all the excitement of personal peril. The rock-fowler who would lay in a good store of eggs must be able to find a footing where no goat would venture, creeping along scarcely perceptible ledges on the face of the giddy cliff, where one false step would assuredly prove his last. ... The richest harvest awaits him on the ledges of crags wholly inaccessible save to him who dares venture to let himself down, slung by a strong rope held by his companions on some upper cliffs.

The most trusty sort of rope is a threefold twist, made of strong raw cowhide. This is again covered with sheepskin to protect it from the sharp cutting rocks. Such a rope as this is a precious heirloom—a bride can bring her husband no more valued dower, nor can a man bequeath to his friend, a more excellent legacy, for with fair usage it should last at least two generations.

The fowler thus slung in mid air carries a light pole, terminating in a cup-shaped bag, with which he scoops up the eggs from such recesses as he cannot reach by hand; and then carefully lays his treasure in the big creel which he carried for the purpose.

Notes of a wanderer in Skye—Temple Bar, 1883

I spoke just now of the scarcety of timber which is so marked a characteristic of the Isles. Indeed there are only a few scattered nooks, such as Armadale, Dunvegan and Greshernish where trees make any head at all.

Throughout the Isles it is a rare and precious article, most frequently the gift of ocean. The man who secures a good log of driftwood has obtained a prize worth having. It may have been a brave old tree, tempest torn from its home in some distant forest, carried to the sea by rushing torrents, and perchance tossed by the waves, and wafted to and fro by many a current, ere it drifted to its rest on these far Isles. Or it may be the mast or spars or perchance the cargo of some wrecked vessel—whatever its story, it is treasure-trove, and most deeply valued. Though encrusted with barnacles or riddled by philades, it can all be turned to good account; the smallest piece will make a stool or a settle, or a box, or part of a door; while large timbers become rafters—precious heirlooms, for a young couple cannot wed till they have accummulated enough rafters to support their thatch, and should they have occasion to "flit" the only part of their bothy that commands any pecuniary compensation is the roof, not the wood-work only, but also the heavy thatch saturated with thick greasy peat-reek (in other words with a thick coating of soot). This, when broken up, forms a valuable manure for the unfertile crofts.

Poor indeed are many of these island homes, generally consisting only of two rooms; an outer byre for the cattle, and an inner room for the family; and until recent years all such bothies had a fireplace in the middle of the floor, round which the whole family might gather, and equally share its comfort. But now most houses have the fireplace at one end of the house, and though the smoke generally contrives to wander at will among the rafters, (forming a blue haze stinging to the unaccustomed eyes, and at last resolving itself into the rich browns so dear to the artistic mind) it does sometimes find a wide open chimney prepared for its escape. But more frequently a hole in the thatch is the only means of egress, a hole perhaps crowned with an old herring-barrel in lieu of chimney can; this however, is an elegant superfluity to which few aspire. All, however must take the precaution of tying on their roofs with a network of ropes, and weigh them with large stones, in order to resist the wild gusts of wind, which would carry off any ordinary cottage roof.

I had wandered up this quiet nameless dell, gathering fragrant white and purple orchid and trails of rich honeysuckle which grows so freely among these grey rocks, when I was aware of the scent of burnt oatcakes, mingled with peat-smoke, very pleasant from old association. Presently I espied a light curl of blue smoke, which guided me to a lonely sheeling built as a lean-to against a great boulder of rock. A wealth of kindly honeysuckle had clambered over the heather thatch, and in the bright summer sunlight, with a clear blue sky overhead, it was indeed a study for a painter!

A kindly old wife welcomed me, and bade me enter. She "had no English", (as the phrase is) but human courtesies are unmistakeable, and not even the "savage gutterals" of the Gaelic tongue could fail to convey the meaning, seconded by a cordial grip from a kindly old hand that doubtless had done many a turn of hard work in its day. Within, all was dark and dingy, walls and rafters alike coated with the rich brown peat-reek of many years. The window, not a foot square, was darkened by the honeysuckle so the sole ray of light streamed down the open chimney, revealing the blue smoke, and falling on the white mutch and scarlet tartan shawl of a second kindly-looking old crone who sat spinning in the ingle-neuk, while occasionally turning the large triangular pieces of oat-cake, the fragrance of which had first attracted my notice. It was simple fare, but no Highlander will deem himself ill off so long as there is meal in the kist, and "a wee pickle of taties" (potatoes) safely stored for winter use. But when oats and potatoes fail utterly—as they have done in the present year—when the fish abandon the coast—and when even the peat-stack, which alone represents fuel, is all destroyed by prolonged rains and wild, tempestuous winds, then in truth is felt the pinch of existence which allows no margin, and which at one step sinks from simple sufficiency which secures content, to the cruel pangs of want and starvation, such as now, alas, weigh so heavily in all the Isles and on large districts of the mainland. But the season in which I visited the Isles was one of plenty, so contentment reigned in all those humble homes, and though neither cheerfulness nor alacrity are insular characteristics, the crofters were all busily employed on their tiny patches of land.

Poor indeed is the return for all the labour expended. At the best, the farmer only looks for treble his outlay, and if he sows four bolls of oats, he looks only for a return of twelve bolls; but many a time even this modest hope is disappointed, and he has to wait with sorely-tried patience, while his poor crop lies rotting in the drenching rains that too often continue throughout the season that should be harvest-time.

But if a fair average of sun ripens his grain he carries it to some breezy knoll, and there threshes it with a little flail, and the wind separates the corn from the chaff. Then the grain required for the day's consumption is dried over the fire in an iron pot, and thence transferred to the quern, the primitive old hand mill, such as was used by our ancestors, in common with the people of the far east.

I do not mean to say that these old querns are still in very general use; more modern mills have gradually come into favour, but the humble hand-mills are still used by the very poor. They consist of two hard gritty, flat grindstones laid horizontally one above the other. The grain is poured between them, through a hole in the centre of the upper stone, which is made to revolve rapidly by means of a wooden handle, and the coarsely ground meal passes between the stones, and accumulates on a cloth spread below.

It is said that to the use of such mills in England we owe the well-known saying concerning an idler that "he will never set the Thames on fire"—the old English mill being known as a Thammis, the wood of which sometimes ignited in the hand of a swift worker from friction against the stone.

Some of the old laws, more especially laws ecclesiastical certainly did descend to interfere with the liberty of the subject in wonderously trivial matters. As, for instance when the General Assembly of the Church of Scotland regulated how women should sit in church and prohibited them from covering their heads with the customary fold of the plaid, lest they should take advantage of such a shelter to sleep unobserved ...

It seems that till long after the Reformation there were no pews in church except those set apart for the big magistrates and landowners. Humbler men brought their own benches to kirk with them, and the women ventured to share these hard seats. But the Kirk session of 1597 forbade such familiarity. It was enacted that women must not sit on the forms which men should occupy "All women must sit together in the kirk and sit laigh"—that is to say lowly on the ground ...

It was forcibly recalled to my memory by seeing some of these bonnie Skye lassies, who ignoring the ecclesiastical regulations, ventured to appear in the kirk at Uig with their plaids so folded as to form a hood, a simple and becoming head-gear-oh! how immeasurably superior to the smart bonnets and gaudy imitation flowers which disfigure most of their neighbours.

Very picturesque is a great Sacramental gathering in some lovely valley, selected as being a central position, not to difficult of access to allow of the assembling of a large concorse of the people. Such "preachings" become great openair camp-meetings, and often continue for a week, but where the people contrive to find shelter at night, or in stormy weather, I cannot imagine.

I had been present at such a meeting, where about three thousand persons had assembled on one of the wildest parts of the Ross shire coast. Glancing over the bleak, barren wilderness of brown hills, it seemed as though they could never have yielded so large a congregation. But so it was. Every shepherd's hut, every lowly bothy, or village, or isle within forty miles had sent its inmates—some on foot, others by boat. Not the strong and healthy only, but even poor semi-paralysed sufferers—who had toiled and crawled for many weary days—sometimes even crawling on hands and knees—that they might be present on the great day of the Feast! Not, however, necessarily in the character of communicants, for I noticed on that day, that of the three thousand assembled on the hillside, only eighty (the youngest of whom was a shepherd upwards of forty years of age) drew near to the long table, covered with fair white linen, round which were gathered this handful, passing the sacred cup and bread from hand to hand. All the others, who had assembled from so far to be present, were deterred from a nearer approach by the awful warnings known as "Fencing the Tables" whereby the sick and sad-hearted are too often turned away sorrowing while those only who answer to a human standard of goodness may approach the table of the Great Physician.

It is rare indeed that our grey Isles produce a scene so striking as that great company, seated on the grass, or clustering up the side of the hill, amid russet brackens and grey rocks—the old wives with large white handkerchiefs tied over their clean white frilled caps, many of them overshadowed by large blue cotton umbrellas, to shade them from the really oppressive heat of an unclouded sun. But the men all sat there bareheaded, gazing earnestly at the preacher, as though drinking in and critically weighing every word he uttered. All were dressed alike, in suits of strong dark-blue homespun, and all had broad blue bonnets. (The kilt never seems to have found favour in the Isles where the shepherds, as well as their seafaring kinsmen, have adhered to one uniform garb). On the rocky hill above this human congregation stood groups of rich-coloured rough Highland cattle with wide-spread horns, and large wondering eyes, wonderingly watching the movements of the invaders. At our feet lay the great calm ocean, in which lay mirrored not only the near cliffs but even the grand Skye hills which seemed to float above the hot misty haze. And mingling with the voice of the speaker came the distant cries of sea birds, with now and again the near crow of grouse or blackcock.

W. Maxwell: *Highlands and islands—1884*

To all aboard Loch Fyne was strange. The chart apprized us we had a shoal to pass ... from this perplexity, the civility of a Highland gentleman relieved us. As he passed us in his little schooner, we hailed, to ask some information. The word "strangers" had magical effect. He pressed us to accept mutton, fish, and whisky—seemed disappointed that we were too largely supplied to allow us to avail ourselves of his kindness—and putting one of his own crew on board as pilot, he sent us on our way rejoicing.

From the dinner-table there was an early adjournment to the ball-room; and, as I went late, the festive scene appeared in all its glory. Most of the Highlanders wore their native dress; and many of the fairer sex also, sported their respective tartans. To the latter the plaid was particularly becoming; and I should say, that this arose chiefly from the great simplicity with which it was put on. Not so the costume of the gentlemen; they, with few exceptions, were dressed in bad taste, and overloaded with glittering ornaments.

In the course of the afternoon, our host came off in his boat to bid us welcome. His mansion seemed a fair specimen of a Highland household; and, in many points, it brought our own old roof-tree to my recollection ... and there was comfort without pretense—and kindness, without display. In the morning I shot the muirs with the laird; and in the evening, listened to Scotch ballads sweetly sung, or danced reels with the young ladies.

The most convenient resting place for a tourist to Loch Lomond is the inn at Balloch, placed where the Leven debouches from the lake; and thither, accordingly, I proceeded in a vehicle, which in Scotland, God knows why, is called a "noddy".

It was a young Highland girl, with a small basket on her arm, and attended by a shepherd's dog. She was uncommonly handsome; but the natural grace and symmetry of a figure to which art lent no aid, struck me more forcibly than her beauty. Her dress was merely a boddice and petticoat of home-made cloth. Her feet were bare—but a prettier ankle was never clad in silken hose. She told me she was carrying dinners to her brothers, who were employed in staking peats upon the moor.

I remember, when a boy, killing, as I then believed, a sporting quantity of coal-fish, under the rocky promontory of Old Head. Our mode of fishing was a sort of trolling by leaded-lines and snoods, the latter baited with small fresh water eels prepared like minnows, and towed after a sailing boat, when progressing a couple of knots per hour. I have in manhood, had much amusement in the western lochs of Scotland and the inlets, from the Clyde, taking, in tolerable numbers, the seath with an artificial fly of the rudest construction? The whole requiring nothing but feathers of a sea gull or white duck, to form a temptation too strong for this most simple fish to overcome. But till I visited the Orcades, I remained in blissful ignorance of the exuberant supplies which Heaven has sent, and man avails himself of ...

As the evening advances, innumerable boats are launched, crowding the surface of the bays, and filled with hardy natives of all ages. The fisherman is seated in his light skiff, with an angling rod or line in his hand, and a supply of boiled limpets near him, intended for bait. A few of these are carefully stored in his mouth for immediate use. The baited line is thrown into the water, and a fish is almost instantaneously brought up. The finny captive is then secured, and while one hand is devoted to wielding the rod, another is used for carrying the hook to the mouth, where a fresh bait is ready for it, in the application of which the fingers are assisted by the lips.

The views presented, as we steamed along, were beautiful and varied. The wooded heights of Appin; the romantic opening of Lochs Creran and Leven, on the right; the distant mountains—all, in turn, were seen to great advantage. Among the frowning hill stretching from the Leven to Ballachulish, runs a wild glen of singular interest and beauty. Many rivulets fall into it from the hills, and one stream intersects it—the Cona, so often mentioned in Ossian's song—on whose banks, as tradition asserts, the bard himself was born. Another and more lamentable event has given this romantic glen a sad celebrity—

the ruthless murder of the MacDonalds in 1691 (1692) forming probably the most blood-stained page in British history.

(Inverness) In "The fifteen" (1715) the first coach was introduced by the then Lord Seaforth; and the driver was considered a personage of such superior importance that every bonnet was doffed at his approach. In "forty", the town council were obliged to advertise for a resident saddler; and in "The forty-five" the Prince and the Duke of Cumberland in turn occupied the same apartments in Church Street—the house being the only one in Inverness which could boast a sittingroom, without a bed in it.

From the official returns for the year 1840–41, it appears that above five hundred and fifty thousand barrels of herrings were cured in Britain, out of which enormous total, five hundred thousand were taken and salted upon the Scottish shores. ... In capturing and curing, twelve thousand five hundred boats and decked vessels were engaged manned by fifty-four seamen, and giving lucrative occupation to two thousand three hundred coopers, twenty seven thousand five hundred curers—four-fifths of the number women—six thousand common labourers, and nearly two thousand merchants.

A. Elliot: *Hood in Scotland—1885*

Whenever the weather permitted which was generally when there were no new books to the fore, I haunted the banks and braes, or paid flying visits to the burns, with a rod intended to punish the rising generation amongst fishes called trout. But I whipped in vain. Trouts there were in plenty; but, like obstinate double teeth with a bad operator, they would neither be pulled out nor come out of themselves. Still the sport, if it might be so called, had its own attractions as—the catching excepted—the whole of the Waltonish enjoyments were at my command—the contemplative quiet, the sweet, wholesome country air, and the picturesque scenery, not to forget relishing the homely repast at the shieling or the mill ...

1821 ... My youngest sister is going on a visit to her aunt, Mrs Keay, and will forward this to you, in order that you may provide me with a plaid against my winter campaign. There are such things to be got here, but I apprehend not so good; and I shall be sure to fancy it more for coming bona fide from Scotland as it is such a national article. And, moreover, you will oblige me by choosing me one, and ordering it to be made as follows. To tell you the truth, I have fallen in love with our friend Wyllie's and should like one of the same family—a twin—that is to say, a Stuart; and if that should be troublesome to get, I will put up with a Kyd, or a—(I have forgot this name; but I will ask Wyllie, and write it outside). But I should prefer the Royal Stuart, on account of the romantic and practical associations connected with it. The collar, red shag (or green, if there be green; if not red), the body without sleeves, like Andrew's but not lined; and a large loose cape lined with green—(I must write this outside too); and that is all, except have the goodness to pay for it, for which purpose I enclose £2, which Andrew tells me was about the price of his; but, at all events, we shall settle that. And now about the size. I am about five feet nine inches high, and as thick as a rushlight, and I hope that will be measure sufficient. I think Wyllie calls his a rachan, or some such name, which I cannot pronounce on paper; but I hope you will know what I want, and how large it ought to be ...

I have made a sketch for you that will give you an idea of the prospect from here of the mouth of the Tay. It is a noble river. We are living in the fat of the land. Tom has milk porridge, baps, cookies, jelly and I have good small ale and whisky—and both are much better—greatly so in looks. On Sunday I went to hear her minister—one of those who have seceded. He preaches in the Schoolroom; but at the same time through a window into a large tent adjoining—a temporary accommodation whilst the new church is building in opposition to the old one ...

In Edinburgh, we saw Holyrood the Castle the Anatomical Museum, the Advocates Library and altogether my visit to Scotland has been very gratifying to my feelings, as well as beneficial to my health. Tom made several friends in Edinburgh, and amongst the rest some ladies, who sent him (Tom) short cake—which, of course he wished had been a long one—of their own making.

My wife desires me to send her love and thanks you for your kindness to her boy who, by his own account, was very happy and comfortable, and is loud in his praise of cookies jelly and porridge, not forgetting the beautiful milk and butter. We rather turn up our noses at our breakfasts for even the haddies are far better north.

> "In walking one morning I came to the green,
> Where the manner of washing in Scotland is seen;
> And I thought that it perhaps would amuse, should I write
> A description of what seemed a singular sight.
> Here great bare-legged women were striding around
> And washing clothes that were laid on the ground
> While, on the T'other hand, you the lasses might spy
> In tubs, with their petticoats up to the thigh,
> And, instead of their hands, washing thus with their feet
> Which they often will do in the midst of the street. ...
> There's so very few ways any leisure to spend
> For they ne'er play at cards Commerce. Ombre or Loo
> Though they often are carding of wool. it is true.

And instead of "pianys" Italian sonatas
At their spinning wheels sitting, they whistle like carters. ...
Superstition as yet, though it's dying away
On the minds of the vulgar holds a powerful sway,
And on doors or on masts you may frequently view,
As defence against witchcraft, some horses old shoe
And the mariner's wife sees her child with alarm
Combe her hair in glass, and predicts some alarm
Tales of goblins and ghosts that alarmed such a one,
By tradition are handed from father to son ...
Some markets for cattle, or fairs, are held here,
On a moor near the town, about thrice in a year.
So I went to the last, found it full to my thinking
Of whisky and porter, of smoking and drinking.

Elliot: While residing at Errol he had the opportunity of witnessing a Scotch fair of the old school. Errol market and races, generation after generation were looked forward to by the inhabitants within a radius of twenty miles as an annual event, in which holiday-making, marketing, horse-couping, and horse-racing were all mixed together ... Hood was immensely tickled with this rural gathering ...

Campbell: *Popular tales from the West Highlands, taken from his introduction—1890*

On the stormy coasts of the Hebrides, amongst seaweed and shells, fishermen and kelp-burners often find certain hard, light, floating objects, somewhat like flat chestnuts, of various colours—grey, black, and brown, which they call sea-nuts, strand-nuts, and fairy-eggs. Where they are most common, they are used as snuff-boxes, but they are also worn and preserved as amulets, with a firm or sceptical belief in their mysterious virtues. Old Martin who wrote of the Western Isles in 1703, calls them "olluka beans", and tells how they were then found, and worn, and used as medicine; how they preserved men from the evil eye, and cured sick cattle by a process as incomprehensible as mesmerism. Practical Highlandmen of the present day call the nuts trash, and brand those who wear them like their ancestors a hundred and fifty years ago, as ignorant and superstitious; but learned botanists, too wise to overlook trifles, set themselves to study even fairy-eggs; and believing them to be West Indian seeds stranded in Europe, they planted them and some of them (from the Azores) grew. Philosophers, having discovered what they were, used them to demonstrate the existence of the Gulf Stream, and it is even said that they formed a part of one link in the chain of reasoning which led Columbus to the New World.

An account given by Mr Hector Maclean ... Islay.

In the island of Barra, the recitation of tales during the long winter nights is still very common. The people gather in crowds to the houses of those whom they consider good reciters to listen to their stories ... Henry Urquhart.

"In my native place Pool-Ewe Ross shire when I was a boy, it was the custom for the young to assemble together on the long winters nights to hear the old people recite the tales of the sgeulachd, or which they had learned from their fathers before them. In these days tailors and shoemakers went from house to house making our clothes and shoes. When one of them came to the village we were greatly delighted, whilst getting new kilts at the same time. I knew an old tailor who used to tell a new tale every night during his stay in the village; and another, an old shoemaker, who, with his large stock stories about ghosts and fairies, used to frighten us so much that we scarcely dared pass the neighbouring churchyard on our way home. It was also the custom when an aoidh, or stranger celebrated for his store of tales, came on a visit to the village, for us, young and old, to make a rush to the house where he passed the night, and choose our seats, some on beds some on forms, and others on three legged stools etc and listen in silence to the new tales; ... The goodman of the house usually opened with the tale ... and then the stranger carried on after that ...

Such a log I lately saw in South Uist. No tool mark was on it; it had lost its own foliage but was covered with a brown and white marine foliage of sea weed and dead barnacles, and it was drilled in all directions by these curious sea-shells which are supposed by the people to be embro geese. It was sound though battered, and a worthy Celtic smith was about to add it to the roof of a cottage which he was making of boulders and turf ... Another such tree I saw in Benbecula with bark still on its roots. ... An old dame in a tall white mutch with a broad black silk band, a red cloak, and clean white apron ... Every horse I met on the road stopped on his own accord. Everyman asked me "whence I was walking" where I lived and why I came? Saddles were often sacks, stirrups a loop of twisted bent, bridles the same, and bits occasionally of wood. Dresses were coarse, but good; but there was an air of kindly politeness over all, that is not to be found in homespun dresses in any other country that I know ... His name is MacPhee; he lives at the north end of South Uist, where the road ends at a sound, which has to be forded at the ebb to get to Benbecula. The house is built of a double wall of loose boulders, with a layer of peat three feet thick between the walls. The ends are round, and the roof rests on the inner wall, leaving room for a crop of yellow gowans. A man might walk round the roof on the top of the wall. There is but one room with two low doors, one on each side of the house. The fire is on the floor; the chimney is a hole above it; and the rafters are hung with pendants and festoons of shining black peet reek. They are of birch from the mainland, American drift wood or broken wreck. They support a covering of turf and straw, and stones and heather ropes, which keep out the rain well enough.

The house stands on a green bank, with grey rocks protruding through the turf; and the whole neighbourhood is pervaded by cockle shells, which indicate the food of the people and their fishing pursuits. In a neighboring kiln there were many cartloads about to be turned, to make lime which is so durable in old castles ...

"In those days, when the people killed their Marte cow they kept the hide, and tanned it for leather to themselves. In those days every house was furnished with a wheel and a reel; the women span, and got their webs woven by a neighbouring weaver; also the women were dyers for themselves, so that the working class had their leather, their linen and their cloth of their own manufaturing; and when they required the help of a shoemaker, or tailor, they would send for them. The tailors and shoemakers went from house to house to work wherever they were required ...

While the above does not really come into travel yet it does give an authentic picture of the life of the West Highlands.

Alex Monfries: *Memoirs of James Drummond Carmichael, Arthurstone (ed.) printed 1884*

The inn we were now in possession of consists of a thatched hut, with a "but and ben" that is, two rooms, one on either side of the door. The "ben" is a room of twelve feet square, in which are two box-beds, seven deal chairs, two deal tables, a chest of drawers, and a cupboard; all these articles in so small a room leave but small space for moving about in. The walls are adorned by gorgeous pictures from the Illustrated London News, Punch and in case the ventilation is not sufficient, a large hole is left at each corner of the room! The porter looked and tasted as if it had been made of "dilutes shoe-blacking", and while we were laughing over it, the daughter of our hostess entered to inquire "Wud ye like eggs on your flesh?" which remarkable query was thrice repeated before we would answer. ... Soon after this our "eating" was served. It consisted of burnt ham, scones, salt butter, and oat cakes, with the addition of a glass of grog which we were obliged to take to wash down the dry viands.

On turning the corner of a bluff, a busy and animated scene of industry burst in view from amidst general desolation. For four or five miles a level plain stretches along to the head of the loch, backed in the distance by the hills of Drumochter. In the foreground were congregated two large flocks of sheep—those shorn, and those about to be operated upon. About twenty men, women, and boys were busy shearing, collecting and gathering the sheep, tying up the fleeces. Not being quite sure of the nearest road, and glad to see a human being, we approached the shearers. Immediately on our arrival a good-looking Highlander approached us with a bottle and a glass, and said something in Gaelic, which was Greek to us. On seeing we did not comprehend the ghillie's meaning, the farmer himself came forward, and told us he was offering us something to drink. We bowed, and each received a glass of genuine "mountain dew" which we quaffed to the donor's health. The farmer, who was a fine if not the finest-looking man we ever saw, a perfect beau ideal of a Gael (clad in kilt and shooting coat) fully six feet high, and with a great quantity of dark-grey hair, then spoke to us of our route—said it was not often they saw strangers; and, after some more talk we parted, bowing. Truly the old Highland hospitality lingers among these hills.

We all took the four o'clock steamer from Bannavie to Ballachulish. She is a fine boat, and paddled rapidly down Loch Eil. There were crowds of passengers on board, who had come down the Caledonian Canal ... The loch narrows as we approach Corran Ferry which is, in fact the southern end of Loch Eil. After this the shores recede and the sea widens out into the Linnhe Loch. ...

We did not sail far down Loch Linnhe, but turned aside into Loch Leven, another of its branches. Loch Leven is a fine arm of the sea, which stretches inland for about twelve miles, and divides Inverness from Argyleshire. We sailed up for about a mile, and then stopped at Ballachulish pier, opposite the New Hotel. Here we disembarked and bade farewell ... Though the distance from the pier to the hotel was only a quarter of a mile, there was a large brake ready to convey passengers. Arrived at the hotel we found it to be a palace; magnificent dining-rooms and bedrooms, worthy of the "Grand Hotel du Louvre in Paris".

After tea, we went out to explore Ballachulish and its prolific slate-quarries. The road along the shore of the loch is very picturesque, winding in and out by bays and headlands. There were numerous sloops and barges waiting to complete their cargoes, and then to convey the useful material wherever houses require good roofs. This is certainly a slaty neighbourhood, for, besides its legitimate use, we saw whole villages built from it, also tombstones and toy figures. Lead is also very abundant here. We walked rapidly through Ballachulish in the direction of the "Corry-head" the entrance to Glencoe. Loch Leven presents at every mile a fresh landscape—in fact, it equals any maritime or inland loch in the variety and beauty of its scenery. Behind Ballachulish towers the sharp cone of one of the hills at the entrance to Glencoe. This glen is doubly celebrated, both for the wild and savage character of its scenery, and for the inhuman massacre of its inhabitants—the unfortunate MacDonalds—by order of William III in 1692. We arrived at the Corry-head

Looking towards Fort William and Ben Nevis.

just as twilight had commenced, and each of the wild rocky hills was covered with a shroud of mist. Oh it was grand and majestic. Glencoe stretches for ten miles in a southerly direction and is without a single habitation. Most of the hills on its sides consist of bare rock inaccessible to human feet, and which form the eyries of the wild eagle and the bittern. On the south side Buichaille Etive is the principle summit, and separated Glencoe from the valley of Loch Etive . . . Next morning we rose by six o'clock and bidding adieu to Ballachulish and Loch Leven embarked on board the "Mountaineer" steamer for Oban . . . The mouth of Loch Creran is protected seawards by the large Island of Lismore, which is ten miles in length, and forms part of the parish of Appin. This island is also famous for its horses. Before we sighted Loch Creran the steamer had stopped at Appin, a little town possessed of a pier and some shipping.

W. Scott Dalgleish: *The cruise of the "Dunnotter Castle"—1890*

The Trishnish Islands are covered with rich grass, which makes excellent pasture. The Laird of Calgary fattens his muttons there during the summer months, and sends out a yacht once a fortnight to capture two or three for use. As the animals are as wild and as swift as deer, capturing them is no easy task. They are generally driven by a contracting line of men and boys into a trap made with spars and a sail between two rocks on the shore; but they often break through the cordons, and even leap sometimes over the heads of the drivers.

John Sinclair: *Scenes and stories of the North of Scotland—1891*

Let me first sketch the outward features of a single dwelling. The walls of a cottage belonging to the crofter or fisherman are usually about six feet high or a little more. They have an outer and inner face built of rough stones of all sizes and shapes, and the space between filled with earth or rubbish. On top of this wall, which is often four feet thick and more, there are built up layers of turf which forms a broad ledge all round the base of the roof, like the rim of a strong boot along the edge of the upper. This flat wall-top, covered with grass and weeds, is a promenade and feeding ground for the sheep and poultry, and often a look-out for the women who expect husbands or brothers home from sea. The roof proper starts from the inner edge of the wall head. The rafters are often few and thin, because all wood for such purposes must be imported from the mainland and is therefore high in price. After the framework is up, layers of turf are laid upon the beams, and over these again a thick coating of grey thatch. To make all tight and fast, straw ropes are thrown over the rounded ridge and their ends whipped firmly round large stones which serve and are known as anchors, to moor the roof in a storm. If anything more be needed, a harrow thrown over a damaged corner may check further mischief for a time. Some of the houses are very short and small; but others are long and roomy. All appear diminutive and squat-looking so much so that an old writer of playful humour remarks that one could put his hand down the smoke hole in the roof and unlatch the door. This is a quiet and harmless joke, no doubt; but if anyone were foolish enough to make the attempt, the result might be serious—for him.

A Lewis village is usually a cluster of closely-packed dwellings, which from a height or from a distance look like groups of grey mole-hills in a patch of rough grass. Only narrow causeways, always tough and often very filthy, separate wall from wall or gable from gable. At some places a few cottages straggle along the roadside, while here and there, on moorland or shore, a few stand apart and alone. ...

The interior was of the type most common in Lewis, and deserves a few words of description. The house was divided into three distinct compartments. The door by which we entered opened into the byre, where there were two or three stalls for cows on the gable end, and in front of these the usual gutter with its usual contents. Then came two dwarf walls some five or six feet high, with an opening between them, but no door to fill it. This was the entrance to the central and most important division of the dwelling—the scene of the active indoor life of the inmates. On a raised hearth in the centre of the floor burned a merry, kindly-looking peat fire with its soft fringe of white and orange ashes. On either side, against the opposite walls, were broad benches, which could easily accommodate a large family and one or two visitors besides. Beyond this compartment again, was the door—really a door this time—of the spare or best room, a small chamber with a mahogany table, box beds, and one or two chests painted in green and red. The smoke of the peat fire in the middle division rose reluctantly upwards, and was drawn out by a wide aperture on the ridge of the roof, while, as part of the same arrangement, another hole just over the wall-head in a far corner, created as much draught as was needed. If the current of air became too strong, a wisp of straw stuffed into the said hole just prevented excess ventilation. One custom, peculiar, so far as I have heard, to the Lews, must here be mentioned. The crofters and fishermen take the thatch and turf off the roofs of their houses every year or two and use them for manure, for which purpose they are said to be most valuable. No wonder, therefore, that the inmates are rather pleased than otherwise to have their roofs blackened and saturated with peat smoke, which supplies the most valuable ingredients in the fertilising process. Within doors in a Lewis dwelling, the prevailing atmosphere is a misty blue, light in colour but dense in quality ...

In outlying districts of the island, marriages do not always arise from love ... The whole matter is, to a large extent one of business or covenance. It hinges very much on the all important question whether the lady is an adept in handling and bearing the 'creel". ... It is used to carry out to the fields the piled-up manure-heap of the byre—an annual piece of work; to carry loads of peats from the moors; to bring great burdens of seaweed from the shore; to convey food to the cattle in the airidh, or green shealing among the hills; ... Hence arises the high value set upon the ability to work the creel. A young man's courtship very often originates with his parents. An elderly man ... commonly addresses his spouse after this fashion ... "Well Maggie, you have always been a good and faithful wife to me. I am afraid, however, that you are not so strong as you once were. Your diligence and industry with the creel have broken your strength. You deserve some measure of relief and rest. We must ask our son Donald to get married, and his wife will take the heavy burden off your shoulders".

Then the guidman and his wife discuss over the fire what fair buxom maiden would be a suitable bride for the excellent young man Donald. Half the robust girls of the neighbourhood pass in review before their minds. By-and-by Donald himself is informed of his parents' ideas; and whatever his personal feelings may be, he considers it his duty to exercise self-denial, and to please his father and mother. The next step is to order a bottle of whisky from Stornaway; and several days may elapse before its arrival. When the liquor has come, the old man and his son wend their way to the dwelling of the young woman who is first-favourite. The bottle is stowed away out of sight. For a time they chat and gossip pleasantly with the family, and by-and-by the purpose of their visit is disclosed. The girl's parents may be well pleased, perhaps even flattered; but she herself may be coy and reluctant ... If any signs of hesitation thus appear, Donald and his father consider their proposal rejected, and at once rise to leave the house ... Once outside, the father and son hold a hurried consultation, and soon decide to visit another dwelling ... This time their fond hopes are realised. Mary had fled when she discovered their errand; but her mother draws her from her hiding place. The young lady's scruples are overcome by maternal persuasions, and she consents to have Donald, as her husband. Then at last the bottle is produced, and amid much cordial good cheer arrangements are made for an early wedding.

The marriage day is a great occasion. Omitting the mere ceremony, let me mention some other features of the gathering. There are graduations of honour and of treatment among the company. If there is a room-end in the house, that contains the inner and upper circle. Among the select guests may be numbered a few of the elders of the kirk, the schoolmaster if he is popular, and those friends who have come greatest distances. The table is adorned with plates, forks, and knives, which have been borrowed for the occasion. Here, too, among other specialities, are some loaves of bread and a stack of broad barley scones. In this room is deposited the jar of whisky, which is under the absolute control of the master of ceremonies. It is kept in the bed, and is guarded by two or three persons, who sit upon the edge of the coverlet. Out of the jar there is poured a sufficient quantity of the pure stuff for the wants of the favoured company in this best room. Then the jar is filled up with water . . . Thus replenished, it is sent, with much show of liberality, to those gathered in the common room or kitchen, in the centre of which the peat fire is burning gloriously. Under a smoky canopy of blue, the guests arrange themselves around the walls. They are provided with bowls or other convenient vessels of a miscellaneous kind out of which to sup their food. There are, of course, large piles of barley scones, while the chief delicascy in this compartment is substantial quantity of beef cut into minute fragments of various shapes, as if intended for a dish of hash. This pièce de resistance is committed to the care of young women . . . Still lower as to the degree of attention paid to them, are a third class, who dare not intrude upon the other two, but are allowed to shift as best they can for themselves. They may locate themselves in the barn; or, if there is no barn, on the manure-heap between the kitchen and the cows, and in either case are well content. They get food of a quality superior to any they indulge in at home, and even the adulterated whisky is to them quite a luxury.

Even on these high occasions, instrumental music is seldom employed, being accounted sinful in no ordinary degree. This is largely due to the influence of one popular preacher, who a generation ago, denounced and resisted the practice. Even to this day, tender consciences are afraid to allow or countenance the use of the fiddle or bagpipe at marriage festivities. The guests have dancing, however, and a pleasant musical accompaniment as well. The young girls sing songs, usually duets, of native composition, and these are set to tunes which suit the various steps of the lively exercise.

There are three classes of anciant inhabitants of Lewis of whom I should like to say a few words . . . The first class is, of course the sweet "fairies or guid folk"—fewer far than they once were, and far more shy of human society . . . Another class, once common enough, but now rarely to be seen, were the Roman Catholic "sisters" or "nuns" . . . The third class of beings are, strange to say, modern as well as ancient. They are called "Fir Chreig" or the false men. You ask Who or What are these? They are remarkable standing stones of venerable age, and are now named "false men" because of their fancied resemblance perhaps in mist or darkness, to men of large stature.

Fergusson: *Rambles in Breadalbane—1891*

The kind-hearted guidewife in a jiffey had the tidy, well-scoured white kitchen table loaded with nice "sappy" barley bannocks, and well-baked, crispy oatmeal cakes, plenty of fine, tasty, powdered butter, a big kebbuck of old cheese, and lots of sweet milk just as it "cam' frae the coo", together with the familiar and never failing big bellied black bottle, filled with the real, genuine, and well-matured Tom-a-choachain whisky, Entire, for which not a single rap of duty had ever been paid into the Queen's exchecker, and which would likely be about six or seven years old, but still standing off and on about beed No 7 or 5.3 o.p. It would have a nice yellow tinge of colour with "real age" a fine mellow peat-reek flavour, and would slip over one's craigie just like a drop of sweet milk, without causing the least gasp or grin. After a few "drams" of it quietly over, how it would warm and brighten up the sometimes dour, dull mororse inner man, to new life and jolly, jovial, buyant spirits!

This widely-famed medicinal beverage used to be often highly recommended by some of the old experienced "lady" doctors in the district, for the squeakin' "skirlin" baby of a few hours or days old, as well as for the wheezing, tottering, old man or woman bordering on five score. Indeed it seemed to be well suited for all constitutions in any stage of life—from the cradle to the grave. A very different medicinal beverage from some of the mixy-maxy blends one so often meets with nowadays and sees advertised in all the newspapers, flashy circulars, &., and said to be pure Islay and Campbeltown with a little Glenlivet, or "Long John" added to help to bring up the flavour . . .

Mrs MacTavish, residing in one of the cottages . . . had suddenly taken ill, and to all appearances had not many hours to live . . . There was no doctor—and, I believe at the time no clergyman—within ten or twelve miles . . . The dying woman seemed anxious . . . to have someone to offer up a prayer on her behalf . . . In the emergency a consultation of all the old women of the hamlet was held resulting in a deputation . . . being sent to Iain Mhor to ask him to go Mrs Mactavish's cottage to offer up a prayer. He at first refused . . . but being urgently pressed . . . he reluctantly consented . . . On entering the old woman's apartment . . . he was about to kneel down . . . Mrs MacTavish sat up in bed held up her hands in horror and gasped out "Oich, oich, pity me pity me to see the biggest sinner in a' Breadalbane come to pray for me . . ."

At Tullyporie . . . Here is . . . two large handsom-looking shops where one can have almost any article from a needle to an anchor, and at very moderate rates indeed. I had occasion to call at one of these shops one day, and told the lad at the counter that I wanted two or three common nails about two inches long. "We don't sell less than a quarter of a pound, sir" quoth he "Oh indeed," I said, "and what's the cost of that quantity" Just a hapney sir" "Oh, well" I said 'I'll just take the lot, although I require only a few to mend a rustic garden seat on which I enjoy a pipe".

The marriage ceremony, as a rule was performed at the Killin Parish Manse—the only Manse there in my boyhood days. The bride, with her friends and party, the bridegroom, his friends and party, often started from different parts of the district, each party having their own pipes—usually two or three marching proudly at the head of the procession, the gaudy varied-coloured ribbons attached to the drones of their bagpipes flaunting and waving in the fresh mountain breeze, and, as previously arranged, met at the Parish Manse. After the knot was solemnly and securely tied, both parties joined and returned in one grand possession. Guns firing, and flags waving along the route towards the bride's father's house, where rejoicings were usually continued for several days. A wedding had taken place at the house of one of our neighbours, a small farmer.

D. Logie: *Stirling to Ben Nevis—1896*

After passing Dalry, about a mile beyond, our train reached Tyndrum station. After passing Tyndrum on the hill to the left called Clifton, above the hotel, there used to be a lead mine worked by Lord Breadalbane. When open it did not prove remunerative, and was in consequence abandoned; but in 1839 it was reopened, and under a hundred workmen employed in it, under the guidance and experience of German miners. A copper mine was subsequently opened in the neighbourhood. . . .

Ever since leaving Crianlarich we have been travelling through a country consecrated to sport, of which fact a significant illustration is to be seen in the little rattling squares of tin hung at intervals along the telegrah wires, and particularly at the openings of glens. These are known as "grouse protectors", and are hung there in order that their noise in the wind may warn the grouse of the existence of a danger, and prevent them hurling themselves in full flight against the telegraph wires . . .

On reaching the summit, (of Ben Nevis) Mr Gibson at once went to the telegraph office to dispatch a telegram to their friends in Stirling . . . Without any previous warning or intimation, a terrible thunderstorm burst over the summit, the first flash of lightening striking the hotel and displacing the corrugated iron roofing, which covered the hotel immediately above their heads. The deafening peal of thunder that followed was awful, and each sat silently looking at one another, and wondering what was going to happen next . . . The two servant girls in the hotel, who were close to the room, became deadly white. The electricity was flying through their hair and singeing it. They had to tear down their hair and remove all the hairpins therein, and to allow their tresses to fall down their backs . . .

Some sixty years ago the late Rev Dr McVicar, of Moffat . . . while yet a young man accompanied by the late Sir Walter Trevelyan and some other friends, made an ascent of Ben Nevis. It was on a hot and somewhat hazy day in June also, this month being undoubtedly the worst month in the year for the ascent of any Scotch mountain. About midday, and only a little while after they had got to the summit, a snow-shower from the south-west swept angrily over the mountain. While this shower lasted a singular noise was heard on all sides, a sort of hissing and crackling, such as proceeds from a point on an excited prime conductor or strongly charged Leyden jar. This hissing and crackling in all directions, continued for upwards an hour and a half, and clearly indicated the emission of pencils of electric light, which very probably would have been visible to the eye had the day been only a little cloudier and darker than it was. The electric discharge was noticed on an umbrella belonging to one of the party, as well as on almost all the sharp pointed rocks around.

Lord Oxford: *A Journey through Hertfordshire Lincolnshire and Notts to the Northern Counties of Scotland, (Hist Mss D of Portland)— 1901*

. . . May 11 We left Haddington half an hour after seven this morning and as we pass from it towards Edinburgh through a small village called Trenent we have a view of the Forth at the part of it where the Highlanders got over in 1715 . . .

We leave Hunting tower, the seat of the Duke of Atholl . . . Going by the side of this river towards the Tay, we pass a flock of sheep which were very singular for their horns, some having three and some four. Those which had four horns had two of them growing almost perpendicular, somewhat like a goat's, and the other two turned about like those of common sheep. We ferried over the river Tay just where the water of Almond joins it within about a quarter of a mile of Scone. It is called the boat of Rome, and the ferryman the Pope. We did not take our horses over, but walked up from hence to Scone. . . . That apartment where the Chevalier de St. George lay here in 1715 is a tolerably good one, though it has nothing in it of royal magnificence. In the next room where he lay they show a small piece of the marble chimney-piece which was shot off at that time by one of the pages, who was playing with some pistols which lay in the room and let one of them off. The gentlemen in the next room imagined it had been some treachery and were going to hew the boy in pieces, but that his master stepping in at the instant saved his life.

They value themselves here for fine kid gloves for ladies, and they are so very choice with them, that I could get but three pairs to bring off with me for a pattern to the southern glovers; but I cannot see anything in those I have which should make them so very valuable, except it be my honoured ladies accepting them as the only curiosity I found to traffic in, about the neighbourhood of the Highlands . . .

May 22 At ten o'clock this morning we left Dupplin, and crossed the water of Arne . . . Sir Patrick Murray, an elderly worthy gentleman took his leave . . . after having passed the river with us, which he was to ford back again immediately in order to go his way home. I wondered that being an old man, and the passage not so very secure and easy, he would ford the river twice, where I thought there was no occasion for him to do it once; but I found it to be a generous, unalterable principle amongst the Scottish men never to part with their friends at the bank of a river which they must leave him to cross; especially if there be any danger in the passing of it, but go through with him and then take their leave and return.

May 23 Our being at this place (Alloway nr Stirling) this Sunday morning afforded us an opportunity of a sight which was curious enough for a stranger. It was the meeting or Assembly of the members of the Presbyterian Kirk, which is by them termed an Occasion.: and perhaps may be so called because the Celebration of the Sacrament is the occasion of such assembling together. There is notice given some time before hand when and where this Occasion is to held, at which time and place (which is generally one of the kirks most commodious for its largeness) the ministers of several "Parochs" to the number of ten, twenty, or perhaps thirty sometimes, are desired to attend and give their assistance, according as their several parts are allotted to them of praying or preaching which is to continue without any intermission both within the kirk and without it in some field adjoining for this whole day from morning to night. St Ninians was the place appointed for this day's solemnity, and we went forth to observe it; both the church and field they were met in being within a bowshot of our inn. We first walked into that part of the open ground where they met to the number of many hundreds, and disposed themselves on a shelving ground facing their preacher, who held forth at the lower part of it, from a tent erected for that purpose. This part of the occasional assembly seemed to be altogether made up of the very meanest sort of people that this country could show. It was a rainy day, but they sat or stood it out with great patience and attention to what the twentieth part of them could not possibly hear words of or rather indeed I should say one sentence. ...

The field exercise seems to be contrived only as an entertainment and amusement to keep those people together, who cannot get into the church till room be made for them by the retirement of some of those who crowd within it, so that they make a continual succession ... We got into the body of the church by the favour of a porter who kept the door constantly shut, but when people had occasion to come out or enter in ... Master Loggin the parish minister was just upon the conclusion of this sermon, which was the first that day, and called the Earnest sermon; after which, having sung a psalm he gave the discharge, that is, he generally pronounced the several sort of sinners whom he discharged or forbid from partaking of the Sacrament ... After then he came down from the pulpit into the body of the church ... where some boards were laid for the whole length of it from west to east about two feet wide and the height of a table, and covered over with an ordinary linen cloth. The persons who were first to communicate about fifty or more, sat on each side ... The minister stood about the middle of it, and ... When this was done the persons thereunto appointed went down on each side of the long table I before mentioned, and received the tickets from every person, that was sat down in order to communicate for without producing such a ticket ... no person was admitted.

Hammerton: *Tony's Highland tour—1901*

... I know many people who are delighted with pipe-music. They are all English people or, at least, English people who would fain be Scots. It is a constant source of amusement to notice how many such there are. At one time I was a member of a "Scottish society" in a certain English town. We had a roll of about three hundred, and I discovered soon after joining that of these some fifty were true Scots; the rest fancied they were, because either their mothers or fathers or their grandmothers or grandfathers had been born in Scotland, or they themselves had been born there while their parents were on a visit. Some were known to have claimed membership on the ground that they kept Scotch terriers. The leading spirit of the society was a podgy little fellow named Shufflebottom—how's that for a Scots cognomen?—who used to turn out in a kilt—he called it "kilts"—at the annual ball, and would ooze joy from every pore when the pipes were playing. He would even try to cry "hooch" and if you ventured to question his right to enthuse over the music of the Highlands, he would scowl on you like any Gruamach, and say his "Ighland blood was hup". I have no violent objection to bagpipes; I like to hear them up among the hills— when I am down in the valley.

Eriskay and Prince Charles—Blackwoods Magazine, February 1901

The scene is almost weird. It is an evening in the early autumn. The house is long and low, it has neither floor nor ceiling; but the walls are thick, and the thatch of divots, or sods of grass, fastened on with heather ropes, is an excellent protection from cold and draught. A peat-fire burns in a hollow in the clay floor, and the smoke seeks escape through an opening in the roof. A kettle, singing gaily, is suspended from an iron chain, and round flat cakes, supported by stones, are arranged in a circle about the fire. The scant furniture of the house has been cleared to one side, and three long planks, supported table-wise at either end, so as to slope towards the door, occupy the open space. Chairs are scarce, but forms and boxes are placed so as to seat the women who are to do the work of the evening. Ten big muscular young women they are, with bare arms, and long coarse aprons over their gowns. They take much heed to the right height and firmness of their seats, as indeed the violent exercise they are about to enter upon requires. The house is already well filled with humanity, and but ill-ventilated, while two or three smoking paraffin-lamps further subtract from the available oxygen. Later we learn to be thankful for the additional reek of peat and tobacco, for the climax of ill-savour is not reached till the hostess brings in the web of cloth freshly dipped in some nauseous compound which contends with its original smell of fish and hot sheep,—fish oil and tallow being the most fragrant of the various dressings applied to the wool, from which the process of fulling is to cleanse it.

Five to each side they sit, and the dripping cloth is passed from hand to hand, while the moisture runs down the sloping boards to the floor. The movements of the women, at first slow, are in perfect rhythm, and, like all co-ordinated movement in these islands, their direction is dessil—sunwards. It is only at first that we can observe the details of their operations, for soon the process becomes so rapid that we can distinguish nothing but the swaying of their figures, and the rapid thud of the cloth, keeping time to the rhythm of their song.

And what strange singing it is! deep-toned and monotonous, the rhythm very marked, the thud of the wet cloth regular as the beat of a drum, the melody seldom extending beyond five notes, each syllable having its separate note, and no pause made from beginning to end of the song, which is necessarily in four times. The verses are couplets, and each is sung first by one woman alone, and then taken up by all.

The course of the web along the board describes a series of zigzags, each woman's movement forming the letter V, of which she herself is the base, and each point thus marked by the loud thud of the cloth upon the board, always in four time. At one she receives the cloth from her neighbour on the right, leaning forward and throwing it down at arm's length; at two she draws herself upright and brings it down again immediately in front of her, twisting it as she does so; at three she passes it, again at arm's length, to her neighbour on the left; and at four, once more upright, she brings her hands again in front of her, still beating time, and is thus ready for one da capo, for the rhythm is ceaseless.

Each song averages about eight minutes, and is about fifty couplets in length. As each one is finished, the women throw down the web and their arms drop. They are exhausted and breathless, as well they may be, for to sing and work as they do throwing themselves violently forward so that the cloth they are handling becomes absolutely hot in the process, is not light work.

In a minute or two they begin again. A "songless" web (clobodaich) is unlucky, and without any pre-arrangement, another strikes up an air. Like the last, it is a love song its sentiment of the most florid description. After this we have another in which the rival merits of two adjacent islands are discussed, and then the women, having worked more than half an hour, examine the cloth. It is carefully measured: a piece of cloth must always be finished at a sitting, and in the course of fulling it should shrink an inch to every foot of length. The women measure on the back of the hand, occasionally verifying their estimate on a half-yard wand—eight feet to the yard being the Highland measure.

"It will take three or four songs more", they say and the picturesque phrase seems in keeping with the scene about us.

While the work has gone on, more visitors have strolled in. The hostess is moving about, now that the cessation of work makes movement possible in the cramped space. The dogs have clustered about the fire, relieved at the stopping of the singing. The hens are complaining on the beams overhead; the cat, who has climbed to the top of one of the cupboard beds, is expressing disgust as only a cat can. With every hair of her fur she protests against the crowd, the smell—above all, the noise; but it is better to bear the ills she has than to run the gauntlet of the dogs. Now they begin again: the women are rested, and the singing becomes more vigerous, the melody is marked and rapid, the asperates of the Gaelic breathe an audible excitement. Four long and short syllables go to a line, and the accent this time is very definite, and the thud of the cloth takes on a sharper sound as the web dries. The very first couplet reveals why the song is one which they sing with special gusto. Morag is the old secret name in Gaelic for Prince Charles.

If over seas thou hast gone from us
May it be soon thou wilt return
. . .

The song is finished, and the women exhausted lean forward on the table. The sudden cessation of sound and movement is almost painful. The discontented cat shakes a disgusted paw, the dogs look hopefully towards the door. The fulling is over, the cloth lies reeking on the table . . . The ceremony is not yet ended. Two of the women stand up and roll the cloth from opposite ends till they meet in the middle, and then, still keeping time, four of them fall upon the roll and proceed to pat it violently, straightening out the creases, and those unemployed strike up another song, this time of different metre. This finished, one standing up calls out "The rhymes the rhymes" And those who have been working reply "Three rhymes, four rhymes, five and a half rhymes"

This is a very mysterious—probably the last remains of some forgotten ceremony.

Then the table is unwound, and again very carefully rolled up, this time into one firm bale, and then all rise and stand in reverent silence while the leader of the fulling-women pronounces the quaint, old-world grace with which their work concludes. Laying one hand on the cloth she says:

"Let not the Evil Eye afflict, let not be mangled
The man about whom thou goest, for ever
When he goes into battle or combat   .
The protection of the Lord be with him".

And then some man of the party—it would not be etiquette for a woman—turns to the owner and says with emphasis "May you posses it and wear it" And the cloth is fulled.

J. Garry: *A Hebridean holiday—Temple Bar 1901*

Here there is none of the painful, inhuman punctuality that is so conspicuous a virtue in the more frequent routes. The steamer starts again "somewhere outside an hour", and no one is particular as to the limits of that outside age, least of all the passengers who are glad to stretch their cramped limbs along the romantic-looking road, that runs like a drab ribbon with green embroidered edges between the two Tarbets ...

What a merry little township we passed through that golden morning! A bright cascade not ten yards from the village street, babbled musically over its track of mossy boulders recklessly scattering diamonds down banks of rag-wort and bracken on its way to the mill stream. Two or three slim Highland lasses, bare-headed, short-skirted, coyly demure, carried in each hand a miniature water-barrel with handles, to be replenished at a spring which trickled from the uplands through a hole in the drystane fence. The process of filling was slow, but not tedious to these maidens in their springtime, who with the privilege of water-drawers since Time began, beguiled the waiting with jest and happy laughter ...

In a hollow beneath, a hundred yards or so away, lay a little bright mountain loch, rimmed with rushes and set like a shimmering bowl of silver in the green of that vast hill-side: Grouped round its margin were a dozen or so of red-deer stooping to the water absorbed in the pleasure of quenching their mid-day thirst, with every delicate limb, every bent head on the alert for hostile scent or sound. Above, in the dazzling blue a hawk hung, poised motionless; not a breath stirred the tiniest spear of grass; it was a rare moment of Nature's supreme absolute calm.

We intended leaving the island in a few days, but its quiet unconventional charm seized on us, and, in spite of some minor discomforts, and midges as big and bloodthirsty which came out for a daily meal of human flesh regularly at 6 p.m. we stayed to the end of our holiday ...

A whole Highland village! "Something to see by Baccus" quoted Kit, who had tramped with me several weary miles on a former holiday to look at one, almost deserted "Highland House". For these primitive dwellings are growing scarce in days of sanitary laws and cheap transport of cheap materials; they are disappearing from Scotland as surely as the otter. But they are a link with the long past; they have been built by the crofters from materials that Nature gave their hands; rough, unhewen, unshaped boulders; the interstices filled in with turf or heather; thickly piled turf and heather over the unplastered rafters, securely weighed with heavy stones, makes a snug weather-proof roof. Very small windows suffice; and a circle of cobble stones in the centre of the floor serves for the glowing mass of peats that warm and cheer the long winter evenings. Crofters have an inborn passionate love of the land; in many cases they have reclaimed from mountain side or rotting quagmire the small fields and holdings that give bread in due season to themselves and their children; they are essentially sons and daughters of the soil, with a distaste for the sea and its dangers; a whole-hearted love for their earth-mother, from whom they have for generations received their scanty, hard-wrung sustenance direct. They are a picturesque people, an outgrowth of the land, so to speak, and in spite of hard conditions under which they live, there is none of the squalor or dirt that give to the Irish hovel its painful distinction ...

It was early evening when, after crossing a footpath, through a field of swaying barley, we wound round a protecting ridge of rock, and crossing the stepping stones of a tiny burn found ourselves within the village, which at that hour looked solemn and brown and silent. Several houses, from twelve to twenty perhaps, stood in a clump; no rows but dotted down here and there as one would pitch tents. No back yards; no front gardens; dwelling and cowhouse and fowl-house built in one, some of drystone, a few mortared, but all roofed with heather. Windows were few and small; in almost every house a narrow stone passage led up to the rooms; one or two possessed chimneys, but the greater number got rid of smoke from "central fires" by a hole in the roof. A few apple trees lent a gracious touch to what might have otherwise looked somewhat sordid; the crofts, marked clearly out by the differing nature of the crops, lay ripening to the harvest, and in the waning light of that summer eve the whole scene was strangely weird and unelfing. Not a person was visible; the fowls were all at roost; only an occasional deep low from the houses indicated that the cattle had been brought home from pasture.

We knocked at a door fortified with the thought that we had come on business. After waiting some time, a neat old woman answered it, who might have been a brownie so tiny was she, so wizened her wrinkled face, so queer and odd her manner—we put our question. She made some faint, unintelligible reply—in Gaelic I presume—and fled—and for a moment we half-repented coming. But while taking counsel as to our next proceedings, a man appeared at the end of one of the house passages and looked interrogatively towards us.

Here was our primaeval man after all! Tall and straight, clean-limbed and muscular, with wide kind blue eyes unclouded by the craft of cities, full of simple fine sincerity that no contact with a cunning world had ever tainted. We stated our business and after consulation with an unseen individual at the far end of the passage, he came back to tell us that our quest was successful.

Mrs. D. Christie: *Dugald Christie of Manchuria—1932*

Glencoe—1855–1862

Amid the lonely mountains at the head of Glencoe, looking out to the wastes of the moor of Rannoch, there stands an ancient change-house, the Kingshouse Inn. Here in the middle of last century a little fair curly-haired boy, Dugald Christie, was running wild on the moors and learning the lore of the hills. He was the ninth and youngest child of Malcolm Christie, who had come from Glen Dochart, where his fathers had been "tacksmen" for centuries, and of Janet MacCallum of Glen Falloch.

Kingshouse was then a large and prosperous sheep-farm, as well as a rest-house for chance travellers and a posting station for the coaches which passed daily in summer. When Dugald was still an infant his father died, but the widow kept on the farm, and here the child spent those formative years, the first seven of his life, while the wild surroundings, the solitudes and silences, and the sounds, entered deep into his Celtic soul.

Being the youngest, he was the favourite of the servants, with his fair curls, blue eyes, and winning smile, his happy nature, quick temper, and hot enthusiasms. His earliest recollection is of being lulled to sleep by the Gaelic songs of his old nurse, for she and most of the farm-servants spoke only Gaelic. Another vivid memory is the ghost stories told in Gaelic in the kitchen, the children listening in fascinated terror, till they feared to go along the dark passages of the old house, lest ghostly hands should stretch out from the gloom and clutch them.

The winters were long and lonely. Coaches ceased to run, and news was carried only by wandering tinkers and pedlars. Every farm had a barn or loft for wayfarers, and the more lonely the place the surer were they of a night's lodging. Occasionally weeks would pass without even this communication with the outer world. Snow lay at time five or six feet deep, blocking the doors and darkening the windows. A path was cut to the river, and ice broken for the animals to drink. The shy hares became tame, and the deer came down from their fastnesses and invaded the garden, their eeries roaring breaking in on the stillness.

The large family and the shepherds of Kingshouse formed a little community sufficient unto themselves. Almost everything in use was home-made. The women spun the wool of the sheep, made it into yarn, knitted it, or sent it to Ballachulish to be woven into cloth. The dyes were made from home-grown herbs. In the long winter evenings the work was done to the accompaniment of Gaelic songs or stories, the women at their spinning-wheels, the men making shoes, or household articles of wood. Sometimes as the evening wore on, work was thrown aside and all joined in the spirited choruses, waving time vigorously with their handkerchiefs.

In the summer the special excitement was the daily passing of the coach and the changing of the horses. It was driven four and sometimes six-in-hand, with red-coated, high-booted postillions, the the guard wound his horn as they careered up and down the steep hills and round the sharp corners of the narrow Glencoe road. The horses were the children's pride each boy having his own special one on whose back he rode to and from the stables. It was a red-letter day to Dugald when he was first allowed to hold the reins of the team, and believed himself to be driving the coach.

One favourite horse had an adventure which brought home vividly to the little boy the dangers of the treacherous Moor. One evening this horse failed to return home with the others from grazing, and search parties could find no trace of him, so it was feared that he had been swallowed up in some peaty quagmire. A few days later a farm worker crossing the Moor descried the head and shoulders of a horse protruding from a moss-hag. All the grass and heather within reach were cropped close, and the poor beast was in the last stages of starvation and exhaustion. By means of ropes he was soon drawn to firm ground, and a few days tending restored his stength. But on the childish mind the impression never faded, of the ruthless cruelty of those bogs.

... One summer day a new wonder was revealed in Kingshouse. Over the crest of the Blackmount there came in sight a man carrying a strange box, with a strap over his shoulders. It was the first barrel-organ ever seen there, a poor, old fashioned thing, but to the boy who listened a miracle ...

Education was something of a problem to so isolated a homestead, but Malcolm Christie had determined that his children should have their chance, and his widow carried out his plans. The nearest school was at Ballachulish, thirteen miles distant, so a little house was rented near that village, where some of the family stayed under the care of a trusted servant. When Dugald was about six years old he was sent to join them there, while the older boys went to Glasgow to the High School.

The Christies were devoted supporters of the Free Church of Scotland, and every Sunday when it was possible a waggonette took the family down to Ballachulish, where they attended a Gaelic service of two hours and another in English. There was little in those to attract a childish mind, for Highland religion last century was of a stern and rigid character.

It is an interesting fact that the wave of religious awakening which passed over Scotland in 1859 reached in time to remote Glencoe, and was noticeable enough to imprint itself on the memory of a child of six. How "The Revival" was brought there is not recorded, but hymns began to be sung by shepherds and in the farm kitchen, and down in the Glen there were little gatherings for prayer and Bible study. In later years he often recalled his first conscious contract with this movement.

Peter the coachman was down at Ballachulish one day with the dog-cart, and brought Dugald back with him. On the way they went into the house of Donald the joiner, and the little fellow heard, wondering, the talk of how this one and that one was "converted" ...

Collected by Henryk Opiesnski, translated by E. Voynich: *Chopin's letters—1932*

London Monday July 17. . . . My Scottish ladies are kind, but they bore me so that I don't know what to do. They want to insist that I should go to their homes in Scotland; that's all right, but nowadays I have no heart for anything. Here, whatever is not boring is not English ...

There is a very beautiful park here, and the owner of the castle must also be called a very charming person: so I feel as happy here as is permitted to me at all. . . . Here I have the utmost material peace, and spend my time on the beautiful Scottish songs; I should like to compose a little, and even could do so if only to give pleasure to these kind ladies, Mrs Erskine and Miss Sterling. . . .

The population here is ugly, but apparently good-natured. On the other hand the cows are magnificent, but apparently inclined to gore people. The milk, butter and eggs are irreproachable and so are their usual companions the cheese and chicken ...

Now, leaving London 10 days ago, I was met at the train for Edinburgh by a gentleman who introduced himself as coming from Broadwood and gave me instead of one seat, two (the second opposite so that no one should crowd me); also, in the same coach he had put a certain Mr Wood, an acquaintance of Broadwood, who knew me too, (he had seen me at Lipinski's at Frankfort in 1836), and who has his own music firm in Edinburgh and Glasgow. Broadwood has also arranged that my Daniel (who is a better person than many gentlefolk, and handsomer than many Englishmen) should travel in the same coach: and I made the 407 English miles from London to Edinburgh, by Birmingham and Carlisle, in 12 hours by express train (the class of train that stops least often) I stopped at Edinburgh where a lodging had been engaged for me in the best hotel (Douglas's) for one and a half days, to rest. I went to look at the exquisite city, of which I send some very poor views on this paper ... I met there some courteous friends of my friends, who took me about in their carriage to see the town. (Everybody is going to Scotland now for the opening of the shooting season. After a rest in Edinburgh, where passing a music shop I heard a blind man playing a mazurka of mine, I got into a carriage harnessed in the English style with a led horse, which Lord Torpichen had sent, and came here, 12 miles from Edinburgh. Lord Torpichen is an old Scotchman, seventy years old, a brother-in-law of Mrs Erskine and Miss Stirling, my excellent Scottish ladies, whom I have long known in Paris, and who take so much trouble for me. I constantly visited them in London, and to them I could not refuse to come here; especially as I have nothing more to do in London, as I need a rest, and as Lord Torpichen gave me a very hearty invitation. The place is called Calder House pronoucned Kolderhaus). It is an old manor surrounded by an enormous park with ancient trees, you can see only lawns, trees, mountains and sky. The walls are 8 feet thick; there are galleries on all sides, dark corridors with endless numbers of ancestral portraits, of various colours, in various costumes, Scotch, some in armour, some in robes; nothing lacking for the imagination. There is even some kind of red cap (ghost) which appears, but which I have not yet seen ... The room which I inhabit has the most beautiful view imaginable ... I must go later to Keir near Stirling, (a district famous for its beauty, near the Lady of the Lake) to Miss Stirling's cousin. These kind Scotch ladies here! There is nothing I can think of that does not at once appear; even the Parisian newspapers are brought to me every day. It is quiet peaceful and comfortable; only I must leave in a week. Lord Torpichen has asked me to come for the whole summer next year. They would let me stay for the rest of my life but what's the use. They have put me far from everyone else so that I can play and do what I like freely; for these people as Bartek will tell you, the first thing to do for a guest is, not to interfere with him. I found a Broadwood piano in my room; in the drawingroom there is a Pleyel, which Miss Stirling brought with her. In England la vie de château is very pleasant. Everyday someone arrives to stay for a few days. The arrangements are most luxurious; libraries horses carriages at your disposal, personal servants, etc. Here they usually meet for lunch ... at 2 oclock everybody eats breakfast in his own room, when and how he pleases, and for dinner at 7. At evening they sit up as long as and how they choose. In the evening I play Scotch songs for the old lord, who hums the tune with me, poor fellow and expresses his feelings to me in French, as best he can. Although everyone in high society speaks French, especially the ladies, the general conversation is mostly in English and I then regret that I don't know the language but I have neither the time nor the desire for it. However I understand simple things; I can't starve or come to grief. . . .

Perthshire Sunday No post, no railway, no carriage, (even for a drive) not a boat, not even a glass of whisky to ...

Very soon I shall forget my Polish, talking only a mixture of French and English—and it is Scottish English I am learning, so I shall be taken for old Jarorka who talked 5 languages at once ...

I have been in Scotland, Walter Scott's beautiful country, among all the reminders of Mary Stuart, of the Charleses, etc. I visited one lord after another. Everywhere I met together with heartiest goodwill and boundless hospitality, superb pianofortes, magnificent paintings famous collections of books. There are also hunting dogs.

Chapter 18   **The '45 Jacobite Rising**

Prince Charles Edward.

The background

The name "Jacobite" comes from "Jacobus" the Latin for James, "Whig" comes from a Covenanting sect known as "Whigamores".

In 1688 William of Orange was invited by the Whig party in England over to Britain. The Stuart king at that time was James VII of Scotland and II of England. James VII was the younger brother of Charles II, and son of Charles I. William had married Mary Stuart the daughter of James VII by his first wife Ann Hyde.

The movement against James was partly political and partly religious. James was a Roman Catholic. His people in England were largely Church of England. In Scotland there were Presbyterians and, in a lesser number, Scottish Episcopalians. Ireland was largely Roman Catholic. Other minority religions looked to James for toleration. The Quakers presented a petition to him, "we are come to testify our sorrow for the death of our good friend Charles, and our joy of thee being made our Governor. We are told thou art not of the persuasion of the Church of England, no more than we; wherefore we hope thou will grant us the same liberty which thou allowest thyself. Which doing, we wish thee all manner of happiness". While James did believe in toleration the country was not ready for such a measure.

Politically Parliament was growing in power, and encroaching on the King's prerogative. The Laws of the Land and the Justice of the Land were the King's. During this struggle they passed to Parliament. It may be mentioned here, that William and his Parliament did not see eye to eye with another. Later, in the reign of George I and George II, as neither spoke the language they did not attend Parliament, and this in turn allowed Parliament to gain further power.

When James had been Duke of York he had worked hard to build up the navy. The present Navy regulations are little changed from those laid down by James. The origin of the midshipmen came from the King's "Letter Boys" who were youngsters who were trained for the sea. James as an Admiral won two naval victories.

When William landed in the South of England, James sent his army to meet him under the command of John Churchill later to become the Duke of Marlborough who deserted and later was to change his opinion and parley with both sides. In Scotland Viscount Dundee (The Bonnie Dundee of the song) raised the Clans for James. James had been in Scotland in 1681 and 1682 as Commissioner from the King to Parliament. He had gained some popularity. Bishop Burnet, who was no friend, said James encouraged trade and was impartial in Justice. (The Princess introduced the first tea to Scotland and the old Palace of Holyrood came to life). James enjoyed playing golf at which he was very good. He also played tennis.

In the Highlands James was held in regard. He had tried to end feudal power and jurisdiction. He had employed Highlanders in his service. His religion was no barrier to Roman Catholic Clans, nor yet to the Episcopal ones. Charles II had helped to end the discord between the Camerons and the MacIntoshes.

The Highlanders' interpretation of the Divine Right of Kings was that shared by the Stuarts. It meant a moral responsibility given by birth, and not an indulgence. It had a religious feeling and was resonable. The Highlanders considered it their duty to God as well as to their King to help restore the rightful King. On their side the Stuarts felt that because they were divinely appointed by birth, it was a duty to deliver their country from foreign domination. This feeling was a factor in the coming to Scotland of Prince Charles Edward.

While Dundee raised the Clans, William sent General Mackay against him. The armies met at Killiecrankie (1689) where Dundee was victorious but unfortunately he died of wounds. No good leader replaced him, and resistance collapsed. This might be called the first Jacobite Rising in Scotland. William continued to fight in Ireland but after the Battle of the Boyne and later at Auchrim in 1691 Irish resistance ended.

The last stronghold James had was the little island off the Berwickshire coast, the Bass Rock which lies about 2 miles out to sea. It had been used as a prison for Covenanters before the arrival of William, and on his taking the Kingdom, these prisoners were released and four of James's supporters were put in the same prison. They were Middleton, Halyburton, Roy and Dunbar. They planned and plotted, and observed that when coal was being landed, all but three or four of the soldiers went to help at the unloading. The four captives managed to overpower their guards, and to train captured guns on the garrison below. These soldiers boarded the boat and sailed away on it. The next night Crawford of Ardmillan and his servant and two Irish joined the garrison. James sent a French ship with supplies. On August 15th the large boat was captured while Ardmillan and Middleton were getting supplies. Roy and Dunbar considered surrendering. Before this was arranged Middleton returned with provisions. Dunbar on shore was taken prisoner when negotiating the surrender, but the Bass was still held.

Two Men of War were sent, but after two days of heavy firing they were so damaged that they had to return to port. It was the custom of the small garrison to seize ships and take what they needed. In August 1693 a French ship with supplies arrived at the Rock, and while supplies were being landed, the ship was attacked and she cut and ran. As there were so few on the Rock, ten of the French sailors helped with the unloading of stores. When their ship left they remained on the Rock. Little food had been landed, and with the extra mouths to feed, supplies ran short. It was decided to call a truce. Halyburton was caught and condemned to be hanged while a Mr. Trotter who had supplied food to the garrison was hanged in sight of the Bass. When the envoys arrived they were well dined and wined. Guns had coats and caps on them to give the appearance of a larger garrison force. The terms offered were excellent for the garrison. A full pardon, all honours of war, swords kept, and the boat with the liberty to go to and from the Rock till the 15th of May 1694 when a ship would carry them to France and all their expenses to be paid.

The regular troops of Dundee went into voluntary exile in France. They served in different garrisons, being paid by Louis XIV. After the French naval defeat off La Hogue, the garrison, men of Dundee's old company volunteered to serve as a private company under their own officers, thus relieving the cost to Louis's purse. They had been men of substance in Scotland and James feared they would find the life hard as indeed they did. Most of them gradually had to sell off the few treasures they had brought to Franch with them. About 120 of them served under Mareschal de Nosilles. They were held in high regard. In the taking of Rosas in Catalinia they did such service that the Governor when surrendering asked the Mareschal where his grenadiers came from, and was told by the Mareschal "Ces sont mes enfants"—they are my children, and added "They are the King of Great Britain's Scottish Officers, who to show their willingness to share his miseries, have reduced themselves to the carrying of arms and chosen to serve under my command". The Governor said it was because of these Scots soldiers that the town was surrendering.

When William became master of the Country, he wished to use his Dutch troops and the resources of his new kingdom to further his Continental War, taking troops from Britain without fear of further Risings. He tried to bribe the Highland Chiefs, but this failed. Then he offered an amnesty to all who had fought against him, if they took an oath of Allegiance before the 31st of December 1691. MacIain the Chief of the MacDonalds of Glencoe took the oath after that date, so Stair, the then Secretary of State for Scotland used this as an excuse to get William to sign an order for the extermination of the MacDonalds of Glencoe. In the original plan, this was to be extended to the lands of Lochiel, Keppoch, Glengarry, and the Appin Stuarts as well as the Glencoe MacDonalds. The Massacre of Glencoe took place on the 13th of February 1692. (The story of it is told in "A short history of Glencoe").

William died as the result of a fall from his horse when it tripped over a mole hill, and among the Jacobites it was a custom to drink to "the little gentleman in black velvet".

In 1708 King Louis of France fitted out an expedition to restore James, the son of James VII and II. The French fleet returned to France without landing James when it was threatened by the British navy. James pleaded in vain to be landed. With the great unrest in Scotland at the Union of the Parliaments, he might well have succeeded in regaining his throne for there were many ready to come to his aid and support his Cause.

In 1715 the Earl of Mar raised the Standard for James VIII and III, at Braemar. Mar captured Perth and then met the government forces under the Duke of Argyll at Sheriffmuir. Mar had much the larger army, for many had joined him. But he was no general and handled his men and the situation so badly that Glenbucket a noted Jacobite and Gordon from the North-East, was heard to say, "Oh! for an hour of Dundee". This is the Battle referred to in the song "we ran and they ran, etc." The Battle was indecisive since each side suffered defeat in one wing. But Argyll held the Forth. James landed in Scotland. But by the time he got here the position of his army had deteriorated. There is some possibility that he was actually crowned when in Scotland. Jacobite ladies had parted with jewellery for a crown and Bishop Rochester in a letter preserved in the Stuart papers refers to 3rd of February as "the anniversary of your Majesty's Coronation". Shortly afterwards James returned to France. In the meantime a body of men had risen in the Lowlands and in Cumberland. They joined forces but were defeated at Preston. Among those who were executed for their part was a cousin of James the Earl of Derwentwater, who was much loved by his own people. From Scotland Viscount Kenmure, Lord Nairn and others were captured and executed. The Earl of Nithsdale was captured and due for execution but was rescued from the Tower by the cleverness of his wife.

James sent money to Argyll before leaving Scotland to compensate country people whose cottages had been burnt during the war.

The rescue of a princess

After the failure of the '15, his adherents advised James to marry to continue the Royal line. James chose Charles Wogan to select his bride. Wogan had been out in the '15 and had escaped after capture at Preston. He was an Irishman of good family. He reported to James on the Princesses of Europe. "The Princess of Furstenberg had a red nose, the Princess of Saxony was too old, and the Princess of Baden was a dwarf." But at the Court at Ohlau in Silesia there were three princesses. The eldest Casimire "bristling with etiquette and astonishingly solemn" Charlotte, "beyond all measure gay free and familiar" and Clemintina "the darling of the family ... in point of sense, discretion, and evenness of temper, and a very becoming modesty. She was seventeen years of age, low stature, with light brown hair, very pretty black eyes, and genteel little features with a good shape—very devout and no manner of airs or variety of humor ... a good mixture of haughtiness in her composition, but cunning enough to disguise it upon occasion". Wogan's choice fell upon this last princess. From her childhood Princess Clemintina had shown great regard and sympathy to the exiled Stuarts and had said she would be "Queen of England" one day.

Wogan returned to Rome where James wished to send him to negotiate with Prince James Sobieski for the hand of his daughter. This Prince was the son of King John Sobieski who turned the Turks at Vienna. There was much rivalry and jealousy in the exiled court. The fact that Wogan was a Catholic caused some to have it that a Protestant should make the negotiations with the Polish prince. So John Murray a Protestant Scot was sent. The consent of Prince James Sobieski having been given, Princess Clemintina and her mother set off for Italy. Owing to the delay, the British Government heard of the proposed marriage. The British Government threatened the Emperor who was a cousin of the Princess, that if she travelled through his domain, his Sicilian plans would be resisted. The Princess and her Mother were arrested and put in a Convent at Innsbruck where they were guarded with great care.

When he heard the news James considered the possibility of arranging another marriage and had even consulted the Pope as to whether he could do this after a betrothal. But when Wogan heard of the arrest he saw James and asked permission to rescue the Princess. James gave his consent, and handed him the fine pearls that had belonged to Mary of Modena (his mother) as a gift to his bride. There is a short verse preserved in the Stuart papers which the princess wrote to James:

I doe love none but only one,
And you are only He
Doe you love none but only one
Thane lett that one be Mee.

Clemintina Marie Sophia Sobieski.
J'ay tout quittez pour vous suivre.

From Dillon's Irish Regiment Wogan collected three friends. They were Major Gaydon, Captain O'Toole, and Captain Misset. Mrs. Misset came too. It was felt that none of the Princess's ladies were suited for the adventure so Mrs. Misset went as chaperone though she was expecting her first child. Mrs. Misset had her maid with her, Jeanneton (sometimes referred to as Jenny). She was to take the place of the Princess. There was also a servant Mitchell recommended by King James as Mitchell had been a helper in the escape of Lord Nithsdale. Wogan saw the Princess then got the necessary permission from her Father without which the Princess would not stir. Prince James Sobieski wrote to his daughter "My dearest daughter—I have always found that you carry out your duties so scrupulously that I have no doubt but that you will follow my wishes without question, in accomplishing that which the Chevalier Wogan tells you to do without delay. My blessing comes with this proof of your obedience as well as the token of the great affection your Father has for you."

Wogan got a berline or post-chaise for four and a pillion as strong as could be got, and to this he added some strong rope in case of need.

The party set off from Strasburg on the 17th of April 1719. They made for Kempten on the frontier. From here Misset and Mitchell set off to tell Chateâudeau the Gentleman usher of the Princess that they had arrived. The others remained two stages away at Nazereith. Chateâudeau sent them word that by now the Mother of the Princess had become anxious especially as on the night of the rescue April 27th the snow was falling. But Wogan persuaded her that the bad weather was in their favour. Wogan and his party arrived when it was dark. The Princess herself was greatly excited and had even got herself a rope ladder which luckily was not needed. The plan was to smuggle Jeanneton into the building and have her take the place of the Princess and maintain the deception for as long as possible. Under the disguise of a love affair Chateâudeau got permission from the gate porter to bring Jeanneton into the Convent.

There had been some trouble with Jeanneton. She was tall and wore high heels, the Princess was not much over five feet. It was necessary for Jeanneton to wear sandals to reduce her height, and this roused her to a considerable fury. She got nervous as the time came nearer, especially when someone accidentally said the word "princess". Hitherto she had been told that O'Toole was trying to rescue a lady who was being forced to marry an old man. However she was told the word "princess" was used because the lady was so beautiful. The Princess got out of the Convent without difficulty, carrying her luggage in an apron, some pious books and the pearls that were her gift from James. Wogan met her, in the excitement she stepped into a gutter and lost her shoe. They got to the inn and joined the rest of the party. Mrs. Misset took off the Princess's wet stockings, and dried her as best she could, and got the muffs which belonged to Wogan and Gaydon and put them on the Princess's feet. They set off in the berline, but when they had gone halfway to the next stage Princess Clemintina remembered that she had left the parcel with the jewels in it at the inn. O'Toole went back for them; he was a man of great strength and lifted the door off its hinges and got in, recovered the jewels, and was away again without wakening anyone.

Trouble met them at Brixton for when they arrived at five in the evening they found that the Princess of Baden and her son had travelled just in front of them, and she had taken all the post horses. In one of George I's efforts to prevent the marriage of James and Clemintina he offered to increase Princess Clemintina's dowry by £10,000 if she would marry the Prince of Baden. When he heard this the Prince of Baden visited Clemintina and on her remaining constant to James the Prince of Baden went on to make a visit to Italy. Twice the berline broke down, and the second time it had to be left for repair and the journey was carried on in a calash which Mitchell had managed to find. This was something like a cart. The women rode in it, while Wogan and Gaydon walked beside them. They continued till they reached Sery which was into Venitian territory. They arrived there on the 31st of April at 5 a.m. Clemintina went to Mass at 6 o'clock to thank God for her escape.

Captain Misset and Captain O'Toole stayed behind the main party to watch for pursuit. When the first courier overtook them they made friends with him. They laced his wine with brandy till he was in no fit state to continue. O'Toole left to see about the horses, while Misset remained with the courier. The courier had been on his way to Trent with papers telling the Governor to stop the progress of the Princess to Italy. After this all the party met up at Sery. With the Princess of Baden's party the inns were crowded but the postmaster had seen Clemintina and Mrs. Misset at Mass and offered them hospitality. Not only were the party altogether but the berline was repaired and they continued their journey reaching Bologna on the second of May 1719.

During the journey the Princess had hardly slept or eaten. Owing to the travelling of the Princess of Baden and her party there had been little food and what there was was very bad. Also it was Lent and the Princess was very strict over the observance. Wogan had brought some cooked chicken but the Princess would not eat it, the others said it was extremely tough. They had been able to get some tea made in an oil can and which tasted of rancid butter, and some terrible soup. The Princess remained cheerful throughout and asked many questions about Britain, the way the women dressed and stories of the '15.

At Bologna the Princess was shown the four pistols which had been carried to defend her in case of need. She put her hand to her lips and touched each of the pistols. She remained incognito but received "toylet, artificial flowers, and other little things" from the Cardinal. She was married by proxy to James. Murray standing proxy for the King who was in Spain at that time.

When Clemintina reached Rome she visited the Pope who received her as a Queen. Her devotion to the Church and her personal charms were seen and felt by many. James met his bride on the 25th of August 1719. Their marriage was solemnized. Wogan was made a baronet, and the three others knighted, James got the commissions in the Spanish army as Colonels. Wogan fought well and with 1300 Spanish he kept 15,000 Moors in check. He was made Governor of La Mancha. Lady Misset stayed in Rome with the Queen, her husband serving the Pope but later going to Spain and died there in 1733 as Governor of

Oran. Chateâudeau was imprisoned till August then allowed free. Jeanneton joined her mistress in Rome.

The reason why James was not in Italy to greet his bride was because he had been in Spain, for 1719 was the year of the Spanish expedition to Scotland when about 300 Spanish soldiers and weapons were landed in the North West. The Jacobite forces were defeated at Glenshiel. James remained in Spain where he had tried to help his adherents who escaped from Scotland getting them placed in Spain where he could.

Our present National Anthem was treasonable in 1714. As first written, as a Jacobite song, it was "God save the King, I pray, God bless the King I pray, God save the King. Send him Victorious, Happy and glorious, soon to reign over us, God save the King. This is why we still sing "Send him victorious" as a part of the original now without point.

The birth of the prince

On the night of the 20th of December 1720 (some authorities give the 31st of December for the date of the Prince's birth, this difference is due to the change in the callender in the 18th century) Princess Clemintina gave birth to a son. At the birth of his Father the Whig propagandists had claimed that the baby was not of royal birth, but a child smuggled into the palace in a warming pan. Hence he was called the Pretender, in his case the Old Pretender while later the Whigs called his son the Young Pretender. The word Pretender is still used apropos Spain in modern times. While in this day and age, not even a very biased Whig would regard the warming pan story as true, in the lifetime of James it was believed by many, and it did harm the Jacobite Cause. The Whigs in general were good at propaganda. With this report on his own birth on his mind, James had as many as seven Cardinals present for the birth of his son.

This happy event raised the hopes of the Jacobites. The signs favoured the birth. That night a storm raged over Hanover, and a new star appeared in the sky. A medal was struck "Spes Britanniae". The infant Prince was christened Charles Edward Louis Phillip Casimer Silvester Maria. By 1722 the first blow had been struck for the young infant. It was known as the "Attenbury Plot". There were many arrests. The Duke of Norfolk being sent to the Tower while the elderly Bishop of Rochester was banished. His chaplain George Kelly burnt papers by a candle flame while he held his enemies back with his sword. Christopher Layer was the only one to meet the death sentence but his was the horrid death of being hung, drawn and quartered. He died bravely.

Spies of the British Government gave out that the child was delicate, deformed, and that death was expected at any moment. Throughout his life spies reported propaganda against him. They reported that Clemintina could have no other child, but a second son was born five years later on 6th March 1725. He was christened Henry Benedict Marie Clement. As with his brother it was the first two that he used. As a small child Prince Charles feared lightning. He was gradually taught to lose this fear. Cardinal Alberoni said "A prince should fear neither man nor devil nor God, as God would rather have us love him than fear him."

For some considerable time there was a rift between James and his Queen. Part of the trouble lay in the differing outlook on the religious instruction of their children. While they were naturally brought up as Roman Catholics. James knowing that if they ever came to the throne they would be in a Protestant country tried to have his son as broadminded as he was himself. James kept two Anglican chaplains for those of his adherents at his court who were of that religion. This with Papal permission. Clemintina was extremely pious and resisted this. The little exiled court was not an easy place. James was greatly busied with letters and other business and usually short of money while Clemintina who had a gay temperament found life dull. She left James for a while and stayed in a convent. This did the Cause immense harm. However after a while the breach was healed and she returned to her husband. She devoted much of her time to pious works and was much loved by the poor.

Often the Prince's spelling has been quoted to show that his education was neglected. Spelling in the 18th century was not standardised as it is today, but Prince Charles was outstandingly poor at it. But he was interested in archaeology and in both ancient and modern history, as well as philosophy. He was musical and played the violoncello with the skill of the professional. He could speak English, French, Italian and Spanish fluently. He is said to have started to play the violin at the age of three. This love of music remained with him all his life, and in exile after Culloden was a source of great pleasure to him when he played French horn and bagpipes. His brother Henry was musical too. They used when they were older to give concerts which had considerable merit. Monsieur de Brosses writes, "Both Princes are devoted to music and understand it thoroughly. The elder plays the violoncello very well, the younger one sings Italian songs with a clear child's voice and in the best taste; they give a concert once a week; it is the best music in Rome and I never miss it. Yesterday I entered whilst they were performing Correlli's famous work, the Notte di Natale, and I expressed my regret at not having arrived in time to hear the whole of it. When it was over and they were about to pass to another piece, the Prince of Wales said, 'No, wait! let us begin again, for I chanced to hear Monsieur de Brosses say he would greatly like to listen to the whole piece'. I gladly inscribe this little incident, as it shows such attention and good-nature". Monsieur de Brosses was a neutral observer, neither Whig nor Jacobite.

Besides music, the Prince played golf, shot and walked endlessly over the Italian hills. To prepare himself for the task of regaining the throne he walked without socks to harden his feet. In the Highlands this training enabled him to keep pace with his Highlanders. As has been mentioned previously, his religious instruction was less happy. The religious views of the little court were mixed. The non Catholic members of his household worshipped in their own way as James kept two Anglican clergy for this purpose. Some of these were inclined to belittle the Catholic faith, and they tried to teach Charles their views. The Catholics pulled the other way. So it is little wonder that he did not have strong religious feelings. However when he was called to see the Pope he was able to acquit himself well and he received the Papal blessing.

In 1734 the Prince was invited to join the Duke of Liria (son of the Duke of Berwick). The Duke was commanding the army of Don Carlos against the Austrians at Gaeta. The young Prince used his Father's old name of Chevalier de St George. The young Prince enjoyed the siege, disregarding the danger in the trenches though cannon balls were fired near him. He was immensely popular with the soldiers, talking to them with ease in their several languages of French, Spanish and Italian. Back in Rome his younger brother aged 9 had thrown away his toy sword in a temper because he could not go to war too. The Duke of Liria wrote of Charles, "The bullets hissed about his ears but he showed not the least concern". Again the Duke wrote, "I wish to God that some of the greatest sticklers in England against the family of the Stuarts had been eye witnesses of the Prince's resolution during the siege, and I am firmly persuaded that they would soon change their way of thinking".

The Prince returned to Rome. In 1735 Princess Clementina died. In 1737 Prince Charles went on a grand tour of Italian cities. He was received with great hospitality. Receptions were given in his honour and in Venice he was treated as royalty when he was received by the Doge and sat on the Bench of Princes when the Grand Council met in assembly. The British government asked the Venetian resident at St. James to leave as a result. At Florence the British envoy made it known that the sending of the Royal carriage to meet the Prince would be frowned on by his government, so caution prevailed but in compensation the aristocracy of Florence made up for this disappointment in their welcome.

The government and its army

At the time of the '45 many of the regular troops were abroad. Cope who was C in C had about 1400 foot soldiers available in various garrisons. He also had some cavalry. However, as was usual in those days, for economical reasons, the horses were out to grass during the summer time and were soft in condition and fat. When Cope marched north he took spare weapons with him, expecting to get further recruits from the men of the Duke of Atholl, Lord George Murray, Glenalmond, MacDonald of Glengarry, and Campbell of Monzie. But he was disappointed and told that men could not be raised in such a hurry, so the spare weapons were returned to Stirling. Cope found that not only did the country people not support him, but they were more than unhelpful. Stores disappeared, and desertions were common, as many as 200 horses disappeared in one night, and with them their drivers. He was misdirected and was in an unfriendly country.

At this date it was the custom for commissions to be bought and sold, or gained by political influence. It was general for the soldiers to be housed in inns rather than housed in barracks. The innkeeper provided bed, beer and food for 4d. per day. Pay was 6d. per day but 2d. was deducted (this did not apply to the Guards). Pay in the Prince's army was 6d. per day with no deductions. The regular army got £30 each year for sickness allowance for each regiment. The doctor got 1gn. a week. A battalion was made up of from 400 to 600 men and a platoon of from 30 men to not more than 48. Discipline was harsh and the army criminal code as severe and as brutal as the civilian one.

The Highland army responded to the pipes, the regular army to the drums and the trumpet. Officers carried a half pike and a sword, the men musket, bayonet and sword. The dragoons were trained to fight on horseback or on foot. They used carbines and pistols when mounted, their swords were used as secondary weapons. Their horses were heavy and very well trained. They would advance at walking pace to the range of the musket. When this was fired the dragoons went to the right and to the left to reform at the rear, while those who had been behind came forward and fired in turn. The drill books of the period gave details of how the reins and sword were held in the left hand, and the carbine in the right when firing, but no contemporary picture shows this. In fact the sword is not shown being held at all when firing. The carbine was protected from the rain by being carried in a bucket under the right pistol holster, the barrel rested on the dragoon's thigh and was made secure with a strap at the front of the saddle. Or it might be hung barrel downwards and secured by a swivel on the belt. Sizing was considered important the tallest were placed in the first and fourth ranks when they formed six deep.

At this date there were neither trained men nor horses to move heavy artillery. Farm horses and farm labourers were pressed for this work. At Falkirk ten guns got bogged down in a lane and never reached the battlefield. At Preston Pans Colonel Whiteford and one old master gunner and some seamen were in charge of the guns, but were overwhelmed after they had fired five rounds. It was after the '15 that General Wade was sent to advise on how to prevent any further Rising, or at least make it less effective. He recommended the Disarming Act. By this weapons were collected, in practice the Jacobite Clans handed in old and useless weapons, hiding those of any value. Faulty and useless guns were even imported from the Continent for the bounty given. The Whig Clans on the other hand gave up their weapons which were good. In the event of the '45 the Whig Clans were not armed but the Jacobite Clans were. Wade advised the building of roads to open up the country, and to allow troops to advance quickly. They being unable to traverse the hills as rapidly as the Highlanders, found themselves at a disadvantage in the Highlands. Wade built 40 bridges and some 250 miles of road. The barracks at Fort Augustus were built in 1716 and were enlarged by Wade. When the '45 came, it was the Jacobite army which used Wade's roads and they were thus able to make their rapid descent on Edinburgh. In 1729 the Government formed the Black Watch, not as regular soldiers, but as a policing force to put down lawlessness and stop cattle lifting. These men wore black instead of the red uniform of the regular soldier. The Black Watch Companies were largely officered by Whig Highlanders, but the force was mixed in sympathy.

Several Jacobites of note joined these companies as they had not expected any Rising. This included Cluny Macpherson the Chief of his Clan. He was later to join the Jacobite forces. In later years the Black Watch became a famous Regiment of the regular army. At this time the Black Watch were enrolled on the understanding that they would not be expected to serve abroad, but when the war with France broke out they were ordered to Flanders. Some deserted on embarkation but they were arrested, tried in London and transported to the Plantations. All the Highland Clans considered this an insult. Many of those thus dealt with had been people of note in their own country, and now sold to slavery.

The clan system; Highland dress; weapons

Up to the end of the '45 a Highland Chief had power and authority over his Clansmen. He might try them and could order the death penalty for crimes which he considered deserved it. He owned the land which was the Clan territory. Some of it he let out to kinsmen, and as Tacksmen they in turn let it out to other Clansmen, keeping some land for themselves and being responsible for such rents as there were. At this date little money changed hands. Much of the rent was paid in kind—hens, cheese, etc. More important was the following the Chief had in time of war. Many, indeed most would be related though perhaps distantly to their Chief. It was usual for him to be consulted for advice on minor and major problems. This ease of approach was helped by the system of fosterage, as the children, especially the likely heir and future Chief, was fostered by some member of the Clan. There he was brought up, by his foster parents along with foster brothers and sisters. In this way he had an insight into the life of the less well off members of his Clan. Throughout his life his foster brothers would help him to the utmost. One Chief of the Macleans was not killed in battle before seven foster brothers had fallen in his defence with a cry of "another for Hector".

Hospitality on a lavish scale was characteristic of the Highlander. It might be a simple black house or in the Castle of the Chief. All travellers account this to be general. Even under extreme conditions the laws of hospitality rarely failed. There was the case of Lamond who killed a Macgregor and who was pursued. Without knowing it, he asked shelter from the bereaved father who had not heard of his loss. When the father heard of the dark deed, his sense of hospitality was such that he did not betray his guest and even helped him to escape. When difficult days overtook the Macgregor he was given hospitality and kindness from the same Lamond.

Each Chief had a number of hereditary retainers. A hereditary piper, a hereditary Bard to recount tales of ancient valour of the Clan, and as important, to recite the descent of the Clan. A Hereditary Standard Bearer and even a hereditary Doctor besides other such retainers. It was not always a case of from father to son, that these hereditary positions descended, it might come from uncle to nephew. In some cases these hereditary positions were held by some one from another Clan as in the case of the Beatons or Macbeths, who were the hereditary doctors to the MacDonalds, up to the end of their great kingdom, and after that the Beatons became doctors to several Highland families—the Macleans of Duart, the MacLeods of Skye, among others. When this hereditary holder of a position was not of the Clan it was usual for them to hold land in the Clan's territory for these offices. The doctor was for the benefit of the whole Clan. In time of scarcity Chiefs would at their own expense import grain.

The Highland dress was usually the philimor or the philibeg. The first is the older form. Here the plaid and kilt are in one piece of tartan some 16 feet long by five feet broad. This is put on the floor on top of a leather belt. The lower half is then pleated. The man lies down on the ground on top of the tartan, fastens the belt stands up and adapts the remaining tartan as he wishes. The bottom half hangs as a kilt, the top may be made into a cloak or carried over the shoulder as a plaid. It can be used as a covering at night. If the work sounds laboured I have seen the putting on of the philimor done in a demonstration and the whole was finished in minutes.

When in Scotland the Prince spoke to the great Gaelic Bard, Alexander MacDonald known in Gaelic as Alasdair Mac Mhaighstir Alasdair. The Prince asked him if he was not cold in the habit (viz. the Highland garb). "I answered I was so habituated to it that I should rather be so if I was to change my dress to any other. At this he laughed heartily and next enquired how I lay with it at night, which I explained to him; he said that my wrapping myself so close in the plaid I would be unprepared for any sudden defence in the case of a surprise. I answered that in such times of danger or during war we had a different method of using the plaid, that with one spring I could start to my feet with the drawn sword and cock'd pistol in my hand without being in the least incumber'd with my bedclothes."

In battle the Chief and his near relations would be in the front rank and be the best armed. He would carry a sword, likely an Andrea Ferrera, pistols likely Scottish though there was a considerable traffic to and from the Continent. Other clansmen might have a pistol that had been cannibalised, i.e. two unsound pistols made into one sound one. The targe was carried in the left arm. It is a large wooden disk covered in leather and studded with brass nails in varying design. (It served as a shield). A sgian dubh, which is a short pointed knife, was carried in the top of the stocking. It rests in a scabbard. A dirk hangs at the right side, but when being used in war it was carried in the left hand with the point coming out by the side of the targe. It carried a small knife and fork used for eating. Some Clansmen might carry a Lochaber Axe. This is a sharp edged blade mounted on a long pole. It has a curved hook at the top; with it a footman could scale a barricade, take a horseman off his horse, with the blade he could kill. The original use for the sporran was to carry meal for food on campaign. It is now used to carry money. The Clan badge worn in the bonnet, is a sprig of a plant, as heather for MacDonald, oak for Cameron.

A Highland charge was alarming even to seasoned troops. The Highlanders first on hearing the pipes play for the advance, each man took off his bonnet and made a short prayer, the bonnet was replaced and they advanced at a run calling out their slogans (Gaelic Clan war cries). They fired their pistols then threw them away and advanced with sword or dirk. The bayonet of the regular soldier often got stuck in the targe leaving the soldier helpless. The speed of the attack and its form caused many well seasoned and more disciplined troops to falter.

Generally, politically, and with religious considerations, the Clans might be regarded as pro-Hanover and Presbyterian or pro-Stuart and Roman Catholic or Scottish Episcopalian. Note that at this date the Scottish Episcopalian Church did not recognise the Hanoverian line and refused to pray for the Hanoverian succession. Since the day of William of Orange it had stood by the claim of the Stuarts. It suffered considerable persecution both by imprisonment and transportations. Services were mostly held in secret and officiated at by itinerant clergy. It was because the Scottish Episcopal church was not at that time in communication with the English Episcopal Church and did not recognise the Hanoverian succession that when the American colonies became independent they sent their clergy to Scotland for the "laying on of hands" as this did not entail taking an oath recognising the King in London. Roman Catholics were likewise persecuted.

The Campbells were a strong Whig Clan. They had risen to power by what many other Clans considered unscrupulous methods and had acquired thus much extra territory and great power. They had got themselves disliked by other Clans and there was a Scottish saying "You never can trust a Campbell". The dislike of this pro-Hanoverian Clan tended to confirm other Clans in their loyalty to the Stuarts. To their old race of Kings they gave unstinting loyalty and under good leaders were splendid soldiers even when the battle odds were against them. Even under poor leaders such as Mar they still fought well.

Prior to the '45 the Highlanders were slowly moving towards more settled times. They were largely a pastoral people whose chief source of wealth was cattle. Lochiel in particular discouraged cattle raiding which had hitherto been a major Highland activity. In these raids, and there were many, and they varied, there was rarely any loss of life except where the owners breathing vengeance came after their beasts. Women were not harmed. The cattle were "lifted" and taken away. The origin of the word "blackmail" stems from the payment of money to keep cattle from being taken. If money was paid for this service your cattle would be guarded, and if taken returned. The origin of the word is from the use of "black" meaning unofficial rent. Rob Roy even had a sliding scale of payments for this service. There was also what is known as tascal money whereby if cattle were stolen a reward would be given to any who restored the cattle and helped to catch the thief. While this sometimes worked when secrecy was guaranteed, Wade reported that the Camerons and some others bound themselves never to take tascal money.

The Highlander had great love for his Chief. After Culloden when many of the estates of the Chiefs were forfeited and themselves in exile, their Clansmen paid as they must the rent to the government representative, and then saved to send a second rent across the sea to their Chief. The government tried to stop this practice. It was due to the non payment of government rent which led to eviction in this area which triggered off the shooting of Colin Campbell the Red Fox which in turn led to the trial of James of the Glen. James of the Glen was a Stuart and was tried at Inveraray (the Campbell stronghold) before a jury of Campbells, he was condemned and hanged at a point near Ballachulish Bridge where his monument stands today. He always maintained his innocence and this has generally been accepted.

Among the Highlanders there was a strong desire for the return of the Stuarts, and with this wish the strongly held belief that a leader would come to them and restore their lost prestige. This belief was the theme of much poetry written by the Gaelic Bards, and they eagerly awaited the coming of their Prince. Mrs. Grant of Laggan writes that the word "Whig" to the Highlander "was used to designate a character of negatives; one who had neither ear for music, nor taste for poetry, no pride of ancestry; no heart for attachment; no soul for honour. One who merely studied comfort and conveniency and was more anxious for the absence of positive evil than the presence of relative good. A Whig, in short was what all Highlanders cordially hated—a cold, selfish, formal character".

The strength of the clans

Here is a list of Clans with their relative strength, and territory shown. Jacobite Clans are marked X, if they were out in the '45 XX. Those who rallied would have done so after the "Fiery Cross" had been sent round the Clan lands. The Fiery Cross was crossed sticks burnt at the end and dipped in blood. The fastest runner ran with it through the territory handing it on in turn to someone fresh. The Clan rallying point would be known to all. It was remarkable how fast the news sped through each clan's territory.

In some cases the Chief was not "out" but their Clansmen fought on the side of the

	Clan	Strength	Territory		Clan	Strength	Territory
	Campbell	3000	Argyll, Breadalbane	XX	Macgregor	500	Perthshire
XX	MacLean	500	Mull, Ardgour	XX	Duke of Atholl Murrays	3000	Perthshire
XX	Maclauchlane	200	Loch Fyne	XX	Farquharson	500	Aberdeen
XX	Stuart of Appin	300	Appin	XX	Duke of Gordon	300	Aberdeen
X	MacDougall	200	Oban	XX	Grants of Strathspey	850	Glenmoriston
X	MacDonald of Sleat	700	Skye	XX	and Urquhart		
XX	MacDonald Clanranald	700	Moidart and Isles	XX	MacIntosh	800	Inverness-shire
XX	MacDonald of Glengarry	500	Glengarry	XX	Macpearson	300	Badenoch
XX	MacDonald Keppoch	150	Keppoch	XX	Fraser	700	Inverness-shire
XX	MacDonald Glencoe	150	Glencoe	XX	Grants of Glenmoriston	100	Glenmoriston
XX	Cameron	800	Lochaber	X	Chisholm	200	Strathglass
XX	Macleod	700	Skye and Isles		Mackenzie	2000	Wester Ross
XX	MacKinnon	200	Skye		Munroe	300	Easter Ross
XX	Duke of Perth	300	Perthshire		Ross	300	North Ross-shire
	Drummond				Sutherland	700	Sutherland
XX	Robertson	200	Perthshire	X	Mackay	500	Sutherland
XX	Menzies	300	Perthshire		Sinclair	500	Caithness
XX	Stewart of Garntilly	200	Perthshire				

Stuarts under cadets or lesser Chiefs. The Murrays of Athol were "out" with Duke William known as Tulliebardine and Lord George Murray. Many of the Gordons fought under Lord Lewis Gordon the brother of the Chief. In the case of the MacIntosh Clan the Chief fought for the government, while his wife raised MacIntosh and Farquharsons (her own Clan) for the Prince.

Preparation

James used to entertain British visitors to Rome. At Dinner he would always choose dishes of British origin such as roast beef rather than Italian dishes. He usually spoke to his two sons in English, and to others in French or Italian. The Jacobites let it be known that there was no law against visiting the exiled Stuarts, and the spies of the British government became uneasy fearing that a "tenderness" as they called it, for the Stuarts might follow.

In 1738 the young Prince asked for his father's permission to make an attempt to regain the throne. At that date his father refused.

James had two agents in Paris to look after his Scottish affairs. They were Lord Semple and Balhaldie. The latter was a nephew of Lochiel, a Macgregor who had taken the name Drummond as his own name was proscribed. Neither of them was reliable. They gave inaccurate and misleading reports of optimistic flavour.

In 1740 James got an excellent agent resident in Scotland, Murray of Broughton who took over from Colonel Urquhart. Murray refused payment for the work he did though it involved him in considerable travel and expense. He tried to unite the Scottish Episcopal clergy when they were divided, he dealt with endless procrastination when he tried to raise money for the Cause from those who professed much loyalty to it. He had helpers who were careless with Cyphers, which in the wrong hands would put others in jeopardy. He was concerned with the purchase of plaids, shoes and hose, which the clansmen would be unable to purchase for themselves, and which their Chiefs would find a heavy expense to provide. There was the problem of targes. Their use had been neglected with the long peace, and while the material was readily available the skill to make them was not so easy to find. Also the work had to be done in secret in order not to alarm the government.

In 1743 Cardinal Fleury was succeeded by Cardinal de Tencin as a guide to French policy. The new Cardinal owed his advancement in part to James and was friendly towards the Stuarts. Officially Britain and France were at peace, so when British troops fought with the Hanoverian troops at Detingen Louis XV was angry. He invited Prince Charles to France and began preparations for an invasion.

James made his son Prince Regent. To his father before his departure he said, "I go, Sir, in search of three crowns, which I doubt not but to have the honour and happiness of laying at your Majesty's feet." Leaving Rome was done in great secrecy not even Henry being in the secret. Officially he was going on a boar hunt. A chaise was at hand with two horses, saddled. After a short while the Prince said he would prefer to ride as he was cold. Murray (John) got himself into a ditch and while being rescued the Prince rode off. The boar hunt carried on and friends in Rome received gifts from this hunt. Someone who resembled the Prince rode through the country and local people were deceived as were the spies of the government of London.

Meanwhile (it was 9th January 1744) the Prince changed into the disguise of a Neapolitan courier and rode through Italy. Disguised as a Spanish officer, he went through Tuscany. Under the name of Graham he reached Paris on the 29th of January. From there he went to Gravelines where he waited in secrecy. His hopes for an invasion were dashed by a great gale which brought disaster to the French fleet.

Not only were ships destroyed but many lives lost. No further fleet was planned for invasion. The Prince continued to live in France staying in Paris sometime with Aeneas MacDonald, a banker who was the brother of MacDonald of Kinlochmoidart. Long weeks of waiting and plotting produced no step further. Louis XV refused to see him.

He was often in want of money and one can imagine bored. In a letter to his father he writes ... "Nobody nose where I am or what is to become of me, so that I am entirely buried as to the public, and cant but say but that it is a very great constrent upon me, for I am obliged very often not to stur out of my room, for fier of somebodys noting my face. I very often think that you would laugh very heartily if you saw me going about with a single servant buying fish and other things and squabling for a penny more or less ..."

Murray went to France in 1744 after the naval disaster of Dunkirk. He met the Prince who told him if no troops were available he would come over to Scotland the following year "though with but a single footman". Murray replied, "but I hoped it would not be without a body of troops." The Prince assured Murray that the English had given the strongest assurance of support. Murray believed he could not depend upon more than 4000 Scots without letting his plan be known and it would be wise to find their attitudes. He believed that some French officers would follow and offered to find out if the Scots Brigade in Holland would do so too. The Prince recognised the unpopularity of a foreign invasion which could unite enemy neutrals and lukewarm friends so was less deterred from coming without troops than Murray.

Back in Scotland Murray tried to organise the Jacobite party in Scotland. Macleod of Macleod expressed great loyalty and declared he would rise for the Prince whether he came with or without assistance. When the time came Macleod not only did not rise, but gave help to the Government. There was a great deal of plotting and meeting in secret in taverns and now that the question came for action MacDonald of Sleat agreed to join and "would endeavour to engage his neighbours". He again did not Rise but helped the Government. The Duke of Perth agreed to Rise whether foreign help came or not, but for the rest of the plotters they wished the Rising postponed. Murray sent the information south to be given to the Prince but it returned to Scotland undelivered. In the meantime Sir Hector Maclean the Chief of the Clan arrived from France and carried with him the details of the arrival of the Prince along with the signals he would give. Maclean had trouble with his feet and in spite of Murray's advice to remain in the country, Maclean stayed in Edinburgh, though attainted for share in the '15, to get special shoes made. He was recognised and arrested. Maclean had suspected Macleod might go back on his word, and if so to challenge him to a duel which he thought Macleod would not fight. With the loss of their Chief the Maclean support weakened, and Macleod did not rise.

Murray writes, "This naturally leads me to observe that no humane, no good benevolent unprejudiced person can reflect upon the Prince for an undertaking which till now perhaps appeared to them rash and inconsiderate, or proceeding from youth and heat of blood, as none will be under the necessity of puzzling his brains why he made the attempt of such consequences to himself and his friends with so small a force."

The Jacobites sent Murray to the West coast to intercept the Prince, he waited all June then returned to the south. The Prince landed never having received the message from the Jacobite to defer the Rising. When he met Murray again the '45 had begun.

Eachdraidh a'phrionnsa na bliadhna thearlaich—The year of the prince
Such was the name given by the Gael to the year 1745.

After the long weary months of waiting, under great secrecy the Prince found Anthony Walsh an Irish merchantman who was prepared to use his ship the Du Teillay to take the Prince over to Scotland. Walsh who came of a Jacobite family arranged that his cousin Walter Rutledge who was in charge of a French frigate, should get letters of marque to sail off the Scottish coast. This second boat was the Elizabeth.

Charles wrote to his father, "... I look upon me to borrow forty thousand from young Waters for to be able to dispatch the messenger back and buying of Broad Swords, which is the only comfort the Prince can give them at present; it is but for such uses that the Prince shall ever trouble the king with asking for money. It will never be for Plate and fine Close; but for arms and ammunition or other things that tend to what I am come about to this country. I therefore wish that the King would pawn all the Princes Jewels, for on this side of the water the Prince would wear them with a very sore heart." The letter is dated 7th March 1745.

The Prince moved to Nantes and stayed there disguised as a student of the Scots college in Paris under the name of Douglas. Other members of the party likewise went to Nantes where they lived in different houses and did not talk to each other in the street.

When finally aboard ship he wrote to his father, "I am to tell you what will be a big surprise to you. I have been, above six months ago invited by our friends to go to Scotland and carry what arms and money I could conveniently get; this being they are fully persuaded, the only way of restoring you to the crown, and them to their liberties ... Your Majesty cannot disapprove a son's following the example of his father. You yourself did the like in 1715."

With the Prince sailed seven men later known as the "seven men of Moidart". They were the Rightful Duke of Atholl who had been attainted for his part in the '15. He was over 60. His Whig brother now owned the estates and went by the name of Duke. So to avoid confusion from here onwards the rightful Duke will be called Tulliebardine, Sir Thomas Sheridan the Prince's old Tutor now 70, the Rev George Kelly who had been involved in the Atterbury Plot, Captain O'Sulivan who was respected as a soldier on the Continent, Sir John MacDonald another Irishman, Aeneas MacDonald the Banker, Colonel Francis Strickland the only Englishman who came of an old family in Westmorland. They waited off Bellisle for their escort and the two ships set sail on 22nd June, 1745.

On the 5th of July the two ships were sailing off the Lizard when they were attacked by a British ship "The Lion". "The Lion" and "The Elizabeth" fought for five hours, the

Prince wished to have the "Du Teillay" go to the assistance of "The Elizabeth" but the Captain refused. After the fight "The Elizabeth" had to return to port as she was so badly damaged. "The Elizabeth" had carried most of the arms. The "Du Teillay" sailed on alone. On the 22nd July they got a pilot at Barra by the name of Macneil. Then sailed to the little Hebridean Island of Eriskay. Before they reached it, Tulliebardine saw a golden eagle, which appeared to follow the ship. He said to the Prince, "Sir I hope this is a good omen and promises good things for us. The King of birds is come to welcome your Royal Highness upon your arrival in Scotland."

They landed on the white sands of Eriskay. The strand of beach is still known as "Coileag a Phrionsa". "The Prince's Strand". As the Prince walked along this strand he scattered some seeds of convolvulus which he had collected on the beach in France before embarking. The seeds scattered thus, germinated, and flowered and seeded in turn, and descendants grow there to this day, though it is not native to the Isles.

The Prince and his party spent the night in a cottage on Eriskay. It was a "black house", that is, a house where the fire is in the centre of the room, and where the smoke escapes where it will, there being no chimney. In some such houses there is a hole in the roof for the smoke to escape, though not directly above the fire, in other houses without this hole the smoke finds its way out through the door or windows or where it can. The Prince not being used to this atmosphere had to go out from time to time to get a breath of fresh air. The owner of the cottage was heard to say, "what a plague is the matter with that fellow, that he can neither sit nor stand still, and neither keep within nor without doors." Later when night fell the Prince went to inspect the bed which was to be used by his old tutor Sherridan. The owner of the cottage said, "That it was so good a bed and the sheets so good that a Prince need not be ashamed to lie on them." Food was in short supply but some flounders were caught to add to the scanty fare.

Messages were sent to Alexander MacDonald of Sleat and to MacDonald of Boisdale at Kilbride in South Uist. The latter knew that Sleat was not going to rise, and suggested to the Prince that he should go home. Whereupon the Prince said, "I am home."

On the 25th of July the "Du Teillay" sailed to Loch nan Uamh. While the boat lay at anchor it was visited by many. Among others was the great Gaelic Bard Alexander MacDonald. He described the scene, "we called for the ships boat and were immediately carried on board, and our hearts were overjoyed to find ourselves so near our long wished for Prince . . . there entered the tent a tall youth of most agreeable aspect in plain black coat with a plain shirt not very clean and a cambrick stock fixed with a plain silver buckle a fair round wig out of the buckle, a plain hatt with a canvas string having one end fixed to one of his coat buttons; he had black stockings and brass buckles in his shoes; at his first appearance I found my heart swell in my very throat . . ."

Kinlochmoidart (another MacDonald) went to the south to get in touch with the Duke of Perth, Lord George Murray, and Cameron of Lochiel. Young Clanranald MacDonald went to Skye to persuade Sleat to rise. He returned to tell of his failure. While the talking was going on about the many aspects of the Rising, and with young Clanranald considering declining to rise, the Prince saw the younger brother of Kinlochmoidart grasp his sword so the Prince turned to him and said, "will you not assist me?" the reply was, "I will and though no other man in the Highlands should draw a sword I am ready to die for you."

It might be well to explain to those not familiar with the Scottish custom of calling people by the name of their lands, as an instance, Donald Cameron Chief of Clan Cameron in 1745 was known as "Lochiel" after his estate of land, just as his successor today's Chief of Clan Cameron is known as Lochiel.

Dr. Cameron the brother of Lochiel came with word that Lochiel thought the Prince should return to France. But Lochiel could not resist visiting the Prince besides he considered it discourteous not to do so, and he was won over, and agreed to call out the Camerons. Had he not done so, it is questionable if there would have been a Rising at all. When word had first reached Achnacary, Lochiel's home, that the Prince had landed, Lochiel was planting trees. These were shouched in, and with the stirring events were never properly planted, so that this avenue of closely growing trees stands as a memorial.

On the 11th of August the party landed from the "Du Teillay". The place was Moidart. Their welcome was enthusiastic and included the dancing of a reel. Today, there is a line of trees, seven in number, planted to commemorate the "seven men of Moidart", those who had come with their Prince from France. If any tree blows down, another is planted to take its place.

The "Du Teillay" was sent off. Shortly afterwards Captain Walsh met two ships off Skye which were laden with oatmeal. He directed the ship to the Prince's service, but though the Highlanders would give their lives, refuse gold in bribes for the Cause, the carrying of meal for the use of the army they would not and little meal was got for the use of the Jacobite army.

Alexander MacDonald the Bard gives a further account of the Prince, "we did our best to give him a hearty welcome to our country, the Prince and all his company with a guard of about 100 men being all entertained in the house of Angus MacDonald of Borradel in Arisaig . . . After we had all eaten plentifully and drunk chearfully, H.R.H. drunk the grace drink in English . . . When it came my turn I presumed to distinguish myself by saying audibly in Erse . . . Deoch Slainte an Righ: H.R.H. understanding that I had drunk the King's health made me speak the words again in Erse and said that he could drink the King's health likewise in that language, repeating my words . . ."

The first skirmish of the campaign was over before the Standard was raised. Cope had

Above: Monument at Glenfinnan.

sent forces from Perth to strengthen the garrison at Fort William. The men were under Captain Scott and Captain Thompson. They marched from Fort Augustus towards Fort William along Wade's road till they came to Highbridge over the river Spean. This was a small bridge where the troops would need to go in a narrow file. A small part of it is still standing. Keppoch sent MacDonald of Tirnadris to hold them while reinforcements were collected. So with 12 men Tirnadris did this. Pipes were heard by the soldiers and Clan slogans. Highlanders were seen and the troops not knowing how many opposed them retreated in disorder. Captain Scott marched his men along Loch Lochy, and when he neared the head of the Loch, the original 12 men under Tirnadris had been joined by others. Scott and his men were halted, there was an exchange of fire, after which Captain Scott surrendered and he and his men were taken prisoners. Scott was wounded and taken to Achnacary, a request with a safe pass was sent to Fort William for a surgeon. This was refused so Scott was sent to Fort William on parole.

Murray of Broughton arrived at Kinlochmoidart around the 18th. In his Memoirs he writes that for three weeks he slept with loaded pistols by his bedside. He conveyed two large boxes of Manifestos he had printed for the Prince whose secretary be became.

The Government having learnt of the Prince's arrival put a reward of £30,000 on his head dead or alive. The Prince would not have wished to retaliate in the same way, but his Highlanders were very insistent that he did so.

The raising of the Standard

The Raising of the Standard was planned for the 19th of August at Glenfinnan which lies at the head of Loch Shiel. When the Prince and his party reached the head of the Loch, not a soul was there to greet him. It was some time before the pipes were heard as the Cameron men and other clansmen arrived. The Banner was of white silk with a red silk surround. Later the words "Tandem Triumphens" were added. It was blessed by Bishop Hugh MacDonald. It was raised by Tulliebardine. The Prince made a short speech in which he said that it would be to no purpose to declaim upon the justice of his Father's title to the throne to people who, had they not been convinced of it, would not have appeared on his behalf, but that he esteemed it as much his duty to endeavour to procure their welfare and happiness as they did to assert his right, that it was chiefly with that view that he had landed. Before that speech Tulliebardine had read out the King's Commission appointing Charles, Prince of Wales, to be sole Regent of his Kingdom of Scotland, England and Ireland.

The description of the Prince on that day was that he was dressed in a duncoloured coat, scarlet breeches and waistcoat, with a yellow bob at his hat. When he had finished speaking and the Banner floated free 1,000 voices called out "Prionnsa Tearlach Righ nan Chaidheil" (Prince Charles King of the Gaels) every sword was raised, bonnets thrown in the air and the pipes skirled.

At the present date, in the little church at Glenfinnan is a plaque in memory of the Prince. One of the later MacDonalds of Glenaladale raised a monument at the head of

Memorial in the Roman

Loch Shiel. Originally raised in memory of those who fought for the Prince it has come to be regarded as a memorial to the Prince himself by common consent. The place is maintained by the National Trust for Scotland. The inscription round the Monument is in Gaelic, English, French and Latin.

In the meantime Cope had left Edinburgh for Stirling. The Prince and his army made its way to Corriearrick. At Abercalder the MacDonalds of Glencoe and the Glengarry MacDonalds and some Grants of Glenmoriston joined. Fraser of Gortuleg arrived with a message from Lord Lovat his Chief, regretting not being in readiness owing to the short notice and the nearness of the Garrisons at Inverness and Fort Augustus.

The Prince marched with his men. He wore Highland dress, and he began to learn Gaelic as he marched. Later when they reached Badenoch a heel came off one of his shoes, his men said they were glad as now they would be able to keep up with him. The long walk over the Italian hills had made it possible for him to out walk his Highlanders. Not only was he good at walking but he was better at mock combat with the claymore (really the Claymore was the older two handed sword, and the broadsword was the weapon of the '45 but the cry of Claymore was still used.)

As the little army approached the Corriearrick the Prince said while tying up his brogues "we will meet with Mr. Cope before I unloosen them." However Cope finding himself in unfriendly country and with a considerable desertion among his men, changed his plans and instead of going to Fort Augustus went off to Nairn and from there to Aberdeen and so to Leith by sea.

At Dalwhinnie a small detachment apprehended Cluny Macpherson. Cluny was a wholehearted Jacobite, but he had become an Officer in the Black Watch. However he needed little persuasion to join the Jacobite army and returned to his home to raise his Clan.

A plan was made to capture Ruthven Barracks but did not succeed. It was noted by Murray of Broughton that while Cope destroyed corn without any compensation the Prince paid for any he took.

On the 13th of August the army reached Blair Atholl. Tulliebardine (the rightful Duke and owner of Blair) had been in exile for 30 years yet from the houses men, women and children came to greet him with great affection some with tears in their eyes. Word had been sent to the castle for it to be ready on their arrival. Mrs. Robertson of Lude arranged for the party to dine at Blair and it was a happy time for Tulliebardine. An interesting sidelight was that at Blair the Prince saw his first pineapple which had been grown at Dunkeld. He had seen none in Italy. He also saw a bowling green for the first time. Some woods were brought and he was shown how the game was played.

On his way to Perth the Prince stopped at Gask. The Laird was a Jacobite but was sorely disappointed with his tenants who did not wish to rise. He was much beloved by them, but it was a byword among them that "Oliphant is King to us". In his annoyance at his tenantry he forbade them to cut the harvest though the corn was ripe. The Prince observed the hanging corn and enquired why it was so, when he heard the reason he cut a few blades with his sword and said, "There, I have broken the inhibition! Now everyman may gather his own."

Perth was reached on September 4th.

Over near Inverness one of the Jacobites' most effective and powerful enemies, Duncan Forbes of Culloden, did much to dissuade many from joining. He had influence over Lovat who had thus forbidden Fraser of Gortuleg from bringing out his 200 men as he had promised. It was Forbes who persuaded MacDonald of Sleat and MacLeod not to rise. However in several clans though the Chief did not rise for the Stuarts their clansmen disobeyed their Chiefs and rose, sometimes under a cadet branch sometimes as individuals. Macleods fought as did Mackenzies though neither Chief was out.

James in Italy sent his second son to France to stay at Avignon to wait for word from the French king. Henry sold his jewels to help his brother's Cause.

At Perth two new outstanding recruits joined. First the Duke of Perth, who was known to be gentle, courteous and kindly. He was a known Jacobite. The Government decided to arrest him. A Mr. Campbell asked to be invited to dinner with the Duke at Drummond Castle, and after dinner he produced his warrant. The Duke saw his guest out of the room first, turned the key in the lock and escaped backstairs and out a window. Outside he found a horse without a saddle but with a halter and on this beast he reached Perth and joined the Prince.

The other new recruit was Lord George Murray who was a younger brother of the Whig Duke of Atholl. A fortnight before joining the Prince he was advising Cope as an ally. His son held a commission in Loudon's Regiment. The change of sides caused some not to trust him, and his haughty overbearing manner did not help. That he did not waver and remained loyal was not fully realised by the men. Again he did not get on well with the Prince. Their temperaments rubbed each other the wrong way. However that was to come. He and the Duke of Perth were both made Lieutenant-Generals by the Prince to command on alternate days.

Perth to Edinburgh

The Jacobite army remained in Perth for some days. The Prince entered the town with 1 guinea left, so a levy was made on the town for £500 which came out of the Common Good Fund. Weapons and targes were required and the wrights were kept busy. One Lindsay by name was paid £30 14s. 6d. for 6 score of targes all of which were paid for. Colonel O'Sullivan was made Quartermaster. However Lord George Murray arranged so far as he could that every man carried a peck of meal and arranged that bread for three days preceded them to Edinburgh. There was some resentment by O'Sullivan over this matter.

While in Perth they were joined by Oliphant of Gask, Lord Strathallan and Lord Ogilvie. Robertson the poet Chief who had fought at Killiecrankie and who was now elderly also joined. One recruit who had meant to join was Mackenzie of Letterewer. He had been out in the '15 and again in the '19 and fully intended to be out in '45, in spite of his wife's remonstrances. To foil him she poured very hot water over his foot, which made it impossible for him to go.

While at Perth the Prince attended an Episcopal service. He showed considerable sympathy for the Protestant religion and wrote his father "I must not close this letter without doing justice to your Majesty's Protestant subjects, who I find are as zealous in your cause as the Roman Catholics, which is what Dr. Wagstaff has often told me I should find them. "In another letter to his father he wrote "I keep my health better in these wild mountains than I used to do in the Campagna Felice, and sleep sounder lying on the ground, than I used to in the Palaces of Rome."

From time to time Councils of War were held to decide the future conduct of the war. At Perth the Council decided to make for Edinburgh. At the Forth they had little opposition. 300 Highlanders were detached from the main body and they made as if to force the bridge so the Gardiners Dragoons were sent to oppose them. Shots were fired, the dragoons went off and the Highlanders retired. meanwhile the main body had crossed the river at a ford.

At Newliston the Prince feared an act of revenge against the house owned by Stair, a descendant of the Stair who ordered the Massacre who had got the house by marriage. Arrangements were made for a guard over the house, the Chief of the MacDonalds of Glencoe came and said his men must do the guard duty, or else go home. "If they were considered so dishonorable as to take revenge on an innocent man they were not fit to remain with honorable men, nor support an honorable Cause." At Corstorphine at the sight of a few Jacobite officers, Gardiners dragoons who had been joined by Hamiltons dragoons from Hamilton, took fright and galloped away as fast as they could. This was known as the Canter of Coltbridge. They continued their flight to Dunbar.

From his camp at Corstorphine the Prince sent a summons to the City Fathers to surrender Edinburgh. There was considerable turmoil in the city. A good portion of the city were either Jacobite supporters or sympathisers. The Provost and his Council wondered when Cope would arrive to remove their difficulty. Word was sent to the Prince to ask for terms, and they were told that all that was required was for the gates of the city to be opened to his army, and to hand over arms and ammunition. They replied they could not answer for the militia which was under control of the castle. They asked leave to consult with the Council and this leave was granted to them. After they left the Prince, he and his council discussed plans to take the city by surprise with as little bloodshed as possible. 500 of Lochiel's men and some Macgregors 900 in all, were to be ready to march. Strict instructions were given "to behave with moderation to the inhabitants and the sogers should not be allowed to taste spirits, and to pay for whatever they got, promising them two shillings each so soon as they rendered themselves Masters of the place". When they got near the city Lochiel had one of his men in a great coat and hunting cape demand admittance at the Gate.

But this was refused. Edinburgh at this date was still a walled town, with suburbs outside the city at Cannongate and Portsburgh. There still remained a little of the Flodden Wall hurriedly built to protect the city after the great defeat. The Jacobite party retired, while it would have been possible to gain the city by force by means of the houses on St. Mary's wynd, but they had been so firmly told to be moderate that they decided to await fresh orders. Before this could be done, a coach was heard approaching the gate. It was the coach that had been used by the Provost's deputy who had been at the Jacobite camp, to ask for time to consider the matter of surrender. The coach was going back to the stables in the Cannongate. The Netherport gates were opened for it, and the Camerons and Macgregors rushed in and took the city by surprise without the shedding of blood. The next morning one of the inhabitants who was up early saw a Highlander beside a cannon, and asked, "surely you are not the same soldiers who were here yesterday" "Och no! she be relieved." It should be stressed the excellent conduct of the Highland army. Whisky was offered freely but no man moved to take it.

Heralds proclaimed James VIII and Charles Prince Regent at the Market cross. The Prince rode into the city between the Duke of Perth and Lord Elcho. He was dressed in a short tartan coat with the star of St. Andrews, red velvet breeches, gold laced bonnet of blue velvet which had a white satin cockade on it. As he was about to enter Holyrood (which was hastily made ready for him) Mr. Hepburn of Keith stepped forward with drawn sword raised, and guided the Prince up the stairs. Mr. Hepburn was held in great regard by Jacobites and Whigs alike for learning and goodness and was known as a keen patriot.

Once the Prince had gained Holyrood he saw to orders for bread to be supplied to his army. Most of the army was quartered at Duddingston.

It was while at Holyrood news reached the Prince that Cope had landed at Dunbar. The Prince said, "Has he by God." On the evening of the 19th it was learnt that Cope had moved from Dunbar and was now at Haddington. Orders were given for the city guard to retire early the next morning while the Prince himself slept with his men at Duddingston.

Before going on to the battle, mention might be made of Bishop Forbes, one of the Scottish Episcopal Bishops. He was arrested as a noted Jacobite and never able to take part in the '45. After his release he collected every bit of information he could of the campaign. He wrote directly to those who took part, and he was meticulous as to details. It is from his notes published by the Scottish History Society (1895) that most of the information of the '45 is gained, particularly information on the Prince's wanderings after Culloden.

Preston Pans

Cope reached Dunbar on the 17th and finished disembarking on the 18th. By the 19th the Prince had moved to Duddingston a village near Edinburgh. The guards who moved out of the city on the morning of the 20th and joined the main army brought with them by order, some surgeons and coaches for the wounded, this because there was every prospect of a battle. As the Prince stood at the head of his army he said, "Gentlemen I have thrown away the scabbard, with Gods assistance I don't doubt of making you a free and happy people" as he said this he drew his sword from the scabbard. "Mr. Cope shall not escape us as he did in the Highlands."

By the afternoon of the 20th the two armies faced each other. The Highlanders were on the high ground but there was a morass of bog and moor and dyke between the Highland army and Cope. Kerr of Hepburn made a reconnaissance and reported it was impassable. At 10.30 that evening a Council of war was held and ways of attack considered. The position was difficult to attack. There was some friction among the Clans. It had previously been agreed that the Clans would draw lots as to which position they would have in the line of battle. Unfortunately the MacDonald Clans who wished to fight together drew the left. Since they had fought on the right side at Bannockburn they expected this honour as a matter of right. The Camerons had drawn the right wing but Lochiel stopped the difficulty and let the MacDonalds have the right. It should be explained it was not the MacDonald leaders who objected to the left wing but their clansmen.

That night the Prince lay down on the field with his men, and like them wrapped himself in his plaid. At 11.30 a Mr. Anderson a new recruit went to Lord George Murray to tell him that he knew a way through the bog as he often shot snipe there. The Prince and his Chief officers were wakened. A Council of war was hurriedly held and it was decided to attack at dawn. They moved off about 4.15 on a misty morning which hid them from the enemy and they were able to reform when they crossed the marsh. The battle lasted 7 minutes. 500 of Cope's men were killed, 1,000 were prisoners, and 900 wounded. On the Jacobite side losses were light.

The Prince stopped the killing and gave protection to the prisoners and wounded. He helped to attend to the wounded and one of his men came up to him and said, "Sir, these are your enemies at your feet." The Prince replied, "They are my father's subjects." Later he wrote to his father about the victory and said, "They ran like rabets and not a bayonet was bloodstained."

Cope went off the field with his men and rode to Berwick. Lord Mark Kerr remarked that it was the first time that a general had been the first to arrive with the news of his own defeat. In defence of Cope it must be said that he had repeatedly asked the government for further supplies and more men and was quite disregarded. But the story of his defeat is immortalised in the song "Hey Johnie Cope" which ironically is used in the British army.

Most of the prisoners were held at Doune Castle, but many officers were set free after giving their word not to fight again against the Stuarts for a year and a day. Cumberland had many officers break this oath, but some refused to do this.

The Presbyterian ministers were given assurances allowing them to preach as usual. In spite of this, many refused to officiate.

£2,000 to £3,000 was found in the baggage. Besides this arms etc. were taken. Among the baggage some chocolate was found. It was not known to the Highlanders and they thought it was medicine and it became known as Johnie Cope's salve. Cope's coach was given to Struan the Robertson Chief. He, being an old man returned home in triumph. He drove as far as he could, and when the road ended his clansmen carried the coach the rest of the way to their Chief's home.

Some men changed their black Hanoverian cockades to that of the white cockade of the Stuarts after the battle. A fine example of the spirit of the Highlanders was recorded by a watcher who saw an ordinary clansman carry a wounded soldier of the enemy to a house and leave 6d. for his care.

Some in the Prince's army wished to hold prisoners, and send word to London arranging a cartel for the exchange of prisoners, with a threat that if this was not granted there would be no quarter given in later battles. While this could have been an advantage in gaining the support of timid Jacobites, the Prince refused on grounds of humanity.

The Castle of Edinburgh was not captured, it was blockaded and threatened with siege. General Guest governor of the Castle in return fired into the city of Edinburgh, not at the enemy but at the inhabitants so the City council came to ask the Prince to call off the seige for the safety of the people of Edinburgh, which he did.

There was then, and it is still a debated point as to whether the Jacobite army should have continued their march south immediately. Many government troops were still around, and the victory had given a great boost to the army. On the other hand by waiting six weeks it allowed a considerable number of recruits to join the main army. During the wait the numbers doubled. These included Mackinnon of Mackinnon from Skye described as brave, honest, and inured to fatigue. Glenbucket, who had been bedridden for three years, got a new lease of life and rode from Aberdeen to Edinburgh though nearly bent double. Pitsligo a scholar much loved in his own country and known for his kindness. In the Lowlands recruits came from all walks of life as can be seen in the records of the Prisoners of the '45 (Scottish History Society).

For a brief spell the Palace of Holyrood saw balls and Council meetings and came alive when the last of the long line of the Auld Stuarts was in residence. Generally in the morning the Prince held a levee and held court being of easy access. Council meetings were held and often lasted a long while as members frequently had differences of opinion. The Prince dined in public with his officers. After that he always visited his army at Duddingston. He would talk with the men, whether of importance or not (not so usual in the 18th century). He saw the army being drilled. He saw that each denomination had the means of worshipping as they wished. He is said to have been to services in both Episcopalian and Presbyterian churches.

The question arose of the march into England. Some again were for separating England and Scotland, but it is doubtful if English Whigs would have accepted this. The Prince wished to go by Newcastle and fight General Wade whose army was about equal in size. Lord George Murray favoured avoiding battle and making for Carlisle to allow the English jacobites to join. Lord George's plan was adopted.

The Jacobite army left Edinburgh on the first of November and was 6,000 strong. The stay in Edinburgh had allowed the Prince to equip his men with weapons and clothing. A small party went to Glasgow to levy money from that city as well as from Edinburgh.

The march south

All the foot both Lowland and Highland wore tartan and had muskets, broadswords, pistols, dirks, and targes. Many of the regiments carried colours and some their Clan banner on a long pole. The cavalry wore their ordinary clothing except the life guard who wore blue uniforms with red facings, scarlet and gold-laced vest and a high red cap with a fur plume. The Huzzars under the command of Major Baggot wore military style tartan. Some of the money for the campaign came from Jacobites who were too old, or too timid to Rise and sent in gifts of money or horses. Money too was levied on some towns and on the forfeited estates.

It is sad to relate that those few sick who were left behind in Edinburgh as too ill to be moved, received brutal treatment from garrison troops. One man was taken from his sickbed and pulled down the stone stairs by his heels with his head striking the stone steps till he died. Every house where a Highland soldier had stayed was looted or destroyed. Those whom it was thought could stand the journey went with the army on litters.

While the Jacobites had been in Edinburgh, word had come of a French ship which had landed at Montrose. On board were some Scots and Irish officers, some small arms and the Marquis d'Aiguilles as an ambassador. He came to Holyrood and met the Prince. The arms reached the army at Dalkeith on the march south.

According to tradition at Kelso the Prince took time to plant a rose bush at Sunlaws a house some 4 miles from Jedburgh. The rose was known as Prince Charlie's rose. It was reported to be still there at the end of the last century.

To confuse Wade the army was divided into two columns. One led by the Prince would march by Kelso on the Northumbrian road turning towards Carlisle at Jedburgh, and the other under Tulliebardine would go by Peebles, Moffat and Lockerbie.

On the 6th of November the Tweed was forded. On the 8th the Prince crossed onto English soil. Murray of Broughton reports that when the men first crossed onto English soil, without any command or other arrangement they all drew their swords before they crossed the Esk and when on the other side turned and looked back to Scotland.

On the 10th of November Carlisle received summons to surrender. Lieutenant General Folliot was in command but previous to his arrival the garrison had been in the charge of Captain Gilpin who had 80 men made up of invalided soldiers, two companies of militia horse of 70, 3 artillery men and about 80 civilians as volunteer gunners. As the Highland army approached Carlisle, Dr. Waugh, Chancellor of the Diocese tried to bestir the government for help for the city. The government sent one soldier, Colonel Durant and he in turn asked for 500 men and was told "That Carlisle was not, or could not be of consequence enough to put the government to the expense of sending an express on purpose". The militia proved to be reluctant to continue serving. It was about then that word reached the Prince that Wade was coming to the relief of Carlisle. He ordered the army to be ready to march to Brampton 7 miles north east of Carlisle. The garrison rejoiced to think that the siege had taken off, but when the Prince realised that the news was not correct as Wade had returned to his winter quarters he called a Council of War. It was arranged that the Duke of Perth and Lord George Murray should return to resume the siege of Carlisle, while the Prince and the other half of the army remain at Brampton to watch Wade to see if he attempted to march towards them.

Lord George Murray's handling of the siege was admired not only by the Jacobites but also by some of the French who saw it. On the evening of the 14th the Prince got news that the city was prepared to surrender. This was arranged by the Duke of Perth and Murray of Broughton. On the 16th of November King James was proclaimed at the Market Cross, and the Prince entered the city.

There was a most unfortunate difference in the Jacobite army. Lord George Murray resented the fact that he had not been sent to arrange the details of the surrender of the city. He had a proud temperament and he handed in his resignation offering to serve as a volunteer. This was accepted by the Prince. Then Lord George Murray said along with some leaders that the Duke of Perth being a Roman Catholic should not be allowed command in case he prejudiced the English Jacobites. The Duke of Perth resigned his command and only commanded his own regiment while Lord George Murray was reinstated as sole commander.

At Kendal it is told that a blacksmith knocked nails into the Prince's shoes and the Prince remarked, "You are the first of your trade that ever shod the son of a King."

Some idea of the discipline in the Highland army can be got from the Orderly Book of the Appin Regiment. The whole was run very much as regiment and certainly not as an undisciplined force. It was usual in the contemporary British army for an orderly from each company to come to the Regimental H.Q. and write down either by copying or dictation the orders for the day. From this practice comes the word Orderly Sergeant. This same method was used in the Jacobite army. Arrangements were made to give them cloth for a coat, tartan for hose, shoes, two new shirts, and a bonnet. Anyone who was taken sick was to apply to an officer for a horse, if hungry or thirsty it was to be the officer's duty who called for either necessity and to see the housekeeper was satisfied. Each company was to have an officer to stop plundering. Besides all this are the dispositions and directions for all regimental duties, etc.

The fear the English had for the Highlanders was fantastic. The Prince stayed at a house and some gentlemen were with him and they heard a rustling. A child of five or six emerged. The mother when she entered the room called out to God to spare the child, the only one of seven to survive. She was under the impression that Highlanders ate children. The Government had used this propaganda in their campaign.

Recruits did not flock to the Jacobite army, as had been hoped. However Manchester proved to be loyal. A sergeant called Dickson, went ahead of the army with a drummer boy and a girl and they recruited men for the Jacobite army. They raised 250–300. In this town there was a friendly welcome. The ladies appeared in tartan cloaks, and wore white cockades.

The Prince was described in Manchester thus, "Attended by a dozen or more nobles and officers of high rank, all dressed in blue coats faced with red, and wearing gold laced hats, marched with a light elastic step which showed he was not in the least fatigued, a tall, well-proportioned, fair complexioned, handsome young man of some five and twenty, dressed in a highland garb, armed with a broadsword and carrying a target on his shoulder. He wore no star on his breast, no ornament of any kind, merely a white rose in his bonnet and a blue silk scarf, yet his dignified and graceful deportment proclaimed at once that it was Prince Charles Edward. The Prince's frame was full of vigour. His features were regular and delicately moulded, his complexion fair, his eyes bright, and blue. His natural blond locks would no doubt have become him better than the flaxen-coloured peruke that he wore, though it suited him. His expression was exceedingly amiable and engaging, and his youth, grace and good looks produced a most favourable impression upon beholders." Usually his eyes are described as brown or hazel, it would appear they differed in varying lights.

The Jacobite army passed out of Manchester on the 31st of October. When they reached the Mersey the Prince waded the river up to the middle, on reaching the further bank of the river he was met by a welcoming group of Cheshiremen and a very old lady, Mrs. Skyring. Her father had fought for the Stuarts during the Civil War. She had seen Charles II land at Dover. She was a devoted follower of the Stuart family. Each year she had put aside half of her income and sent it across the water to the exiled King. It was done anonymously. When she heard that the Prince had landed in Britain, she sold all her jewels, her plate, and all she had of value, and here at the side of the Mersey she handed over the purse. As she saw the prince she said, "Lord now lettest Thou thy servant depart in peace." The deeply moved Prince let her feel his face as her sight had greatly failed her. Shortly afterwards she died when she heard the news of the retreat from Derby. When the Jacobite army reached Macclesfield it was learnt that Cumberland was only about 17 miles away. Cumberland was the son of George II. He was about the same age as the Prince. He had seen considerable fighting on the Continent. He was in command of the Government forces. A council of War was held. It was decided to avoid Cumberland's army and get to London as fast as possible. Lord George Murray managed this manoeuvre well.

Derby was reached on the 4th December 1745. The men were cheerfully sharpening their weapons ready for action. On the following day another Council of War was held. Lord George Murray and some of the other officers wished to retreat. The threat of Cumberland's army who were veterans of Continental wars, added to them there were some 30,000 men gathered at Finchley to guard London, but these men were quite untrained and had been gathered together in a great hurry with the bribe of £6 for each enlistment. At Wetherby, Wade still remained with his troops.

News had reached the Jacobite army that Lord John Drummond, brother of the Duke of Perth had landed from France with 800 Scots from the French regiments, and 300 Irish also from French regiments and a considerable amount of money. Lord George Murray proposed that these new recruits could march south and join the main army. There had been few recruits in England, and some desertions in the Jacobite force. Prince Charles was in despair at this idea of retreat and pointed out that such an enterprise as theirs must not retreat. Opinion is still divided among those interested in the Period. In London the government was in a panic, George II though an unpleasant person was not a coward, but he had everything in readiness for flight. The banks were paying out money in red hot sixpennies. Only two days after the retreat had begun, word came from the Welsh Jacobites of their willingness to rise where and when they were desired. This from their leader Sir Watkins-Wynn.

Another ship coming from France was captured while carrying money and on board was The Earl of Derwentwater. He had been captured and imprisoned with his elder brother after the '15, but he had managed to escape. His son was with him, as was the son of Lord Nairn. They were all tried and executed.

It must be rare in military history when the troops have to be deceived about their own retreat. But it was so in this case.

All through the forward march the Prince had been the first to be ready for the day's march and encouraging others and rounding up stragglers. After Derby it was no longer so, and he would be among the later starters.

The Duke of Perth was for continuing to London and according to tradition Sir William of Park, and James Moir of Stonywood. Papers in London show that not only were the Welsh lost by retreat but that Louis XV then cancelled an expedition to be sent to Scotland with the Duke of York. O'Sulivan too was in favour of continuing. O'Sulivan in his narrative says that when retreat was first suggested to the Prince "To retire Lord George, to retire, why the Clans kept me quite another language and assured me they were all resolved to pierce or to dye".

Retreat

So the retreat began, the weather was harsh in the dead of winter and the country people who had cheered what was a victorious army harassed one which was retreating. Some of the dragoons of Cumberland joined with some of Wade's dragoons and came after the retreating army. There was a skirmish at Clifton which Lord George Murray managed well, and there was no further harassments from the dragoons. When Carlisle was reached there was considerable debate as to whether to leave a garrison there or not. At that point there was still a considerable hope of a return after joining with the newly arrived forces from France. So finally it was decided to leave the garrison which was what the Prince wished. The Manchester regiment volunteered for this job. They were less keen to go to Scotland. Frances Townley was in command, his adjutant Captain Syddall wrote, "it was the opinion of everyone in the garrison who had been on foreign service, that the place was tenable for many days." Charles had received two letters at Carlisle, one from the French King and the other from Lord Strathallan. The former advised against a direct battle till he sent extra troops from France, from Strathallan came the news that the army in Perth were in good form and better than the one that was invading England. There was also Lord John Drummond and his men. The Prince had wished (before leaving Scotland) to have someone at Perth to deal with expected large reinforcements and made Strathallan Commander-in-Chief of the North. Both letters had been very slow to reach the Prince, these two letters must certainly have encouraged him to leave the garrison in Carlisle. The Jacobite army never did return to Carlisle and after the garrison surrendered their treatment by the whig forces was dreadful, some being disembowled while still alive. A foretaste of the aftermath of Culloden.

When the Jacobite army reached the Esk it was flooded and running very high. The Highlanders stood shoulder to shoulder with arms linked. While the Prince was crossing one man was swept away. He was caught by the Prince who called out in Gaelic "cobhair cobhair" meaning help. This shows that his Gaelic had progressed well and was not limited to the weather and such topics.

The Jacobite army reached Glasgow on Christmas day. A levy was made on the city for shoes, stockings and shirts. Glasgow was then a very Whiggish city (now it is said to be the largest Gaelic speaking city). Not only had they refused to pay the full levy demanded before the Jacobite advance (they had only paid £5,500 of £15,000 demanded), they had raised 700 men for the Hanoverians. This body of troops however marched off to Stirling when the news of the Highland army's approach reached them. The citizens of Glasgow jeered and sneered at the Jacobite army and exasperated them. There was traditionally a threat to sack the city. Lochiel stood out against any such course. He is said to have been thanked by the Glasgow magistrates and they promised that whenever the Chief of Clan Cameron visited Glasgow the bells would ring out in welcome. This in fact was done in recent times. The Jacobite army left Glasgow on the 2nd of January after a review of the army.

They marched north. Stirling was reached on the 8th of January 1746. The next battle was fought on the 17th January at Falkirk. The commander of the government forces was General Hawley known to his men as "Hangman Hawley". Before the battle Hawley was entertained by the Countess of Kilmarnock. She had strong Jacobite sympathies, her husband was "out" with the Prince. She delayed Hawley's departure to the field with considerable skill. The Highland army won the race to the top of the hill. Hawley's cavalry fled. This battle is noteworthy in military history as a case where infantry charged cavalry. The victory went to the Prince. The government losses were 280 and the Jacobite losses were 32 killed and 130 wounded. It is said that when Cope heard the news he was able to smile again for the first time since Preston Pans. He also won money on a wager as to the result.

After the victory Lord George Murray called for further retreat. The Prince wished to wait and meet Cumberland there. However he yielded to the ruling of the Chiefs and Lord George Murray saying, "if you are resolved upon it I must yield; but I take God to witness that it is with the greatest reluctance and I wash my hands of the fatal consequences which I foresee but cannot help."

One of the reasons why the Chiefs considered the retreat necessary was that unfortunately there had been a shooting accident and young Angus MacDonnel of Glengarry was killed by one of Keppoch's men. This caused desertions from the Glengarry regiment.

The Jacobite army retreated north, some small skirmishes and victories were won by them, but these were wiped out in the last battle.

At one point the Prince stayed at Moy Hall the seat of the Macintosh Chief. The Chief himself was fighting for the government but his wife who was a keen Jacobite had raised some of her own Clan the Farquharsons and with some of the Jacobite Macintoshes for the Prince. While the Prince stayed with her, Lord Loudon with 1,500 men set out from Inverness to capture the Prince. Lady Ann however had had some of her men watching, and as well as this news of the intended attack was brought to her by a young boy. The Prince was hurried to safety, and the watchers—seven men and a piper dealt with Loudon. They shouted slogans and the piper played, a few shots rang out. Loudon's men did not know the size of the force that opposed them and they fled in disorder back to Inverness. This was known as the Rout o' Moy.

Lady Ann Macintosh had a fine character. After Culloden, Colonel Cochrane came to drive off the Moy cattle. The local parson came to give warning, but arrived after the soldiers, he looked at his watch, a soldier snatched it from him. Lady Ann offered to buy it to restore it, and had her purse snatched from her. It was all she had, £50. A soldier said she had more money which she denied, he struck her in the breast with his bayonet. More would have been done but another soldier came to her rescue, Lady Ann had saved this second soldier from a flogging.

The Prince took ill as a result of the night alarm at Moy. It was pneumonia and there was considerable anxiety for him. He was nursed back to health by Mrs. Anderson. She was an ancestor of Lang the historian. Lang writes that the Prince asked Mrs. Anderson how he could reward her. She asked for a post in the customs for her son. In some way the Prince managed to do this for her.

There is a story too taken from the British Journal of Surgery that the Prince sent a white rose from Rome to the Lady of Nethermurlands (Elrick) and that in 1899 it was still alive but now though the original tree is dead, a shoot was accepted by Her Majesty (now the Queen Mother) for Balmoral. The article was written in 1945.

Culloden, 16th April 1746

The Brahan seer, one Kenneth Mackenzie who lived in the seventeenth century and who was outstanding for his prophesies far into the future, said when going between Inverness and Petty and seeing Millburn, "The day will come when the wheel shall be turned for three successive days by water red with human blood; for on the banks of the lade a fierce battle shall be fought, at which such blood shall be spilt." Again at another time he said, "Oh! Drummossie, thy bleak moor shall, ere many generations have passed away, be stained with the best blood of the Highlands. Glad am I that I will not see the day, for it will be a fearful period; heads will be lopped off by the score, and no mercy will be shown or quarter given on either side." Drummossie was the old Highland name for Culloden.

To counteract the swift Highland charge a new drill was formed and used at Culloden. Previously the third line fired then the centre and the front line last. The front rank knelt and the second and third stood. The left foot of the second and third rank was placed inside the right foot of the men in front. This was called locking. The muskets were fired over the right shoulder of the man in front, after firing, the impetus of the Highland charge broke through this rather cumbersome method so a new drill was practised in 1746 before Culloden. In this new way every soldier covered his neighbour. When done correctly the soldier thrust his bayonet towards the enemy on the right and not straight ahead, thus he did not meet the targe as before, but got the swordsman's uplifted arm. In spite of this and heavy artillery the Highlanders broke through the lines in two places. Belford's firing at Culloden of the heavy artillery was an important role in the battle. It is perhaps noteworthy that no British regiment now carries battle honours for Culloden.

Misfortune had befallen the Jacobite army, money was in short supply, and the men were being paid in meal—and not in great measure, so it was a case of short commons. Many dispersed to look for food.

On the night of the 15th April (it was Cumberland's birthday), the Jacobite army Council headed by the Prince, Lord George Murray and the Chief officers decided on making a night attack on the Hanoverian forces. They started to march at 8 o'clock in the evening. There were delays and at 2 in the morning Lord George Murray decided they would not reach the camp before morning though they had only 4 miles to go, and the ground was easier and they should surely have made it in 2 hours. The first that the Prince knew of the retreat back to Culloden was when he met some of the Duke of Perth's men returning. The Prince saw the Duke of Perth who told him Lord George Murray had returned some three-quarters of an hour ago. So they returned back to the moor. The Prince did not want to fight that day but was over-ruled. There are other accounts saying he did wish battle. After such a defeat as followed and this lapse of time, proof is difficult, but in the Lyon in Mourning, the Rev, George Innes states definitely that he did not wish to fight that day. The Jacobite army was hungry and tired for any battle. Many slept through the battle. It was over in twenty minutes and was a total defeat for the Jacobites. A word should be said of the gallant behaviour of the Irish Pickets who covered the retreat of many.

At Culloden the MacDonalds were not given the right wing. For many years historians claimed that as a result the Clan sulked and did not charge. However within recent years the Forestry Department came on the MacDonald graves which showed they had fought and died on the battlefield.

The treatment given to the Jacobite wounded and prisoners was dreadful. Prisoners were given no food or water for the first two days. Many had been stripped of their clothes and some died of cold, some from starvation. The dead and dying were left till there were a number to bury. Some forty wounded Jacobites took refuge in a barn and they were burned alive. Jacobite prisoners who were wounded received no care. The trials were all held in England.

The Chief of Keppoch fell on the battlefield, and so did the Chief of the Macgillivrays. After the battle his waistcoat was stripped off him and taken by a soldier. His Colonel met him wearing it and said, "I met in the field of battle the brave man who wore it and it shall not now be degraded." The first that Clan MacLauchlan knew of the disaster and death of their Chief was when his riderless horse returned to Castle Lauchlan in the Loch Fyne area.

The Duke of Perth was badly wounded but escaped and died on board a ship on the way back to France. Lochiel was badly wounded but escaped to France where he died in 1748. Lord George Murray escaped to the Continent and died in 1760. Glenbucket escaped to Norway and died in 1750. Donald Robertson of Woodsheal who led the Robertsons escaped. Lord Pitsligo stayed in Scotland and had many adventures, and was nearly captured many times. Sir Thomas Sheridan died in 1746 on the Continent. Donald Macleod of Bernera was 51 in 1715 when he was out, and was again out in 1745 and died aged 90.

The following were executed, Lord Lovat, Lord Balmarino and Lord Kilmarnock. Hereditory jurisdiction was ended and many estates forfeited, and some restored in 1784.

The banners of most of the Clans were captured at Culloden and burnt by the public hangman in Edinburgh. The Banner of the Appin Stewarts was saved and returned to Appin. It is now on view in the Museum at Edinburgh Castle. The Banner of the Ogilvie Regiment was also saved and is now in the Museum in Dundee. The Macpherson Clan Museum has a Banner which may have been used in 1745, the Clan being "out" but not at Culloden. The Cameron Banner was saved and is at Achnacarry Castle. A Glenaladale MacDonald Banner is to be seen in the little Roman Catholic Church at Mingarry in the Moidart Peninsula. It can't be claimed that it is the actual Banner of the '45 but is of interest. The 1745 association has a replica of the Banner flown at Glenfinnan but with motto added.

The Government measures to the Highlanders not on the battlefield were harsh in extreme. They had a bad fright and reacted strongly. Cattle were driven off the homes burned, corn destroyed, old men flogged and children killed. Often this happened to those who had taken no part in the Rising. Many were transported. Everywhere the Scots and particularly the Highlanders were hard hit. This again affected not only the Jacobite Clans but Whig Clansmen as well. Even as late as the early days of this century when children went to school from Gaelic speaking homes knowing no English, they were thrashed if they used Gaelic not only in the classroom but even in the playground.

The wearing of Highland dress was prohibited, regardless of which tartan, Whig or Jacobite. People were liable to be transported if seen wearing tartan or Highland dress. Where other clothes were to be got and paid for among the poor crofters and what hardship it must have entailed can be imagined. It was not until 1782 that the ban on the wearing of the tartan and Highland dress was lifted, this through the efforts of Graham, Marquis of Montrose.

There is an anniversary service held at Culloden each year on the 16th of April. The whole battle area is now under the care of the National Trust for Scotland.

Dr. Johnson in his day said, "If England was fairly polled the present King would be sent away tonight and his adherents hanged tomorrow." In our day Culloden would appear to be an end of any chance of the Restoration of the Stuarts, but that is using hindsight. In the 18th century the government was always at the ready and watching. There were a number of Jacobite plots and plans which did not come off. By the way there is a suggestion first raised by Hazlett in his essay, "Of Persons one would wish to have seen" as to where Dr. Johnson was in the years 1745 and 1746. "He did not write any thing that we know of, nor is there any account of him in Boswell during these two years—He seems to have passed through the scenes in the Highlands in company with Boswell with lack-luster eyes yet as if they were familiar to him, or associated in his mind with interests that he durst not explain."

The hunted prince: Part 1—The mainland

The first place that the Prince and his small party made for was Gortuleg in the Stratherick district about ten miles from Fort Augustus. It was one of the outposts of Clan Fraser, and here they met the Chief of the Clan, Simon Fraser, Lord Lovat. He was preparing a banquet for the anticipated victory of the Jacobite army. Throughout his life he had played a dubious part, dealing first with one party and then with the next. He was not greatly trusted by either, nor in fact by any outside his own Clan. Among his own clansmen he was highly thought of, he was extremely hospitable to all his Clan from the greatest to the least important. At heart he was a Jacobite, and the Clan had been out under his son. When he learnt from the party of the terrible disaster that was Culloden, he did what he could for the fugitives and tried to put fresh heart into them, speaking of the eleven reverses that Bruce had sustained before the victory of Bannockburn.

After leaving Gortuleg the Party divided. Lord Elcho and the Prince's ADC Alexander Macleod left the rest, and others consisted of the Prince, Sheridan O'Neal, O'Sulivan and Edward Burke who acted as guide. Ned Burke was born in South Uist. He had been a sedan chair carrier in Edinburgh. To him and to many painfully poor people there was never the slightest temptation to claim the £30,000 offered by the government for betrayal. The party made for Invergarry, which they reached in the early morning of the 17th. Ned Burke found two salmon which he boiled with some oatcakes which gave them a meal.

We now come to the complexities of differing information. On the 16th in the evening the Prince had written to Cluny "You have heard no doubt ere now of the ruffle we met with this afternoon. We have suffered a good deal; but we hope we shall soon pay Cumberland in his own Coin. We are to review tomorrow at Fort Augustus the Frasers, Camerons, Stewarts, Clanranald and Keppoch people. His R.H. expects your people will be with us at furthest Friday morning. Dispatch is the more necessary that his Highness has something in view which will make an ample amends for this day's ruffle—I am, Dear Sir, Yours etc. Gortuleg April 16, 9 at night." Other sources speak of rallying at Ruthven, or that no rendezvous had been previously planned. On the afternoon of the 17th they rode into Cameron Country to Glen Pean and stayed the night with Donald Cameron. They were joined later by Father Allan MacDonald. It was here that the Prince received a letter from Lord George Murray. In it he bitterly reproached the Prince for the whole enterprise and said it should not have been begun without French help. He handed in his resignation. It was likely that it was this letter that shattered the hopes that the Prince had for rallying the Clans and that he must first get to France to get help to save Scotland. In "The Lyon of Mourning" a Captain O'Neil says that the Prince had said Fort Augustus as rendezvous and that he waited there on the 17th. It was after the receipt of Lord George's letter that the Prince wrote to the Clans to have every man fend for himself.

The Prince and his party moved towards the West Coast and met with other fugitive Jacobites. It was at this time that the Prince first met Donald Macleod. Neither he nor his Chief had been "out". Donald had gone on a visit to Inverness to get meal to take to Skye. When he was there the Jacobite army marched into the town. Shortly afterwards he was captured by the MacDonalds of Glencoe. His sword was demanded of him, but the MacKinnon Chief who knew Donald said he was a good man, and so he was allowed to keep it. Donald became committed to the Cause and he and Aeneas MacDonald went to collect gold which had been landed at Barra.

When Donald landed in Borrowdale he met the Prince who asked him "Are you Donald Macleod of Gualtergill in Skye?" Donald replied, "Yes, I am the same man, may it please your Majesty, at your service. What is your pleasure with me?" The Prince said, "Then you see Donald I am in distress. I therefore throw myself into your bosom, and let you do with me what you like. I hear you are an honest man and fit to be trusted."

The first thing that the Prince wished Donald to do was to go with letters to Sir Alexander MacDonald and the Chief of the Macleods under the impression that these two would help him. However Donald refused to do this commission and said "Does your excellency know that these men have played the rogue with you altogether and will you trust them for a' that? Na you mauna do't."

There was a rumour at this time that the Prince was on St Kilda, and warships were sent to the island. The inhabitants had never heard of the Prince and all they knew of the great outside world was that their Chief had been at war "with a great woman abroad" probably Maria Theresa.

As the next thing that the Prince asked of Donald was to go to the Isles, this was made somewhat easier by so many ships being sent to St Kilda. Donald was a fine sailor though over 70 years. The party to cross consisted of the Prince, O'Neil, Ned Burke, O'Sulivan, Father Allan MacDonald and a crew of seven, Donald Macleod and his young son Murdoch. Murdoch had been a school boy at Inverness, but had run away from school and had got hold of a pistol, sword and dirk to fight at Culloden and was thus now in the heather along with his father.

The boat which Donald got had belonged to the son of MacDonald of Borrowdale who had been killed at Culloden. They set off on the 26th of April. Donald foretold a coming gale and was reluctant to make the crossing however the Prince pressed him to carry on. A storm raged. It was not possible to return to land and Donald said "It is not as good for us to be drowned in clean water, as to be dashed in pieces on a rock and drowned too." As they passed Arisaig point their bowsprit broke. The distance to the Isles was about 70 miles and they sailed on without a compass in a dark night. At the beginning of day they could see the Isles. They are known as the Long Island and stretch from the Butt of Lewis to Barra Head with several interruptions by the sea. Though very sea sick the Prince bore up well and never lost courage. They landed on Rossinish on the Island of Benbecula on 27th of April.

In the meantime Murray of Broughton had not made his escape but had stayed to deal with gold which had come from France. This treasure known as the Loch Arkaig treasure caused great trouble among Jacobites. Some think there may still be gold buried there, but generally most of it appears to have been accounted for. Murray was a woefully sick man. He was captured. He had worked hard for the Cause but he did give evidence against Lovat Fraser. Whether Lovat would have been proved guilty without this evidence is not certain. From then on Murray was without friends and called Mr. Evidence Murray—yet none who had truly served the Cause was betrayed by him. Ned Burke later returned to his old job in Edinburgh.

The hunted prince: Part 2—In the Isles

At Rossinish the party, all of them drenched, found an empty hut where they made a fire to dry their clothes. A cow was killed and its flesh boiled in a pot Donald had brought. The sail of the boat was spread on the floor of the hut, and they all slept upon it. Word was sent to old Clanranald who advised that the Prince and his party should go to Stornoway in the disguise of shipwrecked seamen from the Orkneys. On the 29th of April they set off and got to Scalpay off the Island of Harris. The tenant of the Island was a Campbell, notwithstanding his name he proved a friend. He had married a MacDonald. A Presbyterian minister the Rev. Macaulay (grandfather of the historian) heard of the arrival of the Prince and wished to get the reward, sent word to his father in Harris, who in turn alerted the minister in Lewis. Macaulay made an attempt to capture the Prince while on Scalpay but was prevented by Donald Campbell. While he was on Scalpay, one of Donald Campbell's cows got stuck in a bog. Young Kenneth, Donald's son went to her rescue but without any success so the Prince flung off his coat and joined in the rescue wading into the peaty bog and got the beast out safely.

Meanwhile Donald Macleod set off for Stornoway in Campbell's boat to get a boat to go to the Mainland. He made arrangements and word was sent to the party at Scalpay. By boat they got to Loch Seaforth, and from there they walked. The guide lost his way and they walked 38 miles over the Lewis moors. Finally, near Stornoway they rested and the guide was sent to Donald to bring food. He came with this and then took them to the home of Mrs. Mackenzie of Kildun who befriended them. They had some much needed sleep. It was while the party was at Kildun that Donald returned to Stornoway. The people there had heard that the Prince had an army of 500 men with him, whereupon Donald told them that the Prince had two companions, and that when he joined them there would be three. The Stornoway men, mostly Mackenzies, had Jacobite sympathies but their Chief had not been out. They did not wish the Prince harm, nor to claim any reward, but they wished him gone and would not let him have the use of the boat bought for £500. Donald returned with the news. One of Mrs. Mackenzie's cows was killed and she had to be pressed to take money for it. When they left she gave them bread, butter and beef, meal, brandy and sugar. A platter was already in the boat for making dough. Two of the boatmen had gone home, but Campbell's boat being lighter than Donald's they managed. They went to the deserted island of Iuhbard. It was used by fishermen, and they saw some there drying fish. The fishermen went off afraid that the new boat was that of the pressgang. The Prince and his party stayed there for four days. The fish were eaten but money was left to pay for them. It was the Prince who cooked the fish and he used some of the butter given by Mrs. Mackenzie which had come between two fardles of bread. When the bannocks were being made by Ned the Prince told him to "take the brains of the cow and mingle them well in amongst the meal and when making the dough" this was done then "he gave orders to birsle the bannocks well, or else it would not do at all". Donald thought the new mixture was very good. From this little island they moved off, and with no wind rowing had to be done. The Prince sang and kept up their hearts, later a wind rose, and the sail could be used. The only food was dramach which is oatmeal and water, in this case, salt water. They had three nights on an island off Benbecula. They had been pursued by a war ship. The island where their shelter was as Burke said "we came to a poor grass keeper's bothy or hut, which had so laigh a door that we digged below the door and put heather below the Prince's knees, he being tall, to let him the easier into the poor hut". Word was sent to Clanranald and he and Neil MacEachain from Corrodale who advised a stay in that wild area.

Next night they set off being guided by MacEachain they went about 20 miles while Donald took the boat round by sea. The Prince and his party remained at Corrodale for 22 days. Donald went off to get some of the Loch Arkaig gold. The time passed reasonably. The Prince was a good shot, soon he became good at fishing for lythe or rock cod. For short spells he enjoyed sitting in the sun on a rock. At times he was melancholy, at others he was gay and danced Highland reels to music which he whistled. During his wandering he enjoyed smoking. His clay pipes broke easily but he mended them using the quills of birds, putting one into the other, making a long enough stem for a cool smoke. He was visited by MacDonalds while at Corrodale. But their refuge became less secure when two armed sloops, "The Furnace" under Captain Fergusson and the Baltimore, which were armed with troops, and along with them were many government boats, cruising between the Long Island and Skye. His friends were afraid for the safety of their Prince. At Corrodale help had come from his official enemies. Sir Alexander MacDonald of Mugstatt was in the militia but his wife was a Jacobite and sent information and newspapers. Also in the militia was MacDonald of Armadale. He had a stepdaughter Flora. She usually lived in South Uist with her brother where she was then, but she often visited her mother in Skye. It is not certain who first planned that Flora would take the Prince to Skye in the disguise of her servant "Betty Burke". At first Flora hesitated for fear she would bring trouble on her friends, but once she had accepted the task she never faltered.

Neil MacEachain (the father of one of Napoleon's Marshals, Duke of Tarentum), along with O'Neil led the Prince to near Ormaclete where Flora's brother had his shieling. She agreed to help and left to get a passport for "Betty Burke" MacEachain and herself. When she went to cross the Ford between South Uist and Benbecula it was guarded. She had no pass and was arrested. She had arranged to send word back where to meet. When no word came, the Prince sent MacEachain to find out what had happened. He too was arrested. Both were brought before the Captain of the Militia who was Flora's stepfather. He made out the passports and wrote to his wife "I have sent your daughter from this country lest she should be frightened by the troops lying here. She has got one Betty Burke, an Irish girl, who she tells me is a good spinner. If her spinning please you, you may keep her till she spins all your lint or if you have any wool to spin you may employ her."

At Nunton (home of Lady Clanranald) Flora and Lady Clanranald set to make a dress suited to the Prince's size, he was 5′ 10″ and no suitable dress was available. Flora decided the Prince should stay at Rossinish till the dress was finished. It was a troublesome job for the Prince and MacEachain to get there. They took refuge in a hut, but during the day they had to move out as the militia called for milk. The Prince lay on a rock alternately lashed by heavy rain or when that stopped eaten by midges. When the place was clear they returned to the hut where a good fire warmed them and dried their clothes. O'Neil had gone with a guide to escort the two women, and act as go-between between them and the Prince, the guide returned with a chicken. Word came from the boatmen that they were ready for the Skye trip. The Prince was cooking supper, when Flora and Lady Clanranald arrived. A small dinner party started, but it came to an end hurriedly when word came that soldiers were only three miles from the hut. They got in the boat and got to the side of Loch Uskavagh at five in the morning. The remains of the dinner served as breakfast. Then they heard that Captain Ferguson was at Nunton demanding to see Lady Clanranald. She returned home at once saying she had been to a sick child. Now it was time for O'Neil to take leave, as he had no passport. On the 28th June the Prince dressed in his disguise which he found awkward to put on. At 8 o'clock that evening they set off by boat and ran into a storm. During the voyage the Prince kept up the spirits of all by singing and telling stories. Flora afterwards used to tell how he guarded her from any disturbance when they moved about the boat to attend to it. She spoke too of his courtesy to her.

When they reached Skye, Flora through caution went to the house of Lady Margaret MacDonald. She left "Betty Burke" on the shore taking with her MacEachain as her Servant. When she got there, she found Lady Margaret had guests, these included Mrs. MacDonald of Kirkibost (who had prepared her hostess), Mr. Macdonald of Kingsburgh, factor to Sir Alexander MacDonald (husband of hostess) and Lieutenant Macleod, Son of Balmeanach who was Captain of the Militia, of the area. Macleod had four men with him. Flora had to stay and talk. Lady Margaret, on pretext of business, got Kingsburgh alone and told him her problem. It was decided that the Prince should stay over night with Kingsburgh and to go to Portree next day, and from there to Raasay. Donald Roy was asked to help. he had been "out" and in spite of a wound in the foot he rode off to make arrangements. Kingsburgh went to find the Prince and discuss plans. He met a tall ungainly woman striding to meet him. After a brief meal they set off for Kingsburgh which was a distance away. The Prince's stride made it rather obvious he was in disguise and Kingsburgh said "they may call you the Pretender but I never saw anyone so bad at your trade." When they came to a burn the Prince lifted his petticoat high but at the next he let them float on the water.

It was late at night when they reached Kingsburgh. Flora had already arrived on horseback. Mrs. MacDonald was in bed but sent down word that Miton's daughter was to use what she wished. Mrs. MacDonald's small daughter ran up to her mother and said, "the most muckle ill-shaken-up wife she had seen in all her life was walking up and down in the hall." Kingsburgh himself came up to see her, Mrs. MacDonald asked, "do you think the stranger will know anything of the Prince?" her husband said, "my dear, it is the Prince himself." "Then we shall all be hanged" to which he replied, "we can die but once, could we ever die for a better cause." Kingsburgh then said for her to get bread and cheese. The idea of sitting at a table with her lawful sovereign shook her more than did the danger, and the standard of the meal for such an occasion distressed her too. But to the Prince the pleasure of being with friends and fire and food must have been very welcome. He slept that night in a bed and did not waken till mid-day. As he had arrived at the house as "Betty Burke" so he left it thus and changed when some way away. He went with Neil MacEachain and a herd boy as guide. Flora rode to Portree about 7 miles away. At Portree, Donald Roy had met Rona and Murdoch Macleod sons of Macleod of Raasay. They were more than willing to help. The plan was for Rona and two boatmen to bring a boat to a place about a mile from Portree. Flora and Donald Roy waited at the only inn. When it was dark the Prince arrived soaking wet. He had some food, dry clothes and tobacco and was to say farewell to Flora and set off. On the way to the boat they met Captain Malcome Macleod of Brae who had fought under Macleod of Raasay.

On reaching Raasay the Prince stayed in a hut while young Raasay went for food. The Prince expressed a liking for oatbread which he called his own country's bread. The arrival of a stranger on Raasay caused the Prince to go to MacKinnon country on Skye. With Captain Macleod landing 2 miles from Portree. That night the party of the Prince, 3 Macleods and 2 servants dined on bread and cheese. During the night the Prince had a troubled sleep and called out Oh God Oh! Scotland! and sometime Oh! poor England, but later he slept peacefully. With Captain Macleod for company the Prince assumed the name of Lewis Caw. The real Lewis Caw had been "out" and was in Skye at the time. As Lewis Caw the Prince acted the part of servant to Macleod. They made for Macleod's brother-in-law's home who had been "out". Mrs. MacKinnon was not told who he was, but she said, "there was something about the lad she liked unco well." Macleod met his brother-in-law John MacKinnon who with Macleod decided that a boat should be got to take the Prince to the Mainland. MacKinnon set off to arrange this, and met his Chief on the way. Though the Chief was not a young man but somewhere between 60 and 70 he insisted on going with his Prince to the mainland, so with the chief and 4 boatmen and John MacKinnon, Mallaig was reached.

The hunted prince: Part 3—The mainland again
After landing on the mainland MacKinnon went to find Old Clanranald, who refused help, distressing MacKinnon more than the Prince. They saw MacDonald of Morar whose home being burnt now lived in a bothy. He and his family welcomed them and gave them a meal, after that MacDonald took them to a cave, and himself went to see old Clanranald, he returned less cordial but got them a guide to Angus MacDonald of Borrowdale where they were truly welcomed. He was living in a cave and recovering from wounds received at Culloden, but he still wished to serve.

The two MacKinnons left for home, both were arrested and imprisoned till 1747. Borrowdale's nephew MacDonald of Glenaladale was told of the Prince being in the area, and a more inaccessible cave was chosen. Then Borrowdale's son-in-law, Angus MacEachain told them that it was known the Prince was in the area and he suggested it would be safer if he moved to Meoble in the Morar district. They spent a night there, that is Glenaladale, Borrowdale and Borrowdale's son John. MacEachain was able to tell them young Clanranald was near and offered a refuge. Borrowdale set off to find food and reported that General Campbell and six men of war were in Loch Nevis and Captain Scott had landed at Arisaig, an encircling movement had begun. In haste the small party made up of the Prince, MacDonald of Glenaladale, his brother John and John Borrowdale's son, made off to the North East. Troops were at Loch Arkaig so a new route was taken. It was known that Donald Cameron of Glen Pean was in the area and as he knew the area well his help would be asked. John MacDonald had gone to get news but before either met up with the party, a warning that 100 Argyll militia were at the foot of the hill, made them set off at once.

By chance they met Donald Cameron of Glen Pean. He told them of 27 small camps at half mile intervals from Loch Eil to Loch Hourne. The camps were connected by sentries who were within call of one another. At night large fires were built which made it difficult to pass unseen through the line. Under the guidance of Glen Pean they walked through the night, resting by day on a hill known as Sgor Choileam and were joined by Glenaladale's brother John. They moved off in the evening and reached Coire nan Gall in the early morning, and from there to Meall an Spardan in Knoidart. They rested in a crevasse. The area had many troops, and in spite of the glowing fires they tried to get through the line of troops, passing so near them that troops could be seen and heard. Donald Cameron led across the glen and up a ravine. When they came to a burn which poured down a precipice the Prince slipped while crossing and Glen Pean managed to catch him. A little cheese and oatmeal which John had brought was their only food, which they ate hungrily. From here a guide was needed as well as food, Glenaladale went to look for both. He got salty cheese and butter which was gladly eaten.

They went through Glen Shiel with a guide, Donald MacDonald, using Wade's road till through the pass, then took to the moor. In the morning they were on a hill in Strath Clunie where midges tormented them, followed by heavy rain. In the evening they moved to Glenmorriston. It was there that the Prince joined the seven men of Glenmorriston. These men had banded together after seeing the treatment given to those who surrendered.

The Cairn at Loch nan Uamh. It was from this place the Prince left Scotland.
The Cairn was built by the 1745 Association.

Many of their clansmen had done so, and had been shipped to the plantations (that means sold into slavery) all the possessions of theirs and kinsfolk taken, besides the many put to death. The Prince stayed with these men for three weeks. They told afterwards how he improved their cooking and reproved their swearing. While the Prince stayed in Glenmorriston, a young man, Roderick Mackenzie who resembled the Prince was surrounded and as he was attacked called out "vilans you have killed your King" his head was cut off by the soldiers who took it for identification to claim the reward. While this was pending it gave the Prince a much needed breathing space.

The seven men were 2 MacDonalds, 3 Chisholms, a Macgregor and a Grant. They were later joined by Hugh Macmillan. The Prince joined them on July 18th and he stayed with them in first one cave and then another. He was in the Strathglass country of the Chisholms. On August 15th they reached Loch Arkaig, having travelled by Glenmorriston and Glengarry, MacDonald of Lochgarry joined them. He offered the opinion that the clans might rally again. The plan was raised to Cluny and Lochiel and Lochgarry returned with Dr. Cameron to say neither thought there was any possibility of a rally at this date.

When Dr. Cameron, Lochiel's brother and the Rev. John Cameron, Presbyterian chaplain at Fort William saw the Prince he described him as "barefooted, had an old black kilt coat on, philabeg and waistcoat, a dirty shirt and a long red beard, a gun in his hand, a pistol and dirk by his side. He was very cheerful and in good health, and in my opinion fatter than when he was in Inverness."

It was suggested that the Prince stayed in "Cluny's Cage" in Benalder. This was reached on the 15th of September. It was hidden from view and was described by Cluny's brother "there were first some rows of trees laid down in order to level a floor for the habitation, and as the place was steep this raised the lower side to equal height with the other; and these trees, in the way of jests (sic joists) or planks, were entirely well levelled with earth and gravel. There were betwixt the trees, growing naturally on their own roots some stakes fixed in the earth, which with the trees, were interwoven with ropes made of heath and birch twigs all to the top of the cage, it being of a round or rather oval shape, and the whole thatched and covered with foge (sic foge; moss little dried grass). This whole fabric hung, as it were, by a large tree, which reclined from the one end all along the roof to the other, and which gave it the name of the Cage; and by chance there happen'd to be two stones at a small distance from other in the side next to the precipice resembling the pillars of a bosom chimney, and here was the fire placed. The smoke had its vent out there, all along a very stony plat of the rock, which, and the smock were all together so much of a colour that any one could make no difference in the clearest day, the smock and stones by and through which it passed being of such true and real resemblance. The cage was no larger than to contain six or seven persons, four of which number were frequently employed in playing cards, one idle looking on, one becking, and another firing bread and cooking."

From the Cluny Charter Chest it is described as having two rooms, the upper a "salle-a-manger" and bed chamber while the lower contained liquor and other necessities. The whole construction was screened by a dense thicket of hollies. During the Prince's stay he enjoyed the company as did those around him. He stayed there till September 13th. Then he left the area for Moidart. On the 19th of September he left Scotland never to return. The name of the boat he sailed on was ironically called "L'Heureux". The year of the Prince was over. At Loch nan Uamh there is a Cairn at the point of departure. It was put up by the 1745 Association, which is an Historical Association open to those interested in Scottish History in general, but more particularly to the Jacobite period.

Grant Francis who had access to the Cluny Charter Chest found information which appeared in his book "The Romance of the White Rose" that the Prince collected as much money as he could for the relief of those Jacobites who were in need in Scotland. The Prince raised £750 plus plate and jewels to be sold for the same cause. Cluny was told of the hiding place of the Loch Arkaig treasure which was also to be used. The Prince asked him to stay in Scotland to distribute money.

Flora MacDonald was imprisoned at Dunstaffnage and then in a boat off Leith, then London. On her release she returned to Skye where she married Allan MacDonald. They emigrated to America in 1774 but returned to Scotland in 1778. Dr. Johnson met Flora. Of her he said, "A name that will be mentioned in history, and, if courage and fidelity be virtues, mentioned with honour." Lady Ann Macintosh mounted on horse was taken to Inverness. On the road she saw dead and dying men, women and children left by Colonel Cockayne's men. She received better treatment than most and was given as much bread as she wanted, and with this she saved many from starvation.

In England the plant Sweet William was named for the Butcher, while in Scotland ragwort got its name Stinking Billy. Said to have first reached Scotland in the fodder of Cumberland's cavalry.

The Prince landed at Roscoff in Brittany. He did not return to Scotland though he did visit London at least once. Plots and counter plots continued throughout his life and the British Government remained watchful.

In Scotland many songs in Gaelic and Scots recall his visit among them the sad but hopeful "Will ye no come back again".